Beginning Microsoft Office 2010

9 8 7 6 5 4 3 2 1

D1511400

Guy Hart-Davis

Apress®

Beginning Microsoft Office 2010

Copyright © 2010 by Guy Hart-Davis

ISBN-13 (pbk): 978-1-4302-2949-0

ISBN-13 (electronic): 978-1-4302-2950-6

9 8 7 6 5 4 3 2 1

President and Publisher: Paul Manning
Lead Editor: Steve Anglin
Development Editor: Douglas Pundick
Technical Reviewers: Greg Kettell and Edward Mendelson
Editorial Board: Clay Andres, Steve Anglin, Mark Beckner, Ewan Buckingham, Gary Cornell, Jonathan Gennick, Jonathan Hassell, Michelle Lowman, Matthew Moodie, Duncan Parkes, Jeffrey Pepper, Frank Pohlmann, Douglas Pundick, Ben Renow-Clarke, Dominic Shakeshaft, Matt Wade, Tom Welsh
Coordinating Editor: Laurin Becker
Copy Editors: Andy Rosenthal and Katie Stence
Compositor: Mary Sudul
Indexer: BIM Indexing & Proofreading Services
Artist: April Milne
Cover Designer: Anna Ishchenko

Distributed to the book trade worldwide by Springer Science+Business Media, LLC., 233 Spring Street, 6th Floor, New York, NY 10013. Phone 1-800-SPRINGER, fax (201) 348-4505, e-mail orders-ny@springer-sbm.com, or visit www.springeronline.com.

For information on translations, please e-mail rights@apress.com, or visit www.apress.com.

Apress and friends of ED books may be purchased in bulk for academic, corporate, or promotional use. eBook versions and licenses are also available for most titles. For more information, reference our Special Bulk Sales–eBook Licensing web page at www.apress.com/info/bulksales.

This book is dedicated to the memory of Mark Linkous.

Contents at a Glance

Contents vi

About the Author xxv

About the Technical Reviewers xxvi

Acknowledgments xxvii

Introduction xxviii

Chapter 1: Getting Started with Office 2010 1

Chapter 2: Head in the Cloud: Experiencing Software as a Service 23

Chapter 3: Learning Common Tools Across the Office Suite 33

Chapter 4: Working with Text and Graphics 71

Chapter 5: Customizing Office to Suit You 117

Chapter 6: Entering Text and Using Views 135

Chapter 7: Adding Style: Formatting Your Documents 159

Chapter 8: Creating Complex Documents and Layouts 199

Chapter 9: Revising and Reviewing Documents 233

Chapter 10: Printing, Finalizing, and Sharing Documents 263

Chapter 11: Creating Workbooks and Entering Data 283

Chapter 12: Formatting Your Worksheets...311

Chapter 13: Crunching Numbers with Formulas and Functions 345

Chapter 14: Creating Powerful and Persuasive Charts...................................369

Chapter 15: Creating and Using Excel Database Tables 393

▓ **Chapter 16: Starting to Build a Presentation** **413**

▓ **Chapter 17: Creating Clear and Compelling Slides** **439**

▓ **Chapter 18: Adding Life and Interest to a Presentation** **465**

▓ **Chapter 19: Delivering a Presentation Live or Online** **491**

▓ **Chapter 20: Making the Most of E-mail** **511**

▓ **Chapter 21: Keeping Your Contacts in Order** **555**

▓ **Chapter 22: Managing Your Calendar** **579**

▓ **Chapter 23: Working with Tasks and Notes** **597**

▓ **Chapter 24: Taking Notes** **615**

▓ **Chapter 25: Organizing, Synchronizing, and Sharing Your Notes** **639**

▓ **Chapter 26: Making OneNote Work Your Way** **657**

Index **681**

Contents

Contents at a Glance...iv

About the Author xxv

About the Technical Reviewers xxvi

Acknowledgments xxvii

Introduction xxviii

Chapter 1: Getting Started with Office 2010 1

Meeting the Office Programs and Learning What You Can Do With Them 1

    Microsoft Word 1

    Microsoft Excel 2

    Microsoft PowerPoint 3

    Microsoft Outlook 4

    Microsoft OneNote 5

Understanding the Common Features of the Programs...6

    The Title Bar and Minimize, Maximize, and Close Buttons.....................................7

    The Control Menu and the Quick Access Toolbar...8

    The Ribbon...9

    Backstage...9

    The Status Bar 10

Opening Programs 11

    Opening a Program the Standard Way 11

    Making a Program Easy to Run 12

    Making a Program Launch Automatically..12

Creating a Document 13

Saving a Document...15

Closing a Document..17

Opening a Document 18

Closing a Program 21

Summary 21

■ **Chapter 2: Head in the Cloud: Experiencing Software as a Service**.................23

Coming to Grips with Software as a Service 23

Understanding What Software as a Service Is 23

Understanding the Office Web Apps, Windows Live, and SkyDrive..........................23

Deciding Whether Software as a Service Meets Your Needs 25

Getting Started with the Office Web Apps 25

Signing Up for the Office Web Apps 25

Opening an Office Web App..26

Saving Changes to a Document in the Office Web Apps 28

Transferring Documents Between SkyDrive and Your PC 29

Saving Documents to SkyDrive from the Desktop Office Programs.......................29

Copying Documents from Your PC to SkyDrive 30

Downloading Documents from SkyDrive to Your PC 32

Summary 32

■ **Chapter 3: Learning Common Tools Across the Office Suite**.......................33

Using the Ribbon..33

Giving Commands from the Ribbon 35

Minimizing the Ribbon..35

Controlling the Ribbon with the Keyboard 36

Using Backstage 37

Sharing a Document with Other People..39

Sending a Document via E-mail 39

Saving a Document to SkyDrive 41

Saving a Document to a SharePoint Server...42

Saving Time and Effort with AutoCorrect 43

Choosing Options on the AutoCorrect Tab of the AutoCorrect Dialog Box 45

Choosing AutoFormat As You Type Options..45

Choosing Math AutoCorrect Options...48

Creating AutoCorrect Entries 49

Creating AutoCorrect Exceptions 50

Working with Actions..51

Checking Spelling and Grammar 53

Checking Spelling...54

Checking Grammar in Word and Outlook 57

Taking Control over Spelling Checks with Custom Dictionaries..64

Printing Documents 67

Summary 69

Chapter 4: Working with Text and Graphics 71

Entering Text in Your Documents 71

Entering Text in Documents Using Copy and Paste...71

Entering Text by Scanning a Document and Using Optical Character Recognition 71

Entering Text by Using Speech Recognition...72

Inserting Symbols in a Document...72

Navigating with the Keyboard and Selecting Objects...75

Applying Direct Formatting to Text and Objects 76

Using Cut, Copy, and Paste..79

Using Standard Cut, Copy, and Paste in the Office Programs 79

Using the Office Programs' Clipboard 79

Using Paste Options...81

Setting Paste Options in Word 83

Using Find and Replace 84

Locating Text with Find 84

Replacing Text with Replace 86

Using Data Validation to Check for Invalid Entries..................................326

Formatting Quickly with Table Formatting and Styles..............................329

   Formatting with Table Formatting..329

   Formatting with Styles 329

Adding Headers and Footers to Your Worksheets 334

Printing Your Excel Worksheets and Workbooks 335

   Telling Excel Which Part of the Worksheet to Print 336

   Checking the Page Layout and Where the Page Breaks Fall....................336

   Printing a Worksheet or Workbook...339

Sharing Your Workbooks with Your Colleagues......................................339

   Protecting a Workbook or Some of Its Worksheets 340

   Sharing a Workbook So That Your Colleagues Can Edit It......................342

   Working in a Shared Workbook 343

   Resolving Conflicts in a Shared Workbook..344

Summary 344

Chapter 13: Crunching Numbers with Formulas and Functions 345

Understanding the Difference Between Formulas and Functions 345

Referring to Cells and Ranges in Formulas and Functions.......................346

   Referring to a Cell...346

   Referring to Ranges...347

   Referring to Named Cells and Ranges...348

Performing Custom Calculations by Creating Formulas 349

   Meeting Excel's Calculation Operators...349

   Using the Calculation Operators...351

   Understanding the Order in Which Excel Evaluates Operators..................354

   Nesting Parts of Formulas to Override Operator Precedence...................355

   Entering Formulas Quickly by Copying and Using AutoFill 355

   Troubleshooting Common Problems with Formulas.................................356

Performing Standard Calculations by Inserting Functions........................360

   Understanding Function Names and Arguments.....................................360

Inserting Functions with the Function Drop-Down List 361

Finding the Functions You Need with the Insert Function Dialog Box 363

Inserting Functions with the Function Library 364

Providing the Arguments for the Function..365

Inserting Functions by Typing Them into a Worksheet..367

Summary 368

Chapter 14: Creating Powerful and Persuasive Charts...............................369

Learning the Essentials of Charts in Excel...369

Understanding Embedded Charts and Chart Sheets 369

Understanding the Components of a Chart..371

Understanding Excel's Chart Types and Choosing Which to Use 373

Creating, Laying Out, and Formatting a Chart 374

Creating a Chart..375

Changing a Chart from an Embedded Chart to a Chart Sheet 377

Changing the Chart Type 378

Switching the Rows and Columns in a Chart 378

Changing the Source Data for a Chart 378

Choosing the Layout for the Chart..379

Changing the Order of the Data Series...380

Adding a Separate Data Series to a Chart 380

Applying a Style to a Chart 381

Adding a Title to a Chart...382

Adding Axis Titles to the Chart 383

Changing the Scale or Numbering of an Axis 384

Adding a Legend to a Chart 386

Adding Axis Labels from a Range Separate from the Chart Data 386

Adding Data Labels to the Chart..386

Choosing Which Gridlines to Display 387

Formatting a Chart Wall and Chart Floor 388

Naming an Embedded Chart...390

Formatting Individual Chart Elements 390

Copying Chart Formatting..391

Reusing Your Own Designs by Creating Custom Chart Types 392

Summary 392

Chapter 15: Creating and Using Excel Database Tables 393

Understanding What You Can and Can't Do with Excel Database Tables...................393

Creating a Database Table and Entering Data..394

Creating a Database Table 394

Customizing the Database Table's Looks...397

Entering Data in a Database Table 398

Resizing a Database Table..401

Sorting a Database Table by One or More Fields...402

Sorting Quickly by a Single Field 402

Sorting a Database Table by Multiple Fields 402

Identifying and Removing Duplicate Records in a Database Table 404

Filtering a Database Table 406

Summary 411

Chapter 16: Starting to Build a Presentation 413

Creating a Presentation 413

Changing the Slide Size or Orientation 418

Navigating the PowerPoint Window..419

Add Content to a Slide 420

Adding, Deleting, and Rearranging Slides 420

Adding a Slide...421

Deleting a Slide 422

Rearranging Slides 422

Using Views to Work on Your Presentation..423

Creating Your Slides in Normal View 423

Rearranging Your Slides in Slide Sorter View..423

Creating Notes Pages in Notes Page View 425

Viewing a Presentation in Reading View 425

Running a Presentation in Slide Show View..426

Opening Extra Windows to See Different Parts of the Presentation 427

Creating the Outline of a Presentation...427

Organizing Your Slides into Sections...428

Collaborating on a Presentation with Your Colleagues................................430

Editing a Presentation Simultaneously with Your Colleagues 431

Comparing Two Copies of the Same Presentation 435

Summary 437

Chapter 17: Creating Clear and Compelling Slides 439

Planning the Slides in Your Presentation..439

Choosing Slide Layouts to Suit the Contents 440

Using PowerPoint's Built-in Slide Layouts..440

Creating Custom Slide Layouts...441

Formatting Text on Your Slides...442

Changing the Font, Font Size, and Alignment 442

Changing the Indentation and Line Spacing of Text....................................443

Rotating Text 444

Using Bulleted Lists 447

Adding Tables, SmartArt, Charts, and Hyperlinks to Slides...........................451

Adding Tables to Slides 451

Adding SmartArt Graphics to Slides 456

Adding Charts to Slides 457

Adding Hyperlinks to Slides...462

Summary 463

Chapter 18: Adding Life and Interest to a Presentation...........................465

Adding Pictures to a Presentation 465

Creating a Photo Album 466

Adding Movies and Sounds to a Presentation 469

Adding a Movie to a Slide 469

Adding a YouTube Video to a Slide 473

Adding a Sound to a Slide 474

Adding Transitions to Slides 475

Adding Animations to Slides 478

Understanding the Essentials of Animations 478

Adding an Animation to an Object 479

Changing the Order of Animations..480

Using Animation to Display Bulleted Paragraphs One at a Time 481

Animating SmartArt Graphics, Charts, and Tables 483

Keeping Extra Information Up Your Sleeve with Hidden Slides 486

Creating Custom Slide Shows within a Presentation...486

Opening the Custom Shows Dialog Box 487

Creating a Custom Slide Show 487

Playing a Custom Slide Show 488

Editing or Deleting a Custom Slide Show 489

Summary 489

▓ **Chapter 19: Delivering a Presentation Live or Online** 491

Getting Ready to Deliver a Presentation in Person 491

Setting Up Your Display and Choosing the Resolution 491

Using Presenter View 493

Practicing Your Presentation 495

Rehearsing Timings for Slides..495

Delivering a Presentation to a Live Audience 496

Starting a Presentation..496

Displaying the Slides You Need..496

Annotating the Slides 498

Controlling a Presentation Using the Keyboard 499

Displaying a White Screen or Black Screen 500

Creating a Handout for a Presentation 501

Recording Narration into a Presentation 502

Exporting and Sharing a Presentation 504

Broadcasting a Slide Show...505

Publishing Slides to a Slide Library or a SharePoint Site 508

Summary 510

Chapter 20: Making the Most of E-mail 511

Setting Up Outlook..511

Changing the Default Settings for an E-mail Account 514

Meeting the Outlook Interface 518

Using the Ribbon 519

Using and Customizing the Navigation Pane...520

Using and Customizing the Message List and Reading Pane.............................523

Using and Customizing the Reading Pane...527

Using and Customizing the To-Do Bar..529

Using and Customizing the People Pane 531

Sending and Receiving Messages...534

Sending an E-mail Message..534

Receiving and Reading Messages...542

Sending and Receiving Attachments 543

Sending a File As an Attachment...543

Receiving a File as an Attachment 544

Replying to and Forwarding Messages..546

Deleting, Storing, and Organizing Messages...547

Moving a Message to a Mail Folder...548

Creating a New Mail Folder 548

Adding Consistent Closings to Your Messages with Signatures..........................550

Dealing with Spam...552

    Removing Non-Spam Messages from the Junk E-mail Folder...552

    Marking Spam Messages as Junk...553

Summary 553

Chapter 21: Keeping Your Contacts in Order 555

Creating Contacts 555

    Creating a Contact from Scratch 555

    Importing Contacts from Other Address Books 561

    Mapping Custom Fields When Importing Contact Data 570

Working with Contacts..571

    Viewing and Sorting Your Contacts 571

    Editing Contact Information..576

    Communicating with Your Contacts 577

Summary 578

Chapter 22: Managing Your Calendar 579

Meeting the Calendar Interface 579

    Displaying the Dates You Want..581

    Customizing the Calendar Settings 583

    Understanding Appointments, Events and Meetings..584

    Understanding and Using the Calendar Views..585

Creating Appointments and Events..587

    Creating One-Shot Appointments 587

    Creating Repeating Appointments..589

Scheduling Meetings 591

    Setting Up a Meeting 591

    Tracking the Status of Meeting Invitations You've Sent..594

    Dealing with Invitations to Meetings 595

Summary 595

Chapter 23: Working with Tasks and Notes 597

Creating Tasks 597

Meeting the Tasks Interface 597

Viewing the Task List 599

Creating One-Shot Tasks...601

Creating Recurring Tasks 604

Managing Your Tasks 606

Assigning Tasks to Other People 609

Dealing with Tasks Other People Send to You..610

Taking Notes 610

Meeting the Notes Interface 610

Creating a Note...611

Viewing and Using Your Notes...612

Summary 613

Chapter 24: Taking Notes...615

Getting to Grips with the OneNote Interface 615

Working with Notebooks, Section Groups, Sections, and Pages 618

Working with Notebooks 618

Working with Sections and Section Groups 620

Working with Pages...624

Entering Notes on a Page 629

Understanding Which Types of Information You Can Save in OneNote 630

Adding Text to a Page..630

Adding Graphics to Pages..632

Capturing Screen Clippings in Your Notebooks 632

Creating Drawings on Pages 632

Creating Tables..632

Printing to OneNote 633

Sending Outlook Items to OneNote 634

Sending Web Content to OneNote 634

Inserting a Scanner Printout..634

Performing Calculations 635

Using Views, Windows, and Side Notes..635

Using Normal View, Full Page View, and Dock to Desktop View 636

Opening Extra Windows..637

Working with Side Notes 637

Summary 638

Chapter 25: Organizing, Synchronizing, and Sharing Your Notes..................639

Organizing Your Pages, Sections, and Notebooks 639

Moving Pages, Sections, and Section Groups 639

Merging Sections Together 640

Splitting a Section into Two..641

Merging and Splitting Notebooks 641

Changing the Display Name for a Notebook..641

Searching for Information 642

Protecting Your Notes with Passwords 644

Unlocking a Password-Protected Section 645

Locking Password-Protected Sections Manually 646

Removing Password Protection from a Section of a Notebook 646

Sharing Notebooks and Creating Shared Notebooks.............................647

Creating a New Shared Notebook 647

Sharing an Existing Notebook 648

Opening a Shared Notebook...649

Working in a Shared Notebook..649

Reviewing Changes to a Notebook 650

Choosing How to Update a Shared Notebook 652

Using Different Versions of Pages 654

Viewing or Recovering an Earlier Page Version......................................654

Getting Rid of Old Page Versions to Save Space 655

Storing Notes on the Web 655

Summary 656

Chapter 26: Making OneNote Work Your Way 657

Choosing Essential OneNote Options 657

   Choosing Display Options 657

   Choosing Save & Backup Options 659

   Choosing Send to OneNote Options 661

   Choosing Advanced Options 663

   Choosing Audio & Video Options 666

Recording Audio and Video into Your Notebooks 669

   Recording Audio into a Notebook 669

   Recording Video into a Notebook 670

   Exporting or Removing an Audio or Video File 670

   Searching for Words in Audio and Video Recordings 670

Printing Your Notebooks 671

   Using Print Preview 671

   Printing 673

Using OneNote with the Other Office Programs 673

   Exporting a Page or Section to a Word Document 673

   Exporting Data to an Excel Worksheet or a PowerPoint Presentation 675

   Creating an Outlook Message from OneNote 675

   Creating an Outlook Task from OneNote 675

   Transferring a OneNote Notebook to Another PC 677

   Retrieving Material from the Notebook Recycle Bin 678

Summary 680

Index 681

About the Author

 **Guy Hart-Davis** is the author of more than 60 computer books on subjects that range from Microsoft Office to programming Visual Basic for Applications and networking both PCs and Macs.

About the Technical Reviewers

 **Greg Kettell** is a professional software engineer with a diverse career that has covered everything from game programming to enterprise business applications. He has written and contributed to several books about software applications, operating systems, web design, and programming. Greg, his wife Jennifer, and their two children currently reside in upstate New York.

 **Edward Mendelson** has been a contributing editor of PC Magazine since 1988, and has written about every version of Microsoft Office released in the past twenty years. When he is not writing about computers, he is a professor of English at Columbia University.

Acknowledgments

My thanks go to the many people who helped create this book:

- Steve Anglin for signing me to write the book.
- Ben Renow-Clarke and Douglas Pundick for developing the manuscript.
- Edward Mendelson and Greg Kettell for reviewing the manuscript for technical accuracy and contributing helpful suggestions.
- Katie Stence for editing the manuscript with care.
- Nancy Wright for formatting the chapters.
- Laurin Becker for coordinating the book project and keeping things running.
- Mary Sudul for laying out the chapters of the book.
- BIM Indexing & Proofreading Services for creating the index.

Introduction

Do you need to get your work done with the Office programs—smoothly, easily, and quickly?
If so, you've picked up the right book.

Who Is This Book For?

This book is designed to help beginning and intermediate users get up to speed quickly with the Office 2010 programs and immediately become productive with them.

If you need to learn to use Word, Excel, PowerPoint, Outlook, and OneNote to accomplish everyday tasks, at work or at home, you'll benefit from this book's focused approach and detailed advice. You can either start from the beginning of the book and work through it, or use the Table of Contents or the Index to find the topic you need immediately, and then jump right in there.

What Does This Book Cover?

This book contains six parts that cover the shared Office features and the five leading programs.
Part I of the book brings you up to speed with the common features that the Office programs share:

- Chapter 1, "Getting Started with Office 2010," introduces you to the five main Office programs—Word, Excel, PowerPoint, Outlook, and OneNote—and what you can do with them. You'll learn how to open and close the programs; you'll meet key features such as the Ribbon and Backstage; and you'll create, save, close and reopen documents.

- Chapter 2, "Head in the Cloud: Experiencing Software as a Service," tells you what you need to know about the Office Web Apps—the online versions of Word, Excel, PowerPoint, and OneNote—and explains how software as a service works. You'll find out how to get a Windows Live ID, how to start using the Office Web Apps, and how to transfer documents to and from the SkyDrive storage system.

- Chapter 3, "Learning Common Tools Across the Office Suite," shows you how to control the Office programs using the Ribbon and how to access Backstage and use its document-management features. It also explains Office's common ways of sharing a document with others, how to make the most of the AutoCorrect and AutoFormat features, and how to use the Spelling checker and Grammar checker. You'll also learn how to print documents.

- Chapter 4, "Working with Text and Graphics," shows you how to do everything from entering text (using the keyboard or other means) to creating tables and adding graphical objects such as pictures, shapes, and diagrams. Along the way,

CHAPTER 1

Getting Started with Office 2010

You're probably in a hurry to start being productive using Office 2010, so this chapter gets you moving quickly. First, you'll meet each of the programs, find out what you can do with them, and come to grips with key features like the Ribbon and Backstage. I'll then show you how to launch the programs or make them launch themselves. Finally, you'll look at how to create, save, and close documents, and then reopen them when you need to work on them again.

Meeting the Office Programs and Learning What You Can Do With Them

Microsoft Office 2010 Home and Business Edition includes five main programs, which this section briefly introduces.

For ease of use and to save time, the programs share many features, from the ways in which you create, save, and open documents to common actions you perform in them, such as copying text from one part of a document and pasting it in at another part.

Part 1 of this book discusses these common features. Parts 2 through 6 of the book then examine each of the programs in turn.

Microsoft Word

Microsoft Word (see Figure 1-1) is a word processing program that you can use to create everything from a single-page letter to a thousand-page book complete with a table of contents, an index, and cross-references between different parts of the book.

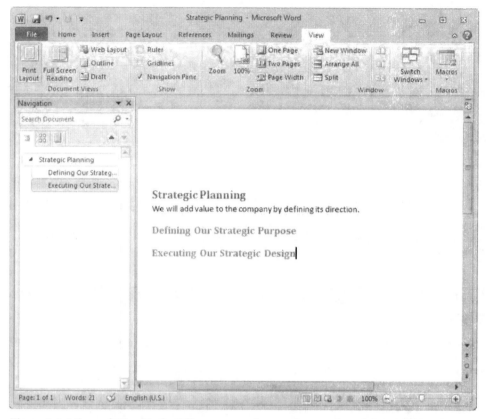

Figure 1-1. Microsoft Word is the Office program for creating text-based documents.

Part 2 of this book explains how to make the most of Microsoft Word.

Microsoft Excel

Microsoft Excel (see Figure 1-2) is a spreadsheet program that you can use to record, calculate, and analyze data. Excel includes features for creating many different types of chart, including the business-oriented PivotCharts and PivotTables.

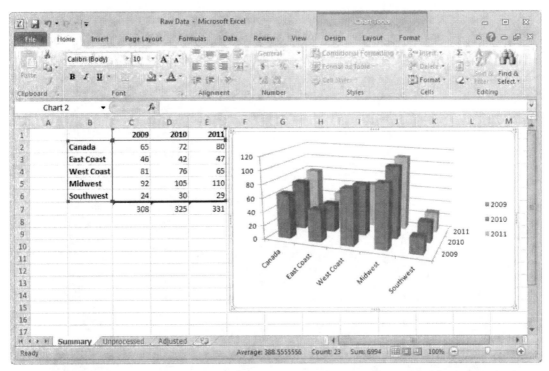

Figure 1-2. *Each Microsoft Excel workbook contains as many worksheets as you need for entering and analyzing your data.*

Part 3 of this book shows you how to work quickly and effectively in Microsoft Excel.

Microsoft PowerPoint

Microsoft PowerPoint (see Figure 1-3) is a program for creating and delivering presentations. Each presentation consists of slides, to which you can add any data from straightforward text to charts and movies. You can also add animations and transition effects to provide visual interest.

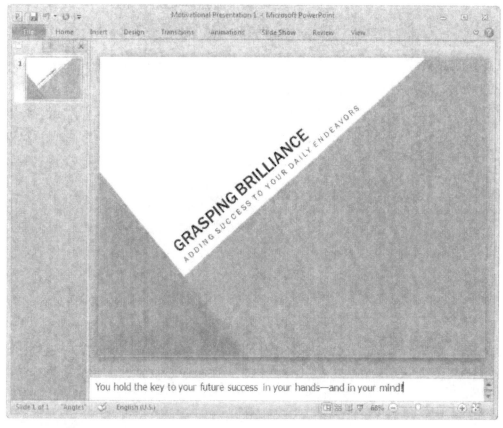

Figure 1-3. In Microsoft PowerPoint, you create slides and organize them into slide shows.

Part 4 of this book covers creating persuasive presentations in PowerPoint and delivering them to your audience either in person or online.

Microsoft Outlook

Microsoft Outlook (see Figure 1-4) is a program for e-mail and managing your contacts, calendar, and task list. If you have multiple e-mail accounts, you can manage them all within the single program, which saves large amounts of time and effort.

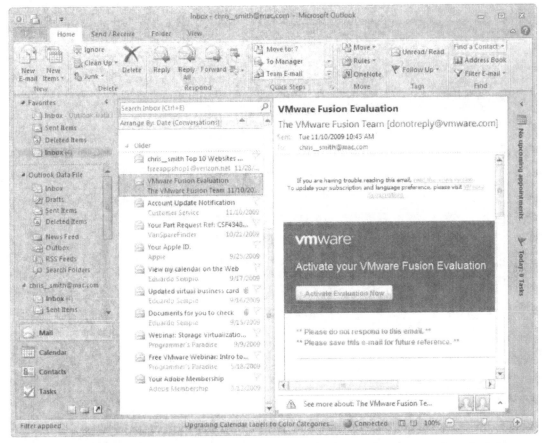

Figure 1-4. Microsoft Outlook makes it easy to work with multiple e-mail accounts and to schedule your business and home life.

Part 5 of this book shows you how to send e-mail and organize your life with Outlook.

Microsoft OneNote

Microsoft OneNote is a program for capturing, organizing, and sharing information (see Figure 1-5). You can create a single notebook or as many notebooks as you need, add to it any type of digital information from text and pictures to audio and video, and organize it into different tabs, sections, and folders. You can keep a notebook strictly to yourself or share it with your colleagues.

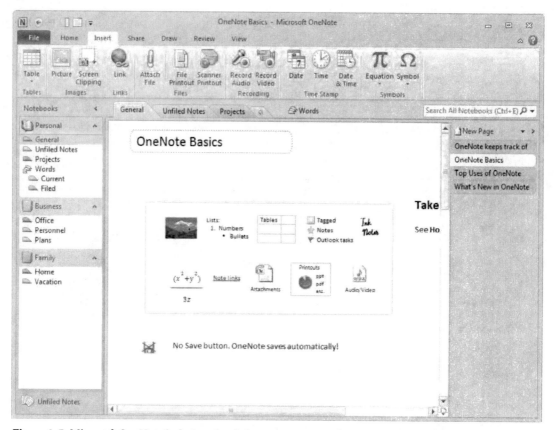

Figure 1-5. Microsoft OneNote is designed to help you capture and organize notes on any topic.

Part 6 of this book explains how to take notes in OneNote, organize your data, and share it with other people or other Office programs.

Understanding the Common Features of the Programs

As you can see from the figures on the last few pages, the Office programs share a common look and several common features. Some of the features are probably familiar from other Windows programs you've used, but some are peculiar to the Office programs.

Figure 1-6 shows the Word window with a document open and the major features labeled. The following sections explain what the features are and what you use them for.

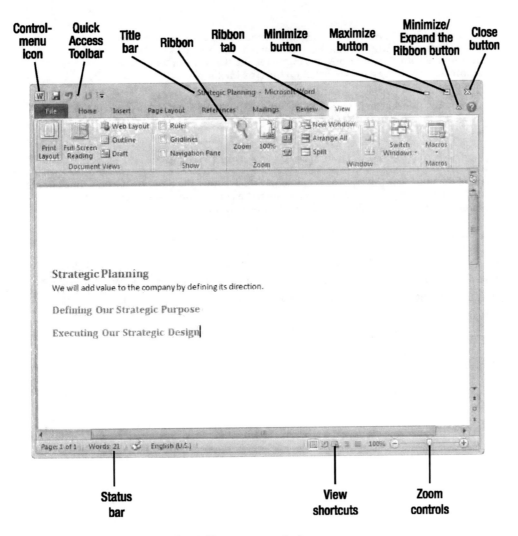

Figure 1-6. The major features of an Office program window

The Title Bar and Minimize, Maximize, and Close Buttons

The title bar at the top of the window shows the name of the open document (if there is one) and the program's name—for example, "Strategy Report—Microsoft Word."

At the right end of the title bar are the following three buttons:

- *Minimize*: Click this button to minimize the window to the program's icon on the taskbar.

- *Maximize*: Click this button to make the window take up the whole screen. When you maximize the window, the Restore Down button replaces the Maximize button. Click the Restore Down button to restore the window to the size it was before you maximized it. When you do this, the Maximize button replaces the Restore Down button.

- *Close*: Click this button to close the window. If this is the last window open in the program, the program closes too.

The Control Menu and the Quick Access Toolbar

At the left end of the title bar is the control-menu icon, which shows the program's icon—for example, the Microsoft Word icon. You can click this icon to open the control menu (see Figure 1-7), which provides commands for closing, resizing, and moving the window.

Note The control menu is a feature that has clung on from earlier versions of Windows. All of its functions are available elsewhere in the programs, so there's no need to use it—but you may find it handy because it puts several widely used commands in a small space. Its most useful feature is that you can double-click the icon to close the window.

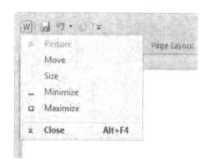

Figure 1-7. Click the program's icon at the left end of the title bar to open the control menu.

To the right of the control-menu icon is the Quick Access Toolbar, which keeps a small number of essential commands, such as Save and Undo, always available at the click of your mouse. You can customize the Quick Access Toolbar so that it contains exactly the buttons you need (see Chapter 5 for details).

The Ribbon

Below the title bar, the Ribbon runs across the top of the application window. The Ribbon is a control bar that contains multiple tabs. You can display one tab's contents at a time by clicking the tab at the top.

Each Office program has a Home tab that contains some of the most widely useful commands, and each of the main programs has a View tab that contains buttons for changing the view, zooming, and similar moves. Beyond these tabs, each of the programs has other tabs to cover its needs. For example, PowerPoint's tabs include the Slide Show tab, the Transitions tab, and the Animations tab, none of which Word, Excel, OneNote, or Outlook need.

Note When you don't need the Ribbon, you can hide it by double-clicking the tab that's currently active. You can then pop up the Ribbon temporarily by clicking a tab. When you click a button on the Ribbon, the Ribbon then hides itself again. Double-click the active tab to display the Ribbon all the time. You can also hide the Ribbon by clicking the Minimize the Ribbon button and restore it by clicking the Expand the Ribbon button that replaces it. From the keyboard, press Ctrl+F1 to toggle the display of the Ribbon.

Each tab contains several groups of controls, divided up into different types of actions. For example, the Home tab in Outlook includes a New group (for creating a new e-mail message or other item), a Delete group (for deleting items, ignoring items, and dealing with junk mail), a Respond group (for replying, replying to all, or forwarding), and so on.

You'll look at the details of how to use the Ribbon in Chapter 3, but the basic method is straightforward: You click the tab for the type of action you want to take, and then click the button or control for the action you want to take. For example, to insert a picture in a Word document, you click the Insert tab to display its contents, and then click the Picture button in the Illustrations g in the Illustrations group.

Backstage

The leftmost tab in the Ribbon is called File, and it's different than the other tabs. Clicking the File tab opens what Microsoft calls Backstage, a behind-the-curtain set of actions you can take on the document itself.

Backstage is like the File menu that many Windows programs have (and the Office programs used to have), but on steroids. Rather than just displaying a menu or a different set of controls on the Ribbon, Backstage takes up the whole of the document window, as you can see in Figure 1-8, which shows Backstage for an Excel workbook.

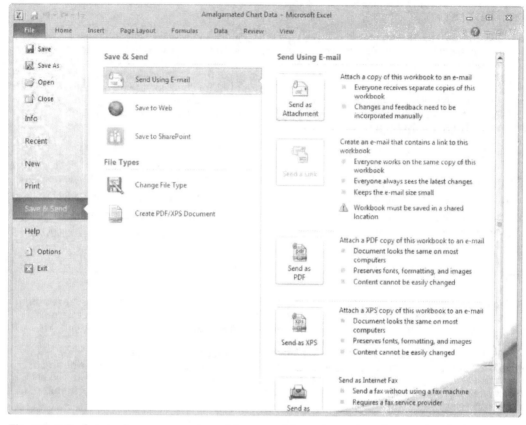

Figure 1-8. Backstage gives you access to a wide range of document actions, from saving the document to sharing it via e-mail or online.

Backstage includes essential commands such as Save, Open, Close, Print, and Exit, so you'll most likely use it frequently. You'll see how to use the other Backstage commands in the chapters on each application.

The Status Bar

At the bottom of the program window is the status bar, which shows information about the document and what you're currently working on and provides controls for changing the view and zooming in or out. For example, in Word, the status bar shows the current page number, the number of words in the document, and the language used. You can customize the status bar so that it shows the information you find most useful.

■ **Note** OneNote doesn't have a status bar.

Opening Programs

To get anything done in the Office applications, you'll need to open and close programs. This section shows you the most useful ways of opening and closing programs.

Opening a Program the Standard Way

The standard way of opening a program is to go through the Start menu to the Microsoft Office folder like this:

1. Click the Start button to open the Start menu.

2. Click All Programs to open the All Programs list.

3. Click the Microsoft Office folder to display its contents (see Figure 1-9).

4. Click the program you want. For example, click Microsoft Word 2010.

■ **Note** If you're using the Classic version of the Start menu, choose Start ➤ Programs ➤ Microsoft Office to reach the Office programs.

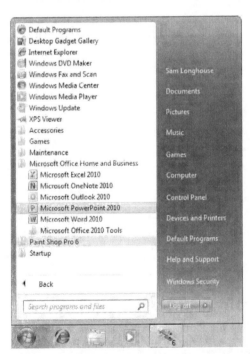

Figure 1-9. The standard way of launching an Office program is to use the Microsoft Office folder on the All Programs section of the Start menu.

■ **Note** Depending on the version of Microsoft Office you have, you may see a different selection of programs than appear in Figure 1-9.

■ **Note** The Start menu shows a yellow highlight on any program or program folder that you haven't yet run.

Making a Program Easy to Run

If you need to open a program frequently, you can pin it to either the Taskbar or the Start menu. Pinning the item makes it always appear on the Taskbar or in the upper-left area of the Start menu, so you can click it that much more easily.

■ **Note** You can pin an item to the Taskbar only in Windows 7, not in Windows Vista or Windows XP. You can pin an item to the Start menu in all these versions of Windows as long as you're using the regular Start menu rather than the Classic Start menu.

To pin an item, follow these steps:

1. Click the Start menu.
2. Click All Programs.
3. Click the Microsoft Office folder.
4. Right-click the program and choose Pin to Taskbar or Pin to Start Menu, depending on which you want.

■ **Tip** You can also pin an item to the Taskbar or the Start menu by dragging it to the Taskbar or the pinned area of the Start menu. When Windows adds a Pin to Taskbar ScreenTip or a Pin to Start Menu ScreenTip to the icon, release the mouse button.

Making a Program Launch Automatically

If you use one or more of the Office programs every time you run Windows, set the program to run automatically when you log on. For example, you may want to run Word, Outlook, and OneNote all the time so that you can work on documents, check your e-mail, and take notes.

Closing a Program

When you have finished using a program, close it. Closing the program removes it from your PC's memory, so your PC can use the memory to run other programs.

The standard way of closing a program is to click the File tab, and then click Exit in the Backstage pane; you can also press Alt+F4. This is usually the best way to close a program because there's no ambiguity about what you're doing: The Exit command closes any documents that are open and then closes the program itself.

You can also close a program by closing its last open window. For example, if you have two documents open in Word, closing the first document leaves the second document open. But closing the second document closes Word as well.

If you have any documents open that contain unsaved changes, the program prompts you to close them.

Note If you plan to use a program again later, you can simply minimize the program until you need it again rather than close it and restart it. The easiest way to minimize a program is to click its Taskbar icon. Click again to display the program's window again. You can also minimize a program by clicking the Minimize button in the upper-right corner of the window.

Summary

Now that you know how to launch the Office programs and create documents in them, you're ready to get to work in the programs.

In the next chapter, you'll learn how the Office programs enable you to save your documents on the Internet so that you can open and edit them using any computer that has an Internet connection—even if the computer doesn't have Office installed.

If you're concentrating on using the Office programs on your PC rather than online, you may prefer to skip ahead to Chapter 3, which shows you how to work quickly and smartly with common tools in the Office programs.

CHAPTER 2

∎∎∎

Head in the Cloud: Experiencing Software as a Service

In this chapter, I'll introduce you to the Office Web Apps, the online versions of four of the Office programs—Word, Excel, PowerPoint, and OneNote—and explain how software as a service works.

I'll start by quickly going over what software as a service is, what it's for, and how to decide whether it's suitable for your needs. I'll then show you how to get a Windows Live ID if you don't already have one, how to start using the Office Web Apps, and how to transfer documents to and from the SkyDrive storage system on the Windows Live site.

Coming to Grips with Software as a Service

In this section, you'll look at what software as a service is, how the Office Web Apps work, and what Windows Live and SkyDrive are. I'll also suggest how to decide whether you should try the Office Web Apps.

Understanding What Software as a Service Is

Software as a service is a term used to describe running software on Internet sites rather than installing it directly on a computer. For example, most of the software that Google produces—such as the Gmail e-mail service and the Google Docs online productivity programs—run on Internet servers rather than as programs on your PC. Your data is stored on the servers too, or in Internet parlance "in the cloud" (the cloud is the standard symbol used to represent the Internet in network diagrams).

You typically access software as a service through a web browser, which means that you can use any computer that has an Internet connection and a web browser—anything from an Internet-capable mobile phone (such as an iPhone or a phone running Google's Android operating system) to a laptop or a desktop computer. As long as the computer has a compatible web browser (such as Internet Explorer, Firefox, or Safari), it doesn't matter which operating system it's running.

Understanding the Office Web Apps, Windows Live, and SkyDrive

Microsoft's Office Web Apps are online versions of Word, Excel, PowerPoint, and OneNote. The Office Web Apps run in a web browser, so you don't need to install them on your computer (or whichever computer you're using). The Office Web Apps are free and compete with other online document programs such as Google Docs (http://docs.google.com) and Zoho Office (http://www.zoho.com).

▓ **Tip** For best performance, make sure that Microsoft's Silverlight media player is installed on the computer you're running Office Web Apps on. If you enjoy watching videos or listening to audio through your browser, you may well have Silverlight installed already; if not, you can download Silverlight for free from the Microsoft web site (`http://www.microsoft.com/silverlight/`).

To use the Office Web Apps, you must be a member of Microsoft's Windows Live online service (here, "live" rhymes with "jive," not with "give"). Windows Live is also free, and you can sign up at any time by providing a small amount of information and—as usual—agreeing to a user agreement.

The Office Web Apps store your documents on a Microsoft Internet site called SkyDrive. SkyDrive is part of the Windows Live service and gives you 25 GB of storage for free—plenty for storing even the heftiest Office documents.

As well as creating documents on SkyDrive with the Office Web Apps, you can save documents to SkyDrive from the desktop versions of the Office programs. You can also use the desktop versions of the Office programs to open the documents you've created on SkyDrive with the Office Web Apps.

▓ **Note** Microsoft describes the Office Web Apps as companions for the desktop versions of Office—Microsoft doesn't intend the Office Web Apps as a substitute for the desktop versions, although if your needs are modest, you may be able to get away with using only the Office Web Apps. The Office Web Apps provide only the essential features of the programs, so if you're used to the desktop versions of the programs, you'll notice that many features are missing. How much these missing features bother you will depend on which types of documents you create: Generally speaking, the more complex the documents you create, the more you'll need the desktop versions.

The Office Web Apps use standard web technologies such as the JavaScript programming language, so they work in most web browsers on Windows, Mac OS X, or Linux. If you create a document using Microsoft Word on your PC in your office, you can save the document to SkyDrive and then edit it using a browser on your Mac at home.

▓ **Caution** The Office Web Apps can edit only files that use the latest Office file formats: the Word Document format (with the .docx file extension), the Excel Workbook format (with the .xlsx file extension), and the PowerPoint Presentation format (with the .pptx file extension). You can open documents that use the older formats—for example, the Word 97–2003 Document format or the Excel 97–2003 Workbook format—in the Office Web Apps, but you can't edit them.

- On the New screen that your browser displays (for example, the New Microsoft Excel Workbook screen), type the name you want to save the document under, and then click the Create button. SkyDrive creates the document and then opens it in the Web App.

Figure 2-2 shows a new Excel workbook open in the Excel Web App. As you can see, the Web App looks similar to the desktop version of Excel, in that it has Backstage (the File tab), the Ribbon, multiple worksheets, and so on. But you'll also notice that it has only some of Excel's features, as you can see by the small number of Ribbon tabs.

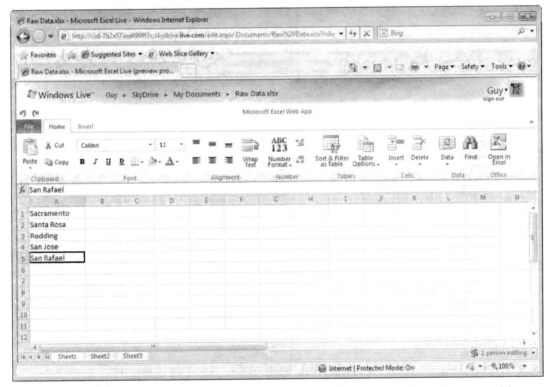

Figure 2-2. After opening a new document in an Office Web App, you can work it in using many of the same techniques as in the desktop version of the program.

Opening an Existing Document on SkyDrive

To open an existing document on SkyDrive, follow these steps:

1. Open your web browser, go to SkyDrive (www.skydrive.com), and then log in.

2. Navigate to the folder that contains the document, and then click the document (see Figure 2-3).

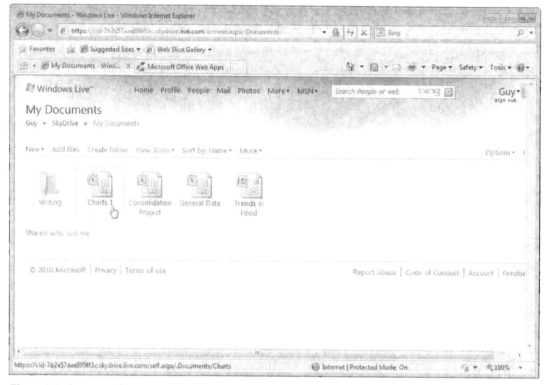

Figure 2-3. Steer your browser to SkyDrive, log in, and then click the document you want to open.

3. SkyDrive then displays the options for the document (see Figure 2-4).

4. Click the Edit link under the document's name to open the document. The browser opens the relevant Office Web App and loads the document in it.

Saving Changes to a Document in the Office Web Apps

After you have saved a document and given it a filename, Excel, PowerPoint, and OneNote automatically save the changes you make to the document. In Word, you need to save the changes explicitly by clicking the Save button on the Quick Access Toolbar or by choosing File ➤ Save.

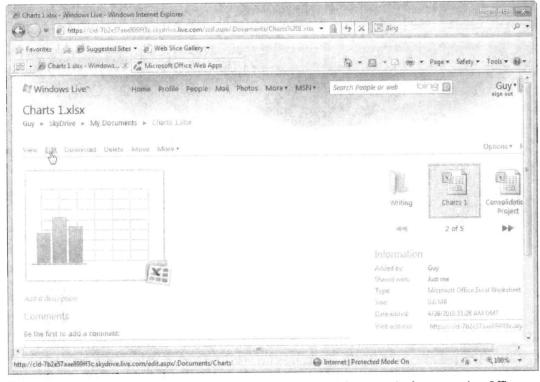

Figure 2-4. *On the document's page, click the Edit link to open the document in the appropriate Office Web App.*

Transferring Documents Between SkyDrive and Your PC

If you have created documents on your PC that you want to be able to use with the Office Web Apps, you need to put those documents on SkyDrive, either by saving them there from the desktop versions of the programs or by copying them to SkyDrive. If you've created documents on SkyDrive, you may want to download them to your PC so that you can work with them while offline.

Saving Documents to SkyDrive from the Desktop Office Programs

To save a document to SkyDrive from the desktop version of Word, Excel, PowerPoint, or OneNote, follow these steps:

1. Open the document in the program as usual.

2. Click the File tab to open Backstage.

3. Click the Save & Send item in the left column to display the Save & Send pane.

4. In the Save & Send column, click the Save to Web item to display the Save to Windows Live SkyDrive pane (shown in Figure 2-5 after you have signed in).

Figure 2-5. In the Save to Windows Live SkyDrive pane in Backstage, choose the SkyDrive folder in which you want to save the document, and then click the Save As button.

5. If the Sign In button appears in the SkyDrive pane, click it. Type your user name and password in the Windows Security dialog box, and then click the OK button. The program signs you into SkyDrive.

6. In the My Folders box in the Save to SkyDrive pane, click the folder you want to use.

7. Click the Save As button. The program displays the Save As dialog box.

8. Change the document name if necessary, and then click the Save button. The program saves the document to SkyDrive.

Copying Documents from Your PC to SkyDrive

Saving a document to SkyDrive using an Office program (as just described) works fine, but you can also simply copy files from your PC to SkyDrive. To do so, follow these steps:

1. Open your web browser, go to SkyDrive, and log in.

2. Click the Add Files link to display the Select a folder to store your files screen.

3. Click the folder to which you want to copy the files. Your browser displays the Add files screen (see Figure 2-6).

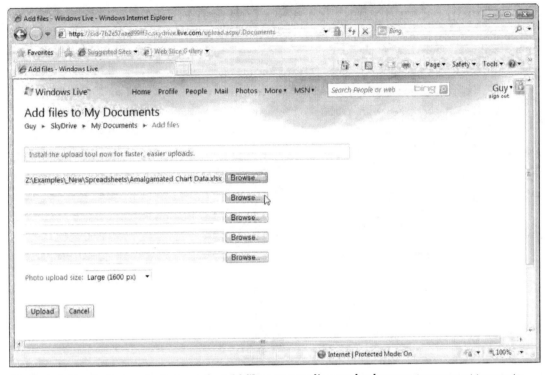

Figure 2-6. *Use the Browse buttons on the Add files screen to line up the documents you want to copy to SkyDrive.*

4. Click the first Browse button to display the Choose File to Upload dialog box, click the file, and then click the Open button. The browser adds the filename to the box.

5. Repeat the previous step to specify up to four more files to upload.

■ **Tip** If you need to upload many files, click the Install the upload tool link on the Add files screen to install the upload tool, which simplifies the upload process.

---

6. Click the Upload button. Your browser uploads the files to SkyDrive. Keep the Uploading files window open until the browser displays the folder to which you uploaded the documents, and you can see that all the files have been transferred successfully.

Downloading Documents from SkyDrive to Your PC

To copy files you've created on SkyDrive to your PC so that you can work with them whether you're online or offline, follow these steps:

1. Open your web browser, go to SkyDrive, and log in.

2. Navigate to the folder that contains the document you want to download.

3. Click the document to display its control screen.

4. Click the Download link. Your browser displays a download dialog box such as the File Download dialog box (see Figure 2-7).

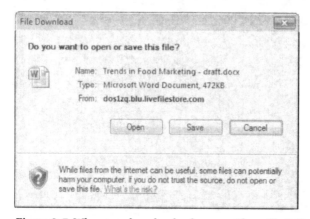

Figure 2-7. When you download a document from SkyDrive, your browser displays its normal dialog box for a file download. Click the button for saving the file, and then choose the folder in which to save it.

5. Click the button for saving the file. For example, in the File Download dialog box that Internet Explorer displays, click the Save button.

6. If the browser displays a Save As dialog box, choose the folder in which to save the file, and then click the Save button. The browser downloads the file and saves it.

Summary

In this chapter, you've learned how the Office Web Apps work and how to decide whether to use them. You now know how to sign up for a Windows Live ID, how to find and launch the Office Web Apps, and how to transfer documents to and from SkyDrive.

In the next chapter, you'll start looking at the common features of the Office programs, beginning with essential features such as the Ribbon and Backstage. Turn the page when you're ready to start.

Press the key for the tab you want. The program displays the tab and shows on it the letters you need to press to give a particular command, as shown in Figure 3-5.

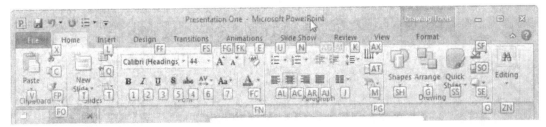

Figure 3-5. After you press the letter for the tab, the program shows the letters you can press for the commands.

■ **Note** Some of the Ribbon access keys remain the same as the menu access keys in earlier versions of Office and other programs. For example, you can press the Alt key, F, O (in sequence) to give the File ➤ Open command, press the Alt key, F, S to give the File ➤ Save command, or press the Alt key, F, X to give the File ➤ Exit command (closing the program). You can also press many (but not all) of the shortcuts that drove the menus in earlier versions. For example, you can press the Alt key, T, O in sequence to display the program's Options dialog box, because this is the key sequence for choosing Tools ➤ Options from the menus in Office 2003 and earlier versions.

Using Backstage

Backstage, also referred to as the Backstage view of a document, is what used to be the File menu in earlier versions of Office. Unlike the File menu, Backstage takes up the whole of the program window and provides not just a menu of actions but a whole different view of the document.

■ **Note** Backstage contains features for taking action with the contents of the document—for example, saving it to a different format, printing it out, or choosing settings for collaborating with other people on it. The rest of the Ribbon contains the features you use to create the content of your documents, such as entering text or pictures, applying formatting, or checking spelling.

To open Backstage, click the File tab on the Ribbon (or press the Alt key, F). When you first open Backstage, the program selects the Info item in the pane on the left and displays a screenful of information about the document, along with actions you can take on it. For example, in Figure 3-6, which shows Backstage for Word, the info screen shows command buttons for protecting the document, checking the document for issues before sharing it with others, and managing different versions of the document.

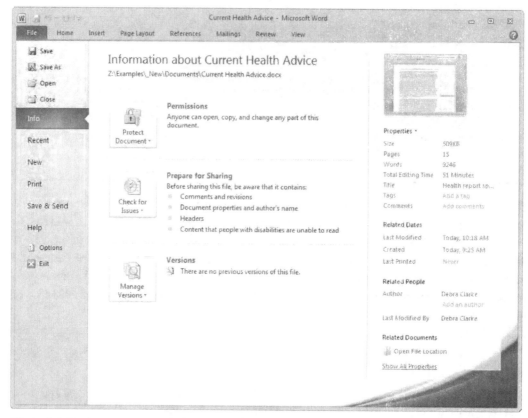

Figure 3-6. Backstage opens with the Info screen displayed.

From here, you can take an action by clicking one of the buttons, or you can click another item in the left pane to either display information associated with it or to run the command. Backstage has a different set of commands and items for each of the programs, but most of the programs have the following commands and items:

- *Save.* Saves the document. If you've never saved the document before, the program displays the Save As dialog box so that you can name the file and choose which folder to store it in.

- *Save As.* Displays the Save As dialog box so that you can save the file under a different name, in a different folder, or both.

- *Open.* Displays the Open dialog box so that you can open a document.

- *Close.* Closes the active document.

- *Info.* Displays information about the active document.

- *Recent.* Displays a screen of recent documents, so that you can quickly open one.

- *New.* Displays a screen of options for creating a new document—for example, by basing it on a template or on an existing document.

- *Print.* Displays a screen for printing the document (see the discussion later in this chapter).

- *Share.* Displays a screen for sharing the document with other people—for example, by sending it via e-mail or saving it to the Windows Live SkyDrive storage site or to a SharePoint site (SharePoint is a Microsoft networking technology used by many companies).

- *Help.* Displays a screen for searching for help, checking for updates, or consulting other resources.

- *Options.* Displays the Options dialog box for setting options in the program.

- *Exit.* Closes all open documents and the program itself.

▨ **Tip** If you're used to an earlier version of Office, and you find you've lost a command you used to use, look first in Backstage. Microsoft has integrated a wide variety of different features and commands into Backstage, and it can take a while to find out where everything you need is.

Sharing a Document with Other People

Word, Excel, and PowerPoint all enable you to share a document with other people in several different ways. This section covers the three ways common to all three of these programs:

- Send Using E-mail

- Save to SkyDrive

- Save to SharePoint

▨ **Note** For coverage of the other ways of sharing documents that the individual programs offer, see the chapters on those programs.

Sending a Document via E-mail

You can send a document by e-mail by starting a message in Outlook (or another program) and then attaching the document's file. But if you're working from one of the Office programs and have the document open, you can start a message directly from the program. This saves a bit of time and effort.

To send a document using e-mail, follow these steps:

1. Make the document the active document. If the document is already open, click in its window; if the document isn't open, open it.

2. Click the File tab to open Backstage, and click Save & Send in the left column to display the Save & Send options (see Figure 3-7).

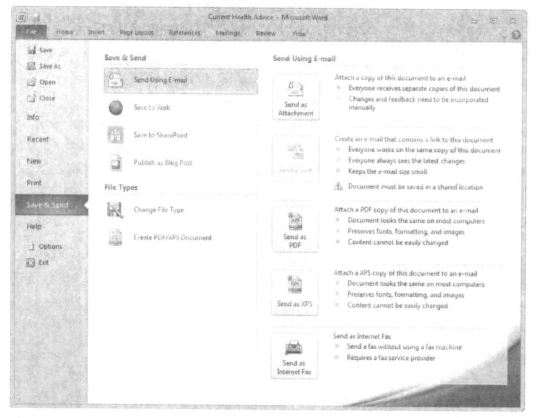

Figure 3-7. From the Save & Send screen in Backstage, you can send a document via e-mail.

3. In the Save & Send list, click Send Using E-mail if this item is not already selected.

4. In the Send Using E-mail area, click the button for the way you want to send the document:

   • **Send as Attachment.** Click this button to send the document attached to an e-mail message. This is the option you'll probably want to use most frequently.

   • **Send a Link.** Click this button if you just want to send a link to the network or Internet server on which the document is located. The recipient can then open or download the document from there.

- **Send as PDF.** Click this button to create a Portable Document Format (PDF) file containing a version of the document, and then send that file via e-mail. A PDF is good for sharing a document you want other people to be able to read but not edit, or for sharing with people who may not have Office.

- **Send as XPS.** Click this button to create an XML Paper Specification (XPS) file containing a version of the document, and then send that file via e-mail. (XML is the abbreviation for Extensible Markup Language, one of the standard technologies used for Internet documents.) XPS is good for sharing a document with other Windows 7 or Windows Vista users in a format that they can read but not edit. Windows XP may or may not have an XPS reader, depending on the updates installed.

Note PDF is much more widely used than XPS. Unless you know your intended recipient has an XPS reader, or your company prefers XPS, PDF is a safer choice.

- **Send as Internet Fax.** Click this button to send the document as a fax using an Internet service fax provider. You must sign up with such a provider before you can use this features.

5. For any of the four Send as options, the program opens Outlook (or your default e-mail program), creates a message, and attaches the file or enters the link. Address the message, type any text needed, and then click the Send button to send it.

Saving a Document to SkyDrive

If you have a Windows Live account (including a Hotmail account or an MSN account), you can save documents to SkyDrive, Microsoft's online document service. You can use SkyDrive either to share documents with other people (who have Windows Live accounts too) or to access and work on your documents from other computers.

Note You can sign up for a free Windows Live account at the Windows Live website (http://home.live.com).

To save a document to SkyDrive, follow these steps:

1. Make the document the active document. If the document is already open, click in its window. If the document isn't open, open it.

2. Click the File tab to open Backstage, and click Save & Send in the left column to display the Save & Send options.

3. In the Save & Send column, click the Save to Web Item to display the Save to Windows Live SkyDrive (shown in Figure 3-8 after signing in).

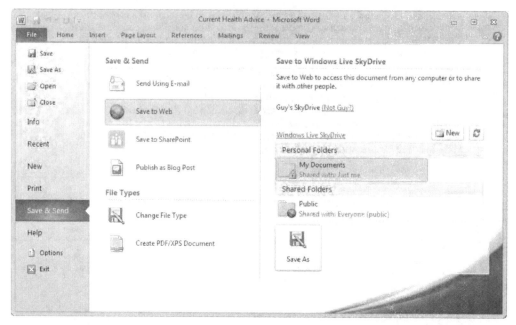

Figure 3-8. When saving a document to SkyDrive, you can choose between putting it in your Public folder (which you share with everyone) or a private folder such as your My Documents folder.

4. If you have not yet signed in to SkyDrive, click the Sign In button, and follow through the login procedure.

5. In the My Folders list, select the folder you want to save the document in. At first, SkyDrive gives you a Public folder (which you share with everyone) and a private My Documents folder. You can create other folders as needed by clicking the New Folder button.

6. Click the Save As button. The program displays the Save As dialog box.

7. Choose the file name and folder as usual, and then click the Save button to save the document to SkyDrive.

Saving a Document to a SharePoint Server

If your company or organization has a SharePoint server, you can save documents to it to share them with your colleagues.

To save a document to a SharePoint server, follow these steps:

1. Make the document the active document. If the document is already open, click in its window; if the document isn't open, open it.

2. Click the File tab to open Backstage, and then click Save & Send in the left column to display the Save & Send options.

3. In the Share column, click the Save to SharePoint item to display the Save to SharePoint options (see Figure 3-9).

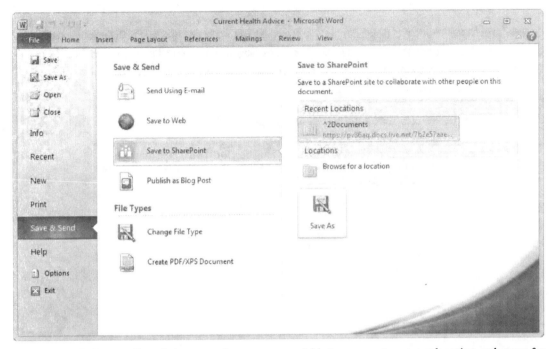

Figure 3-9. The Save to SharePoint screen lets you save quickly to a current or recent location, or browse for a different SharePoint location.

4. If the SharePoint location you want appears in the Current Location list or the Recent Locations list, click it. Otherwise, click the Browse for a Location button.

5. In the Save As dialog box, choose the folder in which to save the document, and then change the file name if necessary.

6. Click the Save button to save the document.

Saving Time and Effort with AutoCorrect

As you work in a document, the AutoCorrect feature watches the characters you type and springs into action if it detects a mistake it can fix or some formatting it can apply. This feature can save you a lot of time and effort, and can speed up your typing substantially—but you need to set it up to meet your needs. AutoCorrect also has some features that can cause surprises, so you will want to choose settings that suit the way you work.

To set up AutoCorrect, open the AutoCorrect dialog box like this:

1. Click the File tab to open Backstage, and then click Options to open the Options dialog box.

2. In the left pane, click the Proofing category to display the Proofing options.

■ **Note** To open the AutoCorrect dialog box in Outlook, choose File ➤ Options to open the Outlook Options dialog box, then click the Mail category in the left pane. Click the Spelling and AutoCorrect button to open the Editor Options dialog box with the Proofing category selected, and then click the AutoCorrect Options button.

3. Click the AutoCorrect Options button to display the AutoCorrect dialog box.

4. If the AutoCorrect tab isn't at the front, click it to display it. Figure 3-10 shows the AutoCorrect tab of the AutoCorrect dialog box for Word. This dialog box has one more tab and a couple more options than the AutoCorrect dialog box for the other programs.

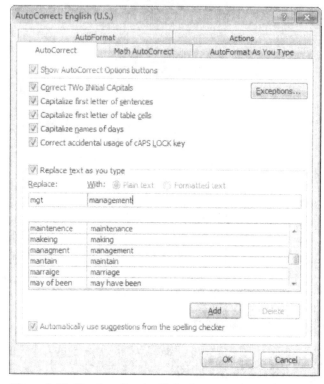

Figure 3-10. *The AutoCorrect dialog box contains options that can save you plenty of time but also give you surprises.*

If you do use Math AutoCorrect, select the Use Math AutoCorrect rules outside of math regions check box if you want to use Math AutoCorrect anywhere in your documents. If you want to use Math AutoCorrect only in math areas, clear this check box.

Figure 3-12. If you include math in your documents, choose whether to restrict Math AutoCorrect to math regions and decide which items to replace as you type.

Creating AutoCorrect Entries

If you use the Replace text as you type feature on the AutoCorrect tab of the AutoCorrect dialog box, make the most of this powerful feature by creating a list of entries that will save you time and effort.

■ **Tip** You can create AutoCorrect entries up to 255 characters long—enough for several sentences. Longer AutoCorrect entries are great for quickly entering boilerplate text, such as addresses, company names, set phrases, or standard text for documents such as business letters or contracts.

The basic way of creating an entry is to type the error or short version in the Replace text box and the replacement text in the With text box, and then click the Add button. You can create an entry faster by pasting in the replacement text, which is especially handy if it's long.

■ **Note** The quickest way of creating an AutoCorrect entry for a typo is by using the AutoCorrect option when checking spelling, as discussed elsewhere in this chapter.

Regular AutoCorrect entries are plain text, but in Word, you can create formatted AutoCorrect entries as well. A formatted AutoCorrect entry can contain not only formatted text but also other objects, such as tables, graphics, or equations. To create a formatted AutoCorrect entry, follow these steps:

1. In a document, create the entry as you want to be able to enter it. For example, type text and format it, add a graphic, or add a table.

2. Select everything you want to include in the AutoCorrect entry.

3. Open the AutoCorrect dialog box as described earlier. The first part of your selection appears in the With text box.

4. Make sure the Formatted text option button is selected. (If not, click it.)

5. Click the Add button to add the entry.

■ **Note** Word stores formatted AutoCorrect entries in the Normal template, Normal.dotm. Depending on the options you've chosen for Word, you may see a prompt to save Normal when exiting Word after creating a formatted AutoCorrect entry. If you receive this prompt, click the Yes button to save the changes to Normal.

Creating AutoCorrect Exceptions

As well as AutoCorrect entries, you can create AutoCorrect exceptions—specific terms when you don't want AutoCorrect to replace text when it normally would. To create AutoCorrect exceptions, follow these steps:

1. On the AutoCorrect tab of the AutoCorrect dialog box, click the Exceptions button. The AutoCorrect Exceptions dialog box opens. Figure 3-13 shows the AutoCorrect Exceptions dialog box for Word and Outlook, which has one more tab (Other Corrections) than Excel, PowerPoint, and OneNote.

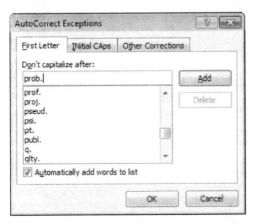

Figure 3-13. *In the AutoCorrect Exceptions dialog box, you can create lists of terms that you want AutoCorrect to ignore.*

2. Click the tab for the type of exception you want to work with:

   - **First Letter.** On this tab, list the terms that end with periods but after which you don't want the next word to start with a capital letter. Office starts you off with a list of built-in terms, such as vol. and wk.

   - **INitial CAps.** On this tab, list the terms that start with two initial capital letters that you don't want AutoCorrect to reduce to a single capital—for example, IPv6.

   - **Other Corrections.** This tab appears only in Word and Outlook. On it, list other terms that you don't want AutoCorrect to fix.

3. Add and delete exceptions as needed:

   - **Add an exception.** Type it in the Don't Correct text box, and then click the Add button.

   - **Delete an exception.** Click it in the list box, and then click the Delete button.

4. In Word or Outlook, select the Automatically add words to list check box if you want the program to automatically add exceptions when you undo a correction it has made.

5. When you have finished working with exceptions, click the OK button to close the AutoCorrect Exceptions dialog box.

Working with Actions

An action is a little button that an Office program inserts automatically in a document where it identifies specific forms of content. The action provides a pop-up menu of actions tailored to that type of content.

Figure 3-14 shows an example of an action on a PowerPoint slide. PowerPoint has identified the text "220 miles" as a distance, so it displays a dotted purple underline under it. When you move the mouse pointer over the underlined text, PowerPoint displays the smart tag button, as in the figure.

Figure 3-14. An action button pops up when you move the mouse pointer over text that the Office program has identified as a candidate for your performing actions on it.

When you move the mouse pointer over the button, the program displays a drop-down arrow that you can click to access a menu of actions—for example, converting the measurement to different units (see Figure 3-15).

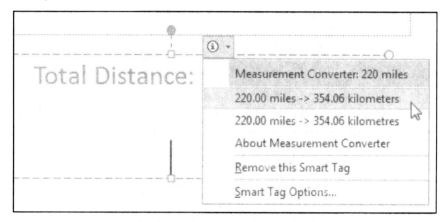

Figure 3-15. You can click the button and choose an action from the menu that appears.

For example, when a document contains a person's name in a format that the program can identify, the program adds an action button that gives you options such as creating a contact for that person.

■ **Note** OneNote doesn't include actions.

To use actions in your documents, you must first turn them on like this:

1. Click the File tab to open Backstage, and then click the Options button. The Options dialog box opens.

2. In the left pane, click the Proofing category to display the Proofing pane.

3. Click the AutoCorrect Options button to open the AutoCorrect dialog box.

4. Click the Actions tab to display its contents. Figure 3-16 shows the Actions tab for Outlook.

Figure 3-16. Turn on actions by selecting the Enable additional actions in the right-click menu check box on the Actions tab of the AutoCorrect dialog box.

5. Select the Enable additional actions in the right-click menu check box.

6. In the Available actions list box or the Recognizers list box, select the check box for each action you want to use.

7. If you've finished choosing options in the AutoCorrect dialog box, click the OK button to close it. Then click the OK button to close the program's Options dialog box.

Checking Spelling and Grammar

To check that your documents are as correct as possible, you can check the spelling in them. Each of the Office programs lets you use the spell checker, which is shared among the programs. Word and Outlook also have a grammar checker.

■ **Note** Computers are great at checking spelling, because in most cases, each word is either spelled correctly or incorrectly—there are few gray areas, and the program doesn't need to understand what the text means to evaluate the spelling. So in most cases it's a good idea to use the spell checker to remove spelling mistakes from your documents.

Checking Spelling

In all of the Office programs except Excel, you can have the spell checker check spelling either as you type or when you're ready to check the whole document. Excel doesn't offer on-the-fly checking, only full checking.

Checking Spelling as You Type

Word, PowerPoint, OneNote, and Outlook can all check your spelling as you type. If you leave this checking turned on, the spell checker puts a wavy red underline beneath any word whose spelling it thinks is wrong.

To check the spelling of a queried word, right-click the word, and then make one of the following choices from the context menu (see Figure 3-17):

- *Replace the word.* Click one of the suggested words at the top of the context menu.

- *Ignore.* Ignore this instance of the apparently misspelled word, but question other instances.

- *Ignore All.* Ignore all instances of the apparently misspelled word in this document.

- *Add to Dictionary.* Add this word to your custom dictionary, so that the spell checker never queries it again.

- *AutoCorrect.* Create an AutoCorrect entry that will fix this typo in future. Click or highlight the AutoCorrect item on the context menu, and then click the correct word on the submenu. The program creates the AutoCorrect entry and corrects the word in the document.

- *Language.* Tell the spell checker that the word is in a different language. Click or highlight the Language item on the context menu, and then click the language on the submenu. If the language doesn't appear, click Set Proofing Language to open the Language dialog box, click the language, and then click the OK button.

- *Spelling.* Launch a full-scale spelling check (see the next section).

- *Look Up.* Click or highlight the Look Up item on the context menu, and then click the research tool (for example, Bing or Encarta Dictionary) on the submenu.

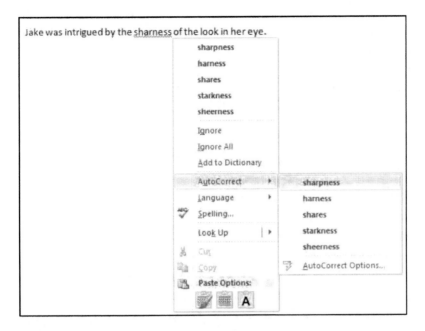

Figure 3-17. *When checking spelling as you type, create an AutoCorrect entry for any spelling mistake you think you may repeat.*

Checking Spelling in the Whole Document

Instead of checking spelling as you type (or as well as doing so), you can run a spell check at any time.

Before you start, position the insertion point or selection where you want to start the check. For example:

- *Word.* Press Ctrl+Home to move the insertion point to the start of the document.

- *Excel.* Click the cell in which you want to start the spell check.

- *PowerPoint.* Click the slide at which you want to start the spell check.

Open the Spelling and Grammar checker by pressing the F7 key or going to the Review tab and giving the appropriate command:

- *Word:* Choose Review ➤ Proofing ➤ Spelling & Grammar.

- *Excel:* Choose Review ➤ Proofing ➤ Spelling.

- *PowerPoint:* Choose Review ➤ Proofing ➤ Spelling.

- *OneNote:* Choose Review ➤ Spelling ➤ Spelling.

- *Outlook:* Choose Review ➤ Proofing ➤ Spelling & Grammar in a message window.

The spell checker displays its first query.

Figure 3-18 shows the Spelling and Grammar dialog box in Word. The Spelling dialog box in Excel, PowerPoint, and OneNote has most of the same features.

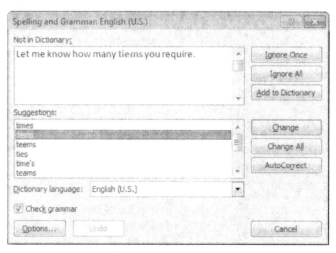

Figure 3-18. *The Spelling dialog box or Spelling and Grammar dialog box suggests ways to fix any problems it finds.*

■ **Note** If the spell checker finds nothing to query, it displays a dialog box telling you that the check is complete. Click the OK button to dismiss the dialog box.

You can now choose how to deal with each query. These are your options:

- *Ignore Once.* Click this button to ignore this instance of the word.

- *Ignore All.* Click this button to ignore all instances of the word in this document (but query it in other documents).

- *Add to Dictionary.* Click this button to add the word to your custom dictionary so that the spell checker never queries it again.

- *Change.* In the Suggestions list box, click the word with which to replace the queried word, and then click this button to change this instance.

- *Change All.* In the Suggestions list box, click the replacement word, and then click this button to change all instances in the document.

- *AutoCorrect.* In the Suggestions list box, click the replacement word, and then click this button to create an AutoCorrect entry and to correct this instance.

> ■ **Tip** When you check spelling, create an AutoCorrect entry for any misspelling you think you may repeat. Each AutoCorrect entry may help only a little, but taken together, they can make a huge improvement in your typing speed and accuracy.

- *Options.* Click this button to open the Proofing pane in the program's Options dialog box.
- *Undo.* Click this button to undo the last spelling change you made.
- *Cancel.* Click this button to end the spelling check before you've dealt with all the queries.

When you've dealt with one query, the spell checker displays the next query. When the spell checker reaches the end of the document after starting anywhere but the beginning, it asks whether you want to continue at the beginning. Figure 3-19 shows the dialog box you'll see in Excel. Click the Yes button or the No button, as appropriate.

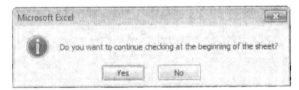

Figure 3-19. *If you start checking from the middle of a document, the spell checker prompts you to continue at the beginning.*

When you have dealt with every spelling query, the spell checker lets you know that the check is complete (see Figure 3-20).

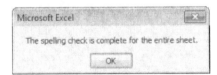

Figure 3-20. *The spell checker confirms that the check is complete.*

Checking Grammar in Word and Outlook

For documents you create in Word or outgoing messages you write in Outlook, you can check the grammar as well as the spelling. As with spelling, you can either check grammar as you type or in a separate operation when you're ready to review your document.

■ **Caution** Before using the grammar checker, make sure you understand how severe its limitations are. The grammar checker doesn't understand the meaning of the text, but it tries to identify the different parts of speech (nouns, verbs, and so on) and their relationship to each other. Many of the grammar checker's suggestions will not improve your documents. Its best features are identifying minor problems such as unsuitable words or missing punctuation.

If you choose to use on-the-fly grammar checking, the grammar checker puts a wavy green underline under any text that it queries. This may be a word, a phrase, or an entire sentence or more, depending on what the query is. You can then right-click the underlined text and choose from the context menu (see Figure 3-21) what to do:

- *Replace the text with a suggestion.* If the grammar checker offers one or more suggestions at the top of the menu, as in the figure, click the one you want to use.

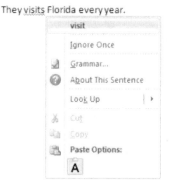

Figure 3-21. When using on-the-fly grammar checking, right-click a query to see what the problem is and whether the grammar checker has a solution.

- *Ignore Once.* Click this item to ignore this instance of the issues.
- *Grammar.* Click this item to open the Spelling and Grammar dialog box.
- *About This Sentence.* Click this item to open a Help window explaining the error the Grammar checker has identified.

When you check grammar along with spelling, the grammar checker runs in tandem with the spell checker, so you see queries from both of them in the Spelling and Grammar dialog box. Figure 3-22 shows an example of a grammar query.

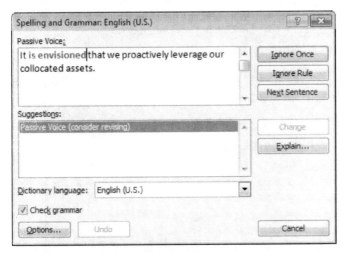

Figure 3-22. If you choose to check grammar, the grammar checker runs alongside the spell checker and displays queries in the Spelling and Grammar dialog box.

From the Spelling and Grammar dialog box, you can take the following actions:

- *Edit the text.* Click in the upper-left text box, and then type your fix for the problem. Click the Change button to apply the change in the document.

- *Ignore Once.* Click this button to ignore this grammar issues once.

- *Ignore Rule.* Click this button to ignore this grammar rule in this document.

- *Next Sentence.* Click this button to move to the next sentence, even if you haven't dealt with the current query.

- *Change.* If the Suggestions box contains a suitable suggestion, click it, and then click this button to replace the text.

- *Explain.* Click this button to open a Help window showing an explanation of the rule.

- *Undo.* Click this button to undo the last change you've made.

- *Cancel.* Click this button to cancel the spelling and grammar check.

Controlling How the Spelling Checker Works

To make the most of the Office programs' spell checker, spend a few minutes customizing its settings. Follow these steps:

1. Choose File ➤ Options to open the Options dialog box.

■ **Note** You can also open the Proofing options by clicking the Options button in the Spelling and Grammar dialog box (in Word and Outlook) or the Spelling dialog box (in the other programs).

---

2. In the left column, click the Proofing category to display the Proofing pane. Figure 3-23 shows the Proofing pane for Word, which has several more options than the other programs.

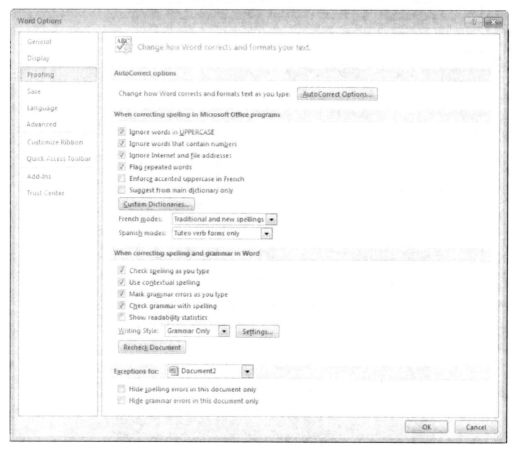

Figure 3-23. You can choose custom settings for the spell checker and grammar checker in the Proofing pane in the Options dialog box.

■ **Note** In Outlook, click the Mail category in the left column to display the Mail pane. Then click the Spelling and AutoCorrect button to display the Editor Options dialog box. Click the Proofing category in the left column.

3. Choose options in the When correcting spelling in Microsoft Office programs area:

   - *Ignore words in UPPERCASE.* Select this check box if you want the spell checker to skip words that appear in uppercase. This is usually helpful, as it helps you avoid queries on technical terms.

   - *Ignore words that contain numbers.* Select this check box to have the spell checker skip any word that includes numbers (for example, IPv6). Clear this check box if you tend to get number typos in words.

   - *Ignore Internet and file addresses.* Select this check box to make the spell checker ignore any URLs (for example, www.apress.com) and file addresses (for example, \\server2\reference\manual.pdf). This option too is usually helpful.

   - *Flag repeated words.* Select this check box to allow the spell checker to query a word that appears twice in succession. This option is good at picking up useless duplication, though you may sometimes need to approve a deliberate repetition.

   - *Enforce accented uppercase in French.* Select this check box if your documents use a French dialect (such as Canadian French) that retains accents on uppercase letters rather than removing the accents (as in standard French).

   - *Suggest from main dictionary only.* Select this check box if you want spelling suggestions only from Office's main dictionary file, not from custom dictionaries you create. Usually, you'll want to clear this check box so that the Spelling checker uses your custom dictionaries.

   - *French modes.* In this drop-down list, choose which spelling type you want the spell checker to use: Traditional and new spellings, Traditional spelling, or New spelling.

   - *Spanish modes.* In this drop-down list, choose whether to use the Tuteo verb forms, the Voseo verb forms, or both for the second person. The choices are Tuteo verb forms only, Tuteo and Voseo verb forms, and Voseo verb forms only.

   - *Dictionary language.* (Excel only.) In this drop-down list, choose the language you want to use—for example, English (US).

4. For all the programs except Excel, you can choose further options in the When correcting spelling in *Program* area (for example, the When correcting spelling in OneNote area). This area contains the following options:

   - *Check spelling as you type.* Select the check box if you want the spell checker to check spelling continually as you type. The spell checker puts a wavy red underline under any word it queries. Clear this check box if you prefer to check spelling in a separate operation.

   - *Use contextual spelling.* Select this check box if you want the spell checker to try to check words in their contexts rather than just on their own. The spell checker puts a wavy blue underline under a word that has a contextual spelling query. OneNote doesn't have this setting.

■ **Note** Contextual spelling is worth using, but it doesn't work consistently because of the complexity of the English language, so don't rely on it. For example, if you write "She bought there car," the spell checker correctly suggests replacing "there" with "their." But the spell checker raises no query with "She wrecked there car."

- *Mark grammar errors as you type.* (Word and Outlook only.) Select this check box if you want the grammar checker to raise queries as you work. The grammar checker puts a wavy green underline under items it queries. On-the-fly grammar checking tends to be distracting, so you'll probably want to clear this check box.

- *Check grammar with spelling.* (Word and Outlook only.) Select this check box if you want to use the grammar checker. Otherwise, clear it.

- *Hide spelling errors.* Select this check box if you want to hide spelling errors in the document. Outlook doesn't have this option. In Word, this option is called Hide spelling errors in this document only; Word also has a Hide grammar errors in this document only check box for hiding grammar queries.

- *Show readability statistics.* (Word and Outlook only.) Select this check box if you want the Spelling checker to display the Readability Statistics dialog box when it finishes a spelling check.

■ **Tip** Don't bother with the readability statistics. The counts of words, characters, paragraphs, and sentences can be useful, but you can get the first three more easily in the Word Count dialog box (choose Review ➤ Proofing ➤ Word Count). The averages of sentences per paragraph, words per sentence, and characters per word have little relevance. The Passive Sentences, Flesch Reading Ease, and Flesch-Kincaid Grade Level are computed statistics that don't accurately assess how easy or hard the document is to read. If you want to know whether a document is hard to understand, ask a colleague to read it.

5. For Word and Outlook, you can also choose grammar and style options. See the next section for details.

6. When you've finished choosing options for the Spelling checker, click the OK button to close the Options dialog box.

Choosing Grammar and Style Options for Word and Outlook

When choosing proofing options for Word and Outlook in the Proofing pane of the Options dialog box, you can also choose options for the grammar checker.

If you turn on the grammar checker by selecting the Check grammar with spelling check box (and the Mark grammar errors as you type check box if you want ongoing error checking as well), you can choose the type of checking you want in the Writing Style drop-down list:

- *Grammar Only.* The grammar checker checks to grammatical problems such as fragments of sentences (rather than complete sentences), misused capitalization and punctuation, and verbs not agreeing with their subjects (for example, "if they buys eggs").

- *Grammar & Style.* The grammar checker also tries to assess your document for clichés, gender-specific words, passive sentences, unclear phrasing, and a dozen or so other potential problems.

This is the overall setting, but if you use the grammar checker, you'll probably want to choose exactly which grammar or style items the grammar checker attempts to analyze. To do so, click the Settings button to the right of the Writing Style drop-down list, and then choose settings in the Grammar Settings dialog box (see Figure 3-24).

Figure 3-24. *Use the Grammar Settings dialog box to control which grammar and style issues the grammar checker raises when checking your documents.*

The Writing style drop-down list at the top shows the setting you chose in the Writing Style drop-down list in the "Options" dialog box. You can change it here if necessary. This acts as the master control for the check boxes in the Style area of the Grammar and style options list box (this area appears below the Grammar area, which you can see in the figure). When you choose Grammar & Style in the Writing style drop-down list, the program selects all the check boxes in the Style area; when you choose Grammar Only, it clears all the check boxes.

The most useful options here are the three in the Require area:

- *Comma required before last list item.* Choose the Always setting to make the grammar checker check for the serial comma (for example, "Peter, Paul, and Mary" rather than "Peter, Paul and Mary"), as is widely used in US English. Choose the Never setting if you don't want to check for the serial comma. Choose the Don't check setting if you don't want to check for this.

- *Punctuation required with quotes.* Choose the Inside setting to make the grammar checker check that punctuation appears inside quotes. Choose the Outside setting to make the grammar checker check that punctuation appears outside quotes. Or choose the Don't check setting to skip checking punctuation placement around quotes.

- *Spaces required between sentences.* Choose the 1 setting to make the grammar checker enforce one space between sentences, as is widely used. Choose the 2 setting to use two spaces between sentences, as some style guides recommend. Choose the Don't check setting to prevent the grammar checker from checking this.

In the Grammar area, clear the check box for any grammar item you don't want the grammar checker to check.

In the Style area, select the check box for each type of check you want to use, and clear the check box for each type of check you want to omit.

When you have finished choosing grammar and style options, click the OK button to close the Grammar Settings dialog box.

Taking Control over Spelling Checks with Custom Dictionaries

The spell checker uses a dictionary file for the language you've chosen (for example, US English). The dictionary file consists of a list of words that are spelled correctly; unlike a conventional dictionary, the file doesn't contain definitions for the words.

You can't change the main dictionary file, but you can add to it by creating custom dictionaries containing words you don't want the spell checker to query. For example, you may need to include technical terms in your documents that the main dictionary file doesn't contain.

Understanding How Custom Dictionaries Work

Office starts you off with a custom dictionary named Custom.dic (Windows associates the .dic file extension with dictionary files). Office stores this dictionary in your user profile in Windows, in a subfolder of the AppData folder in your user folder, and sets the Office applications to add words to it automatically during spelling checks. So when you give the Add to Dictionary command as described earlier in this chapter, the spell checker adds the word to your custom dictionary.

You can stick with using just Custom.dic if you want, but it's often useful to create extra custom dictionaries that contain different types of terms. You can then choose which custom dictionaries to load for a particular project. For example, you may work on some technical documents that need the Spelling checker to accept various technical terms, but you may want the Spelling checker to query the same terms in your other documents.

Normally, you'll just add words to your custom dictionaries, but you may sometimes need to remove words you've added and no longer want the spell checker to accept

Coming to Grips with Your Custom Dictionaries

Office provides the Custom Dictionaries dialog box for creating, editing, and managing custom dictionaries. Here's how to open the Custom Dictionaries dialog box:

1. Click the File tab, and then click Options to open the Options dialog box.

2. In the left column, click the Proofing category to display the Proofing pane.

3. Click the Custom Dictionaries button. The Custom Dictionaries dialog box opens (shown in Figure 3-25 with several dictionaries already added).

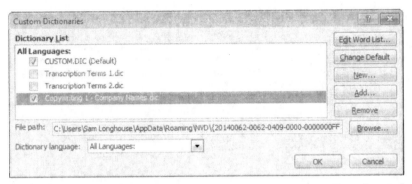

Figure 3-25. Use the Custom Dictionaries dialog box to create, edit, and manage your custom dictionaries.

Creating a Custom Dictionary

To create a new custom dictionary, follow these steps in the Custom Dictionaries dialog box:

1. Click the New button to open the Create Custom Dictionary dialog box. Except for its name, this dialog box is the Save As dialog box that you're familiar with.

2. In the File name text box, type the name you want to give the new dictionary. You can use pretty much any name you want as long as there's no file of that name in the folder you use.

3. If necessary, change the folder. The default folder, the \Microsoft\UProof folder in your user profile, is usually the best place unless you need to share the dictionary with others.

4. Click the Save button. The program closes the Create Custom Dictionary dialog box and creates the dictionary. The dictionary appears in the Dictionary List box in the Custom Dictionaries dialog box.

5. Select the check box next to the dictionary.

The dictionary is now ready for use, but you may need to take one or other further steps.

- *Change the dictionary's language.* The Office programs set the dictionary for use with all languages. If you want to restrict the dictionary to a particular language, click it in the Dictionary List box, and then choose the language from the Dictionary language drop-down list.

- *Make the dictionary the default.* To make this dictionary the one to which the spell checker adds words, click the dictionary, and then click the Change Default button.

■ **Note** If you already have a custom dictionary file (for example, one your company has created), click the Add button in the Custom Dictionaries dialog box. In the Add Custom Dictionary dialog box, select the dictionary file, and then click the Open button. The dictionary then appears in the Dictionary List box in the Custom Dictionaries dialog box, and you can select its check box to make it active.

Adding Words to or Removing Words from a Custom Dictionary

Normally, you'll build a custom dictionary one word at a time by using the Add to Dictionary command when checking spelling. But you can also open a custom dictionary file for editing so that you can make wider-ranging changes to it. This is useful when you need to add a whole list of words to the dictionary or when you need to remove a word that you've added by mistake.

To edit a custom dictionary, follow these steps from the Custom Dictionaries dialog box:

1. Click the custom dictionary in the Dictionary List box.

2. Click the Edit Word List button to open the dictionary for editing. The title bar of the editing dialog box shows the dictionary's name, as you can see in Figure 3-26.

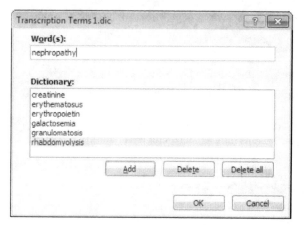

Figure 3-26. When you need to remove words from a custom dictionary or add many words to it, open the dictionary for editing.

■ **Note** You must select the custom dictionary's check box in the Dictionary List box before you can edit the dictionary.

---

3. Add or delete words as necessary:

   • *Add a word.* Type it in the Word(s) text box, and then press the Enter key or click the Add button. You can also paste in a word by pressing Ctrl+V or right-clicking and choosing Paste from the context menu.

■ **Note** The editing dialog box automatically sorts the custom dictionary's contents into alphabetical order.

- *Delete a word.* Click the word in the Dictionary list box, and then click the Delete button. You can also delete the entire contents of the dictionary by clicking the Delete all button, and then clicking the OK button in the confirmation dialog box.

4. Click the OK button to close the editing dialog box.

Turning Off, Removing, or Deleting a Custom Dictionary

When you want to stop using a custom dictionary for the time being, clear its check box in the Dictionary List box is the Custom Dictionaries dialog box. The dictionary remains in the list, and you can start using it again at any point by selecting its check box.

If you want to remove a custom dictionary from the list, click it in the Dictionary List box, and then click the Remove button. The program removes the dictionary from the list, but its dictionary file remains in its current folder. If you need to start using the dictionary again, you can add it by clicking the Add button.

If you want to dispose of a custom dictionary, remove it as just described, and then click the Add button to open the Add Custom Dictionary dialog box. Right-click the dictionary file, and then click Delete on the context menu. Click the Cancel button to close the Add Custom Dictionary dialog box.

Printing Documents

These days, you'll probably share documents with others via e-mail frequently, but there will still be times when you need to print out hard copies of documents to share. For example, you may need to print letters or papers you write in Word, print a page of an Excel spreadsheet, or print a handout for a PowerPoint presentation.

In each of the Office programs, you can choose from a wide range of printing options to make the printout look the way you want. In Word, Excel, PowerPoint, and Outlook, you can use the print preview integrated into Backstage to see at a glance how your document will look when printed.

▓ **Note** OneNote uses an old-style Print dialog box and has a separate Print Preview feature. We'll examine OneNote printing in Chapter 26.

Click the File tab to open Backstage, and then click Print to display the print options. Figure 3-27 shows the Print settings in Backstage in Word, but printing in the other programs works similarly.

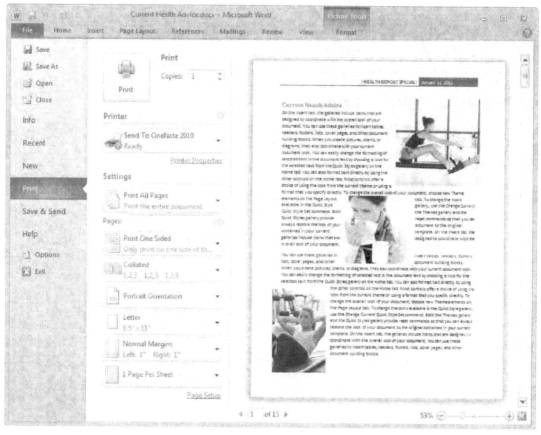

Figure 3-27. The Print item in Backstage gives a built-in preview of the document.

From here, check the preview on the right side to make sure the document looks the way you want it to:

- *Move from page to page.* Click the Previous Page button or Next Page button at the bottom left corner of the preview to move to the previous page or next page. To jump to a page by its number, type the number in the text box and press the Enter key. You can also scroll up and down the document as needed.

- *Zoom in or out.* Use the Zoom Out (–) button or the Zoom In (+) button to zoom by increments, or drag the Zoom slider to zoom freely.

- *Display the whole page.* Click the Zoom to Page button in the lower-right corner of the window.

If the preview looks right, choose options for printing the document. The selection of options varies depending on the program you're using, but these are the main options you'll usually see:

- *Print.* Click this button to print the document with its current settings.

- *Copies.* In this text box, enter the number of copies you want. Either click the spin buttons to adjust the number, or simply type in the number.

- *Printer.* In this drop-down list, select the printer you want to print to. If the list shows no printer you want to use, you can click the Add Printer item to start the process of adding another printer.

▨ **Note** If you need to create a print file for printing the document on a different printer (for example, at a print shop), click the Print to File item at the bottom of the Printer drop-down list.

- *Print What.* In this drop-down list, choose the items you want to print. For example, choose Print All Pages to print all the pages of a Word document, or choose Print Custom Range, click in the Pages text box, and type the range of pages you want (for instance, 3–10).

- *Collated.* When you're printing multiple copies, choose Collated from this drop-down list to print each copy in order, or choose Uncollated to print all the copies of the first page together, all the copies of the second page together, and so on. Uncollated is normally more useful unless you plan to have other people put the pages in order.

- *Orientation.* In this drop-down list, choose Portrait to print with the paper's longer dimension vertical. Choose Landscape to print with the longer dimension vertical.

- *Margins.* In Word and Excel, choose the type of margins from this drop-down list. For a quick change, choose one of the presets, such as Normal, Wide, or Narrow. To adjust the margins manually, choose Custom Margins, and then work on the Margins tab of the Page Setup dialog box.

When you choose a change that affects how the document looks, the preview shows the change. (By contrast, the preview can't show changes such as the number of copies or whether they're set for collation.)

When you've finished choosing settings, click the Print button to print the document. The program sends it to the Windows print queue that serves the printer you chose, and Windows handles the print job from there.

Summary

In this chapter, you've learned how to use several common features of the Office programs. You now know how to control programs using the Ribbon, how to open Backstage to reach its features for managing your documents, and how to share your documents quickly and easily with other people in formats they can read.

We've also looked at ways to save time and effort by using the AutoCorrect feature and those AutoFormat options that you find helpful (while turning off any options that cause unpleasant surprises as you work). You can now choose settings for the spell checker and grammar checker, run one or both, and choose which of its suggestions to accept and which to reject. And you know how to preview your documents and print them.

In the next chapter, I'll show you further vital skills for making the most of the Office programs: How to work with text; use Office's powerful version of Cut, Copy, and Paste; and create tables, shapes, and hyperlinks.

CHAPTER 4

Working with Text and Graphics

In this chapter, I'll show you how to work with text and graphics in the Office programs. As you'll see, the operations are almost the same for each of the programs, so once you've learned to work with text and graphics in one program, you'll be able to work with them in each of the other programs too.

You'll start at the coal face with entering text itself by using the keyboard or other means. Then you'll move along to navigating with the keyboard and selecting objects. You'll then be ready to learn to apply direct formatting to text and objects; use the Cut, Copy, and Paste features; and use the core Find and Replace features that the programs share. I'll then show you how to create tables and add pictures and shapes to your documents. Finally, you'll learn to add to your Office documents hyperlinks that lead the user to another document, take them to a website, or start a new e-mail message automatically.

Entering Text in Your Documents

The main way of entering text in your Office documents is by typing it with the keyboard, but you can also paste text from other documents, scan documents and have your PC identify the text in them, or use speech recognition. You will most likely need to insert symbols in your documents.

Entering Text in Documents Using Copy and Paste

To enter text using Copy and Paste, copy the text from the document that contains it, and then paste it into the Office document. See the section "Using Cut, Copy, and Paste," later in this chapter.

Entering Text by Scanning a Document and Using Optical Character Recognition

If you have a document that contains the text you want to use in an Office document, you can scan the text using a scanner, and then use optical character recognition (OCR) to get the text out of the picture file that the scanner produces.

■ **Caution** To use the text from a hard-copy document in a document of your own, you will typically need to get permission from the copyright holder.

If you have custom scanning software (for example, a program that came with your scanner), use that software. Otherwise, follow these general steps:

1. Open OneNote.

2. Use the Insert ➤ Files ➤ Scanner Printout to scan the document into OneNote.

3. Right-click the scanned picture and choose Copy Text from Picture to recognize the text in it.

4. Switch to the program you want to use the text in, and then paste the text in.

■ **Caution** When you use OCR to recognize a document, always read through the resulting text and compare it to the original. While OCR does its best to recognize the text accurately, it often introduces errors—sometimes surprising ones.

Entering Text by Using Speech Recognition

If your version of Windows includes speech recognition, you can use it both to control the Office programs and to insert text in them.

■ **Tip** Always use a headset microphone for speech recognition, because you will get much better results from having the microphone positioned consistently close to your mouth to pick up your voice clearly. Place the microphone to the side of your mouth rather than in front of it so that it doesn't pick up your breath stream.

To see whether your version of Windows includes speech recognition, click the Start button, click Control Panel, and then choose View by ➤ Small icons or click the Switch to Classic view link. If the Speech Recognition item appears, open it by clicking or double-clicking it (depending on the version of Windows), and then follow the instructions for connecting a microphone and setting up and training Speech Recognition.

Once you have done this, you can dictate into the Office programs.

■ **Caution** When you use speech recognition, proofread your documents closely to catch substitutions of words and phrases. Simple mistakes like substituting "can" for "can't" are usually easy enough to catch, but if Speech Recognition replaces a whole phrase, you may have a hard time working out how the text should actually read.

Inserting Symbols in a Document

By typing, you can easily insert any characters that appear on your keyboard—but many documents need other symbols, such as letters with dieresis marks over them (for example, Ä or ë) or ligatures that bind two characters (for example, Æ).

You can quickly insert one or more symbols in a document by using the Symbol drop-down panel or the Symbol dialog box.

The Symbol drop-down panel is an extra feature that Word, Outlook, and OneNote provide to give you instant access to a shortlist of symbols. This panel starts with a default list of widely used symbols, and then gradually adds the symbols you use most. To reach this panel, choose Insert ➤ Symbols ➤ Symbol. You can then click the symbol you want on the panel (see Figure 4-1).

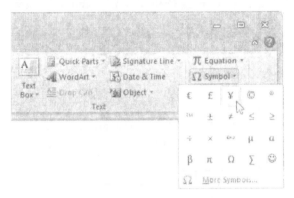

Figure 4-1. In Word, Outlook, and OneNote, you can use the Symbol drop-down panel to quickly insert a symbol. If the symbol doesn't appear on the Symbol drop-down panel, click More Symbols to open the Symbol dialog box.

If the symbol you want doesn't appear on the Symbol drop-down panel in these programs, click the More Symbols item at the bottom. This opens the Symbol dialog box, which you open directly in Excel and PowerPoint by choosing Insert ➤ Symbols ➤ Symbol. Figure 4-1 shows the Symbol dialog box for Word and Outlook; this dialog box includes the AutoCorrect button and the Shortcut Key button, which don't appear in the Symbol dialog box in Excel, PowerPoint, and OneNote.

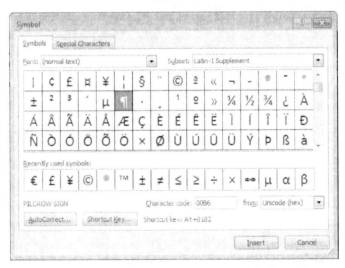

Figure 4-2. The Symbol dialog box lets you quickly choose from a wide range of symbols and special characters.

To find the symbol character you want, first choose the font in the Font drop-down list. The item named "(normal text)" that appears at the top of the list shows the symbol characters in the font you're using.

If the Subset drop-down list appears in the dialog box, you can choose a subset of characters in that font. For example, the Arrows subset contains various arrows, while the Enclosed Alphanumerics subset contains numbers in circles.

In the main box, click the symbol character you want to insert, and then click the Insert button to insert it at the position of the insertion point. Alternatively, double-click the symbol character to insert it without clicking the Insert button. You can then insert further symbol characters as needed.

■ **Tip** In Word, Outlook, and OneNote, you can continue to work in the document while the Symbol dialog box is open. For example, you can type some text in the document, or reposition the insertion point, then click in the Symbol dialog box and use it to insert another symbol character. In Excel and PowerPoint, you must close the Symbol dialog box before you can resume work in the document.

In Word and Excel, the Symbol dialog box includes the Special Characters tab (see Figure 4-3). Click this tab when you need to insert widely used symbols, such as the em dash (—), the paragraph symbol (¶), or special spaces such as the en space (the width of an *n* character in the font).

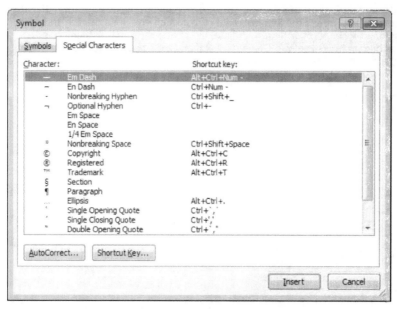

Figure 4-3. *The Symbol dialog box in Word and Excel includes the Special Characters tab, which gives you quick access to widely used symbols such as em dashes and en dashes, optional hyphens, and set-width spaces.*

When you have finished inserting symbols, click the Close button to close the Symbol dialog box. The Close button replaces the Cancel button when you insert a symbol.

Navigating with the Keyboard and Selecting Objects

In Windows, the main means of moving around in a document is by using the mouse. For example, you can click an object to select it, drag the scroll box down the scroll bar to move down the document, or click to place the insertion point where you want to type text.

When you're typing in a document, you may find it handier to use the keyboard to move the insertion point. Table 4-1 explains the standard keyboard shortcuts you can use to move the insertion point in the Office programs.

■ **Note** Because Excel's worksheets consist of cells rather than containing paragraphs, many of the keyboard shortcuts have different effects in Excel.

Table 4-1. Keyboard Shortcuts for Moving the Insertion Point in the Office Programs

Press These Keys	To Move the Insertion Point Like This
Left arrow	One character to the left
Right arrow	One character to the right
Up arrow	Up one line, paragraph, or cell
Down arrow	Down one line, paragraph, or cell
Home	To the start of the line or object
End	To the end of the line or object
Ctrl+Home	To the start of the document
Ctrl+End	To the end
Ctrl+Left arrow	To the beginning of the current word (if the insertion point is in a word) or to the beginning of the previous word
Ctrl+Right arrow	To the beginning of the next word

To work with text or an object in a document, you select that text or object by using the mouse or the keyboard:

- *Select with the mouse*: Click at the beginning of what you want to select, hold down the mouse pointer, and then drag to the end of the selection.

- *Select with the mouse and keyboard*: Click to place the insertion point at the beginning of what you want to select. Hold down the Shift key and click at the end of the selection.

- *Select with the keyboard*: Move the insertion point to the beginning of the selection, hold down the Shift key, and then move the insertion point to the end of the selection (for example, by pressing the arrow keys).

■ **Tip** In Word, you can also select multiple items at once. Select the first item as usual, using either the mouse or the keyboard. Then hold down Ctrl as you select each of the other items with the mouse.

Applying Direct Formatting to Text and Objects

Each of the Office programs lets you apply a wide range of formatting to the text and objects you add to your documents. Each program has different types of formatting suited to its needs, but all the programs support direct formatting—formatting that you apply directly to text or to an object, such as boldface and italic.

■ **Note** Direct formatting is easy to use, but in Word, Outlook, Excel, and OneNote, you can save time by formatting with styles instead. A *style* is a collection of formatting that you can apply in a single click. Not only can you apply formatting more quickly with styles, but you can also change the style's formatting and have the program automatically apply the change to the text that uses the style. This saves even more time and keeps your documents consistent.

You can apply some direct formatting by using the Mini Toolbar that appears automatically when you make a selection. The formatting commands on the Mini Toolbar vary from one program to another, but those for Word (the Mini Toolbar shown in Figure 4-4) are largely typical.

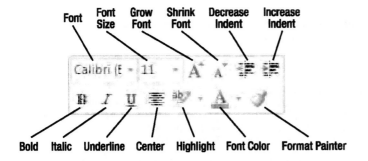

Figure 4-4. The Mini Toolbar, which appears automatically when you make a selection, contains commands for applying widely used direct formatting. This is the Mini Toolbar for Word, but those in the other Office programs are similar.

For a wider range of direct formatting, turn to the Home tab of the Ribbon (or, in an Outlook message window, the Format Text tab). In most of the programs, this tab includes the Font group and the Paragraph group that provide direct formatting commands; in OneNote, the Home tab contains the Basic Text group, which provides some of the same commands, whereas Excel's Home tab includes the Font group and the Alignment group.

Figure 4-5 shows the Home tab for Word with the controls in the Font group and the Paragraph group labeled. As with the Mini Toolbar, the commands vary by program, but each program provides largely similar functionality.

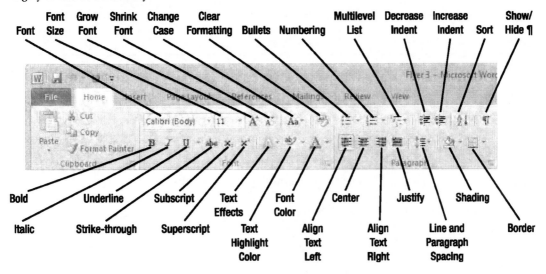

Figure 4-5. In most of the programs, the Home tab of the Ribbon provides a wide range of direct formatting.

With a few exceptions, the controls in these groups are for applying direct formatting. And they're easy to use: In most cases, you select the text or other object you want to affect, and then click the button. For example:

- *Apply boldface*: Select the text you want to affect, or click in a single word. Then click the Bold button to apply boldface. Click again to remove boldface.

- *Change the font*: Select the text you want to affect. Click the Font drop-down list, and then click the font name you want.

- *Change the font size*: Select the text you want to affect, then click the Font Size drop-down list and click the point size you want: 8, 9, 10, 11, 12, 14, 16, 18, 20, or whatever. For a quick change, click the Grow Font button to move up one of the steps in the Font Size drop-down list (for example, from 9 to 10 points, or from 18 to 20 points) or click the Shrink Font button to move down one size.

- *Change the alignment*: Click in the paragraph or click the object you want to affect, and then click the Align Text Left button, the Center button, the Align Text Right button, or the Justify button, as needed.

■ **Note** In an Outlook message window, the Message tab contains the Basic Text group, which contains essential formatting commands.

You can also apply widely used direct formatting by using keyboard shortcuts. Table 4-2 lists the most useful keyboard shortcuts for applying direct formatting.

Table 4-2. Keyboard Shortcuts for Applying Direct Formatting

Formatting Type	Keyboard Shortcut
Boldface	Ctrl+B
Italic	Ctrl+I
Underline	Ctrl+U
Subscript	Ctrl+=
Superscript	Ctrl++ (in other words, Ctrl+Shift+=)
Grow font by one increment	Ctrl+Shift+>
Shrink font by one increment	Ctrl+Shift+<
Align left	Ctrl+L
Align right	Ctrl+R
Center	Ctrl+E

Using Cut, Copy, and Paste

If you've worked with Windows programs before, you're almost certainly familiar with Windows' Cut, Copy, and Paste features. You can use these features as usual in the Office programs, but you can also use the special Clipboard the programs share.

Using Standard Cut, Copy, and Paste in the Office Programs

You can use Cut, Copy, and Paste as usual in the Office programs by using either keyboard shortcuts or the controls in the Clipboard group on the Home tab of the Ribbon (see Figure 4-6):

- *Cut*: Click the Cut button in the Clipboard group or press Ctrl+X.

- *Copy*: Click the Copy button in the Clipboard group or press Ctrl+C.

- *Paste*: Click the Paste button in the Clipboard group or press Ctrl+V.

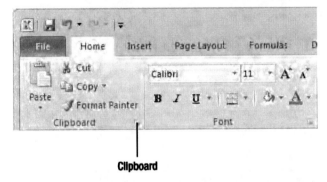

Clipboard

Figure 4-6. You can perform Cut, Copy, and Paste operations by using the controls in the Clipboard group of the Home tab of the Ribbon. For more options, click the Clipboard button in the lower-right corner.

Using the Office Programs' Clipboard

Whereas the Windows Clipboard stores only one item at a time, the Office programs have a special Office version of the Clipboard that can store up to 24 items. To display the contents of this hidden Clipboard, choose Home ➤ Clipboard ➤ Clipboard (clicking the little Clipboard button in the lower-right corner of the Clipboard group on the Home tab of the Ribbon). The program displays the Clipboard task pane (see Figure 4-7).

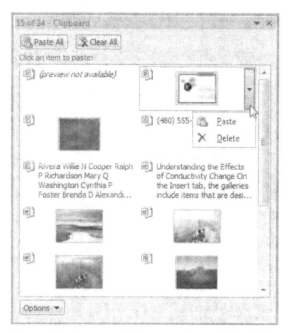

Figure 4-7. Open the Clipboard task pane in an Office program when you need to work with multiple items you've copied. The icon to the left of each item shows the program in which you copied or cut the item.

■ **Tip** Most of the task panes in the Office programs appear *docked*—fixed to one side of to the program window. If you want to position such a task pane freely, click its title bar and drag it away from the side of the window. The task pane becomes free-floating, and you can move it to a different position and resize it by dragging its borders. To dock the task pane again, double-click its title bar.

From here, you can take the following actions:

- *Paste all the items*: Click the Paste All button to paste all the items from the Clipboard into your current document. This can be a handy move if you clear the Clipboard of data first (as described next) and then copy or cut each of the items in the order you want to paste them.

- *Clear the data off the Clipboard*: Click the Clear All button to delete all the data off the Clipboard. Deleting the data is useful when you need to free up the Clipboard for fresh data.

- *Paste an item*: Click the item to paste it at the position of the insertion point. You can also move the mouse pointer over the item, click the drop-down button that appears, and then click Paste.

- *Delete an item*: Move the mouse pointer over the item, click the drop-down button that appears, and then click Delete.

The Options button at the bottom of the Clipboard task pane lets you how control how the Clipboard task pane behaves:

- *Show Office Clipboard Automatically*: Click this item (placing a check mark next to it) to make the Office programs display the Clipboard when you copy or cut an item.

- *Show Office Clipboard When Ctrl+C Pressed Twice*: Click this item (placing a check mark next to it) to make the Office programs display the Clipboard when you press the Ctrl+C shortcut for Copy twice in immediate succession. (This setting makes a double Ctrl+C key press a handy shortcut for displaying the Clipboard.)

- *Collect Without Showing Office Clipboard*: Click this item (placing a check mark next to it) to enable yourself to copy or cut multiple items without the Office programs automatically displaying the Clipboard.

- *Show Office Clipboard Icon on Taskbar*: Click this item (placing a check mark next to it) to make the notification area of the Taskbar display an icon for the Office Clipboard. This icon can be useful for quickly accessing the Office Clipboard.

- *Show Status Near Taskbar When Copying*: Click this item (placing a check mark next to it) to make the Office Clipboard icon in the notification area of the Taskbar display a message saying "Item collected" when you copy or cut an item in the Office programs.

Using Paste Options

When you perform a straightforward Paste operation, the program inserts the copied or cut material at the destination using such formatting as the material has. For example, if you copy an italic paragraph from an e-mail message and paste it into a document, the document receives the italic formatting because it's included in what was copied.

Many times, this type of pasting works well; but other times, you'll want to paste only some of the information copied. To do so, the Office programs provide Paste Options, which lets you control whether the destination document receives both the pasted data and its formatting, just the data, just the formatting, or some other option (depending on the program you're using).

You can use Paste Options in either of two ways:

- *Choose the appropriate option when pasting the data*: If you know that a straightforward Paste operation will give results other than those you want, choose Home ➤ Clipboard ➤ Paste, and then click the appropriate button in the Paste Options area of the Paste panel (see Figure 4-8).

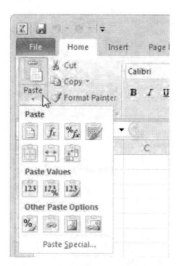

Figure 4-8. When pasting data, you can choose the appropriate option from the Paste panel. Hold the mouse pointer over one of the buttons to see a preview of the effect.

- *Change the paste option after pasting the data*: Often, it's easiest to paste the data, see what result you get, and then choose a different option if necessary. Click the button that the program displays after the pasted data (see Figure 4-9), and then choose the different type of paste option needed.

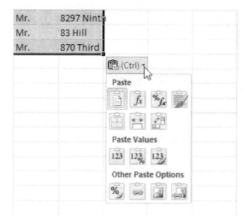

Figure 4-9. You may find it easier to paste the data and then use the Paste Options drop-down menu to change the type of paste operation if necessary.

Setting Paste Options in Word

If you frequently need to choose a different Paste Option after pasting material in Word, change the default settings for Paste Options. Follow these steps:

1. Choose Home ➤ Clipboard ➤ Paste ➤ Set Default Paste to display the Advanced category of the Word Options dialog box.

2. Scroll down to the Cut, copy, and paste section (see Figure 4-10).

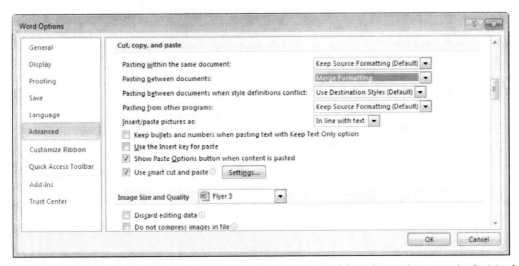

Figure 4-10. Use the options in the Cut, copy, and paste section of the Advanced category in the Word Options dialog box to control how Word handles pasting material within the same document and between documents.

3. In the Pasting within the same document drop-down list, choose the setting you want:

    *   *Keep Source Formatting*: Choose this setting to make the pasted text keep its original formatting. This is usually the best setting for pasting within the same document.

    *   *Merge Formatting*: Choose this setting to make the pasted text receive the formatting of the paragraph into which you paste it.

    *   *Keep Text Only*: Choose this setting to paste the text without formatting.

4. In the Pasting between documents drop-down list, choose the setting you want. The options are the same as for the Pasting within the same document drop-down list, but for pasting between documents, Merge Formatting is usually a better choice.

5. In the Pasting between documents when style definitions conflict drop-down list, choose the setting you want when pasting material from a different document that uses the same style names as the destination document— for example, when you're pasting a Heading 1 paragraph into a document in which the Heading 1 style looks different from the style in the source document.

   • Your choices are Keep Source Formatting, Use Destination Styles, Merge Formatting, and Keep Text Only.

   • The Use Destination Styles item is usually the best choice, as it makes the pasted material take on the look of the destination document.

6. In the Pasting from other programs drop-down list, choose the setting you want for text you cut or copy from another program and paste into Word. The choices are Keep Source Formatting, Merge Formatting, and Keep Text Only. Usually, Merge Formatting is the best choice, but you may prefer Keep Text Only depending on the types of documents you work with.

7. Further down the list, make sure the Show Paste Options button when content is pasted check box is selected. This setting makes Word display the Paste Options button so that you can choose a different Paste Option if needed.

8. Click the OK button to close the Word Options dialog box.

Using Find and Replace

When you need to locate specific text quickly in an Office document, use the Find feature. And when you need to replace specific text with other text, use the Replace feature.

In Word, Excel, and in Outlook's message windows, you access the Find and Replace features primarily through the Find and Replace dialog box, which lets you switch quickly between these two useful features. PowerPoint has a Find dialog box and a Replace dialog box that appear separate but are in fact different manifestations of the same dialog box.

▪ **Note** Each Office program has different Find and Replace functionality to suit its needs. This section covers the common features and introduces you to the basics of using Find and Replace. As well as the Find and Replace dialog box, Word also includes the Navigation Pane for finding text and moving around your documents; see Chapter 7 for details. OneNote handles Find differently (see Chapter 24 for details) and doesn't have a Replace feature.

Locating Text with Find

To use Find, follow these steps:

1. Open the Find and Replace dialog box with the Find tab at the front (or, for PowerPoint, the Find dialog box). Figure 4-11 shows the Find tab of the Find and Replace dialog box for Excel.

- • *Word*: Choose Home ➤ Editing ➤ Find ➤ Find.
- • *Excel*: Choose Home ➤ Editing ➤ Find & Select ➤ Find.
- • *PowerPoint*: Choose Home ➤ Editing ➤ Find.
- • *Outlook*: Choose Format Text ➤ Editing ➤ Find.

■ **Tip** In Excel, PowerPoint, and in Outlook message windows, you can press Ctrl+F to display the Find tab of the Find and Replace dialog box or (in PowerPoint) the Find dialog box. In Word, press Ctrl+F to display the Navigation Pane.

Figure 4-11. *Use the Find tab of the Find and Replace dialog box to quickly locate text in a document. This is the Excel version of the Find and Replace dialog box.*

2. In the Find what box, type or paste the text you want to find.

■ **Tip** If you've performed a search earlier in this session of working with this program, you can open the drop-down list on the Find what box and select the term again.

3. If you need to use any other options, choose them:
   - • *Word or Outlook*: Click the More button to expand the dialog box.
   - • *Excel*: Click the Options button to expand the dialog box (see Figure 4-12).

Figure 4-12. If you need to use further options such as Match case or limiting the search, expand the dialog box by clicking the Options button in Excel or the More button in Word or Outlook.

- *PowerPoint.* Choose the options in the lower part of the Find dialog box.

4. Click the Find Next button to find the next instance of the search term.

5. Click the Close button when you've finished finding items.

Replacing Text with Replace

To replace text in an Office document, follow these steps:

1. Open the Find and Replace dialog box with the Replace tab at the front (or, for PowerPoint, open the Replace dialog box). Figure 4-13 shows the Replace tab of the Find and Replace dialog box for Word.

- *Word*: Choose Home ➤ Editing ➤ Replace.

- *Excel*: Choose Home ➤ Editing ➤ Find & Select ➤ Replace.

- *PowerPoint*: Choose Home ➤ Editing ➤ Replace.

- *Outlook*: Choose Format Text ➤ Editing ➤ Replace.

Figure 4-13. Set up the replacement operation on the Replace tab of the Find and Replace dialog box. This is the Find and Replace dialog box for Word.

▦ **Tip** You can press Ctrl+H to quickly display the Replace tab of the Find and Replace dialog box in Word, Excel, and Outlook, or to display the Replace dialog box in PowerPoint.

---

2. In the Find what box, type or paste the text you want to find.

3. In the Replace with box, type or paste the replacement text.

▦ **Tip** If you've performed a search earlier in this session of working with this program, you can open the drop-down list on the Find what box and select the term again. If you've performed a replacement, you can open the drop-down list on the Replace with box and select the term again.

---

4. If you need to use any other options, choose them:

   - *Word or Outlook*: Click the More button to expand the dialog box (see Figure 4-14).

   - *Excel*: Click the Options button to expand the dialog box.

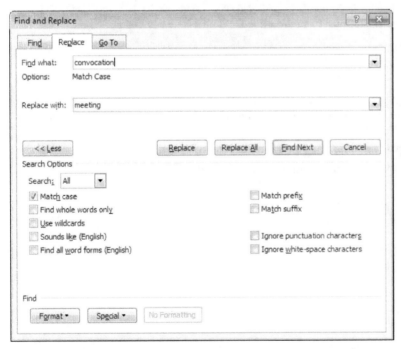

Figure 4-14. If you need to use further options such as Match case or limiting the search, expand the dialog box by clicking the More button in Word or Outlook or the Options button in Excel.

5. Click the button for the operation you want to perform:

   - *Find Next*: Click this button to find the next instance of the search term.

   - *Replace*: Click this button to replace the current instance of the search term with the replacement term and find the next instance of the search term.

   - *Replace All*: Click this button to replace every instance of the search term with the replacement term.

6. When you have finished searching, click the Close button to close the Find and Replace dialog box or the Replace dialog box. The Close button replaces the Cancel button when you start replacing items.

Creating Tables

When you need to lay out data in a regular grid, create a table. A table consists of cells, rectangular areas formed by the intersection of rows and columns. Each table can contain one or more rows and one or more columns.

■ **Note** You can use tables in Word, PowerPoint, OneNote, and Outlook. Excel's worksheets already have a grid structure, so you don't need to create tables for layout in Excel; instead, Excel uses the term *table* to mean a database laid out on a worksheet (see Chapter 15 for details).

Inserting a Table

The most straightforward way of adding a table to a document is to insert it. Inserting a table gives you a regular table with the number of rows and columns you choose.

To insert a table, follow these steps:

1. Position the insertion point where you want the table to appear.

2. Choose Insert ➤ Table ➤ Table, opening the Table panel (see Figure 4-15).

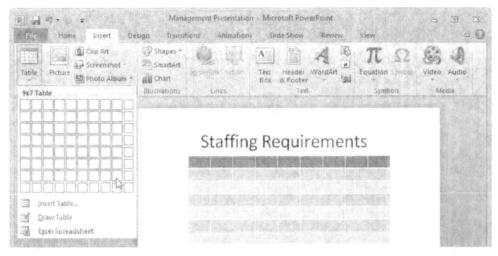

Figure 4-15. Move the mouse pointer over the grid in the Insert Table area of the table panel to display a preview of the table, then click the square for the table you want to insert.

3.   Move the mouse pointer over the grid in the Insert Table area. The program shows a preview of the type of table; for example, five rows of three columns.

4.   When the preview shows the number of rows and columns you want, click the square the mouse pointer is over. The program inserts the table.

▓ **Note** Instead of using the grid on the Table panel, you can click the Insert Table command to display the Insert Table dialog box, and then specify the number of columns and rows in this dialog box. In PowerPoint and OneNote, the Insert Table dialog box has no advantage over the table grid, but it Word and Outlook, the Insert Table dialog box contains options for setting the AutoFit behavior of the table—whether the column widths are fixed, automatically change to fit their contents, or automatically change to fit the window.

Drawing a Table

Inserting a table as described above is usually the easiest way of creating a regular table, but you may also need to create irregular tables by drawing tables instead. You can do this in Word, PowerPoint, and Outlook, but not in OneNote.

To draw a table, choose Insert ➤ Table ➤ Table ➤ Draw Table, and then use the drawing cursor to draw the table layout you want (see Figure 4-16).

- *Draw a cell*: Click with the pen pointer and drag to draw a cell.

- *Erase a line*: Choose Table Tools ➤ Design ➤ Draw Borders ➤ Eraser to change the pen pointer to an eraser, and then click the line you want to erase. Choose Table Tools ➤ Design ➤ Draw Borders ➤ Draw Table when you want to switch back to the pen for drawing more cells.

- *Stop drawing*: Choose Table Tools ➤ Design ➤ Draw Borders ➤ Draw Table to un-press the Draw Table button and turn off the pen pointer.

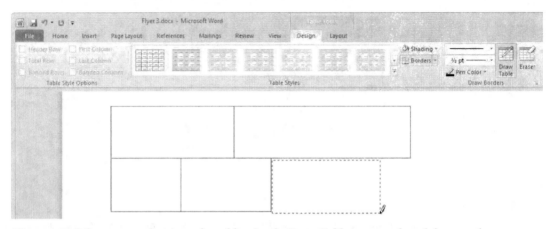

Figure 4-16. When you need an irregular table, give the Draw Table command, and then use the pen pointer to draw the table layout you need.

Merging and Splitting Cells in a Table

To change the layout of the table, you can merge cells together to form a larger cell or split a cell into several smaller cells.

To merge cells together, select the cells, and then choose Table Tools ➤ Layout ➤ Merge ➤ Merge Cells. The program turns the selected cells into a single cell. Any contents of the previous cells appear as separate paragraphs in the merged cell.

To split a cell into multiple cells, click in the cell, and then choose Table Tools ➤ Layout ➤ Merge ➤ Split Cells. In the Split Cells dialog box that the program displays (see Figure 4-17), enter the number of columns and rows you want to create within the cell, and then click the OK button.

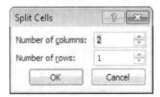

Figure 4-17. Use the Split Cells dialog box to split one existing cell into two or more new cells.

Adding Content to a Table

The most straightforward way to add content to a table is by clicking in the destination cell and then typing the text. Press the Tab key the insertion point to the next cell, or press Shift+Tab to move the insertion point to the previous cell.

You can also paste text into a table you've created. Simply click in the cell, and then paste the text (for example, choose Home ➤ Clipboard ➤ Paste or press Ctrl+V).

▓ **Tip** In Word and Outlook, you can copy text that's laid out with a tab between each separate item, and then paste it into multiple cells at once. Copy the text from the source, switch to Word or Outlook, select the appropriate number of cells in the table, and then give the Paste command.

Formatting a Table

To make a table look the way you want, you format it. You can apply formatting either quickly by using a table style or manually by applying only the formatting the table needs.

To apply a table style, click anywhere in the table, and then choose Table Tools ➤ Design ➤ Table Styles ➤ Quick Styles, choosing the style you want either from the Quick Styles box or from the Quick Styles drop-down panel (see Figure 4-18).

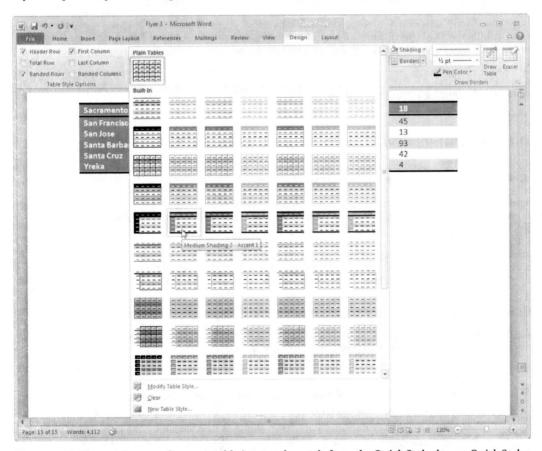

Figure 4-18. The quick way to format a table is to apply a style from the Quick Styles box or Quick Styles drop-down palette on the Design tab of the Ribbon.

After applying a table style, you can customize it by selecting or clearing the check boxes in the Table Style Options group on the Design tab of the Ribbon. For example, select the Header Row check box to apply different formatting to the table's first row so that it looks like a header, or select the First Column check box to apply different formatting to the first column if it contains headings.

If you prefer not to use a table style, you can format a table manually. These are the main techniques you'll need:

- *Borders*: Click the table, choose Table Tools ➤ Design ➤ Table Styles ➤ Borders, and then click the border style you want.

- *Shading*: Click the table, choose Table Tools ➤ Design ➤ Table Styles ➤ Shading, and then click the shading color.

- *Font formatting*: Select the cell or cells you want to format, and then use the controls in the Font group of the Home tab of the Ribbon as for other text.

Using Pictures and Shapes in Your Documents

To give your documents visual interest, you can add various types of graphical content—graphics themselves (I'll use the term to cover all kinds of pictures and images), shapes (anything from a simple arrow or circle to a complex shape), charts, and even movies.

▪ **Note** See Chapter 14 for instructions on creating charts in Excel.

Understanding How You Position Graphical Objects

Even though an Office document appears to be flat, it actually consists of multiple separate layers. Until you add objects to a layer, the layer is transparent, so you see right through it to whatever is underneath. One layer contains the text; the other layers contain graphical objects. Having these multiple layers enables you to position graphical objects either in front of the text layer or behind the text layer. You can also position a graphical object in front of another graphical object; for example, to superimpose one graphical object on another.

Each of the Office programs lets you position graphical objects in the graphics layers, where you can move them freely. Word and Outlook also let you position graphical objects as inline characters in the text layer. When you do this, the program places the graphical object just like a character in the document's text. If you then insert text before the graphical object, it moves further down the document.

Choosing Where to Insert a Graphical Object

Before inserting a graphical object, you need to place the insertion point or selection where you want to insert the object. Place the insertion point or selection like this:

- *Word, OneNote, or Outlook*: Place the insertion point where you want to insert the object.

- *Excel*: Click the cell where you want to place the upper-left corner of the object.

- *PowerPoint*: Click the slide on which you want to insert the object, or select the placeholder in which you want to place the object. If the placeholder is a standard placeholder, you can click one of the three icons at the bottom—the Insert Picture from File icon on the left, the Clip Art icon in the middle (see Figure 4-19), or the Insert Media Clip icon on the right—to start inserting a graphical object.

Figure 4-19. Click the Clip Art icon in a standard placeholder on a PowerPoint slide to start inserting a clip art item in that placeholder.

Inserting Clip Art

When you need a quick illustration in a document, you can insert a clip art item. Office includes a modest but useful set of clip art pictures, videos, and sounds that you can use in your documents. The Clip Organizer can also search a much larger database of clip art items at the Office.com website and download the items you choose.

To insert a clip art item in a document, follow these steps:

1. Position the insertion point where you want to insert the item.

2. Choose Insert ➤ Illustrations ➤ Clip Art to display the Clip Art task pane (shown in Figure 4-20 after a search that has found some results).

Figure 4-20. Use the Clip Art task pane to insert clip art items, photos, movies, or sounds in your Office documents. You can hold the mouse pointer over a search result to see notes about it.

3. In the Search for box, type your search term or terms; for example, farming.

4. Open the Results should be drop-down list, and then select the check box for each file type you want to find: Clip art, Photographs, Movies, and Sounds. Select the All media types item if you want to find everything that matches the keywords.

5. Select the Include Office.com content check box if you want to search online as well. As long as you have an Internet connection, this is usually a good idea.

6. Click the Go button to start the search.

7. Browse through the clip art items that appear in the Clip Art task pane, and then click the one you want to insert in the document. The program inserts the clip art item at its default size; you can resize it as described later in this chapter.

Instead of inserting a clip in the document, you can take several other actions. To do so, move the mouse pointer over the clip art item so that a drop-down button appears, click this button, and then click the appropriate command on the drop-down list (see Figure 4-21).

Figure 4-21. To access further commands for the clip art items you've found, hold the mouse pointer over an item, and then click the drop-down button that appears.

- *Insert*: Click this item to insert the item. Usually, it's easier simply to click the item.

- *Copy*: Click this item to copy the clip art item to the Clipboard so that you can paste it into another program.

- *Delete from Clip Organizer*: Click this item to delete an item you've added to the Clip Organizer. You can't delete the items that come with the Clip Organizer.

■ **Note** To open the Clip Organizer program for managing your clip art, choose Start ➤ All Programs ➤ Microsoft Office ➤ Microsoft Office Tools ➤ Microsoft Clip Organizer.

- *Copy to Collection*: Click this item to display the Copy to Collection dialog box (see Figure 4-22), which you use to add the clip art item to a particular collection in the Clip Organizer. You can do this only for clip art items that are stored on your PC, not those on Office.com.

Figure 4-22. *In the Copy to Collection dialog box, choose which clip art collection to store a clip art item in. You can create a new collection by clicking the New button and working in the resulting dialog box.*

- *Make Available Offline*: Click this item to copy an online clip art item to your PC so that you can use it later whether you're online or offline. The program displays the Copy to Collection dialog box; choose the collection to which you want to add the clip art item, and then click the OK button.

- *Move to Collection*: Click this item to display the Move to Collection dialog box, which you use for moving one of your clips (rather than one of Office's clips) to a different collection. The Move to Collection box is a renamed version of the Copy to Collection dialog box.

- *Edit Keywords*: Click this item to display the Keywords dialog box (see Figure 4-23), in which you can add or edit keywords for a clip you've added to the Clip Organizer. You can't edit the keywords for the Office clips.

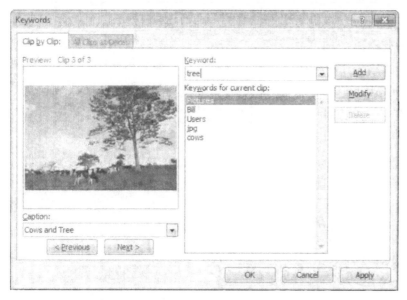

Figure 4-23. Use the Keywords dialog box to add keywords to a clip you've added to the Clip Organizer.

- *Preview/Properties*: Click this item to display the Preview/Properties dialog box showing the clip art item (see Figure 4-24). Use this dialog box to get a better look at an image.

Figure 4-24. Open the Preview/Properties dialog box when you want to get a closer look at an image.

Inserting Pictures in Your Documents

You can insert your own pictures in your Office documents easily too. Follow these steps:

1. Position the insertion point or the selection where you want to insert the picture.

2. Choose Insert ➤ Illustrations ➤ Picture to display the Insert Picture dialog box.

3. Navigate to the folder that contains the picture, and then click the picture to select it.

4. Click the Insert button to close the Insert Picture dialog box. The program inserts the picture.

LINKING A PICTURE TO A DOCUMENT

As discussed in the main text, the normal way of putting a picture in a document is by inserting it. When you do this, the program adds a copy of the picture to the document. The program saves the picture in the document, so even if you move the document, the picture stays in it.

If you need to keep the document's file size down, or if you need to be able to update the picture easily, you can link the picture instead. In the Insert Picture dialog box, click the drop-down button on the Insert button, and then click Link to File on the drop-down menu instead. Instead of inserting a copy of the picture in the document, the program adds a link to the picture file. When you open the document, the program loads the current version of the picture from the file. But if you move the document to a different computer, the link will no longer work, because the program will be unable to find the picture file.

To solve the problem of broken links, the Insert drop-down menu also contains the Insert and Link command. This command both inserts a copy of the picture in the document *and* links it back to the original picture. When you open the document, the program checks to see if the linked version is available. If so, the program loads the linked picture; if not, it displays the version saved in the document.

Adding and Formatting a Shape

If a document needs a drawing, you can create it from scratch by using Office's shapes. Office provides a wide variety of shapes, from arrows and basic shapes through to stars, banners, and callouts.

To insert a shape, follow these steps:

1. Display the area of the document where you want to add the shape. When adding a shape, you don't need to position the insertion point or make a selection.

2. Choose Insert ➤ Illustrations ➤ Shapes to display the Shapes drop-down panel (see Figure 4-25), and then click the type of shape you want to insert.

Figure 4-25. Choose the type of shape from the Shape drop-down panel in the Illustrations group of the Insert tab of the Ribbon. Hold the mouse pointer over a shape to see a ScreenTip showing its description.

3. When you click the shape, the program changes the mouse pointer to a crosshair. With this crosshair, click where you want to place one corner of the shape, and then drag to the opposite corner (see Figure 4-26). It doesn't matter which corner you place first, as you can drag in any direction, but placing the upper-left corner first is usually easiest.

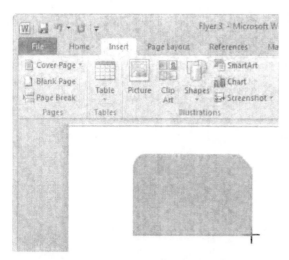

Figure 4-26. Click and drag with the crosshair to place and size the shape you're inserting.

When you release the mouse button, the shape appears with selection handles around it, so you can work with it as described in the following sections. When the shape is selected, the program adds the Drawing Tools section to the Ribbon, which gives you access to the controls on the Format tab.

Applying a Style to a Shape

After inserting a shape, you can apply a style to it from the Shape Styles box or drop-down panel in the Shape Styles group on the Format tab of the Drawing Tools section of the Ribbon. If the style you want appears in the Shape Styles box, click it; otherwise, click the More button (the drop-down button at the right side of the Shape Styles box), and then click the style on the drop-down panel (see Figure 4-27).

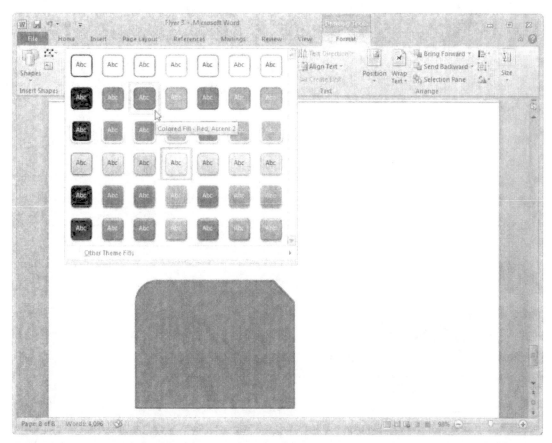

Figure 4-27. *To change a shape's style, open the Shape Styles drop-down panel on the Format tab of the Drawing Tools section of the Ribbon, and then click the style you want.*

To refine the shape, open the Shape Fill drop-down panel, the Shape Outline drop-down panel, or the Shape Effects drop-down panel in the Shape Styles group, and then click the option you want. For example, choose Drawing Tools ➤ Format ➤ Shape Styles ➤ Shape Effects ➤ 3-D Rotation, and then click one of the 3-D rotation effects (see Figure 4-28).

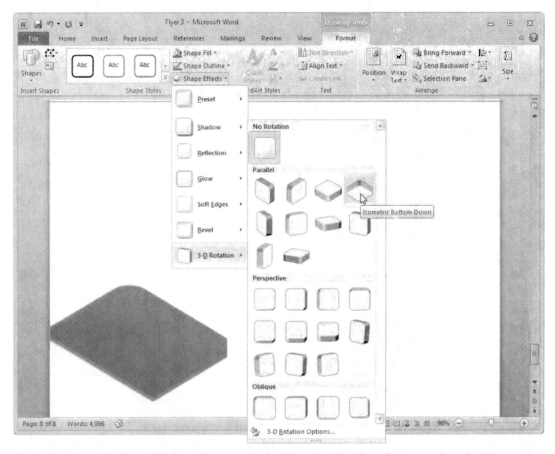

***Figure 4-28.** Use the Shape Fill drop-down panel, the Shape Outline drop-down panel, or the Shape Effects drop-down panel (shown here) to make the shape look the way you want it to.*

Rotating a Graphical Object

After inserting a graphical object, you can rotate it as needed. Click to select the object, and then drag the green handle to the left to rotate counterclockwise (see Figure 4-29) or to the right to rotate clockwise.

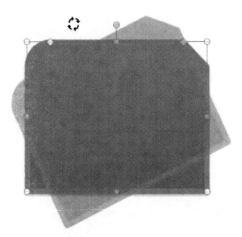

Figure 4-29. Drag the green rotation handle to the left or right to rotate a graphical object.

Positioning a Graphical Object

If you don't get a graphical object in precisely the right position when you insert it, you can easily move it afterward.

The quick way to reposition a graphical object is to click it and then drag it to where you want it. This works well most of the time, but for more precision you can also click the object to select it, and then press an arrow key (for example, the Left arrow key) to nudge it a small distance in the arrow's direction.

When you need to control exactly where the object appears, right-click the object, and then click Size and Position on the context menu to display the Size category in the Format dialog box for the object. Click the Position item in the left panel, and then use the controls in the Position category to control where the object appears. Figure 4-30 shows the Position category in the Format Shape dialog box, which you use for formatting a shape.

Figure 4-30. Use the controls in the Position category of the Format dialog box for an object to position the object precisely.

Choosing Text Wrapping in Word and Outlook

In Word and Outlook, you can place a graphical object either inline with the text or in the graphics layers. If you can't move a graphical object freely, it's most likely because it's inline.

To change how the object appears in Word, click the object, choose Format ➤ Arrange ➤ Position, and then click the position you want on the Position drop-down panel (see Figure 4-31). You can then choose Format ➤ Arrange ➤ Wrap Text, and then click the appropriate option: In Line with Text, Square, Tight, Through, Top and Bottom, Behind Text, or In Front of Text. Click Edit Wrap Points to set up custom text wrapping by placing your own wrap points around the object.

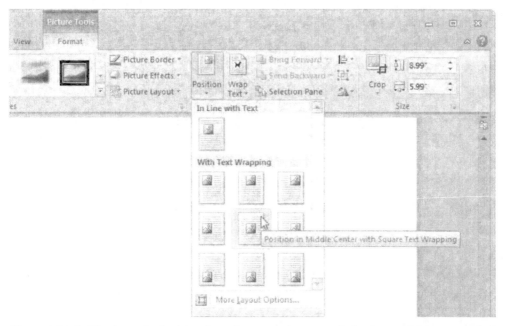

Figure 4-31. *In Word, use the Position drop-down panel to control whether an object appears in line with text or with text wrapping.*

To change how the object appears in an Outlook message, click the object, choose Format ➤ Arrange ➤ Wrap Text, and then click the appropriate option: In Line with Text, Square, Top and Bottom, Behind Text, or In Front of Text.

In either Word or Outlook, you can also click More Layout Options at the bottom of the Wrap Text panel to display the Text Wrapping tab of the Layout dialog box (see Figure 4-32), which provides controls for wrapping the text exactly as you need it.

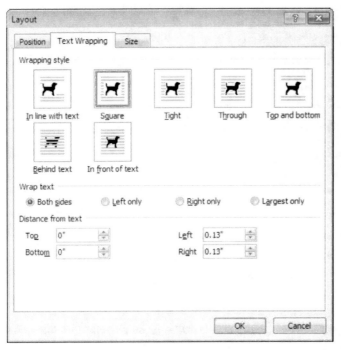

Figure 4-32. Use the Text Wrapping tab of the Layout dialog box to take precise control of how Word or Outlook wraps text around an object.

Making a Picture Look the Way You Want It

After you insert a picture, you can use the controls that appear on the Format tab of the Picture Tools section of the Ribbon to make the picture look the way you want it. You can adjust the picture's colors, apply a picture style to the picture, or crop the picture so that only part of it shows.

Adjusting a Picture's Sharpness, Brightness, Contrast, and Colors

To adjust the sharpness, brightness, or contrast in a picture, click the picture to select it, then choose Picture Tools ➤ Format ➤ Adjust ➤ Corrections to open the Corrections drop-down panel (see Figure 4-33). Click the color correction you want.

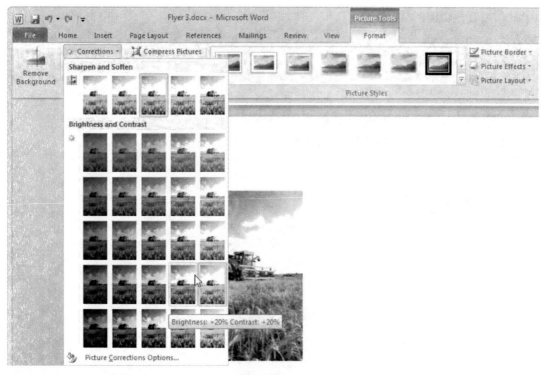

Figure 4-33. To fix problems with a picture's sharpness, brightness, or contrast, open the Corrections drop-down panel and choose the look you want.

To change the colors in a picture, click it, choose Picture Tools ➤ Format ➤ Adjust ➤ Color, and then click the effect you want. The Color drop-down panel has different sections for Color Saturation, Color Tone, and Recolor (for example, Grayscale or Sepia).

To apply an effect such as paint strokes or a light screen to a picture, click the picture, choose Picture Tools ➤ Format ➤ Adjust ➤ Artistic Effects, and then click the effect you want.

To reset a picture to its original look, choose Picture Tools ➤ Format ➤ Adjust ➤ Reset Picture.

▒ **Tip** If you need to replace a picture you've worked on with another picture, choose Picture Tools ➤ Format ➤ Adjust ➤ Change Picture, and then use the Insert Picture dialog box to pick the replacement picture. The program retains any cropping or effects you've applied to the picture in the document, which saves you from having to reapply them.

Applying a Picture Style

To apply a picture style to a picture, click the picture, click the Format tab of the Picture Tools section of the Ribbon to display it, and then click the picture style you want. If the picture style appears in the Quick Styles box in the Picture Styles group, click it there; otherwise, click the More button (the drop-down button at the right side of the Quick Styles box) and then click the picture style on the Quick Styles drop-down panel (see Figure 4-34).

Figure 4-34. *Choose the picture style from the Quick Styles box or drop-down panel in the Picture Styles group of the Format tab of the Ribbon.*

Cropping a Picture

If you need the document to show only part of a picture rather than the whole picture, you can crop off the parts you don't want.

The Office programs let you crop a picture in several ways, but this way is usually the easiest:

1. Click the picture to select it. The program adds the Picture Tools section to the Ribbon.

2. Click the Format tab on the Picture Tools section of the Ribbon if the program has not displayed it.

3. Choose Picture Tools ➤ Format ➤ Size ➤ Crop, clicking the top part of the Crop button rather than the drop-down button. The program displays crop handles on the picture (see Figure 4-35).

Figure 4-35. *The quick way of cropping is to drag the crop handles until they encompass the part of the picture you want to keep.*

4. Drag the crop handles to make the cropping area contain the part of the picture you want to show:

   • Shift+drag to crop the image proportionally.

   • Ctrl+drag to crop the image evenly about its center point.

   • Ctrl+Shift+drag to crop the image proportionally about its center point.

░ **Tip** If you make the crop area exactly the size you need, you can click and drag within the crop area to make a different part of the picture appear in it.

---

5. Click the Crop button again to turn off the Crop tool, or click elsewhere in the document to deselect the picture. The program applies the cropping to it.

▓ **Note** For more cropping options, choose Picture Tools ➤ Format ➤ Size ➤ Crop, clicking the Crop drop-down button rather than the top part of the button. On the drop-down menu that appears, choose Crop to Shape if you want to make the picture fit into a shape; choose Aspect Ratio if you want to crop the picture to a specific aspect ratio, such as 4:3 or 3:5.

Inserting SmartArt

When you need to create an illustration such as an organization chart, a flow chart, or a Venn diagram, use Office's SmartArt feature. Follow these steps:

1. Position the insertion point or the selection where you want to insert the SmartArt object.

2. Choose Insert ➤ Illustrations ➤ SmartArt to display the Choose a SmartArt Graphic dialog box (shown in Figure 4-36 with settings chosen).

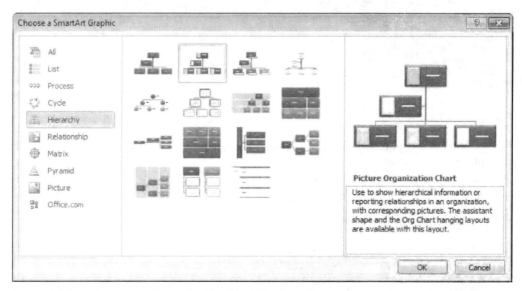

Figure 4-36. In the Choose a SmartArt Graphic dialog box, choose the type of SmartArt graphic you want to create.

▓ **Note** In PowerPoint, if you're inserting the SmartArt on a slide that has a standard placeholder, click the Insert SmartArt Graphic icon in the placeholder to display the Choose a SmartArt Graphic dialog box. Otherwise, choose Insert ➤ Illustrations ➤ SmartArt as in the other programs.

3. In the left list box, click the category of graphic you want; for example, choose Hierarchy if you want to create an org chart.

4. In the main pane, click the type of graphic; for example, Picture Organization Chart.

5. Click the OK button to close the dialog box. The program inserts the SmartArt graphic, displays the Type your text here window next to it, and adds the SmartArt Tools section to the Ribbon (see Figure 4-37).

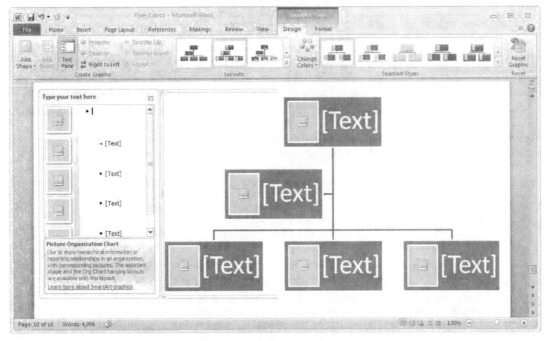

Figure 4-37. When you insert a SmartArt graphic, the program displays the Type your text here window next to it and adds the SmartArt Tools section to the Ribbon.

■ **Note** If the program doesn't display the Type your text here window, choose SmartArt Tools ➤ Design ➤ Create Graphic ➤ Text Pane to display it.

6. Type the text for each item in the Type your text here window. As you do, the program adds the text to the SmartArt graphic (see Figure 4-38).

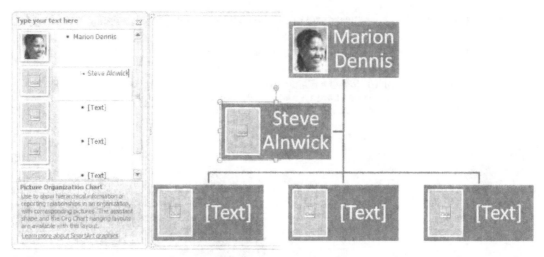

Figure 4-38. Add the text to the SmartArt graphic by typing in the Type your text here window. To add other items, such as the pictures shown here, click the placeholder and use the dialog box that opens.

7. Add any other items the SmartArt graphic needs. For example, add pictures to a Picture Organization Chart by clicking each picture placeholder in turn and then, in the Insert Picture dialog box that opens, selecting the picture to use. Click the picture placeholder in the Type your text here window once to open the Insert Picture dialog box; double-click the picture placeholder in the SmartArt graphic itself.

8. Resize the SmartArt graphic to suit the slide best. For example, you may want to make it as big as will fit on the slide to enable the audience to read it easily.

9. If you need to change the layout of the SmartArt graphic, choose another layout from the Change Layout box or Change Layout drop-down panel in the Layout group of the Design tab on the SmartArt Tools section of the Ribbon.

10. Apply a style to the SmartArt graphic by choosing a style from the Quick Styles box or the Quick Styles drop-down panel in the SmartArt Styles group of the Design tab.

When you have finished creating the SmartArt graphic, save the document as usual.

Arranging Graphical Objects to Control Which Is Visible

When you have placed multiple graphical objects in the same area of a document, you may need to arrange the order in which they appear in the document's layers to control how they appear in relation to each other. For example, you may need to move a particular object to the front of the stack of document layers, so that it appears on top of the other objects, or move another object back so that it appears behind one of its companion objects.

To change where an object appears in the layers, follow these steps:

1. Click the object to select it. The program adds the appropriate section to the Ribbon—for example, the Drawing Tools section if you click a shape.

▨ **Note** If the object is obscured so that you can't click it, click another object to add the section to the Ribbon, click the Format tab, and then choose Arrange ➤ Selection pane to display the Selection and Visibility pane. In the list of objects, click the object you want to affect. To turn off the display of an object, clear the check box to the right of it.

2. Make sure the Format tab of the Ribbon is displayed. If not, click it.

3. Go to the Arrange group on the Format tab, and then click the appropriate control:

   • *Bring Forward*: Click this button to bring the object forward by one layer. To bring it all the way to the front, click the Bring Forward drop-down button, and then click Bring to Front.

   • *Send Backward*: Click this button to send the object backward by one layer. To send the object all the way to the bock, click the Send Backward drop-down button, and then click Send to Back.

▨ **Note** You can also move an object forward or back by right-clicking it and using the Bring to Front command and submenu and the Send to Back command and submenu on the context menu. For example, to send an object backward, right-click it and choose Send to Back ➤ Send Backward.

Creating Hyperlinks

As you know from browsing the web, a *hyperlink* is text or an object on a web page that's linked to another location—for example, to another web page or to another place on the same web page. You can insert a hyperlink in just about any Office document—a Word document, an Excel workbook, a PowerPoint presentation, or an e-mail message or task you're creating in Outlook.

You can create both text hyperlinks and object hyperlinks. A text hyperlink appears as underlined text. An object hyperlink appears as just the object; for example, a picture or a shape. For either type of hyperlink, you can choose whether to display a ScreenTip when the user holds the mouse pointer over the hyperlink, as in the text hyperlink shown in Figure 4-39.

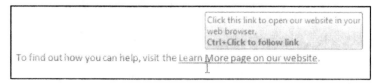

Figure 4-39. When you create a hyperlink, you can include a ScreenTip that appears when the user holds the mouse pointer over the hyperlink.

To insert a hyperlink, follow these steps:

1. Choose the type of hyperlink you want to insert:

    - *New text hyperlink*: Position the insertion point where you want the hyperlink to appear.

    - *Hyperlink that displays existing text*: If the document already contains text that you want to use as the display text for the hyperlink, select that text.

    - *Object hyperlink*: Insert the object in the document, and then select it. For example, you can insert a graphic by using the technique explained earlier in this chapter.

2. Choose Insert ➤ Links ➤ Hyperlink to display the Insert Hyperlink dialog box (see Figure 4-40).

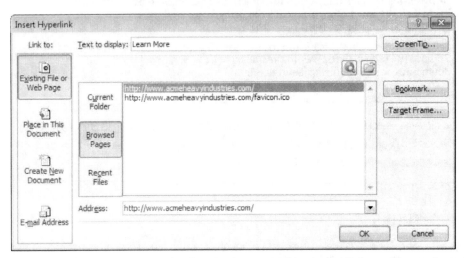

Figure 4-40. *Use the Insert Hyperlink dialog box to quickly create a link to a file, a web page, an e-mail address, or a document.*

3. In the Link to column on the left, click the button for the link destination you want to use:

    - *Existing File or Web Page*: Click this button when you want the hyperlink to point to a file on your PC or network or to a web page. For a file, click either the Current Folder button or the Recent Files button, and then browse to the file you want. For a web page, click the Browsed Page button, and then either click the page in the list or type or paste its URL into the Address box.

    - *Place in This Document*: Click this button to make the hyperlink lead to a different point in the document. In Word or Outlook, you can make the hyperlink point to the top of the document, to a heading, or to a bookmark. In Excel, you can choose a cell reference (for example, cell A1 on the current worksheet) or a range you've named. In PowerPoint, you can make the hyperlink point to a slide, to a title on a slide, or to a custom slide show that you have set up.

■ **Note** Hyperlinks work differently in OneNote than in the other Office programs. In OneNote, choose Insert ➤ Links ➤ Link, and then work in the Link dialog box. You can make the link point to a URL, to another file, or to a location in OneNote.

- *Create New Document*: Click this button if you want to make the link lead to a new document that you create either now or later. Usually, it's easiest to link to an existing file to avoid slip-ups.

- *E-mail Address*: Click this button if you want to make the link start a new e-mail message to the address you specify in the E-mail address box (see Figure 4-41). You can type a suggested subject in the Subject box; the sender can change the subject, but entering a default helps avoid you receiving messages with blank subject lines by accident.

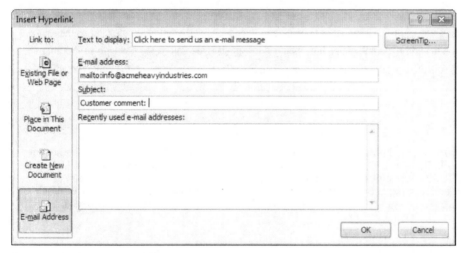

Figure 4-41. *Click the E-mail Address button in the Link to bar to insert a hyperlink that starts a new message to an e-mail address you specify.*

4. In the Text to display box, enter the text that you want the document to display for the hyperlink.

   - If you selected text in the document in step 1, that text appears here.

   - If you selected an object in step 1, the Text to display box shows <<Selection in Document>> and is not available for change.

5. To add to the hyperlink a ScreenTip that appears when the user holds the mouse pointer over it, click the ScreenTip button. In the Set Hyperlink ScreenTip dialog box (see Figure 4-42) that opens, type the ScreenTip, and then click the OK button.

Figure 4-42. You can add a ScreenTip to a hyperlink to provide a more detailed explanation of where the link goes or why the user may want to click it.

6. When you have finished specifying the details of the hyperlink, click the OK button to insert it in the document.

You can now test your hyperlink by Ctrl+clicking it.

■ **Note** To edit a hyperlink, right-click the text or object, and then click Edit Hyperlink on the context menu; the Office program opens the Edit Hyperlink dialog box, which is the Insert Hyperlink dialog box with a different name. To remove a hyperlink, right-click the text or object, and then click Remove Hyperlink on the context menu.

Summary

In this chapter, you've learned how to work with text and objects in the Office programs. You now know how to navigate with the keyboard; select objects using the mouse, the keyboard, or both; and apply the most widely used types of formatting to text and objects. You can also use the Cut, Copy, and Paste features; find and replace text; and add tables, graphical objects, and hyperlinks to your documents.

In the next chapter, I'll show you how to customize the Office programs to suit your needs.

CHAPTER 5

Customizing Office to Suit You

How the Office programs look and behave when they are first launched is the result of many focus groups. If the programs' default looks and behavior don't suit you, you can easily change the programs' looks and behavior to suit your needs.

Microsoft lets you customize the Office programs in many ways. This chapter shows you the most important customizations you can perform in all the programs or most of the programs. Later chapters cover other customizations.

We'll start with the Quick Access Toolbar, which you'll almost certainly want to customize with the buttons most useful to you. You can also customize the Ribbon by adding and removing groups of controls or entire tabs. You can even change the items that each program displays on the status bar, which can be a great help in making the information you need available to you.

Beyond these direct customizations to the user interface, each program has hundreds of settings you can use to change how the programs work. In the second half of this chapter, we'll look at two key areas of options common to the programs: The General options, which control vital aspects of the programs' looks and behavior, and the Save options, which control the default format and folder that the programs use to store your documents.

Customizing the Quick Access Toolbar, Ribbon, and Status Bar

To put the controls and information you need at your fingertips, you can customize the Quick Access Toolbar, the Ribbon and the Status Bar.

Customizing the Quick Access Toolbar

The best place to start customizing the Office programs is the Quick Access Toolbar. This is the short row of buttons that appears at the left end of the title bar in the program window, just to the right of the control-menu icon.

By customizing the Quick Access Toolbar, you can put the commands you find most useful right where you can reach them with a single click of the mouse.

You can customize the Quick Access Toolbar in four ways:

- *Add a frequently used button*. The programs make it easy to add any of a dozen or so frequently-used buttons to the Quick Access Toolbar.

- *Add any command from the Ribbon.* Instead of choosing from the list of frequently-used buttons, you can quickly add any command that's on the Ribbon.

- *Add any other command.* Some commands don't appear on the Ribbon, but you can add them to the Quick Access Toolbar easily enough.

- *Move the Quick Access Toolbar to below the Ribbon.* You can display the Quick Access Toolbar below the Ribbon instead of in the title bar.

Adding Buttons for Frequently Used Commands to the Quick Access Toolbar

The fastest way to customize the Quick Access Toolbar is to add buttons for frequently-used commands. To customize the Quick Access Toolbar like this, follow these steps:

1. Click the Customize Quick Access Toolbar button at the right end of the Quick Access Toolbar to display the Customize Quick Access Toolbar menu (see Figure 5-1).

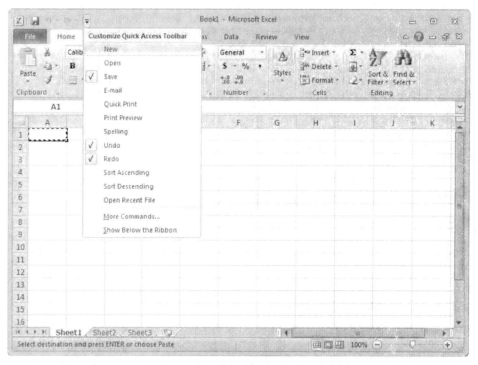

Figure 5-1. Use the Customize Quick Access Toolbar menu to quickly add buttons for frequently-used commands to the Quick Access Toolbar.

2. Click the item you want to add to the menu or remove from it:

- When you click an item that's not currently displayed, a check mark appears next to the item.

- When you click an item that's on the Quick Access Toolbar, the check mark disappears from next to it.

3. If you need to add or remove other items, repeat steps 1 and 2 until you've finished.

Adding a Ribbon Command to the Quick Access Toolbar

The menu of frequently used commands makes it easy to customize the Quick Access Toolbar a little, but you'll probably want to add other buttons to the Quick Access Toolbar as well. The easiest way to do so is to add the buttons from the Ribbon. This prevents you having to locate the button by name in the Options dialog box, which the next method requires.

Simply right-click the button on the Ribbon, and then click Add to Quick Access Toolbar on the context menu. The program adds the button to the right of the last button on the Quick Access Toolbar.

To remove a button you've added to the Quick Access Toolbar, right-click it, and then click Remove from Quick Access Toolbar on the context menu.

■ **Note** Customizing the Quick Access Toolbar using this technique makes the change for all documents rather than for just the active document. To make the change for just the active document, use the technique described in the following section.

Adding Buttons for Other Commands to the Quick Access Toolbar

If you really want to dig into customizing the Quick Access Toolbar, or if you want to rearrange the icons that appear on it, work in the Options dialog box for the program. Follow these steps:

1. Right-click anywhere in the Quick Access Toolbar, and then click Customize Quick Access Toolbar on the context menu. The program opens the Options dialog box and selects the Quick Access Toolbar item in the left column. Figure 5-2 shows the Word Options dialog box.

Figure 5-2. Use the Options dialog box when you want to customize the Quick Access Toolbar extensively.

2. In Word, Excel, and PowerPoint, click the Customize Quick Access Toolbar drop-down list in the upper-right corner of the Options dialog box, and then choose the item you want to affect:

- *For all documents (default).* Select this item to make your changes apply to all the documents you create (except for documents that you customize separately). This is what you'll normally want to do.

- *For document.* Select this item to make your changes affect only the active document. Customizing a document like this can be useful when you plan to distribute it on its own. For example, you may want to put all the commands the document needs on the Quick Access Toolbar so that readers don't need to use the Ribbon.

3. Open the Choose commands from drop-down list and choose the category of commands you want to use:

- *Popular Commands.* These are the commands that appear on the Customize Quick Access Toolbar menu. So if you've already used that menu to customize the Quick Access Toolbar, you'll probably want to select a different category.

- *Commands Not in the Ribbon*. This choice gives you access to commands that don't appear in the Ribbon, which is what you'll often want.

- *All Commands*. This choice gives you the full range of commands available. The list is long, but you can be sure the command you need is somewhere on it.

- *Macros*. If you record or write your own macros, select this category when you want to put buttons on the Quick Access Toolbar that run the macros.

- *File Tab*. This category gives you access to the Backstage commands.

- *Home Tab and other tabs*. These categories display all the commands associated with these tabs.

4. In the left list box, click the command you want to add to the Quick Access Toolbar.

5. In the right list box, click the command you want to add the new command after.

6. Click the Add button to add the command to the right list box.

■ **Note** To remove an item from the Quick Access Toolbar, click it in the right list box, and then click the Remove button.

---

7. If you want to position the Quick Access Toolbar below the Ribbon rather than in the title bar, select the Show Quick Access Toolbar below the Ribbon check box.

8. If you want to rearrange the buttons on the Quick Access Toolbar, select a button in the right list box, and then click the up arrow button or the down arrow button until the button appears where you want it.

9. When you have finished customizing the Quick Access Toolbar, click the OK button to close the Options dialog box.

Resetting the Quick Access Toolbar to Its Default Buttons

If you need to restore the default set of buttons to the Quick Access Toolbar, follow these steps:

1. Right-click anywhere in the Quick Access Toolbar, and then click Customize Quick Access Toolbar on the context menu. The program opens the Options dialog box and selects the Quick Access Toolbar item in the left column.

2. In the lower-right corner, click the Reset drop-down button, and then choose Reset only Quick Access Toolbar from the menu. The program displays the Reset Customizations dialog box (see Figure 5-3).

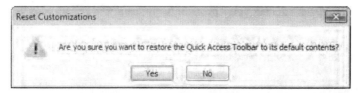

Figure 5-3. You can wipe out any customizations you've made to the Quick Access Toolbar by resetting it.

3. Click the Yes button. The program resets the Quick Access Toolbar.

4. Click the OK button to close the Options dialog box.

Moving the Quick Access Toolbar to Below the Ribbon

When the Quick Access Toolbar is in the title bar, you need to keep the number of buttons it contains low so that it doesn't take over the title bar. To give yourself more space, you can move the Quick Access Toolbar to below the Ribbon so that it stretches the full width of the program window.

To move the Quick Access Toolbar, click the Customize Quick Access Toolbar button at the right end of the Quick Access Toolbar, and then click Show Below the Ribbon on the menu that appears.

To put the Quick Access Toolbar back in the title bar, click the Customize Quick Access Toolbar button again, but this time choose Show Above the Ribbon.

Customizing the Ribbon

While you'll almost certainly want to customize the Quick Access Toolbar, you may not want to customize the Ribbon—for two reasons.

- First, the Ribbon's standard layout works well for many people. You do have to learn where to find the commands you need, but in general, Microsoft has done a good job of laying out the commands by what they do.

- Second, you can customize the Ribbon only in limited ways. You might want to knock out existing buttons that you don't need and replace them with buttons for commands that you do find useful. But you can't. Instead, you can customize the Ribbon only in larger strokes: by adding a new tab, by adding a new group to which you can then add the buttons you want, or by removing a complete group. This makes sense, as it deals with an entire tab or a horizontal section of a tab, but it may not give you the level of control you'd like to have.

If you do want to customize the Ribbon, follow these steps:

1. Right-click anywhere in the Ribbon, and then click Customize the Ribbon on the context menu. The Office program displays its Options dialog box with the Customize Ribbon item selected in the left pane. Figure 5-4 shows the Customize Ribbon pane for Word with customization underway.

Figure 5-4. *Use the Customize Ribbon pane in the Options dialog box to create new Ribbon tabs and Ribbon groups.*

2. In the Customize the Ribbon drop-down list, choose the tabs you want to change:

   - *Main Tabs.* This is usually the best place to start, because it shows the regular set of tabs—Home, Insert, View, and so on.

   - *All Tabs.* Choose this item to display the full list of tabs.

   - *Tool Tabs.* Choose this item to display the list of tool tabs, such as the SmartArt Tools tab, the Chart Tools tab, and the Picture Tools tab.

3. To add a new tab, follow these steps:

   - In the list of tabs in the large box on the right, click the tab after which you want to add the new tab.

   - Click the New Tab button. The program adds the new tab, names it New Tab (Custom), and creates a new group in it called New Group (Custom).

- Click the New Tab (Custom) name, and then click the Rename button to display the Rename dialog box for tabs. Type the tab name in the Display name text box, and click the OK button.

▦ **Note** You can also add a new group to an existing tab. Double-click the tab to display this groups, and click the group you want to add the new group after. Click the New Group to add a new group named New Group (Custom), and then rename the group as described nearby.

- Click the New Group (Custom) name, and then click the Rename button to display the Rename dialog box for groups (see Figure 5-5).

Figure 5-5. Type the name for a custom group in the Display name text box in this Rename dialog box.

- If you want to assign an icon to the group, click it in the Symbol box.
- Type the name for the group, and then click the OK button.

4. To add items to the group, follow these steps:

- In the Choose commands from drop-down list, select the source of commands. For example, choose All Commands if you want access to every single command, or choose Macros if you want to add buttons for running macros.
- In the right list box, click your new group. If you've already added buttons to the group, click the command you want to add.
- Click the command in the left list box.
- Click the Add button. The program adds the button to the group.

- If necessary, you can arrange buttons in a group by clicking the button and then clicking the up arrow button or the down arrow button.

5. To remove a group from a tab, click the group in the right list box, and then click the Remove button.

6. When you have finished customizing the Ribbon, click the OK button to close the Options dialog box.

Resetting the Ribbon to Its Default Settings

If you find that your Ribbon customization doesn't meet your expected results, you can reset either a tab or all customizations. All customizations include changes you've made to the Quick Access Toolbar, so be prepared to lose these as well when you reset the Ribbon.

If you need to reset the Ribbon, follow these steps:

1. Right-click anywhere in the Ribbon, and then click Customize Ribbon on the context menu. The program opens the Options dialog box and selects the Customize Ribbon item in the left column.

2. To reset a tab, click it in the right list box, click the Reset drop-down button in the lower-right corner, and then click Reset only selected Ribbon tab. The program resets the tab without confirmation.

3. To reset all of the Ribbon and the Quick Access Toolbar, click the Reset drop-down button in the lower-right corner, and then choose Reset all customizations. In the confirmation dialog box that the program displays (see Figure 5-6), click the Yes button.

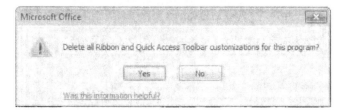

Figure 5-6. *Resetting all the changes you've made to the Ribbon also resets the Quick Access Toolbar.*

4. Click the OK button to close the Options dialog box.

Sharing Customizations with Other PCs

After customizing the Quick Access Toolbar and Ribbon on one PC, you can easily share the customizations with another PC. To do so, follow these steps:

1. In the program that contains the customizations, right-click anywhere in the Ribbon, and click Customize Ribbon on the context menu. The program opens the Options dialog box and selects the Customize Ribbon item in the left column.

2. In the lower-right corner, click the Import/Export drop-down button, and click Export All Customizations. The program opens the File Save dialog box.

3. Either accept the suggested name (for example, PowerPoint Customizations) or type another name over it.

4. Click the Save button. The program saves the file.

5. Click the Cancel button to close the Options dialog box.

6. Transfer the customizations file to another computer. For example, put it on a network drive or a USB stick, or send it via e-mail.

7. On the other computer, open the same program and open the Customize Ribbon pane as described in step 1.

8. Click the Import/Export drop-down button, and then choose Import Customization File. The program displays the File Open dialog box.

9. Choose the customizations file, and then click the Open button. The program displays a confirmation message box (see Figure 5-7).

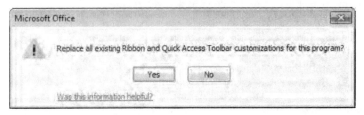

Figure 5-7. You can quickly import customizations on another PC.

10. Click the Yes button. The program imports the customizations.

11. Click the OK button to close the Options dialog box.

Customizing the Status Bar

The status bar at the bottom of each program window shows information about the document you're currently using and what you're doing. For example:

- *Word*. The status bar shows the page readout (such as "Page: 1-of-10"), the number of words, the spelling status (whether the document contains spelling errors) and the language used.

- *PowerPoint*. The status bar shows the slide readout (such as "Slide 2-of-21"), the theme used for the slide, the spelling status and the language used.

■ **Note** Unlike Word, Excel, PowerPoint, and Outlook, OneNote doesn't have a status bar.

The status bar also provides buttons for changing views (for example, changing among Normal view, Page Layout view, and Page Break Preview in Excel) and for zooming in and out.

You can change the selection of items that appear on the status bar like this:

1. Right-click anywhere in the status bar. The program displays the Customize Status Bar menu. Figure 5-8 shows the Customize Status Bar menu for Excel.

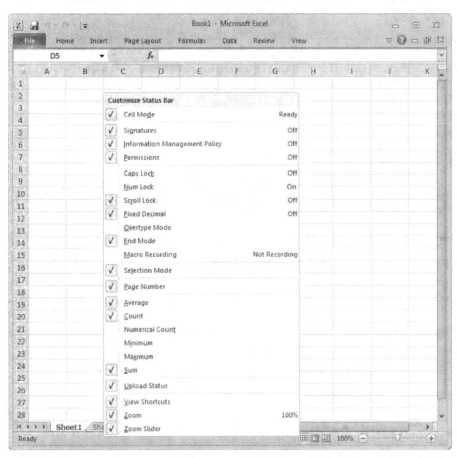

Figure 5-8. *Use the Customize Status Bar menu to control exactly which items appear on a program's status bar.*

■ **Note** Even when you select the check boxes, many of the items you can display in the status bar appear only when the circumstances are right. For example, the Signatures item appears only if the document has a digital signature applied to it, and the Information Management Policy item appears only if the document has Information Rights Management (IRM) applied.

2. The check marks indicate which items are set to appear on the menu. Click an item to switch its check mark on or off.

3. When you're ready to close the menu, click the status bar or anywhere in the document area.

Choosing Essential Options

Each of the Office programs includes several hundred options—many more than we can cover in detail here. So this section concentrates on those settings that are common to several (or all) of the programs and make a big difference in the way that the programs behave.

■ **Note** You'll find information on options peculiar to individual programs in the chapters on those programs, later in the book.

To work through this section, you'll need to have the Options dialog box open. Open it like this:

1. Open the program if it's not already running.

2. Click the File tab to open Backstage.

3. Click the Options button to display the Options dialog box.

Choosing General Options

Click the General category in the left column to display the General pane. Figure 5-9 shows the General pane for Excel, but the other programs have similar sets of options.

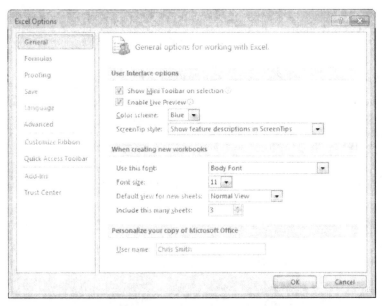

Figure 5-9. A program's General options include choosing whether to show the Mini Toolbar and ScreenTips, whether to enable Live Preview, and which color scheme to use.

These are the common features you can set here:

- *Show Mini Toolbar on selection*. Select this check box if you want the program to display the floating Mini Toolbar when you make a selection. This toolbar shows buttons for applying frequently used formatting, such as font formatting and indentation. Figure 5-10 shows the Mini Toolbar for Word.

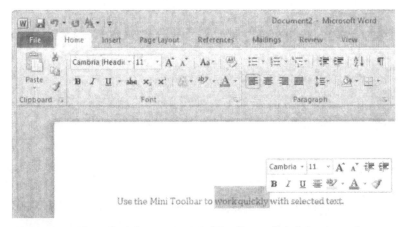

Figure 5-10. If you find the pop-up Mini Toolbar unhelpful or intrusive, you can turn it off in the General pane of the Options dialog box.

- *Enable Live Preview*. Select this check box to have the program display previews of formatting changes so that you can see them in place before you actually apply them. This is a great feature. The only reason to turn it off is if it makes your PC run slowly.

- *Color scheme*. In this drop-down list, select the overall color scheme you want the Office applications to have: Blue, Silver, or Black. Office uses this color scheme for all programs—you can't have different programs use different colors.

- *ScreenTip style*. In this drop-down list, choose how you want ScreenTips to appear. To start with, you'll probably want to use the Show feature descriptions in ScreenTips setting, which shows the feature's name and a short description of what the feature does. Once you know your way around, you may prefer the Don't show feature descriptions in ScreenTips setting, which shows just the feature's name. Or you can choose the Don't show ScreenTips setting to turn ScreenTips off altogether.

- *User name*. Make sure your name appears the way you want in this text box. Office uses this setting, and the Initials setting, for each of the programs.

- *Initials*. Check that this text box shows your initials. (Excel doesn't have this text box, so you need to set the initials in one of the other programs.)

Choosing Save Options in Word, Excel, and PowerPoint

When you're customizing Word, Excel, and PowerPoint, spend a few minutes setting the program's Save options. In the left column of the Options dialog box, click the Save category to display the Save pane. Figure 5-11 shows the Save pane of the Word Options dialog box; in Excel and PowerPoint, the Save pane also has the options discussed here, but it has some other program-specific options as well.

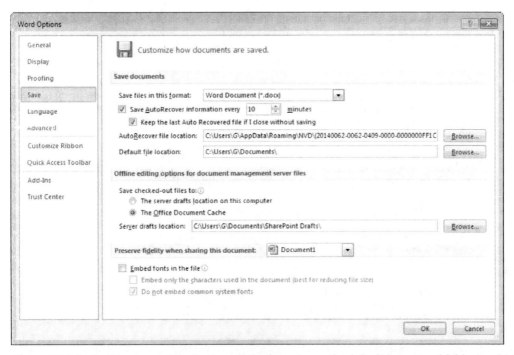

Figure 5-11. *In the Save pane of the Options dialog box, choose the default format and folder in which to save documents, and choose whether to save AutoRecover files.*

Choosing the Default Format for Saving Documents

Word, Excel, and PowerPoint can each save documents in several different formats. Each program comes set to save documents in its preferred format. For example, PowerPoint uses the latest PowerPoint Presentation format by default. But to make sure other people can open the documents you share with them, you may need to change the format. For example, you may need to use a Word document format that colleagues using Office 2003 can open.

To change the default format, open the Save file in this format drop-down list, and then choose the format you want.

These are the formats you're most likely to need for Word:

- *Word Document.* Use this format if your colleagues have Office 2010, Office 2007 for Windows, or Office 2008 for Mac. Anyone with Office 2003 for Windows or Office 2004 for Mac will need to install converter filters to be able to open the documents.

- *Word 97–2003 Document.* Use this format if your colleagues have Office 2003 for Windows, Office 2004 for Mac, or an earlier version of Office. You can also use this format for greater compatibility with other word processors, such as OpenOffice.org Writer or Google Docs.

- *Rich Text Format.* Use this format if you're creating text-based documents that you need to ensure are fully readable in almost any word processor.

These are the formats you're most likely to need for Excel:

- *Excel Workbook.* Use this format if your colleagues have Office 2010, Office 2007 for Windows, or Office 2008 for Mac. Anyone with Office 2003 for Windows or Office 2004 for Mac will need to install converter filters to be able to open the workbooks.

- *Excel Macro-Enabled Workbook.* Use this format if you need to include macros in your workbooks to perform custom actions. Again, your colleagues will need to have Office 2010, Office 2007 for Windows , Office 2007 for Mac, Office 2003, or Office 2004 with filters installed to open these workbooks.

- *Excel Binary Workbook.* Use this format if you create large and complex workbooks and need to improve performance. Once more, your colleagues will need to have Office 2010, Office 2007 for Windows, Office 2007 for Mac, Office 2003, or Office 2004 with filters installed to work with these workbooks.

- *Excel 97–2003 Workbook.* Use this format if your colleagues have Office 2003 for Windows, Office 2004 for Mac or an earlier version of Office. You can also use this format for greater compatibility with other spreadsheet programs, such as OpenOffice.org Calc or Google Docs.

These are the formats you're most likely to need for PowerPoint:

- *PowerPoint Presentation.* Use this format if your colleagues have Office 2010, Office 2007 for Windows or Office 2008 for Mac. Anyone with Office 2003 for Windows or Office 2004 for Mac will need to install converter filters to be able to open the workbooks.

- *PowerPoint Presentation 97–2003.* Use this format if your colleagues have Office 2003 for Windows, Office 2004 for Mac, or an earlier version of Office. You can also use this format for greater compatibility with other presentation programs, such as OpenOffice.org Impress, Google Docs, or Apple Keynote.

■ **Note** If you need to change the format only for a particular document, you can change it when you're saving that document. But if you need to create all your documents in a different format, change the default format in the Options dialog box.

Choosing AutoRecover Settings

Next, choose whether to keep AutoRecover files and, if so, where to save them. AutoRecover is a safety net that automatically saves a copy of each open document every few minutes in case the program closes unexpectedly and loses the changes you've made. After the program restarts automatically, or you restart it manually, the program opens the latest AutoRecover files for you so that you can choose which versions to keep. If you save your documents and then exit the program, it gets rid of the saved AutoRecover files.

▓ **Caution** Don't rely on AutoRecover as protection against disasters. When AutoRecover works, it can save your bacon. But you should always save your documents frequently while working on them, just in case AutoRecover doesn't work. You can save a document at any time by pressing Ctrl+S or clicking the Save button on the Quick Access Toolbar.

To use AutoRecover, select the Save AutoRecover information every N minutes check box, and then set the number of minutes in the text box. The default setting is 10 minutes, but if you work quickly and prefer not to save your documents manually, it's a good idea to reduce the interval to two or three minutes.

Select the Keep the last Auto Recovered file if I close without saving check box if you want to prevent the program from deleting the last AutoRecover file it has saved when you close a program without saving changes. This setting can be very helpful.

The AutoRecover file location text box shows the folder in which the program is storing your AutoRecover files. You don't need to open AutoRecover files manually, because the program automatically opens them for you, so normally there's no need to change this folder.

▓ **Note** For Excel, you can select the Disable AutoRecover for this workbook only check box to turn off AutoRecover for the current workbook. You may want to do this when you're working on an especially large workbook and you find that AutoRecover takes so long that it interrupts your work.

Choosing the Default File Location

Next, check the folder shown in the Default file location text box. This is the folder the program suggests saving your documents in. If you find you frequently need to change folders in the Save As dialog box, you may want to change the default location.

You can type a different location in the text box, but it's usually easier to paste it in:

1. Open a Windows Explorer window to the folder you want to use.

2. Click in the address bar to display and select the folder path.

3. Right-click in the selection, and then choose Copy from the context menu.

4. Switch to the Office program, right-click in the Default file location text box, and then choose Paste from the context menu.

Summary

In this chapter, you've learned essential techniques for customizing the Office programs. You now know how to load the Quick Access Toolbar with the buttons you find most useful, and you can add and remove Ribbon groups—or even entire Ribbon tabs—if you need to make wider-ranging changes. And you know how to reach the treasure trove of settings in each program's Options dialog box, how to set

General options to control key aspects of how the programs look and behave and how to use Save options to choose the default format and folder in which to save your documents.

This is the end of the first part of the book. You're now familiar with the most important tools and techniques that the programs share, so it's time to dig into using the individual programs. We'll start with Microsoft Word.

CHAPTER 6

Entering Text and Using Views

In this chapter, I'll show you how to enter text quickly in Word documents by using extra features that Word provides. You'll see how to select text in advanced ways with the mouse and the keyboard, how to move around your documents using keyboard shortcuts and the mysterious "browse object," and how to tell Word where to find your custom templates.

You'll also learn how to control Word with your own custom keyboard shortcuts, make Word automatically create backup documents so that you can recover from disastrous edits or other mishaps, and how to exploit the possibilities offered by Word's five different views of a document.

Entering Text in Your Word Documents

In Word, you can enter text in your documents by typing it in as usual, but you can often save time by entering text in other ways:

- *Paste*: If you have the text in another document or e-mail, copy it, and then paste it into the Word document.

- *Scan*: If you have the text in a hard-copy document, you can scan it and recognize it using OneNote, then export the page as a Word document. See Part 6 of this book for details.

- *Inserting a file*: If you have the text in a Word document or a text file, you can insert it quickly in a Word document. See the first subsection for details.

- *Using AutoCorrect*: After creating AutoCorrect entries as described in "Saving Time and Effort with AutoCorrect" in Chapter 3, you can insert their contents by just typing their names. AutoCorrect is great for entering sections of boilerplate text with just a few keystrokes.

- *Using AutoText*: As well as AutoCorrect, Word provides AutoText, which is another easy way of inserting preexisting blocks of text. See the second subsection for details.

Inserting the Text from a File in a Document

When you need to put all the text from one document in another document, you can use the Insert ➤ Object ➤ Text from File command instead of opening the document, copying the content, closing the document, and then pasting the content. Follow these steps:

- Place the insertion point where you want to insert the text.

- Choose Insert ➤ Text, click the Object drop-down button, and then click Text from File on the drop-down menu. Word displays the Insert File dialog box.

- Navigate to the document you want to insert, and then click it.

- Click the Insert button. Word inserts the document's text.

■ **Tip** You can also insert the contents of a bookmark from another document. In the Insert File dialog box, select the document, and then click the Range button. In the Enter Text dialog box that appears, type the bookmark's name, and then click the OK button. Click the Insert button in the Insert File dialog box as usual.

Inserting Prebuilt Blocks of Text with AutoText

If some or many of your documents will include some of the same sections of text, you may be able to save time by using AutoText. This feature gives you an easy way to store prebuilt sections of text so that you can reuse them in your documents. AutoText is like AutoCorrect in a way, but it doesn't replace text automatically—instead, you choose when to insert each AutoText entry, although you can have Word prompt you with available AutoText entries if you like.

An AutoText entry consists of as much text as needed, plus any other objects, such as graphics or tables. Word includes prebuilt AutoText entries as part of its Building Blocks that lets you quickly insert prebuilt elements such as headers and footers, tables, cover pages, and text boxes.

To use AutoText, you first create one or more AutoText entries that contain the text and elements you want. You can then insert these entries as needed in your documents.

To create a new AutoText entry, follow these steps:

1. In your document, enter the material that you want to include in the AutoText entry:

   - Type in the text and apply any formatting it needs.

   - Add other elements such as graphics or tables.

■ **Tip** Unless you're highly organized, you may find it easier to create AutoText entries when you realize that part of a document you've created would be useful again in future. If you need to modify the material before creating an AutoText entry from it, copy that part of the document, paste it into a new document, and then change itfor example, removing specific information that you will fill in each time you reuse it. When the material is ready, select it, and then create an AutoText entry.

---

2. Select the material.

3. Choose Insert ➤ Text ➤ Quick Parts to open the Quick Parts drop-down menu.

4. Click or highlight AutoText to open the AutoText submenu, and then click Save Selection to AutoText Gallery at the bottom of the menu to open the Create New Building Block dialog box (see Figure 6-1).

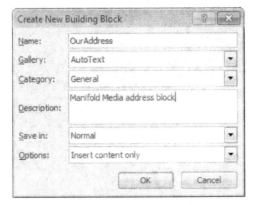

Figure 6-1. Use the Create New Building Block dialog box to create a new AutoText entry from the text or other material you've selected in the document.

5. In the Name text box, type the name you want to give the AutoText entry.

■ **Tip** As you'll see in a moment, the easiest way to insert an AutoText entry is by typing enough of its name to identify it. This means it's best to give your AutoText entries distinctive names that describe their contents, so that you can type the names without having to look up the entries.

---

6. In the Gallery drop-down list, make sure that AutoText is selected. (It should be selected because you opened the Create New Building Block dialog box from the AutoText submenu.)

7. In the Description text box, type a description of the AutoText entry. This description is to help you identify the entry, so make it as helpful as possible.

8. In the Save in drop-down list, choose Normal.

9. In the Options drop-down list, choose the appropriate item:

   • *Insert content only*: Select this item to make Word insert the AutoText entry just as it is at the position of the insertion point.

   • *Insert content in its own paragraph*: Select this item to make the AutoText entry a separate paragraph even if it doesn't include its own paragraph mark.

   • *Insert content in its own page*: Select this item to make the AutoText entry a free-standing page.

10. Click the OK button. Word closes the Create New Building Block dialog box and adds the AutoText entry.

After creating your AutoText entries, you can insert them at the insertion point using either the Ribbon or the keyboard:

- *Ribbon*: Choose Insert ➤ Text ➤ Quick Parts ➤ AutoText, and then click the entry on the drop-down menu.

- *Keyboard*: Type the first four characters of the name, or enough to identify it uniquely among your AutoText entries. When Word displays a ScreenTip containing the first part of the AutoText entry (see Figure 6-2), press Enter to insert it.

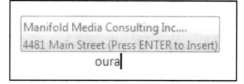

Figure 6-2. *Word displays a ScreenTip containing the first part of the AutoText entry when you type enough of the name to identify it uniquely. Press Enter to insert the entry.*

■ **Tip** If Word doesn't display a ScreenTip prompting you to press Enter to insert the AutoText entry, type the whole name (or enough to identify it uniquely) and then press F3 to enter it.

Selecting Text in Word-Specific Ways

Apart from the ways of selecting text that you learned in Chapter 4, you can use several shortcuts for selecting text in Word. You can use the mouse, the keyboard, or both.

Selecting Text with the Mouse

When you're using the mouse to move around a document, you can quickly select text by moving the mouse pointer to the left of the text area so that the pointer changes to an arrow pointing up and to the right. You can then use this selection pointer like this:

- *Select a line*: Click next to the line you want to select.

- *Select multiple lines*: Click to place the insertion point anywhere in the line at which you want to begin the selection. Then Shift+click in the left margin at the line on which you want to end the selection.

- *Select a paragraph*: Double-click next to the paragraph you want to select.

- *Select the whole document*: Triple-click or Ctrl+click. (Again, you click to the left of the text area, not in the text.)

- *Select a column of text*: Sometimes it's useful to select not whole lines but part of several lines—for example, to select the first few blank characters at the beginning of several lines of text you've pasted so that you can delete them all at once. You can do this by Alt+dragging with the mouse (see Figure 6-3). When you've selected the text you want, you can format it or delete it.

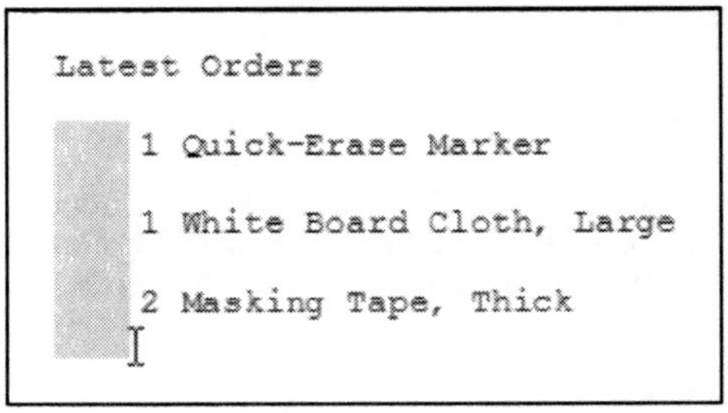

```
Latest Orders

   1 Quick-Erase Marker

   1 White Board Cloth, Large

   2 Masking Tape, Thick
   I
```

Figure 6-3. Alt-drag when you need to select part of the text on each of several lines—for example, to delete unwanted blank space.

Selecting Text with the Extend Selection Feature

You can select text in Word using the standard keyboard selection methods discussed in Chapter 4, but Word also provides an odd feature called Extend Selection. You put Word into Extend mode by pressing F8, and you can then continue selecting like this:

- Keep pressing F8. Press once more to select the current word. Press twice more to select the current sentence. Press three more times to select the current paragraph. Press four more times to select the whole document.

- Press the character to which you want to extend the selection. For example, press M to extend the selection to the next letter *m*, press . (the period key) to extend the selection to the end of the sentence, or press Enter to extend the selection to the end of the paragraph.

- Press Right Arrow to extend the selection by a single character, or press Left Arrow to reduce the selection by a single character. Press Down Arrow to extend the selection by a line, or press Up Arrow to reduce the selection by a line.

▓ **Note** You can also extend the selection by using Find and searching for particular text or by pressing cursor-movement keys (such as the arrow keys).

- With the mouse, click or right-click at the point to which you want to extend the selection.

- Press Esc when you've finished selecting and want to work with the selection.

▒ **Note** The Extend Selection feature can be useful, but it's fine if you decide it's too odd to use. But if Word starts behaving oddly and selecting sections of text you're not trying to select, you may have switched on Extend mode by accident. If so, press Esc to switch it off again.

Selecting Multiple Items at Once

Sometimes in Word, it's useful to select multiple items at the same time. To do so, select the first item using the keyboard, the mouse, or both. Then hold down Ctrl and select the other items with the mouse.

After you've selected multiple objects, you can apply most types of formatting to them all at the same time.

Moving with Keyboard Shortcuts and the Browse Object

As well as the standard keyboard shortcuts discussed in Chapter 4, you can move around a document by using the keyboard shortcuts listed in Table 6-1.

Table 6-1. Keyboard Shortcuts for Moving the Insertion Point in Word

Press These Keys	To Move the Insertion Point Like This
Ctrl+Up Arrow	If the insertion point is in a paragraph, to the start of that paragraph. If the insertion point is at the start of a paragraph, to the start of the previous paragraph.
Ctrl+Down Arrow	To the start of the next paragraph.
Ctrl+Home	To the start of the document.
Ctrl+End	To the end of the document.
Ctrl+Page Down	To the next page (or the next browse object).
Ctrl+Page Up	To the previous page (or the previous browse object).

▒ **Tip** To reveal more scroll options, right-click the vertical scroll bar. You can then click Scroll Here on the context menu to scroll to the point you clicked, click Top or Bottom to scroll to the top or bottom, click Page Up or Page Down to move by a page, or click Scroll Up or Scroll Down to scroll by an amount other than a page.

To move about a document with the mouse, you can click the scroll arrows or drag the scroll box as usual, but you can also use the three buttons that appear below the vertical scroll bar on the right side of the Word window:

- *Previous button*: This is the button with a double arrow pointing upward.

- *Select Browse Object button*: This is the button with a round gray dot on it. The *browse object* is the type of item by which Word is currently set to move through a document—for example, pages, headings, or tables.

- *Next button*: This is the button with a double arrow pointing downward.

When you first open a document, the arrows on the Previous and Next buttons appear in black. This means that the buttons are Previous Page and Next Page. Click the buttons to display the previous page or the next page.

When you search using Find, Word automatically switches the Previous and Next buttons to Previous Find and Next Find, and changes the arrows to blue to indicate that it's using a different browse object. You can click the Previous button and Next button to move to the previous or next instance of your search term (if the search term appears more than once).

Similarly, you can move among ten other types of objects in a document, such as comments, tables, and graphics. Table 6-2 explains these items.

Table 6-2. Word's Twelve Browse Objects

Browse Object	Explanation
Page	Browse from page to page in the document. This is the default setting until you use Find or otherwise change the browse object.
Section	Browse from one section to the next. See Chapter 8 for information on sections.
Comment	Browse from one comment attached to text (or another object) to the next. See Chapter 9 for information on comments.
Footnote	Browse from one footnote to the next. A footnote is a note that appears at the foot of the page that refers to it. See Chapter 8 for information on footnotes.
Endnote	Browse from one endnote to the next. An endnote is a note that appears at the end of a section or document. See Chapter 8 for information on endnotes.
Field	Browse from one field to the next. See Chapter 8 for details on how to use fields.
Table	Browse from one table to the next. See Chapter 8 for information on creating tables.
Graphic	Browse from one graphic to the next.
Heading	Browse from one heading to the next. This works with any paragraph you've given a Heading style (see Chapter 7 for details).
Edits	Browse back and forth among the last four edits you've made in the document.

Browse Object	Explanation
Find	Browse to the next instance of the search term (or other object, such as formatting) you've entered in Find or to the previous instance.
Go To	Move to the next item you've set on the Go To tab of the Find and Replace dialog box. The Go To tab (choose Home ➤ Editing ➤ Find ➤ Go To) lets you move among pages, sections, lines, bookmarks, comments, footnotes, endnotes, fields, tables, graphics, equations, objects, and headings, giving you more flexibility than the Select Browse Object panel does.

▬ **Tip** You can also move the insertion point to your last four edits by pressing Shift+F5 once, twice, thrice, or four times.

To choose the browse object, click the round button between the Previous button and the Next button below the vertical scroll bar. This is the Select Browse Object button, and it displays the Select Browse Object panel shown in Figure 6-4. Click the item you want, and you can then click the Previous button and the Next button to move among the instances of that item. You can also press Ctrl+Page Down to move to the next item or Ctrl+Page Up to move to the previous item.

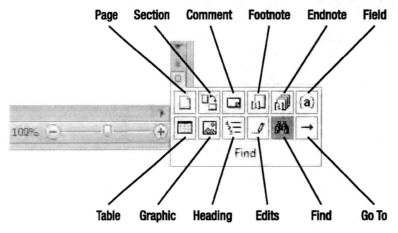

Figure 6-4. To browse through a document by comments, fields, or another object, click the Select Browse Object button, and then click the object you want.

▓ **Tip** To open the Select Browse Object panel from the keyboard, press Ctrl+Alt+Home. You can then use the arrow keys to select the object you want to browse by, and press Enter to close the panel and start browsing by that object.

Telling Word Where to Find Your Templates

If you have your own custom templates, you may need to tell Word where they're located, or you may need to move them into the templates folder that Word is already using so that you can use them from the New pane in Backstage.

▓ **Note** Word uses two template folders, the User templates folder and the Workgroup templates folder. When you install Office, the installer automatically sets the User templates folder for you to a folder on your PC. For a normal installation, the installer normally does not set the Workgroup templates folder. If you share templates with others on your network, you can set the Workgroup templates folder manually to point to this folder by using the technique described in this section.

To set your templates folders, or to check which folders Word is using for them, follow these steps:

1. Click the File tab to open Backstage.
2. Click the Options item in the left column to display the Word Options dialog box.
3. In the left column, click the Advanced category to display the Advanced pane.
4. Scroll down all the way to the bottom of the pane.
5. Click the File Locations button to display the File Locations dialog box (see Figure 6-5).

Figure 6-5 Use the File Locations dialog box to check or change the folder in which Word stores your templates.

6. In the File types list box, click the type of file for which you want to see or change the path. For example, click the User templates item.

7. Click the Modify button to display the Modify Location dialog box. The address box shows the full address of the folder.

■ **Tip** If you need to open the folder in a Windows Explorer window so that you can move your templates to it, click the address box in the Modify Location dialog box. Word displays the folder path (for example, C:\Users\Jan\AppData\Roaming\Microsoft\Templates in Windows 7) and selects it. Press Ctrl+C or right-click and choose Copy to copy the address to the Clipboard. Click the Start button, right-click the Search box and choose Paste, and then press Enter to open a Windows Explorer window showing the folder.

---

8. To change the folder, navigate to the folder you want to use, click it, and then click the OK button. Word closes the Modify Location dialog box and displays the new path (or as much of it as will fit) in the File Locations dialog box.

9. Change any other file paths (for example, you may want to set the Workgroup templates path), and then click the OK button to close the File Locations dialog box.

10. Click the OK button to close the Word Options dialog box.

Customizing Keyboard Shortcuts in Word

To work quickly in Word, you can use keyboard shortcuts. Word lets you use most of the Office-wide keyboard shortcuts, such as Ctrl+S for saving the active document and Ctrl+O for displaying the Open dialog box, and you can press Alt as usual to display the letters for giving Ribbon commands from the keyboard. But what you may also want to do is create your own custom keyboard shortcuts so that you can instantly run commands.

To customize Word's keyboard shortcuts, follow these steps:

1. Right-click any tab of the Ribbon, and then click Customize the Ribbon on the context menu to open the Customize Ribbon pane in the Word Options dialog box.

2. Click the Customize button at the bottom to display the Customize Keyboard dialog box (shown in Figure 6-6 with settings chosen).

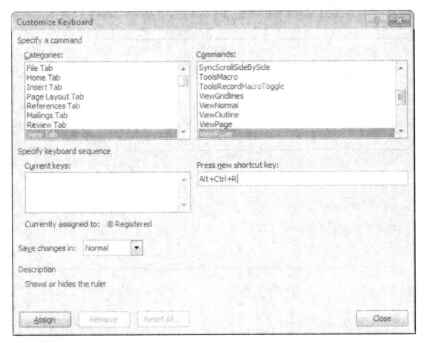

Figure 6-6. *The Customize Keyboard dialog box lets you create keyboard shortcuts for the commands you use most often.*

3. In the Save changes in drop-down list, choose the document or template to save the keyboard shortcuts in. The following are your choices:

   - *Normal*: Select this item to save the changes in Word's Normal template. Word loads Normal each time you start the program, making the keyboard shortcuts available in every document. Usually, this is the best choice.

   - *Template attached to the active document*: Select the template's name that appears in the drop-down list—for example, Invoice (or Invoice.dot, if Windows is set to display file extensions). Keyboard shortcuts you store in the template are available when the template itself is open or when a document that has the template attached is open.

   - *Active document*: Select the document's name that appears in the drop-down list. Keyboard shortcuts you save in a document are available only when that document is open.

4. In the Categories list box, click the category of command you want to create a keyboard shortcut for.

   - *Ribbon tabs*: Click a Ribbon tab to display its commands in the Commands list box.

   - *Commands Not in the Ribbon*: Click this category to see only the commands that don't appear in the Ribbon.

   - *All Commands*: Click this category to see the full list of Word commands. There are more than 1,000, so working with this list is slow going.

   - *Macros, Fonts, Building Blocks, Styles, Common Symbols*: Click the category for the type of item. For example, click Macros to display the list of macros in the Commands list box.

5. In the Commands list box, click the command. Word displays information about the command:

   - *Current keyboard shortcuts*: The Current keys list box shows any keyboard shortcuts currently assigned to the command (some commands have several shortcuts). If this command has any shortcuts, check that you know them and decide whether you need to create another.

   - *Description*: This area shows the description of the command. Read it to make sure you've picked the command you intended. Some command names are clear, but others can be confusing.

6. Click in the Press new shortcut key text box.

7. Press the keyboard shortcut you want to assign:

   - You can use the Ctrl, Ctrl+Alt, Ctrl+Alt+Shift, Ctrl+Shift, or Alt+Shift modifier keys and key combinations.

   - You can use pretty much any key on the keyboard—letters, numbers, function keys, and so on.

8. A normal shortcut consists of a modifier or modifiers plus one key—for example, Ctrl+Alt+T. But you can also create modifiers that use two keys in sequence—for example, Ctrl+Alt+T, S—by pressing the extra key after the key combination. This lets you create many more keyboard and is good for related

commands. For example, you could use the "Ctrl+Shift+S, 1" keyboard shortcut for one style, the "Ctrl+Shift+S, 2" keyboard shortcut for another, and the "Ctrl+Shift+S,3" keyboard shortcut for a third.

9. Check the Currently assigned to area to see if the keyboard shortcut is currently used. If so, press another keyboard shortcut if you don't want to overwrite it.

10. Click the Assign button. Word assigns the keyboard shortcut to the command.

11. When you've finished assigning keyboard shortcuts, click the Close button to close the Customize Keyboard dialog box, then click the OK button to close the Word Options dialog box.

At this point, you've created the keyboard shortcuts, but you haven't saved them in the document or template. Save them like this:

- *Normal template*: Close Word by choosing File ➤ Exit. If Word displays the dialog box shown in Figure 6-7 telling you that "Changes have been made that affect the global template, Normal," click the Save button.

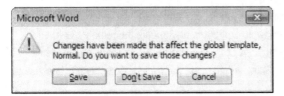

Figure 6-7. If this dialog box appears when you exit Word after creating custom keyboard shortcuts, click the Save button to save the shortcuts.

■ **Note** Word prompts you to save changes to the Normal template if you have cleared the Prompt Before Saving Normal Template check box in the Advanced category of Word options. See the next section for details.

- *Document or template*: Save the document by pressing Ctrl+S or clicking the Save button on the Quick Access Toolbar. For a template, click the Yes button in the dialog box that prompts you to save the changes.

Creating Backup Documents and Recovering from Disaster

Like the other Office programs, Word automatically saves versions of your documents as you work and offers you the chance to recover them when Word restarts after closing unexpectedly (see Chapter 5). But to keep your documents safe, it's a good idea to also turn on Word's feature for creating automatic backups. When you do so, you can also check that a couple of other important options are set correctly. Follow these steps:

1. Click the File tab to open Backstage.

2. Click the Options item in the left pane to open the Word Options dialog box.

3. In the left column, click the Advanced category to display the Advanced pane.

4. Scroll down most of the way to the bottom so that you can see the Save heading.

5. Select the Always create backup copy check box.

6. If you want Word to automatically save changes you make to the Normal template, such as the keyboard shortcuts discussed in the previous section, make sure the Prompt before saving Normal template check box is cleared. Select this check box if you want Word to ask you to decide whether to save changes.

7. Select the Allow background saves check box if you want Word to enable you to keep working while it saves a document. You'll probably want to select this check box if you save documents to SkyDrive, where saving can take a while because saving across an Internet connection is much slower than saving to your PC's hard disk or to a network drive.

▨ **Note** If you work with documents on SkyDrive or another drive you access across an Internet connection, you may also want to select the "Copy remotely stored files onto your computer, and update the remote file when saving" check box. This setting makes Word store a working copy of the file on your PC and save changes to it there, then copy the updated file back to the remote drive. This method helps you avoid losing changes because of interruptions to the Internet connection.

---

8. Click the OK button to close the Options dialog box.

Now that you've selected the Always create backup copy check box, Word keeps one backup of each document. Here's how it does it:

- The first time you save, Word saves the document as normal. There's no backup.

- Each time you save the document after that, Word changes the name of the latest saved version of the document to the backup name, and then saves the current version under the document name.

Word names the backup file *Backup of* and the document's name, gives it the .wbk file extension (which Windows associates with the Microsoft Word Backup Document file type), and keeps it in the same folder as the document. So if you create a document named Merlot Tasting.docx, Word names the backup file Backup of Merlot Tasting.wbk.

If a document becomes corrupted, or if you delete a vital part of it and save the change, you can recover your work by opening the backup document. To open the backup document, follow these steps:

1. Click the File tab to open Backstage.

2. Click the Open button to display the Open dialog box.

3. In the drop-down list above the Open button, choose All Files.

4. Click the backup document.

5. Click the Open button.

Using Views and Windows to See What You Need

To work quickly and comfortably in your documents, you need to understand the five different views that Word provides and know when to use each of them. You may also need to open multiple windows on the same document so that you can work in different parts of it. Or you may want to split a single document window into two panes so that you can view the document differently in each.

Picking the Right View for What You're Doing

Each of Word's five views has a distinct purpose, but you can use each view as much or as little as you want. Most likely, you will find some views much more useful than others for the types of documents you create and the PC you work on.

You can switch from view to view in these ways:

- *Status bar*: Click the five View Shortcuts button on the status bar (see Figure 6-8).

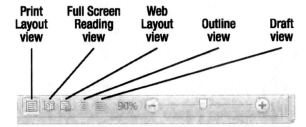

Figure 6-8. To change view quickly with the mouse, click the View Shortcuts buttons on the status bar.

- *Ribbon*: Click the View tab, go to the Document Views group, and then click the button for the view you want.

- *Keyboard*: Press Ctrl+Alt+P for Print Layout view, Ctrl+Alt+O for Outline view, and Ctrl+Alt+N for Draft view (which used to be called Normal view).

Using Print Layout View to See How a Document Will Look When Printed

Word opens at first in Print Layout view (see Figure 6-9), which shows you the document as it will appear on paper. You can see each printable element in the document—text, tables, graphics, equations, and so on—in the positions they occupy on the page, along with the white space of the page margins. If you have added headers or footers to the document, you see them too.

▦ **Tip** In Print Layout view, you can hide headers, footers and white space by double-clicking the space between pages. This trick lets you concentrate on your document's text as it is laid out without viewing the extra elements. When you want to display these items again, double-click the divider line between the pages.

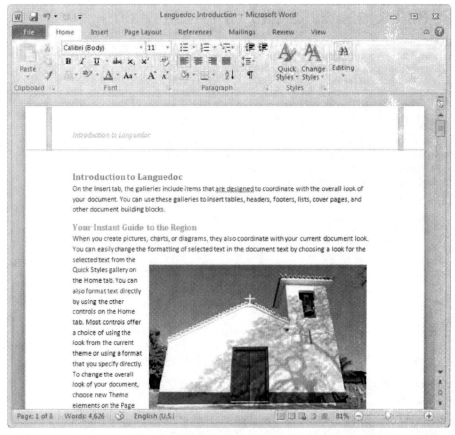

Figure 6-9. Print Layout view shows the document with headers and footers, margins, and graphics all in the positions they occupy on paper.

Using Full Screen Reading View to See More of a Document

As its name suggests, Full Screen Reading view is designed for reading documents. In Full Screen Reading view, Word maximizes the window and hides the Ribbon and displays only essential controls on the Quick Access Toolbar, dedicating as much space as possible (see Figure 6-10). Word displays two pages of the document as large as they will go, to show you as much text as possible.

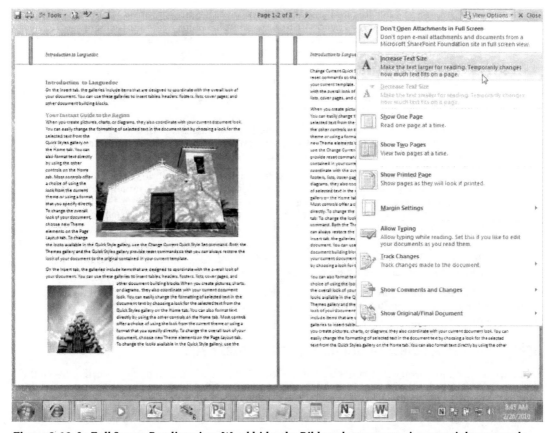

Figure 6-10. *In Full Screen Reading view, Word hides the Ribbon, but you can give essential commands from the View Options drop-down menu.*

If the text isn't big enough to read, click the View Options drop-down button in the upper-right corner of the window and choose Increase Text Size from the drop-down list. Repeat the command as needed until the text is a comfortable size. (If the text is too big, choose View Options ➤ Decrease Text Size one or more times.)

You can customize the view further as needed using the other options on the View Options drop-down menu:

- *Show One Page*: Click this item to show only one page. This is good for small screens.

- *Show Two Pages*: Click this item to switch to viewing two pages. This is how Full Screen Reading view normally opens.

- *Show Printed Page*: Click the item to display the pages as they will appear when printed. If you've changed the text size or the margins, Word restores them.

- *Margin Settings*: Click this item and then click Show Margins, Suppress Margins, or Automatically Decide, as needed. Suppress Margins helps make the text large enough to read. Automatically Decide lets Word choose between Show Margins and Suppress Margins depending on the page size and screen size.

- *Allow Typing*: Click this item to turn on editing. Full Screen Reading view starts with editing turned off so that you can concentrate on reading. But if you have a large enough screen, Full Screen Reading view can be a good way to edit a document, as you can see more of it at once.

- *Track Changes*: Click this item to turn on the Track Changes feature for marking revisions (see Chapter 9 for details). Click the arrow button to display a submenu for accessing Track Changes options or changing your user name.

- *Show Comments and Changes*: Click this item to display a submenu of the comments and markup you can show or hide for the document: Comments, Ink, Insertions and Deletions, Formatting, and Markup Area Highlight. Click the Reviewers item on the submenu to reveal a further submenu you can use to choose which reviewers' changes you see.

- *Show Original/Final Document*: Click this item to display a submenu of the document versions you can view: Final, Final with Markup, Original, and Original with Markup. Again, see Chapter 9 for details on the markup tools.

To leave Full Screen Reading view, click the Close button in the upper-right corner of the Word window, or press Esc. Word returns you to the view you were using before you switch to Full Screen Reading view.

Using Web Layout View to Get a Preview of Web Pages

Web Layout view shows you how the document will look if you save it as a web page. Word hides all the items that don't appear on web pages—headers and footers, margins, and page breaks—and wraps the lines to the width of the window, just as a web browser does (see Figure 6-11).

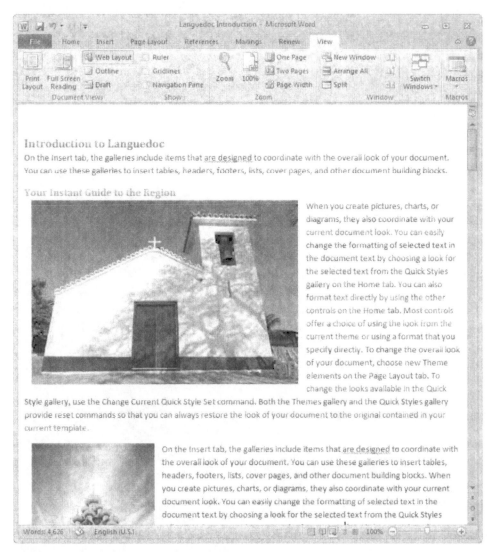

***Figure 6-11.** Web Layout view displays the page as if it were in a web browser, with no headers and footers, margins, or page breaks.*

Developing a Document in Outline View

Outline view is a powerful tool for developing the outline and structure of a document. Outline view displays the document as a structure of headings, each of which you can collapse or expand as needed (see Figure 6-12). See Chapter 8 for instructions on using Outline view.

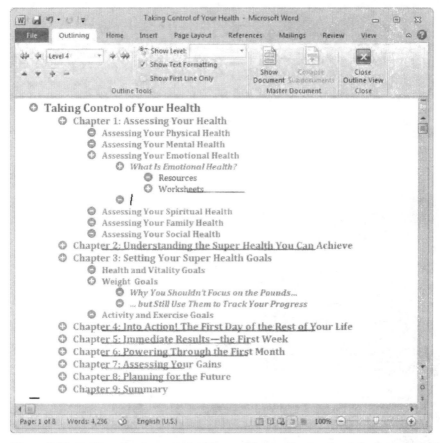

Figure 6-12. *Outline view is a great tool for working on the structure of a document. You can expand different sections of the document to different levels as needed.*

Using Draft View

Draft view, which used to be called Normal view, is great for working with the body text of a document. You see all the text, but Word hides items such as headers and footers, margins, and objects. Figure 6-13 shows Draft view.

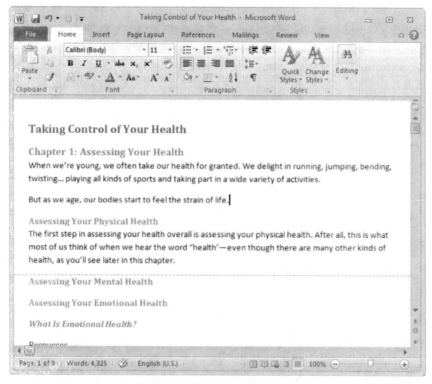

Figure 6-13. Draft view enables you to concentrate on the text of the document without worrying about layout elements such as headers and footers.

Opening Extra Windows

At first, Word displays a single window of each document. For short documents, this is all you need, but for long or complex documents, you may find it helpful to open extra windows so that you can see two or more parts of the document at once or use different views.

For example, when you're writing a lengthy report, you may benefit from seeing the introduction as you write the conclusion, to make sure you nail each of your main points. Or you may want to open a window showing the outline of a document so that you can add headings and change its structure even as you write regular text in one of its sections.

Here's how to open and work with extra windows:

- *Open a new window*: Choose View ➤ Window ➤ New Window. Word adds : 1 to the document's name in the title bar of the original window to indicate that it's now the first window of the document. The second window's name includes : 2—for example, **Linguistics Report: 2**.

- *Arrange your Word windows*: Click and drag the windows to where you need them. To arrange the windows side by side, minimize all other windows, right-click the notification area, and then choose Show Windows Side by Side from the context menu.

▨ **Note** Word includes an Arrange All command (View ➤ Window ➤ Arrange All), but it tiles the Word windows horizontally, which usually isn't what you want. In most cases, the Show Windows Side by Side command is more useful, even though it includes windows from other programs if they're not minimized.

- *Switch from window to window*: If you can see the window you want, click it. Otherwise, choose View ➤ Window ➤ Switch Windows, and then click the window you want.

▨ **Tip** Press Ctrl+F6 or Alt+F6 to display the next window (of any open Word document, not just the one that has multiple windows open). Press Ctrl+Shift+F6 or Alt+Shift+F6 to display the previous window.

- *Close a window*: Click the window's Close button (the × button). The document remains open until you close its last window.

Splitting the Document Window into Two Panes

Sometimes it's useful to split the document window into two panes so that you can work in two different parts of the same document at once. Splitting the document window is like opening a new window except that you don't need more space.

To split the document window into two equal parts, double-click the split box just above the scroll arrow at the top of the vertical scroll bar (see Figure 6-14). You can then adjust the split by dragging the split bar up or down as needed.

▨ **Note** To split the document window unequally from the start, choose View ➤ Window ➤ Split. You can then click the split box and drag it to where you want the split bar to appear. You can also press the up arrow or down arrow to move the split bar, and press Enter when you're ready to lock it in position.

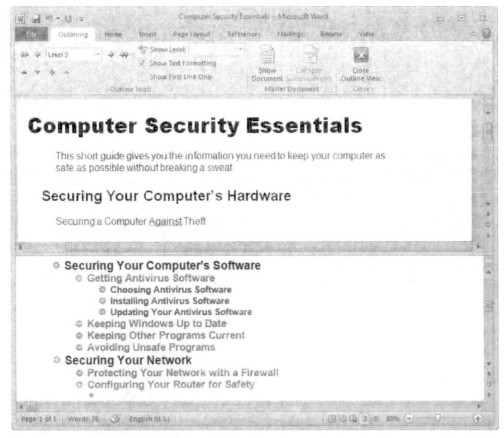

Figure 6-14. You can split a window into two panes so that you can use two different views at once or work in different parts of the document.

Once you've split the window, you can scroll each pane separately, so you can display a different part of the document in each pane. You can also use a different view in each pane—for example, display the document's outline in Outline view in one pane while you write the introduction or summary in Normal view in the other pane.

To switch to the other pane, click in it or press F6.

◼ **Tip** You can also zoom out in one pane to get an overview of the document as a whole, and zoom in using the other pane so that you can see the detail of a section.

When you want to remove the split, take one of these actions:

- *Mouse*: Double-click the split bar. Alternatively, drag it to the top (to keep the lower pane) or to the bottom (to keep the upper pane).
- *Keyboard*: Press Ctrl+Alt+S.
- *Ribbon*: Choose View ➤ Window ➤ Remove Split.

Summary

In this chapter, you've learned new tricks for inserting text quickly and easily in Word document, including how to insert the text from an existing document and how to create AutoText entries to reuse boilerplate text. You've also grasped how to select text using the Alt+drag maneuver and the Extend Selection feature and learned new ways of navigating around a document using keyboard shortcuts and the browse object.

Better yet, you now know how to create custom keyboard shortcuts so that you can use the keyboard to make Word jump in the ways you prefer. And you know how to get Word to make automatic backups of your documents, how to make the most of Word's five views, and how to open extra windows or split a single window into two panes.

In the next chapter, you'll learn how to save any amount of time by formatting your documents the right way—by using Word's powerful styles.

CHAPTER 7

Adding Style: Formatting Your Documents

To make your documents look good, you must apply formatting to the text and other elements in them.

That's easy to say, but Word gives you such a wide range of formatting options that it's easy to use the wrong ones. This chapter teaches you the right way to format a document quickly and consistently by using styles—collections of formatting—rather than by applying direct formatting bit by bit. It also shows you how to use the Navigation pane and the Find feature to navigate your documents, and how to make the most of the versatile Replace feature.

Before we start, a word of warning: Styles are an extremely powerful tool that can save you huge amounts of time—but you will need to invest some time and effort in understanding how they work before you can harness all their power. To complicate things, Word provides six different tools for working with styles, and the way these tools interact and overlap takes some getting used to. But once you get the hang of them, you'll find that you can work swiftly and effectively with them

Understanding Word's Many Types of Formatting

Word gives you such a wide variety of formatting that it's easy to waste time by using the wrong ones for your needs. This section explains the different types of formatting and shows you the best and fastest way to use them.

Understanding Direct Formatting and When to Use It

Where most people start is by using direct formatting, the kind of formatting that you can apply by using the controls in the Font group and the Paragraph group on the Home tab of the Ribbon (see Figure 7-1). For example, you can create a heading paragraph by changing to a different font, increasing the font size, changing the font color, giving it an "outdent" so that it sticks out into the margin, and adding extra space before and after the paragraph.

Figure 7-1. *You can easily apply direct formatting such as font formatting and paragraph formatting using the Font group and Paragraph group controls on the Ribbon, but you can save time and effort by applying styles from the Styles group first.*

Each part of this formatting is easy enough to apply—click this, click that, click the other—but it takes time. And if you need to create another heading of the same type, you need to do it all over again. Or you can copy and paste the formatted text and type the new heading over it (as many people do) or use Word's clever Format Painter feature (which you'll learn about later in this chapter).

Because direct formatting takes extra time and effort, you'll do best to apply it only when you have formatted your documents almost completely using better tools, as discussed next.

Understanding Styles and When to Use Them

To save you time, Word includes a feature called styles. A *style* is a collection of formatting that you can apply all at once. So once you've set up a style for the heading that contains exactly the formatting you want, you can apply it in a single click.

In fact, in many cases you don't even need to create the styles yourself. Word comes with many styles built in to its Normal template and other templates. So as soon as you create a document based on one of these templates, you can start applying styles, formatting your documents swiftly and consistently.

Word gives you different types of styles:

- *Paragraph style.* This is a style you apply to a whole paragraph at a time—you can't apply it to just part of a paragraph. A paragraph style contains a full range of formatting for that paragraph—everything from the font name, size, and color through to the indentation and spacing for the paragraph, and the language used. For example, many documents use a Body Text style that gives the distinctive look to the body paragraphs.

- *Character style.* This is a style you apply to individual characters within a paragraph, usually to make it look different from the style of the rest of the paragraph. For example, within a paragraph that uses the Body Text style, you can apply an Emphasis character style to a word to make it stand out.

- *Linked paragraph and character style.* This is a style that works either for a paragraph as a whole or for individual characters within a paragraph. Word applies the linked style as a paragraph style if you either place the insertion point in the paragraph or select the whole of the paragraph. If you select just part of the paragraph, Word applies the style as a character style. Both the paragraphs formatted with the paragraph style and the text formatted with the character style appear at the same level in the table of contents.

- *Table style.* This is a style you can apply to a Word table. Like a paragraph style, the style can contain font and paragraph formatting, but it can also contain table formatting such as borders and shading.

- *List style.* This is a style you can apply to one or more paragraphs to make them into a list—a numbered list, a bulleted list, or a multilevel list. A list style usually contains font formatting and numbering formatting.

Styles enable you not only to apply formatting quickly, but you can also change it quickly in three ways:

- *Apply the same style from a different set.* Some Word templates include different sets of styles called Quick Styles. Each set contains styles with the same names but different looks. You can change the set of Quick Styles the document is using, changing the look of each styled paragraph in moments.

- *Modify the style.* If the style doesn't look right, you can modify it. Each paragraph to which you've applied the style takes on the changes you make immediately.

- *Replace one style with another style.* You can replace every instance of one style with another style in moments, making sweeping changes right through a document.

Formatting Your Documents the Best Way

Here's the best way to format your documents:

- First, format each paragraph with either a paragraph style or a linked paragraph and character style. This style gives the whole paragraph its overall look. If the paragraph is a heading, the Heading style tells Word to include the paragraph in the document's outline.

- Next, use a character style or the character aspect of a linked paragraph and character style to add extra formatting needed within paragraphs. For example, use a character style such as Emphasis to add impact to a word or phrase that you want to stand out.

- If the document contains lists, apply the appropriate list style to each list. For example, apply a numbered list style to a list than needs numbers, or a bulleted list style to a list that needs bullets.

- If the document contains tables, apply a suitable table style to each table.

UNDERSTANDING WHERE WORD KEEPS STYLES

Word keeps styles in templates and documents. As you learned in Chapter 1, a template is a file that contains the basic structure of a document—for example, the structure of a business letter. When you create a new document, you can choose whether to base it on a particular template or on the Normal template that Word uses for "blank" documents.

The styles available from the Styles group and the Styles panel when you first open Word are the ones stored in the Normal template. You can customize these styles as needed, but be aware that the changes carry through to all documents based on the Normal template.

When you create or open a document based on a template other than the Normal template, Word makes that template's styles available in the Styles group and the Styles panel. If the template is one that comes with Word, or one that you've downloaded from the web, it will most likely contain its own styles. You can modify these styles if you need to.

When you create a new template, you can create all the custom styles you need. You can also import styles from other templates or documents to save time.

Even though each document picks up the details of the styles from the attached template, the document itself contains information about the styles. This enables Word to display the document correctly when the template is not available.

When you're working in a document and modify a style, you can choose whether to save the changes in that document or in the template attached to the document. Normally you'll want to save the changes in the template, making them available to all existing documents based on the template and any new documents you create based on the template. By contrast, changes you save in the document are available only to that document (and to other documents you base on it).

Applying Styles to a Document

The easiest way to get started with styles is to apply styles by using the Quick Styles gallery on the Home tab of the Ribbon. Follow these steps:

1. Click in the paragraph to which you want to apply the style. If you want to apply the style to several paragraphs at once, select all or part of each paragraph.

2. Preview the style:

    • If the style name is in the part of the Quick Styles gallery that appears in the Styles group, hold the mouse over it for a moment (see Figure 7-2).

    • If the style name doesn't appear in the Styles group, click the More button (the drop-down button at the right end of the Quick Styles box) to display the Quick Styles gallery. Then hold the mouse pointer over the style name.

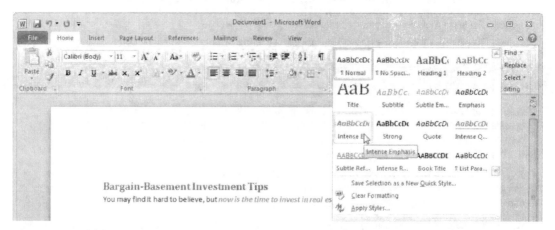

Figure 7-2. Hold the mouse pointer over a style name in the Quick Style gallery to preview the effect on the current paragraph or the selection. Click the style name to apply the style.

░ **Note** If Word doesn't display a preview of the style when you hold the mouse pointer over the style name, choose File ➤ Options. In the General pane of the Word Options dialog box, select the Enable Live Preview check box, and then click the OK button.

3. When you've found the style you want, click to apply it. If you had opened the Quick Styles gallery, Word closes it.

░ **Tip** Never use the Normal style as the formatting for the body of your documents. The problem is that Word uses the Normal style as the default, so it can be hard to tell whether you've applied the Normal style or Word has applied it because you haven't applied another style. For the body text in your documents, use a style such as Body Text instead, keeping the Normal style only for text you still need to give a style. You can then search (as described later in this chapter) for the Normal style and apply another style to each instance of it as needed.

Applying Different Quick Styles, Colors, Fonts, or Paragraph Spacing

When you've applied a style to each paragraph (and perhaps to individual words), you've defined what the different parts of the text are—the headings, the body text, and so on. If you want to change the way the whole document looks, you can now change the look of the styles, apply different colors, use different fonts, or alter the paragraph spacing.

Start by choosing Home ➤ Styles ➤ Change Styles ➤ Style Set, and highlighting each of the named items on the Style Set submenu (see Figure 7-3). As you move through Clean, Default, Distinctive, Elegant, and the other style sets, Word previews the styles on the document as a whole. Click the style set you want to use.

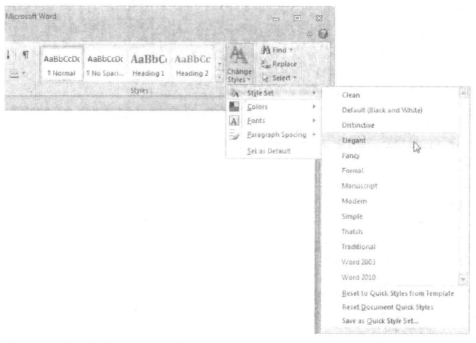

Figure 7-3. *Use the Change Styles drop-down menu in the Styles group on the Home tab of the Ribbon to change a style set, colors, fonts, or paragraph spacing.*

Next, choose Home ➤ Styles ➤ Change Styles ➤ Colors, and then choose the set of theme colors you prefer for the document. Again, Word gives you a preview, so you can see what will look best for the document.

If you need further changes, choose Home ➤ Styles ➤ Change Styles ➤ Fonts, and choose the set of fonts you want to use. The Fonts menu gives a wide range of sets, from the sober-looking Office set to the dramatic Arial Black and Newsprint sets.

If you want to change the paragraph spacing, choose Home ➤ Styles ➤ Change Styles ➤ Paragraph Spacing, and click the spacing you want. The top item is the default for the Quick Style set you're using. The Built-In section of the list provides a range of choices, from No Paragraph Space (none at all) to Compact (no extra spacing between lines, but some between paragraphs), to Double (widely spaced for a manuscript-like look).

▪ **Note** If you want to use the Quick Style look you've chosen as your standard look, choose Home ➤ Styles ➤ Change Styles ➤ Set as Default.

Changing the Styles in the Quick Style Gallery

The Quick Style gallery includes a selection of styles to get you started. But if you apply styles frequently from the Quick Style gallery, as is handy, you may want to customize the selection of styles.

You can customize the Quick Style gallery like this:

- *Remove an existing style.* In the Quick Style gallery, right-click the style, and then click Remove from Quick Style Gallery on the context menu.

- *Create a new style and add it.* Format some text with the formatting you want the new style to have, then choose Home ➤ Styles ➤ More ➤ Save Selection as a New Quick Style (the More button is the drop-down button at the right end of the Quick Style box in the Styles group). In the small Create New Style from Formatting dialog box (see Figure 7-4), type the style name, and then click the OK button. (There's also a larger version of the Create New Style from Formatting dialog box, as you'll see later in this chapter.)

Figure 7-4. You can use the small Create New Style from Formatting dialog box to create a Quick Style from formatting and add the style to the Quick Style gallery.

░ **Note** When creating a new style (as described later in this chapter), select the Add to Quick Style List check box if you want to add the style to the Quick Style gallery.

- *Add one of Word's styles.* Choose Home ➤ Styles ➤ Styles (click the little button with the arrow in the lower-right corner of the Styles group) to open the Styles pane. Right-click the style, and then click Add to Quick Style Gallery on the context menu.

Using the Apply Styles Pane

The Quick Style gallery is usually the easiest way of applying styles with the mouse, but if you need to apply styles throughout an existing document, you may prefer to use the Apply Styles pane (see Figure 7-5). To open this pane, click the More button (the drop-down button at the right end of the Quick Style box), and then click Apply Styles at the bottom of the Styles pane. This pane is small enough that you can comfortably keep it open as you work, which is useful if you hide the Ribbon.

Tip You can also open the Apply Styles pane by pressing Ctrl+Shift+S.

Figure 7-5. You can also apply styles by using the Apply Styles pane, which you open by choosing Home ➤ Styles ➤ Apply Styles.

The Style Name box in the Apply Styles pane shows the style applied to the current paragraph; if you have selected multiple paragraphs with different styles, the Style Name box shows the style applied to the last paragraph.

To apply another style, open the Style Name drop-down list, and then click the style you want to apply.

To reapply the same style, removing any extra formatting you have added to the style, click the Reapply button.

When you have finished working in the Apply Styles pane, click the Close button (the × button) to close it.

Note You can also apply styles from the Styles pane, which you'll meet later in this chapter.

Applying Styles Using the Keyboard

You can also apply styles by using keyboard shortcuts, which is useful when you're typing. Table 7-1 shows standard keyboard shortcuts, which work in Word's Normal template and in many other templates.

Table 7-1. Standard Keyboard Shortcuts for Applying Styles in Word

Style	Keyboard Shortcut
Normal	Ctrl+Shift+N
Heading 1	Ctrl+Alt+1
Heading 2	Ctrl+Alt+2
Heading 3	Ctrl+Alt+3
List Bullet	Ctrl+Shift+1

■ **Tip** If you want to apply other styles from the keyboard, create keyboard shortcuts for them as discussed in Chapter 5.

See Which Styles a Document Uses

To see which style a particular paragraph uses, you can click in the paragraph and look at the style selected in the Apply Style pane or in the Quick Style gallery (but you may need to open the Quick Style gallery to see the name). You can also look in the Styles pane (but you may have to scroll to see the style name, so this isn't very practical) or in the Style Inspector or the Reveal Formatting pane, which you'll meet later in this chapter.

To see the style applied to each paragraph, you can open the style area, a vertical strip at the left side of the Word window that displays the style applied to each paragraph (see Figure 7-6). You can display the style area only in Draft view and Outline view, not in any of the views that displays the page as it will appear when laid out.

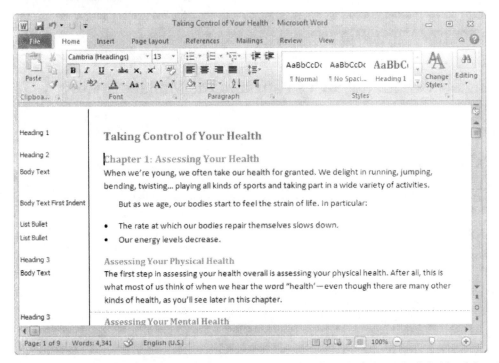

Figure 7-6. In Draft view and Outline view, you can display the style area on the left side of the window to see the style applied to each paragraph.

To display the style area, follow these steps:

1. Click the File tab to open Backstage.

2. Click the Options item to display the Word Options dialog box.

3. Click the Advanced item in the left pane to display the Advanced category.

4. Scroll down to the Display heading, about halfway down.

5. In the Style area pane width in Draft and Outline views text box, type a width such as 1" for the style area. (The default setting hides the style area.)

6. Click the OK button to close the Word Options dialog box.

Now click the Draft button in the View Shortcuts area on the status bar to switch to Draft view. The style area appears on the left of the screen, and you can easily see which style each paragraph has.

Tip To change the width of the style area, move the mouse pointer over the line that divides the style area from the text. When the pointer changes to a double-headed arrow, click and drag the line to the width you want. Drag the line all the way to the left to close the style area.

Managing Styles with the Styles Pane and the Manage Styles Dialog Box

For managing your styles, Word provides the Styles pane and the Manage Styles dialog box.

Working with the Styles Pane

To open the Styles pane (see Figure 7-7), choose Home ➤ Styles ➤ Styles or press Ctrl+Alt+Shift+S. The Styles button is the tiny button with the arrow at the lower-right corner of the Styles group on the Home tab of the Ribbon.

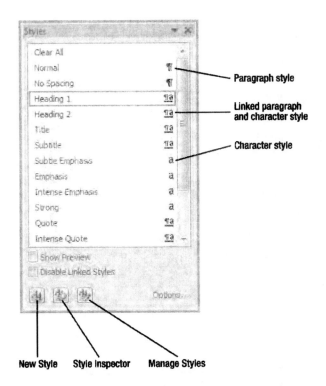

Paragraph style

Linked paragraph and character style

Character style

New Style   Style Inspector   Manage Styles

Figure 7-7. From the Styles pane, you can apply a style, inspect a style, start creating a new style, or manage your styles.

■ **Note** At first, the Styles pane shows only a selection of styles that Word recommends for frequent use. To display more styles in the Styles pane, click the Options button in the lower-right corner. Once the Style Pane Options dialog box opens, click the Select styles to show drop-down list, and then click All styles. You can also open the Select how list is sorted drop-down list and choose Alphabetical if you want the Styles pane to show the styles in alphabetical order. Click the OK button to close the Style Pane Options dialog box.

The Styles pane shows a list of styles sorted in the way selected in the Style Pane Options dialog box. To the right of each style appears a symbol showing whether it's a paragraph style (the ¶ or pilcrow), a character style (the letter *a*), or a linked paragraph and character style (¶a), as you can see in the figure.

From the Styles pane, you can take various actions. The following are the most useful:

- *Apply a style.* Click in the paragraph or select the text, and then click the style in the Styles pane.

- *View a preview of your styles.* Select the Show Preview check box to make the Styles pane show the styles with their font formatting rather than as a plain list. This makes the styles easier to identify.

- *Unlink linked styles.* Select the Disable Linked Styles check box to turn off the linkage between paragraph and character styles, so that character styles don't appear in the outline.

- *Start creating a new style.* Click the New Style button to display the larger version of the Create New Style from Formatting dialog box.

- *Open the Style Inspector.* Click the Style Inspector button.

- Open the Manage Styles dialog box. Click the Manage Styles button.

- *Change all instances of one style to another.* Right-click the style, and then click the Select All command. Word selects all the instances of the style. Click the style you want to apply instead of the current style.

- *Modify a style.* Right-click the style, and then click Modify to display the Modify Style dialog box.

■ **Tip** If you need to change heading styles to different heading levels, you may find it easier to promote or demote the headings in Outline view rather than change the styles as described here. See Chapter 8 for instructions on using Outline view.

Working with the Manage Styles Dialog Box

To open the Manage Styles dialog box (see Figure 7-8), click the Manage Styles button in the Styles pane.

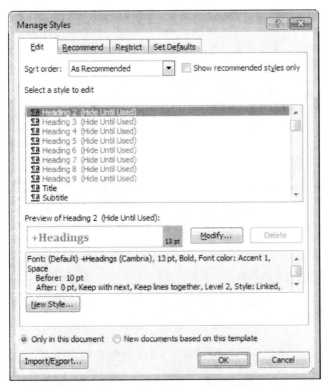

Figure 7-8. *You use the Manage Styles dialog box to edit existing styles, start creating new styles, recommend styles for use or restrict them from use, and to set default styles.*

The Manage Styles dialog box lets you take a wide range of advanced actions with styles. These are the actions you'll probably find most useful:

- *Change the sort order.* On the Edit tab, click the Sort order drop-down list, and then choose the sort order you want—for example, Alphabetical or By type.

- *Open a style to modify it.* On the Edit tab, click the style, and then click the Modify button to display the Modify Style dialog box.

- *Recommend styles.* On the Recommend tab, build a list of the styles you want Word to display in the Recommended list.

■ **Note** A typical Word template has so many styles that wading through the full list is awkward. By setting up the Recommended list with the styles you normally use, you can apply styles faster and more easily.

- *Restrict styles.* On the Restrict tab, build a list of the styles to restrict when you protect a document for formatting changes.

- *Set the default font, size, color, paragraph position, and paragraph spacing.* Use the controls on the Set Defaults tab to choose the default settings.

- *Export or import styles.* To import styles from or export styles to another document or template, click the Import/Export button at the bottom of any tab in the Manage Styles dialog box, and then work on the Styles tab of the Organizer dialog box that Word opens.

Creating Custom Styles

If you find that Word's styles don't meet your needs, you can either create custom styles of your own or customize the built-in styles to make them suitable.

The easiest way to create a custom style is by example, and that's the way we'll look at here. Along the way, you'll also see how to create a new style by specifying its formatting in the Create New Style from Formatting dialog box.

Creating a Custom Style by Example

To create a custom style by example, you set up a paragraph or other object with the formatting you want. Then tell Word to create a style from that formatted text, so you can then reapply the style wherever you need it.

Type a paragraph of text to use as a sample, or pick an existing paragraph in the document. If Word has an existing style that's similar to the style you want to create, apply that style first, so you don't need to make as many formatting changes.

Choosing the Font Formatting for a Style

Often, you'll want to start by choosing the font formatting for the style. You can do so by using any of the standard tools:

- *Font group.* Use the controls in the Font group of the Home tab of the Ribbon.

- *Mini Toolbar.* Select the paragraph or text, and then use the pop-up Mini Toolbar to adjust the formatting.

- *Font dialog box.* Choose Home ➤ Font ➤ Font (clicking the small button with the arrow at the lower-right corner of the Font group), or press Ctrl+D, to open the Font dialog box. On the Font tab (see Figure 7-9), choose the font, font style, size, color, underline, and other effects you need (for example, small caps). Click the OK button when you've finished.

Figure 7-9. You can quickly choose font formatting on the Font tab of the Font dialog box.

Note On the Advanced tab of the Font dialog box, you can change the scaling, spacing, and position of fonts. For example, you can change the spacing to spread the letters farther apart, or choose the Raised position to create a superscript. You can also work with features such as ligatures (two letters joined together), which you'll normally need only if you're typesetting a document.

Choosing the Paragraph Formatting for the Style

You can set some paragraph formatting for your sample paragraph by using the controls in the Paragraph group on the Home tab of the Ribbon, but you'll usually want to open the Paragraph dialog box so you can reach all the most useful types of paragraph formatting.

To choose paragraph formatting, follow these steps:

1. Choose Home ➤ Paragraph ➤ Paragraph (clicking the small button with the arrow at the lower-right corner of the Paragraph group) to open the Paragraph dialog box.

2. On the Indents and Spacing tab (see Figure 7-10), choose settings like this:

- *Alignment.* Choose Left, Centered, Right, or Justified, as needed. Justified text is aligned with both margins.

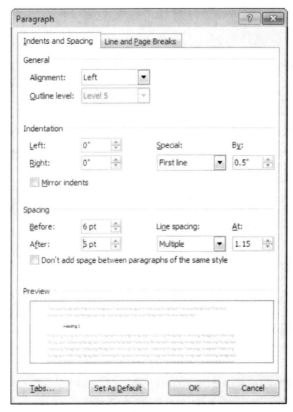

Figure 7-10. *Choose alignment, indentation, and spacing on the Indents and Spacing tab of the Font dialog box.*

- *Outline level.* If you want Word to treat this style as a type of heading, click the appropriate level, from Level 1 (a top-level item) down to Level 9. Choose Body Text if you want Word to treat paragraphs of this style as regular body text.

- *Indentation.* In the Left box and the Right box, set any indentation needed from the margins. To create a first-line indent, choose First line in the Special drop-down list, and then set the distance in the By box. You can also create a hanging indent (also known as an "outdent") by choosing Hanging in the Special drop-down list.

■ **Note** Select the Mirror indents check box if you want to produce facing pages that have outside indents that match each other and inside indents that match each other.

- *Spacing before and after paragraphs.* In the Before box and the After box, set the number of points of empty space you want before or after each paragraph that uses this style. Select the Don't add space between paragraphs of the same style check box if you want to suppress space between successive paragraphs that use the same style (for example, Body Text style).

■ **Note** A point (pt) is $\frac{1}{72}$-inch. Try six points after single-spaced paragraphs if you want a small gap, or 12 points for a larger gap. Body text doesn't usually need space before it, but you will probably want to add 12–24 points of space before a heading to separate it from the text above it, and around 12 points to separate it from the text below.

- *Line spacing.* In the Line Spacing drop-down list, choose the line spacing you want: Single, 1.5 lines, Double, At least, Exactly, or Multiple. For the At least setting or the Exactly setting, set the number of points in the At box. For the Multiple setting, set the number of lines in the At box—for example, use 3 to set three-line spacing.

3. Click the Line and Page Breaks tab to display it (see Figure 7-11), and then choose settings like this:

   - *Widow/Orphan control.* Select this check box if you want to avoid a single line appearing at the top of a page (a widow) and a single line appearing at the end of a page (an orphan), each separated from the rest of its paragraph. Normal typesetting practice is to suppress both widows and orphans.

Figure 7-11. *On the Line and Page Breaks tab of the Paragraph dialog box, you can tell Word whether to keep a paragraph with the next paragraph or add a page break before it.*

- *Keep with next.* Select this check box to make Word keep the paragraph on the same page as the next paragraph. Typically, you'll set this option for a heading style to prevent Word from putting it at the bottom of a page with the following paragraph on the next page.

- *Keep lines together.* Select this check box to make Word keep all the lines of a paragraph on the same page rather than breaking the paragraph across pages. This setting is useful for headings and display paragraphs, but not for body text.

- *Page break before.* Select this check box to have Word start a new page each time the style occurs. You'd normally use this only for styles such as chapter headings.

■ **Note** The Formatting exceptions area of the Line and Page Breaks tab contains settings for suppressing line numbers (in automatically numbered documents such as legal papers) and preventing hyphenation. Both these options are for specialized use only.

4. If you want to set tabs for the style, click the Tabs button at the bottom of the Paragraph dialog box to display the Tabs dialog box (see Figure 7-12). You can then set tabs like this:

- *Change the default spacing.* Adjust the value in the Default tab stops text box. For example, if you want Word to move one inch each time you press Tab in a paragraph that has this style, enter 1".

- *Set a new tab stop.* In the Tab stop position text box, type the position for the tab—for example, 1". Click the appropriate option button in the Alignment area—for example, the Left option button. If you want to use tab leader characters, click the appropriate option button in the Leader area. Then click the Set button.

- *Delete an existing tab stop.* Click the tab in the Tab stop position list box, and then click the Clear button. Click the Clear All button if you want to delete all the tabs.

- *Move or change a tab stop.* Delete the tab stop you want to change, and create a new tab stop with the position and alignment you want.

5. When you've finished setting tabs for the style, click the OK button to close the Tabs dialog box.

Figure 7-12. Use the Tabs dialog box to set any custom tab stops that the style needs.

6. Click the OK button to close the Paragraph dialog box.

Adding Bullets or Numbering to the Style

If you're creating a list style, add whichever bullets or numbering it needs.

The quick way to add bullets or numbering is to use the first three controls in the Paragraph group on the Home tab of the Ribbon. Click the Bullets drop-down button, the Numbering drop-down button, or the Multilevel List drop-down button in the Paragraph group to open the panel, hold the mouse pointer over a list style to preview it, and click the style you want to apply. Figure 7-13 shows the Numbering panel.

■ **Note** You can also apply the default style of bullets, numbering, or multilevel list by clicking the button itself (for example, the Bullets button) rather than the drop-down button.

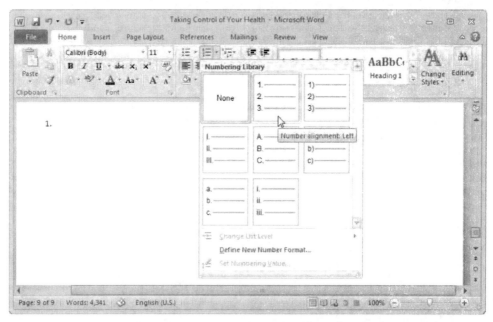

Figure 7-13. *You can quickly apply bullets, numbering, or a multilevel list by using the Bullets drop-down button, the Numbering drop-down button, or the Multilevel List drop-down button in the Paragraph group of the Home tab.*

Adding Borders and Shading to the Style

Next, add any borders or shading that the style needs.

You can apply individual borders by clicking the Home ➤ Paragraph ➤ Border drop-down button and then clicking the border you want in the drop-down panel, but you can get greater control by choosing Home ➤ Paragraph ➤ Border ➤ Borders and Shading to display the Borders and Shading dialog box.

To add borders, display the Borders tab (see Figure 7-14), and then work like this:

1. In the Apply to drop-down list, choose Paragraph if you want to apply the border to the whole paragraph. Choose Text if you want to put the border only around the text.

2. To apply a standard border, click Box, Shadow, or 3-D in the Setting area. To create a custom border, click the borders in the diagram in the Preview area to place borders where you want them.

3. Change the border's appearance by using the Style list, the Color drop-down list, and the Width drop-down list.

■ **Note** To move the borders closer to the text or farther away from it, click the Options button. In the Borders and Shading Options dialog box that opens, adjust the Top, Bottom, Left, and Right measurements, and then click the OK button.

4. Click the OK button to close the Borders and Shading dialog box.

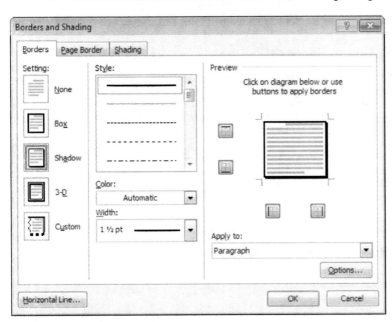

Figure 7-14. Use the Borders tab of the Borders and Shading dialog box to quickly apply borders to a paragraph.

■ **Note** A paragraph border is usually the most useful kind of border for a style, but if you're creating a style that will occupy most (or all) of a page, you may want to create a page border in the style. In this case, click the Page Border tab in the Borders and Shading dialog box, select the appropriate document part in the Apply to drop-down list (for example, This section), and then work with the border controls in the same way as for applying a paragraph border.

To apply shading to a style, click the Shading tab in the Borders and Shading dialog box, and then follow these steps:

1. In the Apply to drop-down list, choose Paragraph if you want to apply the shading to the whole paragraph. Choose Text if you want to apply the border only to the text.

2. In the Fill drop-down list, choose the shading color you want.

3. In the Style drop-down list, choose the shading style—for example, 25% shading or Dk Trellis shading.

4. In the Color drop-down list, choose the pattern color.

5. Click the OK button to close the Borders and Shading dialog box.

Adding Language Formatting to the Style

The final type of formatting that you can include in the style is language formatting. Unlike almost all the other types of formatting, language formatting isn't visual formatting. Instead, it tells Word to treat the text as being in a particular language. For example, if you're writing a paper on French poets, you could create a style for block quotes and set its language to French. The spell checker would then refrain from querying the words as not being in the English language.

■ **Note** The text doesn't actually have to be in the language you specify, but you're telling Word to treat it as if it is.

To apply language formatting to text, follow these steps:

1. Choose Review ➤ Language ➤ Language ➤ Set Proofing Language to display the Language dialog box (see Figure 7-15).

Figure 7-15. *In the Language dialog box, you can specify the language used for the text. You can also turn off spelling and grammar checking for the style.*

2. In the Mark selected text as list box, select the language you want to use. Your current language appears at the top of the list to save you from having to scroll to find it.

3. If you want to tell spell checker and grammar checker not to check the text, select the Do not check spelling or grammar check box.

4. Click the OK button to close the dialog box.

Creating the Style

Once you have set up the paragraph with all the formatting it needs, you can create a style like this:

1. Select the paragraph.

2. Choose Home ➤ Styles ➤ More ➤ Save Selection as a New Quick Style to display the small Create New Style from Formatting dialog box.

3. Type the name for the style in the Name text box.

4. Click the Modify button to display the large Create New Style from Formatting dialog box (see Figure 7-16).

Figure 7-16. In the large Create New Style from Formatting dialog box, choose the style type and the style for the next paragraph. Select the New documents based on this template option button if you want to make the style available to other documents.

5. In the Style type drop-down list, choose the style type: Paragraph, Character, Linked (paragraph and character), Table, or List.

6. In the Style for following paragraph drop-down list, choose the style you want Word to apply automatically to the next paragraph when you press the Enter key at the end of a paragraph with this style. For a display style (such as a heading), you will normally want a body style next; for a body style, you will probably want to continue with the same body style.

7. Select the Add to Quick Style list check box if you want Word to include this style in the Quick Style gallery. Otherwise, clear this check box.

8. Clear the Automatically Update check box unless you want Word to update the style without consulting you when it thinks you've altered the style.

9. Tell Word where to store the style by selecting the appropriate option button:

   • *Only in this document.* Select this option button to store the style in the document.

- *New documents based on this template.* Select this option to store the style in the template, from which it will be available to all documents you create based on the template. This is normally the better choice.

10. Click the OK button to close theCreate New Style from Formatting dialog box.

Modifying an Existing Style

You can modify an existing style either by opening it in the Modify Style dialog box and working from there. You can also change the formatting of a paragraph of text that uses the style and then making the style pick up your changes.

Changing a Style Using the Modify Style dialog Box

The more formal way of modifying an existing style is to open the style in the Modify Style dialog box, which is a renamed version of the large Create New Style from Formatting dialog box. You can then use the formatting controls and the options on the Format drop-down list to adjust the style exactly as you need it.

You can open the Modify Style dialog box from the Styles pane, the Quick Style gallery, or the Apply Styles pane:

- *Styles pane.* Right-click the style name, and then click Modify on the context menu.

- *Quick Style gallery.* Right-click the style name, and then click Modify on the context menu.

- *Apply Styles pane.* Select the style, and then click the Modify button.

Updating a Style with New Formatting

Instead of modifying an existing style as described in the previous section, you can apply a style, change its formatting, and then update the style to match the new formatting. This method can be useful when you're developing a template and you need to keep adjusting styles to make everything look and fit right.

Apply the style using whichever tool you prefer (for example, the Apply Styles pane), and reformat the text as needed. When you're ready, select the paragraph, right-click in the selection, click or highlight Styles on the context menu, and then click Update *Style Name* to Match Selection on the submenu.

Applying Direct Formatting on Top of Styles

After you've applied the style each paragraph needs, and you've applied list styles and character styles as needed, you can finish off the formatting by applying direct formatting to any parts of the document that need it. For example, you may need to apply different font formatting to pick out special display elements or add more space before some paragraphs.

■ **Note** To get the most out of Word's automatic formatting features, use direct formatting as little as possible. If you need to apply the same direct formatting to several different items, consider creating a style with that formatting so you can apply it instantly in future. If you will need to use the same direct formatting and text, save it as an AutoText entry (see Chapter 6 for instructions).

To apply direct formatting, use the tools you've met earlier in this chapter for setting up font formatting, paragraph formatting, bullets and numbering, and so on. For example:

- *Font formatting.* Use the controls in the Font group on the Home tab of the Ribbon, on the mini toolbar, or in the Font dialog box.

- *Paragraph formatting.* Use the controls in the Paragraph group on the Home tab of the Ribbon or in the Paragraph dialog box.

- *Bullets and numbering.* Use the controls in the Paragraph group on the Home tab of the Ribbon.

■ **Tip** To remove direct formatting from text, select the text, and then press Ctrl+spacebar.

Copying and Pasting Formatting Using the Format Painter

When you've painstakingly applied direct formatting to text or another object, you may want to reuse that direct formatting for other text or another object. The straightforward way to do so is to copy the text (or object), paste it in, and then type the new text over it. This works fine for new text items or objects (unless you forget to replace the pasted text), but it's not efficient if the text is already there.

Instead, you can use Word's Format Painter. This feature enables you to pick up the formatting for a selection and then "paint" it on other text or another object. Follow these steps:

1. Select the text or object that contains the formatting you want to copy.

2. Choose Home ➤ Clipboard ➤ Format Painter (the brush icon) or press Ctrl+Shift+C to copy the formatting. Word changes the mouse pointer to a brush icon.

■ **Tip** If you want to apply the formatting to multiple items, double-click the Format Painter button in the Clipboard group. The mouse pointer becomes the Format Painter brush until you turn it off by clicking the Format Painter button again or pressing the Esc key.

3. Drag the brush over the text or object to which you want to apply the formatting. Word applies the formatting and restores the mouse pointer.

Seeing Which Formatting You've Applied to Text

Because Word uses both styles and direct formatting, you'll often need to check exactly what formatting a paragraph or some text uses—especially if you've received the document from someone else rather than formatting it yourself.

As you saw earlier in this chapter, you can view the paragraph style by looking in the Apply Styles pane or other panes for applying styles. In Draft view and Outline view, you can also display the style area on the left of the Word window to see at a glance which style each paragraph uses.

But to really dig into the details of the formatting, you need to use two other tools that Word provides: the Style Inspector and the Reveal Formatting pane.

Using the Style Inspector to Examine a Style

When you need to see whether a paragraph uses only style formatting or has direct formatting applied to it as well, open the Style Inspector (see Figure 7-17) by clicking the Style Inspector button in the Styles pane.

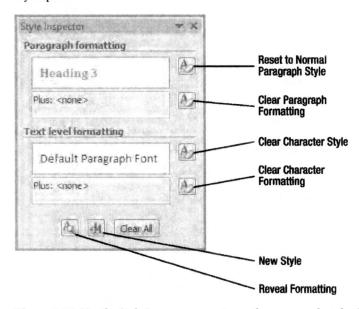

Figure 7-17. Use the Style Inspector pane to see the paragraph style, the text level formatting, and any additional formatting added.

You can quickly change the formatting of the paragraph and text by using the four buttons on the right side of the Style Inspector:

- *Reset to Normal Paragraph Style.* Click this button only if you want to apply the Normal style to the paragraph. Doing this is usually not helpful.
- *Clear Paragraph Formatting.* Click this button to remove from the paragraph all the extra paragraph formatting listed in the Plus box. For example, if you've applied double line spacing or indents to the paragraph manually, clicking this button removes them, restoring the style's usual paragraph formatting.

- *Clear Character Style.* Click this button to remove character styles from the paragraph. Doing this is sometimes helpful, but what you'll frequently want to do is leave the character styles in place, but remove direct formatting.

- *Clear Character Formatting.* Click this button to remove any extra formatting you've applied to the paragraph's text (as opposed to the paragraph as a whole). For example, if you've changed the font or font color using direct formatting, clicking this button restores the default font.

■ **Note** Click the Clear All button if you want to wipe out all the paragraph, style, and direct formatting and apply the Normal style to the paragraph. Doing this is occasionally useful if someone has laid on the direct formatting with a trowel and you need a quick way to remove it. After clicking this button, use the Apply Styles pane, the Quick Style gallery, or another method to apply the style you want the paragraph to have, and then apply any character styles needed.

As you can see in the figure, the Style Inspector contains two more buttons:

- *Reveal Formatting.* Click this button to open the Reveal Formatting pane.

- *New Style.* Click this button to open the large Create New Style from Formatting dialog box.

Seeing Formatting Details with the Reveal Formatting Pane

To see exactly what formatting a paragraph uses, and perhaps sort out problems with it, open the Reveal Formatting pane by clicking the Reveal Formatting button in the Style Inspector.

Figure 7-18 shows the Reveal Formatting pane with different views of the same formatting information:

- The screen on the left shows the Reveal Formatting pane as it normally opens, showing the details of the font formatting and paragraph formatting (in expanded lists) and offering details of the section formatting (in a collapsed list).

- The screen on the right shows the Reveal Formatting pane with the Distinguish style source check box selected. Selecting this check box makes the Reveal Formatting pane break down each list to show which formatting comes from styles and which comes from direct formatting. For example, here you can see that the Subtle Emphasis character style provides italics and a font color, but that the underline, dark blue font color, and shadow effect come from direct formatting applied on top of the style.

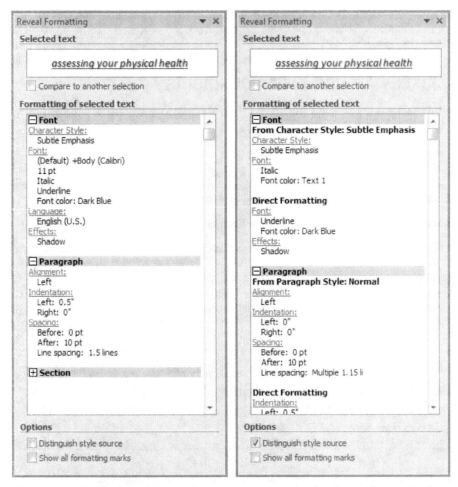

Figure 7-18. Use the Reveal Formatting pane to see exactly what formatting a selection uses (left) or to see how that formatting differs from the styles applied (right).

▓ **Tip** To see how the formatting of your current selection compares to other text, you can select the Compare to another selection check box. Next, click in or select the text that you want to compare it with. The Reveal Formatting pane displays a list of the formatting differences, which you can use to remove unwanted formatting from the selection.

Click the – sign to the left of the Font list or the Paragraph list to collapse that list, or click the +sign next to the Section list to expand that list.

Within each list, you can click the links to open the dialog box or pane for adjusting that type of formatting. For example, click the Alignment link in the Paragraph section to open the Paragraph dialog box with the Indents and Spacing tab at the front.

Navigating Quickly Around Your Documents

To help you navigate quickly around your documents, Word provides the Navigation pane, the Find and Replace feature, and the Go To feature.

Using the Navigation Pane

The Navigation pane is a pane that appears by default docked to the left side of the Word window. If you want, you can drag it to the right side of the Word window and dock it there, or drag it elsewhere to use it as a floating pane.

To open the Navigation pane, choose View ➤ Show ➤ Navigation Pane, selecting the Navigation Pane check box.

As you can see in Figure 7-19, the Navigation pane has a Search box at the top, with three tabs below it:

- *Headings tab.* Click this tab (shown on the left in the figure) to view your document as an outline of collapsible headings. If a heading contains subheadings, a triangle appears next to it. Click the triangle to display the headings or to hide them again. Click the heading you want to display.

Tip To control which levels of headings appear on the Headings tab, right-click any heading, highlight Show Heading Level, and then click the heading level you want—for example, Show Heading 3. From the context menu, you can also take other actions, including promoting and demoting the current heading, creating a new heading before or after it, or creating a subheading.

- *Pages tab.* Click this tab (shown in the middle of the figure) to view thumbnail pictures of your document's pages. Click the thumbnail for the page you want to display.

- *Search Results tab.* Click this tab, type a search term in the Search box, and then press the Enter key to see the results. Hold the mouse pointer over a result to display a ScreenTip giving the page number and the heading section the result is in. Click a result to display it in the document. Click the Previous button (the up arrow) to go to the previous search result, or click the Next button (the down arrow) to go to the next search result.

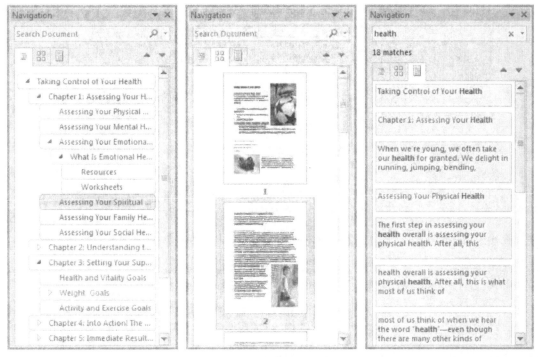

Figure 7-19. *The Navigation pane contains three tabs for browsing the document by headings (left), pages (middle), and search results (right).*

■ **Note** You can search using any of the tabs in the Navigation pane. After you search, the Headings tab highlights any headings that match the search, and the Pages tab shows only the pages that match the search. Click the X button in the Search box when you want to clear the search.

When you have finished using the Navigation pane, click the Close button (the × button) to close it.

Using Find

As you saw in the previous section, you can search using the Navigation pane rather than the Find and Replace dialog box. But you can also open the Find and Replace dialog box when you want to use complex searches to find specific parts of a document or when you want to replace text, formatting, or both.

You can open the Find and Replace dialog box in any of these ways:

- *From the Ribbon.* Choose Home ➤ Editing ➤ Find ➤ Advanced Find to display the Find and Replace dialog box with the Find tab at the front, or choose Home ➤ Editing ➤ Replace to display the Find and Replace dialog box with the Replace tab at the front.

- *From the Navigation pane.* Choose Home ➤ Editing ➤ Find to open the Navigation pane, then click the drop-down button to the right of the Search box and click 'Advanced Find on the menu. This method leaves the Navigation pane open, so you may prefer the previous method.

- *With the keyboard.* Press Ctrl+H to open the Find and Replace dialog box with the Replace tab at the front. To display the Find tab, click it.

With the Find and Replace dialog box open, you can search for regular text by using the techniques explained in Chapter 4. But you can also click the More button to display the hidden part of the dialog box (see Figure 7-20) and then choose other search options as described here.

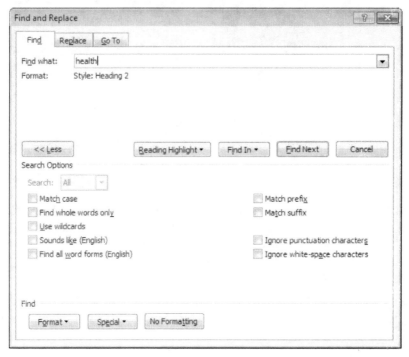

Figure 7-20. *After expanding the Find and Replace dialog box by clicking the More button (which changes to Less), you can search with wildcards and special characters. You can also search for particular formatting or for styles. The area below the Find what box shows the search options you're using.*

▒ **Tip** You can work in the document while the Find and Replace dialog box is open—just click in the document and edit it as needed, then click in the dialog box when you want to start using it again. This means you can leave the Find and Replace dialog box open until you've finished searching and making any changes needed to what you find.

Displaying Reading Highlights

To make Word highlight all the instances it has found, click the Reading Highlight button, and then click Highlight All on the menu. Click the Reading Highlight button again and choose Clear Highlighting when you want to get rid of the highlights.

Searching Only Part of the Document

When you need to search in just part of the document, select it. Click the Find In button and make sure Current Selection is selected (if not, click it). Click the Find In button again and choose Main Document when you want to search in the whole document again.

Changing the Search Direction

When you first search, Word searches from the position of the insertion point to the end of the document, wraps round automatically to the beginning, and continues till it gets back to the insertion point.

If you want to search upward rather than downward, open the search drop-down list and choose Up; at the beginning of the document, Word asks if you want to continue. To search downward, and have Word ask at the end of the document if you want to continue, choose Down. Choose All to search through the whole of the document without prompting.

Finding Search Terms That Match the Case You Type

Normally, Find ignores the case of characters, so it finds the search term no matter what capitalization it uses. If you want Find to find only results that match the case you type, select the Match case check box.

Restricting the Search to Whole Words

If you want to find your search term only as a whole word rather than as part of other words, select the Find whole words only check box. For example, you may need to find the word "any" rather than "many" or "anywhere." This option works only for single words; as soon as you type a space in the Find what box, Word makes this check box unavailable.

Using Wildcards to Find Variable Text

To give your searches more flexibility, select the Use wildcards check box. A *wildcard* is a character or group of characters that represents other characters—a bit like your being able to use a joker as another card in some games or a blank tile at Scrabble. Table 7-2 explains the wildcards you can use for searching in Word.

Table 7-2. Wildcard Characters for Searching in Word

Use This Wildcard	To Find This Text	Example
?	Any character	**r?de** finds *rede*, *ride*, *rode*, and *rude*.
*	Any characters, or none	**force*** finds *force, forced, forceps,* and *forces*.
[*characters*]	Any one of the characters you've specified	**b[aeiou]ll** finds *ball, bell, bill,* and *bull*.
[*character1– character2*]	Any one of the characters in the alphabetical range you've entered	**b[a-j]t** finds words such as *bat, bet,* and *bit*. It does not find *but*, because *u* is not in the range.
[!*character1– character2*]	Any one character that's not in the alphabetical range you've entered	**b[!a-jt]** finds *bot* and *but*, but doesn't find *bat, bet,* and *bit*.
character{*number*}	The number of occurrences of the character	**20{4}** find *20,000*, because it has four zeroes.
character{*number1, number2*}	From *number1* instances to *number2* instances of the character	**20{1,4}** finds *20, 200, 2000, 20000,* and similar numbers.
character@	One or more instances of the character	**0@in** finds *10in, 100in,* and other text with one or more zeroes followed by *in*.

Finding Words That Sound Like Other Words

If you need to find words that sound like other words, select the Sounds like check box. This feature is worth trying if you work in documents that may have unintentional word substitutions (for example, documents entered using speech recognition), but overall it's too hit-and-miss to rely on.

Finding All Forms of a Word

Select the Find all word forms check box if you need to find each different form of the search text. For example, if you search for "go," Find finds "went" and "gone" as well.

Searching for Special Characters

If you need to search for a character that you can't type with the keyboard, such as a paragraph mark (the normally hidden character that ends a paragraph) or an em dash (—), click the Special button, and then click the item you want on the pop-up menu (see Figure 7-21). Word enters the appropriate code in the Find what text box, and you can then run the search.

Figure 7-21. Use the Special drop-down menu in the Find and Replace dialog box to enter a special character, such as the code for a paragraph mark or a graphic.

Searching Only at the Start or End of a Word

To make Word search for your search text only at the start of words, select the Match prefix check box. For example, you can search for "after" at the beginning of words to find *afterward* and *afternoon*.

Similarly, you can select the Match suffix check box to search for your search term only at the end of words—for example, finding "after" in *hereafter* or *rafter*.

Ignoring Punctuation and White Space

If you want Word to ignore any punctuation that may appear in a word, select the Ignore punctuation characters check box. Ignoring punctuation is useful when you need to find text that may contain a comma, apostrophe, or other punctuation.

Similarly, you can select the Ignore white-space characters to make Word ignore spaces and tabs when searching. For example, when ignoring white space, searching for "nobody" also finds "no body."

Finding Formatting

As well as finding text, Word enables you to find formatting—either formatting applied to particular text or formatting on its own. For example, you can search for instances of the word industry with the Subtle Emphasis style applied to it, or you can search for any text formatted with both bold and italic.

To search for formatting, follow these steps:

1. Type your search text in the Find what box like you've done before. If you want to search for just formatting, delete anything that's in the Find what' box.

2. Click the Format button, and then click the type of formatting on the drop-down menu (see Figure 7-22).

Figure 7-22. Use the commands on the Format drop-down menu in the Find and Replace dialog box to specify the formatting you want to find.

3. In the dialog box that opens, set up the type of formatting. For example, in the Find Style dialog box, click the style name, and then click the OK button.

■ **Note** The Highlight item on the Format drop-down menu doesn't display a dialog box—it just switches on searching for Highlight text. Choose Format ➤ Highlight again to search for Not Highlight; choose Format ➤ Highlight a third time to remove Highlight from the search.

Click the No Formatting button when you want to remove the formatting criteria from the search.

Replacing Text, Formatting, and Styles

Finding text or formatting is great, but what you'll often need to do is replace it with other text, formatting, or both. To replace items, choose Home ➤ Editing ➤ Replace or press Ctrl+H to display the Replace tab of the Find and Replace dialog box.

The Replace tab (shown in Figure 7-23 with settings chosen for replacing direct formatting with a style) works in much the same way as the Find tab. For a straightforward replacement, type the search text in the Find what box and the replacement text in the Replace with box. For a complex replacement, click the More button to display the lower part of the dialog box, and then choose the options you want.

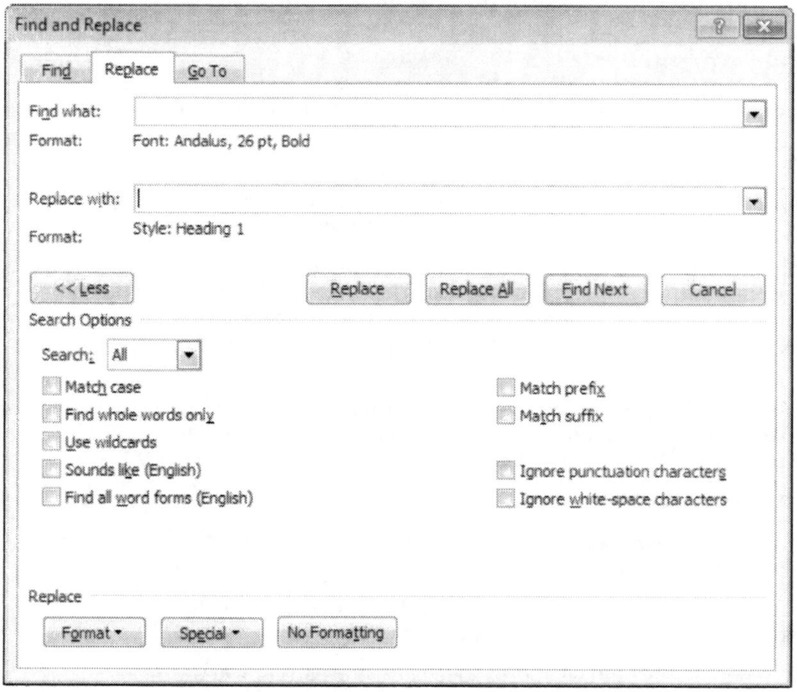

Figure 7-23. One of the Replace tool's most useful tricks is to replace direct formatting with a style.

Once you've set up the replacement, use the Replace button, Replace All button, and Find Next button to run it:

- *Find Next.* Click this button to find the next instance of the search term.

- *Replace.* Click this button to replace the instance Word has found and to find the next instance.

- *Replace All.* Click this button to replace every instance. If you've chosen Up or Down rather than All in the Search drop-down list, Word asks if you want to continue when it reaches the beginning or end of the document.

Replacing Text

To replace text, simply type the replacement in the Replace with box. But you can also make Word insert the contents of the Clipboard or the Find what box:

- *Insert the contents of the Clipboard.* Type ^c in the Replace with box to make Word insert the contents of the Clipboard in place of whatever you're searching for. You can use this trick to insert a table, image, or a section of text that you've copied to the Clipboard.

- *Insert the contents of the Find what box.* Type ^& in the Replace with box to make Word insert the contents of the Find what box (or what the contents represents). For example, you can type wildcards in the Find what box, and then have the Replace with box insert text plus whatever expression matched the wildcards.

Replacing Formatting or Styles

When you need to reformat documents, you can use Replace to replace formatting. You can replace formatting in several ways:

- *Replace text and formatting.* Sometimes you may need to find given text that's formatted in a particular way and replace it with other text formatted differently. (You can also replace it with the same text formatted differently.)

- *Replace text with formatting.* You can find text that's formatted in a particular way and replace it with formatting, getting rid of the text. This approach is useful if you create documents in a text editor (for example, on a portable device) and need to apply formatting in Word. For example, you can replace the text *h1* with the Heading 1 style.

- *Replace formatting only.* You can replace one type of formatting with another type—for example, replacing bold italic 20-point text with a Heading 2 style. Or you can replace one style with another style.

To replace formatting or styles, follow these steps:

1. Open the Replace tab of the Find and Replace dialog box. Choose Home ➤ Editing ➤ Replace or press Ctrl+H.

2. In the Find what box, enter any text you want to find. If you're searching for formatting, delete anything that's in the Find what' box.

3. With the insertion point in the Find what box, specify the formatting you want to find. Click the Format drop-down button; click Font, Paragraph, Tabs, Language, Frame, or Style and use the dialog box that opens to specify the

details. When you click the OK button, the Format line under the Find what box shows your choices.

4. In the Replace with box, enter any replacement text. To replace only with formatting, delete anything that's in this box.

5. With the insertion point in the Replace with box, specify the replacement formatting. Use the same techniques as in Step 3.

6. Run the replacement as usual. For example, click the Replace All button to replace all instances of the formatting.

Navigating with Go To

If you want to get about your documents quickly, it's well worth learning how to use the Go To feature. Go To overlaps with browsing by different objects using the Select Browse Object button (as discussed in Chapter 6), but it can be a handy way of getting around a document.

To use Go To, open the Go To tab of the Find and Replace dialog box (see Figure 7-24) in one of these ways:

- *Mouse.* Click the Page readout at the left end of the status bar.

- *Ribbon.* Choose Home ➤ Editing ➤ Find ➤ Go To.

- *Keyboard.* Press Ctrl+G.

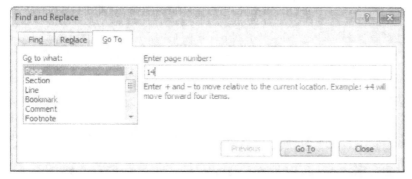

Figure 7-24. The Go To tab of the Find and Replace dialog box is great for moving quickly to a page by number or for going from one equation or bookmark to another.

In the Go to what box, click the type of object you want to move by: Page, Section, Line, Bookmark, Comment, Footnote, Endnote, Field, Table, Graphic, Equation, Object, or Heading.

░ **Note** A bookmark is an invisible marker you set in the text to mark a point you want to be able to access easily (see Chapter 8). An object is an item such as an audio file or video file that you insert in the document.

Once you've done this, you can move from one object of that type to another in either of these ways:

- If you just want to move to the next or previous object, click the Next button or the Previous button. (The Next button replaces the Go To button until you identify the object.)

- In the box on the right, identify the number or name of the object you want. This box changes depending on the object you've chosen. For example, type a page number or choose a bookmark name; type + and a number (for example, +5) to move forward by that number of objects or – and a number (for example, –50) to move backward by that number of objects. Then click the Go To button.

When you've finished using the Go To feature, click the Close button to close the Find and Replace dialog box.

Summary

In this chapter, you've learned the best way to format your Word documents—by using styles from start to finish, and then adding only such little direct formatting as is absolutely necessary. You've seen how to apply Word's existing styles, how to create custom styles of your own, and how to modify a style either directly or by updating it to match an example.

You now also know how to navigate around your documents using the Navigation pane, Find, and Go To. And you've learned how to find any document item you need, from plain text to characters you can't type—and how to replace it if necessary.

In the next chapter, I'll show you how to create complex documents and complex layouts. Turn the page when you're ready to start.

CHAPTER 8

Creating Complex Documents and Layouts

Once you've mastered the art of formatting your documents with styles (as described in Chapter 7), you're ready to create long or complex documents in Word.

In this chapter, you'll learn first how to use the extra table features that Word provides over those that the Office programs share. Then I'll show you how to break a document into multiple sections; how to add headers, footers, and page numbers; and how to create newspaper-style columns of text.

After that, you'll see how to mark important parts of a document with bookmarks, and how to insert cross-references back to these bookmarks or to other parts. Finally, you'll learn how to develop your documents using Word's powerful Outline view and how to add footnotes and endnotes to your documents.

Working with Word's Extra Table Features

In Word, you can create tables in the following three ways:

- *Insert a table:* As discussed in Chapter 4, choose Insert ➤ Table ➤ Table, and then click the table arrangement you want on the Insert Table grid—for example, five rows of three columns each. This is good for creating regular tables, ones that have the same number of cells in each row.

- *Draw a table:* Also as discussed in Chapter 4, choose Insert ➤ Table ➤ Table ➤ Draw Table, and then use the drawing cursor to draw the table layout you want. Drawing a table is good for creating irregular tables.

- *Convert existing text to a table:* If the document already contains the text you want to create the table from, you can convert the text into a table, as discussed next.

Converting Existing Text into a Table

Converting existing text to a table is usually faster than creating a table and moving existing data into it.

First, you need to make sure that the material is laid out regularly, with its contents separated using one of these four items:

- *Tabs:* This is usually the easiest way of separating material, as you can see the different columns that the table will create. Figure 8-1 shows a table laid out with tabs. Notice that because the tab stops aren't optimally positioned, the columns don't align in each row. This doesn't matter as long as there's only one tab between each item destined for a cell.

Department → Position·Needed   →   Manager   →   Target·Hire·Date¶

Sales·and·Marketing → Administrative·Assistant   →   Renee·Williams·4·January·2011¶

Operations   →   Director·of·Operations·→Mauro·Flaherty·11·January·2011¶

HR   →   Administrative·Support·[Hiring·Manager]   →   11·January·2011¶

Figure 8-1. When using tabs to lay out text you plan to turn into a table, use only one tab between the contents of each cell. Press Ctrl+Shift+8 to display the invisible characters including the tabs and paragraph marks.

Note When converting tabbed material into a table, you must make sure of two things. First, check that each item is separated only by one tab, not by two or more tabs—otherwise, you'll get the wrong number of columns. Second, check that the material for each cell is not broken onto multiple lines—otherwise, you'll get the wrong number of rows.

- *Paragraphs*: If each cell's data appears in a separate paragraph, you can quickly convert it to a table. Make sure the data contains no unnecessary blank paragraphs.
- *Commas*: If you have data separated by commas, such as a comma-separated values export from a spreadsheet, you can use a comma as the separator character for a table.
- *Other character*: If your data is separated consistently by another character (for example, * or |), you can specify that character as the separator character. You need to make sure that this character doesn't appear as part of the regular text, only as the separator character.

When your data is in good order, convert it to a table like this:

1. Select the paragraphs of data. Select right from the start up to the paragraph mark at the end of the last paragraph. (If Word is hiding paragraph marks, you'll appear to have selected a chunk of blank space at the end of the last paragraph.)

2. Choose Insert ➤ Table ➤ Table ➤ Convert Text to Table to display the Convert Text to Table dialog box (see Figure 8-2).

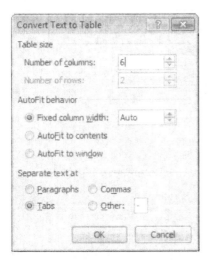

Figure 8-2. *In the Convert Text to Table dialog box, make sure that Word has chosen the right separator character (for example, tabs), and choose the AutoFit behavior you want.*

3. In the Separate text at area, make sure that Word has picked the right separator character. If not, select the Paragraphs option button, the Commas option button, the Tabs option button, or the Other option button as appropriate; for the Other option button, type the separator character in the text box.

4. In the Table size area, make sure that the number of columns is right:

   - If you're using tabs as the separator character, and the number of columns is wrong, one or more of the paragraphs contains an extra tab (or is missing a tab). Click the Cancel button, find the extra or missing tab, and then start the conversion again.

   - If you're using paragraphs as the separator character, you must tell Word how many paragraphs to use for each row. Enter this number in the Number of columns box.

5. In the AutoFit behavior area, choose whether to fit the column widths automatically to their contents:

   - *Fixed column width:* Select this option button to use a fixed width for each column. You can then choose Auto to have Word allocate the space equally among the columns or type the fixed width you want.

   - *AutoFit to contents:* Select this option button to let Word adjust each column's width to fit its contents. You may need to adjust the widths afterward.

   - *AutoFit to window:* Select this option button to have Word make the table automatically fit the window's width.

6. Click the OK button to close the Convert Text to Table dialog box. Word converts the text to a table. Figure 8-3 shows the text from the example in Figure 8-1 converted into a table.

Department¤	Position·Needed¤	Manager¤	Target·Hire·Date¤	¤
Sales·and·Marketing¤	Administrative·Assistant¤	Renee·Williams¤	4·January·2011¤	¤
Operations¤	Director·of·Operations¤	Mauro·Flaherty¤	11·January·2011¤	¤
HR¤	Administrative·Support¤	[Hiring·Manager]¤	11·January·2011¤	¤

Figure 8-3. The table that Word creates from the tabbed text in Figure 8-1.

Converting a Table to Text

Word also lets you convert a table back to text. This move is useful when you've received material in table form that you need to convert to a different layout.

To convert a table to text, follow these steps:

1. Click anywhere in the table. You don't need to select it.

2. Choose Table Tools ➤ Layout ➤ Data ➤ Convert to Text to display the Convert Table to Text dialog box (see Figure 8-4).

Figure 8-4. When converting a table back to text, you can separate the cells with paragraph marks, tabs, commas, or another character of your choice.

3. In the Separate text with area, choose the character with which to separate the cell contents: Select the Paragraph marks option button, the Tabs option button, the Commas option button, or the Other option button (and type the character in the text box).

4. Select the Convert nested tables check box if you want to convert nested tables as well. This check box is available only when you're using paragraphs as the separator character.

■ **Note** Word converts a nested table to paragraphs of text like the rest of the table. The nested table's paragraphs appear in their cell order between the paragraphs for the table cells that surround them.

---

5. Click the OK button to close the Convert Table to Text dialog box and perform the conversion.

Nesting One Table Inside Another Table

When you need to create a complex layout, you can nest one table inside another, so that one cell of the outer table contains however many cells the inner table has. Figure 8-5 shows an example of a nested table.

To nest a table, click in the cell in which you want to nest the table, and then insert the table as usual.

Department	Coverage		Contact Information
Anthropology	Biological Anthropology	1-8	
	Cultural Anthropology	1-4	
	Linguistic Anthropology	5-12	
	Social Anthropology	1-12	
Biology			
Chemistry			

Figure 8-5. You can nest one table inside another table to create complex layouts.

Tip You can nest tables several levels deep if necessary, but the further you nest tables, the more confusing working with them tends to become. If you're considering several levels of nesting, see if merging and splitting cells could give you a similar result with less fuss.

Creating Complex Documents with Multiple Sections

When you need to create documents that use multiple layouts, you have to put each layout in a separate section. Here are examples of documents that use multiple layouts:

- A newsletter may need different numbers of columns on different pages.

- A report may require different headers and footers for different chapters.

- A business letter may need to contain an envelope page as well.

Word's sections are highly useful, but they're tricky both to see and to grasp. Word makes matters worse by automatically creating sections when your documents need them—for example, when you apply columns to part of a document, as discussed later in this chapter—but not making clear what it's doing.

The following are the essentials:

- *Each new blank document has a single section at first*: When you create a new blank document, Word creates it as a single section until you add further sections. By contrast, documents you create based on a template contain however many sections the template has.

- *When you need to give part of the document a different layout, you create a new section*: For example, if you need to create a landscape page in a document that uses portrait orientation, you put the landscape page in a separate section so that you can change the layout.

- *A section can start on the same page or on a different page*: Word gives you four kinds of section breaks.

    - *Continuous*: The new section starts on the same page as the previous section. This type of break is useful for creating multi-column layouts on part of a page.

    - *Next page*: The new section starts on the next page after the previous section ends. This is the kind of break you use for putting a new chapter on a new page or for changing layout from portrait to landscape.

    - *Even page*: The new section starts on the next even page after the previous section ends. This may mean having a blank page in the printed document.

    - *Odd page*: The new section starts on the new odd page after the previous section ends. This too may mean a blank page appears in the printed document.

- *A section break divides one section from the next:* When you create a section (or Word creates one automatically for you), you add a section break to the document. A section break is normally hidden, but if you display paragraph marks and other invisible characters, it appears as a dotted double line with the words Section Break and the type in the middle—for example, Section Break (Continuous).

Once you know all this, inserting a section break is simplicity itself:

1. Place the insertion point where you want the new section to start. It's best to put the insertion point at the beginning of a paragraph.

2. Choose Page Layout ➤ Page Setup ➤ Breaks to open the Breaks panel, and then click the section break type you want: Next Page, Continuous, Even Page, or Odd Page. Word inserts the break.

To see the break in Print Layout view, Web Layout view, or Full Screen Reading view, choose Home ➤ Paragraph ➤ Show/Hide ¶. In Draft view or Outline view, Word displays the break all the time.

When you start using sections in a document, add the Section readout to the status bar to give you a heads-up on which section you're working in. Follow these steps:

1. Right-click any blank part of the status bar to display the Customize Status Bar menu.

2. Click the Section item to place a check mark next to it.

3. Click anywhere outside the Customize Status Bar menu to hide the menu again.

The Section readout appears at the left end of the status bar, showing the section number—for example, **Section: 2**.

Adding Headers, Footers, and Page Numbers

If you're planning to print out a multipage document, or to distribute it as a PDF or XPS file, it's often a good idea to add headers, footers, and page numbers to make the pages easy to identify.

Adding Headers and Footers to a Document

A *header* appears across the top of a page, and a footer appears across the bottom of a page. You can use headers and footers to add information such as the document name and file name, author name, date, and page numbers—or any other information that you need to make available to the reader.

Word gives you plenty of flexibility with headers and footers. If a document needs the same header (or footer) all the way through, you can quickly add one. But you can also use different headers or footers on the odd pages of the document to the even pages, and use different headers and footers from one section of the document to the next. You can also prevent the header or footer from appearing on the first page of a document, which is useful for documents such as letters.

Word's templates come with built-in headers and footers that you can quickly add to give your documents a standard look. These headers and footers range from the straightforward Blank one to stylish designs that can look good in a variety of documents. Many of the headers and footers come with odd-page and even-page versions so that you can create effective page spreads.

■ **Note** If you want to create a header or footer completely from scratch, choose Insert ➤ Header & Footer ➤ Header ➤ Blank. In Print Layout view, you can also simply double-click in the header area at the top of the page.

To insert a built-in headers or footers, follow these steps:

1. If the document has multiple sections, click in the section you want to add the header or footer to.

2. Choose Insert ➤ Header & Footer ➤ Header or Insert ➤ Header & Footer ➤ Footer to open the Header panel or the footer panel.

■ **Note** Word doesn't preview headers or footers for you, but you can hold the mouse pointer over a header or footer in the Header panel or Footer panel to view a ScreenTip describing the header or footer.

---

3. Click the header or footer you want. Word then does the following:

   - Inserts the header or footer in the document.

   - Switches to Print Layout view if the document is in any other view.

   - Displays the header or footer area with the header or footer ready for editing. Figure 8-6 shows a header added to a page. The Header tab shows that you're working in the header; if you're in a particular section of the document rather than the document as a whole, the tab shows that too.

- Adds the Header & Footer Tools section to the Ribbon and displays the Design tab.

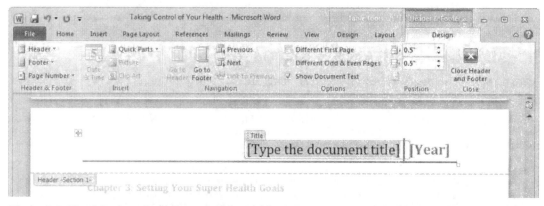

Figure 8-6. *Word displays the Design tab of the Header & Footer section of the Ribbon so that you can work with the header or footer that you've inserted. The Header tab includes the section number if the document uses multiple sections.*

4. Fill in the placeholders in the header or footer. For example, in the "Type the document title" placeholder shown, type the title that you want the header to show. Or click the drop-down list button that appears when you click the Year placeholder, and then click the date in the panel that opens.

5. If necessary, adjust the position or alignment of the header:

   - To change the header's position relative to the top of the page, alter the value in the Header from Top box in the Position group of the Design tab of the Header & Footer Tools section of the toolbar.

■ **Note** When the Word window is too narrow for the labels to fit, the Header from Top box, the Footer from Bottom box, and the Insert Alignment Tab button appear unmarked. Hold the mouse pointer over the controls in the position group to display ScreenTips identifying each button.

   - To change the footer's position relative to the bottom of the page, alter the value in the Footer from Bottom box in the Position group.

   - To change the alignment, click the Insert Alignment Tab in the Position group. In the Alignment Tab dialog box that opens, click the Left option button, the Center option button, or the Right option button, as appropriate. In the Align relative to drop-down list, click Margin to make the alignment relative to the margin, or click Indent to make it relative to the indent. Click the OK button to close the Alignment Tab dialog box.

6. Choose Design ➤ Close ➤ Close Header and Footer to close the header and footer area and return to the main document. You can also press Alt+Shift+C or double-click in the main text area.

Creating Different Headers and Footers for Different Pages

Many documents either don't need a header (or footer) on the first page or need a different one there. Likewise, many documents need a different header or footer on their odd pages than on their even pages.

To set up different headers and footers for the first page or for odd and even pages, follow these steps:

1. Open the header area or footer area in one of these ways:

   • In Print Layout view, double-click in the header area or footer area.

   • Choose Insert ➤ Header & Footer ➤ Header ➤ Edit Header or Insert ➤ Header & Footer ➤ Footer ➤ Edit Footer.

2. To create a different first page header or footer, select the Different First Page check box in the Options group on the Design tab of the Header & Footer Tools section of the Ribbon.

3. To create different headers and footers for odd pages and even pages, select the Different Odd & Even Pages check box in the Options group.

4. Use the Previous button and Next button in the Navigation group on the Header & Footer Tools tab to move from one header or footer to another, entering the material you want each to have. If you're using Word's built-in headers or footers, try the Odd Page and Even Page ones for your odd and even pages.

Using Different Headers and Footers in Different Sections of a Document

If you break a document into separate sections, you can create different headers and footers in each section or continue headers and footers from one section to the next. As well as each section being different from the other sections, you can also create different first-page and odd- and even-page headers and footers within sections as needed.

Create your sections as described earlier in this chapter, then go to the beginning of the document and open the header area or footer area. Give the first section the headers and footers it needs, and then go through the remaining sections.

Word automatically carries through the headers and footers from one section to the next until you tell it to stop by giving the Header & Footer Tools ➤ Design ➤ Navigation ➤ Link to Previous command, "unpressing" the button so that the Link to Previous feature is no longer on.

Delete a Header or Footer

When you want to get rid of a header or footer, you can open it for editing and then delete its contents. This is easy if the header or footer is only text, but may take longer if the header or footer contains various types of objects.

Instead, choose Insert ➤ Header & Footer ➤ Header ➤ Remove Header or Insert ➤ Header & Footer ➤ Footer ➤ Remote Footer to get rid of the header or footer in one move.

Inserting Page Numbers in a Document

To help your readers (or perhaps yourself) keep the pages of a document in the right order, it's often useful to add page numbers. The best way to add page numbers in Word is to put a page number field in the header or footer. Word then repeats the page number on each page, inserting the correct value.

■ **Note** If you need to insert in the body of a document a page number that's in fact a reference to another page, insert a cross-reference as discussed later in this chapter. You can refer to either an item such as a heading, table caption, or graphic, or to a bookmark that you place exactly where you need it.

To add page numbers to a header or footer, follow these steps:

1. Choose Insert ➤ Header & Footer ➤ Page Number to display the Page Number drop-down menu.

2. Highlight or click the position you want—Top of Page, Bottom of Page, or Page Margins—to display a submenu of the different options.

3. Highlight an option in the submenu to display a ScreenTip about it.

4. Click the style of page number you want to use. Word inserts the page number and opens the header area or footer area so that you can work with the page number.

5. If you want to change the way the page number appears, follow these steps:

   • Choose Header & Footer Tools ➤ Design ➤ Header & Footer ➤ Page Number ➤ Format Page Number to display the Page Number Format dialog box (see Figure 8-7).

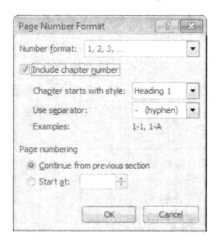

Figure 8-7. *Use the Page Number Format dialog box to change the formatting of a page number you've already inserted in a document.*

- Open the Number format drop-down list and click the number formatting you want—for example, 1, 2, 3; A, B, C; or i, ii, iii.

- If your document has chapters and you want to include the chapter number in the page numbering, select the Include chapter number check box. Then open the Chapter starts with style drop-down list and click the style that marks the beginning of each chapter—for example, Heading 1 or a Chapter Title style you've added. Last, open the Use separator drop-down list and choose the separator character to use between the chapter number and the page number. Your choices are a hyphen, a period, a colon, an em dash (a long dash), or a en dash (a short dash but longer than a hyphen).

6. In the Page Numbering area, choose how to control the numbering. Click the Continue from previous section option button to have the page numbers follow those in the previous section. To start again, or start at a specific number, click the Start at option button and enter the number in the text box.

7. Click the OK button to close the Page Number Format dialog box. Word applies your choices.

■ **Note** To remove the page numbers from a document, choose Insert ➤ Header & Footer ➤ Page Number ➤ Remove Page Numbers.

Creating Newspaper-Style Columns of Text

If you create newsletters or similar publications, you may want to create multicolumn layouts. Word can do this well, but there are a couple of tricks you need to learn.

■ **Tip** Only Print Layout view and Full Screen Reading view show the columns on screen, so it's best to use these views to work with columns. Print Layout view is the easiest choice.

To create simple columns, follow these steps:

1. If you want to turn only part of the document into columns, select that part. For example, select existing text, or select a blank paragraph at the point where you want to start the columns.

■ **Note** If you want to turn the whole document into columns (and the same number of columns throughout), click anywhere in the document.

---

2. Choose Page Layout ➤ Page Setup ➤ Columns to open the Columns panel, and
    then click the type of columns you want (see Figure 8-8). Word turns your
    selection into columns.

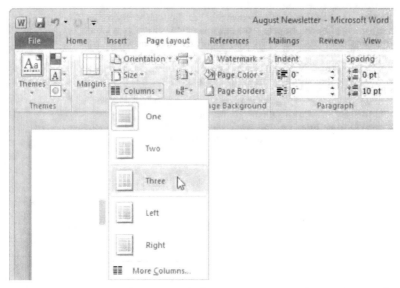

*Figure 8-8. From the Columns panel, choose One, Two, or Three columns. Choose Left for a narrow left
column and a wide right column, and Right for wide left and narrow right. Click More Columns for
further options.*

If you need to create other types of columns than appear on the Columns panel, such as four
columns or columns with a vertical line between them, follow these steps:

1. Select the part of the document you want to apply the columns to.

2. Choose Page Layout ➤ Page Setup ➤ Columns ➤ More Columns to display the
    Columns dialog box (see Figure 8-9).

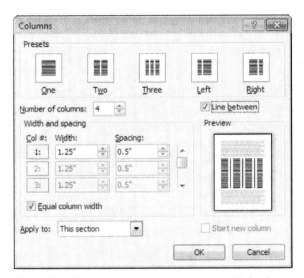

Figure 8-9. *Use the options in the Columns dialog box to create more complex column layouts in your Word documents.*

3. Choose the type of columns you want:

   • To use one of the presets in the Presets area, click it.

   • To specify a different number of columns, enter it in the Number of columns box.

4. If you want a vertical line between the columns, select the Line between check box.

5. Set up the column width and spacing:

   • To make each column the same width, select the Equal column width check box. On the Col # 1 line of controls, set the width and spacing for the columns.

   • To set each column to the width you want, clear the Equal column width check box, and then set the width for each column in the Width box and the spacing in the Spacing box. If you have four or more columns, you'll need to scroll down to reach the last ones.

6. Make sure the Apply to drop-down list shows the right part of the document—Selected text to affect only the selection, This section to affect only the current section, This point forward to affect the rest of the document from here on, or Whole document to affect the whole document.

7. If you chose This point forward, you can select the Start new column check box if you want to create a new column layout from the current position of the insertion point.

8. Click the OK button to close the Columns dialog box. Word creates the columns using your choices. Figure 8-10 shows a three-column layout with vertical lines between the columns.

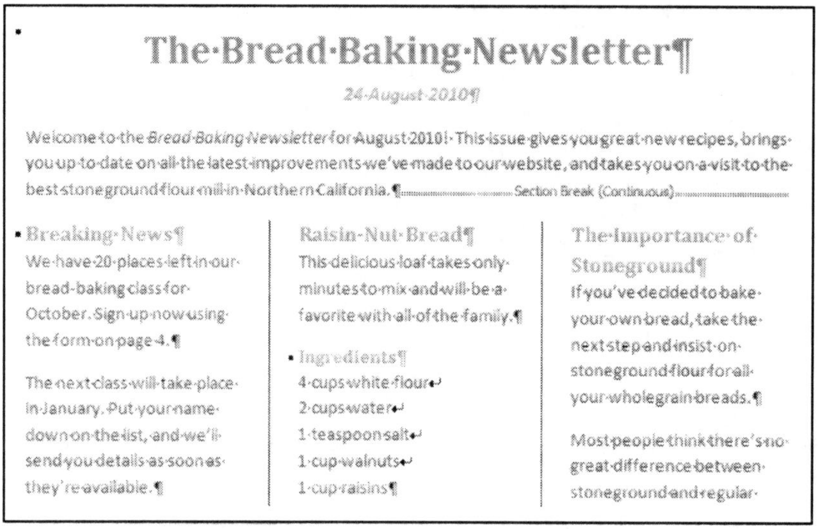
The Bread Baking Newsletter

24 August 2010

Welcome to the *Bread Baking Newsletter* for August 2010! This issue gives you great new recipes, brings you up to date on all the latest improvements we've made to our website, and takes you on a visit to the best stoneground flour mill in Northern California. Section Break (Continuous)

Breaking News

We have 20 places left in our bread-baking class for October. Sign up now using the form on page 4.

The next class will take place in January. Put your name down on the list, and we'll send you details as soon as they're available.

Raisin-Nut Bread

This delicious loaf takes only minutes to mix and will be a favorite with all of the family.

Ingredients

4 cups white flour
2 cups water
1 teaspoon salt
1 cup walnuts
1 cup raisins

The Importance of Stoneground

If you've decided to bake your own bread, take the next step and insist on stoneground flour for all your wholegrain breads.

Most people think there's no great difference between stoneground and regular

Figure 8-10. You can include vertical lines between the columns to make a multicolumn layout easier to read.

Breaking Your Columns with Column Breaks

After you've created the columns, Word automatically flows the text down each column as you enter it. When the first column reaches the bottom of the text area on the page, Word flows it to the start of the second column, and so on.

To end a column early, you can insert a column break. Position the insertion point where you want the break, then choose Page Layout ➤ Page Setup ➤ Breaks ➤ Column. Word inserts the column break and moves the insertion point to the top of the next column.

If you need to remove a column break, delete it. Choose Home ➤ Paragraph ➤ Show/Hide ¶ or press Ctrl+* to display invisible characters so that you can see the column break, which appears as a row of dots with the words Column Break in the middle. Position the insertion point before the column break, and then press Delete to delete it.

Removing Multiple Columns from a Section or Document

If you want to change a multiple-column section or document back to a single column, click in the section or document, and then choose Page Layout ➤ Page Setup ➤ Columns ➤ One. Word restores the text to a single column.

Using Bookmarks, Fields, and References

In long documents, you'll often need to mark parts of the document so that you can find them easily or refer to them. You may also want to insert pieces of information that Word can automatically update for you, such as the date and time or the name of the last person to save a document. And you may also find it useful to be able to refer easily to another part of the document and have Word keep its page number, name, or contents automatically updated.

Marking Important Parts of a Document with Bookmarks

To identify parts that you want to return to or refer to, you can place bookmarks in your Word documents. A bookmark is an electronic marker that you can place either at a single point in text (between two characters or other objects) or around text or an object.

■ **Note** Use a single-point bookmark when you need to move the insertion point to a particular point or refer to a page number. Use a bookmark with contents when you need to refer to the specific contents—for example, to make a reference automatically display the text that appears in the bookmark.

Insert a Bookmark to Mark Part of a Document

To insert a bookmark, follow these steps:

1. Click the point where you want to place the bookmark, or select the text or other object you want the bookmark to contain.

2. Choose Insert ➤ Links ➤ Bookmark to display the Bookmark dialog box (see Figure 8-11).

Figure 8-11. Create a bookmark when you need to mark a specific point or an area of content in a document.

3. Type the name for the bookmark in the Bookmark name text box. You must start the name with a letter, but after that you can use any letters, numbers, and underscores as needed. You can't use spaces or symbols in the name.

4. Click the Add button to add the bookmark and close the dialog box.

▨ **Note** If you need to move a bookmark to a different point in a document, position the insertion point in or select the new location. Then open the Bookmark dialog box, click the bookmark name, and click the Add button. Word changes the bookmark to the new location without comment.

Navigating from Bookmark to Bookmark

After placing a bookmark, you can move the insertion point to the bookmark. Follow these steps:

1. Choose Insert ➤ Links ➤ Bookmark to display the Bookmark dialog box.

2. In the Bookmark name list box, click the bookmark.

3. Click the Go To button. If the bookmark is a single point, Word moves the insertion point to it; if the bookmark has contents, Word selects them.

4. Click the Close button to close the Bookmark dialog box.

Seeing Where Bookmarks Are in Your Documents

Word hides the bookmarks in your documents unless you set it to display them. When you're editing a document, it's often useful to display the bookmarks to avoid deleting them by accident. You may also need to display the bookmarks to make sure that they're in the right place.

To display bookmarks, follow these steps:

1. Click the File tab to open Backstage.

2. Click the Options item in the left column to open the Word Options dialog box.

3. Click the Advanced item in the left column to display the Advanced pane.

4. Scroll down about halfway to the Show Document Content heading.

5. Select the Show bookmarks check box.

6. Click the OK button to close the Word Options dialog box.

For a single-point bookmark, Word displays a black I-beam in the document. For a bookmark that contains text or another object, Word displays brackets around the contents. Figure 8-12 shows one single-point bookmark (between "Aerobic" and "Exercise") and two bookmarks with contents ("aerobics class" and the illustration).

How to Get the Most Out of Your Aerobic Exercise

Aerobic exercise—such as jogging, cycling, or taking an aerobics class—is vital to your health.

That means it's essential for you to do it the right way.

Figure 8-12. Word displays a black I-beam for a single-point bookmark marker and a pair of black brackets around the text or object in a bookmark that has contents.

Deleting a Bookmark You No Longer Need

When you no longer need a bookmark, delete it like this:

1. Choose Insert ➤ Links ➤ Bookmark to display the Bookmark dialog box.
2. In the Bookmark name list box, click the bookmark.
3. Click the Delete button.
4. Click the Close button to close the Bookmark dialog box.

Inserting Automated Information with Fields

Many documents need automated items of information that Word can provide for you, such as the date or time, page numbers (discussed earlier in this chapter), or the file name. To add such information to your documents, you use fields—codes that tell Word to insert the information you want and whether to update it automatically.

Inserting a Field

To insert a field in a document, follow these steps:

1. Choose Insert ➤ Text ➤ Quick Parts ➤ Field to display the Field dialog box (shown in Figure 8-13 with the full list of fields displayed).

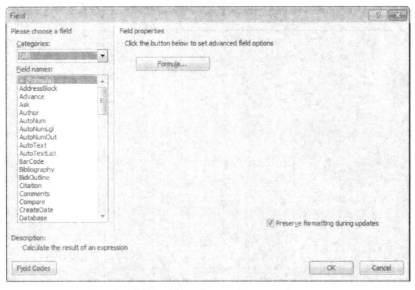

Figure 8-13. *The Field dialog box includes a wide range of fields. Normally, you'll want to start by choosing the type of fields in the Categories drop-down list.*

2. In the Categories drop-down list, choose the category of fields you want (see the list below). In the example, I use the Date & Time category as an easy example.

- *(All))*: Lists all the fields. This is useful when you know the field's name but not the category that contains it.

- *Date and Time*: Contains fields for entering dates and times, such as the current date or the time the document was last saved, in various formats. You can also insert a date, time, or both more easily by choosing Insert ➤ Text ➤ Date & Time and using the Date and Time dialog box.

- *Document Automation*: Contains fields for automating movement about the document, running macros, printing, and similar actions.

- *Document Information*: Contains fields for inserting information contained in the document's properties, such as the author name or file name.

- *Equations and Formulas*: Contains fields for inserting equations and formulas. Use these when the Insert ➤ Symbols ➤ Equation menu doesn't contain what you need.

- *Index and Tables*: Contains fields for creating indexes and content tables (such as tables of contents and tables of figures). The References tab of the Ribbon contains controls for inserting these fields more easily.

- *Links and References*: Contains fields for inserting links (such as hyperlinks) or cross-references. The Insert ➤ Links ➤ Hyperlink, Insert ➤ Links ➤ Bookmark and Insert ➤ Links ➤ Cross-reference commands provide easier access to these fields.

- *Mail Merge*: Contains fields for creating mail-merge documents. The Mailings tab of the Ribbon gives you an easier way to insert these fields.

- *Numbering*: Contains fields for inserting automatic numbering in a document. For creating page numbers, it's easier to work in the header or footer, as described earlier in this chapter.

- *User Information*: Contains fields for inserting the user's name, initials, or address.

3. In the Field names list box, click the field you want. In the example, I've clicked the SaveDate field, which inserts the date the document was last saved. The Field properties panel then shows the field's properties, and the Field options panel shows any options that are available for it (see Figure 8-14).

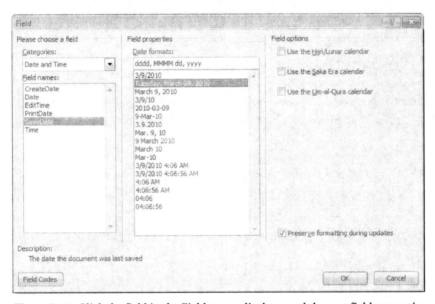

Figure 8-14. *Click the field in the Field names list box, and then set field properties and field options as needed.*

4. In the Field properties panel, choose the file properties you want. The available properties depend on the field you've chosen, but for date fields such as SaveDate, a Date formats list appears in which you click the format you want.

5. In the Field options panel, choose any options you want. Again, these depend on the field: Some fields have no options, while the SaveDate field lets you use various esoteric calendars that you will seldom need.

6. Select the Preserve formatting during updates check box if you want to keep the field's formatting when you update it. This behavior is normally useful.

7. Click the OK button to close the Field dialog box and insert the field.

Examining and Updating a Field

Now that you've inserted a field, you can examine it. At first, the field displays the field results—the information that the field produces. For example, the SaveDate field displays a date in the format you chose.

Normally, the field result appears like normal text until you click in it or select it, at which point Word displays gray shading behind it to indicate that it's a field (see Figure 8-15). To update the field, right-click it, and then click Update Field on the context menu.

Last saved date: Thursday, June 24, 2010

Figure 8-15 .When you click a field result, Word displays gray shading to indicate that it is a field.

■ **Note** If you want to see field shading all the time, click the File tab, and then click the Options item to display the Word Options dialog box. Click the Advanced item in the left pane, open the Field shading drop-down list in the Show document content area, and click Always. You can also select the Show field codes instead of their values check box if you want to display field codes all the time. Click the OK button to close the Word Options dialog box.

If you want to see the field code that's producing the field result, right-click anywhere in the field and choose Toggle Field Codes. Word displays the field code, as shown in Figure 8-16. Again, when you've selected the field, Word displays an Update Update button.

Last saved date: { CREATEDATE \@ "dddd, MMMM dd, yyyy" * MERGEFORMAT }

Figure 8-16. If you want to see the code that produces a field result, right-click in the field and then click Toggle Field Codes on the context menu. Repeat this move to show the field result again.

■ **Note** To change a field you've inserted in your document, right-click the field, and then click Edit Field on the context menu. Word displays the Field dialog box, and you can edit the field using the same techniques as when you inserted it.

Adding Cross-References to Other Parts of a Document

When you create formal documents, you often need to refer from one part to another. To do so, you can create cross-references to any of several different types of item, including headings, bookmarks, figures, and tables.

To insert a cross-reference, follow these steps:

1. Position the insertion point where you want the reference.

2. Choose Insert ➤ Links ➤ Cross-reference to display the Cross-reference dialog box (shown in Figure 8-17 with settings chosen for referring to a bookmark).

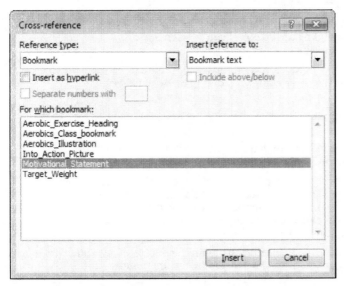

Figure 8-17. In the Cross-reference dialog box, you can insert a cross-reference to a bookmark, heading, table, or other item in the document.

3. Open the Reference type drop-down list and choose the type of item you want to refer to:

- *Numbered item*: An item to which you have applied Word's automatic numbering. For example, a paragraph in a numbered list.

- *Heading*: A paragraph you have formatted with one of Word's Heading styles.

- *Bookmark*: A bookmark you have inserted in the document (as described earlier in this chapter).

- *Footnote*: A footnote you have created in the document, as discussed later in this chapter.

- *Endnote*: An endnote you have created in the document, as discussed later in this chapter.

- *Equation*: An equation you have inserted with the Insert ➤ Symbols ➤ Equation command or as a field.

- *Figure*: A figure that you have marked with an automatically numbered caption using the References ➤ Captions ➤ Insert Caption command.

- *Table*: A table that you have marked with an automatically numbered caption using the References ➤ Captions ➤ Insert Caption command.

4. In the For which list box, click the item you want to refer to. (The name of this list box changes to reflect the type of item you've selected—for example, "For which numbered item" when you select Numbered item, or "For which caption" when you select Table.)

5. Open the Insert reference to drop-down list and choose the item you want to refer to. The options vary depending on the object you're referring to, but these are the options for a bookmark to give you an idea:

   - *Bookmark text*: Inserts the bookmark's contents (whatever that may be). Use this for bookmarks that have contents rather than for single-point bookmarks.

   - *Page number*: Inserts the page number on which the first part of the bookmark appears.

   - *Paragraph number*: Inserts the paragraph number in which the start of the bookmark appears. Use this only with numbered paragraphs.

   - *Paragraph number (no context)*: Inserts the numbering for the paragraph in which the start of the bookmark appears, without any other numbering involved in the multilevel list. For example, if you have a three-level list, and the bookmark appears in paragraph 2. a. (ii), this choice inserts the (ii) part without the rest of the numbering.

   - *Paragraph number (full context)*: Inserts the numbering for the paragraph in which the start of the bookmark appears, including the full number—for example, 2. a. (iii).

   - *Above/below*: Inserts "above" if the start of the bookmark appears earlier in the document than the reference, or "below" if it appears later in the document. This is occasionally useful, but see the next paragraph for a better alternative.

6. If you choose a page number or paragraph number in the Insert reference to drop-down list, you can select the Include above/below check box if you want to add "above" or "below" to the end of the reference to indicate whether the item falls before or after the reference.

7. Select the Insert as hyperlink check box if you want the reference to appear as a hyperlink. The reader can Ctrl+click the hyperlink to jump to the referenced item.

8. Click the Insert button to insert the reference in the document. The Cancel button changes to a Close button.

9. Click the Close button to close the Cross-reference dialog box.

▪ **Note** A cross-reference is a field code, so you can update it by clicking in the field and then clicking the Update button that appears.

▓ **Note** If you create a new blank document and switch it straight to Outline view, Word automatically applies Heading 1 style to the first paragraph. You can then start creating your outline immediately.

Promoting and Demoting Headings

You can quickly promote or demote headings by using the buttons in the Outline Tools group:

- To move the current paragraph down to the next heading level, click the Demote button.
- To change a paragraph to body text, click the Demote to Body Text button.
- To move the current paragraph up to the next heading level, click the Promote button.
- To promote the current paragraph to Heading 1, click the Promote to Heading 1 button.

▓ **Tip** From the keyboard, press Tab to demote the current paragraph or Shift+Tab to promote it. You can also select a section and then drag it to the left to promote it or to the left to demote it, but doing so sometimes requires a steady touch.

Expanding and Collapsing the Outline and Headings

One of Outline view's strongest features is that you can expand the outline to different levels so that you can see exactly what you need to. Figure 8-19 shows a section of outline with three levels of heading displayed and some sections expanded.

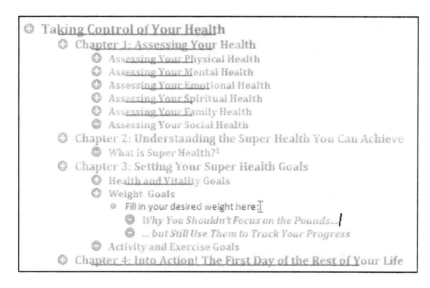

Figure 8-19. You can expand an outline to different levels so that you can see exactly what you need.

To choose the overall level of outline levels displayed, open the Show Level drop-down list and click the level you want. Your choices are from Level 1 to Level 9, or All Levels if you want to display every paragraph. For much of your work in Outline view, you'll likely want to show several levels of headings—for example, Levels 1, 2, and 3.

Once you've chosen the outline level, you can double-click the + sign next to a heading to display or hide the headings and other contents below it. A – sign next to a heading indicates that it has no lower-level headings or body text below it, as is the case with the "Activity and Exercise Goals" heading in Chapter 3.

The dotted underline that appears under some headings indicates that the heading has collapsed subheadings under it. The underline starts at the indentation level of the first subheading, so you can see which level this is at.

If you want to expand or collapse multiple sections at once, select the sections, and then click the Expand button or the Collapse button.

Tip If you want to zero in on the text of your outline without distractions, clear the Show Text Formatting check box in the Outline Tools group on the Outlining tab. Clearing this check box makes Word show all the text in a standard font that lets you see more of the outline at once.

When you display all of the text of the document, you may find you lose many of the advantages of Outline view. But you can select the Show First Line Only check box in the Outline Tools group of the Outlining tab to make Word display only the first line of each paragraph (ending with an ellipsis to show that the rest is hidden). This feature lets you follow the gist of the paragraphs in the document without displaying the full text.

Moving Paragraphs Up and Down the Document

When you have displayed the outline level you want, you can quickly move paragraphs up and down the outline.

Click a + sign to select that item and all its subordinate items, or click and drag in the selection bar to select multiple items. You can then move them up or down the outline in these ways:

- *Ribbon*: Click the Move Up button or the Move Down button to move the selection up or down by one displayed paragraph at a time.

- *Keyboard*: Press Alt+Shift+Up arrow or Alt+Shift+Down arrow to move the selection up or down by one displayed paragraph at a time.

- *Mouse*: Drag the selection up or down as far as necessary. Word displays a line between paragraphs to indicate where the selection will land when you drop it.

Returning from Outline View to Your Previous View

To return from Outline view to the previous view you were using, choose Outlining ➤ Close ➤ Close Outline view.

Alternatively, switch to another view by clicking a view button in the View Shortcuts area of the status or in the View ➤ Document Views group.

Tip If you need to create very long documents, look into Word's Master Document feature. This feature, which is beyond the scope of this book, enables you to create a kind of super-document that consists of multiple subdocuments. You can work with the master document in Master Document view, which is similar to Outline view.

Adding Footnotes and Endnotes

If you create professional or academic documents, you may need to add footnotes or endnotes to provide extra information or show your sources.

A *footnote* is a note that appears at the foot of the page that refers to it, while an *endnote* is a note that appears at the end of a section or document. Use footnotes when it's likely the reader will want to read the information and the chunks of information are short enough to fit at the bottom of pages. Use endnotes for information that you think only a few readers will need to consult or for longer pieces of information.

Tip You can convert footnotes to endnotes, or endnotes to footnotes, if necessary. So it's not a disaster if you start with one type of note and then realize you need the other type.

Adding a Footnote

To add a footnote to a document, follow these steps:

1. Place the insertion point immediately after the last word of the text you want the footnote to refer to.

2. Choose References ➤ Footnotes ➤ Insert Footnote to insert a superscript footnote number or mark and open the footnote area.

    • In Print Layout view, Word shows the footnote area at the bottom of the page, separated by a horizontal line, as shown in the upper part of Figure 8-20. The footnote area shows only the footnotes that appear on that page.

    • In Draft view, Outline view, or Web Layout view, Word shows the footnote area as a separate pane, as shown in the lower part of Figure 8-20. The footnote pane shows a list of all the footnotes in the document.

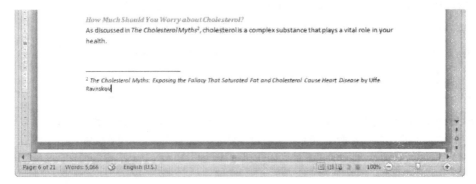

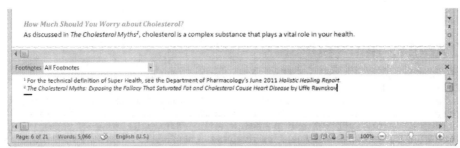

Figure 8-20. In Print Layout view, the footnote area appears at the bottom of the page (above). In Word's other views, the footnote area appears as a separate pane (below).

3. Add the text or other material for the footnote—for example, by typing it in or pasting it.

4. Click in the main text of the document again to resume work in it. You can either leave the footnote pane open so that you can work with other footnotes in it or close it in one of these ways:

- Click the Close button (the × button) at its right end.
- Double-click the bar that separates the pane from the main window.
- Press Alt+Shift+C.

Adding an Endnote

To add an endnote to a document, follow these steps:

1. Place the insertion point immediately after the last word of the text you want the footnote to refer to.

2. Choose References ➤ Footnotes ➤ Insert Endnote to insert a superscript endnote number or mark and open the endnote area.

   - In Print Layout view or Web Layout view, Word shows the endnote area on the last page of the document or section, separated by a horizontal line, as shown in the upper part of Figure 8-21.

   - In Draft view or Outline view, or Web Layout view, Word shows the endnote area as a separate pane, as shown in the lower part of Figure 8-21. The endnote pane shows a list of all the endnotes in the document.

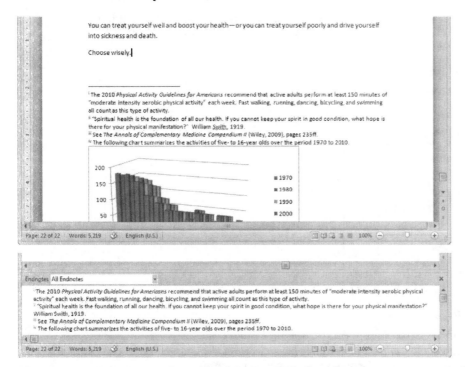

Figure 8-21. In Print Layout view and Web Layout view, the endnote area appears at the bottom of the final page of the document or section (above). In Draft view and Outline view, the endnote area appears as a separate pane (below).

3. Type or paste in the text or other material for the endnote.

4. Click in the main text of the document again to resume work in it. In Draft view or Outline view, you can either leave the endnote pane open for further use or close it in one of these ways:

    •   Click the Close button (the × button) at its right end.

    •   Double-click the bar that separates the pane from the main window.

    •   Press Alt+Shift+C.

Customizing Footnotes and Endnotes to Suit Your Document

Word automatically numbers footnotes and endnotes and inserts them using its default placement—footnotes at the foot of the page, and endnotes at the end of the document. The default settings work well for many documents, but for others, you may want to change the numbering or the placement. To do so, follow these steps:

1. Click in the section of the document for which you want to change the footnotes or endnotes. (If the document has only a single section, click anywhere in it.)

2. Choose References ➤ Footnotes ➤ Footnote & Endnote (click the little button with the arrow at the lower-right corner of the Footnotes group) to display the Footnote and Endnote dialog box (see Figure 8-22).

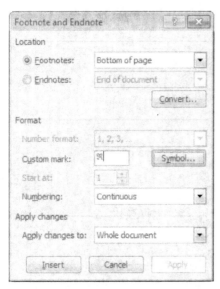

Figure 8-22. *Use the Footnote and Endnote dialog box to set up custom numbering or placement for footnotes or endnotes, or to convert footnotes to endnotes (or vice versa).*

3. In the Location area, select the Footnotes option button or the Endnotes option to tell Word which type of notes you want to affect.

4. Choose where to place the notes in the document:

   • *Footnotes*: In the Footnotes drop-down list, choose Bottom of page (the default) or Below text. Below text gives an odd look but helps make the footnotes more obvious to the reader.

   • *Endnotes*: In the Endnotes drop-down list, choose End of document (the default setting) or End of section.

5. In the Format area, choose the numbering you want for the notes whose option button you've selected:

   • *Number format*: In this drop-down list, click the numbering format to use: "1, 2, 3"; "a, b, c"; "A, B, C"; "i, ii, iii"; "I, II, III"; or a series of symbols.

   • *Custom mark*: To use a custom note mark, click the Symbol button. In the Symbol dialog box, click the symbol you want, and then click the OK button. The symbol appears in the Custom Mark box; delete it if you want to return to regular numbering.

   • *Start at*: In this box, enter the starting number to use for numbering. The default is the first character of the number format—for example, 1, i, or A.

   • *Numbering*: In this drop-down list, choose Continuous if you want to use the numbering sequence throughout the document. Choose Restart each section to start afresh with each section (this is useful for a document with endnotes at the end of each chapter). Choose Restart each page if you want to restart footnote numbering on each page (you can't use this option for endnotes, as it wouldn't make sense).

6. Click the Apply button to apply your choices.

7. Click the Close button to close the Footnote and Endnote dialog box.

Converting Footnotes to Endnotes or Endnotes to Footnotes

To convert footnotes to endnotes, endnotes to footnotes, or each kind of note to the other at the same time, follow these steps:

1. Choose References ➤ Footnotes ➤ Footnote & Endnote (click the little button with the arrow at the lower-right corner of the Footnotes group) to display the Footnote and Endnote dialog box.

■ **Caution** Before converting the footnotes or endnotes in a long or complex document that contains many notes, create a fresh backup of the document. The conversion seldom goes wrong, but when it does, the notes can become severely scrambled.

---

2. Click the Convert button to display the Convert Notes dialog box (see Figure 8-23).

Figure 8-23. *Use the Convert Notes dialog box to convert footnotes to endnotes, endnotes to footnotes, or switch each kind of note to the other.*

3. Click the Convert all footnotes to endnotes option button, the Convert all endnotes to footnotes option button, or the Swap footnotes and endnotes option button, as needed.

4. Click the OK button to close the Convert Notes dialog box and perform the conversion.

5. Click the OK button to close the Footnote and Endnote dialog box.

Navigating Among and Viewing Footnotes or Endnotes

You can navigate from one footnote or endnote to another by using the References ➤ Footnote ➤ Next Footnote button and drop-down menu. Click the Next Footnote button to move to the next footnote; to move to another note, click the drop-down button, and then click Previous Footnote, Next Endnote, or Previous Endnote, as appropriate.

Once you've located a footnote mark or endnote mark, you can preview the footnote or endnote by holding the mouse pointer over the footnote mark or endnote mark until Word displays a ScreenTip containing the text of the footnote or endnote (see Figure 8-24).

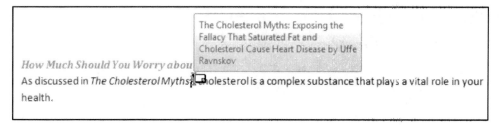

Figure 8-24. *The quick way to view a footnote is to preview it in a ScreenTip.*

If the note is short and text only, this may be all you need to do. But if the note is longer or contains other types of contents (such as graphics, tables, or charts), double-click the footnote mark or endnote mark to display the footnote area or endnote area and jump directly to the note whose mark you double-clicked.

You can then move from note to note in the footnote area or endnote area. As you move the insertion point to another note, Word displays the corresponding part in the main document.

■ **Note** You can also display the footnote or endnote area by choosing References ➤ Footnotes ➤ Show Notes. If Word displays the View Footnotes dialog box, click the View footnote area option button or the View endnote area option button as appropriate, and then click the OK button. (If the document contains only one kind of notes, Word displays the area for that kind of notes.)

Summary

In this chapter, you've learned how to create complex documents and complex layouts. You now know how to convert existing text in a Word document into a table; how to add headers, footers, and page numbers to a document; and how to create a multicolumn, newsletter-style layout.

You've also seen how to insert bookmarks to enable yourself easily to access and refer to parts of a document, and how to insert cross-references to bookmarks or other document elements. And you've learned to develop a document's outline swiftly and easily in Outline view plus the techniques for adding footnotes and endnotes to your documents.

In the next chapter, I'll show you how to revise, review, and finalize your documents.

CHAPTER 9

Revising and Reviewing Documents

Chances are that you'll create some documents on your own, but for other documents you'll need to work with other people—either sharing the documents on a network or via the Internet, or using e-mail to send the documents back and forth.

Word includes strong features for working together on documents. In this chapter, I'll start by reviewing your different options so that you're clear about the different choices. After that, I'll show you how to work on a document simultaneously with your colleagues—if you have the technology required—and how to share documents but work on them one person at a time.

Next, you'll learn how to use the Track Changes feature, also called revision marking, to track all the edits you and your colleagues make to a document so that you can keep an audit trail. You can then review the changes and decide which to keep and which to remove.

After that, I'll show you how to add comments to a document, how to compare two documents to identify their differences automatically, and how to incorporate changes from two or more copies of a document into a single file. Lastly, you'll learn how to dig into Word's archives to recover an old version of a document after something horrible happens to the current version.

Understanding How You Can Work on Documents with Your Colleagues

In Word, you can work on documents with your colleagues either together or separately:

- *Work on the same copy of the document simultaneously*: If you have a SharePoint site or you store documents on Windows Live, you and your colleagues can store the document on the site, each open it at the same time, and work on it together. Microsoft calls this *coauthoring*.

- *Work on separate copies of the document*: If you don't have a SharePoint site, Word warns you when you're opening a document that someone else is using. When this happens, you can decide whether to wait until your colleague stops using the document or whether to open a separate copy and then integrate any changes you make back into the main copy.

- *Circulate a copy of the document, and each work on it in turn*: This method is easiest, as you use only a single copy of a document, and each person has free rein when they're editing it—but it usually takes longer than the other methods. To see clearly which changes each person has made to the document, you'll normally use Word's Track Changes feature, as discussed in this chapter.

■ **Note** If you have a SharePoint site, chances are you will want to try simultaneous editing and see how well it works for you. But if you find that running into conflicting changes creates more problems than it solves, you may be better off using the older means of collaboration. Coauthoring is technically very impressive and it can be great in the right situation, but it's not suitable for everyone.

Whichever way you work, you can use four main features for revising and reviewing documents with your colleagues:

- *Track Changes*: When you turn on this feature, Word tracks the insertions, deletions, formatting changes, and most other changes to the document. You can then view the changes, accept the changes you want to keep, and reject the others.

- *Comments*: You and your colleagues can attach comments to items in the document to offer opinions or suggest changes, without actually changing the text itself. You can then view the comments and remove them once you've dealt with them.

- *Document Compare*: This feature makes Word analyze and mark up the differences between two versions of the same document. Document Compare is useful when you need to amalgamate changes from two or more different versions in which you haven't tracked changes.

- *Versions*: Word stores different versions of a document within the same file. You may sometimes need to go back to a previous version of a document to recover text that you or a colleague has deleted.

Editing a Document Simultaneously with Your Colleagues

Word's most advanced way of working on a document with your colleagues is for each of you to open the same copy of the document at the same time, and all work on it together. Here's what happens:

- *Create the document*: You create the document as normal (for example, by using a template) and store it on your SharePoint site or on Windows Live SkyDrive.

■ **Caution** Unless you have a fast and reliable Internet connection, simultaneous editing of a large document stored on Windows Live SkyDrive can be slow enough to make collaboration difficult.

- *Open the document*: The first person opens the document as normal. When another person opens the document, they see a pop-up message (see Figure 9-1) telling them about the other people already editing the document. The first person also receives a pop-up as soon as Word notices that other authors have joined in the fray.

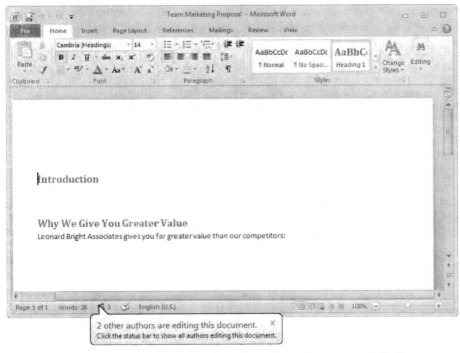

Figure 9-1. When you open a document that others are working on, Word displays a pop-up to let you know they're editing it. The Save button on the Quick Access Toolbar shows green arrows to indicate that it's acting as an Update button rather than as a regular Save button.

- *See who's editing the document*: The status bar displays an icon showing the number of people editing the document. (This number includes you.) You can click the icon to see who the people are (see Figure 9-2). For more detail, click the File tab to open Backstage, and then look at the People Currently Editing readout at the top of the Info pane.

Figure 9-2. To see who the other authors are, click the Authors icon on the status bar.

■ **Tip** In the People Currently Editing area of the Info pane in Backstage, there's a Send a Message button you can click to display a drop-down menu for sending either an e-mail message or an instant message to all the other people editing the document. For example, you could give them a ten-minute warning of the deadline by which you must finish the document, or you could ask them to get out of the paragraph you need to edit next.

- *Edit the document*: You can work pretty much as normal in Word, except that only one person can edit a particular paragraph or other element at a time. As you work, Word shows you which parts of the document other authors are working on by placing a line to the left of the items and displaying a name box (see Figure 9-3).

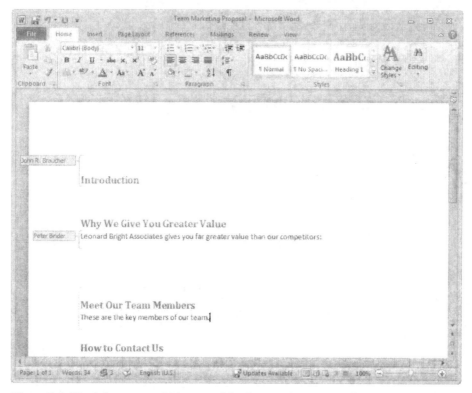

Figure 9-3. Word shows you which parts of the document your coauthors are working on at the moment. The Updates Available button on the status bar lets you know that updates from your coauthors are available.

- *Update the document*: When you're ready to save changes and get any updates that are available, you press Ctrl+S or click the Save button on the Quick Access Toolbar as usual. The Save button displays a pair of curving arrows to indicate that it's acting as an Update button. Word then updates the copy of the document you're viewing with the changes the others have made (Figure 9-4 shows an example using the same document as before), applies shading to the changes to draw your attention to them, and makes your changes available to your coauthors.

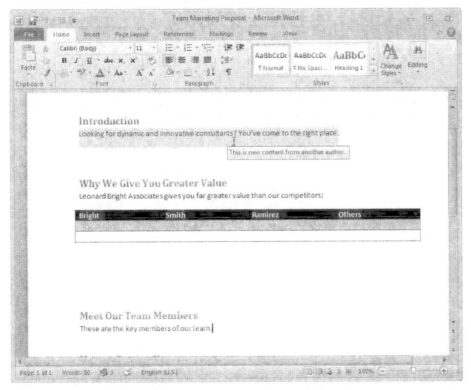

Figure 9-4. When you save your changes, Word merges in updates your coauthors have saved. Word displays the new items with shading (as in the paragraph under the Introduction heading here).

- *Resolve conflicts*: Word does its best to show you and your coauthors who's working where, but sooner or later, two or more of you may change the same part of the document in the same cycles of saving and updating. When this happens, Word displays the Upload Failed bar (see Figure 9-5) to the author who tried to save changes over changes another author had already saved. In the Conflicting changes pane that Word displays, right-click the conflict, and then choose Accept Conflict or Reject Conflict, as appropriate. Word displays the Conflicts Resolved bar when you have resolved all the conflicts; click the Save and Close View button to save the changes and close the Conflicting changes pane.

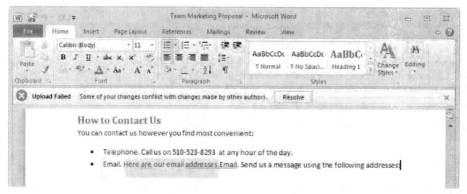

Figure 9-5. Word warns you of any conflicting changes when you try to save the document. Click the Resolve button on the Upload Failed bar to deal with the highlighted conflicts.

- *Close the document*: When you have finished working with the document, save any unsaved changes, and then close it as usual.

Sharing Documents with Your Colleagues on a Network

You can also share documents with your colleagues on a network without using SharePoint. In this case, you save the document in a shared folder on the network. From there, anyone permitted to use the folder can open the document, edit it, and save it—but only one person can open the document at the same time.

If you try to open a document that someone else has already opened, Word displays the File in Use dialog box (see Figure 9-6). From here, you can take four actions:

- *Cancel opening the document*: Click the Cancel button to cancel your request to open the document. You can then try again at a convenient time.

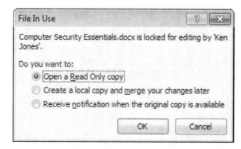

Figure 9-6. From the File in Use dialog box, you can open the document as a read-only file, create a copy on your PC and merge your changes later, or wait until the document is free.

- *Open a read-only copy of the document*: Select the Open a Read-Only copy option button and click the OK button to open the document in a read-only state. Read-only means that you can't save changes to the network copy of the document, but you can save it under a different name. If you want to integrate those changes into the network copy, you'll need to do so either manually or by using the Document Combine feature (discussed later in this chapter).

- *Create a local copy and merge your changes later*: Select the Create a local copy and merge your changes later option button and click the OK button if you need to go ahead and make changes to the document now rather than waiting. When the document becomes available for editing, Word offers to merge your changes into it; click the Merge button to do so.

- *Have Word tell you when the document becomes available*: Select the Receive notification when the original copy is available option button and click the OK button to make Word keep tabs on the document and tell you when the other person has finished with it. When Word displays the File Now Available dialog box (see Figure 9-7), click the Read-Write button to open the document for editing.

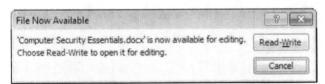

Figure 9-7. *Word displays the File Now Available dialog box when the file you've requested is available for editing. Click the Read-Write button to open the document so that you can edit it.*

▤ **Note** When you tell Word to notify you when a document becomes available, bear in mind that other people may be ahead of you in the notification list. So even if you persuade the person mentioned in the File in Use dialog box that it's your turn to edit the document, Word may offer it first to someone else—and they may take their time working on it.

Tracking the Changes in a Document

When you need to work with other people on creating or revising a document, use Word's Track Changes feature. Track Changes can automatically tracks almost all the changes in the document so that you can review them, see who made which changes when, accept the changes you want to keep, and reject the rest.

You can choose which types of changes to track and which to ignore. For example, you may want to track only the edits to the text of a document and let your colleagues handle the formatting.

Choosing Which Changes to Track

To choose which types of changes Word tracks in a document, follow these steps:

1. Choose Review ➤ Tracking ➤ Track Changes ➤ Change Tracking Options to display the Track Changes Options dialog box (see Figure 9-8).

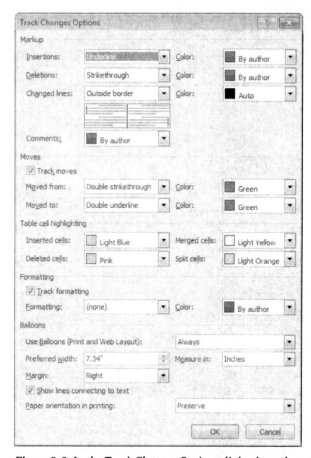

Figure 9-8. *In the Track Changes Options dialog box, choose how to show markup, track moves, and handle changes to table cells and formatting. You can also choose whether to use balloons to display changes.*

2. In the Markup area, choose how to mark insertions, deletions, changed lines, and comments:

   • *Insertions*: Open the Insertions drop-down list, and then click the type of markup you want for inserted text. Your choices are (none), Color only, Bold, Italic, Underline, Double Underline, or Strikethrough. Use the Color only setting when you need a subtle indication of added text; use Underline or Double Underline when you need a stronger indication. Open the topmost Color drop-down list and choose By author if you want Word to use a different color for each reviewer's additions; to use a specific color or shading for all added text, click that color or shading.

- *Deletions*: Open the Deletions drop-down list, and then click the type of markup to use for deleted text. Your choices are (none), Color only, Bold, Italic, Underline, Double Underline, Strikethrough, Hidden, ^ (Word displays a single caret mark to show where text has been deleted), # (Word shows a single pound sign where text has been deleted), or Double strikethrough. Open the middle Color drop-down list and choose By author if you want Word to use a different color for each reviewer's deletions; to use a specific color or shading for all deletions, click that color or shading.

▨ **Tip** The (none) item can be a good choice for deletions, as it makes the deleted items disappear from the document, leaving only the text that hasn't been deleted and the text that has been added.

- *Changed lines*: Open the Changed lines drop-down list and whether (and, if so, where) you want Word to display a vertical line in the margin next to each line that has changed. These changed lines help you locate changes in documents that contain changes on only some lines, but if most every line has changed, the changed lines are little use. Choose (none) to skip using changed lines, Left border to put them in the left margin, Right border to put them in the right margin, or Outside border to put the lines in the left margin on left pages and the right margin on right pages. Open the third color drop-down list and choose the color or shading you want; the Auto item applies the default text color and is often the best choice.

- *Comments*: Open the Comments drop-down list and choose the color or shading to give to each reviewer's comments. Choose the By author item to have Word use different colors for each reviewer.

3. In the Moves area, select the Track moves check box if you want Word to track text you've moved within a document separately from insertions and deletions. If you select this check box, you can choose settings as follows:

- *Moved from*: Open the Moved from drop-down list and choose how to mark the text that is no longer there because it has been moved to a different location in the document. Your choices are the same as for Deletions, but you'll want to use a different marking so that you can identify moved text. For example, use Strikethrough for Deletions and Double Strikethrough for Moved From text. Open the Color drop-down list and choose By author or the color or shading you want.

- *Moved to*: Open the Moved to drop-down list and choose how to mark the moved text in its new location. Your choices are the same as for Insertions, but you'll want to use a different marking so that you can distinguish the moved text; for example, Underline for Insertions and Double Underline for Moved To text.

■ **Note** Word's feature for tracking moved text separately from insertions and deletions works only for documents that use the Word Document format (with the .docx file extension), not for documents that use the older Word 97–2003 Document format.

4. In the Table cell highlighting area, choose the colors with which to shade cells that have been inserted, deleted, merged, or split in a table. Usually, you'll want to use a different color for each of these changes to a table's structure.

■ **Caution** Word provides the By author setting for the four drop-down lists in the Table cell highlighting area of the Track Changes Options dialog box, but it's best not to use this setting. Otherwise, while you can see who changed the table's structure, you need to dig deeper to see what damage the person inflicted on the table. Usually, it's easier to see how the table has changed, and then find out who made the changes only if you need to.

5. In the Formatting area, select the Track formatting check box if you want to track changes to formatting. This is usually a good idea. You can then open the Formatting drop-down list and choose the marking for formatting changes (for example, Bold or Italic), and open the Color drop-down list and choose the color.

6. In the Balloons area, choose whether to use balloons and the comments pane to display details of tracked changes and comments. These are the settings you can choose:

   • *Use Balloons (Print and Web Layout)*: Open the Use Balloons drop-down list and choose Always if you want to use balloons for all markup, Never if you don't want to use balloons, or Only for comments/formatting if you want to use balloons for comments and formatting but not for other tracked changes. If you choose Never, skip the rest of this sublist, as the options don't apply.

   • *Preferred width*: Set your preferred width for the markup area, using the measurement type specified in the Measure in drop-down list; for example, 2" or 25% of the page width.

   • *Margin*: Choose Left to display the markup area on the left, or Right to display it on the right (the default position).

   • *Show lines connecting to text*: Select this check box to make Word show a line connecting each balloon to the text it refers to. Usually, you'll want to show these lines unless the document is so full of markup that it's hard to follow the lines. Even if you turn the lines off, Word displays a line connecting the currently selected comment to its reference.

- • *Paper orientation in printing*: Choose the orientation to use when printing a document with its markup. Choose Auto to stay with Word's default orientation, Preserve to use the orientation set in this section of the document, or Force Landscape to print all the pages in landscape orientation.

7. Click the OK button to close the Track Changes Options dialog box.

Turning On Track Changes for a Document

To turn on Track Changes for a document, choose Review ➤ Tracking ➤ Track Changes, clicking the top part of the Track Changes button so that the button appears pressed in. (You can also click the bottom part of the button and then click Track Changes on the drop-down menu, but there's no point.)

■ **Tip** From the keyboard, press Ctrl+Shift+E to toggle Track Changes on or off.

When you need to turn Track Changes off again, choose Review ➤ Tracking ➤ Track Changes again, so that the button no longer appears pressed in.

■ **Tip** To give yourself an easy way to turn Track Change on and off, right-click blank space on the status bar to display the Customize Status Bar menu. Click the Track Changes item to put a check mark next to it, then click the status bar to close the menu. The status bar then displays a Track Changes readout that you can click to toggle Track Changes on or off.

Ensuring Your Colleagues Use the Track Changes Feature

Track Changes is a great feature, but anyone can turn off tracking and rampage through the document making untracked changes unless you force them to use Track Changes. You can do this by using Word's Restrict Formatting and Editing feature. Follow these steps:

1. Open the document and click the File tab to open Backstage. Word displays the Info pane by default.

2. Click the Protect Document button and then click Restrict Editing on the drop-down menu to display the Restrict Formatting and Editing pane (shown in Figure 9-9 with settings chosen).

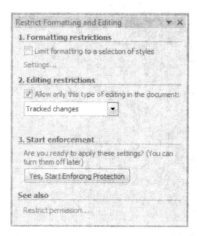

Figure 9-9. Use the Restrict Formatting and Editing pane to ensure that your colleagues use Track Changes when editing the document.

3. If you want to prevent others from applying direct formatting, follow these steps:

   • Select the Limit formatting to a selection of styles check box.

   • Click the Settings link to display the Formatting Restrictions dialog box (see Figure 9-10).

Figure 9-10. To prevent your colleagues from messing up a document using direct formatting, use the Formatting Restrictions dialog box to limit them to applying styles you approve.

- Make sure the Limit formatting to a selection of styles check box is selected.

- In the Checked styles are currently allowed list box, select the check box for each style you want to allow your colleagues to apply. You can click the None button to clear all the check boxes so that you can quickly select just a few, click the All button to select all the check boxes so that you can clear just a few, or click the Recommended Minimum button to see Word's best guess of the styles your colleagues will need.

- In the Formatting area, clear the Allow AutoFormat to override formatting restrictions check box unless you want to AutoFormat to apply styles as it thinks necessary. (This is seldom a good idea.)

- Select the Block Theme or Scheme switching check box if you want to ensure your colleagues don't change the document's overall look. (This is usually a good idea.)

- Select the Block Quick Style Set switching check box if you want to prevent your colleagues from changing the set of Quick Styles used. (This too is usually a good idea.)

- Click the OK button to close the Formatting Restrictions dialog box and return to the Restrict Formatting and Editing pane.

▒ **Note** If Word displays a dialog box saying that the document may contain formatting or styles that aren't allowed check box and offering to remove them, click the Yes button. After you finish setting up the formatting and editing restrictions, check through the document for paragraphs whose style Word has replaced with Normal style. Apply to each paragraph a suitable style from the list of styles you've approved for the document.

---

4. In the Editing restrictions area, select the Allow only this type of editing in the document check box, and then choose Tracked changes in the drop-down list.

▒ **Tip** You can also use the Allow only this type of editing in the document drop-down list to restrict your colleagues to using comments (discussed later in this chapter), using the document as a form (beyond the scope of this book), or preventing them from making any changes.

---

5. In the Start enforcement are, click the Yes, Start Enforcing Protection button. Word displays the Start Enforcing Protection dialog box (see Figure 9-11).

▒ **Note** The User authentication option button in the Start Enforcing Protection dialog box is available only if you've set Word up to use Information Rights Management (IRM).

Figure 9-11. In the Start Enforcing Protection dialog box, apply a password to the document to prevent your colleagues from turning off the formatting and editing restrictions.

6. Select the Password option button, and then type a password in the Enter new password box and then Reenter password to confirm text box. Make the password at least eight characters long, mix upper- and lowercase letters, and include numbers and symbols.

7. Click the OK button to close the Start Enforcing Protection dialog box. Word protects the document and updates the Restrict Formatting and Editing pane (see Figure 9-12).

Figure 9-12. In the Restrict Formatting and Editing pane, you can see which restrictions you've applied to the document. You can also stop the protection.

8. Click the Close button (the × button) to close the Restrict Formatting and Editing pane.

9. Save the document. For example, click the Save button on the Quick Access Toolbar.

Working in a Document with Track Changes On

After you turn on Track Changes for a document, you can work in it much as normal. Word tracks your insertions, deletions, and other changes and displays such markup as you've chosen to show.

For example, in Print Layout view, Web Layout view, and Full Screen Reading view, Word normally displays the markup area and balloons, as shown in Figure 9-13.

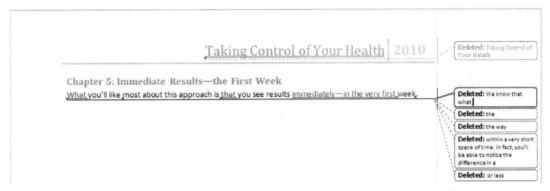

Figure 9-13. In Print Layout view, Web Layout view, and Full Screen Reading view, Word displays the markup area with balloons detailing the changes.

■ **Tip** To switch quickly among the settings for markup balloons, choose Review ➤ Tracking ➤ Show Markup ➤ Balloons, and then click the command you want: Show Revisions in Balloons, Show All Revisions Inline, or Show Only Comments and Formatting in Balloons.

In Draft view and Outline view, Word shows the changes inline, using the markup specified in the Track Changes Options dialog box; for example, applying an underscore to each insertion and strikethrough to each deletion, as shown in Figure 9-14.

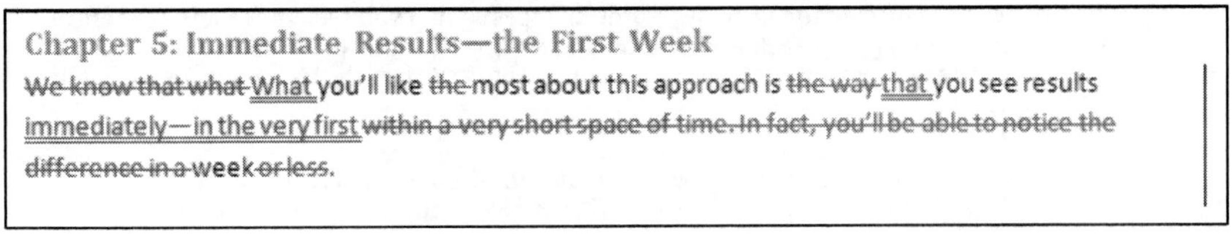

Figure 9-14. Depending on the markup options you've chosen and the view you're using, Word can mark insertions and deletions inline.

To see information about a change in Draft view or Outline view (or in one of the other views when you have chosen not to use the markup area), hold the mouse pointer over the change. Word displays a ScreenTip showing the details of the change (see Figure 9-15).

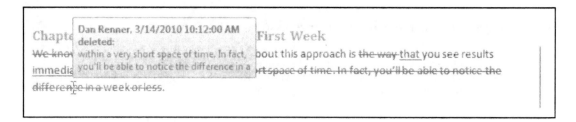

Figure 9-15. Hold the mouse pointer over a tracked change to display a ScreenTip showing the details.

Choosing How to View the Document's Changes and Markup

As you work with Track Changes on, you may find it helpful to change how Word displays the markup for review. For example, you can show the document as it will appear with all the markup accepted, or show the document's original version to see how it was.

To choose how to view the document's markup, choose Review ➤ Tracking ➤ Display for Review, and then click the setting you want on the Display for Review drop-down menu:

- *Final: Show Markup*: Choose this item to see the document's final text with all the markup displayed. This is the default setting, and the one you'll probably want to use most of the time while marking up the document.

- *Final*: Choose this item to see the document's final text with no markup appearing. Use this view when you want to read the document without the visual distraction of markup.

- *Original: Show Markup*: Choose this item to see the document's original text with the markup displayed. Use this view when you want to focus on the changes made to the original text.

- *Original*: Choose this item to see the document's original text before any of the changes were made.

Controlling Which Changes Word Displays

When a document contains many changes, or when you want to focus only on one aspect of the changes, you may want to turn off the display of some changes so that you see only others. To control which changes Word displays, choose Review ➤ Tracking ➤ Show Markup. On the Show Markup drop-down menu, select the check box for each item you want to see, and clear the check box for each item you want to hide.

These are your options:

- *Comments*: Choose whether to show comments inserted in the document (as discussed in the section "Adding Comments to a Document," later in this chapter).

- *Ink*: Choose whether to show ink markup added to the document using Windows' handwriting support.

- *Insertions and Deletions*: Choose whether to show text and other items inserted in the document, deleted from it, or moved from one place in the document to another.

- *Formatting*: Choose whether to show changes to formatting; for example, the application or a style or the addition of direct formatting.

- *Markup Area Highlight*: Choose whether to show shading on the markup area rather than displaying it as the document's normal background color.

- *Balloons*: In this submenu, choose whether Word uses balloons (Show Revisions in Balloons), displays revisions in the text (Show All Revisions Inline), or shows comments and formatting changes in balloons but all other changes inline (Show Only Comments and Formatting in Balloons). These settings are mutually exclusive: you can choose only one at a time.

- *Reviewers*: In this submenu, choose All Reviewers to display comments from all reviewers. Otherwise, clear the All Reviewers check box, and select the check box only for each reviewer whose changes you want to see.

- *Highlight Updates*: Choose whether to have Word highlight the latest updates to the document so that you can identify them more quickly.

- *Other Authors*: Choose whether to mark updates by other authors.

Integrating Tracked Changes into a Document

When everyone has made their edits to the document, you can go through the changes and accept those you want to keep and reject the others.

To go through the changes, use the controls in the Changes group on the Review tab. First, select a change by clicking the Next button or the Previous button, clicking the balloon in the markup area, or clicking the change in the Reviewing pane.

You can then accept changes by using the Accept button and its drop-down menu:

- *Accept the selected change and select the next change*: Click the upper part of the Accept button (or click the lower part and then click Accept and Move to Next on the drop-down menu).

- *Accept the selected change*: Click the lower part of the Accept button, and then click Accept Change.

- *Accept all changes shown with your Show Markup options*: When you've chosen to show only some markup, click the lower part of the Accept button, and then click Accept All Changes Shown to accept all that markup but not markup that's hidden. For example, if you've chosen to show Formatting but not show Insertions and Deletions, clicking Accept All Changes Shown accepts all formatting changes.

- *Accept all the changes in the document*: If the document contains changes light enough that you can review them all without dealing with individual changes along the way, click the lower part of the Accept button, and then click Accept All Changes in Document.

Similarly, you can reject one or more changes at once:

- *Reject the selected change and select the next change*: Click the upper part of the Reject button (or click the lower part and then click Reject and Move to Next on the drop-down menu).

- *Reject the selected change*: Click the lower part of the Reject button, and then click Reject Change.

- *Reject all changes shown with your Show Markup options*: When you've chosen to show only some markup, click the lower part of the Reject button, and then click Reject All Changes Shown to reject all that markup but not markup that's hidden.

- *Reject all the changes in the document*: To get rid of all the changes, click the lower part of the Reject button, and then click Reject All Changes in Document.

When you've finished accepting or rejecting changes, save the document. You may want to save it under a different name if the document is now ready for another stage in its evolution.

■ **Tip** You can also accept or reject a change by using the context menu. Right-click the change in the text, in the markup area, or in the Reviewing pane, and then click Accept Change or Reject Change on the context menu.

Using Track Changes in Full Screen Reading view

If you like to work in Full Screen Reading view, you can work with Track Changes in it too. Click the View Options button and then use the last four items on the drop-down menu to control editing and tracking:

- *Allow Typing*: Click this item to start editing the document in Full Screen Reading view.

- *Track Changes*: Click this item to toggle Track Changes on or off. Click the arrow button to display a submenu with Track Changes, Change Tracking Options, and Change User Name commands.

- *Show Comments and Changes*: Click this item to display a submenu with commands for controlling which markup items Word shows (see Figure 9-16).

- *Show Original/Final Document*: Click this item to display a submenu with commands for switching among Final, Final with Markup, Original, and Original with Markup displays.

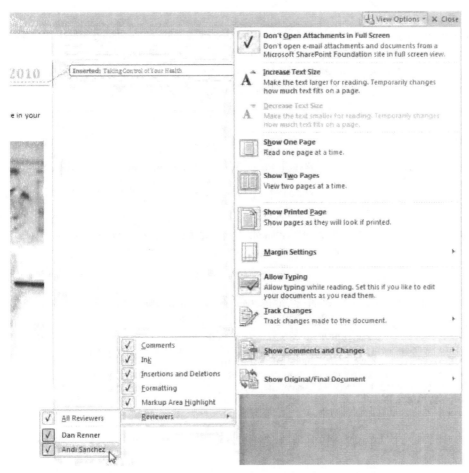

Figure 9-16. In Full Screen Reading view, you can control Track Changes using the commands at the bottom of the View Options drop-down menu.

Adding Comments to a Document

When you need to give your input on a document without making changes to the text, use Word's comments. A *comment* appears in a floating balloon attached to a word or another object in text, enabling you to comment easily and clearly on a specific item.

Note If you want to ensure your colleagues use comments on a document rather than altering its text, open the Restrict Formatting and Editing pane as discussed in the section "Ensuring Your Colleagues Use the Track Changes Feature," earlier in this chapter. Select the Allow only this type of editing in the document check box, and then click Comments in the drop-down list. Click the Yes, Start Enforcing Protection button.

Adding a Comment

To add a comment to a document, select the text or object you're commenting on, and then choose Review ➤ Comments ➤ New Comment.

Note If you want to attach a comment to a single word, just click in that word. When you insert the comment, Word automatically puts the comment parentheses around the word.

Word then adds colored parentheses around your selection to indicate that it has a comment attached. The way Word displays the comment depends on the view you're using:

- *Print Layout view, Web Layout view, or Full Screen Reading view*: Word displays the comments pane at the right side of the page and opens a comment balloon for you to type the comment in. The comment balloon is attached to the comment markers by a thin line, so you can see which part of the document each comment belongs to. Figure 9-17 shows the comments pane open with two comments inserted.

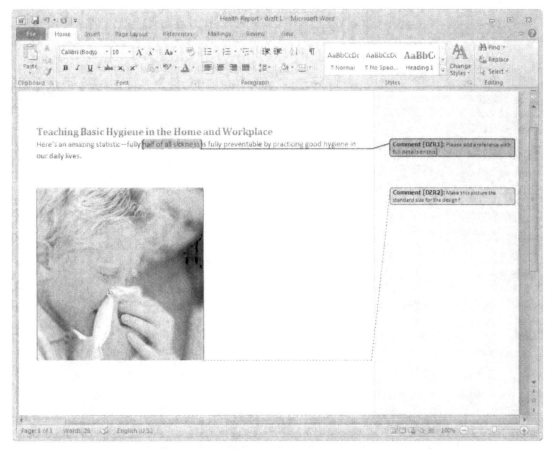

***Figure 9-17.** In Print Layout view, Web Layout view, or Full Screen Reading view, Word displays comments in the comments pane to the side of the document.*

- *Draft view or Outline view*: Word opens the Reviewing pane, which you use for reviewing comments and other markup. Figure 9-18 shows the Reviewing pane open in Draft view.

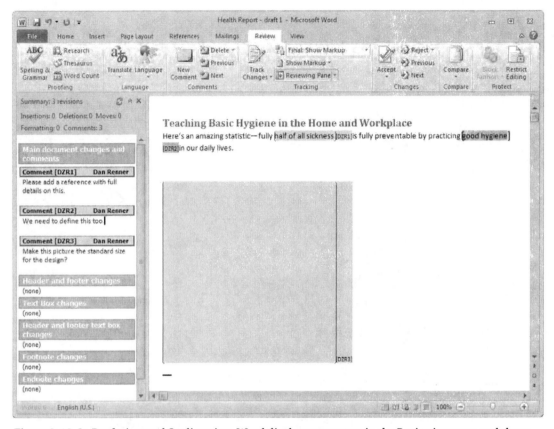

Figure 9-18. In Draft view and Outline view, Word displays comments in the Reviewing pane and shows the commenter's initials and the comment number in brackets after the commented item.

Type (or paste) the text of the comment either in the comment balloon or in the comment's area in the Reviewing pane. Most people leave comments as plain text, but you can apply formatting to a comment if you want. For example, you can apply boldface or a style to a word that you want to emphasize. You can also insert elements such as tables and graphics in comments.

In Draft view or Outline view, click the Close button (the × button) at the upper-right corner of the Reviewing pane when you've finished using it. You can also choose Review ➤ Tracking ➤ Reviewing Pane to toggle the display of the Reviewing pane.

■ **Tip** If you find the Reviewing pane takes up vital space at the side of the Word window, choose Review ➤ Tracking ➤ Reviewing Pane ➤ Reviewing Pane Horizontal to switch it to horizontal placement. Choose Review ➤ Tracking ➤ Reviewing Pane ➤ Reviewing Pane Vertical to put it back.

Viewing and Reviewing Comments

To review comments, you normally use the comments pane and comment balloons (in Print Layout view, Web Layout view, and Full Screen Reading view) or the Reviewing pane.

You can also hold the mouse pointer over commented text or the comment mark to display a ScreenTip showing the text of the comment, as shown in Figure 9-19.

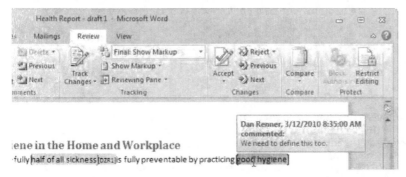

Figure 9-19. *Hold the mouse pointer over commented text or a comment mark to display a ScreenTip showing the text of the comment.*

Most people find the comments pane and comment balloons easy unless a document has a huge number of comments, but if you find the balloons awkward, you can turn them off like this:

1. Choose Review ➤ Tracking ➤ Track Changes ➤ Change Tracking Options to display the Track Changes Options dialog box.

2. In the Balloons area at the bottom, open the Use Balloons (Print and Web Layout) drop-down list and choose Never.

3. Click the OK button.

Even when the comments pane is open, you can display the Reviewing pane by choosing Review ➤ Tracking ➤ Reviewing pane.

■ **Tip** You can browse comments by using the browse object. Click the Select Browse Object button between the Previous button and Next button below the vertical scroll bar, and then click Comment on the panel. You can then click the Previous button and Next button to move from comment to comment.

Deleting Comments

You can delete a comment by right-clicking it in the text, in the comment pane, or in the Reviewing pane, and then clicking Delete comment on the context menu.

Alternatively, click the comment in the text, in the comment pane, or in the Reviewing pane, and then choose Review ➤ Comments ➤ Delete (clicking the top part of the Delete button).

To delete all the comments from the document, choose Review ➤ Comments ➤ Delete ➤ Delete All Comments in Document. Word doesn't confirm the deletion, but you can use Undo if you give the command by accident.

Comparing or Combining Different Versions of the Same Document

When you need to follow and review the changes in a document, the best approach is to use Track Changes (as described earlier in this chapter) on a single document that each reviewer works on in turn. This way, Track Changes records all the information you need about the changes made to a document and gives you the tools to review the changes and incorporate them easily.

Other times, you may need to circulate a document to various colleagues at the same time; for example, to get the review done more quickly. This method gives you multiple copies of the same document containing their different edits marked by Track Changes. To incorporate all the different edits into a single copy of the document, you can use Word's Document Combine feature.

You may also need to compare two copies of a document in which the changes haven't been tracked. For this, you can use the Document Compare feature. This feature isn't as good as Track Changes used consistently, but it's a huge improvement over spending hours poring over different document files and trying to integrate the best changes into a single version.

To use Document Compare to compare or combine two documents, follow these steps:

1. If either or both of the document is open, close it. Starting with both documents closed is usually easier than starting with either or both open.

2. Give the command for comparing or combining, as needed:

    • *Compare*: Choose Review ➤ Compare ➤ Compare to display the Compare Documents dialog box (shown in Figure 9-20 expanded to display all its settings).

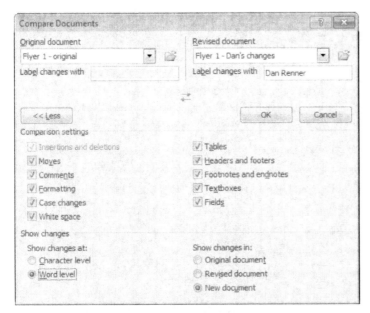

Figure 9-20. Use the Compare Documents dialog box or the related Combine Documents dialog box to identify the changes between two documents based on the same document.

- *Combine*: Choose Review ➤ Compare ➤ Combine to display the Combine Documents dialog box, which is almost identical to the Compare Documents dialog box apart from the title.

3. Choose the documents you want to compare:

- Either open the Original Document drop-down list and click the document in the list; or click the Open button next to the drop-down list, click the document in the Open dialog box, and then click the Open button.

- Similarly, either open the Revised Document drop-down list and click the document in the list; or click the Open button next to the drop-down list, click the document in the Open dialog box, and then click the Open button.

4. Tell Word how to label the changes to the document:

- The left Label Changes With text box shows the name of the original document's last reviewer who used revision marks. Type a different name if necessary. If the text box is blank and unavailable, the document contains no tracked changes.

- The right Label Changes With text box shows the last reviewer of the revised document. Again, you may need to type a different name.

5. Click the More button to display the lower part of the dialog box so that you can choose comparison settings.

6. In the Comparison settings area, clear the check box for any items you don't want to integrate. For example, if you want to omit the changes to fields, clear the Fields check box. Usually, you'll want to leave most of the check boxes selected.

7. On the Show changes at side of the Show changes area, select the Word level option button to make Word analyze changes at the word level. If you need to dig deeper, you can select the Character level option button instead, but for many documents this produces more detail than you need.

8. On the Show changes in side of the Show changes area, select the New document option button if you want to merge the changes into a new document. This is usually clearest, but you can select the Original document option button or the Revised document option button instead if you prefer.

9. Click the OK button to close the dialog box and make Word analyze the changes.

10. If Word displays the dialog box shown in Figure 9-21, warning you that it will treat the tracked changes in the documents as having been accepted so that it can make the comparison, click the Yes button. (The alternative is to click the No button, go back into the documents, and accept or reject the revisions before you compare or combine the documents.)

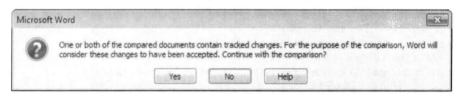

Figure 9-21. If Word displays this dialog box when you're comparing or combining documents, click the Yes button to proceed.

Word then displays the result of the comparison or combination; for example, a new compare document together with the source documents that produced it, with the Reviewing pane showing a list of the differences (see Figure 9-22).

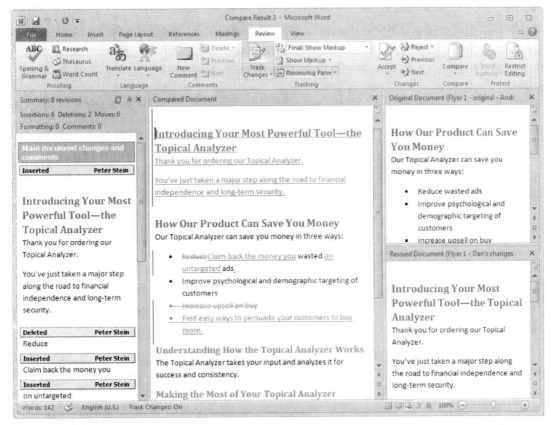

Figure 9-22. After you compare documents, Word displays the resulting document (the document named Compare Result 3 here) plus the source documents. The Reviewing pane shows a list of the changes.

If you don't need to see the source documents as you review the result of the comparison, click the Close button (the × button) button on each of the source document panes or choose Review ➤ Compare ➤ Compare ➤ Show Source Documents ➤ Hide Source Documents. The Show Source Documents submenu also gives you commands for opening the compared document's source documents again if you need them.

Save the changes to the compared or combined document if you want to keep them.

Using Word's Document Versions

As you work, Word automatically saves AutoRecover files of your documents in case your PC crashes, Word disagrees with itself, or you make a major edit that you later regret. To stop these files from cluttering up your PC's hard drive, Word automatically deletes the AutoRecover files when you save all your documents and exit Word. But if things go wrong while you're editing a document, you may be able to open an earlier version of the document and recover what you've lost.

■ **Note** If you don't want Word to save AutoRecover files of your documents, click the File tab, click Options, and then click the Save item in the left pane of the Word Options dialog box. Clear the Save AutoRecover information every *N* minutes check box, and then click the OK button to close the Word Options dialog box.

To see which versions of a document are available, click the File tab to open Backstage with the Info pane showing. Then look at the Versions area (see Figure 9-23), which lists the versions (or tells you there are none).

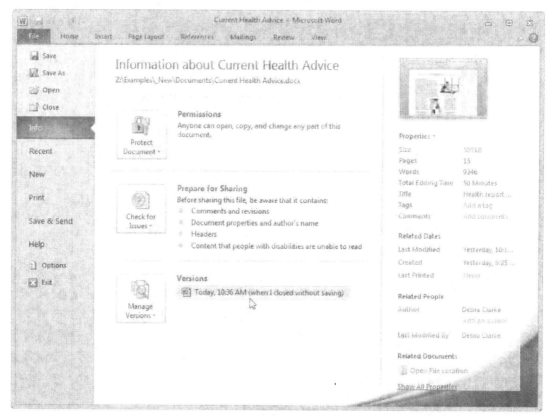

Figure 9-23. *Use the Versions readout in the Info pane in Backstage to see which versions are available for a document. To open a version, click the Manage Versions button, and then click Recover Draft Versions.*

To open a version, click it. Word opens the version and displays the Autosaved Version bar at the top to make sure you're clear that this is an older version of the document (see Figure 9-24).

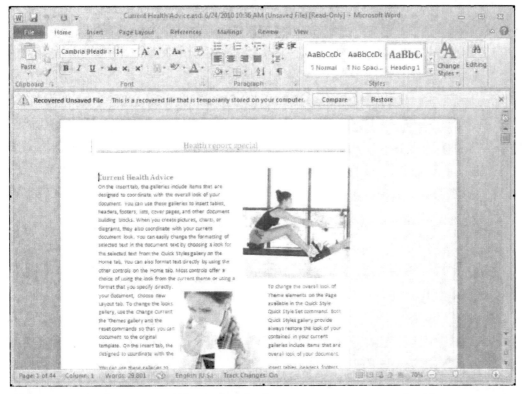

Figure 9-24. When you open an older version of a document, you can compare it to the current version or restore it to its former glory.

If you know that your most recent version is wrecked, you can go ahead and click the Restore button to restore the version. But what you'll often want to do is compare the version to your current version of the document to see if there's material you can recover. To do so, click the Compare button, and follow through the comparison process, as described in the previous section.

Summary

In this chapter, you've learned essential techniques and tools for revising and reviewing documents. You've learned how to edit a document simultaneously with your colleagues and how to share documents via a network. You know how to set up Track Changes to mark the changes you want to track, how to make your colleagues use Track Changes, and how to accept or reject the changes that Word records. You can use comments to add suggestions or requests to documents, and you can use the Document Compare feature and Document Combine feature to analyze documents and automatically incorporate different edits in them.

Finally, you've learned how to locate earlier versions of a document that has suffered damage so that you can recover missing information from it.

In the next chapter, I'll show you how to finalize, print, and share your Word documents.

CHAPTER 10

Printing, Finalizing, and Sharing Documents

In this chapter, you'll look at how you can share your documents with other people. You'll start by seeing how to print an entire document or the relevant pages or sections of it, how to choose whether to include markup, and how to print other parts of the document, such as markup and document properties. After that, I'll show you how to finalize your Word documents by removing sensitive information, applying any restrictions the document needs, and then marking it as final.

Next, you'll learn how to deal with issues in making a Word 2010 document compatible with earlier versions of Word. Last, I'll show you how to create electronic versions of a document suitable for distributing online or taking to a print shop for specialist printing.

Using Word's Features for Printing Documents

You can print your Word documents by using the standard techniques discussed in Chapter 3, but Word also offers extra features that you may want to use, such as printing a custom range of pages, printing markup with its document or without its document, or printing a document's properties, styles, or custom key assignments.

To use these extra printing features, you use the Print What drop-down menu (see Figure 10-1) in the Print place in Backstage. Here's how to open the Print What drop-down menu:

1. Click the File tab to open Backstage.

2. Click the Print item in the left column to display the Print place.

3. Click the Print What drop-down button to display the Print What drop-down menu.

Note You can also press Ctrl+P to go straight to the Print place.

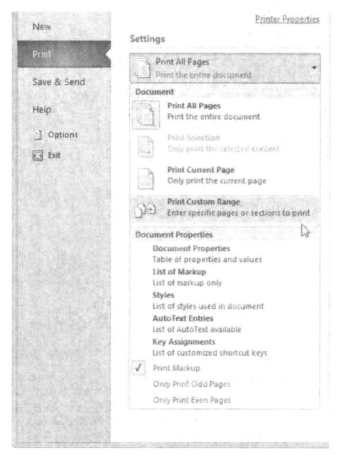

Figure 10-1. From the Print What drop-down menu in the Print place in Backstage, you can print a custom range of the document, print markup, print properties, or other items.

Printing a Custom Range of Pages

After correcting a document, you may need to print a custom range of pages from a document; for example, pages 3, 5, 8–10, 15, and 20. To do so, open the Print What drop-down menu, and then click Print Custom Range. Word replaces the Print What button with the Print Custom Range button and displays the Pages box below it.

Type in the details of the range you want to print, using the conventions shown in Table 10-1. For example, 3,5,8-10,15,20 prints the pages mentioned in the previous paragraph. Then click the Print button.

Table 10-1. Specifying a Custom Range of Pages to Print

To Print These Pages	Type This	Example
Consecutive pages	Starting page number, hyphen, ending page number	8-10
Individual pages	Page number, comma, page number	7,11,15
Sections	s and section number	s1,s3
Range of sections	s and starting section number, hyphen, s and ending section number	s1-s3
Pages within sections	p and page number, s and section number	p3s5-p8s7

■ **Note** Printing by sections is most useful if you've split up a document into different sections, each of which starts on a new page.

Choosing Whether to Print Markup—Or Only Markup

When you print a document, you can choose whether to print any markup and comments it contains or whether to print the document as it appears without the markup and comments.

To tell Word which you want, open the Print What drop-down menu in the Print place in Backstage. At the bottom, click the Print Markup item, placing a check mark next to it, if you want to print the markup. If you don't want the markup, make sure the Print Markup item has no check mark next to it.

■ **Note** Sometimes it's useful to print only the markup for a document. To do so, open the Print What drop-down menu in the Print place in Backstage, click List of Markup, and then click the Print button.

Printing Document Properties, Styles, AutoText Entries, and Key Assignments

In the same way that you can print only the markup in a document, you can also print four other items by choosing them on the Print What drop-down menu in the Print place in Backstage:

- *Document Properties*: Select this item to print a page showing the document's properties—the filename, directory (folder), template, title, subject, author, and so on.

- *Styles*: Select this item to print pages listing the styles used in the document and their formatting.

- *AutoText Entries*: Select this item to print a list of the AutoText entries stored in the document's template.

- *Key Assignments*: Select this item to print a list of the custom key assignments in the document (there may not be any).

Finalizing a Document

When you have finished creating, editing, and reviewing a document, you can make it final. Finalizing a document has three main parts:

- Removing sensitive or surplus information from the document.

- Marking the document as being final.

- Signing the document with a digital signature to prove it hasn't been altered.

You may also need to encrypt the document with a password or otherwise limit the people who can open, edit, or print the document. You'll look at these topics along the way.

Removing Sensitive Information from a Document

Quite apart from any confidential contents, a Word document can include sensitive information about who worked on it, who last saved it, and who added and deleted which parts of it. Before you distribute a document, use Word's tools for cleaning up a document to make sure it doesn't contain anything that will come back to bite you.

To remove potentially sensitive information from a document, follow these steps:

1. Click the File tab to open Backstage. Word displays the Info pane.

▓ **Note** If you've protected the document (as described later in this chapter), you must remove protection before using the Document Inspector. (If you try to run the Document Inspector without removing protection, Word displays a warning dialog box to let you know the problem.)

---

2. Click the Check For Issues button, and then click Inspect Document on the drop-down menu to open the Document Inspector dialog box (see Figure 10-2).

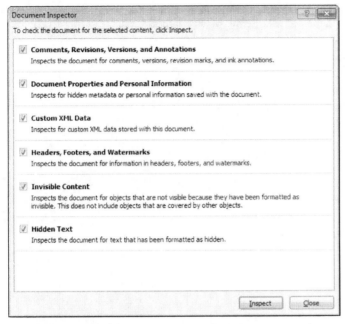

Figure 10-2. In the Document Inspector dialog box, choose the types of metadata and hidden content you want to scan the document for.

3.   Select the check box for each content type you want to scan the document for:

   • *Comments, Revisions, Versions, and Annotations*: Select this check box to scan for comments, tracked changes, earlier versions of the document, and ink annotations.

   • *Document Properties and Personal Information*: Select this check box to scan for potentially sensitive document properties and personal information about you or other people who have worked on the document.

   • Custom XML Data: Select this check box to scan for custom XML tags and mappings. (XML is an advanced feature used for manipulating data automatically.)

   • *Headers, Footers, and Watermarks*: Select this check box to have Word check the headers, footers, and any watermarks you've applied. These may contain information that you want to remove or update before sharing the document. For example, you may need to remove a Draft watermark or add a Confidential watermark.

   • *Hidden Text*: Select this check box to scan for text formatted to be hidden from view using hidden font formatting. Hidden text is easy to miss when you're looking through a document, but anyone you share the document with can display the hidden text.

4. Click the Inspect button to run the inspection for the items you chose. Word then updates the Document Inspector with details of what it found (see Figure 10-3).

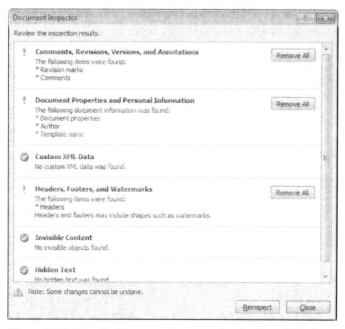

Figure 10-3. After the Document Inspector has inspected the document, click the Remove All button for each item you want to remove.

5. For each category of items, read through what the Document Inspector has found, and click the Remove All button if you want to remove those items.

6. To double-check the document, click the Reinspect button.

7. When you're satisfied with the results the Document Inspector produces, click the Close button to close the dialog box.

8. Go through your document visually to check that the items you've removed haven't left any holes.

9. Save the document, and then finalize it as described next.

Marking a Document as Final

To indicate that a document is finished rather than being in draft, you can mark it as finished. Doing so makes the document read-only, so nobody can make changes to the document without deliberately opening it up for editing.

To mark a document as final, follow these steps:

1. Click the File tab to open Backstage. Word displays the Info pane.

2. Click the Protect Document button, and then click Mark as Final on the drop-down menu. Word displays a confirmation dialog box (see Figure 10-4).

Figure 10-4. You can mark a document as final to ensure that nobody edits it further without knowing that it's finished.

3. Click the OK button. Word closes the dialog box, marks the document as final and read-only, and then saves it.

Word displays a yellow bar across the top of the window to warn you that the document is marked as final (see Figure 10-5). Click the Edit Anyway button if you want to open the document for editing anyway. When you've finished editing the document, repeat the above process to mark it as final again.

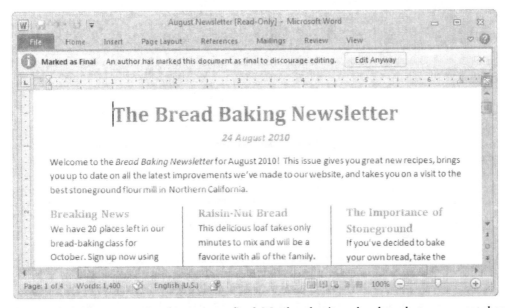

Figure 10-5. After you mark a document as final, Word makes it read-only so that you cannot change it unless you click the Edit Anyway button.

Encrypting a Document with a Password

If you need to keep other people out of a document, or let only approved people open it, you can encrypt the document with a password.

▪ **Caution** Word's encryption is effective only against casual snoopers. An attacker who uses a password-cracking program (which are widely available on the Internet) can open an encrypted document with minimal effort.

To encrypt a document with a password, follow these steps:

1. Click the File tab to open Backstage. Word displays the Info pane by default.

2. Click the Protect Document button, and then click Encrypt with Password on the drop-down menu to display the Encrypt Document dialog box (see Figure 10-6).

Figure 10-6. You can encrypt a document with a password. Doing so provides moderate protection against conventional snoopers.

3. Type the password you want to use; the dialog box shows dots rather than characters, in case someone's peeking over your shoulder. To give the most protection, use eight or more characters, using both capitals and lowercase, and including numbers and symbols. Memorize the password, or write it down somewhere safe.

4. Click the OK button. Word displays the Confirm Password dialog box, which is almost exactly the same as the Encrypt Document dialog box.

5. Type the password again (to make sure you've typed what you intended), and then click the OK button. Word closes the dialog box and changes the Permissions readout in the Info pane in Backstage to show that the document is protected (see Figure 10-7).

Figure 10-7. The Permissions readout shows that opening the document requires a password.

6. Save the document. For example, press Ctrl+S.

After you password-protect a document, it behaves as normal, except that when you try to open it, Word displays the Password dialog box demanding the password. If you type the password and click the OK button (or press Enter), Word opens the document; otherwise, Word tells you it can't open the document.

■ **Note** To remove the password, click the File tab to open Backstage, click the Protect Document button in the Info pane, and then click Encrypt with Password. In the Encrypt Document dialog box, delete the password from the Password text box, and then click the OK button. Word removes the password. Save the document (for example, press Ctrl+S).

Limiting the People Who Can Open, Edit, and Print the Document

Protecting a password can be an effective way of keeping unwanted people out of it, but you can also set permissions on a document so that only certain people can open it. To do this, Word uses Microsoft's Information Rights Management (IRM) tools, which attempt to verify the identity of each user who tries to open a file and make sure they're allowed to do so.

If you're working for a company or organization that has implemented Microsoft's Information Rights Management (IRM), you can use the company's IRM server to authenticate people's credentials. Otherwise, you can sign up to Microsoft's free IRM service, which uses a Windows Live ID for authentication.

If you want to sign up for Microsoft's IRM service, follow these steps:

1. Click the File tab to open Backstage. Word displays the Info pane by default.

2. Click the Protect Document button, click the Restrict Permission by People item on the drop-down menu, and then click Manage Credentials. Word displays the Service Sign-Up dialog box for the IRM service.

3.   Select the Yes, I want to sign up for this free service from Microsoft option button, and then click the Next button. Follow through the Information Rights Management Configuration Wizard, either providing your existing Windows Live ID or signing up for a new one to use.

4.   When you reach the Select User dialog box, in which you identify the user account for creating or opening IRM-protected content, select your user name, and then click the OK button. Word then displays the Permission dialog box, which you normally reach as described next, so that you can set permissions on the document.

When you've set up your IRM credentials, you can set permissions on a document like this:

1.   Click the File tab to open Backstage. Word displays the Info pane.

2.   Click the Protect Document button, click the Restrict Permission by People item on the drop-down menu, and then click Restricted Access to display the Permissions dialog box (shown in Figure 10-8 with settings chosen).

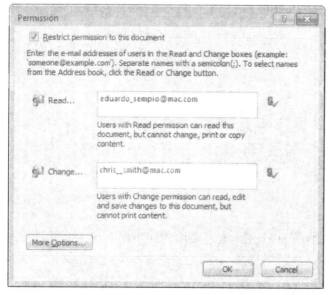

Figure 10-8. You can use Word's Information Rights Management tools to allow only certain people to read or change a document.

3.   Select the Restrict permission in this document check box.

4.   In the Read text box, enter the e-mail address for each person allowed to open the document but not change it, print it, or copy material from it.

   •   You can either type in the addresses, separating them with semicolons, or click the Read button and pick the addresses from your address book.

   •   Click the checkmark button to the right of the Read box to check the addresses.

5. In the Change text box, enter the e-mail address for each person allowed to open the document, edit it, and save changes to it, but not print it.

- As with the Read addresses, you can type the Change addresses, separating them with semicolons, or click the Change button and choose the addresses from your address book.

- Click the checkmark button to the right of the Change box to check the addresses.

6. If you want to let users print the document or copy content, or make the document expire automatically after a time, click the More Options button to display additional controls in the Permission dialog box (see Figure 10-9).

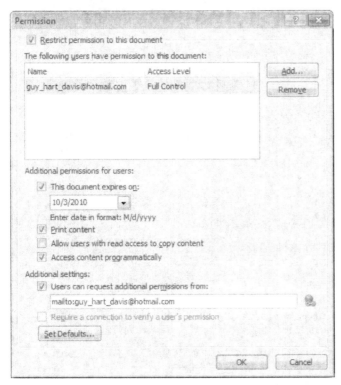

Figure 10-9. *Expand the Permission dialog box to reveal extra options, including settings for making the document expire and allowing users to print the document.*

7. Use the Add and Remove buttons to add users to the list box called The following users have permission to this document.

8. In the Additional permissions for users area, choose permissions as needed:

- *This document expires on*: If you want to make the document unavailable after a certain date, select this check box, open the date picker, and click the date.

- *Print content*: Select this check box if you want users to be able to print the document. This applies to both users with read access and users with change access.

- *Allow users with read access to copy content*: Select this check box if you want users with read access to be able to copy document content (and paste it into other documents or programs).

- *Access content programmatically*: Select this check box if you want users to be able to run macros that manipulate the document.

9. In the Additional settings area, choose settings as needed:

- *Users can request additional permissions from*: Select this check box and type an e-mail address in the text box if you want users to be able to request you upgrade their permissions; for example, from read access to change access.

- *Require a connection to verify a user's permission*: If you're using IRM on a network, you can select this check box to make Word check the user's authentication online. If you're using Microsoft's IRM service, this check box is unavailable.

10. Click the OK button to close the Permissions dialog box.

When anyone tries to open the document after you've restricted access, Word checks their credentials. If they're not on the change access list or the read access list you've provided, Word refuses to open the document.

Signing a Final Document with a Digital Signature

When you need to prove that a document is a final and approved version, apply a digital signature to the document. A *digital signature* is encrypted data saved in the document that verify that the document hasn't been changed since the signature was applied. To create a digital signature, you use a digital certificate, which is a file containing encrypted data that identifies you or your company or organization.

■ **Note** To get a digital certificate, you apply to a certificate authority (CA). Commercial CAs, such as VeriSign (www.verisign.com) or Comodo (www.comodo.com), issue certificates to both companies and individuals. Your company or organization may also run its own CA to provide digital certificates to its employees. You can create a digital certificate of your own for testing by using a tool built into Office, as discussed in a moment, but the self-signed certificates it produces will not inspire trust in other people.

Signing a document with a digital signature authenticates the final document but doesn't protect it; to protect the document, you need to use a password or restrictions, as discussed earlier in this chapter. If somebody changes the document, Word removes the digital signature. If you're the one who changes the document, you can sign it again once you've finalized it.

To sign a document with a digital signature, follow these steps:

1. Click the File tab to open Backstage.

2. On the Info screen that Word automatically displays, click the Protect Document button, and then click Add a Digital Signature on the drop-down menu to display the Sign dialog box (see Figure 10-10).

■ **Note** The first time you give the Add a Digital Signature command, Word displays a Microsoft Office Word dialog box explaining briefly what digital signatures are and what they're useful for. Click the Signature Services from the Office Marketplace button if you want to browse options for getting a digital certificate. Otherwise, select the Don't show this message again check box, and then click the OK button to dismiss the dialog box. Word then displays the Get a Digital ID dialog box, in which you can either select the Get a digital ID from a Microsoft partner option button to get a commercial certificate or select Create your own digital ID option button to open Microsoft's tool for creating a test certificate of your own. Either way, click the OK button.

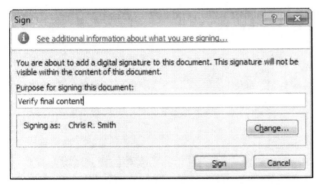

Figure 10-10. Use the Sign dialog box to apply a digital signature to a document to prove it hasn't been changed since you last worked on it.

3. Check that the certificate that appears in the Signing as box is the right one. If not, click the Change button to open the Windows Security: Select a Certificate dialog box, click the right certificate, and then click the OK button. The certificate you chose appears in the Signing as box.

4. If you need to double-check what you're signing, click the See additional information about what you are signing link to display the Additional Information dialog box. Figure 10-11 shows an example of this dialog box. Click the OK button when you have read the warnings and information.

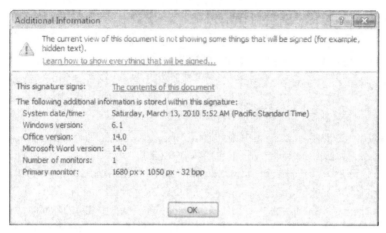

Figure 10-11. Use the Additional Information dialog box to show any warnings about document contents that don't appear in the current view (such as hidden text or markup) and the information the signature will contain.

5. Click the Sign button. Word signs the document, saves it, and displays the Signature Confirmation dialog box (see Figure 10-12).

Figure 10-12. Word displays the Signature Confirmation dialog box to confirm that you have applied a digital signature to the document.

6. Click the OK button to close the Signature Confirmation dialog box. You can select the Don't show this message again check box first if you want to suppress this dialog box in future, but usually it's useful to see.

The document remains signed only until you edit it (or someone else does). If you go to edit the document, Word warns you that editing will remove the signature (see Figure 10-13).

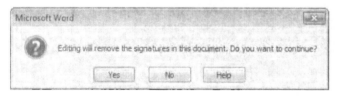

Figure 10-13. Word warns you that editing a signed document will remove the signatures.

Click the Yes button if you're prepared to accept this. Word removes the signature, saves the document, and then displays the Signature Removed dialog box to make sure you're aware of this. Click the OK button, and you can then edit the document freely.

Making a Document You Can Open with Earlier Versions of Word

If you work with people who use versions of Word earlier than Word 2007 for Windows or Word 2008 for Mac, or with people who use other word processing programs, you may need to make versions of your documents that will open in earlier versions of Word. This is because earlier versions of Word used a different file format than Word 2007, Word 2008, Word 2010, and the forthcoming Word for Mac 2011; Word 2003 for Windows and Word 2004 for Mac can open the new file format only if you install file converters (see the nearby Note), and many other word processing programs can open only files in the older format, which is generally referred to as Word 97–2003 on Windows or Word 98–2004 on the Mac.

Note If you need to get the file converters for Windows, steer your browser to the Microsoft Download Center (www.microsoft.com/downloads/) and download the Microsoft Office Compatibility Pack for Word, Excel, and PowerPoint File Formats file. For the Mac, go to the Mactopia Downloads page (www.microsoft.com/mac/downloads) and download the Open XML File Format Converter.

To save a document in a format compatible with earlier versions of Word, follow these steps:

1. If the document contains unsaved changes, save them.

2. Click the File tab to open Backstage.

3. Click the Save & Send item in the left column to display the Save & Send pane.

4. In the File Types area, click the Change File Type button to display the Change File Type pane (see Figure 10-14).

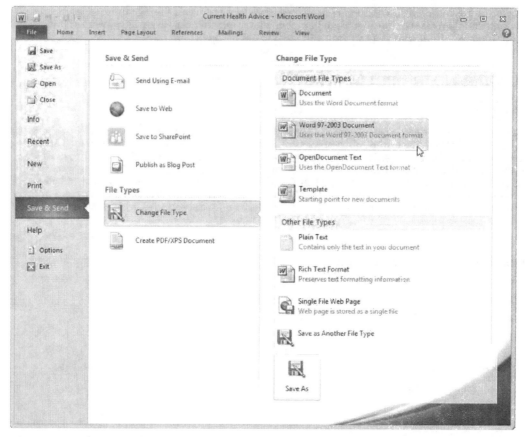

Figure 10-14 The Change File Type pane in Backstage gives you an easy way to choose the file type you want to create.

5. In the Change File Type list, click the type of document you want to create. These are the file types you're most likely to need:

    • *Word 97–2003 Document*: Use this format to create a document readable by older versions of Word and by compatible word processing programs.

■ **Note** The Document format in the Change File Type list is the Word 2010 format. This is the format in which Word 2010 saves documents unless you specify another format—so in most cases you will be changing the document from this format to another format.

    • *Template*: Use this format to create a Word template on which you can base new documents.

- *Rich Text Format*: Use this format to create a document with formatting that most word processing programs and text editors can open successfully.

6. Click the Save As button at the bottom of the Change File Type pane.

7. Word displays the Save As dialog box with the Save as type drop-down list set to the file type you chose.

8. Choose any other settings needed for the new document. For example, you may want to give it a different file name or save it in a different folder.

9. Click the Save button to save the document.

10. If you have finished working with the document, close it.

▒ **Note** You can also save a document to a different format by choosing File ➤ Save As and picking the format in the Save as type drop-down list in the Save As dialog box. The Change File Type pane gives you an easy way to pick the format you want.

Creating Documents for Digital Distribution

When you want to distribute a Word document digitally (as opposed to printing it and distributing the hard copy), you can choose between sending the document in Word format and sending an electronic file that shows the Word document's contents and layout.

Normally, you'll send the Word document only when the recipient needs to edit the document in Word or a compatible word processor. For other purposes, sending a file of the laid-out document is usually better. Word gives you two choices for such a file, PDF and XPS.

▒ **Note** At the time of this writing, PDF is more widely used than XPS. Use PDF if you're not sure which operating system the recipient is using or (if they're using Windows) whether they're using an older version than Windows 7 or Windows Vista. Use XPS if you're sure that the recipient is using Windows 7 or Windows Vista or otherwise has a program that can display XPS files correctly.

To create a PDF file or XPS file from a document, follow these steps:

1. Open the document if it's not already open.

2. Click the File tab to open Backstage.

3. Click the Save & Send item in the left column to display the Save & Send pane.

4. In the File Types area, click the Create PDF/XPS Document item to display the Create a PDF/XPS Document pane.

5. Click the Create a PDF/XPS button to display the Publish as PDF or XPS dialog box (see Figure 10-15).

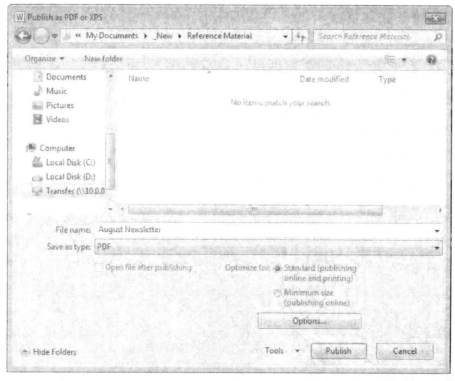

Figure 10-15. In the Publish as PDF or XPS dialog box, choose which type of file to create and decide how to optimize it.

6. In the Save as type drop-down list, choose PDF or XPS Document, depending on the type of document you want to create.

7. Select the Open file after publishing check box if you want Word to open the PDF or XPS file automatically so that you can make sure it looks right. If you're creating a PDF file, and your PC doesn't have a PDF viewer program, this check box is unavailable.

8. In the Optimize for area, select the option button for the quality you want to create:

   • *Standard*: Select this option button if you're planning to publish the file online at full quality or send it to a service for printing.

   • *Minimum size*: Select this option button for a file you will distribute online and for which you're prepared to lower the quality in order to reduce the file size.

9. To choose further options, such as publishing only part of the document, click the Options button. Word displays the Options dialog box for PDF files (see Figure 10-16) or the Options dialog box for XPS files (which has the same

controls except for the bottom section). You can then choose the settings you need, as discussed in the following list. Click the OK button when you're done.

- *Page range*: Select the All option button to print all the pages, or the Current page option button to print just the current page. To print a range of pages, select the Page(s) option button, enter the starting page number in the From box, and enter the ending page number in the To box. To print what you've selected in the document before giving the Publish command, click the Selection option button.

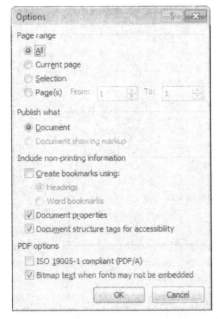

Figure 10-16. *In the Options dialog box for creating PDF files (shown here) or XPS files, choose which pages to publish, whether to include markup, and which non-printing information to include.*

- *Publish what*: Select the Document option button if you don't want to include any markup (such as revision marks and comments) the document contains. Select the Document showing markup option button if you do want to include markup.

- *Include non-printing information*: To make Word create bookmarks in the PDF or XPS file, select the Create bookmarks using check box, and then click the Headings option button or the Word bookmarks option button, as appropriate; headings are usually best. Select the Document properties check box if you want to include extra information that Word stores, such as the author's name. Select the Document structure tags for accessibility if you want to include XML tags that the document includes.

- *PDF options*: For PDF files, you can select the ISO 19005-1 compliant (PDF/A) check box if your PDFs need to meet the ISO 19005-1 standard, which covers long-term preservation of documents. (You may need to do this if you're creating PDFs for a corporation, organization, or government body.) Select the Bitmap text when fonts may not be embedded check box if you want Word to substitute pictures of text for which it's not legal to include the fonts in the PDF. This is usually a good idea for ensuring the PDF is legible, but see the next Note. If you want to encrypt the PDF, select the Encrypt the document with a password check box, and then enter the password in the Encrypt PDF Document dialog box that opens when you click the OK button.

■ **Note** If you select the ISO 19005-1 compliant (PDF/A) check box, Word makes the Bitmap text when fonts may not be embedded check box unavailable.

- *XPS Document options:* For XPS documents, the XPS Document options area contains one option, the Preserve restricted permissions in XPS check box. If you're using Information Rights Management (IRM) to protect your Word documents from unauthorized changes (as discussed earlier in this chapter), you can select this check box to carry the restrictions through to the PDF. If you're not using IRM, this check box is unavailable.

10. Click the Publish button to close the Publish as PDF or XPS dialog box. Word creates the PDF file or XPS document file you specified. If you chose to open the file, Word launches your PC's default PDF viewer (for example, Adobe Acrobat Reader) or XPS viewer (for example, Windows' built-in XPS Viewer) and opens the document in it.

Summary

In this chapter, you've learned how to use Word's extra features for printing documents or parts of them, such as document properties or details of the styles they contain. You've also grasped how to create a final version of a Word document by removing sensitive information, marking the document as final, and signing it with a digital signature if necessary.

You've also learned how to save a Word 2010 document so that it's usable with earlier versions of Word and how to create documents in the PDF and XPS formats that you can take to specialist printing services or distribute across the Internet.

CHAPTER 11

Creating Workbooks and Entering Data

In this chapter, you'll get started quickly with Excel by creating and saving a new workbook. You'll then look at how to navigate the Excel interface and work with worksheets and workbooks. You'll learn how to enter data in worksheets, how to select and manipulate cells, and how to use Excel's various view features to see the worksheet data you need so that you can work easily with it.

Creating and Saving a New Workbook

When you launch Excel, the program creates a new blank workbook for you . You can either start using this workbook and save it, or create a new workbook of a different type; for example, one based on a template. Either way, you'll need to save the workbook to keep the changes you make to it.

Creating a New Workbook

To create a new workbook, you use the New pane in Backstage. Click the File tab to open Backstage, and then click the New item in the left column to display the New pane (see Figure 11-1).

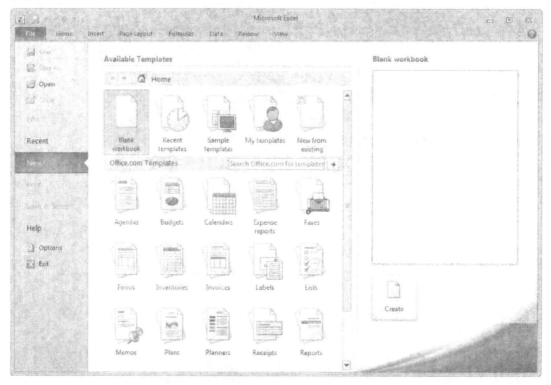

Figure 11-1. From the New pane in Backstage in PowerPoint, you can create a blank workbook, a workbook based on a template, or a workbook based on an existing workbook.

From here, you have five ways to create a new workbook:

- *Blank workbook or Office.com template*: To create a blank workbook, click the Blank workbook item in the top area, and then click the Create button. To create a workbook based on a template from Office.com:

  1. Double-click the category to open it. For example, double-click the Invoices category.

  2. If Excel displays a list of folder, double-click the appropriate folder to open it.

  3. Click the template you want to use.

  4. Click the Download button. Excel downloads the template and then creates a new workbook based on it.

- *Recent templates*: Click the Recent templates item to display a list of the templates you've used recently. Click the template, and then click the Create button.

- *Sample templates*: Click the Sample templates item to display the selection of sample templates, which includes templates such as Blood Pressure Tracker, Personal Monthly Budget, and Sales Report. Click the template you want, and then click the Create button.

- *My templates*: Click the My templates item to open the New dialog box, which shows any templates you have added to your Personal Templates folder. Until you add templates, this folder is empty.

- *New from existing*: Click the New from existing item when you want to create a new workbook based on an existing workbook. In the New from Existing Workbook dialog box that Excel displays, click the existing workbook, and then click the Open button. Excel clones the workbook, and you can then customize its contents.

Saving a Workbook

To save a workbook for the first time, give the Save command in any of the usual ways—by clicking the Save button on the Quick Access Toolbar, by choosing File ➤ Save, or by pressing Ctrl+S. In the Save As dialog box that Excel opens, select the folder in which to save the workbook, type the workbook name, and then click the Save button.

The one complication is the file type. By default, Excel uses the format called Excel Workbook, which Excel 2010 and Excel 2007 for Windows and Excel 2008 and Excel 2011 for Mac can open. Earlier versions of Excel used a different format, called Excel 97–2003 Workbook format on Windows and Excel 98–2004 format on the Mac. Excel 2003 for Windows and Excel 2004 for Mac users can install converters to enable Excel to handle the new file formats, but many people don't have these converters, even though they're available for free from the Microsoft web site.

So if you want to be able to share the workbook with colleagues who use Excel versions released before 2007, open the Save as type drop-down list in the Save As dialog box and click the Excel 97–2003 Format item before you click the Save button to save the workbook. Your colleagues will then be able to open the workbook in Excel 2003 or Excel 2004 without installing the converters.

Navigating the Excel Interface, Worksheets, and Workbooks

When you've created a new workbook or opened an existing one, you see the worksheets in the workbook. Figure 11-2 shows a new workbook with some data entered.

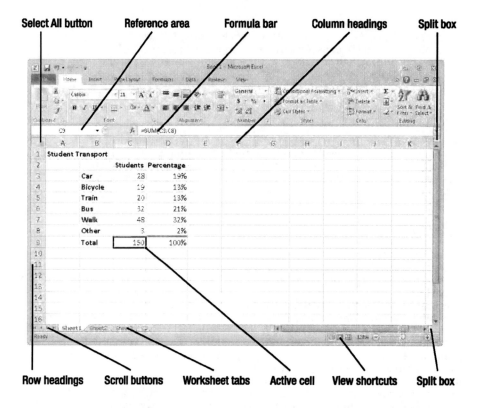

Figure 11-2. The main elements of the Excel program window and a workbook

Apart from regular Windows elements such as the Ribbon, the Quick Access Toolbar, the scroll bars, and the status bar, these are the main elements of the Excel program window and workbooks:

- *Formula bar*: This is the bar below the Ribbon. This area shows the data or formula in the active cell and gives you an easy place to enter and edit data.

- *Reference area*: This area appears at the left end of the formula bar. It shows the active cell's address (for example, B3) or name.

- *Row headings*: These are the numbers at the left side of the screen that identify each row. The first row is 1, the second row 2, and so on.

- *Column headings*: These are the letters at the top of the worksheet grid that identify the columns. The first column is A, the second column B, and so on.

- *Cells*: These are the boxes formed by the intersections of the rows and columns. Each cell is identified by its column letter and row number. For example, the first cell in column A is cell A1, and the second cell in column B is cell B2.

- *Active cell*: This is the cell you're working in. Excel displays a heavy black rectangle around the active cell.

- *Select All button*: Click this button at the intersection of the row headings and column headings to select all the cells in the worksheet.

- *Worksheet tabs*: To display a worksheet, you click its tab in this area.

- *Scroll controls*: Click these buttons to scroll the worksheet tabs that are displayed. Click the leftmost button to scroll all the way back to the first tab, or click the rightmost button to scroll to the last tab. Click the two middle buttons to scroll back or forward by one tab.

- *View Shortcuts*: Click these buttons to switch among Excel's three views: Normal view, Page Layout view, and Page Break Preview. You'll learn how to use these views later in this chapter.

- *Split boxes*: You use these boxes when you need to split the worksheet window into two or four areas. You'll learn how to do this in the section "Splitting the Window to View Separate Parts of a Worksheet," later in this chapter.

Understanding Workbooks, Worksheets, Columns, and Rows

Each workbook consists of one or more worksheets or other sheets, such as chart sheets or macro sheets. To display the worksheet you want to use, you click its tab in the worksheet tab bar (see Figure 11-3); if the worksheet's tab isn't visible in the worksheet tab bar, you click the scroll buttons to display it (unless you've hidden the worksheet).

■ **Tip** If you want to make the worksheet tab bar wider so that you can see more tabs at once, drag the divider bar to the right. Excel makes the horizontal scroll bar smaller to compensate.

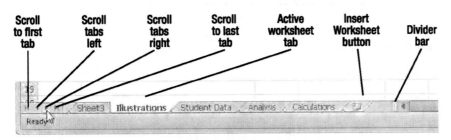

Figure 11-3. Use the worksheet tab bar to display the worksheet you want or to insert a new worksheet. You can drag the divider bar to change the length of the tab bar.

Each worksheet contains 16,384 columns and 1,048,576 rows, giving a grand total of 17,179,869,184 cells. Normally, you'll use only a small number of these cells—perhaps a few hundred or a few thousand—but there's plenty of space should you need it for large data sets.

■ **Tip** You can quickly move to the next worksheet by pressing Ctrl+Page Down or to the previous worksheet by pressing Ctrl+Page Up.

Each column is identified by one, two, or three letters:

- The first 26 columns use the letters A to Z.

- The next 26 columns use AA to AZ, the following 26 BA to BZ, and so on.

- When the two-letter combinations are exhausted, Excel uses three letters: AAA, AAB, and so on.

Each row is identified by a number, from 1 up to 1048576.

Each cell is identified by its column lettering and its row number. For example, the cell at the intersection of column A and row 1 is cell A1, and the cell at the intersection of column ZA and row 2256 is ZA2256.

Moving the Active Cell

In Excel, you usually work in a single cell at a time. That cell is called the *active cell* and receives the input from the keyboard.

You can move the active cell easily using either the mouse or the keyboard:

- *Mouse*: Click the cell you want to make active.

- *Keyboard*: Press the arrow keys to move the active cell up or down by one row or left or right by one column at a time. You can also press the keyboard shortcuts shown in Table 11-1 to move the active cell further.

Table 11-1. Keyboard Shortcuts for Moving the Active Cell

To Move the Active Cell Like This	Press This Keyboard Shortcut
First cell in the row	Home
First cell in the active worksheet	Ctrl+Home
Last cell used in the worksheet	Ctrl+End
Down one screen	Page Down
Up one screen	Page Up
Right one screen	Alt+Page Down
Left one screen	Alt+Page Up
To the last row in the worksheet	Ctrl+Down arrow
To the last column in the worksheet	Ctrl+Right arrow
To the first row in the worksheet	Ctrl+Up arrow
To the first column in the worksheet	Ctrl+Left arrow or Home

To access a cell, click it with the mouse or use the arrow keys to move the selection rectangle to it. Excel makes that cell the active cell, the cell that receives input from the keyboard.

Selecting and Manipulating Cells

To work with a single cell, you simply click it or use the keyboard to move the active cell to it. When you need to affect multiple cells at once, you select the cells using the mouse or keyboard.

Excel call a selection of cells a *range*. A range can consist of either a rectangle of contiguous cells or various cells that aren't next to each other. The left illustration in Figure 11-4 shows a range of contiguous cells, while the right illustration shows a range of separate cells.

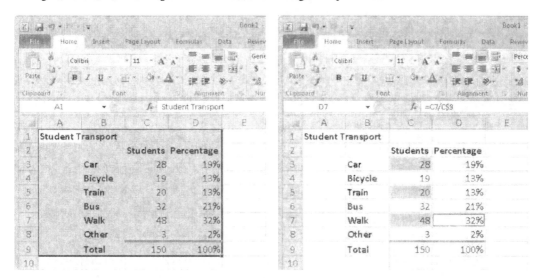

Figure 11-4. *You can select either a range of contiguous cells (left) or a range of individual cells (right).*

You can select a range of contiguous cells in any of these three ways:

- *Click and drag*: Click the first cell in the range, and then drag to select all the others. For example, if you click cell B2 and then drag to cell E7, you select a range that's four columns wide and six rows deep. Excel uses the notation B2:E7 to describe this range—the starting cell address, a colon, and then the ending cell address.

- *Click and then Shift+click*: Click the first cell in the range, then Shift+click the last cell. Excel selects all the cells in between. This technique tends to be easiest when the first cell and last cell are widely separated; for example, they don't appear in the same window.

- *Hold down Shift and use the arrow keys*: Use the arrow keys to move the active cell to where you want to start the range, then hold down Shift and use the arrow keys to extend the selection for the rest of the range. This method is good if you prefer using the keyboard to the mouse.

You can select a range of noncontiguous cells by clicking the first cell, then holding down Ctrl while you click other individual cells or drag through ranges of contiguous cells. Excel uses commas to separate the individual cells in this type of range. For example, the range D3,E5,F7,G1:G13 consists of three individual cells (D3, E5, and F7) and one range of contiguous cells (G1 through G13).

▧ **Note** You can quickly select a row by clicking its row heading or pressing Shift+spacebar when the active cell is in that row. Likewise, you can select a column by clicking its column heading or pressing Ctrl+spacebar. To select all the cells in the active worksheet, click the Select All button (where the row headings and column headings meet) or press Shift+spacebar followed by Ctrl+spacebar.

To deselect a range you've selected, click anywhere outside the range.

Entering Data in Your Worksheets

You can enter data in your worksheets by typing it, by pasting it, or by using drag and drop to move or copy it. Excel also includes a feature called AutoFill that automatically fills in series data for you based on the input you've provided.

Typing Data in a Cell

The most straightforward way to enter data is to type it into a cell.

Once you make a cell the active cell by clicking it or moving the selection rectangle to it, you can start typing in it. When you start typing, Excel displays an insertion point in the cell.

When you've finished typing the contents of the cell, move to another cell in any of these ways:

- *Press Enter*: Excel moves the active cell to the next cell below the current cell.

- *Click another cell*: Excel moves the active cell to the cell you click.

- *Press an arrow key*: Excel moves the active cell to the next cell in the direction of the arrow. For example, press the right arrow key to move the active cell to the next cell to the right.

▧ **Tip** To change the direction Excel moves the active cell when you press Enter, choose File ➤ Options. In the Excel Options dialog box, click the Advanced item in the left column to display the Advanced options. In the Editing options area at the top, open the Direction drop-down list, and then choose Down, Right, Up, or Left, as needed. Click the OK button to close the Excel Options dialog box.

Editing a Cell

When you need to edit the existing contents of a cell, open it for editing in one of these ways:

- Double-click the cell. Excel displays an insertion point in the cell.

- Move the active cell to the cell, and then press F2. Excel displays an insertion point in the cell. Figure 11-5 shows an example of editing in a cell.

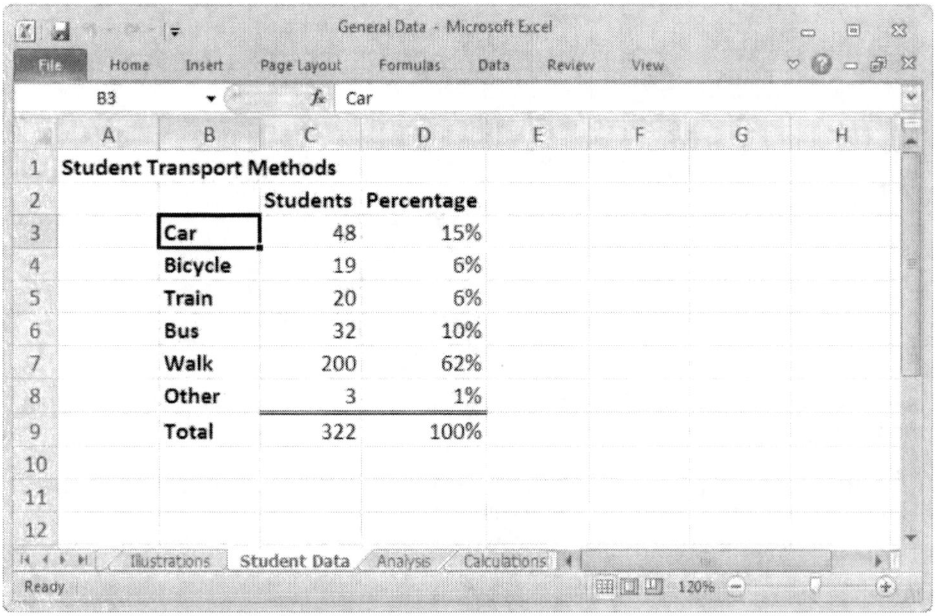

Figure 11-5. Double-click in a cell to edit its contents in place. In this example, cell B3 is open for editing.

- Click the cell (or move the active cell to it), and then click the cell's contents in the formula bar. Excel displays an insertion point in the formula bar (see Figure 11-6).

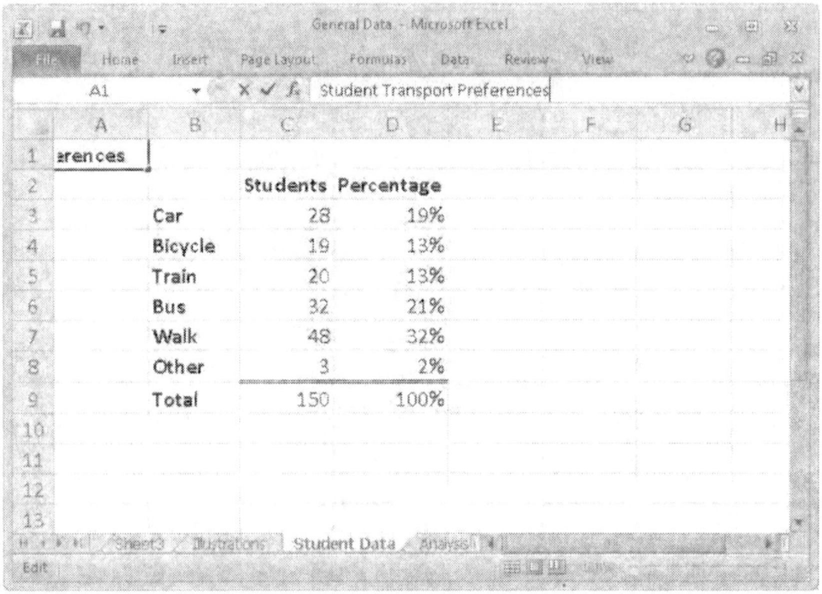

Figure 11-6. You can also edit a cell by clicking in the formula bar. This method is often easier for editing entries longer than their cells.

When you're editing a cell in the cell, pressing an arrow key moves the insertion point within the cell rather than finishing the entry and moving to another cell:

- *Left arrow key*: Press this key to move left by one character.

- *Right arrow key*: Press this key to move right by one character.

- *Down arrow key*: Press this key to move to the end of the cell's contents.

- *Up arrow key*: Press this key to move the insertion point back to where it was before you moved to the end of the cell's contents.

To finish editing a cell, press Enter, click the check mark on the formula bar, or click another cell. To cancel editing a cell and restore its previous contents, press Esc or click the cross on the formula bar.

■ **Note** Instead of editing a cell's existing contents, you can simply replace them by making the cell active and then typing new contents. Replacing tends to be faster than editing when a cell contains a short entry that you can easily retype.

Entering Data Quickly Using AutoFill

When you need to fill in a series of data, see if Excel's AutoFill feature can do the trick. To use AutoFill, you enter the base data for the series in one or more cells, then select them and drag the AutoFill handle in the direction you want to fill. AutoFill checks your base data, works out what the other cells should contain, and fills it in for you.

Using AutoFill's Built-in Capabilities

Open a test workbook, or press Shift+F11 to add a test worksheet to your current workbook, and then try using AutoFill.

Type **Monday** in cell A1, and then drag the AutoFill handle—the black square that appears at the lower-right corner of the selection—down to cell A7. As you drag past each cell, AutoFill displays a ScreenTip showing the data it will fill in that cell (see Figure 11-7). When you release the mouse button on cell A7, AutoFill fills in the days Tuesday through Sunday.

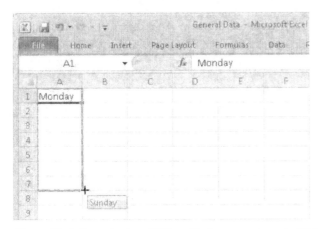

Figure 11-7. Drag the AutoFill handle down or across to fill in a series of data derived from one or more existing entries. In this case, AutoFill fills in the days of the week, and repeats the series if you drag further.

Now drag through the range and press Delete to clear it. Then follow these steps:

1. Click cell B2 and type a date such as **2/15/11** in it.

2. Press Enter, and you'll see that Excel changes it to a full date—for example, 2/15/2011.

3. Right-click the AutoFill handle and drag it to cell G2. As you drag, AutoFill displays dates incremented by one day for each column (2/16/2011, 2/16/2011, and so on), but when you release the mouse button, AutoFill displays a context menu (see Figure 11-8).

4. Click the Fill Months item, and Excel fills in a separate month for each column: 3/15/2011, 4/15/2011, and so on.

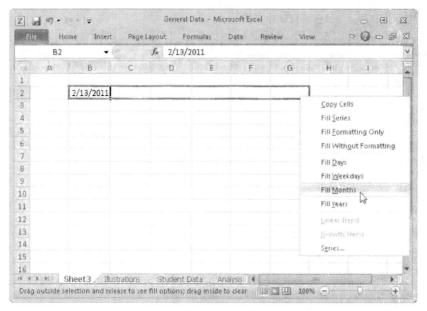

Figure 11-8. To reach more AutoFill options, right-drag the AutoFill handle, and then choose from the context menu.

Now clear your data again, then follow these steps:

1. Click cell A1 and type 5 in it.

2. Press Enter to move to cell A2, type 25 in it, and press Up arrow to move back to cell A1.

3. Press Shift+Down arrow to select cells A1 and A2.

4. Click the AutoFill handle and drag downward. AutoFill fills in a series with intervals of 20—cell A3 gets 45, cell A4 gets 65, and so on—using a linear trend.

Delete the data that AutoFill entered, leaving 5 in cell A1 and 25 in cell A2. Then follow these steps:

1. Select cells A1 and A2.

2. Right-click the AutoFill handle and drag downward. As you drag, you'll see ScreenTips for the same values as in the previous list.

3. Release the mouse button, and then click Growth Trend on the context menu. AutoFill enters a growth trend instead of the linear trend: Because the second value (25) is 5 times the first value (5), Excel multiplies each value by 5, giving the sequence, 5, 25, 125, 625, 3125, and so on.

Note The AutoFill context menu also contains items for filling the cells with formatting only (copying the formatting from the first cell), filling the cells without formatting (ignoring the first cell's formatting), and filling in days, weekdays, and years.

Creating Your Own Custom AutoFill Lists

If you need to enter the same series of data frequently, you can create your own AutoFill lists. Follow these steps:

1. Click the File tab to open Backstage.

2. In the left column, click Options to display the Excel Options dialog box.

3. In the left column, click Advanced to display the Advanced options.

4. Scroll all the way down to the bottom, and then click the Edit Custom Lists button in the Options area to display the Custom Lists dialog box (shown in Figure 11-9 with settings chosen).

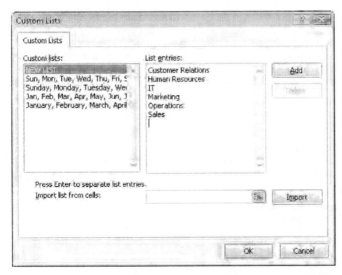

Figure 11-9. You can supplement Excel's built-in AutoFill lists by creating your own data series that you need to enter frequently in your worksheets.

5. In the Custom lists box, click the NEW LIST item.

6. Click in the List entries box, and then type your list, putting one item on each line.

■ **Tip** If you've already entered your list on cells in the worksheet, you don't need to retype it—instead, import it from the worksheet. Click the Collapse Dialog button to the left of the Import button to collapse the Custom Lists dialog box to a shallow Options dialog box, then drag through the list on the worksheet. Click the Collapse Dialog button to restore the Custom Lists dialog box, and then click the Import button.

---

7. Click the Add button to add the list to the Custom lists box.

8. Click the OK button to close the Custom Lists dialog box.

9. Click the OK button to close the Excel Options dialog box.

Pasting Data into a Worksheet

If the data you need to add to a worksheet is already in another document, you can copy it and paste it into the worksheet using the techniques explained in Chapter 4. You can also use Excel's Paste Special command to paste only some of the data; for example, the values of formulas rather than formulas themselves.

Using Paste and Paste Options

To paste data, position the active cell at the upper-left corner of where you want the data to land. You don't need to select the right number of cells for the data, because Excel does that for you automatically.

After positioning the active cell, you can either simply give the Paste command or choose one of the available Paste Options:

- *Paste*: Press Ctrl+V or choose Home ➤ Clipboard ➤ Paste (clicking the top part of the Paste button).

- *Paste Options*: Choose Home ➤ Clipboard ➤ Paste (clicking the drop-down button), and then click the appropriate icon in the Paste Options area. Or right-click the active cell, and then click one of the Paste Options icons.

Which Paste Options are available depends on the data you're pasting, but in most cases you have at least the choice of Keep Source Formatting (retaining the formatting the data had wherever you copied it from) and Match Destination Formatting (making it look like the worksheet you're pasting it on). You can hold the mouse pointer over a Paste Options icon to get a preview of how the data will look with that option.

In many cases, it's easiest to paste the data with a straightforward Paste command, see what result you get, and then use the Paste Options action button (see Figure 11-10) to change it if needed.

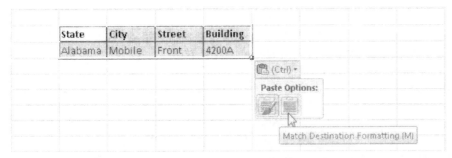

Figure 11-10. If pasted data arrives in the wrong format, open the Paste Options action button and choose a different Paste Option.

Controlling Pasted Data with the Paste Special Command

Sometimes you'll want to paste less than all of the data you've copied. For example, you may need to paste all the data and formatting except for cell borders, or you may want to retain only the values and number formats rather than other information.

For these needs, Excel provides the Paste Special command. You can access most of these options from either the Paste panel in the Clipboard group of the Home tab or from the Paste Special submenu of the context menu (see Figure 11-11), but in most cases it's clearest to use the Paste Special dialog box.

Figure 11-11. The Paste Special submenu of the context menu lets you paste values, formulas, formatting, or other options, but in many cases the Paste Special dialog box is easier to use.

■ **Note** The advantage of the Paste Special icons on the Paste panel and the Paste Special submenu is that you get a preview of the result of the paste operation. The disadvantage is that you have to learn which icon is which or hold the mouse pointer over an icon to display a ScreenTip identifying it.

To display the Paste Special dialog box (see Figure 11-12), choose Home ➤ Clipboard ➤ Paste ➤ Paste Special or right-click a cell and then click Paste Special on the context menu.

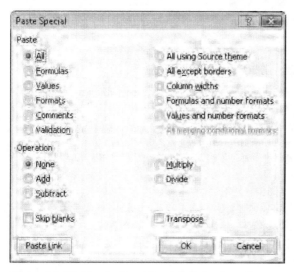

Figure 11-12. Use the Paste Special dialog box when you need to paste only some of the data, when you need to perform an operation on the data, or when you need to transpose its rows and columns.

You then choose the option button you want in the Paste area:

- *All*: Select this option button to paste all the data and all its formatting. Normally, you'll want to do this only if you're using the Skip blanks check box, the Transpose check box, or the Paste Link button.

- *Formulas*: Select this option button to paste in all the formulas and constants without formatting.

- *Values*: Select this option button to paste in formula values instead of pasting in the formulas themselves. Excel removes the formatting from the values.

- *Formats*: Select this option button to paste in the formatting without the data. This option is surprisingly useful once you know it's there.

- *Comments*: Select this option button to paste in only comments. This option is handy when you're integrating different colleagues' takes on the same worksheet.

- *Validation*: Select this option button to paste in data-validation criteria.

- *All using Source theme*: Select this option button to paste in all the data using the theme from the workbook the data came from.

- *All except borders*: Select this option button to paste in all the data and formatting but to strip out the cell borders.

- *Column widths*: Select this option button to paste in only the column widths—no data and no other formatting. This option is useful when you need to lay one worksheet out like another existing worksheet.

- *Formulas and number formats*: Select this option button to paste in formulas and number formatting but no other formatting.

- *Values and number formats*: Select this option button to paste in values (rather than formulas) and number formatting.

- *All merging conditional formats*: Select this option button to copy all data and formatting and to merge in any conditional formatting. See Chapter 12 for details on conditional formatting.

If you need to perform a mathematical operation on the data you're pasting, go to the Operation area of the Paste Special dialog box and select the Add option button, the Subtract option button, the Multiply option button, or the Divide option button, as needed. Otherwise, leave the None option button selected to paste the data without performing math on it.

In the bottom section of the Paste Special dialog box, you can select or clear the two check boxes as needed:

- *Skip blanks*: Select this check box to prevent Excel from pasting blank cells.

- *Transpose*: Select this check box to transpose columns to rows and rows to columns. This option is much quicker than retyping data that you (or someone else) have laid out the wrong way.

When you've chosen the options you want, click the OK button to paste the data.

■ **Note** If you need to link the data you're pasting back to its source, click the Paste Link button in the Paste Special dialog box instead of the OK button. This makes Excel create a link to the source data, so that when the source data changes, the linked data changes too. If the source data is in the same workbook, Excel updates the links automatically. If the source data is in another workbook, Excel updates the data when you open the workbook that contains the links.

Copying and Moving Data with Drag and Drop

When you need to copy or move data within Excel, you can use drag and drop. Follow these steps:

1. Select the data you want to move or copy.

2. Move the mouse pointer over an edge of the section so that the pointer turns into an arrow with a four-headed arrow on it (see Figure 11-13).

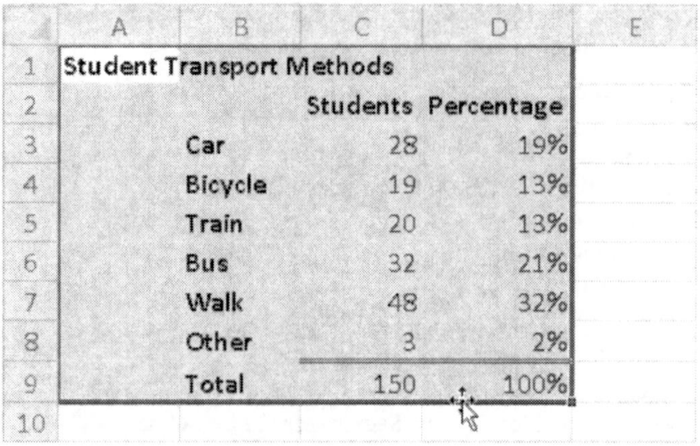

	A	B	C	D	E
1	Student Transport Methods				
2			Students	Percentage	
3		Car	28	19%	
4		Bicycle	19	13%	
5		Train	20	13%	
6		Bus	32	21%	
7		Walk	48	32%	
8		Other	3	2%	
9		Total	150	100%	
10					

Figure 11-13. To move data using drag and drop, select the data, then move the mouse pointer over one of its edges to display the drag-and-drop pointer.

3. Click and drag the data to where you want it to appear. If you want to copy the data rather than move it, Ctrl+drag rather than drag.

Normal drag and drop moves or copies all of the data and all of its formatting, much like pasting the material. To reach more options, such as copying only the values or the formats, or creating a link or a hyperlink to the source, right-click and drag instead of left-clicking and dragging. When you release the mouse button, Excel displays a context menu of choices (see Figure 11-14). Click the choice you want.

Figure 11-14. Use the right-drag context menu to transfer only some of the data or to create a link.

Inserting, Deleting, and Rearranging Worksheets

When you create a workbook, Excel puts three worksheets in it by default. For many workbooks, this may be all you need, but for other workbooks, you'll need to insert further worksheets to give yourself space to work in.

For most workbooks, you'll want to give the worksheets custom names instead of the default names. You may also need to rearrange the worksheets into a different order.

■ **Tip** To change the number of worksheets that Excel includes in a blank workbook, click the File tab to open Backstage, and then click Options. In the General category of the Excel Options dialog box, change the number in the Include this many sheets box to the number of worksheets you want, and then click the OK button.

Inserting and Deleting Worksheets

The easiest way to insert a new worksheet in a workbook is to click the Insert Worksheet button that appears on the tab bar after the last worksheet tab. Excel inserts a new worksheet after the last worksheet. You can then move the worksheet to a different position in the workbook if necessary, using the technique you'll learn in a moment.

You can also insert a new worksheet before a particular worksheet. To do so, follow these steps:

1. Right-click the tab of the worksheet before which you want to insert the new worksheet.

2. On the context menu, click Insert to display the Insert dialog box.

3. On the General tab, click the Worksheet item. (This item may already be selected.)

4. Click the OK button to close the dialog box and insert the worksheet.

■ **Tip** You can also press Shift+F11 to insert a new worksheet after the worksheet that's currently selected.

After inserting a worksheet, double-click its tab to select the default name, type the name you want, and then press Enter. You can use up to 31 characters in the name. If you want to make the tab stand out, right-click the tab again, click or highlight Tab Color, and then click the color for the tab.

To delete a worksheet, right-click its tab, and then click Delete on the context menu. If the worksheet contains any data, Excel displays a dialog box (see Figure 11-15) to double-check that you're prepared to delete it; click the Delete button to go ahead. If the worksheet is blank, Excel deletes it without prompting you.

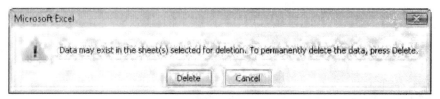

Figure 11-15. When you go to delete a worksheet that contains data, Excel double-checks that you're prepared to lose the data on the worksheet.

Rearranging the Worksheets in a Workbook

You can rearrange the worksheets in a workbook into the order you need.

The quick way to move a worksheet is to click its tab, drag it left or right until Excel displays a downward arrow between the worksheets where you want to place it, and then drop it.

■ **Tip** To move two or more worksheets, select them first. Click the first worksheet's tab, then Ctrl+click each other worksheet's tab in turn. To select a range of worksheets that appear next to each other, click the first worksheet's tab, and then Shift+click the tab for the worksheet at the other end of the range.

This method works well for moving a worksheet a short distance along the tab bar, but for moving larger distances, you may prefer to use the Move or Copy dialog box. Follow these steps:

1. Right-click the worksheet's tab to display the context menu. To move multiple worksheets, select them, and then right-click one of the selected tabs.

2. On the context menu, click Move or Copy to display the Move or Copy dialog box (see Figure 11-16).

Figure 11-16. Use the Move or Copy dialog box to move one or more worksheets further than you can comfortably drag within a workbook or to move or copy worksheets to another open workbook.

3. In the To book drop-down list, make sure the current workbook is selected unless you want to move the worksheet to another workbook—in which case, select that workbook.

4. In the Before sheet list box, click the worksheet before which you want to position the worksheet you're moving.

5. Select the Create a copy check box if you want to copy the worksheet to the destination rather than move it. Copying tends to be most useful when the destination is another workbook, but you can copy within a workbook as well.

6. Click the OK button to close the dialog box. Excel moves or copies the worksheet to the destination you chose.

Making Excel Display Worksheets the Way You Need

To work quickly and easily in your workbooks, you need to know how to make the most of Excel's three views and how to use Full Screen view. You also need to know how to split the window into two or four parts, how to hide windows when you don't need to see them, and how to use Excel's features for freezing parts of a window that you need to keep in sight.

Understanding Excel's Views

Excel gives you three different views for working in your workbooks:

*   *Normal view:* This is the view in which workbooks normally open, and the view in which you'll do most of your data entry, formatting, and reviewing. Normal view is the view in which you've seen Excel so far in this chapter.

*   *Print Layout view:* This view shows your worksheets as they will look when laid out on paper. You use it to adjust the page setup. You'll learn how to do this in Chapter 12.

*   *Page Break Preview:* This view shows where the page breaks will fall when you print the workbook. You use this view to make sure the page breaks are in suitable positions and to move them if they're not. You'll learn how to do this too in the next chapter.

To switch view, click the View Shortcut buttons on the status bar (see Figure 11-17) or click the View tab of the Ribbon, go to the Workbook Views group, and then click the Normal button, the Page Layout button, or the Page Break Preview button.

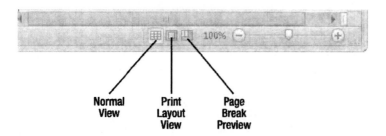

Normal View   **Print Layout View**   **Page Break Preview**

Figure 11-17. Use the View Shortcuts buttons on the status bar to change views quickly.

■ **Tip** When you want to see as much of a worksheet as possible, choose View ➤ Workbook Views ➤ Full Screen. Excel hides the Ribbon and displays the worksheet full screen. You can use Full Screen view in any of the three views. Press Esc when you want to return from Full Screen view to a window.

Splitting the Window to View Separate Parts of a Worksheet

Often, it's useful to be able to see two parts of a worksheet at the same time as you work in it; for example, to make sure that your notes correctly describe your data, or when you're copying information from one part to another.

When you need to see two parts of the worksheet in the same window, you can split the window.

Double-click the horizontal split box to split the window horizontally above the active cell, or double-click the vertical split box to split the window vertically to the left of the active cell. If the active cell isn't in the right place for splitting, click the horizontal split box or the vertical split box, and then drag it till the split bar appears where you want the split.

If you want to split the window into four panes, split it in the other dimension as well. For example, if you've already split the window horizontally, split it vertically as well. Figure 11-18 shows the Excel window split into four panes.

■ **Note** You can also split the window into four panes by choosing View ➤ Window ➤ Split.

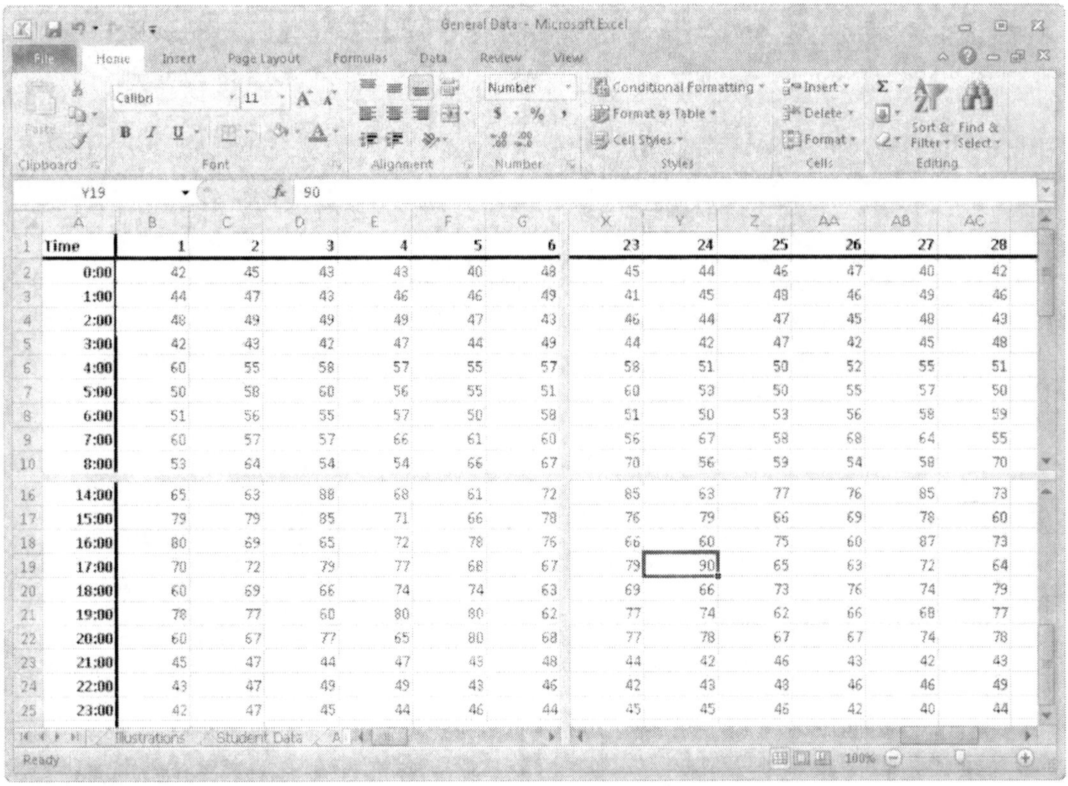
General Data - Microsoft Excel
File Home Insert Page Layout Formulas Data Review View
Calibri 11
Number
Conditional Formatting
Format as Table
Cell Styles
Insert
Delete
Format
Sort & Filter
Find & Select
Clipboard Font Alignment Number Styles Cells Editing
Y19 90
Time 1 2 3 4 5 6 23 24 25 26 27 28
0:00 42 45 43 43 40 48 45 44 46 47 40 42
1:00 44 47 43 46 46 49 41 45 48 46 49 46
2:00 48 49 49 49 47 43 46 44 47 45 48 43
3:00 42 43 42 47 44 49 44 42 47 42 45 48
4:00 60 55 58 57 55 57 58 51 50 52 55 51
5:00 50 58 60 56 55 51 60 53 50 55 57 50
6:00 51 56 55 57 50 58 51 50 53 56 58 59
7:00 60 57 57 66 61 60 56 67 58 68 64 55
8:00 53 64 54 54 66 67 70 56 59 54 58 70
14:00 65 63 88 68 61 72 85 63 77 76 85 73
15:00 79 79 85 71 66 78 76 79 66 69 78 60
16:00 80 69 65 72 78 76 66 60 75 60 87 73
17:00 70 72 79 77 68 67 79 90 65 63 72 64
18:00 60 69 66 74 74 63 69 66 73 76 74 79
19:00 78 77 60 80 80 62 77 74 62 66 68 77
20:00 60 67 77 65 80 68 77 78 67 67 74 78
21:00 45 47 44 47 43 48 44 42 46 43 42 43
22:00 43 47 49 49 43 46 42 43 48 46 46 49
23:00 42 47 45 44 46 44 45 45 46 42 40 44
Illustrations Student Data
Ready
100%

Figure 11-18. *Split the Excel window into two or four panes when you need to work in separate areas of the worksheet at the same time.*

Once you split the window, you get a separate scroll bar in each part, so you can scroll the panes separately to display whichever areas of the worksheet you need.

■ **Note** When you split the window, you may find it helpful to freeze certain rows and columns, as discussed later in this chapter, to keep them visible even when you scroll to other areas of the worksheet.

To reposition the split, click the split bar and drag it to where you want it. If you've split the window into four panes, you can resize all four panes at once by clicking where the split bars cross and then dragging.

To remove the split, either double-click the split bar or click the split bar and drag it all the way to the left of the screen or all the way to the top.

Opening Extra Windows to Show Other Parts of a Workbook

Instead of splitting a window, you can open one or more extra windows to show other parts of the workbook.

Choose View ➤ Window ➤ New Window to open a new window on the active workbook. Excel distinguishes the windows by adding :1 to the name of the first and :2 to the name of the second—for example, General Data:1 and General Data:2.

■ **Note** Opening extra windows has two advantages over splitting a window. First, you can display other worksheets (or workbooks) in the windows if you want rather than just other parts of the same worksheet. Second, you can zoom each window by a different amount as needed, or use a different view in each window.

Changing the Window and Arranging Open Windows

The easiest way to change the window you're working in is to click the window you want to use— either click the window itself (if you can see it) or click its button on the Taskbar. You can also choose Window ➤ Switch Windows to display the list of windows, and then click the window.

When you've opened several windows, you can arrange them by using standard Windows techniques, such as by dragging them to the size and position you want or right-clicking the Taskbar and choosing Show Windows Side by Side from the context menu to arrange open windows from Excel and other programs. You can also use Excel's Arrange Windows dialog box to arrange Excel's windows like this:

1. Choose View ➤ Window ➤ Arrange All to display the Arrange Windows dialog box (see Figure 11-19).

Figure 11-19. *Use the Arrange Windows dialog box to tile or otherwise arrange all the Excel windows or only those from the active workbook.*

2. Click the option button for the arrangement you want:

    *   *Tiled*: Select this option button to make Excel resize all the nonminimized windows to roughly even sizes so that they fit in the Excel window. If you have several windows open, tiling tends to make them too small for working

in, but it's good for seeing which windows are open and closing those you don't need.

- *Horizontal*: Select this option button to arrange all the windows horizontally in the Excel window. This arrangement works well for two windows in which the data is laid out in rows rather than columns.

- *Vertical*: Select this option button to arrange all the windows vertically in the Excel window. This arrangement works well for two windows in which the data is laid out in columns rather than rows.

- *Cascade*: Select this option button to arrange the windows in a stack so that you can see each one's title bar. This arrangement is useful for picking the window you want out of many open windows.

3. To arrange only the windows of the active workbook, select the Windows of active workbook check box. This option is good for the Horizontal and Vertical arrangements.

4. Click the OK button to close the Arrange Windows dialog box. Excel arranges the windows as you chose.

▓ **Tip** When you don't need to see a particular window, you can hide it to get it out of the way. Click the window, and then choose View ➤ Window ➤ Hide Window. To display the window again, choose View ➤ Window ➤ Unhide window, click the window in the Unhide dialog box, and then click the OK button.

Zooming to Show the Data You Need to See

You can zoom in or out on your worksheets to make the data easier to read or to display more of a worksheet at once.

The easiest way to zoom in or out is by using the Zoom buttons and Zoom slider on the status bar. Click the – button or + button to change the zoom by 10 percent per click, or drag the Zoom slider to make larger changes or to set a custom zoom percentage.

When you need to zoom just the right amount to display a particular area of the worksheet as large as it will fit in the window, select the area, and then choose View ➤ Zoom ➤ Zoom to Selection.

▓ **Note** To set a custom zoom percentage, you can use the Zoom dialog box. Choose View ➤ Zoom ➤ Zoom to display the dialog box, type the percentage in the Custom box (which makes Excel select the Custom option button for you), and then click the OK button.

Comparing Two Windows Side by Side

When you need to compare the contents of two open windows, use the View Side by Side command. You can also set the windows to scroll in sync, which makes it easier to compare them. Follow these steps:

1. Click one of the windows you want to compare.

2. Choose View ➤ Window ➤ View Side by Side. If you have only two windows open, Excel arranges them side by side. If you have more windows open, Excel displays the Compare Side by Side dialog box (see Figure 11-20).

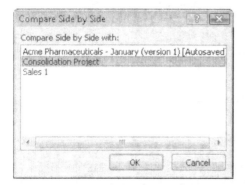

Figure 11-20. In the Compare Side by Side dialog box, select the window you want to compare with the active window.

3. Click the window you want to compare with the active window.

4. Click the OK button to close the Compare Side by Side dialog box. Excel positions the windows side by side, sizing them to share the space in the Excel window, and turns on synchronous scrolling. You'll see that the View Side by Side button and the Synchronous Scrolling button in the Window group both appear pressed in.

You can now compare the data in the two windows as needed. When you scroll one window, Excel automatically scrolls the other window too by the same amount, keeping them synchronized.

If you need to turn off synchronous scrolling, choose View ➤ Window ➤ Synchronous Scrolling (un-pressing the button).

When you have finished the comparison, choose View ➤ Window ➤ View Side by Side to un-press the View Side by Side button and restore the windows to their previous sizes and positions.

Freezing Rows and Columns So That They Stay on Screen

To keep your data headings on screen when you scroll down or to the right on a large worksheet, you can freeze the heading rows and columns in place. For example, if you have headings in column A and row 1, you can freeze column A and row 1 so that they remain on screen.

You can quickly freeze the first column, the top row, or your choice of rows and columns:

*   *Freeze the first column*: Choose View ➤ Window ➤ Freeze Panes ➤ Freeze First Column.

*   *Freeze the first row*: Choose View ➤ Window ➤ Freeze Panes ➤ Freeze Top Row.

- *Freeze your choice of rows and columns*: Click the cell below the row and to the right of the column you want to freeze. For example, to freeze the top two rows and column A, select cell B3. Then choose View ➤ Window ➤ Freeze Panes ➤ Freeze Panes.

Excel displays a black line along the gridlines of the frozen cells. Once you've applied the freeze, the frozen columns and rows don't move when you scroll down or to the right. Figure 11-21 shows a worksheet with rows 1 and 2 and column A frozen.

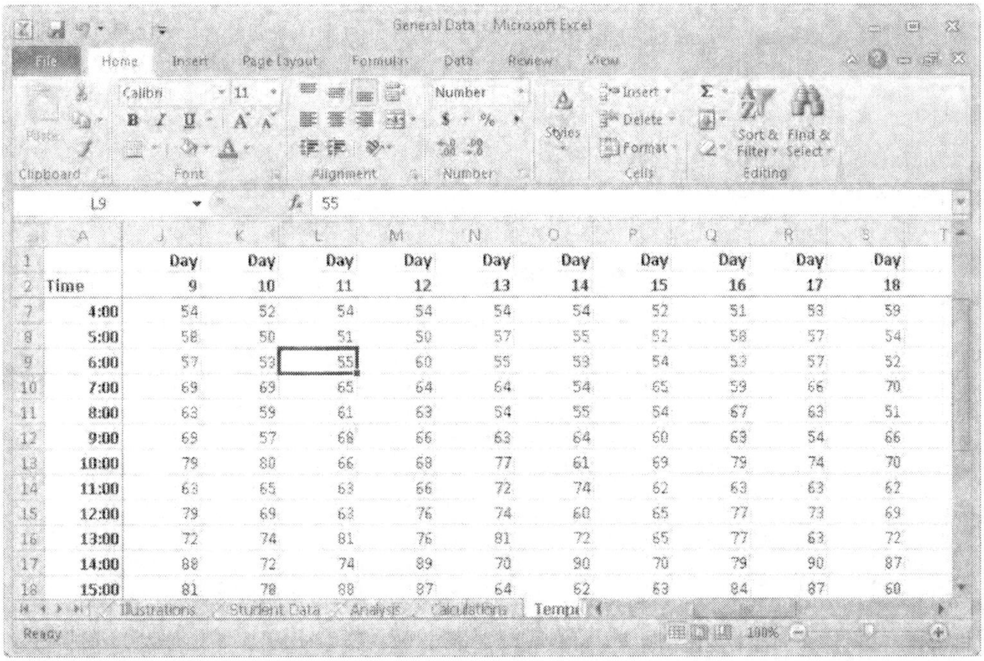

Figure 11-21. Freeze the heading rows and columns to keep them in place when you scroll down or across the worksheet.

When you no longer need the freezing, choose View ➤ Window ➤ Freeze Panes ➤ Unfreeze Panes to remove the freezing.

Summary

In this chapter, you've learned how to create and save a workbook and start entering data in it. You've come to grips with the Excel interface, and you know how to add, delete, and rearrange the worksheets in a workbook. You've also learned how to select cells and ranges, not to mention essential techniques for making Excel display worksheets the way you need them—everything from splitting a window into separate parts to opening and arranging multiple windows and freezing any heading rows and columns you want to keep on screen when you scroll.

CHAPTER 12

Formatting Your Worksheets

In this chapter, you'll learn how to format your worksheets so that they show the information you need and present it clearly.

You'll start by looking at how to work with rows and columns—inserting, deleting, and formatting them so that your worksheet is the right shape. I'll then show you how to format cells and ranges, how to apply conditional formatting to quickly flag values that need attention, and how to use data validation to check for invalid entries.

After that, you'll look at how to format worksheets quickly using table formatting or Excel's styles, how to add headers and footers to worksheets, and how to print worksheets and workbooks.

Lastly, you'll learn to use Excel's features for sharing workbooks with your colleagues. You can protect a workbook against unwelcome changes, and even share a workbook so that both you and your colleagues can edit it at the same time.

Working with Rows and Columns

In this section, you'll learn how to insert and delete rows, columns, and cells; change the width of columns and the height of rows; and hide rows or columns when you don't need to see them.

Inserting and Deleting Rows, Columns, and Cells

To accommodate the data in your worksheets, you'll often need to insert or delete entire columns or rows. Sometimes you may also need to delete a block of cells without deleting an entire column.

To insert a column, click a cell in the column before which you want to insert the new column (or click the column heading), and then choose Home ➤ Cells ➤ Insert ➤ Insert Sheet Columns. To insert more than one column, select cells in that number of columns beforehand, and then give the command.

To insert a row, click a cell in the row before which you want to insert the new row (or click the row heading), and then choose Home ➤ Cells ➤ Insert ➤ Insert Sheet Rows. To insert more than one row, select cells in that number of rows first, and then give the command.

▪ **Tip** You can also insert a column by right-clicking the heading of the existing column before which you want to insert the new column, and then clicking Insert on the context menu. Similarly, you can insert a row by right-clicking the heading of the existing row before which you want to insert the new row, and then clicking Insert on the context menu.

To insert just some cells, follow these steps:

1. Select the area before which you want to insert the cells.

2. Choose Home ➤ Cells ➤ Insert ➤ Insert Cells to display the Insert dialog box (see Figure 12-1).

Figure 12-1. When you insert a block of cells, click the Shift cells right option button or the Shift cells down option button in the Insert dialog box to tell Excel which way to move the existing cells.

3. Select the Shift cells right option button to move the existing cells to the right. Select the Shift cells down option button to move the existing cells down the worksheet. The Entire row option button inserts a whole row, and the Entire column option button inserts a whole column; the methods described earlier are usually easier.

4. Click the OK button to close the Insert dialog box. Excel inserts the cells.

To delete a column, select a cell in it, and then choose Home ➤ Cells ➤ Delete ➤ Delete Sheet Columns. To delete a row, select a cell in it, and then choose Home ➤ Cells ➤ Delete ➤ Delete Sheet Rows.

To delete just some cells, select them, and then choose Home ➤ Cells ➤ Delete ➤ Delete Cells. In the Delete dialog box (see Figure 12-2) that Excel displays, select the Shift cells left option button or the Shift cells up option button, as appropriate, and then click the OK button.

Figure 12-2. When you delete a block of cells, click the Shift cells left option button or the Shift cells up option button in the Delete dialog box to tell Excel how to fill the gap in the worksheet.

Setting Row Height

Excel normally sets the row height automatically to accommodate the tallest character or object in the row. For example, if you type an entry in the a cell, then select the cell and click the Increase Font Size button in the Font group of the Home tab a few times, Excel automatically increases the row height so that there's enough space for the tallest characters. You can also choose Home ➤ Cells ➤ Format ➤ AutoFit Row Height to force automatic fitting if Excel doesn't set the row height automatically.

You can also set row height manually in either of these ways:

- *Drag the lower border of the row heading*: Move the mouse pointer over the lower border of the row heading so that the pointer changes to an arrow pointing up and down, then click and drag the border up (to make the row shallower) or down (to make the row deeper).

- *Use the Row Height dialog box*: Right-click the row heading, and then click Row Height to display the Row Height dialog box (see Figure 12-3). Type the row height you want, and then click the OK button.

Figure 12-3. Use the Row Height dialog box when you need to set a row's height precisely.

▓ **Note** The row height is measured in points. Each point is $^1/_{72}$ inch.

Setting Column Width

Unlike with row height, Excel doesn't automatically adjust column width as you enter data in a worksheet. But you can quickly set column width in any of these ways:

- *AutoFit a column*: Double-click the right border of the column heading. Excel automatically changes the column's width so that it's wide enough to contain the widest entry in the column.

- *AutoFit several columns*: Select cells in all the columns you want to affect, and then double-click the right border of any of the selected column headings. Excel automatically fits each column's width to suit its contents. You can also select the cells and then choose Home ➤ Cells ➤ Format ➤ AutoFormat Column Width.

■ **Tip** AutoFit is usually the best way to resize a worksheet's columns. But if some cells have such long contents that AutoFit will create huge columns, you'll do better to set the column width manually and hide parts of the longest contents.

- *Resize a column by hand*: Drag the right border of the column heading as far as needed.

- *Resize a column precisely*: Right-click the column heading, and then click Column Width on the context menu to display the Column Width dialog box (see Figure 12-4). Type the cell width (measured in standard characters in the font you're using), and then click the OK button.

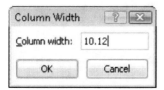

Figure 12-4. Use the Column Width dialog box when you need to set column width precisely.

- *Resize several columns precisely*: Select the columns by dragging through their column headings or by selecting cells in each column. Right-click in the selected column headings, and then click Column Width on the context menu to display the Column Width dialog box. Type the column width, and then click the OK button.

Hiding Rows and Columns

Sometimes it's helpful to hide particular columns and rows so that they're not visible in the worksheet. You may want to do this to hide sensitive data from your printouts, or simply to make the part of the worksheet you're actually using fit on the screen all at once.

To hide a column or row, right-click its column heading or row heading, and then click Hide on the context menu.

■ **Tip** To quickly hide the active row or selected rows, press Ctrl+9. To hide the active column or selected columns, press Ctrl+0.

To unhide a row or column, select the rows above and below it or the columns on either side of it. Then right-click the selected row headings or column headings and click Unhide on the context menu.

■ **Note** You can also hide and unhide items by using the Home ➤ Cells ➤ Format ➤ Hide & Unhide submenu. But usually it's easier to right-click the column heading or row heading.

Formatting Cells and Ranges

In Excel, you can format cells in a wide variety of ways—everything from choosing how to display the borders and background to controlling how Excel represents the text you enter in the cell. This section shows you how the most useful kinds of formatting work and how to apply them.

Each cell comes with essential formatting applied to it—the font and font size to use, and usually the General number format, which you'll meet shortly. So when you create a new workbook and start entering data in it, Excel displays the data in a normal-size font.

■ **Tip** To control the font and font size Excel uses for new workbooks, choose File ➤ Options. In the General category, go to the When creating new workbooks area. Set the font in the Use this font drop-down list and the font size in the Font size drop-down list. Then click the OK button to close the Excel Options dialog box.

Understanding the Three Main Tools for Applying Formatting

Excel gives you three main tools for applying formatting to cells and ranges:

- *Mini Toolbar*: The smaller version of this toolbar (see Figure 12-5) appears when you select text within a cell and right-click the selection. Because in Excel you normally format at least a whole cell rather than part of it, the smaller Mini Toolbar is less useful in Excel than in other Office programs. But the larger version (see Figure 12-6), which appears when you right-click a cell or a selected range of cells, contains enough essential commands to be useful much of the time.

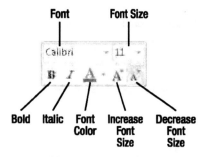

Figure 12-5. The smaller Mini Toolbar provides a few commands for applying widely used formatting.

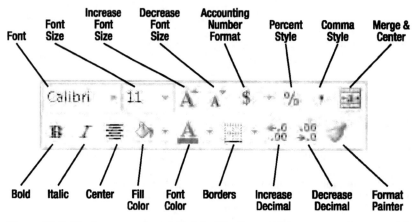

Figure 12-6. The larger version of the Mini Toolbar, which appears when you right-click a cell or selection, contains a good selection of frequently used formatting.

- *Home tab of the Ribbon*: The Font group provides widely used font formatting; the Alignment group offers horizontal and vertical alignment, orientation, indentation, wrapping, and merging; and the Number group gives you a quick way to apply essential number formatting. Figure 12-7 shows these controls labeled.

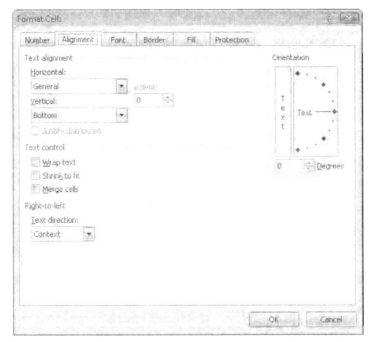

Figure 12-9. The Alignment tab of the Format Cells dialog box lets you rotate text to precise angles when needed.

- *Vertical alignment*: You can align text Top, Center, Bottom, or Justify. You can also choose Distributed to distribute the text vertically, which can be useful when you rotate the text so that it runs vertically.

- *Rotate text*: Use the Orientation box on the Alignment tab of the Format Cells dialog box or the Orientation drop-down list in the Alignment group.

- *Indentation*: You can indent the text as far as is needed.

- *Wrap*: You can wrap the text to make a long entry appear on several lines in a cell rather than disappear where the next cell's contents start.

- *Shrink to fit*: Select this check box on the Alignment tab of the Format Cells dialog box to shrink the text so that it fits in the cell.

- *Merge cells*: Use the Merge & Center drop-down list in the Alignment group to merge selected cells together into a single cell. You can also center an entry across a merged cell.

Choosing Font Formatting

You can quickly format the contents of a cell (or the selected part of a cell's contents) by using the controls in the Font group on the Home tab or the Font tab of the Format Cells dialog box (see Figure 12-10).

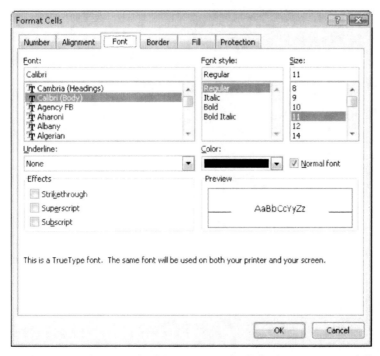

Figure 12-10. *The Font tab of the Format Cells dialog box gives you a full range of font formatting for the current selection.*

Applying Borders and Fills

To apply borders to a cell, open the Borders drop-down list in the Font group on the Home tab of the Ribbon, and then click the border type you want in the Borders section of the list (shown on the left in Figure 12-11). To draw a border, click the appropriate item in the Draw Borders section of the list, and then draw with the resulting pointer.

For more border options, click the More Borders item at the bottom of the list to display the Borders tab of the Format Cells dialog box (shown on the right in Figure 12-11). Use its controls to set up the borders you want, and then click the OK button.

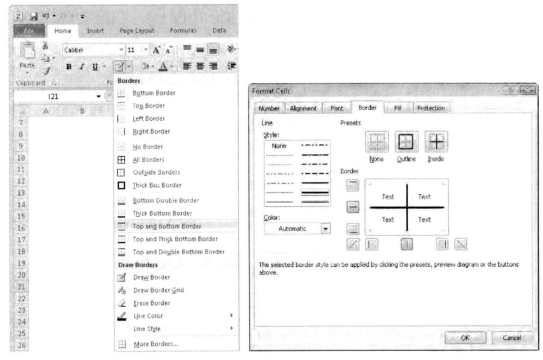

Figure 12-11. *You can quickly apply borders from the Borders drop-down list in the Font group of the Home tab (left) or from the Borders tab of the Format Cells dialog box (right).*

To apply a fill, use the Fill Colors drop-down list in the Font group on the Home tab of the Ribbon or work on the Fill tab of the Format Cells dialog box.

Applying Protection to Cells

The Protection tab of the Format Cells dialog box contains only two controls:

- *Locked*: Select this check box to lock a cell against changes.
- *Hidden*: Select this check box to hide the formula in a cell (the formula's result remains visible).

After selecting either of these check boxes, you must protect the worksheet before the locking or hiding takes effect. You'll learn how to protect a worksheet in the section "Protecting a Worksheet," later in this chapter.

Applying Conditional Formatting to Identify Particular Values

In many worksheets, it's useful to be able to monitor the values in the cells and to pick out values that stand out in particular ways. For example, you may want to see which 10 products are bringing in the most revenue, or you may need an easy way to make unusually high values or unusually low values stand out from the others.

To monitor the values in a cell or a range, you can apply *conditional formatting*—formatting that Excel displays only when the condition is met. For example, if you're monitoring temperatures in Fahrenheit, you could apply conditional formatting to highlight low temperatures (say, below 20F) and high temperatures (say, above 100F). Temperatures in the normal range would not receive any conditional formatting.

Understanding Excel's Preset Types of Conditional Formatting

Excel provides five kinds of preset conditional formatting, which you can apply from the Conditional Formatting panel in the Styles group of the Home tab. Figure 12-12 shows the Conditional Formatting panel with the Icon Sets panel displayed.

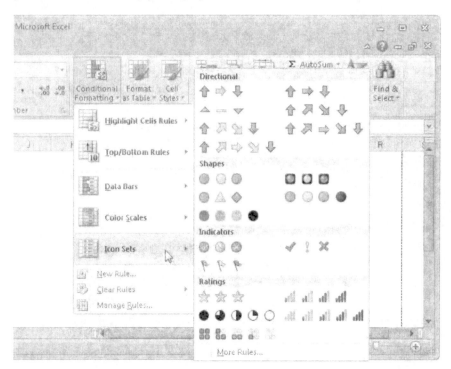

Figure 12-12. The Conditional Formatting panel includes sets of icons you can apply to indicate data trends.

- *Highlight Cells Rules*: This panel gives you an easy way to set up conditional formatting using Greater Than, Less That, Between, Equal To, Text that Contains, A Date Occurring, or Duplicate Values criteria.

- *Top/Bottom Rules*: This panel lets you apply conditional formatting for Top 10 Items, Top 10 %, Bottom 10 Items, Bottom 10 %, Above Average, and Below Average criteria.

- *Data Bars*: This panel enables you to apply different gradient fills and solid fills.

- *Color Scales*: This panel lets you set up color scales using two or three colors—for example, using green, amber, and red to indicate different levels of risk associated with activities.

- *Icon Sets*: This panel provides different sets of icons, such as directional arrows (up, sideways, down) or a checkmark–exclamation point–cross set, for indicating data trends.

Applying a Preset Form of Conditional Formatting

To apply one of these types of conditional formatting, open the Conditional Formatting panel, display the appropriate panel from it, click the type of formatting, and then specify the details. For example:

1. Select the cell or range you want to affect.

2. Choose Home ➤ Styles ➤ Conditional Formatting ➤ Highlight Cells Rules ➤ Greater Than to display the Greater Than dialog box (see Figure 12-13).

Figure 12-13. *Excel's preset conditional formatting types make it easy to apply conditional formatting to cells quickly.*

3. In the Format cells that are GREATER THAN box, enter the comparison. You can either type in the value or collapse the dialog box, click the cell that contains the value, and then restore the dialog box.

4. In the with drop-down list, choose the formatting you want. Excel provides various canned options, but you can also create custom formatting by clicking the Custom Format item at the bottom of the list and working in the Format Cells dialog box that opens.

5. Click the OK button to close the Greater Than dialog box. Excel applies the conditional formatting.

■ **Note** If none of the preset conditional formatting rules meets your needs, you can define conditional formatting rules of your own. To do so, choose Home ➤ Styles ➤ Conditional Formatting ➤ New Rule, and then work in the New Formatting Rule dialog box that opens.

Using Data Validation to Check for Invalid Entries

When you're entering large amounts of data, it's easy to type an incorrect value by mistake. To help avoid errors in your data, you can use Excel's data validation feature to check entries automatically and flag those that may be wrong. For example, if every entry in a range of cells should be between 250 and 1000 (inclusive), you can validate the data to flag any entry that is not in that range.

To apply validation to cells, follow these steps:

1. Click the cell or select the range you want to validate.

2. Choose Data ➤ Data Tools ➤ Data Validation (clicking the top part of the Data Validation button) to display the Data Validation dialog box.

3. Click the Settings tab (shown in Figure 12-14 with settings chosen) to bring it to the front of the dialog box if it's not already there.

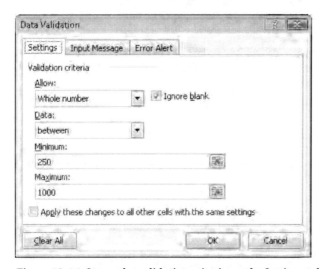

Figure 12-14. Set up the validation criteria on the Settings tab of the Data Validation dialog box. The controls that appear depend on the data type you choose in the Allow drop-down list.

4. In the Allow drop-down list, choose the type of data you want to validate, and then use the controls that appear to set the details.

   • *Any value*: Select this item when you want to turn off validation for the cell or range. Even with this setting, you can use the Input Message tab (discussed later in this list) to display a message about the cell or range.

▓ **Tip** When setting the criteria for your data validation, you can either type in a value or click the Collapse Dialog button and then click the cell that contains the value. Using a value in a cell enables you to change the value easily without editing the conditional formatting.

- *Whole number*: Select this item to set criteria for a whole number—one with no decimal places. For example, in the Data drop-down list, click the between item, and then set the minimum value in the Minimum box and the maximum value in the Maximum box.

- *Decimal*: Select this item to set criteria for a number with decimal places. For example, in the Data drop-down list, click the greater than or equal to item, and then set the minimum value in the Minimum box.

- *List*: Select this item when you need to restrict the cell to a list of valid entries that you specify. You can enter this list in two ways: Either type it in the Source box, separating each entry with a comma, or click the Collapse Dialog button at the right end of the Source box, select the worksheet range that contains the data, and then click the Collapse Dialog button again to restore the dialog box. Select the In-cell drop-down check box to make Excel display a drop-down list with the valid entries in the cell so that the user can enter them easily.

- *Date*: Select this item to set criteria for a date. For example, click the greater than item in the Data drop-down list, and then enter the start date in the Start date box.

- *Time*: Select this item to set criteria for a time. For example, click the not between item in the Data drop-down list, and then enter the start time in the Start time box and the end time in the End time box.

- *Text length*: Select this item to set criteria for a text entry or formula. For example, click the less than or equal to item in the Data drop-down list, and then enter the maximum length in the Maximum box.

- *Custom*: Select this item when you need to enter a formula that returns a logical value of TRUE or FALSE.

5. Select the Ignore blank check box if you want to allow the user to leave the cell blank. Clear this check box to make the user fill in the cell with valid data

6. Click the Input Message tab to display it. The left screen in Figure 12-15 shows the Input Message tab with settings chosen.

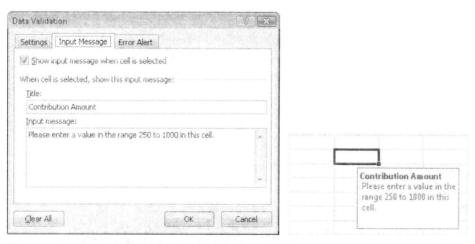

Figure 12-15. *On the Input Message tab of the Data Validation dialog box (left), enter the message you want the user to see when the cell is active (right).*

7. To display a message when the user makes the cell active, select the Show input message when cell is selected check box. Type the title in the Title box and the message in the Input message box. The right screen in Figure 12-15 shows how the message appears.

8. Click the Error Alert tab to bring it to the front. The left screen in Figure 12-16 shows the Error Alert tab with settings chosen; the right screen shows how the error message appears.

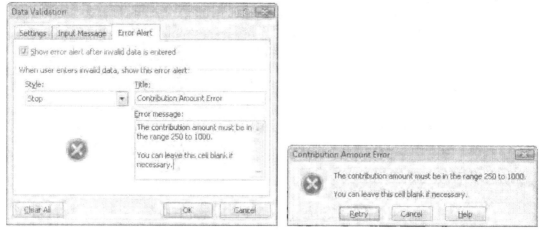

Figure 12-16. *On the Error Alert tab of the Data Validation dialog box (left), set up the error to display when the user enters invalid data in the cell (right).*

9. Select the Show error alert after invalid data is entered check box if you want Excel to display an error message box when the user enters invalid data. Usually, this is helpful.

10. In the Style drop-down list, choose the icon to display—Stop, Warning, or Information.

■ **Caution** To force the user to enter valid data, choose the Stop item in the Style drop-down list on the Error Alert tab of the Data Validation dialog box. If you use the Warning item or the Information item, Excel alerts the user to the problem but allows them to leave the invalid entry in the cell.

---

11. Enter the title and error message for the message box.

12. Click the OK button to close the Data Validation dialog box. Excel applies the validation.

Formatting Quickly with Table Formatting and Styles

To save you time with formatting, Excel provides preset formatting that you can apply to a table to give it an overall look. And to save you the effort of applying many different types of formatting over and over again to different cells, Excel includes styles, collections of formatting that you can apply all at once.

Formatting with Table Formatting

When you need to format a table quickly, see if Excel's preset table formatting will do the trick. Select the table, then choose Home ➤ Styles ➤ Format as Table and click the style you want.

■ **Note** See Chapter 15 for instructions on creating and working with Excel tables.

Formatting with Styles

As you've seen earlier in this chapter, you can give any cell exactly the formatting you want by using the controls in the Font group, Alignment group, and Number group of the Home tab of the Ribbon—or by opening the Format Cells dialog box and working on its six tabs. But applying formatting one aspect at a time—font, font size, alignment, and so on—takes ages, and it's easy to apply it inconsistently.

To save time and ensure your formatting is consistent, you can use Excel's styles. If you're familiar with Word's styles (discussed in Chapter 7), you'll find Excel's styles a snap, as they work in much the same way.

Each style is a collection of formatting that you can apply to one or more cells. The style contains six types of formatting, one for each tab of the Format Cells dialog box:

- *Number*: For example, General, Currency, or Percentage.

- *Alignment*: Horizontal alignment (for example, General, Center, or Justify), vertical alignment (for example, Top, Center, or Bottom), and any trimmings (such as wrapping the text to the window).

- *Font*: The font, font size, font color, and so on.

- *Border*: Any borders you've applied to the style, or No Borders if it has no borders.

- *Fill*: Any fill you've applied to the style, or No Shading if it's plain.

- *Protection*: Locked, Hidden, both, or No Protection.

Most Excel templates contain plenty of styles to get you started, but you can create your own custom styles as well if you need to.

Meeting Excel's Styles

To see which styles are available in a workbook, choose Home ➤ Styles ➤ Cell Styles and look at the Cell Styles panel (see Figure 12-17). This panel lists the styles in the following categories:

- *Custom*: This category appears only when you have created one or more custom styles in the workbook.

Figure 12-17. The Cell Styles panel displays your custom styles at the top and Excel's built-in styles in different categories.

- *Good, Bad and Neutral*: This category has Good, Bad, and Neutral styles that you can use to apply color coding to cells. Here is also where you will find the Normal style that Excel applies to any cell that doesn't have another style.

- *Data and Model*: This category contains the Calculation, Check Cell, Explanatory, Followed Hyperlink, Hyperlink, Input, Linked Cell, Note, Output, and Warning Text styles. Most of these styles are used for data modeling. Excel automatically applies the Hyperlink style to cells containing hyperlinks you have not clicked yet, changing their style to Followed Hyperlink once you have clicked them.

- *Titles and Headings*: This category contains four styles for descending levels of headings (Heading 1, Heading 2, Heading 3, and Heading 4), the Title style for giving a worksheet a title, and the Total style for easily formatting cells that contain totals.

- *Themed Cell Styles*: This category contains six Accent styles (Accent 1 through Accent 6) featuring six of the theme colors, with four degrees of shading for each.

- *Number Format*: This category contains five number formats: Comma (thousands separator, two decimal places), Comma [0] (thousands separator, no decimal places), Currency (currency symbol, thousands separator, two decimal places), Currency [0] (currency symbol, thousands separator, no decimal places), and Percent (percent symbol, multiplies the number by 100).

Applying a Style

To apply a style, choose Home ➤ Styles ➤ Cell Styles, and then click the style on the Cell Styles panel. You can also apply the Currency style, the Percent style, and the Comma style from the Number group on the Home tab of the Ribbon.

Creating Custom Styles

If none of Excel's styles meets your needs, you can create your own styles. To create a style, follow these steps:

1. Format a cell with the formatting you want the style to have.

▓ **Tip** To jump-start your formatting, apply the existing style that's nearest to the look and formatting you want.

---

2. Select the cell you've formatted.

3. Choose Home ➤ Styles ➤ Cell Styles ➤ New Cell Style to display the Style dialog box (shown in Figure 12-18 with settings chosen).

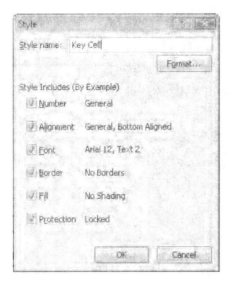

Figure 12-18. In the Style dialog box, you can quickly create a new style based on the formatting of the selected cell. You can change the formatting as needed by clicking the Format button and working in the Format Cells dialog box.

4. In the Style name box, type the name you want to give the style.

5. In the Style Includes (By Example) area, clear the check boxes for any formatting the cell has that you want to omit from the style. For example, clear the Protection check box to leave out the Locked or Hidden formatting.

___

Note If you need to alter the formatting, click the Format button to display the Format Cells dialog box. Make the changes needed, and then click the OK button to return to the Style dialog box.

___

6. Click the OK button to close the Style dialog box and create the style. Excel adds the style to the Custom area at the top of the Cell Styles panel.

___

Tip Instead of creating a new style, you can modify one of the built-in styles. Choose Home ➤ Styles ➤ Cell Styles to display the Cell Styles panel, right-click the style you want to change, and then click the Modify button. In the Style dialog box, click the Format button to display the Format Cells dialog box, and make the changes you need. When you have finished, click the OK button to return to the Style dialog box, and then click the OK button.

___

Copying Styles from One Workbook to Another

If you have styles in one workbook that you want to use in another workbook, you can copy the styles across. Excel calls this *merging styles*. When you merge the styles, the destination workbook receives all the styles from the source workbook—you can't pick and choose (but see the nearby Tip).

To merge the styles, follow these steps:

1. Open the source workbook (the workbook that contains the styles) and the destination workbook.

2. Switch to the destination workbook by clicking in it.

3. Choose Home ➤ Styles ➤ Cell Styles ➤ Merge Styles to display the Merge Styles dialog box (see Figure 12-19).

Figure 12-19. *Use the Merge Styles dialog box to copy all the styles from one workbook into another workbook.*

4. In the Merge styles from list box, click the source workbook.

5. Click the OK button to close the Merge Styles dialog box. Excel copies the styles into the destination workbook, and you can then start using them.

■ **Tip** If you need to copy just one style from one workbook to another, apply that style to a cell. Then copy that cell and switch back to the destination workbook. Right-click a cell you don't mind changing, go to the Paste Options section of the context menu, and click the Formatting icon. Excel pastes the style onto the cell, and you can then use the style in the workbook.

Deleting Styles You Don't Need

If you no longer need a style, you can delete it. Choose Home ➤ Styles ➤ Cell Styles, right-click the style on the Cell Styles panel, and then click Delete on the context menu.

▪ **Note** Excel prevents you from deleting the Normal style.

Adding Headers and Footers to Your Worksheets

Before printing a worksheet or creating a PDF or XPS file from it, you'll probably want to add headers, footers, or both to identify the pages. Excel gives each worksheet a separate header and footer, which you can fill with either preset text or custom text. Each header and footer area consists of a left section, a center section, and a right section.

To add headers and footers to the active worksheet, follow these steps:

1. Choose Insert ➤ Text ➤ Header & Footer to display the header area and reveal Header & Footer Tools section of the Ribbon, which contains the Design tab (see Figure 12-20).

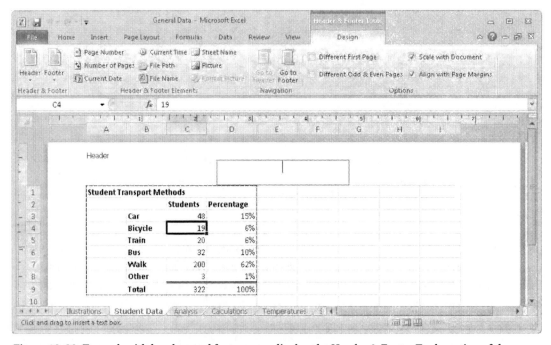

Figure 12-20. To work with headers and footers, you display the Header & Footer Tools section of the Ribbon. Each header and footer consists of three sections—left, center, and right.

2. To insert a preset header that contains workbook information such as the page number, worksheet title, or filename, choose Header & Footer Tools ➤ Design ➤ Header & Footer ➤ Header, and then click the preset header you want. Similarly, you can insert a preset footer by clicking the Footer button in the Header & Footer group, and then clicking the one you want.

3. To move from the header area to the footer area, choose Header & Footer Tools ➤ Design ➤ Navigation ➤ Go to Footer. To go back, choose Header & Footer Tools ➤ Design ➤ Navigation ➤ Go to Header.

4. To add text to the header or footer, click in the section in which you want to place the text—for example, the middle section—and then type the text.

5. To add a predefined element to the current section, click the appropriate button—Page Number, Number of Pages, Current Date, Current Time, File Path, File Name, or Sheet Name—in the Header & Footer Elements group.

6. To add a picture to the current section, click the Picture button in the Header & Footer Elements group, select the picture in the Insert Picture dialog box, and then click the Insert button. To format the picture, click the Format Picture button in the Header & Footer Elements group, and then work on the Size tab and Picture tab of the Format Picture dialog box. For example, set the picture's height and width on the Size tab. Click the OK button when you've finished.

7. Choose options for the header and footer in the Options group:

   • *Different First Page*: If the printout will occupy two or more pages, you can select this check box to put a different header or footer on the first page. When you're working in this header or footer, Excel displays *First Page Header* or *First Page Footer* so that you can easily tell which one you're editing.

   • *Different Odd & Even Pages*: If the printout needs different headers and footers on odd pages than on even pages, select this check box. When you're working in these headers and footers, Excel displays *Odd Page Header*, *Odd Page Footer*, *Even Page Header*, or *Even Page Footer*, as appropriate.

   • *Scale with Document*: Select this check box to have Excel resize the header or footer if you resize the worksheet to fit it on paper when printing. Clear this check box if you want the header or footer to print at full size each time.

   • *Align with Page Margins*: Select this check box to make Excel align the edges of the header and footer with the page's left and right margins. Alignment usually makes for a tidy look, but you may sometimes need to clear this check box to accommodate wider headers or footers.

8. When you finish creating the header or footer, click a cell in the worksheet to return to the worksheet.

Printing Your Excel Worksheets and Workbooks

To print from Excel, you use the Print pane in Backstage, as with the other programs. But before you print, you need to tell Excel which part of the workbook to print. You may also want to check the page setup to make sure that the page breaks fall where you want them to.

Telling Excel Which Part of the Worksheet to Print

As you learned earlier in this chapter, each worksheet contains billions of cells, so normally you don't want to print the whole of the worksheet—you want to print only the range of cells you've used, or perhaps only a small subset of that range. So when you're printing, the first thing to do is tell Excel which part of the worksheet you want to print. Excel calls this setting the print area. You can set a separate print area for each worksheet.

▓ **Caution** Until you set the print area, Excel assumes you want to print all the cells you've used on the worksheet—even if there are huge amounts of blank space between them. So it's a good idea always to set the print area before printing.

To set the print area, follow these steps:

1. Click the worksheet whose print area you want to set.

2. Select the range of cells you want to print.

3. Choose Page Layout ➤ Page Setup ➤ Print Area ➤ Set Print Area. Excel displays a dotted line around the print area to indicate that it is set.

If you need to change the print area afterward, repeat the above steps. If you need to clear the print area so that the worksheet has no print area set, click the worksheet, and then choose Page Layout ➤ Page Setup ➤ Print Area ➤ Clear Print Area.

Checking the Page Layout and Where the Page Breaks Fall

After setting the print area, check the page layout of the worksheet and adjust it as needed. Follow these steps:

1. Switch to Page Layout view in either of these ways:

   - Click the Page Layout View button in the View Shortcuts area in the status bar.

   - Choose View ➤ Workbook Views ➤ Page Layout.

2. Click the Page Layout tab of the Ribbon to show its controls. Figure 12-21 shows a worksheet in Page Layout view with the Page Layout tab displayed.

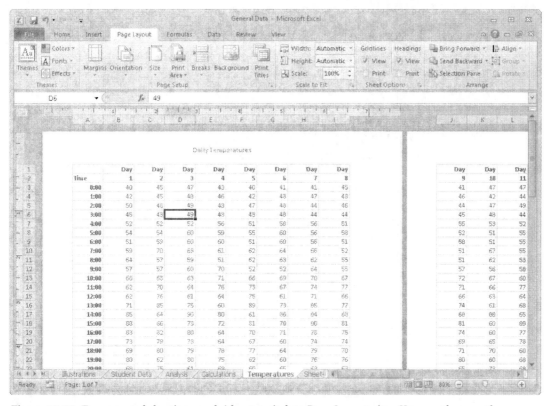

Figure 12-21. *To see a worksheet's pages laid out, switch to Page Layout view. You can then use the controls on the Page Layout tab of the Ribbon to refine the layout.*

3. Use the controls in the Page Setup group to change the page setup as needed:

    -   *Change the margins*: Click the Margins button, and then click Normal, Wide, or Narrow. Or click Custom Margins, work on the Margins tab of the Page Setup dialog box, and then click the OK button.

    -   *Change the orientation*: Click the Orientation button, and then click Portrait or Landscape.

    -   *Change the paper size*: Click the Size drop-down list, and then click the paper size.

    -   *Insert a page break*: Click the column before which you want to insert a manual page break. Click the Breaks button, and then click Insert Page Break.

▬ **Note** If you put a page break in the wrong place, click the column after it, and then choose Page Layout ➤ Page Setup ➤ Breaks ➤ Remove Page Breaks. To restore all page breaks to where Excel had placed them, choose Page Layout ➤ Page Setup ➤ Breaks ➤ Reset Page Breaks.

---

4. To get an overall view of where page breaks fall, and to adjust them, switch to Page Break Preview in either of these ways:

   • Click the Page Break Preview button in the View Shortcuts area in the status bar.

   • Choose View ➤ Workbook Views ➤ Page Layout.

5. In Page Break Preview (see Figure 12-22), click and drag the page breaks as needed. A dotted blue line indicates a page break that Excel has placed, and a solid blue line indicates a page break you've placed.

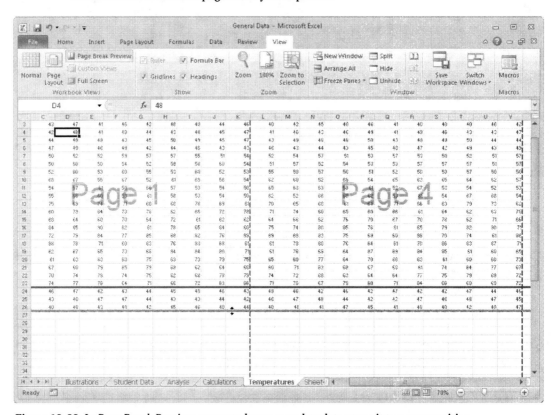

Figure 12-22. In Page Break Preview, you can drag a page break to move it to a new position.

When you have finished laying out the pages, click the Save button on the Quick Access Toolbar to save your workbook.

Printing a Worksheet or Workbook

After you've set the print area for each worksheet you want to print, you can print a worksheet or workbook like this:

1. Click the File tab to open Backstage.

2. In the left column, click Print to display the Print pane.

3. Open the Print What drop-down list and choose what to print:

    - *Print Active Sheets*: Click this item to print all the active worksheets in the workbook—the worksheets that have contents.

    - *Print Entire Workbook*: Click this item to print every worksheet in the workbook. Normally, you'll use this option only for small workbooks.

    - *Print Selection*: Click this item to print only the cells you've selected. This option is useful for printing smaller amounts without resetting the print area.

    - *Ignore Print Area*: Click this item (placing a check box next to it) to override the print area you've set. This option is occasionally useful, but it most cases you'll want to make sure it's cleared.

4. Check that the preview of the printout looks right. If not, use the other options in the Settings area to fix the problems:

    - *Change the orientation*: Click the Orientation button, and then click Portrait Orientation or Landscape Orientation as needed.

    - *Change the margins*: Click the Margins button, and then click the margins you want on the drop-down list.

    - *Scale the printout*: Click the Scaling button, and then click the scaling you want: Fit Sheet on One Page, Fit All Columns on One Page, Fit All Rows on One Page, or No Scaling. For other scaling options, click Custom Scaling Options, and then work on the Page tab of the Page Setup dialog box; click the OK button when you've made your choices.

5. Click the Print button to print the worksheets.

Sharing Your Workbooks with Your Colleagues

You may create some workbooks on your own, but for others, you'll probably need to work with colleagues to collect, enter, and analyze data. You can either share a workbook on the network so that one person can work on it at a time, or turn on Excel's sharing features that enable you and your colleagues to work on the workbook at the same time.

Before sharing a workbook, you may choose to protect it with a password, or to allow your colleagues to make only some types of changes to it.

Protecting a Workbook or Some of Its Worksheets

Before sharing a workbook with your colleagues for editing individually on a network, you may want to restrict the changes your colleagues can make in the workbook or on some of its worksheets. Excel calls this *protecting* the workbook or worksheets.

Protecting a Workbook

To protect a workbook, follow these steps:

1. Choose Review ➤ Changes ➤ Protect Workbook to display the Protect Structure and Windows dialog box (see Figure 12-23).

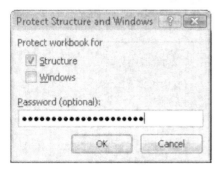

Figure 12-23. When protecting a workbook, you'll normally want to protect the structure but not the windows.

2. Select the Structure check box to prevent your colleagues from inserting, deleting, or otherwise changing whole worksheets.

3. Select the Windows check box only if you need to prevent your colleagues from changing the number or sizes of windows that you're using for the workbook. Normally, you don't need to do this if your colleagues will work conventionally in the workbook.

4. Type a strong password in the Password text box.

5. Click the OK button. Excel displays the Confirm Password dialog box.

6. Type the password again, and then click the OK button to close both the Confirm Password dialog box and then Protect Structure and Windows dialog box.

7. Save the workbook by pressing Ctrl+S or clicking the Save button on the Quick Access Toolbar.

■ **Note** To unprotect a workbook, choose Review ➤ Changes ➤ Protect Workbook. In the Unprotect Workbook dialog box, type your password, and then click the OK button. Save the changes to the workbook.

Protecting a Worksheet

When you need to limit the changes your colleagues can make to a particular worksheet, apply protection to it. Follow these steps:

1. Click the worksheet to activate it.

2. Choose Review ➤ Changes ➤ Protect Sheet to display the Protect Sheet dialog box (shown in Figure 12-24 with settings chosen).

Figure 12-24. *Protect a worksheet when you need to prevent your colleagues from making specific types of changes to it.*

3. Make sure the Protect worksheet and contents of locked cells check box is selected.

4. Type a password in the Password to unprotect sheet text box.

5. In the Allow all users of this worksheet to box, select each check box for actions you want your colleagues to be able to take. Clear each other check box.

6. Click the OK button. Excel displays the Confirm Password dialog box.

7. Type the password again, and then click the OK button to close both the Confirm Password dialog box and then Protect Sheet dialog box.

8. Save the workbook by pressing Ctrl+S or clicking the Save button on the Quick Access Toolbar.

Sharing a Workbook So That Your Colleagues Can Edit It

When you need to be able to share a workbook with your colleagues, follow these steps:

1. Open the workbook.

2. Choose Review ➤ Changes ➤ Share Workbook to display the Share Workbook dialog box. The left screen in Figure 12-25 shows the Editing tab of the Share Workbook dialog box.

Figure 12-25. On the Editing tab (left) of the Share Workbook dialog box, select the Allow changes by more than one user at the same time check box. You can then choose options on the Advanced tab (right).

3. Select the Allow changes by more than one user at the same time check box on the Editing tab.

4. Check the Who has this workbook open now list box. It should show only your name and should include the word "Exclusive" to indicate that you've got sole access to the workbook.

5. Click the Advanced tab to display its contents (shown on the right in Figure 12-25).

6. In the Track Changes area, choose how long to keep the change history for the workbook. Normally, you'll want to select the Keep change history for option button and set the number of days in the days box. The default setting is 30 days, but if you develop your workbooks quickly, you may want to reduce the interval to 7 days or 14 days. The alternative is to select the Don't keep change history option button, but usually it's best to keep change history so that you can unravel any mysterious changes.

7. In the Update changes area, choose when to update the changes to the workbook.

    - The default setting is the When file is saved option button, which generally works pretty well.

    - The alternative is to select the Automatically every option button and set the number of minutes in the minutes box. The default setting is 15 minutes; if you work fast, you may want to shorten the interval to 5 or 10 minutes.

    - If you select the Automatically every option button, you can choose between the Save my changes and see others' changes option button (usually the better choice) and the Just see other users' changes option button.

8. In the Conflicting change between users area, choose how to handle conflicting changes to the workbook. Normally, you'll want to select the Ask me which changes win option button so that you can decide which of the conflicting changes to keep. The alternative is to select the option button called The changes being saved win, which tells Excel to overwrite the conflicting changes with the latest changes.

9. In the Include in personal view area, select the Print settings check box if you want to include print settings in your view of the workbook. Select the Filter settings check box if you want to include filter settings. (See Chapter 15 for instructions on filtering an Excel database table.)

10. Click the OK button to close the Share Workbook dialog box. Excel then displays a dialog box telling you that it will save the workbook.

11. Click the OK button. Excel sets up the sharing and adds "[Shared]" to the workbook's title bar so that you can easily see it's shared.

Working in a Shared Workbook

Once you've shared a workbook, or someone else has shared it, you can perform basic editing in it much as normal. You can enter data and formulas in cells or edit their existing contents, format cells, and use both drag and drop and cut, copy, and paste. You can also insert rows, columns, and even whole worksheets.

Beyond these basics, Excel prevents you from making changes that may cause problems with the sharing. These are the main restrictions:

- *Apply conditional formatting*: If your workbook needs conditional formatting, apply it before sharing the workbook.

- *Insert objects*: You can't insert pictures, SmartArt, charts, hyperlinks, or various other objects. In fact, the only control available on the Insert tab of a shared workbook is the Header & Footer button.

- *Insert or delete blocks of cells*: You can insert or delete a whole row or column, but you can't insert or delete a block of cells. You also can't merge cells together.

- *Delete a worksheet*: You can't delete a worksheet from the shared workbook.

- *Protect a sheet with a password*: Any protection you've applied before sharing the workbook remains in force, but you can't apply protection to a sheet in a shared workbook.

- *Outline the workbook*: Excel's advanced capabilities include creating a collapsible outline from a worksheet. (This book does not cover outlining.) You can't create an outline in a shared workbook.

Resolving Conflicts in a Shared Workbook

If you chose the Ask me which changes win option button when sharing the workbook, Excel prompts you to deal with conflicts that arise between the changes you're saving and the changes that your colleagues have already saved. The Resolve Conflicts dialog box (see Figure 12-26) takes you through each of the changes in turn, showing the change you made and the conflicting change.

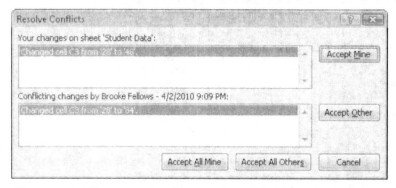

Figure 12-26. When you and another user have changed the same cells, the Resolve Conflicts dialog box walks you through each change in turn. You can accept all your changes, all your colleagues' changes, or some of each.

For each change, you can click the Accept Mine button to accept your change or click the Accept Other button to accept your colleague's change. To clear all the changes at once, click the Accept All Mine button or the Accept All Others button. Excel closes the Resolve Conflicts dialog box automatically when you've finished reviewing the conflicts.

Summary

In this chapter, you've learned how to apply all Excel's most useful types of formatting to a worksheet. You know how to manipulate the worksheet's rows and columns to make it fit your data, how to format cells and ranges, and how to save time and worry by using conditional formatting and data validation.

You've also gone through how to format quickly with table formatting and styles, how to give your worksheets the headers and footers that printouts need, and how to rearrange your worksheet's pages so that they come out right when you print.

Finally, you've learned to protect worksheets and workbooks against changes, and you know how to share your worksheets with colleagues—and how to resolve the conflicts that often occur.

In the next chapter, I'll show you how to turn your data into powerful and persuasive charts. Turn the page when you're ready.

CHAPTER 13

Crunching Numbers with Formulas and Functions

To make your worksheets deliver the information you want, you'll probably need to perform calculations with your data. To perform calculations, you enter formulas and functions in cells, as you'll learn to do in this chapter.

I'll start by going over what functions and formulas are, so that you're clear on the difference between them. Then I'll show you how to create your own formulas using Excel's calculation operators. You'll find it easy to get started, as Excel provides plenty of help, but you'll also look at how to troubleshoot common problems that occur with formulas.

In the second half of the chapter, you'll dig into functions: how to insert them in your worksheets using the various tools that Excel provides, how to find the ones you want, and how to point the functions to the data they need for the calculations.

Understanding the Difference Between Formulas and Functions

In Excel, you can perform calculations in two main ways:

- *By using a formula*: A *formula* is a custom calculation that you create when none of Excel's functions (discussed next) does what you need. The word "formula" may sound imposing, but a formula can be a simple calculation; for example, to subtract 50 from 100, you can type =**100-50** in a cell. Formulas can also be more complex. For example, say you need to add the contents of contents of the cells in the range A1:A6 and then divide them by the contents of cell B1. Excel doesn't have a built-in function for doing this, because it's not a standard calculation. So instead you create a formula such as this: =**SUM(A1:A6)/B1**. (In this example, the / is the keyboard equivalent of the ÷ symbol.)

- *By using a function*: A *function* is a preset formula that performs a standard calculation. For example, when you need to add several values together, you use the SUM() function—for instance, =**SUM(1,2,3,4,5,6)**, which is simpler than =**1+2+3+4+5+6** but has the same effect.

In the following sections, I'll show you how to use each of these methods. But before I do that, let's go over the ways of referring to cells and ranges in formulas and functions.

Referring to Cells and Ranges in Formulas and Functions

To make your formulas and functions work correctly, you need to refer to the cells and ranges you want. This section makes sure you know how to refer to cells and ranges, both when they're on the same worksheet as the formula and when they're on a different worksheet. You can even refer to cells and ranges in another workbook—as long as you're sure where it is.

Referring to a Cell

To refer to a cell on the same worksheet, simply use its column lettering and its row number. For example, use =**A10** to refer to cell A10.

To refer to a cell on a different worksheet, enter the worksheet's name followed by an exclamation point and the cell reference. For example, use =**Supplies!A10** to refer to cell A10 on the worksheet named Supplies. The easiest way to set up such a reference is like this:

1. Start creating the formula. For example, type = in the cell.

2. Click the worksheet tab for the worksheet that contains the cell you want to refer to.

3. Click the cell.

4. Click the worksheet tab on which you're creating the formula.

5. Finish creating the formula as usual.

■ **Note** If the worksheet's name contains any spaces, you must put the name inside single quotes; for example, =**'Sales Results'!A10** rather than =**Sales Results!A10**. You can also use the single quotes on worksheet names that don't have spaces if you find it easier to be consistent.

To refer to a cell in a different workbook, put the workbook's path and file name in brackets, then the worksheet's name, and then the cell reference. For example, the reference =**[Z:\Shared\Spreads\Results.xlsx]Sales!AB12]** refers to cell AB12 on the worksheet named Sales in the workbook Z:\Shared\Spreads\Results.xlsx.

Unless you happen to know the path, filename, worksheet name, and cell, it's usually easiest to set up the reference by using the mouse. Follow these steps:

1. Open the workbook you want to refer to.

2. In the workbook that will contain the reference, start creating the formula. For example, type = in the cell.

3. Switch to the other workbook. For example, choose View ➤ Windows ➤ Switch Windows, and then click the appropriate window. Or if you've tiled the workbooks, simply click the other workbook.

4. Navigate to the worksheet that contains the cell, and then click the cell.

5. Switch back to the workbook in which you're creating the reference, and complete the formula.

▒ **Tip** Sometimes you may need to make the contents of one row or column refer to another row or column. For example, say you need to make each cell in row 25 refer to the corresponding cell in row 4, so that cell A25 refers to cell A4, cell B25 to cell B4, and so on. To do this, click the row heading for row 25, selecting the row. Then type **=4:4** to create the reference to row 4, and press Ctrl+Enter to enter it in all the cells of the selection. Similarly, you can refer to a whole column by entering its letter designation, a colon, and the letter designation again; for example, **E:E**.

Referring to Ranges

To refer to a range that consists of a block of cells, give the cell addresses of the first cell and the last cell, separating them with a colon. For example, to refer to the range from cell P10 to cell Q12, use **=P10:Q12**.

To refer to a range that consists of individual cells, give the address of each cell, separating the addresses with commas. For example, to refer to cell J14, cell K18, and cell Z20, use **=J14,K18,Z20**.

To refer to a range on a different worksheet or in a different workbook, use the techniques explained in the previous section. For example, if you need to refer to the range P10 to Q12 on the worksheet named Stock Listing, use **='Stock Listing'!P10:Q12**.

UNDERSTANDING ABSOLUTE REFERENCES, RELATIVE REFERENCES, AND MIXED REFERENCES

Using cell addresses or range addresses is straightforward enough, but when you start using formulas, there's a complication: If you copy a formula and paste it, you need to tell Excel whether the pasted formula should refer to the cells it originally referred to, or the cells in the same relative positions to the cell where the formula now is, or a mixture of the two. (If you move a formula rather than copy it, Excel keeps the formula as it is.)

To make references clear, Excel uses three types of references:

- *Absolute reference*: A reference that always refers to the same cell, no matter where you copy it. Excel uses a dollar sign ($) to indicate that each part of the reference is absolute. For example, B3 is an absolute reference to cell B3.

- *Relative reference*: A reference that refers to the cell by its position relative to the cell that holds the reference. For example, if you select cell A3 and enter **=B5** in it, the reference means "the cell one column to the right and two rows down." So if you copy the formula to cell C4, Excel changes the cell reference to cell D6, which is one column to the right and two rows down from cell B4. To indicate a relative reference, Excel uses a plain reference without any dollar signs; for example, B4.

- *Mixed reference*: A reference that is absolute for either the column or the row and relative for the other. For example, $B4 is absolute for the column (B) and relative for the row (4), while B$4 is relative for the column and absolute for the row. When you copy and paste a mixed reference, the absolute part stays the same, but the relative part changes to reflect the new location.

If you're typing a reference, you can type the $ signs into the reference to make it absolute or mixed. If you're entering references by selecting cells, click in the reference in cell you're editing or in the Formula bar, and then press F4 repeatedly to cycle a reference through its absolute, relative, column-absolute, and row-absolute versions.

Referring to Named Cells and Ranges

To make your references easier to enter and recognize, you can give a name to any cell or range. You can then refer to the cell or range by the name.

To create a named range, follow these steps:

1. Select the cell or range.

2. Choose Formulas ➤ Defined Names ➤ Define Name (clicking the Define Names button rather than the drop-down button to its right) to display the New Name dialog box (shown in Figure 13-1 with settings chosen).

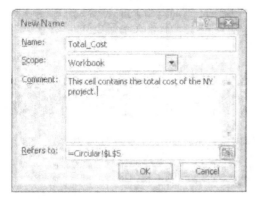

Figure 13-1. Use the New Name dialog box to give a cell or range a name by which you can easily refer to it.

3. In the Name text box, type the name for the range. Follow these rules:

   • The name must start with a letter or an underscore.

   • The name can contain only letters, numbers, and underscores. It can't contain spaces or symbols.

   • The name must be unique in its scope (discussed next); for example, it must be unique in the workbook.

4. In the Scope drop-down list, choose whether to make the name unique within the workbook or only within the worksheet:

   • *Workbook:* In many cases, this is the best choice, as it enables you to refer to the named range from anywhere in the workbook by using just its name rather than having to specify the worksheet name.

- *The current worksheet*: Choose the worksheet in the Scope drop-down list when you need to use the same name on different worksheets in the same workbook; for example, because each sheet has a similar layout.

5. In the Comment text box, type any comment to help you (or your colleagues) identify the cell or range.

6. Make sure that the Refers to box shows the right cell or range. If not, click the Collapse Dialog button, select the right cell or range in the worksheet, and then click the Collapse Dialog button again to restore the dialog box.

7. Click the OK button to apply the name to the range.

After you've named a range, you can use the name in your formulas instead of the cell reference or range reference.

■ **Note** To delete a name from a range, choose Formulas ➤ Defined Names ➤ Name Manager. In the Name Manager dialog box, click the name, click the Delete button, and then click the OK button in the confirmation dialog box that Excel displays. Click the Close button to close the Name Manager dialog box.

Performing Custom Calculations by Creating Formulas

When you need to perform a custom calculation in a cell, use a formula rather than a function. All you need to do is type in a simple formula using the appropriate calculation operators, such as + signs for addition and – signs for subtraction. In this section, you'll meet the comparison operators, try using them in a worksheet, and learn the order in which Excel applies them—and how to change that order.

Meeting Excel's Calculation Operators

To perform calculations in Excel, you need to know the operators for the different operations—addition, division, comparison, and so on. Table 13-1 explains the full set of calculation operators you can use in your formulas in Excel.

Table 13-1. Calculation Operators You Can Use in Excel

Calculation Operator	Operation	Explanation or Example
Arithmetic Operators		
+	Addition	=1+2
–	Subtraction	=1–2
*	Multiplication	=2*2
/	Division	=A1/4
%	Percentage	=B1%
^	Exponentiation	=B1^2 raises the value in cell B2 to the power 2.

Calculation Operator	Operation	Explanation or Example
Comparison Operators		
=	Equal to	=B2=15000 returns TRUE if cell B2 contains the value 15000. Otherwise, it returns FALSE.
<>	Not equal to	=B2<>15000 returns TRUE if cell B2 does not contain the value 15000. Otherwise, it returns FALSE.
>	Greater than	=B2>15000 returns TRUE if cell B2 contains a value greater than 15000. Otherwise, it returns FALSE.
>=	Greater than or equal to	=B2>=15000 returns TRUE if cell B2 contains a value greater than or equal to 15000. Otherwise, it returns FALSE.
<	Less than	=B2<15000 returns TRUE if cell B2 contains a value less than 15000. Otherwise, it returns FALSE.
<=	Less than or equal to	=B2<=15000 returns TRUE if cell B2 contains a value less than or equal to 15000. Otherwise, it returns FALSE.
Reference Operators		
[cell reference]:[cell reference]	The range of cells between the two cell references	A1:G5 returns the range of cells whose upper-left cell is cell A1 and whose lower-right cell is cell G5.
[cell reference],[cell reference]	The range of cells listed	A1,C3,E5 returns three cells: A1, C3, and E5.
[cell or range reference] [space][cell or range reference]	The range (or cell) that appears in both cells or ranges given.	=A7:G10 B10:B12 returns the cell B10, because this is the only cell that appears in both the ranges given.
Text Operator		
&	Concatenation (joining values as text)	=A1&B1 returns the values from cells A1 and B1 joined together as a text string. For example, if A1 contains "New York " (including a trailing space) and B1 contains "Sales", this formula returns "New York Sales." If A1 contains 100 and B1 contains 50, this formula returns 10050.

Using the Calculation Operators

Now that you know what the calculation operators are, try the following example of creating a simple worksheet (see Figure 13-2) that uses the four most straightforward operators—addition, subtraction, multiplication, and division.

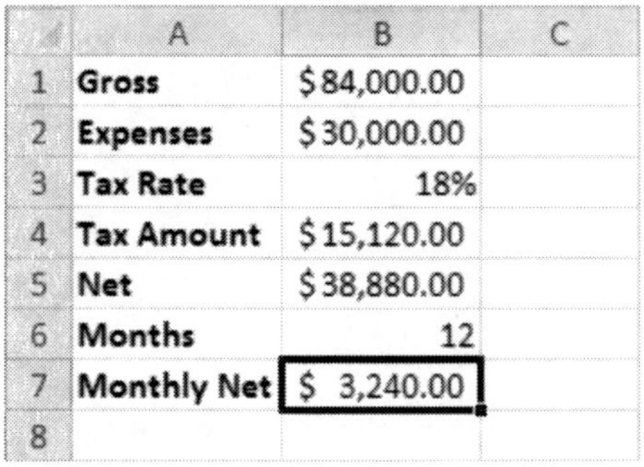

⊿	A	B	C
1	Gross	$ 84,000.00	
2	Expenses	$ 30,000.00	
3	Tax Rate	18%	
4	Tax Amount	$ 15,120.00	
5	Net	$ 38,880.00	
6	Months	12	
7	Monthly Net	$ 3,240.00	
8			

Figure 13-2. Create this simple worksheet to try using Excel's addition, subtraction, multiplication, and division operators.

To create the worksheet, follow these steps:

1. Create a new workbook. The quickest way to do this is to press Ctrl+N.

2. Type the following text in cells A1 through A7:

   - *A1*: Gross
   - *A2*: Expenses
   - *A3*: Tax Rate
   - *A4*: Tax Amount
   - *A5*: Net
   - *A6*: Months
   - *A7*: Monthly Net

3. Apply boldface to column A by clicking the column heading, and then choosing Home ➤ Font ➤ Bold.

4. Apply Currency format to column B by clicking the column heading, and then choosing Home ➤ Number ➤ Number Format ➤ Currency.

5. Type the following text in cells B1 through B3:

   - *B1*: 84000
   - *B2*: 30000
   - *B3*: 0.18

6. Apply Percent style to cell B3 by clicking the cell, and then choosing Home ➤ Number ➤ Percent Style.

7. Now enter the formula **=B1*B3** in cell B3, like this:

   - Click cell B3 to select it.

   - Type = to start creating a formula in the cell.

   - Click cell B1 to enter it in the formula. Excel displays a shimmering dotted blue outline around the cell and adds it to the formula in the cell and to the Formula bar (see Figure 13-3).

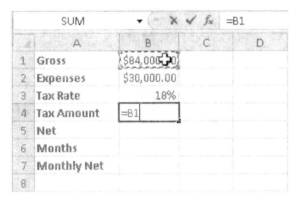

Figure 13-3. *When you click cell B1, Excel adds it to the formula in both the cell and the Formula bar, and displays a dotted blue outline around it.*

   - Type * to tell Excel you want to multiply the value in cell B1. Excel enters the asterisk in the formula and changes the outline around cell B1 to solid blue.

   - Click cell B3 to enter it in the formula. Excel displays a shimmering dotted outline (green this time) around the cell and adds it to the formula in the cell and in the formula bar (see Figure 13-4).

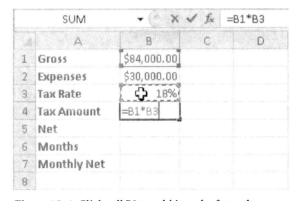

Figure 13-4. *Click cell B3 to add it to the formula.*

- Press Enter or click the Enter button (the checkmark button in the Formula bar) to finish entering the formula in cell B4.

8. Enter the formula =**B1**-(**B2**+**B4**) in cell B5. Follow these steps:

- Click cell B5 to select it. If you pressed Enter to enter the previous formula, Excel may have selected this cell already.

- Type = to start creating a formula in the cell.

- Click cell B1 to add it to the formula.

- Type – to enter the subtraction operator.

- Type (to start a nested expression. (More on this shortly.)

- Click cell B2 to add it to the formula.

- Type + to enter the addition operator.

- Click cell B4 to add it to the formula.

- Type) to end the nested expression.

- Click the Enter button to finish entering the formula.

9. Enter **12** in cell B6 and apply General formatting to it. Follow these steps:

- Click cell B6.

- Choose Home ➤ Number ➤ Number Format ➤ General.

- Type **12**.

- Press Down arrow to enter the value and move the active cell to cell B7.

10. Enter the formula =**B5/B6** in cell B7. This time, simply type the formula in—lowercase is fine—and then press Enter. You'll notice that when you type **b5**, Excel selects cell B5 for confirmation.

Now that you've created the worksheet, try changing the figures in cells B1, B2, and B3. You'll see the results of the formulas in cells B4, B5, and B7 change accordingly. Excel recalculates the formulas each time you change a value in a cell, so the formula results remain up to date.

■ **Note** If you create a workbook with huge amounts of data, automatic recalculation may make Excel run slowly. If this happens, choose Formulas ➤ Calculation ➤ Calculation Options ➤ Manual to turn off automatic recalculation. You can recalculate manually when necessary by pressing Shift+F9 or choosing Formulas ➤ Calculation ➤ Calculate Sheet (to recalculate just the active worksheet), or pressing F9 or choosing Formulas ➤ Calculation ➤ Calculate Now to recalculate the whole workbook.

Understanding the Order in Which Excel Evaluates Operators

In the previous example, you entered the formula =B1-(B2+B4) in cell B5. The parentheses are necessary because the calculation has two separate stages—one stage of subtraction and one stage of addition—and you need to control the order in which they occur.

Try changing the formula in cell B5 to =B1-B2+B4 and see what happens. Follow these steps:

1. Click cell B5.

2. Click in the Formula bar to start editing the formula there. (You can also edit in the cell by double-clicking the cell or pressing F2, but editing in the Formula bar gives you more space, so it's often easier.)

3. Delete the opening and closing parentheses.

4. Click the Enter button on the Formula bar.

You'll notice that the Net amount (cell B5) jumps substantially. This is because you've changed the meaning of the formula:

- =B1-(B2+B4): This formula means "add the value in cell B2 to the value in cell B4, then subtract the result from the value in cell B1."

- =B1-B2+B4: This formula means "subtract the value in cell B2 from the value in cell B2, then add the value in cell B4 to the result."

Click cell B5 and press F2 to open the cell for editing. Position the insertion point before **B2** and type (, then position the insertion point after **B4** and type). As you type the closing parenthesis, notice that the opening parenthesis momentarily darkens to make the pairing clear. In this case, you can easily see the opening parenthesis because the cell's contents are short and simple. But when a cell has complex contents, and contains other nested items, having the corresponding parenthesis darken like this helps you to identify it.

The order in which Excel evaluates the operators is called *operator precedence*, and it can make a huge difference in your formulas—so it's vital to know both how it works and how to override it. Table 13-2 shows you the order in which Excel evaluates the operators in formulas.

Table 13-2. Excel's Operator Precedence in Descending Order

Precedence	Operators	Explanation
1	–	Negation
2	%	Percentage
3	^	Exponentiation
4	* *and* /	Multiplication and division
5	+ *and* –	Addition and subtraction
6	&	Concatenation
7	=, <>, <, <=, >, *and* >=	Comparison operators

When two operators are at the same level, Excel performs the operator that appears earlier in the formula first.

Nesting Parts of Formulas to Override Operator Precedence

You can override operator precedence in any formula by nesting one or more parts of the formula in parentheses. For example, as you just saw, using =**B1**-(**B2**+**B4**) makes Excel evaluate **B2**+**B4** before the subtraction.

You can nest parts of the formula several levels deep if necessary. For example, the following formula uses three levels of nesting and returns 180.

```
=10*(5*(4/(1+1))+8)
```

■ **Tip** Nested formulas can quickly become hard to read. If you find a formula is becoming too complex, break it up into intermediate stages, and place each in a separate cell. Excel gives you almost unlimited space, and it's much better to use more cells than to get the wrong result by creating a formula that's impressively complex but wrong.

Entering Formulas Quickly by Copying and Using AutoFill

In many worksheets, you'll need to enter related formulas in several or many cells. For example, say you have the worksheet shown in Figure 13-5, which lists a range of products with their prices and sales. Column D needs to show the total revenue derived by multiplying the Units figure by the Price value.

	D2	▾		f_x	=B2*C2	
	A	B	C	D	E	
1	**Product**	**Units**	**Price**	**Total**		
2	Emulator	915	$39.99	$36,590.85		
3	Virtualizer	638	$4.99			
4	Video Mule	18	$189.99			
5	Q Leader	1827	$19.99			
6						

Figure 13-5. When a worksheet needs similar formulas in a column or row, you can enter one formula manually and then use AutoFill or Copy and Paste to enter it quickly in the other cells.

Each cell in column D needs a different formula: Cell D2 needs =B2*C2, Cell D3 needs =B3*C3, and so on. Because the formula is the same except for the row number, you can use either AutoFill or Copy and Paste to enter the formula from cell D2 into the other cells as well.

To enter the formula using AutoFill, click the cell that contains the formula (here, cell D2), and then drag the AutoFill handle (the heavy black square at the lower-right corner of the active cell) down through cell D5. Excel automatically fills in the formulas, adjusting each for the change in row.

To enter the formula using Copy and Paste, click the cell that contains the formula, and then give the Copy command (for example, press Ctrl+C.). Select the destination cells, and then give the Paste command (for example, press Ctrl+V).

■ **Note** If you need to copy a formula to a different row or column but have it refer to the original location, create the formula using mixed references. If you need to keep the column the same, make the column absolute (for example, **=$B2**); if you need to keep the row the same, make the row absolute (for example, **=B$2**).

Troubleshooting Common Problems with Formulas

Formulas are great when they work, but a single-letter typo or a wrong reference can prevent a formula from working correctly. This section shows you how to deal with common problems with formulas, starting with solutions to the error messages you're most likely to produce.

Understanding Common Errors—and Resolving Them

Excel includes an impressive arsenal of error messages, but some of them appear far more frequently than others. Table 13-3 shows you eight errors you're likely to encounter, explains what they mean, and tells you how to solve them.

Table 13-3. *How to Solve Excel's Eight Most Common Errors*

Error	What the Problem Is	How to Solve It
#####	The formula result is too wide to fit in the cell.	Make the column wider—for example, double-click the column head's right border to AutoFit the column width.
#NAME?	A function name is misspelled, or the formula refers to a range that doesn't exist.	Check the spelling of all functions; correct any mistakes. If the formula uses a named range, check that the name is right, and that you haven't deleted the range.
#NUM!	The formula tries to use a value that is not valid for it—for example, returning the square root of a negative number.	Give the function a suitable value.
#VALUE!	The function uses an invalid argument—for example, using =FACT() to return the factorial of text rather than a number.	Give the function the right type of data.
#N/A	The function does not have a valid value available.	Make sure the function's arguments provide values of the right type.
#DIV/0	The function is trying to divide by zero (which is mathematically impossible).	Change the divisor value from zero. Often, you'll find that the function is using a blank cell (which has a zero value) as the argument for the divisor; in this case, enter a value in the cell.

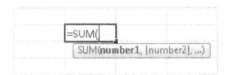

Figure 13-12. When you enter a function in a cell, Excel prompts you to supply the arguments it needs.

The ScreenTip shows that the SUM() function has one required argument, one optional argument. and that you can add further arguments as needed:

- *Required argument:* Each required argument appears in boldface, like the argument *number1* in the ScreenTip. You separate the arguments with commas. For example, you can use SUM() to add the values of cells in a range: SUM(C1:C10).

- *Optional argument:* Each optional argument appears in brackets, like the argument *[number2]* in the ScreenTip. For example, you can use SUM() to add the values of two cells: SUM(C1,C3).

- *Extra arguments:* The ellipsis (…) shows that you can enter extra arguments of the same type. For example, you can use SUM() to add the values of many cells: SUM(C1,C3,D4,D8,E1,XF202).

■ **Note** A few functions take no arguments. For example, you don't need to tell the TODAY() function which day you're talking about. Similarly, the NOW() function needs to arguments to return the current date and time, and the NA() function simply enters #(N/A) in a cell to indicate that the information is not available.

Inserting Functions with the Function Drop-Down List

The quickest and easiest way to enter any of five widely used functions—SUM(), AVERAGE(), COUNT(), MAX(), or MIN()—in your worksheets is to use the Function drop-down list in the Editing group of the Home tab of the Ribbon. Follow these steps:

1. Click the cell you want to enter the function in.

2. Choose Home ➤ Editing ➤ Function (click the drop-down button to the right of the AutoSum button), and then click the function (see Figure 13-13).

■ **Note** You can also use the Function drop-down list to launch the Insert Function dialog box. Just click the More Functions item at the bottom of the drop-down list.

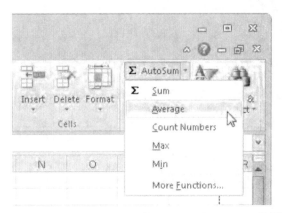

Figure 13-13. Use the Function drop-down list in the Editing group of the Home tab when you need to insert the SUM(), AVERAGE(), COUNT(), MAX(), or MIN() function quickly.

3. Excel inserts the function in the cell you chose and selects the range it thinks you may want to use as the argument. Figure 13-14 shows an example with the AVERAGE() function.

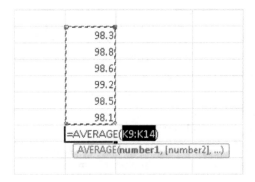

Figure 13-14. When you insert a function from the Function drop-down list, Excel selects a range of data it thinks may be suitable.

4. If you need to change the range, do so in one of these ways:

   • Click and drag to select the right range.

   • Type the range over the range selected within the parentheses.

5. Add another argument to the formula if needed. For example, type a comma, and then click and drag to select another range.

6. When the formula is as you want it, press Enter to enter it in the cell. Excel displays the result of the formula.

Finding the Functions You Need with the Insert Function Dialog Box

Excel includes more than 500 functions that cover a wide variety of needs—everything from calculations that almost everyone uses (such as the SUM() function) to highly specialized functions for statistics (such as the CHISQ.DIST.RT() function for returning the right-tailed probability of the chi-squared distribution) and engineering (such as the various Bessel functions).

When you need to find a function but don't know its name, use the Insert Function dialog box to search for the function. Follow these steps:

1. Open the Insert Function dialog box (see Figure 13-15) in either of these ways:

    •   Choose Home ➤ Editing ➤ Function ➤ More Functions.

    •   Choose Formulas ➤ Function Library ➤ Insert Function.

    •   Open any of the drop-down lists in the Function Library group on the Formulas tab of the Ribbon (except the More Functions drop-down list), and then click the More Functions item that appears at the bottom.

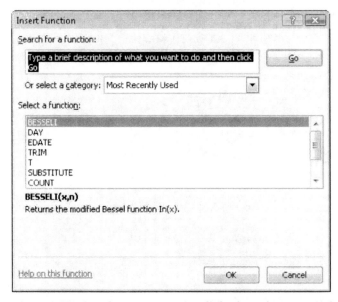

Figure 13-15. *Use the Insert Function dialog box when you need to search for a function by name or description.*

2. With the Insert Function dialog box open, type your search terms in the Search for a Function box, and then press Enter or click the Go button. In the Select a Function list box, click the function you want. When you select a function, Excel displays details of what the function does, so you can tell whether you've made the right choice.

■ **Note** You can also browse for a function by opening the Or select a category drop-down list and choosing the category of function you want. This is sometimes useful, but if you want to view functions by category, the drop-down lists in the Function Library group on the Formulas tab of the Ribbon are usually faster and easier.

---

3. When you've found the function you need, click the OK button. Excel closes the Insert Function dialog box and displays the Function Arguments dialog box. You can then enter the arguments for the function as discussed in the section "Providing the Arguments for the Function," later in this chapter.

Inserting Functions with the Function Library

The third way of inserting functions is to use the controls in the Function Library group on the Formulas tab of the Ribbon. The Function Library group (see Figure 13-16) breaks the functions down into the following categories:

- *AutoSum*: Open this drop-down list when you want to insert one of the five frequently used functions that appears in the Function drop-down list in the Editing group of the Home tab: SUM(), AVERAGE(), COUNT(), MAX(), or MIN(). This drop-down list appears here for convenience.

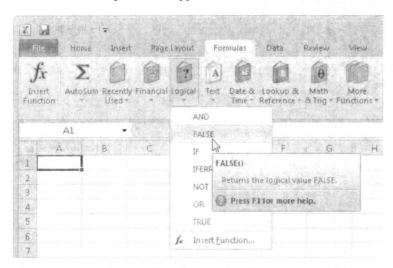

Figure 13-16. Use the controls in the Function Library group on the Formulas tab of the Ribbon to insert functions by category.

- *Recently Used*: Open this drop-down list when you need a function you've used recently. Many spreadsheets need only a small number of different functions, so this list can be a great time-saver if you use it whenever possible.

- *Financial*: Open this drop-down list to insert financial functions; for example, to calculate the payments on your mortgage or the depreciation on an asset. (There are more cheerful financial functions too.)

- *Logical*: Open this drop-down list to insert the AND(), FALSE(), IF(), IFERROR(), NOT(), OR(), and TRUE() functions.

- *Text*: Open this drop-down list to insert functions for manipulating text, such as the TRIM() function (for trimming off leading and trailing spaces) and the LEFT() function, which returns the leftmost part of the value.

- *Date & Time*: Open this drop-down list to insert date and time functions—everything from returning the current date with the TODAY() function to using the WEEKDAY() function to return the day of the week for a particular date.

- *Lookup & Reference*: Open this drop-down list to insert functions for looking up data from other parts of a worksheet or referring to other cells in it.

- *Math & Trig*: Open this drop-down list to insert mathematical functions, such as the SQRT() function for returning a square root, and trigonometric functions, such as the COS() function for calculating a cosine.

- *More Functions*: Open this drop-down menu to reach submenus for the following:

  - *Statistical*: Open this submenu to reach Excel's statistical functions, such as those for calculating standard deviations based on a population or a sample.

  - *Engineering*: Open this submenu to get to the engineering functions, such as the DEC2HEX() function (for converting a decimal number to hexadecimal) and the HEX2OCT() function (for converting a hexadecimal number to octal, base 8).

  - *Cube*: Open this submenu to access functions for working with data cubes.

  - *Information*: Open this submenu to access functions for returning information about data, such as whether it is text or a number.

  - *Compatibility*: Open this submenu to find functions included for compatibility with Excel 2007 (Windows), Excel 2008 (Mac), and earlier versions. It's best to use these functions only for compatibility with these older versions; if you're developing worksheets for Excel 2010 or Excel 2011 (Mac), use the newer functions that these versions support—for example, use the new POISSON.DIST() function rather than the old POISSON() function.

You can hold the mouse pointer over a function's name to see a ScreenTip explaining briefly what the function does. When you've found the function you want, click it. Excel then displays the Function Arguments dialog box, in which you work as described in the next section.

Providing the Arguments for the Function

Whether you use the Insert Function dialog box or one of the drop-down lists in the Function Library to identify the function, Excel displays the Function Arguments dialog box. Figure 13-17 shows the Function Arguments dialog box for the NETWORKDAYS() function, which you use to calculate the net number of working days between two dates.

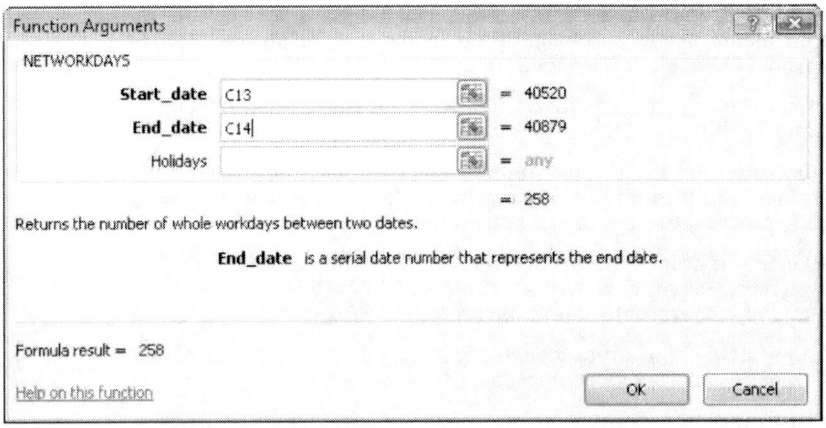

Figure 13-17. Provide the data for each argument in the Function Arguments dialog box. The boldface arguments are required, whereas those in regular font are optional.

■ **Note** If you choose a function that takes no arguments, Excel displays a smaller version of the Function Arguments dialog box telling you so. Click the OK button to insert the function.

Enter the data for each required argument (shown in boldface) and for each optional argument (shown in regular font) you decide to use. For each, you can type a value into the box, type a cell reference or range, or use the mouse to choose the appropriate cell or range in the worksheet. For the last, you can either click the Collapse Dialog button at the right end of the box to move the Function Arguments dialog box out of the way, or simply work around it.

The readout to the right of each box shows the value you've provided, and (when you've provided enough data) the Formula result readout in the lower-left corner shows the result.

Click the OK button to close the Function Arguments dialog box and insert the function in the cell.

■ **Note** To edit a function you've inserted in the worksheet, click the cell, and then choose Formulas ➤ Function Library ➤ Insert Function. Excel displays the Function Arguments dialog box, and you can edit the function as before. For quick fixes, you can also double-click the cell that contains the function, and then edit it right in the cell.

Inserting Functions by Typing Them into a Worksheet

You can also enter functions in your worksheets by typing them into cells. Follow these general steps:

1. Click the cell to select it.

2. Type = to tell Excel that you're creating a formula.

3. Start typing the function's name. Excel displays a list of matching functions (see Figure 13-18).

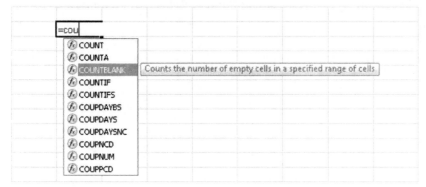

Figure 13-18. When you start typing a function name into a cell, Excel lists matching functions. Select a function to display a ScreenTip explaining it.

■ **Note** You can also keep typing until you've typed enough to identify the function uniquely—or type the whole of the function name if you prefer.

---

4. To view a ScreenTip giving details of a function, press Down arrow or Up arrow to move the highlight to it.

5. To enter a function, move the highlight to it by pressing Down arrow or Up arrow, and then press Enter. Alternatively, double-click the function.

6. Specify the arguments for the function. As you learned earlier in this chapter, you can either type in a value or a reference, or use the mouse to select a cell or range.

Summary

In this chapter, you've learned how to use formulas and functions to perform calculations in your workbooks. You know that a formula is the recipe for a calculation, and you know how to assemble it from its various components—an equal sign, cell or range references, operators, and more. You know how to create the formulas you need, and how to troubleshoot them when they go wrong.

You're now also familiar with functions. You know that a function is a preset formula built into Excel, how to insert functions from the Ribbon or by typing them into cells, and how to furnish functions with the arguments they need to work.

In the next chapter, I'll show you how to create powerful and persuasive charts from your data.

- *Depth axis*: In 3-D charts, this is the axis that provides the third dimension. This axis is also called the *Z-axis*.

Each axis has tick marks that show where the values appear on it.

Categories and Data Series

The *categories* are the subdivisions of data that appear on the horizontal axis. For example, in the sample chart, each weather station is a category.

The *data series* are the sets of data used to create the chart. For example, in the sample chart, the data series contain the rainfall measurements.

Chart Title and Axis Titles

The *chart title* is text that identifies the chart as a whole. Normally, you put the chart title at the top of the chart, but you can place it elsewhere if you want.

The *horizontal axis title* is text that explains what is shown on the horizontal axis; for example, the weather stations in the sample chart.

The *vertical axis title* is text that explains what the vertical axis shows; for example, the amount of rainfall in the sample chart.

A 3-D chart can also have a *depth axis title* that explains what the depth axis shows.

■ **Note** Chart titles and axis titles are optional, so you can include only those your chart needs. Generally, people viewing your charts will benefit from having clear chart titles and axis titles.

Data Markers, Gridlines, and Data Labels

The *data markers* are the points on the chart that show where each data point appears. Each series typically contains several data markers. Depending on the chart type, the data markers may appear as separate points, or they may be linked together.

To make it easy to see how the data markers relate to the axes, you can add *gridlines* to the chart—lines that run across or up from the data markers.

Data labels are text items that display the exact value of data points. You can display data labels when viewers need to see the exact figure for each data point rather than judging the value from the chart.

Understanding Excel's Chart Types and Choosing Which to Use

Excel enables you to create an impressive variety of different types of charts. Some of the charts are widely useful, whereas others are highly specialized. Table 14-1 describes the types of charts that Excel provides and suggests typical uses for them. The table lists the charts in the same order as Excel's Insert Chart dialog box, which you'll meet shortly and which puts the most widely used chart types first.

Table 14-1. Excel's Chart Types and Suggested Uses

Chart Category	Description	Suggested Uses
Column	Displays data in vertical bars.	Comparing equivalent items (such as sales results) or sets of data that change over time (such as rainfall).
Line	Displays each series in a line.	Showing evenly spaced values that change over time, such as temperatures.
Pie	Displays a single data series as a pie divided up by the contribution of each data point.	Showing how much each item contributes to the whole; for example, breaking down expenses by department.
Bar	Displays data in horizontal bars.	Comparing similar items or indicating progress.
Area	Displays data as lines but with the areas between them shaded.	Showing how values have changed over time, especially the contribution of different data points in the series.
X Y (Scatter)	Displays each data point as a point (or cross, or similar marker) on the plot area.	Showing values sampled at different times or that are not directly related to each other.
Stock	Displays each data series as a vertical line or bar indicating three or more prices or measurements (for example, high, low, and closing prices).	Showing the daily prices of stocks. Also suitable for some scientific data.
Surface	Displays the data points as a three-dimensional surface.	Comparing two sets of data to find a suitable combination of them.
Doughnut	Displays the data series as a sequence of concentric rings.	Showing how much each item contributes to the whole—like a pie chart, but it works with two or more data series.
Bubble	Displays the data points as bubbles of different sizes depending on their values.	Showing the relative importance of each data point.
Radar	Displays the combined values of different data series.	Showing how the combined values of separate data series compare to each other; for example, the sales contributions of several different products over several periods of time.

Creating, Laying Out, and Formatting a Chart

In this section, you'll look at how to create a chart from your data, lay it out with the components and arrangement you want, and apply the most useful types of formatting.

Creating a Chart

The easiest way to create a chart in Excel is to use the controls in the Charts group of the Insert tab of the Ribbon. Follow these steps:

1. Select the data that you want to chart, including any row or column headings needed. For example, click the first cell in the data range, and then Shift+click the last cell.

■ **Tip** You can create a chart from either a block range or from a range of separate cells. To use separate cells, select them as usual—for example, click the first, and then Ctrl+click each of the others.

---

2. Click the Insert tab of the Ribbon, and then click the appropriate button in the Charts group: Column, Line, Pie, Bar, Area, Scatter, or Other Charts (which contains the Stock, Surface, Doughnut, Bubble, and Radar chart types).

3. On the panel that opens, click the chart type you want. Figure 14-4 shows the Column panel, which is one of the most widely useful.

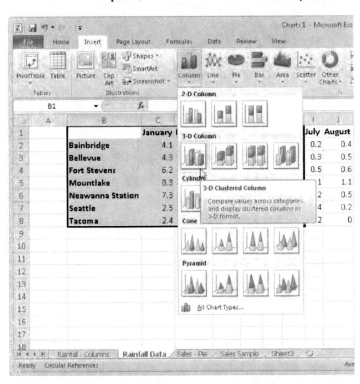

Figure 14-4. The quick way to insert a chart is to click the appropriate drop-down button in the Charts group on the Insert tab of the Ribbon, and then click the chart type you want.

Excel creates the chart as an embedded chart in the current worksheet. If you need to move the chart to a different position, click it and drag it by the border. If you need to move the chart to its own chart sheet, do so as discussed in the next section.

If you prefer to browse through the various types of charts available, use the Insert Chart dialog box rather than the Charts group. Follow these steps:

1. Select the data you want to create the chart from.

2. Choose Insert ➤ Charts ➤ Create Chart (click the little button in the lower-right corner of the Charts group) to display the Insert Chart dialog box (see Figure 14-5).

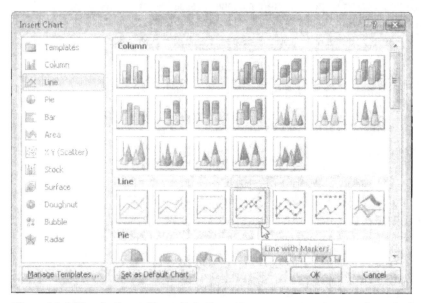

Figure 14-5. Use the Insert Chart dialog box when you want to browse through the many types of charts that Excel offers.

3. In the left column, click the category of charts you want to view. For example, click Column to view the Column chart category, or click Line to view the Line chart category. If you prefer, you can simply scroll down the contents of the dialog box by using the scroll bar on the right.

4. To see the description of a chart type, hold the mouse pointer over it until Excel displays a ScreenTip.

5. Click the chart you want.

6. Click the OK button to close the Insert Chart dialog box. Excel inserts the chart on the active worksheet as an embedded chart.

After inserting the chart, you can reposition it, resize it, or move it as needed:

- *Reposition the chart*: If you want to keep the chart as an embedded chart, move the mouse pointer over the chart border so that it turns to a four-headed arrow, and then drag the chart to where you want it.

- *Resize the chart*: Click to select the chart, and then drag one of the handles that appear. Drag a corner handle to resize the chart in both dimensions; you can Shift+drag to resize the chart proportionally. Drag a side handle to resize the chart in only that dimension; for example, drag the bottom handle to resize the chart only vertically.

- *Move the chart to a chart sheet*: If you want to move the chart to a chart sheet, follow the instructions in the next section.

Changing a Chart from an Embedded Chart to a Chart Sheet

You can change a chart from being embedded in a worksheet to being on its own chart sheet like this:

1. Click the chart on the worksheet it's embedded in.

2. Choose Chart Tools ➤ Design ➤ Location ➤ Move Chart to display the Move Chart dialog box (see Figure 14-6).

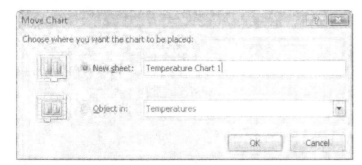

Figure 14-6. Use the Move Chart dialog box to change a chart from being embedded to being on its own chart sheet.

3. Select the New sheet option button.

4. Type the name for the new chart sheet in the New sheet text box.

5. Click the OK button. Excel creates the new chart sheet and moves the chart to it.

■ **Note** You can also use the Chart Tools ➤ Design ➤ Location ➤ Move Chart command to move a chart from a chart sheet to an embedded chart on a worksheet, or to move an embedded chart from one worksheet to another.

Changing the Chart Type

If you realize that the chart type you've chosen doesn't work for your data, you can change the chart type easily. Follow these steps:

1. Right-click the chart and then click Change Chart Type on the context menu to display the Change Chart Type dialog box. This dialog box is the same as the Insert Chart dialog box except for its name.

▓ **Note** To open the Change Chart Type dialog box, you can also click the chart and then choose Chart Tools ➤ Design ➤ Type ➤ Change Chart Type.

---

2. In the left column, click the chart type you want.

3. In the main area, click the chart subtype.

4. Click the OK button to close the Change Chart Type dialog box. Excel applies the different chart type to the chart.

Switching the Rows and Columns in a Chart

When Excel displays the chart, you may realize that the data series are in the wrong place; for example, the chart is displaying months by rainfall instead of rainfall by months.

When this happens, there's a quick fix: Switch the rows and columns by choosing Chart Tools ➤ Design ➤ Data ➤ Switch Row/Column. Excel displays the chart with the series the other way around.

Changing the Source Data for a Chart

Sometimes you may find that your chart doesn't work well with the source data you've chosen. For example, you may have selected so much data that the chart is crowded, or you may have missed a vital row or column.

When this happens, you don't need to delete the chart and start again from scratch. Instead, follow these steps:

1. Choose Chart Tools ➤ Design ➤ Data ➤ Select Data to display the Select Data Source dialog box (see Figure 14-7).

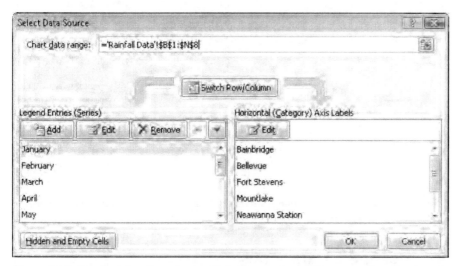

Figure 14-7. Use the Select Data Source dialog box to change the source data the chart is using.

2. In the Chart data range box, enter the data range you want to use:

- Usually, it's easiest to click the Collapse Dialog button to collapse the dialog box, drag on the worksheet to select the right data range, and then click the Collapse Dialog button again to restore the dialog box. (Or you can just work around the Select Data Source dialog box if you prefer.)

- You can also type the data range in the Chart data range box. This is easy when you just need to change a column letter or row number to fix the data range.

3. If you need to switch the rows and columns as well, click the Switch Row/Column button.

4. Click the OK button to close the Select Data Source dialog box. Excel applies the changes to the chart.

Choosing the Layout for the Chart

When you've sorted out the chart type and the source data, it's time to choose the layout for the chart. For each chart type, Excel has a number of preset layouts that control where the title, legend, and other elements appear. After applying a layout, you can customize it further as needed.

To apply a layout, click the chart and choose Chart Tools ➤ Design ➤ Chart Layouts ➤ More (clicking the drop-down button on the Quick Layout box). On the Quick Layout panel that Excel displays (see Figure 14-8), click the layout you want to apply to the chart.

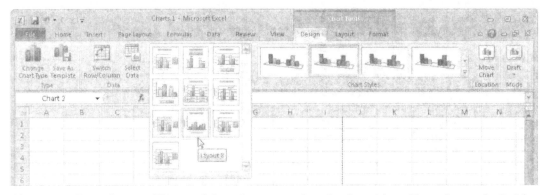

Figure 14-8. To set the overall layout of chart elements, such as the chart title and legend, open the Quick Layout panel and click the layout you want.

Changing the Order of the Data Series

When you create a chart, Excel lays out the data series in the order in which they appear in the source data. Often, this works well, but for some charts, you may want to change the order in which they appear. For example, you may want to place a standout result in the middle of the chart to make the contrast with the other results clearer, or you may want to give elbow room to a modest data point that's crowded by larger neighbors.

One possibility is to go to the data source and shift the columns or rows around so that when Excel automatically updates the chart to reflect the data, the chart appears the way you want it. Often this messes up your data, and it's better to change the way the chart uses the data without changing the data itself.

To change the order of the data series at the chart end, follow these steps:

1. Click the chart to select it.

2. Choose Chart Tools ➤ Design ➤ Data ➤ Select Data to display the Select Data Source dialog box.

3. In the Legend Entries (Series) list box, click the series you want to move.

4. Click the Move Up button to move the series up the list or the Move Down button to move it down the list. (The Move Up button and Move Down button are the two arrow buttons to the right of the Remove button.) Excel rearranges the chart so that you can see what you're doing.

5. When you've finished rearranging the data series, click the OK button to close the Select Source Data dialog box.

Adding a Separate Data Series to a Chart

Sometimes you may find you need to add to a chart a data series that doesn't appear in the chart's source data; for example, to add projections of future success to your current data.

To add a data series, work from the Select Data Source dialog box. Follow these steps.

1. Click the chart to select it.

- *Major unit*: To have Excel decide the interval between major units on the axis, select the Auto option button. To set it yourself, select the Fixed option button, and then type the value in the box. Depending on how big your chart is, you'll probably want between five and ten major units on the scale you've set by choosing the Minimum value and Maximum value.

- *Minor unit*: To have Excel decide the interval between minor units on the axis, select the Auto option button. To set it yourself, select the Fixed option button, and then type the value in the box. You'll normally want between four and ten minor units per major unit, depending on what the chart shows.

- *Values in reverse order*: For some charts, it's helpful to have the values run in reverse order; for example, lowest values at the top instead of the highest. When you need this setup, select this check box.

- *Logarithmic scale*: If you need the chart to use a logarithmic scale rather than an arithmetic scale, select the Logarithmic scale check box, and then enter the logarithm base in the Base box. For example, enter 10 to have the scale use the values 1, 10, 100, 1000, 10000, and so on at regular intervals.

- *Display units*: If you want the chart to show units—Hundreds, Thousands, Millions, and so on—select the unit in this drop-down list. Excel reduces the figures shown accordingly; for example, 1000000 appears as 1, with Millions next to the scale. This helps make the axis easier to read.

3. In the second section, set up the positioning of the tick marks:

- *Major tick mark type*: In this drop-down list, choose Inside to have the tick marks appear inside the chart, Outside to have them appear outside (on the axis side), or Cross to have them appear on both sides. Choose None if you do not want major tick marks.

- *Minor tick mark type*: In this drop-down list, choose how you want minor tick marks to appear—Outside, Inside, Cross, or None.

- *Axis labels*: Choose Next to Axis to have the labels appear next to the axis. Choose High to have the labels appear on the high side of the chart, or choose Low to have them appear on the low side. Choose None to suppress the labels.

4. In the bottom section, choose where to have the horizontal axis cross the vertical axis:

- *Automatic*: Select this option button to have Excel decide. If your chart looks right with Excel's choice, there's no reason to change it.

- *Axis value*: Select this option button if you need to control where the axis crosses. Type the value in the box. For example, for some charts, it's helpful to have the horizontal axis cross at a negative value.

- *Maximum axis value*: Select this option button to make Excel place the horizontal axis at the maximum value.

- When you're satisfied with the axis, click the Close button to close the Format Axis dialog box.

Adding a Legend to a Chart

Many charts benefit from having a legend that summarizes the colors used for different data series. You can add a legend by selecting the chart, choosing Chart Tools ➤ Layout ➤ Labels ➤ Legend, and then clicking the placement you want: Show Legend at Right, Show Legend at Top, Show Legend at Left, Show Legend at Bottom, Overlay Legend at Right, or Overlay Legend at Left.

Each of the "Show" items reduces the chart area to make space for the legend. The two "Overlay" items place the legend on the chart without reducing its size, so they're good for keeping the chart as large as possible.

Whichever placement you use for the legend, you can drag it to a better position as needed. You can also resize the legend by clicking it and then dragging one of the handles that appear around it.

If you need to remove a legend from a chart, either click the legend and then press Delete, or choose Chart Tools ➤ Layout ➤ Labels ➤ Legend ➤ None.

Adding Axis Labels from a Range Separate from the Chart Data

Depending on how the worksheet containing the source data is laid out, you may need to add axis labels that are in separate cells from the chart data. To do this, follow these steps:

1. Click the chart to select it.

2. Choose Chart Tools ➤ Design ➤ Data ➤ Select Data to display the Select Data Source dialog box.

3. On the right side, under Horizontal (Category) Axis Labels, click the Edit button to display the Axis Labels dialog box (see Figure 14-12).

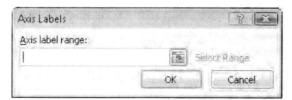

Figure 14-12. Use the Axis Labels dialog box to enter labels in a range that's separate from the chart data.

4. In the Axis label range box, enter the labels by clicking and dragging in the worksheet. (You can click the Collapse Dialog button first, but the Axis Labels dialog box is so small this is hardly worth doing.)

5. Click the OK button to close the Axis Labels dialog box. Excel enters the labels in the Horizontal (Category) Axis Labels box.

6. Click the OK button to close the Select Data Source dialog box. Excel applies the labels to the axis.

Adding Data Labels to the Chart

If viewers will need to see the precise value of data points rather than just getting a general idea of their value, add data labels to the chart. To do so, click the chart, and then choose Chart Tools ➤ Layout ➤ Labels ➤ Data Labels ➤ Show.

■ **Caution** Use data labels sparingly. Only some charts benefit from data labels—other charts may become too busy, or having the details may distract the audience from the overall thrust of the chart.

When you add data labels to a chart, Excel displays a data label for each data marker. If you want to display only some data labels, delete the ones you don't need. To delete a data marker, click it, and then either press Delete or right-click the selection and click Delete on the context menu.

Choosing Which Gridlines to Display

On many types of charts, you can choose whether to display horizontal and vertical gridlines to help the viewer judge how the data points relate to each other and to the axes.

To control which gridlines appear, follow these steps:

1. Select the chart.

2. Choose Chart Tools ➤ Layout ➤ Axes ➤ Gridlines, then click Primary Horizontal Gridlines, Primary Vertical Gridlines, or Depth Gridlines to display the appropriate submenu.

3. Click the menu item for the type of gridlines you want to display:

   - *None*: Click this item to suppress the display of gridlines.

   - *Major Gridlines*: Click this item to display only gridlines at the major divisions in the data series. For example, if your data is in the range 0–25, major gridlines normally appear at 5, 10, 15, 20, and 25.

■ **Tip** When the viewer needs to see clearly where each value falls, use either data labels or major and minor gridlines. If using minor gridlines (with oi without major gridlines) makes the chart look cluttered, use only major gridlines. Normally, it's best not to use both horizontal and vertical minor gridlines, as they tend to make charts look confusingly busy—but sometimes your charts may need them.

   - *Minor Gridlines*: Click this item to display gridlines at the minor divisions in the data series. For example, if your data is in the range 0–25, minor gridlines normally appear at each integer—1, 2, 3, and so on up to 24 and 25.

   - *Major and Minor Gridlines*: Click this item to display both major and minor gridlines. The major gridlines appear darker than the minor gridlines, so that you can see the difference between them. Having both major and minor gridlines is usually clearer than having only minor gridlines.

4. Repeat steps 2 and 3 for each other set of gridlines the chart needs.

> ▪ **Note** To change the values at which the gridlines appear, format the axis, as described in the section "Changing the Scale or Numbering of an Axis," earlier in this chapter.

Formatting a Chart Wall and Chart Floor

Some charts look fine with a plain background, but for 3-D charts, you may want to decorate the chart walls (the areas at the back and the side of the chart) and the chart floor (the area at the bottom of the chart). You can add a solid color, a gradient, a picture, or a texture to the walls, the floor, or both. Figure 14-13 shows a chart that uses a picture for the walls.

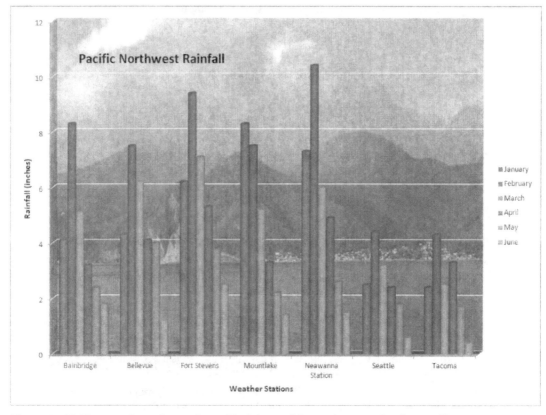

Figure 14-13. You can give a chart a themed look by applying a picture to the chart walls.

▨ **Tip** Usually, the chart walls and floors are the elements that look best with a custom fill (such as a picture). But you can apply a custom fill to many other chart elements as well. To do so, display the Format dialog box for the element, click the Fill category in the left pane, and then make your choices.

To format the chart wall or the chart floor, follow these steps:

1. Click the chart to select it.

2. Choose Chart Tools ➤ Layout ➤ Current Selection ➤ Chart Elements, and then click the item you want to format: Back Wall, Floor, Side Wall, or Walls (to format both the back wall and the side wall).

3. Click the Format Selection button in the Current Selection group to display the Format dialog box for the item you selected. Figure 14-14 shows the Format Walls dialog box with the controls for inserting a picture fill displayed.

Figure 14-14. Use the Fill pane in the Format dialog box to apply a picture fill to objects such as the chart walls or floor.

4. Make sure the Fill item is selected in the left pane.

5. In the Fill pane, set up the fill you want:

   - *No fill*: Select this option button to remove the existing fill.

   - *Solid fill*: Select this option button, and then choose the color in the Color drop-down panel. Drag the Transparency slider to choose how transparent the fill is.

   - *Gradient fill*: Select the Gradient fill option button, and then use the controls in the bottom part of the pane to choose the fill colors, direction, brightness, and transparency.

   - *Picture or texture fill*: Select the Picture or texture fill option button. To use a texture, choose it from the Texture drop-down palette. To use a picture, click the File button, choose the picture in the Insert Picture dialog box, and then click the Insert button. To use clip art, click the Clip Art button, search for and click the picture in the Select Picture dialog box, and then click the OK button.

   - *Pattern fill*: Select the Pattern fill option button, and then click the pattern in the box that appears. Choose the colors in the Foreground Color drop-down panel and the Background Color drop-down panel.

6. Click the Close button to close the Format dialog box.

Naming an Embedded Chart

To make an embedded chart easy to identify within a workbook, you can give it a name. This is useful when you need to refer clearly to the chart, either when discussing it with your colleagues or when you're using Office's programming language, Visual Basic for Applications (VBA), to manipulate it.

To rename an embedded chart, click the chart, then choose Chart Tools ➤ Layout ➤ Properties ➤ Chart Name. Type the new name in the Chart Name text box, and then press Enter.

■ **Note** Excel identifies a chart on a chart sheet by the chart sheet's name. So if you rename your chart sheets (rather than letting Excel name them Chart1, Chart2, and so on), you also rename the charts.

Formatting Individual Chart Elements

You can format any of the individual elements of a chart—for example, the legend, the gridlines, or the data labels—by selecting it and then using its Format dialog box. This dialog box includes the name of the element it affects: the Format Data Labels dialog box, the Format Plot Area dialog box, and so on.

You can display the Format dialog box in either of these ways:

- *Right-click the element, and then click the Format item on the context menu*: This is usually the easiest way of opening the Format dialog box.

- Select the element in the Chart Elements drop-down list, and then click the Format Selection button: If you're finding it difficult to right-click the element on the chart (for example, because the chart is busy), choose Chart Tools ➤ Format ➤

Current Selection ➤ Chart Elements, and then click the element you want on the drop-down list. You can then click the Format Selection button (also in the Current Selection group) to open the Format dialog box for the element.

The contents of the Format dialog box vary depending on the object you've selected, but for most objects, you'll find categories such as these:

- *Fill*: You can fill in a solid shape with a solid color, color gradient, picture, or texture. See the section "Formatting a Chart Wall and Chart Floor," earlier in this chapter, for instructions on creating fills.

- *Border Color*: You can give a shape a color border, gradient border, or no line.

- *Border Styles*: You can choose among different border styles, change the border width, and pick a suitable line type.

- *Shadow*: You can add a shadow to the shape, set its color, and adjust its transparency, width, and other properties.

- *Glow and Soft Edges*: You can make an object stand out by giving it a glow, choosing a color that contrasts with the object's surroundings, and choosing how wide the glow should be. You can also apply soft edges to a shape.

- *3-D Format*: You can apply a 3-D format to different aspects of a shape; for example, setting a different bevel for the top and bottom of the shape.

- *3-D Rotation*: You can apply a 3-D rotation to the object.

- *Alignment*: For text objects, you can choose how to align text and whether to rotate it.

If the chart element contains text, you can format it by using the controls on the Home tab of the Ribbon or keyboard shortcuts. For example, to apply boldface to the data labels, click the data labels, and then choose Home ➤ Font ➤ Bold (or press Ctrl+B).

▓ **Tip** To restore an element to its original formatting, select the element either by clicking it on the chart or by using the Chart Elements drop-down list. Then choose Chart Tools ➤ Format ➤ Current Selection ➤ Reset to Match Style.

Copying Chart Formatting

After you set up a chart with all the formatting you need, you can apply that formatting to another chart by using Copy and Paste. Follow these steps:

1. Click the formatted chart to select its chart area.

2. Right-click the border of the chart, and then click Copy on the context menu to copy the chart and its formatting to the Clipboard.

3. Go to the sheet that contains the chart onto which you want to paste the formatting.

4. Choose Home ➤ Clipboard ➤ Paste ➤ Paste Special to display the Paste Special dialog box.

5. Select the Formats option button.

6. Click the OK button to close the Paste Special dialog box. Excel applies the formatting to the chart.

Reusing Your Own Designs by Creating Custom Chart Types

If you want to be able to reuse a chart design you've created, you can turn it into a custom chart type. Follow these steps:

1. Select the formatted chart either on a chart sheet or on a worksheet.

2. Choose Chart Tool ➤ Design ➤ Type ➤ Save As Template to display the Save Chart Template dialog box. This is a standard Save As dialog box.

3. If you want, change the folder in which to save the chart type. Excel suggests using the Templates\Charts folder in your user profile. This is good for a template only you will use, but if your colleagues will need to use the template too, you may need to store it in a shared folder on the network.

4. Type a descriptive name for the template in the File name box.

5. Click the Save button to save the Save Chart Template dialog box. Excel saves the template in the folder you chose.

To create a chart based on your template, follow these steps:

1. Select the source data for the chart.

2. Choose Insert ➤ Charts ➤ Create Chart, clicking the little button at the lower-right corner of the Charts group, to display the Insert Chart dialog box.

3. In the left pane, click the Templates item to display the My Templates category.

4. Click the template.

5. Click the OK button to close the Insert Chart dialog box. Excel creates the chart.

Summary

In this chapter, you've learned how to create powerful and persuasive charts from your data. You know what the separate components of charts are called, how to create a chart, and how to position it either on a worksheet or on its own chart sheet. You can also make Excel show the components you want for a chart and format them as needed. To save time and effort, you've also learned to reuse your custom chart formatting by either pasting it onto an existing chart or by creating a custom chart template from it.

In the next chapter, I'll show you how use Excel to create powerful databases for storing and manipulating your data. Turn the page when you're ready to start.

CHAPTER 15

Creating and Using
Excel Database Tables

Packed with over sixteen thousand columns and more than a million rows, each Excel worksheet has enough space to contain serious amounts of data—so it's great for creating a database to store information and quickly find the items you need.

In this chapter, you'll learn to use Excel to create databases. Excel refers to databases as *tables*, which can be confusing if you're used to that word's normal meaning in the Office programs. So this chapter refers to these databases as *database tables* for clarity.

The first step is to set up the database table and to tell Excel that you're creating a database table rather than a regular worksheet. The next step is to add your data to the database, either by typing it into the cells as usual or by using a data-entry form.

Once the data is in the database, you can sort the table to reveal different aspects of its contents, or filter it to identify items that match the criteria you specify.

Understanding What You Can and Can't Do with Excel Database Tables

Before you start creating a database table in Excel, it's important to be clear on what you can and can't do with Excel database tables.

As you know, an Excel worksheet consists of rows and columns. To create a database table on a worksheet, you make each row into a *record*—an item that holds all the details of a single entry. For example, in a database table that records your sales to customers, a record would contain the details of a purchase. You make each column a *field* in the database table—a column for the purchase number, a column for the date, a column for the customer's last name, and so on. Figure 15-1 shows part of an Excel database table for tracking sales to customers.

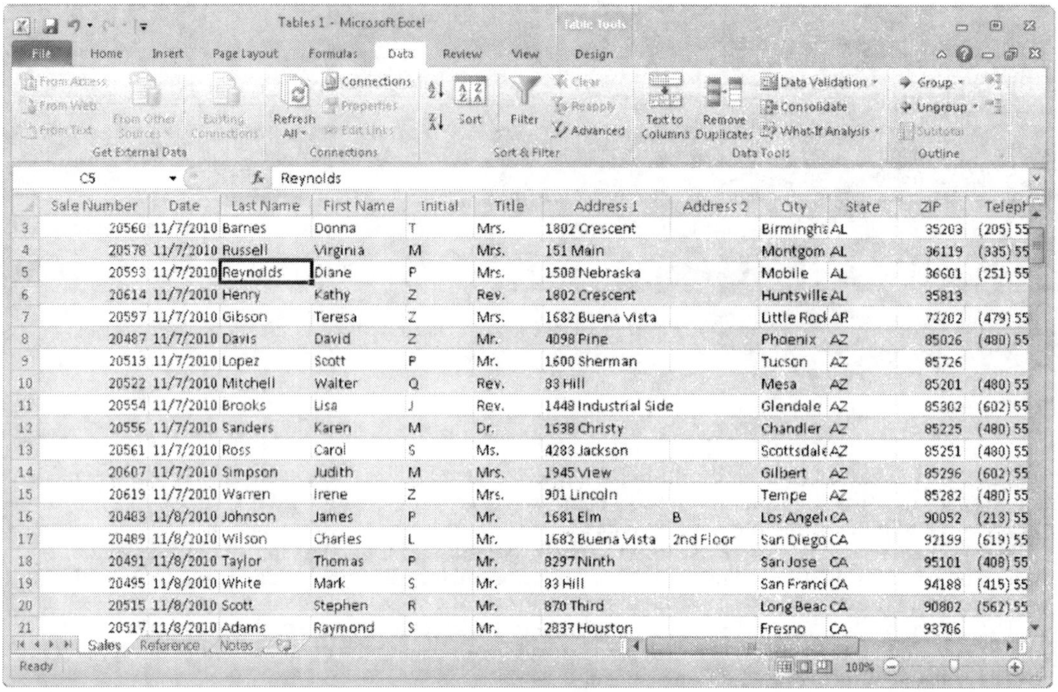

Figure 15-1. *An Excel database consists of a table, with each row forming a record and each column containing a field.*

This is what's called a *flat-file* database: All the data in the database is stored in a single table rather than in separate tables that are linked to each other.

This means that you can use Excel to create any database for which you can store all the data for a record in a single row. Because you've got a million rows at your disposal, you can create large databases if necessary, but they may make Excel run slowly.

What you can't do with Excel is create *relational databases*—ones that store the data in linked tables. A relational database is the kind of database you create with full-bore database programs such as Microsoft Access. In a relational database, every record has a unique ID number or field that the program uses to link the data in the different tables.

Creating a Database Table and Entering Data

In this section, you'll look at how to create a database table and enter data in it by using either standard Excel methods or by using a data-entry form.

Creating a Database Table

To create a database table, follow these steps:

1. Create a workbook as usual. For example, you can:

   - Create a new blank workbook. Press Ctrl+N.

- Create a workbook based on a template or an existing workbook. Choose File ➤ New, and then work in Backstage.

2. Name the worksheet on which you'll create the database table. Double-click the worksheet tab, type the name you want (up to 31 characters, including spaces), and then press Enter to apply the name.

3. Type the headings for the database table. For example, if the database table will contain customer names and addresses, you'd type fields such as Last Name, First Name, Middle Initial, Title, Address 1, and so on.

Note Usually, it's easiest to put the headings in the first row of the worksheet, but if you need to have information appear above the database table, leave rows free for it.

---

4. Select the headings and at least one row below them.

5. Choose Insert ➤ Tables ➤ Table to display the Create Table dialog box (see Figure 15-2).

Figure 15-2. In the Create Table dialog box, make sure that Excel shows the correct range for the database table's data. If your database table has a header row, select the My table has headers check box.

6. Make certain that the Where is the data for your table? box shows the data range you selected. (It always should—but if something has gone wrong, drag in the worksheet to select the correct range.)

7. Make sure that the My table has headers check box is selected (unless you're creating a database table without headers, which is less usual).

8. Click the OK button to close the Create Table dialog box. Excel then does the following:

- Creates the database table and displays the Table Tools section of the Ribbon.

Note When the Table Tools section of the Ribbon isn't displayed, you can display it by clicking in the table.

- Names the database table with a default name, such as Table1 or Table2.

- Turns the header row into headers with drop-down buttons. Excel keeps these headers displayed when you scroll further down the database table—you don't have to freeze the panes the way you do with a regular worksheet.

- Applies a table style with banded shading based on the workbook's theme. You can change these colors later as needed.

9. Choose Table Tools ➤ Design ➤ Properties ➤ Table Name, type the name you want to give the database table instead of the default name, and then press Enter to apply it.

Note As with chart names, the database table name must be unique in the workbook, must start with a letter or an underscore, and cannot contain spaces or symbols.

Figure 15-3 shows a database table with several rows of data added (so that you can see how a database table looks with data in it).

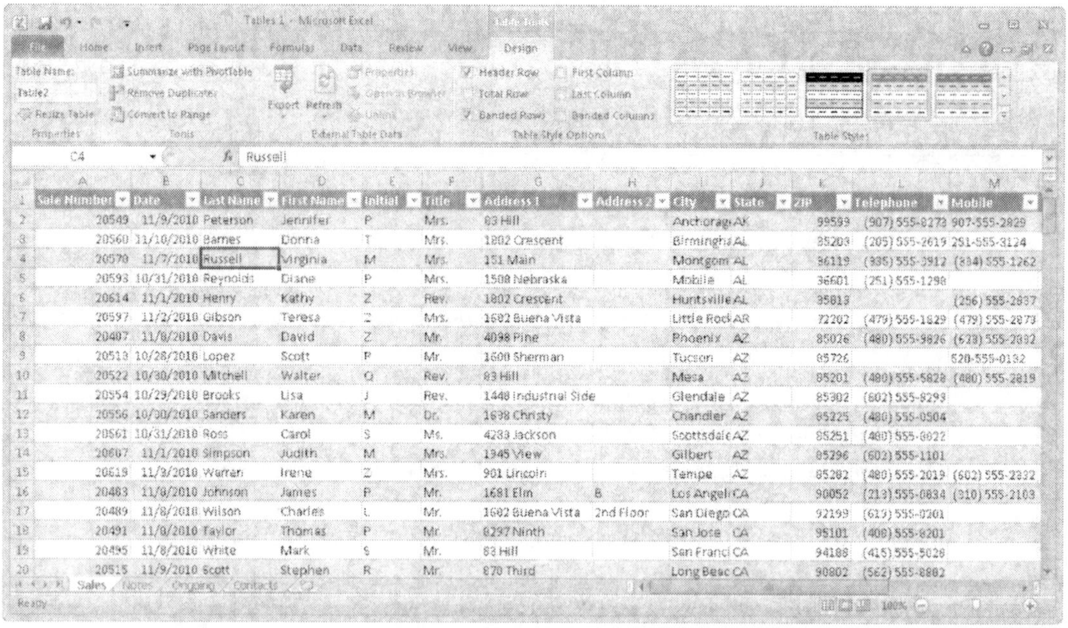

Figure 15-3. *Excel applies a table style based on the workbook's template. You can choose a different style from the Table Styles group on the Design tab in the Table Tools section of the Ribbon.*

Customizing the Database Table's Looks

At this point, you can start entering data in the database table (as discussed next)—but before you do, you may want to change the way it looks. To do so, follow these steps:

1. Click anywhere in the database table to add the Table Tools section to the Ribbon.

2. Choose Table Tools ➤ Design ➤ Table Styles ➤ Quick Styles ➤ More (clicking the drop-down button are the right end of the Quick Styles box) to display the Quick Styles panel.

3. Hold the mouse pointer over a style to preview how it will look applied to the database table.

4. Click the style you want to apply.

5. In the Table Style Options group on the Design tab, select the check box for each table style option you want to use:

    - *Header Row*: Select this check box to display the header row. This is almost always useful.

    - *Total Row*: Select this check box to add a row labeled Total straight after the database table's last row. This is useful when you need to add a total formula or another formula in the last row. To add a formula, click a cell, click the drop-down button that appears (see Figure 15-4), and then click the formula you want on the drop-down list.

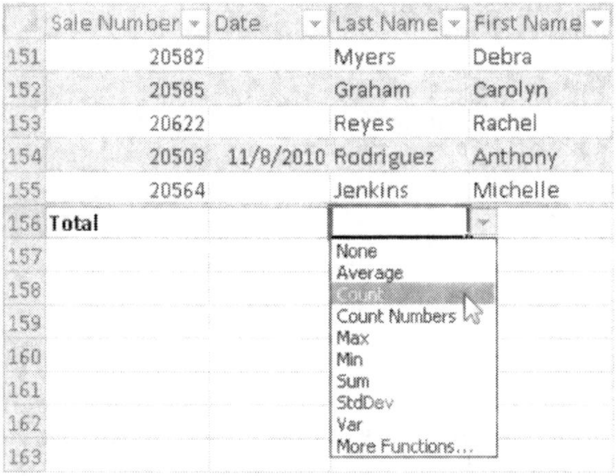

	Sale Number ▼	Date ▼	Last Name ▼	First Name ▼
151	20582		Myers	Debra
152	20585		Graham	Carolyn
153	20622		Reyes	Rachel
154	20503	11/8/2010	Rodriguez	Anthony
155	20564		Jenkins	Michelle
156	**Total**			▼
157			None	
158			Average	
159			Count	
			Count Numbers	
160			Max	
161			Min	
			Sum	
162			StdDev	
			Var	
163			More Functions…	

Figure 15-4. Adding a Total row to a database table lets you quickly insert functions in the row's cells.

Tip The drop-down list in the Total row of a database table gives you instant access to the most widely used functions in databases—Average, Count, Count Numbers, Max, Min, Sum, StdDev (Standard Deviation), or Var (calculating variance based on a sample). You can also click the More Functions item at the bottom of the drop-down list to display the Insert Function dialog box, from which you can access the full range of Excel's functions. For example, you can insert the COUNTBLANK() function to count the number of blank cells in a column. You might do this to ensure that a column of essential data contains no blanks.

- *Banded Rows*: Select this check box to apply a band of color to every other row. This helps you read the rows of data without your eyes wandering to another row.

- *First Column*: Select this check box if you want the first column to have different formatting. You may want to do this if the first column contains the main field for identifying each record (for example, a unique number).

- *Last Column*: Select this check box if you want the last column to have different formatting. Usually, you'll want this only if the last column contains data that is more important in some way than the data in the other columns.

- *Banded Columns*: Select this check box to apply a band of color to every other column. This is sometimes helpful, but usually less helpful than banded rows. (Don't use both—the effect is seldom useful.)

Entering Data in a Database Table

You can enter data in a database table either by typing it in directly or by using a data-entry form. In most cases, the data-entry form is the easier option, as you'll see in a moment.

Entering Data Directly in the Database Table

A database table is essentially an Excel worksheet at heart, so you can enter data in the database table by using the standard techniques you've learned in the last few chapters. In other words, you can click a cell, and then type data into it.

Tip You can quickly select a row, column, or an entire database table with the mouse. To select a row, move the mouse pointer to the left part of a cell in the database table's leftmost column, and then click with the horizontal arrow that appears. To select a column, move the mouse pointer over a column heading, and then click with the downward arrow that appears. To select the whole database table, move the mouse pointer over the upper-left cell in the database table, and then click with the diagonal arrow that appears.

Entering Data Using a Data-Entry Form

Typing directly into the database table tends to be awkward, especially when the database table contains too many columns to fit in the Excel window with the whole content of each column displayed. When your database has grown beyond a few rows, you can usually enter data more easily by using a data form than by typing directly into the database table.

A *data-entry form* may sound forbidding, but it's just a dialog box that Excel automatically tailors to suit your database table. There's one complication, though—Microsoft has chosen to hide the Form command in the Excel interface, so you need to customize Excel to make it available.

ADDING THE FORM COMMAND TO THE QUICK ACCESS TOOLBAR

To add the Form command to the Quick Access Toolbar, follow these steps:

1. Click the Customize Quick Access Toolbar drop-down button at the right end of the Quick Access Toolbar to display the Customize Quick Access Toolbar menu.

2. Click the More Commands item to display the Quick Access Toolbar category in the Excel Options dialog box.

3. In the Customize Quick Access Toolbar drop-down list in the upper-right corner of the Excel Options dialog box, choose For all documents to make this customization available for all your Excel workbooks. (If you want the Data Form command to be available only in your database workbook, open the Customize Quick Access Toolbar drop-down list and click the For [workbook] item, where workbook is the database workbook's name.)

4. Open the Choose commands from drop-down list, and then click Commands Not in the Ribbon to display the list of commands that don't appear on the Ribbon in the left list box.

5. Scroll down to the Form command, click it, and then click the Add button to add it to the bottom of the list in the right box.

6. If you want to move the Form button up the list in the Quick Access Toolbar, click the Move Up button as many times as needed.

7. Click the OK button to close the Excel Options dialog box. The Form button now appears on the Quick Access Toolbar.

Click the Form button on the Quick Access Toolbar to display the Form dialog box. Figure 15-5 shows this dialog box, whose title bar shows the name of the worksheet you're using (here, Sales) rather than the word "Form".

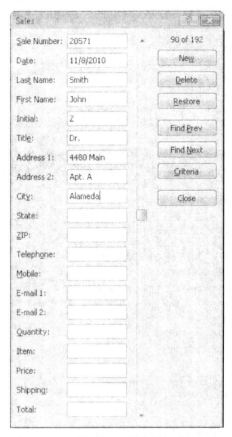

Figure 15-5. *The Form dialog box bears the name of the worksheet your database table is on (here, Sales), and shows each field in the order they appear in the header row.*

To use the data form, you move to the record you want in one of these ways:

- *Create a new record*: Click the New button to create a new record in the database. When you type the data in the fields, Excel adds the new record after the last current record in the database.

- *Move forward or backward through the records*: Click the Find Next button to display the next record, or click the Find Prev button to display the previous record.

- *Scroll through the records*: Drag the scroll box up or down the scroll bar to move quickly through the records.

- *Search for a record*: Follow these steps:

    1. Click the Criteria button to switch to the criteria view of the form. Excel clears any data in the fields.

2. Type your search term in the field by which you want to search. For example, to search for your customers in Arizona, type AZ in the State field (assuming your database has this field).

3. Click the Find Next button to find the next instance, or click the Find Prev button to find the previous instance.

Excel automatically switches the dialog box back to Form view when you search. If you decide you don't need to search after all, click the Form button (which replaces the Criteria button) to return to Form view.

Once you've created or located the record you want to change, type or edit the data in the fields. Excel enters it in the columns for you.

When you've finished using the Form dialog box, click the Close button to close it.

Resizing a Database Table

When you've created a database table, Excel normally resizes it for you automatically when you add or delete rows or columns. For example, when you add a record by using the Form dialog box, Excel expands the database table to include it.

Excel also expands the database table automatically if you add data to the row after the current last row in a database table that doesn't have a totals row. Excel calls this feature Table AutoExpansion. If you don't want Excel to do this, click the AutoCorrect Smart Tag that appears below and to the right of the first cell in the added row, and then click Undo Table AutoExpansion (see Figure 15-6). Click the Smart Tag again, and then click Stop Automatically Expanding Tables.

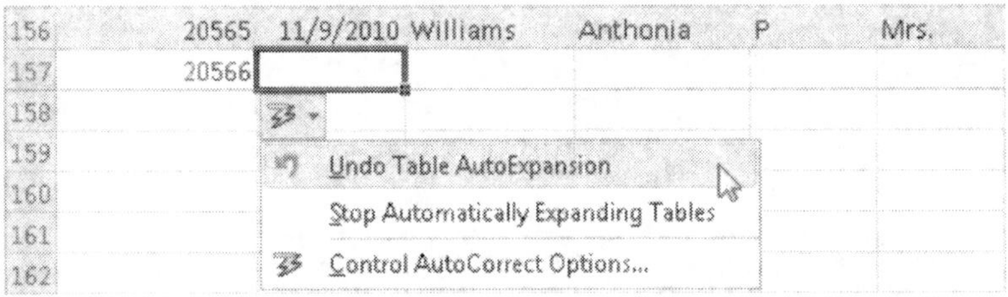

Figure 15-6. You can use the AutoCorrect smart tag both to undo Table AutoExpansion and to turn it off.

■ **Note** To turn Table AutoExpansion back on, choose File ➤ Options. In the Excel Options dialog box, click Proofing in the left column, and then click the AutoCorrect Options button. In the AutoCorrect dialog box, click the AutoFormat As You Type tab. Select the Include new rows and columns in table check box, and then click the OK button to close the AutoCorrect dialog box. Click the OK button to close the Excel Options dialog box.

Sorting a Database Table by One or More Fields

When you need to examine the data in your database table, it's often useful to sort it. Excel lets you sort a database table either quickly by a single field or by using multiple fields.

■ **Tip** If you need to be able to return a database table to its original order, include a column with sequential numbers in it. These numbers may be part of your records (for example, sequential sales numbers for transactions) or simply ID numbers for the records. In either case, you can use AutoFill to enter them quickly. To return the database table to its original order, you can then sort it by this column.

Sorting Quickly by a Single Field

To sort a database table by a single field, click any cell in the column you want to sort by, and then choose Data ➤ Sort & Filter ➤ Sort A to Z or Data ➤ Sort & Filter ➤ Sort Z to A. The Sort A to Z button is the upper button on the left size of the Sort & Filter group; the Sort Z to A button (highlighted in Figure 15-7) is the lower button on the left side of the group.

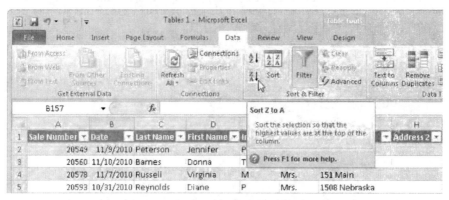

Figure 15-7 . Use the Sort A to Z button or the Sort Z to A button in the Sort & Filter group of the Data tab when you need to sort quickly by the column you've selected.

After you sort, the database table remains sorted that way until you change it.

Sorting a Database Table by Multiple Fields

Often, it's useful to sort your database table by two or more fields at the same time. For example, in a customer database, you may need to sort your customers first by state, and then by city within the state.

To sort by multiple fields, follow these steps:

1. Choose Data ➤ Sort & Filter ➤ Sort to display the Sort dialog box. Figure 15-8 shows the Sort dialog box with two criteria entered and a third criterion under way.

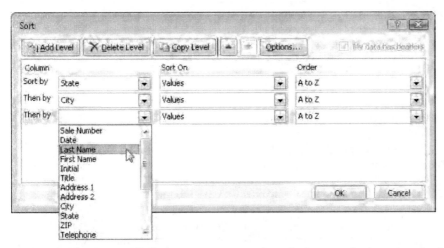

Figure 15-8. In the Sort dialog box, you can set up exactly the sort criteria you need to identify data in your database.

2. Set up your first sort criterion using the controls on the first row of the main part of the Sort dialog box. Follow these steps:

- Open the Sort by drop-down list, and then click the column you want to sort by first. For example, click the State column.

- Open the Sort On drop-down list, and then click what you want to sort by: Values, Cell Color, Font Color, or Cell Icon. In most cases, you'll want to use Values, but the other three items are useful for tables to which you've applied conditional formatting.

- Open the Order drop-down list, and then click the sort order you want. If you choose Values in the Sort On drop-down list, you can choose A to Z for an ascending sort, Z to A for a descending sort, or Custom List. Choosing Custom List opens the Custom List dialog box, in which you can choose a custom list by which to sort the results. For example, you could use a custom list of your company's products or offices to sort the database into a custom order rather than being restricted to ascending or descending order.

- If you need the sort to be case sensitive (so that "smith" appears before "Smith," and so on), click the Options button. In the Sort Options dialog box (see Figure 15-9), select the Case sensitive check box, and then click the OK button.

Figure 15-9. *Select the Case sensitive check box in the Sort Options dialog box if you want to treat lowercase letters differently than their uppercase versions.*

3. Click the Add Level button to add a second line of controls to the main part of the Sort dialog box.

4. Set up the criterion for the second-level sort using the same technique. The only difference is that the first drop-down list is called Then by rather than Sort by. For example, set up a second-level sort using the City column in the database.

5. Set up any other criteria needed by repeating steps 3 and 4.

6. Click the OK button to close the Sort dialog box. Excel sorts the data using the criteria you specified.

■ **Note** When you're sorting data that's not in a database table, there are two main differences. First, the My data has headers check box in the Sort dialog box is available, and you must select it if the data range you're sorting includes a header row. (Otherwise, Excel sorts the headers into the data range.) Second, you can select the Sort left to right option button in the Sort Options dialog box to sort columns rather than rows, a choice that's not available in a data table.

Identifying and Removing Duplicate Records in a Database Table

When you've created a large database table, you may need to check it for duplicate records and remove those you find. Excel provides a Remove Duplicates feature that saves you having to comb the records by hand.

■ **Caution** Two warnings before removing duplicate values. First, make sure you have a backup copy of your database workbook—for example, use Windows Explorer to copy the current version of a file to a safe location. Second, be certain you know which fields in the database table should contain unique values and which can contain duplicate values. For example, a customer ID number field must be unique, because each customer has a different ID number; but a customer last name field can't reasonably be unique, because many customers will likely share last names.

To remove duplicate records from a database table, follow these steps:

1. Click any cell in the database table to add the Table Tools section to the Ribbon.

2. Choose Table Tools ➤ Design ➤ Data Tools ➤ Remove Duplicates to display the Remove Duplicates dialog box (see Figure 15-10).

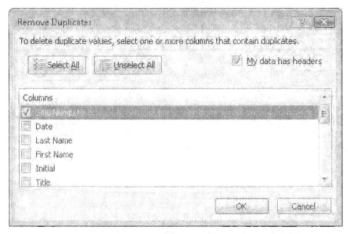

Figure 15-10. Use the Remove Duplicates dialog box to locate duplicate values in columns that should contain only unique values.

3. Make sure the My data has headers check box is selected.

4. Click the Unselect All button to clear all the check boxes in the Columns box.

5. In the Columns box, select the check box for each column you want to check for duplicates.

■ **Tip** Normally, it's best to check a single column for duplicate values at a time. Make sure that the column is one that must contain a unique value.

6. Click the OK button to close the Remove Duplicates dialog box. Excel searches for duplicate values, removes them from the database, and displays a message box telling you the result of the search (see Figure 15-11).

Figure 15-11. Excel tells you how many duplicate values it has removed from the database.

7. Click the OK button to close the message box.

8. Repeat the process with another field if necessary.

Filtering a Database Table

When you need to find records in a database table that match the terms you specify, you can *filter* it. Filtering makes Excel display only the records that match your search terms, hiding all the other records.

■ **Note** You can also search for records by using Excel's Find feature. Choose Home ➤ Editing ➤ Find & Select ➤ Find or press Ctrl+F to display the Find and Replace dialog box, type your search term in the Find what box, and then click either the Find Next button or the Find All button. Filtering displays all the matching records together rather than spread out in the database table, so it's often more convenient than using Find.

To make filtering easy, Excel provides a feature named AutoFilter. To use AutoFilter, follow these steps:

1. Click a cell in the database table to display the Table Tools section of the Ribbon.

2. Click the Data tab of the Ribbon to display its contents.

3. In the Sort & Filter group, make sure that the Filter button is selected, so that it looks pushed in. Excel automatically selects the Filter button when you create a database table, so this button should be pushed in unless you've turned filtering off. Selecting this button makes Excel display a drop-down button on each column heading in the database table.

4. On the column you want to use for filtering, click the drop-down button to display the AutoFilter list. Excel displays a list of filtering criteria (see Figure 15-12).

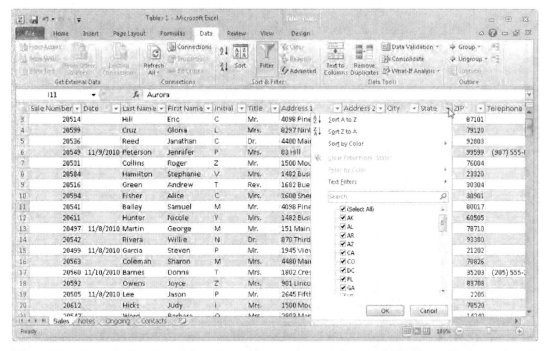

Figure 15-12. To apply filtering, click the drop-down arrow on a column heading (here, the State column), and then click the filtering type you want.

5. Click the type of filtering you want to apply. The choices depend on what the column contains, but these choices are typical:

    • *Sort*: Click the type of sort you want to apply—for example, Sort A to Z or Sort Z to A for text, or Sort Smallest to Largest or Sort Largest to Smallest for numbers.

    • *Text Filters*: Click this item to display a submenu containing comparisons you can apply (see Figure 15-13). Click the type of comparison you want to use. For example, choose Equals to set a filter that picks particular states, or choose Begins With to set a filter than selects cities that start with text you specify. Use the fields in the Custom AutoFilter dialog box (see Figure 15-14) to set up the rest of the comparison.

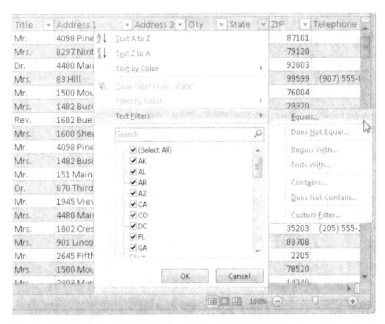

Figure 15-13. From the Text Filters submenu, choose the type of comparison you want to use for the filter; for example, Equals.

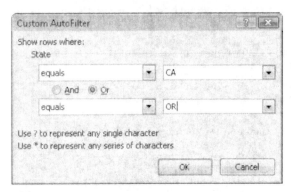

Figure 15-14. In the Custom AutoFilter dialog box, set up the details of the filter. You can use one criterion or two; for example, the State column contains CA or OR.

- *Number Filters*: Click this item to display a submenu containing comparisons you can apply (see Figure 15-15), and then click the type of comparison you want to use. For the Above Average and Below Average items, you need specify no more information; for the other comparisons, use the Custom AutoFilter dialog box to set up the rest of the comparison.

Figure 15-15. *The Number Filters submenu provides comparisons suited to numbers, including Greater Than and Less Than, Between, Top 10, and Above Average and Below Average.*

- *Date Filters*: Click this item to display a submenu containing comparisons you can apply (see Figure 15-16), and then click the type of comparison you want to use. Comparisons that show no ellipsis, such as Yesterday or Last Week, need no further information; for comparisons that do show an ellipsis, you use the Custom AutoFilter dialog box to specify the details.

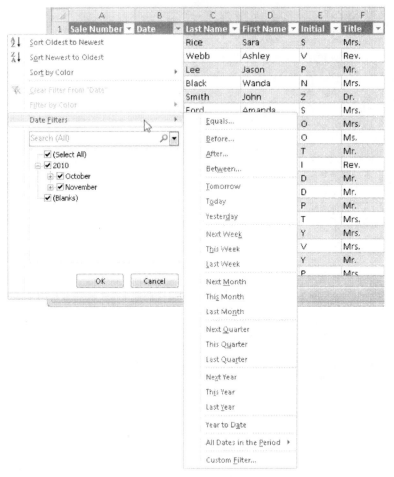

Figure 15-16. Use the Date Filters submenu to quickly filter by either a set period of time, such as a week or a quarter, or by specific dates.

- *Specific items in the list*: The drop-down list includes a check box for each unique item in the column's cells. Select the check box for each item you want to display, and clear the check box for each item you don't want to see.

When you've specified the details of the filter, Excel applies it to the database table and reduces the display to those rows that match the filter. Excel displays a filter symbol in place of the drop-down button on the column that contains the filtering (as on the State column heading in Figure 15-17).

H	I	J	K	L
Address 2 ▼	City ▼	State ▼	ZIP ▼	Telephone ▼
B	Los Angel CA		90052	(213) 555-0834
2nd Floor	San Diego CA		92199	(619) 555-0201
	San Jose CA		95101	(408) 555-8201
	San Franci CA		94188	(415) 555-5028
	Long Beac CA		90802	(562) 555-8882

Figure 15-17. The filter symbol (shown on the State column heading here) indicates that you're filtering the database table by that column.

To remove filtering from a single column, click the filter symbol on the column heading, and then click the Clear Filter item on the drop-down list. This item includes the column's name—for example, Clear Filter from "State" for the State column.

To remove filtering from the database table as a whole, choose Data ➤ Sort & Filter ➤ Filter, un-pressing the Filter button in the Sort & Filter group.

■ **Note** If AutoFilter doesn't give you the flexibility you need, you can also create custom filters manually. To do this, you insert extra rows above the database table to create a criteria range, enter the criteria in the appropriate columns, choose Data ➤ Sort & Filter ➤ Advanced, and then work in the Advanced Filter dialog box. This topic is beyond the scope of this book, but look it up (online or offline) if you need to perform filtering that AutoFilter can't manage.

Summary

In this chapter, you've learned how to create a database table in Excel—a flat-file database rather than the relational type of database that you create with a database program such as Microsoft Access.

You now know how to set up a database table, choose display options for it, and format it to look the way you want. You can add data to the database either by working in the cells as normal or by using a data-entry form to speed the process. You've gained the essential skills of sorting the data into the sort order you need or filtering it to show the records you're interested in.

This is the last chapter in the Excel part of the book. In the next part, I'll show you how to make the most of PowerPoint, Office's easy-to-use presentation program.

CHAPTER 16

Starting to Build a Presentation

In this chapter, you'll learn how to start building a presentation in PowerPoint.

Your first move is to create the presentation document. PowerPoint gives you a wide range of choices, from colorful design templates to sample templates with content that can give your presentation a kick start. You can change the look, colors, or fonts if you don't like what you've got, and you can also customize the slide size and orientation if necessary.

Once you've created the presentation, you add slides to it or customize the sample slides that it contains. A PowerPoint presentation consists of a series of slides that you normally play from start to finish. Each slide can contain any of a wide variety of different types of content, from text titles and bullet points through charts, diagrams, and even movies. You'll look at how to add straightforward content in this chapter and how to add more entertaining content types in the next two chapters.

After making sure you know how to add, delete, and rearrange slides, I'll show you how to use PowerPoint's four views to work efficiently on a presentation, how to develop the outline of a presentation quickly, and how to organize a presentation's slides into different sections for convenience.

Last, I'll show you how to collaborate with your colleagues on creating a presentation in PowerPoint—either all editing the presentation at once, or editing at your leisure and combining the results.

Creating a Presentation

To create a new presentation, you use the New pane in Backstage: Click the File tab to open Backstage, and then click the New item in the left column to display the New pane (see Figure 16-1).

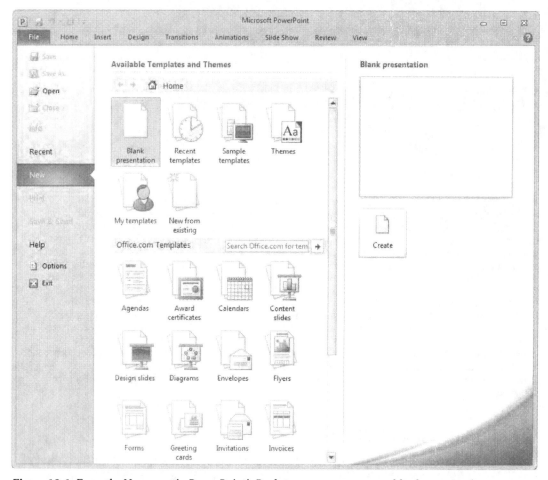

Figure 16-1. From the New pane in PowerPoint's Backstage, you can create a blank presentation or a presentation based on a template, a theme, or on an existing presentation.

From here, you can choose among six ways of creating a new presentation:

- *Blank presentation or Office.com template*: To create a blank presentation, click the Blank presentation item in the top area, and then click the Create button. To create a presentation based on a template from Office.com, double-click the appropriate folder to open it, click the template, and then click the Download button.

- *Recent templates*: Click this item to see a list of the templates you've used recently. Click the template you want to use, and then click the Create button.

■ **Tip** PowerPoint offers so many templates that the Recent templates category can be a real timesaver when you need to create a presentation similar to one you've created before. If the previous presentation wasn't based on a template, use the New from existing command instead to create a new presentation based on the previous one.

- *Sample templates*: Click the Sample templates item to display the selection of sample templates (see Figure 16-2). Click the theme you want, and then click the Create button. PowerPoint creates the new presentation with all the contents of the sample template. You can then customize all the text placeholders, add and delete slides, and make other changes to build the presentation you want.

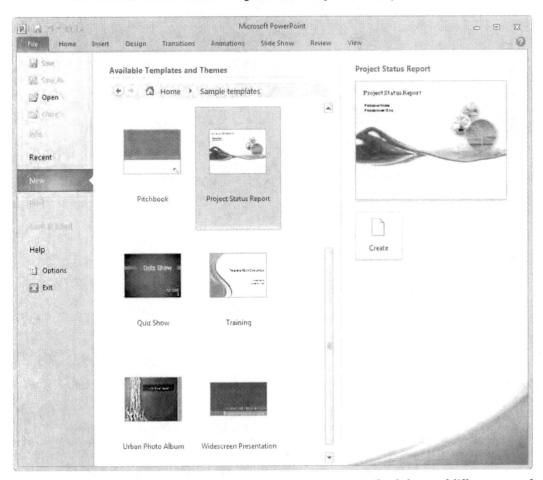

Figure 16-2. The Sample templates folder includes templates containing the skeletons of different types of presentations, such as a project status report, a training session, or a quiz show.

> ▪ **Note** A presentation template includes sample contents that you can use as the basis of your presentation. A presentation theme is a coordinated look for the slides in a presentation but does not contain sample contents.

- *Themes*: Click the Themes item to display PowerPoint's selection of visual themes (see Figure 16-3). Click the theme you want to give your new presentation, and then click the Create button to create the presentation.

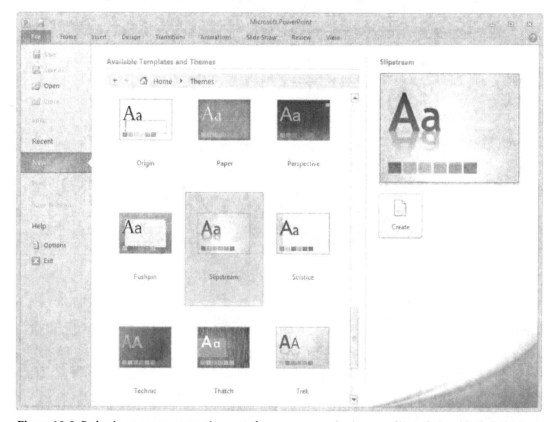

Figure 16-3. *By basing a new presentation on a theme, you can give it a coordinated visual look from the many options that PowerPoint offers.*

- *My templates*: Click the My templates item to display the New Presentation dialog box, which shows any templates you have added to your Personal Templates folder. Until you add templates, this folder is empty.

- *New from existing*: Click the New from existing item when you want to create a new presentation based on an existing presentation. In the New from Existing

Presentation dialog box that PowerPoint displays, click the existing presentation, and then click the Open button.

You can change the look of the presentation by applying a different theme to it. A *theme* is an overall look for a presentation, including a slide background design, a set of colors, a set of fonts, and a set of visual effects for graphical objects such as arrows.

To change the theme, click the Design tab, and then use the controls in the Themes group. Either click one of the themes displayed in the Themes box on the Ribbon, or click the More button (the drop-down button) and then click the theme on the Themes panel (see Figure 16-4).

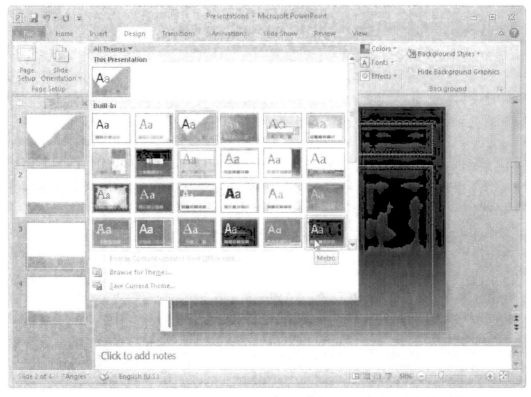

Figure 16-4. *Use the Themes panel in the Themes group on the Design tab to quickly change your presentation's theme. For smaller changes within the theme, use the Colors panel, the Fonts panel, or the Effects panel.*

When you've applied the theme you want, you can make changes within it:

- *Change the colors*: Choose Design ➤ Themes ➤ Colors, and then click the color set you want to use.

- *Fonts*: Choose Design ➤ Themes ➤ Fonts, and then click the fonts set.

- *Effects*: Choose Design ➤ Themes ➤ Effects, and then click the effects set.

Changing the Slide Size or Orientation

For some presentations, you may also need to change the size or orientation of the slides. Most PowerPoint templates start you off with slides sized for displaying on a regular-format screen in a landscape (wider than high) orientation, which is what you'll most often need. But if you need to create widescreen slides, slides sized for printing on paper, or slides in a portrait orientation, you'll need to change the setup.

To change the size or orientation, follow these steps:

1. Choose Design ➤ Page Setup ➤ Page Setup to display the Page Setup dialog box (see Figure 16-5).

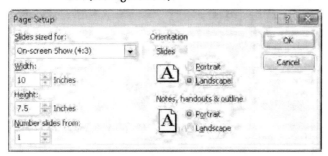

Figure 16-5. Use the Page Setup dialog box to change slide size or orientation. You can also switch the notes, handouts, and outline from portrait orientation to landscape.

2. Open the Slides sized for drop-down list and choose the size you need. For example, the following:

   • Choose On-screen Show (16:9) to create slides sized for a screen with a 16:9 aspect ratio.

   • Choose Letter Paper (8.5x11 in) to create slides sized for printing on letter paper.

3. If necessary, change the slide size in the Width box and the Height box.

4. If you need to change the slide numbering, change the starting number from 1 in the Number slides from box. For example, you may need this presentation's slides to continue the numbering from a previous presentation.

5. In the Slides group box, choose the slide orientation by clicking the Portrait option button or the Landscape option button.

6. In the Notes, handouts & outline group box, choose the orientation for notes, handouts, and outline pages by clicking the Portrait option button or the Landscape option button.

7. Click the OK button to close the Page Setup dialog box. PowerPoint applies your choices to the presentation.

■ **Tip** If you just need to change the slide orientation, choose Design ➤ Page Setup ➤ Slide Orientation, and then click Landscape or Portrait.

Navigating the PowerPoint Window

When you first open a presentation, PowerPoint usually displays it in Normal view. In this view, the PowerPoint window contains three panes, as you can see in Figure 16-6.

- *Slide pane*: This pane shows the current slide. Click the Fit Slide to Current Window button to zoom the slide as large as it will go and still fit in the pane.

- *Navigation pane*: This pane appears on the left and contains two tabs, Slides and Outline. The Slides tab shows a thumbnail picture of each slide that you can click to display the slide in the Slide pane. The Outline tab displays an outline of the presentation that you can use to quickly develop the presentation's text contents. In the Outline tab too, you click a slide to display it in the Slide pane.

- *Notes pane*: This pane appears at the bottom of the window, below the Slide pane. This is where you create notes that you want to accompany the slide.

Tip You can resize the Slide pane, Navigation pane, and Notes pane by dragging the borders that separate them. For example, you may want to widen the Slides pane to make the thumbnail pictures larger so that you can identify the slides more easily.

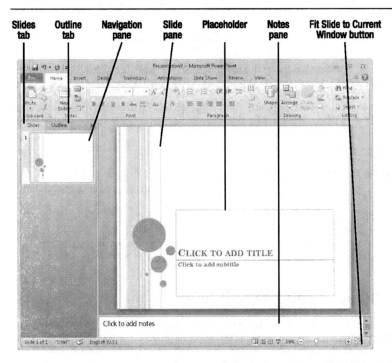

Figure 16-6. In Normal view, the Navigation pane appears on the left and the Notes pane at the bottom of the window, leaving the slide pane taking up most of the space.

▨ **Tip** If you want more room to work on your slide, close the Navigation pane by clicking its Close button (the ×
button) or by dragging its right border all the way to the left side of the window. To display the Navigation pane
again, drag the border back to the right. Similarly, you can hide the Notes pane by dragging its border down to the
bottom of the window and reveal it again by dragging the border back up.

Add Content to a Slide

Once you've created a slide, you can add content to it. As you'll see in Chapters 17 and 18, PowerPoint
slides can contain a wide variety of types of content, from text to audio and movies.

Most slides come with one or more placeholders for adding content. For example, the slide shown
in Figure 16-6 has a title placeholder (where it says "Click to add title") and a subtitle placeholder. Other
slides contain placeholders for other types of content, such as tables or graphics.

▨ **Note** Most themes and templates start you off with one or more slides. If your presentation doesn't have a
slide at this point, choose Home ➤ Slides ➤ New Slide to insert a slide. See the next section for more details on
adding slides.

To add text to a text placeholder, click anywhere in the placeholder. PowerPoint hides the prompt
(the "Click to add" text) and displays an insertion point. Type the text you want, and then click outside
the placeholder to deselect it.

To resize a placeholder, click to select it. You can then drag a corner handle to resize the placeholder
proportionally or drag a side handle to resize it only in one dimension.

▨ **Note** To reset a slide's placeholders to their defaults, choose Home ➤ Slides ➤ Reset. To change the layout of a
slide, click the slide, choose Home ➤ Slides ➤ Layout, and then click the Layout you want on the Layout panel.

To move a placeholder, click to select it. Then move the mouse pointer over a border so that the
pointer changes to a four-headed arrow. Then drag the placeholder to where you want it to appear.

Adding, Deleting, and Rearranging Slides

If you based your presentation on a theme, you'll probably need to add more slides to it now. If you
based the presentation on a sample template, you may have the opposite problem—the presentation
contains too many slides, and you need to delete some of them. Sooner or later, you will likely need to
change the order in which the slides appear in the presentation.

Adding a Slide

To add a new slide, select the slide after which you want to insert the new one. Choose Home ➤ Slides ➤ New Slide (clicking the drop-down button on the New Slide button), and then click the slide design on the panel that opens (see Figure 16-7).

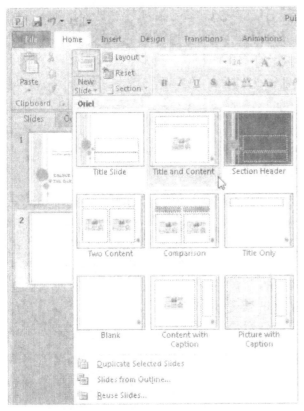

Figure 16-7. *Insert a slide by opening the New Slide panel on the Home tab of the Ribbon and clicking the slide layout you want.*

You can also insert slides in a presentation in three other ways:

- *Duplicate slides from the presentation*: To create new slides based on ones already in your presentation, select those slides, and then choose Home ➤ Slides ➤ New Slide ➤ Duplicate Selected Slides.

■ **Tip** You can quickly duplicate a slide by right-clicking it in the Slides pane or in Slide Sorter view and then clicking Duplicate slide on the context menu. Alternatively, select the slide, and then press Ctrl+D.

- *Insert slides from an outline in a document*: If you've created an outline in a Word document, a rich text format (RTF) document, or a text document, you can create slides based on it. Choose Home ➤ Slides ➤ New Slide ➤ Slides from Outline to open the Insert Outline dialog box, click the document that contains the outline, and then click the Insert button.

- *Copy slides from another presentation*: You can insert slides from another presentation by choosing Home ➤ Slides ➤ New Slide ➤ Reuse Slides, using the controls in the Reuse Slides pane that opens to choose the source of the slides, and then picking the slides to insert.

Deleting a Slide

You can delete a slide in the Slides pane or the Outline pane in Normal view or in the main pane in Slide Sorter view. (You'll learn about these views in a moment.) Use either of these techniques:

- *Context menu*: Right-click the slide, and then click Delete Slide on the context menu.

- *Delete key*: Click the slide, and then press Delete.

■ **Note** You can also delete a slide by selecting it in the Outline pane in Normal view or in the main pane in Slide Sorter view, and then giving a Cut command—for example, choosing Home ➤ Clipboard ➤ Cut. Cutting the slide removes it from the presentation and places it on the Clipboard, from which you can paste it somewhere else if you want to.

Rearranging Slides

You can change the order of the slides in the presentation in either Normal view or Slide Sorter view:

- *Normal view*: In the Slides pane or in Outline pane, click the slide you want to move, and then drag it up or down. When PowerPoint displays a horizontal line between the slides where you want to position the slide, release the mouse button.

- *Slide Sorter view*: Select the slide or slides, and then drag them to the appropriate position. When PowerPoint displays a vertical line between the destination slides, release the mouse button.

Using Views to Work on Your Presentation

So far in this chapter, you've seen only Normal view, though I've also mentioned Slide Sorter view. Altogether, PowerPoint provides five different views to help you work swiftly and easily on your presentations: Normal view, Slide Sorter view, Reading view, Notes Page view, and Slide Show view.
You can switch views in either of these ways:

- *Status bar*: Click the appropriate view button in the View Shortcuts group (see Figure 16-8). This group doesn't contain a button for Notes Page view.

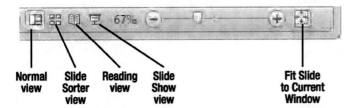

Normal   Slide   Reading   Slide   Fit Slide
view   Sorter   view   Show   to Current
       view   view   Window

Figure 16-8. Click a view button in the View Shortcuts group on the status bar to change views quickly. In Normal view, click the Fit Slide to Current Window button to make the slide fit neatly in the window.

- *Ribbon*: Click the View tab, go to the Presentation Views group, and then click the Normal button, the Slide Sorter button, the Notes Page button, or the Reading View button. To start a slide show from the current slide, choose Slide Show ➤ Start Slide Show ➤ From Current Slide.

Creating Your Slides in Normal View

As you've seen already, Normal view is the view you use to create your slides and work on their contents. Normal view is the view in which PowerPoint usually opens, and you can give yourself more space to work on a slide by hiding the Navigation pane and the Notes aNotes area.

Rearranging Your Slides in Slide Sorter View

When you need to rearrange your slides into a different order, use Slide Sorter view (see Figure 16-9). This view shows a thumbnail picture of each slide laid out in a grid pattern, so you can quickly see where each slide appears in relation to the other slides.

Figure 16-9. In Slide Sorter view, you can quickly drag a slide or a group of slides to a different place in the presentation. Drag the zoom slider to change the size at which the slide thumbnails appear.

■ **Note** To select a slide in Slide Sorter view, click it. To select a range of slides, click the first slide, and then Shift-click the last slide; alternatively, click before the first slide and drag over the slides you want. To select slides that aren't next to each other, click the first slide, and then Ctrl+click each of the others.

The main point of Slide Sorter view is to see the order your slides are in and change the order if it's wrong. To move one or more selected slides, drag them to where you want them to appear. PowerPoint displays a vertical line between the destination slides, so you can tell where the slides will land when you drop them.

Slide Sorter view is also useful for finding the slide you need to edit. Once you've located the slide, double-click it to open the slide in Normal view so that you can edit it.

Creating Notes Pages in Notes Page View

When you need to add notes to a slide, switch to Notes Page view by choosing View ➤ Presentation Views ➤ Notes Page. In Notes Page view (see Figure 16-10), you can type the notes you need for each slide.

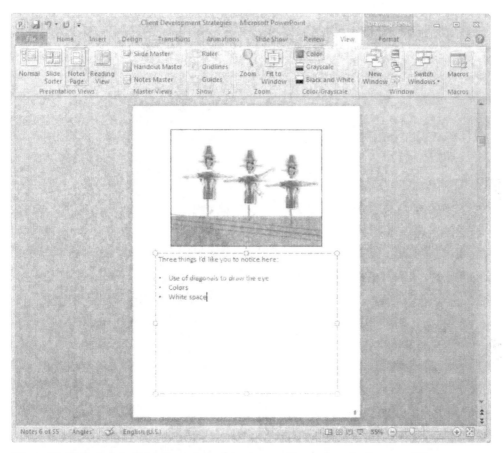

Figure 16-10. Switch to Notes Page view when you need to create notes for your slides.

Viewing a Presentation in Reading View

When you want to read a presentation rather than edit it, use Reading view (see Figure 16-11). This view hides the Ribbon and most of the PowerPoint interface and displays a single slide as large as it will go in the window.

Use the Previous button and Next button at the right side of the status bar to move from slide to slide. Click the Menu button (between the Previous button and the Next button) to display a menu that includes choices for accessing other slides, copying the current slide, switching to full screen, or ending the slide show.

■ **Tip** The advantage of Reading view over Slide Show view is that Reading view displays the slide in a window that you can resize as needed rather than taking up the full screen. This is useful when you need to take notes on a presentation or put together additions for it.

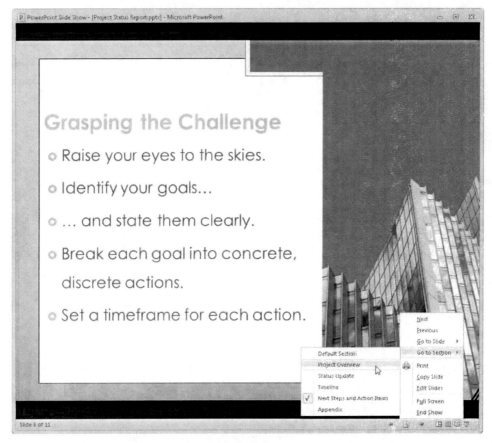

Figure 16-11. Reading view hides almost all of the PowerPoint interface to give you more space to read the slides. Click the Menu button to reach a menu of commands.

Running a Presentation in Slide Show View

PowerPoint's fourth view, Slide Show view, is the view you use when running a presentation. Slide Show view displays the current slide full screen on the screen you're using for the presentation. If you have a secondary screen (for example, because you've connected your PC to a projector), you can choose to show your presenter notes on it to help you with the presentation.

You'll see Slide Show view in action in Chapter 19, which covers running slide shows.

Opening Extra Windows to See Different Parts of the Presentation

Often, it's useful to be able to see two or more different slides at once. The easiest way to do this is to open a new window on the presentation and then display the other slide in that window.

To open a new window, choose View ➤ Window ➤ New Window.

Creating the Outline of a Presentation

When you need to develop the outline of a presentation quickly, work in the Outline tab of the Navigation pane in Normal view. With the presentation open, click the Outline tab in the Navigation pane to display the outline.

The Outline tab (see Figure 16-12) shows the presentation as a sequence of collapsible slides. Each slide appears as a heading with its ordinal number and the text from the title placeholder (if there is any).

You can expand or collapse a slide by double-clicking its icon in the Outline tab. A collapsed slide shows an underline to indicate that material is hidden, as in slides 3 and 4 in Figure 16-12.

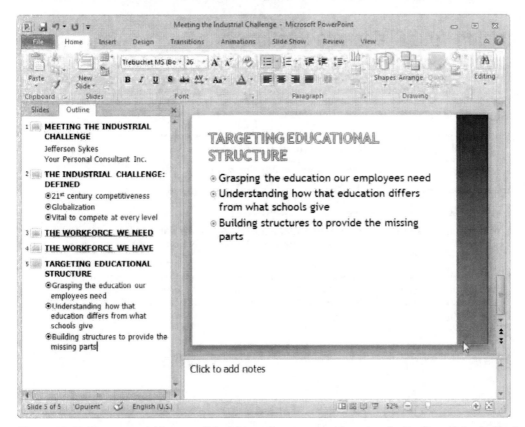

Figure 16-12. You can quickly enter slide titles and text contents by using the Outline tab in the Navigation pane. As you work, PowerPoint enters the information with basic formating on the slide itself; you can fix it later.

Use these techniques for working in the Outline tab:

- *Create a new slide*: Press Enter at the end of a paragraph to start a new paragraph, and then press Shift+Tab one or more times (as needed) to promote the paragraph to a slide title.

- *Create a bulleted paragraph*: After typing a slide title, press Enter to start a new paragraph. Then press Tab to demote the paragraph to the first level. You can demote a paragraph to a lower level if needed (for example, to create second-level bulleted paragraphs).

- *Move a paragraph or selection up or down*: Click at the left end of a paragraph to select it, or click and drag to select multiple paragraphs. You can then drag the paragraph or selection up or down the outline to where you want it to be. For example, you can drag a bulleted paragraph from one slide to another.

- *Paste in text*: You can paste text into the Outline tab, and then promote or demote its paragraphs to the levels at which you want them to appear.

Organizing Your Slides into Sections

When you add many slides to a presentation, it can become difficult to navigate through the presentation. To simplify matters, you can divide the presentation up into two or more sections. Each section can contain however many slides you need it to, and you can expand or collapse sections as needed.

To add a section, follow these steps:

1. Switch to Normal view if you're using any other view. For example, click the Normal view button in the View Shortcuts area of the status bar.

2. Display the Navigation pane if it's not already displayed.

3. Click the Slides tab of the Navigation pane if the Outline tab is displayed.

4. Select the slides you want to put in the section.

5. Right-click in the selection, and then click Add Section on the context menu. PowerPoint creates a new section and names it Untitled Section on the section bar across the top.

6. Right-click the section bar and then click Rename Section on the context menu to display the Rename Section dialog box (see Figure 16-13). Type the section name, and then click the Rename button to close the dialog box and apply the new name.

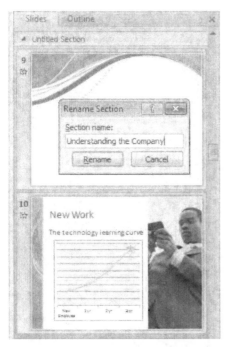

Figure 16-13. *After PowerPoint creates the section and names it Untitled Section, use the Rename Section dialog box to apply the name you want.*

Once you've created your sections, you can manipulate them easily like this:

- *Expand or collapse a section*: Double-click its section heading. You can also click the triangle to the left of the section name.

- *Expand or collapse all sections*: Right-click a section heading, and then click Expand All or Collapse All on the context menu.

- *Move a section up or down the list of sections*: Either click the section heading and drag it to where you want the section, or right-click the section heading, and then click Move Section Up or Move Section Down on the context menu (see Figure 16-14).

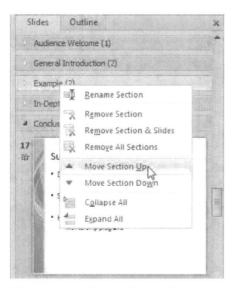

Figure 16-14. *After creating sections, you can use the context menu to rename them, rearrange them, or remove them.*

- *Remove a section but leave its slides*: Right-click the section heading, and then click Remove Section on the context menu. To remove all sections, click Remove All Sections.

- *Remove a section and its slides*: Right-click the section heading, and then click Remove Section and Slides on the context menu.

Collaborating on a Presentation with Your Colleagues

You'll probably create some presentations on your own, but for others you may need to get input from your colleagues. You can do this in several ways:

- *Work on the presentation together at the same time*: PowerPoint's "coauthoring" feature enables you and your colleagues to open the same copy of the presentation from a SharePoint site or from Windows Live and work on together, resolving any conflicts that crop up when two or more people try to change the same part of the presentation at the same time.

- *Work on the presentation in turn*: If you find coauthoring troublesome, or if you don't have a SharePoint site, you may prefer to save the presentation in a shared folder and work on it in turn. PowerPoint doesn't offer revision marks like Word does, so you may want to have your colleagues provide input by adding comments rather than by changing the slides directly.

- Work on separate copies of the presentation, and then compare them: The third option is to use two or more separate copies of the presentation. After you and your colleagues have provided your input, you can use PowerPoint's Compare feature to flag the differences between the copies, and then decide which changes to keep and which to reject.

Working on a presentation in turn requires coordinating the various editors but is otherwise straightforward enough. Coauthoring presentations and comparing presentations are more involved. The first subsection discusses coauthoring, and the second explains comparing presentations.

Editing a Presentation Simultaneously with Your Colleagues

When you need to create a presentation quickly, you can edit the presentation simultaneously with your colleagues. If you can avoid stepping on each other's toes, coauthoring a presentation can be a great way to work.

Tip When coauthoring a presentation, either agree beforehand which slides or which section each person will work on, or use instant messaging to keep in touch as you work. As far as possible, avoid working on the same slide as one of your coauthors—otherwise, it's all too easy to create conflicting changes that you then need to resolve.

Here's how to coauthor a presentation with your colleagues:

- *Create the presentation*: One of you creates the presentation in the normal way—for example, by basing it on a theme, as described earlier in this chapter, or by cloning an existing presentation (likewise). You save the presentation either to a SharePoint site on your local network or to Windows Live SkyDrive.

Note If you have the choice between using a local SharePoint site and using Windows Live SkyDrive, choose the SharePoint site—it'll give much better performance, especially if you create a large and complex presentation.

- *Open the presentation*: The first person opens the presentation as usual. When each other person opens the presentation, PowerPoint displays a pop-up message telling them who else is working on it (see Figure 16-15). The first person also sees a corresponding pop-up message.

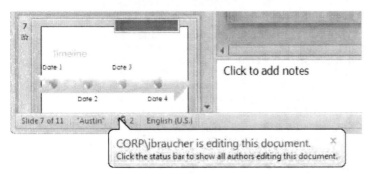

Figure 16-15. The Authors readout on the left side of the status bar shows you when another author opens the presentation for editing.

- *See the current list of editors*: To see the full list of people editing the presentation, click the Authors readout on the status bar to display the Authors editing this document menu. For more detail, click the File tab to open Backstage, and then look at the People Currently Editing readout at the top of the Info pane (see Figure 16-16). From here, you can click the Send a Message button to send an e-mail message or (usually better) an instant message to the other authors.

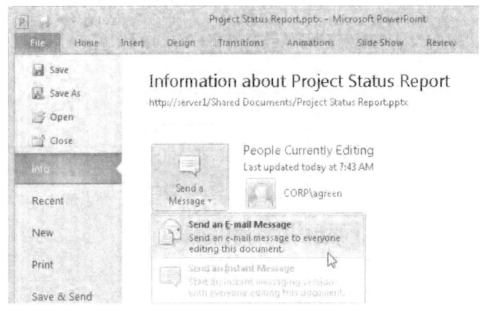

Figure 16-16. From the People Currently Editing area in the Info pane in Backstage, you can click the Send a Message button to start sending an e-mail message or an instant message to the other editors.

- *Edit the presentation*: You can work as normal using almost the full range of PowerPoint's features. The main limitation is that only one person can edit any given element at a time. For this reason, the most practical approach is to work on different slides than your coauthors are editing.

- *Update the presentation*: When you've made changes you want to share with your coauthors, or when you're ready to see what changes they've made, click the Save button on the Quick Access Toolbar or press Ctrl+S to save the presentation. PowerPoint uploads your changes to the document on the SharePoint site or on SkyDrive and merges them with your coauthors' changes; if your changes conflict with a coauthor's changes, you'll need to resolve them, as described later in this chapter. PowerPoint downloads your coauthors' changes and displays them for you.

- *Resolve conflicts*: If you and another author change the same element at the same time, PowerPoint displays the Upload Failed dialog box (see Figure 16-17) to whomever saves the document after the other. Click the Resolve Conflicts button, and then work in the Revisions pane, as described later in this section.

Figure 16-17. If you see the Upload Failed dialog box, click the Resolve Conflicts button, and then us
the Revisions pane to work through the conflicting changes that are preventing PowerPoint from saving
your edits.

- *Review your coauthors' changes*: When you save your changes as described a moment ago, PowerPoint merges your coauthors' changes into the presentation you're viewing and flags them for you. To review the changes and choose which to accept, follow these steps:

  1. Click the Updates Available button on the status bar to open Backstage showing the Info pane.

  2. In the Document Updates Available section at the top, click the Save button, and then click Save and Review on the drop-down menu. PowerPoint displays the Upload Blocked dialog box (see Figure 16-18) prompting you to review the changes that other authors have made.

Figure 16-18. Click the Review Changes in the Upload Blocked dialog box to review the changes that
others have made to the presentation you're collaborating on.

  3. Click the Review Changes button to display the Merge tab of the Ribbon and the Revisions pane (see Figure 16-19). The Slides tab of the Navigation pane shows the slides that contain changes, and the first of these slides appears in the Slide pane.

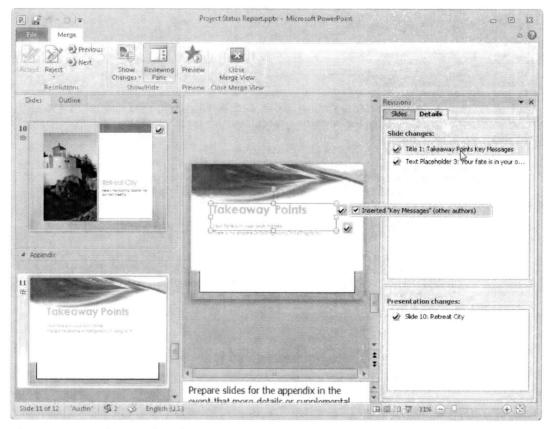

Figure 16-19. Use the controls on the Merge tab and in the Revisions pane to review—and accept or reject—the changes your coauthors have made to the presentation. The Details tab in the Revisions pane displays changes to the current slide (in the Slide changes box) and to the presentation (in the Presentation changes box).

4. In the Revisions pane, click the Details pane, and then click the entry for the change you want to view. PowerPoint displays a marker with details of the change, as you can see in the figure. Leave the check box selected (either in the Revisions pane or on the marker) to keep the change; clear the check box to reject the change.

■ **Note** To start with, PowerPoint displays only the conflicting changes. To see the non-conflicting changes as well as the conflicting ones, choose Merge ➤ Show/Hide ➤ Show Changes ➤ Show All Changes; to switch back to viewing conflicts only, choose Merge ➤ Show/Hide ➤ Show Changes ➤ Show Only Conflicts.

5. Move to each revision in turn and deal with it. You can click the Previous button or Next button in the Resolutions group of the Merge tab to move to another revision, or click it in the Revisions pane.

6. To make sweeping changes, click the drop-down button on the Accept button or the Reject button in the Resolutions group. You can then click Accept All Changes to the Current Slide, Accept All Changes to the Presentation, Reject All Changes to the Current Slide, or Reject All Changes to the Presentation, as needed.

7. Click the Close Merge View button to close the merge view and return to editing the presentation.

- *Close the presentation*: When you have finished working with the presentation, save any unsaved changes that you want to keep, and then close the presentation as usual—for example, choose File ➤ Close.

Comparing Two Copies of the Same Presentation

If you use two or more copies of the same presentation to gather input, use PowerPoint's Compare feature to compare the copies and identify the differences so that you can review them.

▓ **Tip** When comparing presentations, keep the original presentation clean (unedited) as the basis for the comparison. You can then compare each edited version in turn to the original presentation and identify all the changes. The result is much clearer than comparing one person's edited version with your edits of the original version.

To compare two copies of a presentation, follow these steps:

1. Open one copy of the presentation in PowerPoint as usual.

2. Choose Review ➤ Compare ➤ Compare to display the Choose File to Merge with Current Presentation dialog box. This dialog box is the Open dialog box under a different name.

3. Navigate to the other copy of the presentation, and then click it.

4. Click the Merge button to close the dialog box. PowerPoint merges the changes from the second presentation into the first presentation and displays the Revisions pane. Figure 16-20 shows a presentation with changes merged into it and the reviewing process underway.

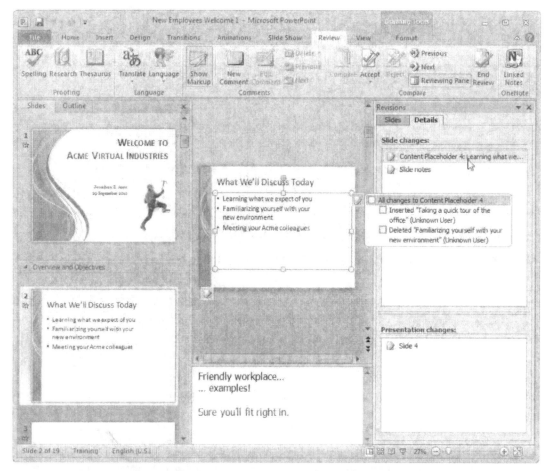

Figure 16-20. *Click the slide you want to review, then click an entry in the Revisions pane to display the change on the slide. Select a change's check box to accept the change; clear the check box to reject the change.*

5. In the Slides pane or the Outline pane, click the slide you want to review.

6. In the Revisions pane, click the change you want to display. PowerPoint selects the changed item in the Slide pane and displays a pop-up window with details of the changes.

7. Select a change's check box to accept the change, or clear the check box to reject the change. You can also use the Accept button or the Reject button in the Compare group on the Review tab of the Ribbon.

8. When you have finished reviewing the changes, choose Review ➤ Compare ➤ End Review to stop the review. You can then save the presentation.

Make sure you review all the changes before you save the presentation. Otherwise, PowerPoint displays the dialog box shown in Figure 16-21 warning you that saving will end the review, losing all unaccepted changes. Click the Don't Save button if you want to check through the changes again, accepting those you want to keep and rejecting the others.

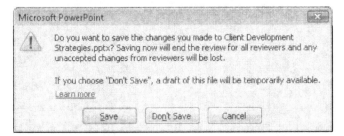

Figure 16-21. *If PowerPoint displays this dialog box when you try to save the presentation, you'll usually want to click the Don't Save button so that you can go back and review the remaining changes.*

Summary

In this chapter, you've learned how to create a new PowerPoint presentation by basing it on a sample template, on a design theme, or on an existing presentation. You've seen how to add slides to the presentation, rearrange them, and delete ones that aren't needed. You've grasped the techniques for adding content to slides, developing the outline of a presentation, and organizing slides into different sections.

I've also shown you how to use PowerPoint's powerful collaboration features to work on presentations with your colleagues—either sharing the same copy of the presentation or working on separate copies and then integrating the changes from each.

In the next chapter, we'll look at how to create compelling slides by making the layouts and the contents work effectively together.

C H A P T E R   17

Creating Clear
and Compelling Slides

In this chapter, I'll show you how to create slides that convey your meaning clearly and powerfully to your audience.

I'll begin where you'll probably want to start your presentation—by looking at how to plan the slides it will contain. Then you'll see which of PowerPoint's built-in slide layouts suits which type of content—and how you can create a custom slide layout when none of the built-in layouts fits the bill.

After that, you'll learn how to add text to your slides and format it to look good. Finally, I'll show you how to add tables, charts, SmartArt graphics, and hyperlinks to your slides.

Planning the Slides in Your Presentation

As you plan your presentation, and as you create the slides for it, keep the audience in mind. Whether you'll deliver the presentation in person, via an Internet broadcast, or by distributing digital copies of the presentation, you'll want to make sure that your slides are easy to read, are attractive to look at, and convey your meaning clearly.

For most presentations, follow these general rules when planning and creating your slides:

- *Keep your text concise*: Some presentation experts suggest following the "6×6 rule" for text slides—each slide should have around six bullet points of around six words each. The name is catchy, but the exact numbers are less important than the wider point: it's fine to have anywhere from four to eight bullets, as long as each of them is fairly short and your slide is easy to read.

- *Keep your slides uncluttered*: If you need to choose between fitting in more information on an existing slide and adding a slide, it's usually best to add the extra slide. Don't feel you need to fill up each slide—it's fine to leave blank space on a slide. You're not short-changing the audience by making the presentation easy for them to assimilate.

- *Illustrate your points*: When you make a point, drive it home by illustrating it with an example than catches your audience's imagination. For example, don't just say that you're now selling half a million gizmos a year—point out that's enough for everyone in Albuquerque to have one.

- *Use your strongest material—not all your material*: Many presentations suffer from too much detail. Usually, you can convince your audience that you have the facts and figures with just a couple of well-chosen examples; you don't need to numb them with a complete run-down of the data.

▦ **Tip** You may find it useful to keep extra material in reserve by using hidden slides or by creating custom slide shows that lets you show a series of extra slides when you need to. See Chapter 18 for details on both these topics.

- *Provide visual interest—but don't overdo it*: Even with the liveliest presenter, a text-only presentation can be dull as ditchwater. As you'll see in this chapter and the next, PowerPoint makes it easy to add tables, charts, graphics, videos, and animations to your slides, so it's a good idea to include visually interesting and relevant information to give the audience something to look at. You can also use audio in your presentations.

Choosing Slide Layouts to Suit the Contents

To get your material onto a slide, and to make it look good, you need to choose a suitable layout. You can either use one of PowerPoint's built-in slide layouts or create a custom layout of your own.

Using PowerPoint's Built-in Slide Layouts

You'll probably want to start by using the nine standard slide layouts that PowerPoint provides on the Home ➤ Slides ➤ New Slide drop-down panel. Table 17-1 lists these layouts and explains when to use each.

Table 17-1. PowerPoint's Standard Slide Layouts and When to Use Them

Slide Layout	When to Use It
Title Slide	To start your presentation or to introduce a new section of it.
Title and Content	To display a content item such as a table, chart, or picture.
Section Header	To start a new section of the presentation. In most designs, this slide has a substantially different look from other slides to suggest the change.
Two Content	To display two content items—for example, two pictures or two tables—but without necessarily comparing them to each other.
Comparison	To display two content items (for example, two charts) and compare them to each other. The Comparison layout is like the Two Content layout but has an extra text box above each item that you can use to highlight the differences.

Slide Layout	When to Use It
Title Only	To add only a title to a slide, or to have a title followed by content you place manually.
Blank	To create your own layout, or if you need to insert a blank slide as a pause in your presentation.
Content with Caption	To display a content item (such as a table or chart) over most of the slide, with a title and explanatory text alongside it.
Picture with Caption	To display a picture over most of the slide, with a title and explanatory text alongside it. The Picture with Caption layout is almost identical to the Content with Caption layout but is customized for pictures rather than other content types.

You can change a slide's layout at any time by clicking the slide, choosing Home ➤ Slides ➤ Layout, and then clicking the layout you want. And you can snap a slide's layout back to its default settings by choosing Home ➤ Slides ➤ Reset.

Note If you change a slide's layout by applying a layout that has fewer placeholders than the number of containers you're currently using, PowerPoint leaves the extra containers on the slide so that you can deal with them.

Creating Custom Slide Layouts

When none of PowerPoint's built-in slide layouts is exactly what you want, you can create a custom slide layout in either of two ways:

- Apply the closest slide layout to what you want, and then customize it. For example, you can delete a placeholder by clicking it and then pressing Delete, or copy a placeholder by clicking it and then Ctrl+dragging to where you want the copy.

- Start with a blank slide layout, and then add the objects you need.

Tip After you create a custom slide layout, you can reuse it by selecting the slide and choosing Home ➤ Slides ➤ New Slide ➤ Duplicate Selected Slides.

Formatting Text on Your Slides

You can format text on PowerPoint slides quickly by using the controls in the Font group and the Paragraph group on the Home tab of the Ribbon. You'll be familiar with most of these controls from the first part of the book, but Figure 17-1 points out several key controls and PowerPoint-specific controls that you'll use in this section.

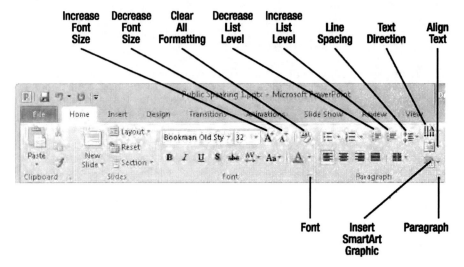

Figure 17-1. You can format most text quickly by using the controls in the Font group and Paragraph group on the Home tab of the Ribbon.

░ **Note** To change the formatting of all the text in a placeholder, select the placeholder itself. To change the formatting of just some of the text, select that text.

Changing the Font, Font Size, and Alignment

You can easily change the font, font size, and alignment of text:

- *Change the font size*: Click the placeholder that contains the text, and then click the Increase Font Size button or the Decrease Font Size button in the Font group on the Home tab, or open the Font Size drop-down list and click the size you want.

- *Change the font*: Click the placeholder, open the Font drop-down list in the Font group on the Home tab, and then click the font you want. Alternatively, choose Home ➤ Font ➤ Font (clicking the little button in the lower-right corner of the Font group), and then work in the Font dialog box.

■ **Note** To use the full range of font options, click the Font button (the little button at the lower-right corner of the Font group) and work in the Font dialog box. The Font tab in the Font dialog box contains most of the options, but if you need to space characters farther apart or place them closer together, use the Character Spacing tab.

- *Change the alignment*: Click the placeholder or click in the paragraph you want to affect, and then click the Align Text Left button, the Center button, the Align Text Right button, or the Justify button in the Paragraph group on the Home tab of the Ribbon.

KEEPING YOUR TEXT EASY TO READ

Like most Windows programs, PowerPoint gives you such a wide variety of fonts that it's easy to make poor choices.

When choosing fonts and font sizes for your slides, put clarity foremost. If the audience can't read the text on a slide because you've chosen an unsuitable font or too small a font size, your words of wisdom will be wasted. After creating a slide, make sure that even the smallest text on it will be easy to read from the back of the audience—and by someone with less than perfect eyesight.

Often, it's tempting to use a striking or "design-y" font to look different. But in most cases, the best fonts are those that people barely notice because they're simply easy to read, such as the Calibri font used in the Office design. Unless you're presenting to designers, you're usually better off with straightforward fonts rather than fonts that set out to catch the eye.

Changing the Indentation and Line Spacing of Text

To make text look right on a slide, you'll often need to adjust its indentation and line spacing. You can change these as follows:

- *Change the indentation*: Click the Decrease Indent button or the Increase Indent button. To take direct control, click the Paragraph button (the little button at the lower-right corner of the Paragraph group) to display the Paragraph dialog box (see Figure 17-2), and then use the controls in the Indentation area.

- *Change the line spacing*: Click the Line Spacing button, and then make your choice from the panel: 1.0, 1.5, 2.0, 2.5, or 3.0. For greater control, click the Line Spacing Options item on the panel to display the Paragraph dialog box, and then use the controls in the Spacing area.

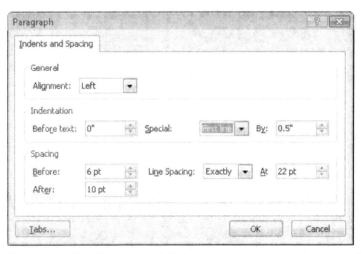

Figure 17-2. Use the Paragraph dialog box when you need close control over the indentation and spacing of paragraphs.

Rotating Text

For some slides, you may want to rotate text either in two dimensions or in three dimensions.

To rotate text simply, click the text placeholder, choose Home ➤ Paragraph ➤ Text Direction, and then click one of the directions on the panel (see Figure 17-3).

- *Horizontal*: Choose this item to restore text to normal horizontal orientation.

- *Rotate all text 90 degrees*: Choose this item to turn the text on its side, so that it reads from top to bottom.

- *Rotate all text 270 degrees*: Choose this item to turn the text on its side, so that it reads from bottom to top.

- *Stacked*: Choose this item to make the text read from top to bottom but without rotating the letters. This arrangement is good for adding narrow labels to graphical items.

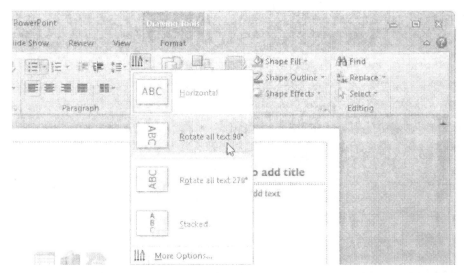

Figure 17-3. *Use the Text Direction panel in the Paragraph group on the Home tab of the Ribbon to turn text sideways or make it run in a stack down a slide. For other types of rotation, click the More Options button to open the Text Effects dialog box.*

■ **Note** Use text rotation only for special effects. Don't rely on rotated text to convey important points, as the audience may find it difficult to read.

If you need rotate text in other ways, follow these steps:

1. Choose Home ➤ Paragraph ➤ Text Direction ➤ More Options to display the Format Text Effects dialog box.

2. In the left column, click the Text Box item to display the Text Box pane (see Figure 17-4).

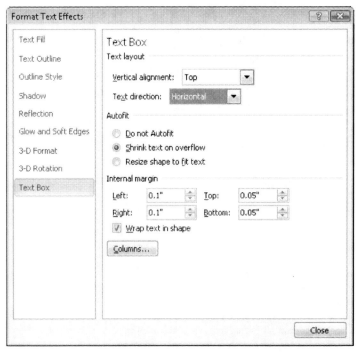

Figure 17-4. In the Text Box pane of the Format Text Effects dialog box, open the Text direction drop-down list and choose the text direction you want.

3. In the Text Layout area at the top, open the Vertical alignment drop-down list and choose the alignment for the text—Top, Middle, Bottom, Top Centered, Middle Centered, or Bottom Centered.

4. Open the Text direction drop-down list and choose the direction for the text—Horizontal, Rotate all text 90 degrees, Rotate all text 270 degrees, or Stacked.

5. In the left column, click the 3-D Rotation item to display the 3-D Rotation pane.

6. Set up the 3-D rotation you want by using the Presets drop-down list and the controls in the Rotation area. See Chapter 4 for details on rotating shapes.

7. In the Text area, make sure the Keep text flat check box is cleared so that PowerPoint rotates the text rather than just the shape around it.

8. Click the Close button to close the Format Text Effects dialog box.

■ **Tip** If you need to display text upside down, put it in its own container, and then rotate the container so that it is upside down.

Using Bulleted Lists

Many PowerPoint slides use bulleted lists, as they can be a great way of presenting your content clearly—provided you get them right.

This section shows you how to handle the mechanics of bulleted lists and suggests ways to make your content easy for your audience to grasp.

Creating a Bulleted List

Creating a bulleted list couldn't be easier. When you start typing text in a placeholder that has bullets applied, PowerPoint automatically gives the paragraph a bullet. When you press Enter to create the next paragraph, PowerPoint displays a bullet for that paragraph too.

To move the current paragraph down to the next lower level of bulleted list, press Tab at the beginning of the paragraph or choose Home ➤ Paragraph ➤ Increase List Level. Figure 17-5 shows a slide with three levels of indentation.

To move the current paragraph up to the next higher level, press Shift+Tab at the beginning of the paragraph or choose Home ➤ Paragraph ➤ Decrease List Level.

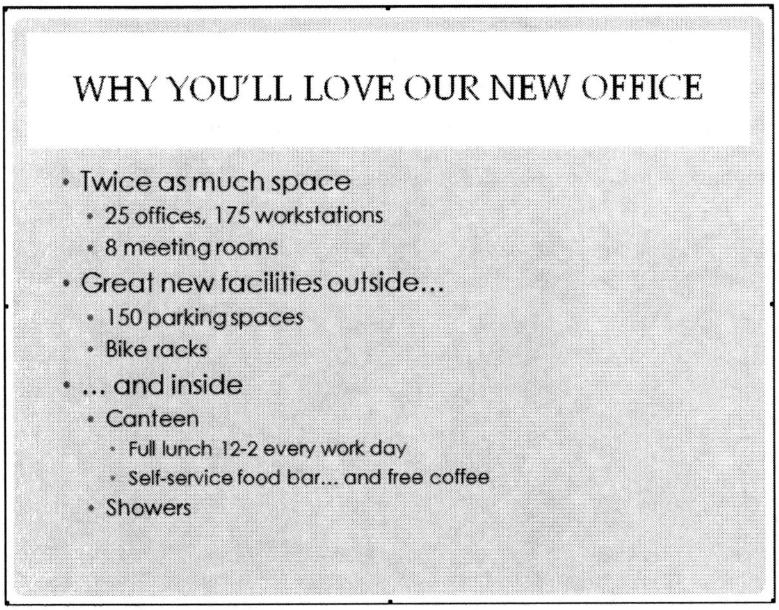

Figure 17-5. You can create a sublist by pressing Tab or by choosing Home ➤ Paragraph ➤ Increase List Level.

Making Sure Your Bulleted Lists Are Readable

The fonts and font sizes PowerPoint uses for text depend on the slide design. Many bulleted slides start off in a small enough font size to enable you to type five or six bullets of two lines each—so if you have fewer bullets on a slide, or if each is less than a single line, it's often a good idea to increase to font size to make the word easy to read.

When you start a sub-bulleted list, PowerPoint reduces the font size. This makes the hierarchy of the bullet points clear, but it can easily make the text too small to read. You may need to increase the font size of the sub-bullets as well to keep them readable. The extra indentation and different bullets will still indicate the hierarchy.

■ **Caution** PowerPoint lets you create pretty much as many levels of sub-bullets as you want—just keep pressing Tab at the start of a line or clicking the Increase List Level button to go to the next level. But if you go past two levels of bullets, that should raise a red flag to indicate that your slide is becoming too complex. If some content is that far subordinate, either cut it, or break the material up onto several slides.

Livening Up Your Slides with Custom Bullets

One way to make your slides look different is to change from the default bullet characters. PowerPoint provides a wide range of bullet characters, but you can also create your own.

To customize bullets, follow these steps:

1. Click the text placeholder in which you want to use the bullets.

2. Choose Home ➤ Paragraph ➤ Bullets, clicking the drop-down button, and then click Bullets and Numbering on the Bullets panel. PowerPoint displays the Bullets and Numbering dialog box with the Bulleted tab at the front (see Figure 17-6).

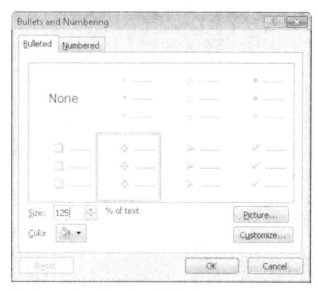

Figure 17-6. Use the Bulleted dialog box to set up custom bullets for a list.

3. If you want to create a custom bullet based on an existing bullet, follow these steps:

   • In the box of bullets, click the bullet style you want to start with.

   • Use the Size box to increase or decrease the bullet's size relative to the text. For example, set the bullet to 150% of text to make the bullet one and a half times the base height of the text.

   • Click the Color drop-down button, and then click the color you want on the color palette. To choose a color that doesn't appear, click the More Colors button, and then work in the Colors dialog box; click the OK button when you've chosen the color.

4. If you want to use a different bullet character, follow these steps:

   • Click the Customize button to display the Symbol dialog box (see Figure 17-7).

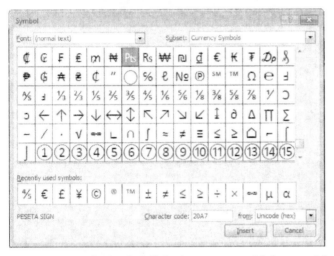

Figure 17-7. In the Symbol dialog box, you can pick from a wide range of symbol characters available in the various fonts. If the Subset drop-down list appears, you can select a subset of characters.

   • In the Font drop-down list, choose the font whose symbols you want to see.

⬛ **Tip** Fonts that include a good selection of symbols include the Symbol font, the Webdings font, the Wingdings font, the Wingdings 2 font, and the Wingdings 3 font.

   • Click the symbol of your choice.

   • Click the OK button to close the Symbol dialog box. PowerPoint returns you to the Bulleted tab of the Bullets and Numbering dialog box, where it displays the symbol you chose.

- Use the Size box and the Color drop-down palette to change the symbol's size and color as needed.

5. To use a picture as a bullet, follow these steps:

- Click the Picture button to display the Picture Bullet dialog box (see Figure 17-8).

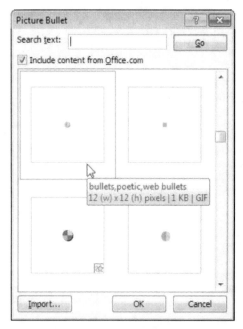

Figure 17-8. Use the Picture Bullet dialog box to find a picture bullet that meets your needs or to import a picture you can use as a bullet. Hold the mouse pointer over a bullet if you want to see information about it. For example, what it's supposed to show.

- Either browse through the bullets that appear in the list box, or type a search term (for example, nature or artsy) in the Search text box and click the Go button.

- Click the bullet you want.

■ **Note** To create a bullet from a picture, click the Import button. In the Add Clips to Organizer dialog box that appears, click the picture, and then click the Add button. You can then click the added picture in the Picture Bullet dialog box. You can use most graphics file types, including .gif, .jpg, .png, and .tif.

- Click the OK button to close the Picture Bullet dialog box and return to the Bullets and Numbering dialog box.

6. Click the OK button to close the Bullets and Numbering dialog box and apply the bullet you chose to the placeholder.

Adding Tables, SmartArt, Charts, and Hyperlinks to Slides

PowerPoint makes it as easy as possible to add graphical content to your slides. If the slide has a content placeholder (see Figure 17-9), click the appropriate icon in it, and then use the dialog box or pane that PowerPoint opens to identify the item you want. If the slide doesn't have a content placeholder, use the commands on the Insert tab of the Ribbon. Choose Insert ➤ Tables ➤ Table to insert a table, choose Insert ➤ Images ➤ Picture to insert a picture, choose Insert ➤ Illustrations ➤ Chart to insert a chart, and so on.

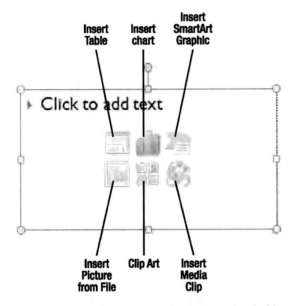

Figure 17-9. Click one of the six icons in a placeholder to start adding that type of content, or click the "Click to add text" prompt to start typing text.

Adding Tables to Slides

You can create a new table on a slide, but you can often save time by importing a table from Word or OneNote or by creating it from cells in an Excel worksheet.

Creating a Table from Scratch

To create a table from scratch, follow these steps:

1. Click the Insert Table icon in a placeholder to display the Insert Table dialog box (see Figure 17-10).

▪ **Note** If the slide doesn't have a content placeholder, choose Insert ➤ Tables ➤ Table, and then choose the table dimensions on the grid.

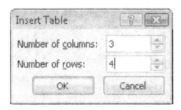

Figure 17-10. To insert a new table, click the Insert table icon in a placeholder, and then specify the number of columns and rows in the Insert Table dialog box.

2. In the Number of columns box, set the number of columns. Unless each data item is very short, you'll usually need to keep the number low (for example, three or four columns) to make sure the text is readable.

3. In the Number of rows box, set the number of rows. You can add further rows as needed, so it's fine to start with just a few.

4. Click the OK button to close the dialog box. PowerPoint inserts the table and gives it a design that works with the presentation's color theme.

5. Type the contents of the table, pressing Tab to move from one cell to the next. Figure 17-11 shows a table with simple data entered.

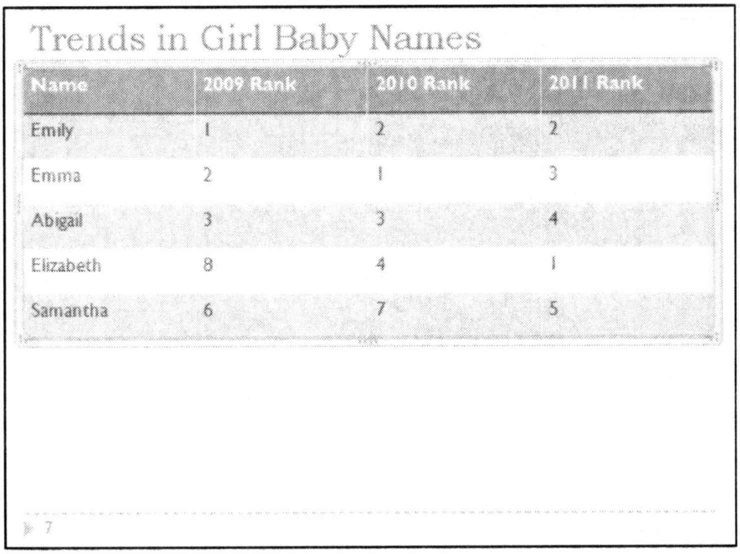

Name	2009 Rank	2010 Rank	2011 Rank
Emily	1	2	2
Emma	2	1	3
Abigail	3	3	4
Elizabeth	8	4	1
Samantha	6	7	5

Figure 17-11. At its default size, table data is often too small for comfortable reading from a distance.

6. Resize the table and its contents as needed. For example, the following

- If the table occupies only part of the slide, drag the handle at the bottom of its container downward, or drag the lower-right handle down and to the right, to expand the table. PowerPoint increases the row height to take up the extra space.

- With the table container selected, adjust the fonts to make the text easy to read. For example, click the Increase Font Size button a few times to pump up the font size. Figure 17-12 shows the same table taking up the full slide and with the text at a better size.

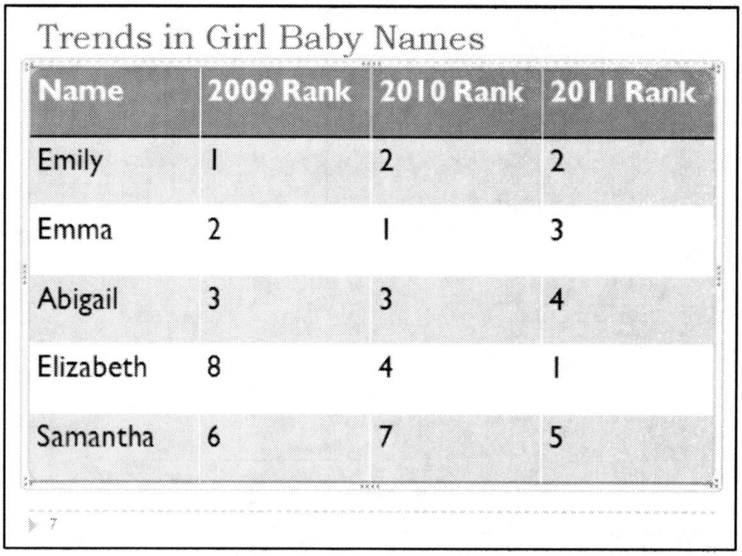

Trends in Girl Baby Names

Name	2009 Rank	2010 Rank	2011 Rank
Emily	1	2	2
Emma	2	1	3
Abigail	3	3	4
Elizabeth	8	4	1
Samantha	6	7	5

▶ 7

Figure 17-12. To make a table more readable, give it as much of the space on the slide as it needs, then increase the font sizes.

7. Change the design of the table as needed. For example, choose Table Tools ➤ Design ➤ Tables Styles, and then click the table style you want to apply.

Importing a Table from Word or OneNote

If the table you need to use in PowerPoint is already in a Word document or a OneNote notebook, you can quickly reuse it in PowerPoint—but you may need to reformat it. Follow these general steps:

1. In Word or OneNote, open the document or notebook that contains the table.

2. Select the table, and then copy it to the Clipboard. For example, right-click in the table, and then choose Table ➤ Select Table. Then right-click again and click Copy on the context menu.

3. In PowerPoint, right-click the slide on which you want to place the table, and then click the appropriate icon in the Paste Options section. As you move the mouse pointer over the icons, PowerPoint shows a preview of how the table will appear, as you can see in Figure 17-13. These are the options, from left to right:

   • *Keep Source Formatting*: Click this icon to keep the original formatting the table has in Word or OneNote.

   • *Use Destination Styles*: Click this icon to make the table pick up styles from the design you're using. This is often the best choice.

   • *Embed*: Available in Word only, click this icon to embed the Word table in the PowerPoint slide so that you can edit it as a Word document from within PowerPoint.

- *Picture*: Click this icon to embed the table as a picture. Use this option when you've got the table looking just right in Word or OneNote and you don't want to change it at all in PowerPoint (beyond resizing the picture).

- *Keep Text Only*: Click this icon to paste only the text from the table. You can then create a PowerPoint table containing that text (or use it to create bulleted points if that's what you need).

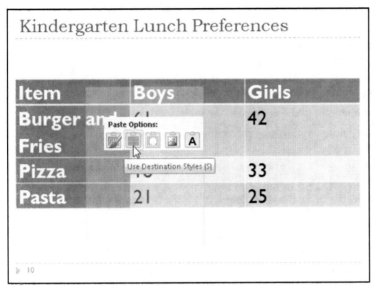

Figure 17-13 . Use the Paste Options icons on the context menu to control how PowerPoint inserts a table you've copied from Word or OneNote.

4. Format the table as needed in PowerPoint. For example:

    - Resize the table's container to the size you need.

    - Choose Table Tools ➤ Design ➤ Table Styles, and then click the style you want to apply.

    - Still on the Design tab, choose options in the Table Style Options group. For instance, select the Total Row check box if the table needs different formatting for a total row at the bottom.

    - If necessary, use the controls in the Font group on the Home tab of the Ribbon to change the font sizes. For instance, you may need to increase the font sizes to make the table readable in PowerPoint, because tables in Word and OneNote typically use smaller font sizes.

Creating a Table from Excel Worksheet Data

When a PowerPoint slide needs a table of data that you have in an Excel worksheet, copy the data across and paste it in. Don't waste time retyping the data and maybe introducing mistakes into it.

To create a PowerPoint table from Excel worksheet data, follow these steps:

1. In Excel, select the cells you want, and then copy them. For example, right-click in the selection, and then click Copy on the context menu.

2. In PowerPoint, select the slide on which you want to place the data.

3. Insert a table in one of these ways:

   - If the slide has a placeholder displaying the content icons, click the Insert Table icon. Either set the exact number of rows and columns your Excel selection will occupy, or insert a smaller table; for example, 2 columns by 2 rows. Click the OK button. PowerPoint automatically adjusts the number of columns and rows to fit the data you pasted.

   - Choose Insert ➤ Tables ➤ Table, and then click the table size. Again, either set the right number of rows and columns or (easier) create a smaller table.

4. Click to place the insertion point in the first cell in the table.

5. Right-click to display the context menu, and then choose one of these items in the Paste Options area:

   - *Keep Source Formatting*: Click this item to keep the cells' current formatting.

   - *Use Destination Styles*: Click this item if you want the table to take on the formatting from the design of the slide. Often, this is the best choice for integrating the slide into the presentation.

6. Format the table as needed in PowerPoint. For example:

   - Resize the table's container to occupy more of the slide.

   - Choose Table Tools ➤ Design ➤ Table Styles, and then click the style you want to apply.

   - On the Design tab of the Ribbon, choose options in the Table Style Options group.

   - Open the Home tab of the Ribbon and use the controls in the Font group on the Home tab of the Ribbon to change the font sizes as needed. For most slides, you'll need to increase the font size considerably to make the data easy to read in PowerPoint.

Adding SmartArt Graphics to Slides

You can add a SmartArt graphic to a slide by using the techniques explained in Chapter 3. For example, you can add an org chart like this:

1. Select the slide on which you want to add the SmartArt graphic. Create a new slide if necessary.

2. If there's a content placeholder, click the Insert SmartArt Graphic icon to display the Choose a SmartArt Graphic dialog box. Otherwise, choose Insert ➤ Illustrations ➤ SmartArt.

3. In the left list box, click the category of graphic you want. For example, choose Hierarchy if you want to create an org chart.

4. In the main pane, click the type of graphic; for example, Picture Organization Chart.

5. Click the OK button to close the dialog box and insert the SmartArt graphic.

6. If PowerPoint doesn't display the Type your text here window, click the double arrow button on the left side of the SmartArt graphic's container to display the window.

7. Type the text for each item in the Type your text here window.

8. Add any other items the SmartArt graphic needs. For example, add pictures to a Picture Organization Chart by clicking each picture placeholder in turn and then selecting the picture to use.

9. Resize the SmartArt graphic to suit the slide best. For example, you may want to make it as big as will fit on the slide to enable the audience to read it easily.

Adding Charts to Slides

A chart can be a great way of presenting complex or detailed information in a manner that's instantly clear on a slide. PowerPoint lets you add a chart to a slide in two ways:

- *Create a chart on an embedded worksheet*: Click the Insert Chart icon in a content placeholder, and then choose the chart type in the Insert Chart dialog box. PowerPoint then opens Excel for you and creates a new workbook so that you can enter the chart data and create the chart. The workbook is embedded in the PowerPoint presentation, so it becomes part of that file.

- *Copy a chart from an Excel workbook*: Create your chart in Excel using the techniques described in Chapter 13. Then copy the finished chart and paste it into your PowerPoint slide. You can choose whether to embed the chart's workbook in the PowerPoint presentation, to link the chart back to its source data in the Excel workbook, or just to insert it as a picture.

Here's how to choose when to create a new embedded workbook, embed an existing workbook, link back to a workbook, or insert a picture:

- *Create a new embedded workbook*: Do this when you don't yet have the data for the chart in Excel and you need to keep the chart's data with the PowerPoint presentation. For example, you'll send the presentation to someone else who will need to work on the chart data too.

- *Embed an existing workbook*: Do this when you have the data for the chart, or the chart itself in a workbook in Excel and you need to keep the chart's data available in the PowerPoint presentation.

- *Link back to a workbook*: Do this when you want to be able to change the chart or its source data in Excel and then automatically bring those changes into PowerPoint by updating the chart. Linking requires the workbook to stay in the same relative place in the computer's file system to the presentation so that the presentation can find the updated data. Moving the presentation to a different computer breaks the link.

- *Insert a picture*: Do this when you don't need to keep the connection between the chart and its source data and you will not need to edit the chart in the presentation.

Creating a Chart in a New Embedded Workbook

To create a chart on a worksheet in a new workbook embedded in your PowerPoint presentation, follow these steps:

1. On the slide where you want to create the chart, click the Insert Chart icon in a placeholder. If there's no placeholder, choose Insert ➤ Illustrations ➤ Chart instead. Either way, PowerPoint displays the Insert Chart dialog box (see Figure 17-14).

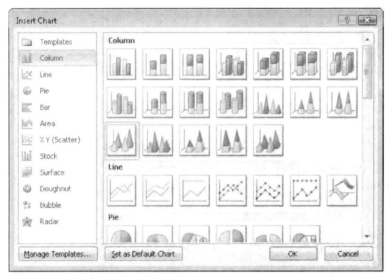

Figure 17-14. In the Insert Chart dialog box, click the chart type you want to create, and then click the OK button to launch Excel.

2. In the left column, click the category of chart you want to create; for example, Column.

3. In the main area, click the chart type.

4. Click the OK button. PowerPoint creates a chart of that type on the slide and launches Excel, which creates a new workbook, embeds it in the presentation, and gives it a name such as Chart in Microsoft PowerPoint.

5. Change the chart range and the sample data (see Figure 17-15) to the data your chart needs. PowerPoint automatically updates the chart to match the data in the Excel worksheet.

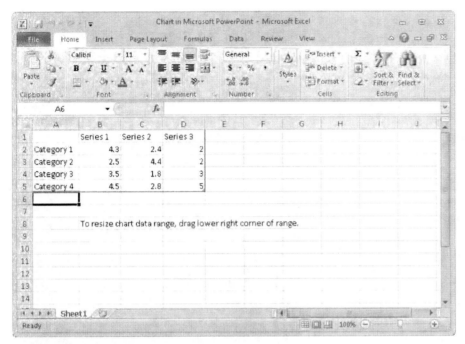

Figure 17-15. Excel enters sample data on the first worksheet in the embedded workbook. Change this data to create your chart.

6. When you have finished changing the data, close Excel. For example, click the Close button (the × button).

7. Use the controls in the Chart Tools section of the Ribbon to format the chart the way you want it. Figure 17-16 shows a slide containing a chart with formatting under way.

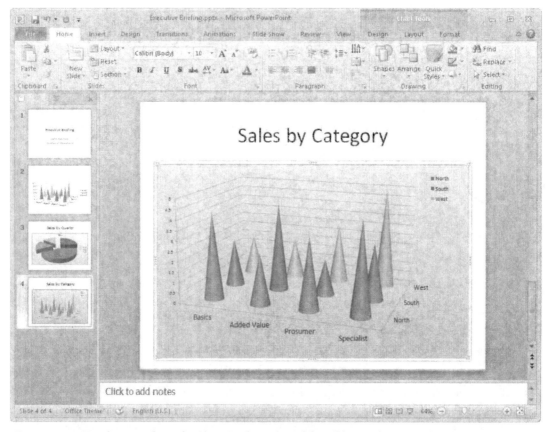

Figure 17-16. *Use the controls on the Chart Tools section of the Ribbon to format a chart you've created using an embedded workbook.*

8. Save your presentation.

■ **Note** To edit the data on your chart again, choose Chart Tools ➤ Design ➤ Data ➤ Edit Data. PowerPoint opens Excel, which displays the embedded worksheet.

Pasting a Chart from Excel into a PowerPoint Slide

If you have a chart already created in Excel, or if you have a workbook containing the data from which you will create the chart, you can paste the chart into PowerPoint. Follow these general steps:

1. Create the chart using the techniques explained in Chapter 13.

2. Click the chart to select it.

3. Copy the chart to the Clipboard. For example, choose Home ➤ Clipboard ➤ Copy, or right-click the selection and then click Copy on the context menu.

4. Switch to PowerPoint, and then select the slide on which you want to insert the chart.

5. Right-click the slide, and then click the appropriate icon in the Paste Options section of the context menu (see Figure 17-17):

   • *Keep Source Formatting & Embed Workbook*: Click this item to insert the chart using an embedded workbook, but to retain the chart's current formatting.

   • *Use Destination Theme & Embed Workbook*: Click this item to insert the chart using an embedded workbook, changing the chart's formatting to match the presentation's current theme.

   • *Keep Source Formatting & Link Data*: Click this item to link the chart back to the Excel workbook and retain the chart's current formatting.

   • *Use Destination Theme & Link Data*: Click this item to link the chart back to the Excel workbook, changing the chart's formatting to match the presentation's current theme.

   • *Picture*: Click this item to insert the chart as a picture, without embedding the workbook or linking the chart back to the Excel workbook.

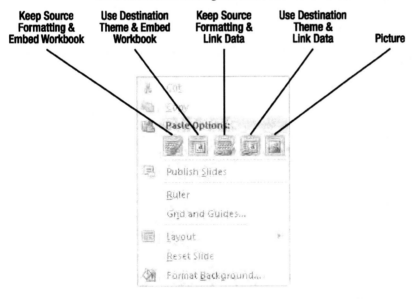

Figure 17-17. When pasting a chart from Excel into a PowerPoint slide, choose how to paste the chart by clicking the appropriate icon in the Paste Options section of the context menu.

6. Use the controls in the Chart Tools section of the Ribbon to format the chart the way you want it.

7. Save the presentation.

To edit the data in either an embedded or linked chart, choose Chart Tools ➤ Design ➤ Data ➤ Edit Data.

To update a linked chart, choose Chart Tools ➤ Design ➤ Data ➤ Refresh Data.

Adding Hyperlinks to Slides

You can add hyperlinks to PowerPoint slides using the standard technique explained in detail in Chapter 4.

1. Place the insertion point where you want to insert the hyperlink.

2. Choose Insert ➤ Links ➤ Hyperlink to display the Insert Hyperlink dialog box.

3. Choose the destination for the hyperlink, and specify the text to display on the slide.

4. Click the OK button to close the Insert Hyperlink dialog box and insert the hyperlink.

In your presentations, you'll typically use hyperlinks on slides for two purposes:

- *Link to other slides in the presentation*: To make it easy for the presenter or someone browsing the presentation to move to another slide, add a hyperlink to it. Follow these steps:

    1. In the Link to box on the left, click the Place in This Document button.

    2. In the Select a place in this document box (see Figure 17-18), click the slide you want to display.

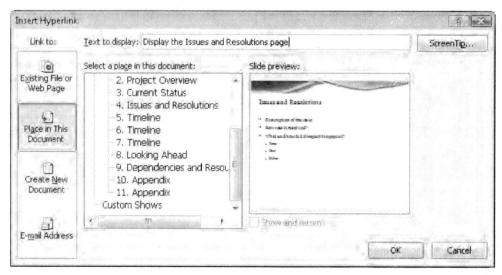

Figure 17-18. From the Insert Hyperlink dialog box, you can quickly create a link to another slide in the same presentation. This is a great way of enabling the viewer to navigate quickly about the presentation.

3. Edit the text in the Text to display box as needed.

4. If you need to provide additional information about the hyperlink, click the ScreenTip button, type ScreenTip text in the Set Hyperlink ScreenTip dialog box, and then click the OK button.

5. Click the OK button to close the Insert Hyperlink dialog box and insert the hyperlink.

- *Link to a web site*: You'll often want to include a link to your web site. In a live presentation, you can click the hyperlink to display your web site directly from a slide. In a presentation you share with others, they can click the hyperlink to go to the web site or to find out how to contact you.

Summary

In this chapter, you've learned how to plan and put together attractive and compelling slides. You now know how to use PowerPoint's built-in slide layouts effectively, how to create your own custom layouts, and how to add graphical elements such as table, charts, and SmartArt to your slides.

In the next chapter, I'll show you how to add graphics, movies, and sounds to your presentations; how to animate the objects on a slide; and how to apply transitions between slides.

CHAPTER 18

Adding Life and Interest to a Presentation

In the previous two chapters, you've learned how to create a presentation and how to fill it with good-looking slides that convey the message you want.

In this chapter, you'll look at how to inject life and interest to a presentation by adding graphics, movies (including movies straight from YouTube) and sounds, animations, and transitions. You'll also learn to hide slides so that they don't appear during a slide show, allowing you to keep them in reserve, and how to create custom slide shows within a presentation so that you can show only specific parts of it.

Adding Pictures to a Presentation

Many slides benefit from having pictures—graphics or photos—to illustrate or offset their text content. You can easily add a picture in these ways:

- *Use a content placeholder*: If the slide includes a content placeholder, click the Insert Picture from File icon to display the Insert Picture dialog box. Click the picture file, and then click the Insert button.

- *Use the Insert ➤ Images ➤ Picture command*: If the slide doesn't have a content placeholder, choose Insert ➤ Images ➤ Picture to open the Insert Picture dialog box. Click the picture file, and then click the Insert button.

Note To add a clip art picture, choose Insert ➤ Images ➤ Clip Art. In the Clip Art pane, locate the picture you want (for example, search for it by typing a term in the Search for box and clicking the Go button), and then click the picture to insert it.

Once you've added a graphic or photo to a slide, you can work with it using the techniques discussed in Chapter 4. For example, you can resize the picture, drag it to a different position (see Figure 18-1), change its contrast and brightness by using the Picture Tools ➤ Format ➤ Adjust ➤ Corrections command, or apply an artistic effect to it by using the Picture Tools ➤ Format ➤ Adjust ➤ Artistic Effects command. (The Artistic Effects command is not available for images such as drawings.)

Figure 18-1. After inserting a graphic or photo, resize it and reposition it as needed. You may also want to correct the picture's contrast and brightness or apply an artistic effect.

Creating a Photo Album

When you need to insert many pictures in a presentation all at once and in a regular layout, use PowerPoint's New Photo Album command like this:

1. Choose Insert ➤ Images ➤ Photo Album (clicking the top of the Photo Album button) to display the Photo Album dialog box (shown in Figure 18-2 with settings chosen).

▓ **Note** You don't need to create a new presentation before giving the New Photo Album command. PowerPoint automatically creates a new presentation for you.

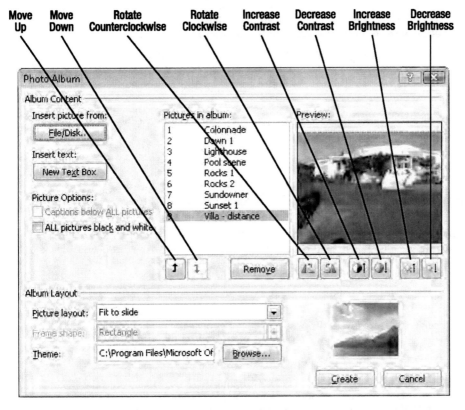

Move Up **Move Down** **Rotate Counterclockwise** **Rotate Clockwise** **Increase Contrast** **Decrease Contrast** **Increase Brightness** **Decrease Brightness**

Figure 18-2. Use the Photo Album dialog box to quickly create a new presentation based on a sequence of pictures.

2. Click the File/Disk button to display the Insert New Pictures dialog box.

3. Navigate to the folder or camera that contains the pictures, and then select the pictures:

   - Click a picture to select it. Shift+click to select from the current picture to the picture you click. Or Ctrl+click to add a picture to the selection.

   - Click to drag a box around a group of adjacent pictures.

4. Click the Insert button to close the Insert New Pictures dialog box and add the list of pictures to the Pictures in album list box in the Photo album dialog box.

5. Adjust each picture as needed by following these steps:

   - Click the picture in the Pictures in album list box. The picture's preview appears in the Preview box.

   - If the picture needs rotating, click the Rotate Counterclockwise button or the Rotate Clockwise button, as appropriate.

467

- If the picture's contrast needs adjustment, click the Increase Contrast button or the Decrease Contrast button, as appropriate.

- If the picture is too dark or too bright, click the Increase Brightness button or the Decrease Brightness button.

Note To make extensive color corrections to a picture, you may find it easier to use the Picture Tools ➤ Format ➤ Adjust ➤ Corrections panel after creating the album.

---

6. Arrange the pictures in the Pictures in album list box into the order you want for the album. Click a picture to select it, and then click the Up button or the Down button to move the picture up or down.

7. Add any text slides the presentation will need. In the Pictures in album list box, click the picture after which to insert the text box, then click the New Text Box button. PowerPoint adds to the Pictures in album list box an entry called Text Box. After you create the photo album, you can add text to it.

8. In the Album Layout area of the Photo Album dialog box, choose how the album should look:

   - Open the Picture layout drop-down list and choose the general layout: Fit to slide, 1 picture, 2 pictures, 4 pictures, 1 picture with title, 2 pictures with title, or 4 pictures with title. The graphic above the Create button gives you an idea of how this layout looks.

   - If the Frame shape drop-down list is available, open it and then click the frame shape you want: Rounded Rectangle; Simple Frame, White; Simple Frame, Black; Compound Frame, Black; Center Shadow Rectangle; or Soft Edge Rectangle. This drop-down list is not available when you choose the Fit to Slide layout.

   - If you want to apply a theme to the presentation, click the Browse button, click the theme in the Choose Theme dialog box that opens, and then click the Select button.

9. In the Picture Options Area, select the Captions below ALL pictures check box if you want to add a caption to each picture.

10. Also in the Picture Options area, select the ALL pictures black-and-white check box if you want to convert all the pictures to black and white.

11. Click the Create button to create the presentation from the photos you've chosen.

12. Enter your own text to fill in the placeholders for the presentation name, slide titles, and captions.

Adding Movies and Sounds to a Presentation

Graphics and photos can make a big difference to a presentation, but you may also want to add movies and sounds.

You can even add a video from YouTube, as long as the computer playing back the presentation will have an Internet connection.

Adding a Movie to a Slide

You can add a movie file to a slide so that you can play the movie as needed during the presentation. To add a movie file to a slide, follow these steps:

1. Select the slide on which you want to add the movie. Add a new slide if necessary.

2. If the slide has a content placeholder, click the Insert Media Clip icon to display the Insert Video dialog box. If not, choose Insert ➤ Media ➤ Video (clicking the top part of the Video button) to open this dialog box.

3. Navigate to the folder that contains the movie file, and then click the file to select it.

4. Insert the video file or link it, as appropriate:

    • *Insert the video file*: Click the Insert button. PowerPoint adds the whole of the video file to the presentation.

    • *Link the video file*: Click the Insert drop-down button, and then click Link to File instead. PowerPoint adds a link to the video file.

▨ **Note** Insert the video file when you want to include it in the presentation so that you can move the presentation to another computer. Link the video file when you're sure you will give the presentation from this computer and you want to keep the presentation's file size down.

---

5. Adjust the video file's appearance as needed by using the controls in the Video Tools ➤ Format tab of the Ribbon (see Figure 18-3):

    • Click the video file to select it, and then drag it into the right position on the slide.

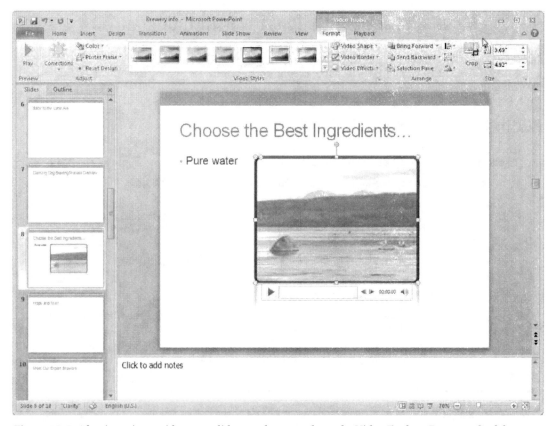

Figure 18-3. After inserting a video on a slide, use the controls on the Video Tools ➤ Format tab of the Ribbon to make it appear the way you want.

- If necessary, resize the video frame by dragging a corner handle. You can also crop it by choosing Video Tools ➤ Format ➤ Size ➤ Crop, and then dragging a corner handle with the cropping pointer.

- To correct the video's brightness and contrast, choose Video Tools ➤ Format ➤ Adjust ➤ Corrections, and then click the balance of brightness and contrast you want.

- To change the video's color balance, choose Video Tools ➤ Format ➤ Adjust ➤ Color, and then click the color option you want. For example, you can apply a sepia hue or make the video black and white.

- To choose which frame of the video appears on the slide until you play the video, use the playback controls to move the video to the frame you want. Then pause the video and choose Video Tools ➤ Format ➤ Adjust ➤ Poster Frame ➤ Current Frame.

▓ **Tip** Instead of using a frame from the video, you can use a still picture as the poster frame for the video. Choose Video Tools ➤ Format ➤ Adjust ➤ Poster Frame ➤ Image File, select the picture in the Insert Picture dialog box, and then click the Insert button.

- To put the video in a frame, choose Video Tools ➤ Format ➤ Video Styles ➤ More (clicking the drop-down button on the Video Styles box), and then click the frame you want.

- To change the video shape, choose Video Tools ➤ Format ➤ Video Styles ➤ Video Shape, and then click the shape you want.

- To customize the border for the shape, choose Video Tools ➤ Format ➤ Video Styles ➤ Video Border, and then click the type of border you want.

- To apply a video effect, choose Video Tools ➤ Format ➤ Video Styles ➤ Video Effects. On the menu that appears, click the type of effect, and then choose the specific effect from the panel that opens. For example, you can display a shadow under the video, or you can perform a 3-D rotation on it.

6. Click the Playback tab in the Video Tools section of the Ribbon, and then choose playback options.

- To place a bookmark marking a point in the video that you want to be able to access easily, move the Playhead across the clip's control bar until you reach the right point in the video. Then choose Video Tools ➤ Playback ➤ Bookmarks ➤ Add Bookmark. The bookmark appears as a dot that you can click. You can remove a bookmark by clicking it and then choosing Video Tools ➤ Playback ➤ Bookmarks ➤ Remove Bookmark.

- To trim the video so that only part of it plays, choose Video Tools ➤ Playback ➤ Editing ➤ Trim Video. In the Trim Video dialog box that opens (see Figure 18-4), drag the green beginning marker and the red end marker to specify where to start and stop the video, and then click the OK button.

Figure 18-4. *In the Trim Video dialog box, move the start and end markers to set the part of the video clip you want to play.*

- To fade the video in or out, set the timing in the Fade In box or Fade Out box in the Fade Duration area of the Editing group.

- To choose how to start the video, choose On Click or Automatically in the Start drop-down list in the Video Options group.

- To make the video play full screen rather than at the size you've given it on the slide, select the Play Full Screen check box in the Video Options group. This setting is useful for giving the video full impact without devoting a full slide to it.

- To hide the video when it's not playing, select the Hide While Not Playing check box in the Video Options group.

- If you want the video to keep playing in a loop until you stop it, select the Loop until Stopped check box in the Video Options group.

- If you want the video to rewind to the beginning so that you can easily play it again, select the Rewind after Playing check box in the Video Options group.

7. Click the Play button (Video Tools ➤ Playback ➤ Preview ➤ Play) to play the video and check that everything is how you want it to be.

Adding a YouTube Video to a Slide

If you don't have a copy of the video you need to play, but it's available on YouTube, you can add it to a slide directly from YouTube.

Note For the YouTube video to play back correctly, the PC must be connected to the Internet. So if you'll give the presentation at a client's office, check that you'll have an Internet connection available.

To add a YouTube video to a presentation, follow these steps:

1. Find the video on YouTube. For example, open Internet Explorer, go to www.youtube.com, and browse to find the video.

2. Click the <Embed> button to display the embedding pane (see Figure 18-5).

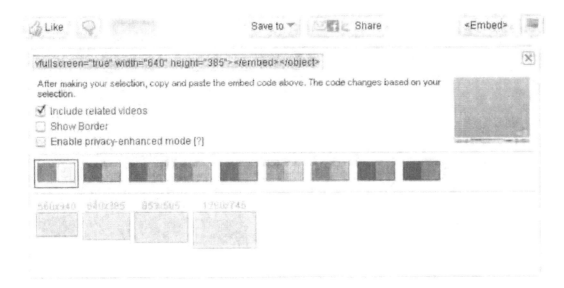

Figure 18-5. *Before you copy the embed code for a YouTube video, click the Customize button and choose the video size and other options.*

3. Choose the settings you want for the video:

    • Select or clear the Include related videos check box, the Show Border check box, and the Enable privacy-enhanced mode check box, as needed.

    • Click the color scheme you want.

    • Click the video size you want.

4. Select the contents of the Embed box and press Ctrl+C to copy it to the Clipboard.

5. Go back to PowerPoint and select the slide you want to insert the video on. Create a new slide if necessary.

6. Choose Insert ➤ Media ➤ Video ➤ Video from Web Site to display the Insert Video from Web Site dialog box (see Figure 18-6).

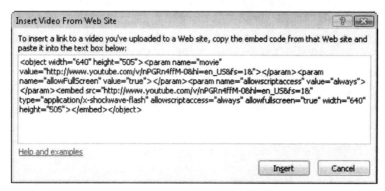

Figure 18-6. Use the Insert Video From Web Site dialog box to set up a slide to play a video directly from YouTube.

7. Right-click in the box, and then click Paste on the shortcut menu to paste in the embed code you copied.

8. Click the Insert button to insert the embed code.

9. Click the Slide Show button in the View Shortcuts group on the status bar to view the slide as it will appear in the slide show.

10. Select the video item on the slide, and then click the Play button. Make sure the video plays as you want it to.

Adding a Sound to a Slide

To add a sound to a slide, follow these steps:

1. Select the slide on which you want to add the audio.

2. Choose Insert ➤ Media ➤ Audio ➤ Audio (clicking the top part of the Audio button) to display the Insert Audio dialog box.

3. Navigate to the folder that contains the file you want to insert, and then click the file.

■ **Tip** You'll find various Windows sounds in the \Windows\Media\ folder on your PC's boot drive—usually drive C:.

---

4. Click the Insert button. PowerPoint inserts an audio icon (see Figure 18-7) representing the sound.

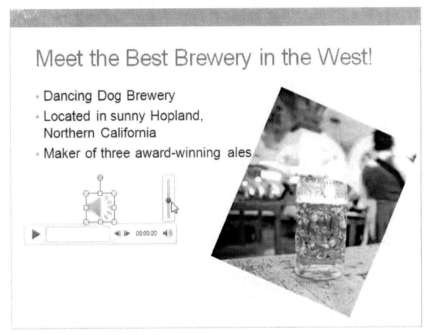

Figure 18-7. PowerPoint inserts an audio item as a speaker icon. Click the icon to display controls for testing the audio and setting the volume.

5. Select the icon by clicking it, and then drag it to where you want it to appear.

6. With the icon selected, use the pop-up controls to test the audio clip and set the volume at which you want it to play.

Adding Transitions to Slides

Instead of having a straightforward switchover from one slide to the next, you can set PowerPoint to play a *transition*—an effect that smoothes, animates, or dramatizes the change of slides. You can set a different transition for each side if necessary. You specify the transition by selecting the slide and choosing the transition to play when the slide appears (as opposed to setting the transition for when PowerPoint changes the slide to the next).

PowerPoint provides a wide range of transitions that you can apply from the Transitions tab of the Ribbon (see Figure 18-8).

Figure 18-8. The Transitions tab of the Ribbon gives you one-stop access to the key controls for setting up transitions between slides.

■ **Note** Depending on the presentation template or design you're using, some or all of the slides in the presentation may already have transitions applied to them.

PowerPoint breaks up the transitions into three categories:

- *Subtle*: Use these transitions when you don't need to draw the audience's attention to the transition. The first transition in the Subtle category is the None transition, which you apply when you don't want a transition effect between slides.

- *Exciting*: Use these transitions when you want to make sure the audience notices the transition. For example, you can use an effect such as Vortex or Shred to dramatize the switchover from one slide to another than uses a similar look and so might be mistaken for the previous slide.

- *Dynamic Content*: Use these transitions when you want to draw attention to the transition. For example, the Ferris Wheel transition makes the incoming slide go around as if it were moving on a Ferris wheel.

■ **Tip** PowerPoint's transitions are easy and fun to apply, but don't go hog wild with them. In a typical presentation, not every slide benefits from a transition; and when you do use a transition, one of the Subtle transitions often gives the best effect. Keep the Exciting and Dynamic Content transitions for those rare occasions when you actually want to draw your audience's attention to the transition rather than to the content of the slides.

To apply a transition, follow these steps:

1. Click the slide to which you want to apply the transition. PowerPoint will play the transition between the previous slide and this slide.

2. Click the Transitions tab to display its contents.

3. Preview and apply the transition you want:

   - Hold the mouse pointer over a transition to preview its effect.

   - If the transition appears in the Transition Scheme box, click it. The Transition Scheme box is the long box in the Transition to This Slide group.

- Otherwise, click the More button (the drop-down button) at the right side of the Transition Scheme box, and then click the transition on the panel that appears (see Figure 18-9).

Figure 18-9. *Open the Transition Scheme drop-down panel to access the full range of transitions all at once.*

4. To choose options for the transition, choose Transitions ➤ Transition to This Slide ➤ Effect Options, and then click the option you want on the panel that opens.

   - The choices on this panel vary depending on the transition you've selected. For example, the Ripple transition has five directional options (Center, From Bottom-Left, From Bottom-Right, From Top-Right, and From Top-Left), while the Honeycomb transition has no options.

   - You can preview an option by holding the mouse pointer over it.

5. To preview the transition again, choose Transitions ➤ Preview ➤ Preview.

6. If you want to add a sound to the transition, choose Transitions ➤ Timing ➤ Sound, and then click the sound on the drop-down list. You can make the sound keep playing until the next sound starts (click the Loop Until Next Sound to place a check mark next to it), but this is not usually a good idea.

■ **Note** To use a sound other than PowerPoint's built-in sounds, choose Transitions ➤ Timing ➤ Sound ➤ Other Sound, click the sound file in the Add Audio dialog box, and then click the OK button.

---

7. If you want to change the duration of the transition, set it in the Duration box in the Timing group of the Transitions tab. PowerPoint automatically sets the duration to a suitable length for the transition you choose, but you may need to change it to make your presentation's timing work.

8. In the Advance Slide section of the Timing group on the Transitions tab, choose how to advance the slide to the next slide:

   - *On Mouse Click*: Select this check box if you want to click the mouse to move to the next slide.

   - *After*: To display the next slide automatically, select this check box, and then set the timing in the text box.

9. Preview the transition again to make sure it gives the effect you want, and then click the Save button on the Quick Access Toolbar to save your changes.

Adding Animations to Slides

When you need to bring a slide to life, you can animate one or more of the objects on it. For example, you may need to make an object appear on a slide, draw attention to itself at a key point, or disappear from view when its role is over—or all three.

You can also use animations to reveal only part of a slide, or part of an object at a time, which can help keep the audience focused on your current point rather than reading ahead to the end of the slide

Understanding the Essentials of Animations

To add an animation to a slide, you apply it to an object on the slide—for example, a picture or a text placeholder. Any object can have one or more animations, and you can arrange them into the order you need.

■ **Caution** As with transitions, it's easy to go over the top with animations. Resist the temptation: animations will have more effect in your slides if you use them sparingly and only at the appropriate times.

PowerPoint provides a wide range of animations in four categories:

- *Entrance*: These animations bring the object onto the slide. For example, the Appear animation makes the object appear in place, while the Swivel animation makes the object appear and swivel several times.

- *Emphasis*: These animations help draw the audience's attention to the object. For example, the Pulse animation makes the object pulse visibly, and the Spin animation makes the object revolve around its axis.

- *Exit*: These animations remove the object from the slide. For example, the Disappear animation makes the object vanish, while the Shrink & Turn animation makes the object turn sideways as it disappears into the distance.

- *Motion Path*: These animations make the object move around, and then return to its original position.

The next section shows you how to add a straightforward animation to an object. The section after than shows you how to create more complex animations.

Adding an Animation to an Object

To add a straightforward animation to an object on a slide, follow these steps:

1.   Click the object to select it.

2.   Click the Animations tab to display its controls.

3.   In the Animation group, click the More button at the right end of the Add Animation box, and then click the animation on the drop-down panel (see Figure 18-10).

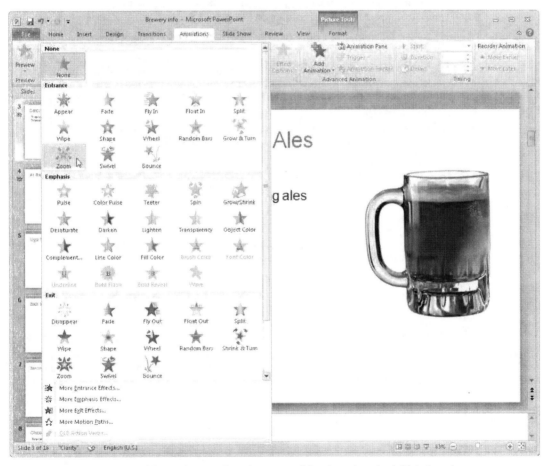

Figure 18-10. *You can quickly apply an animation to an object by using the Add Animation drop-down panel.*

■ **Note** PowerPoint automatically plays a preview of the animation effect you're working on to help you see how it is. To turn off this automatic preview, choose Animations ➤ Preview ➤ Preview ➤ AutoPreview (removing the check mark from the AutoPreview item on the Preview drop-down menu); repeat the command to turn the automatic preview back on. When the automatic preview is off, choose Animations ➤ Preview ➤ Preview (clicking the upper part of the Preview button) to preview the current animation.

4. To choose options for the effect, choose Animations ➤ Animation ➤ Effect Options, and then click the option you want. The options available depend on the effect you've chosen; for example, many animations offer direction options such as From Bottom, From Bottom-Left, From Left, From Top-Left, From Top, From Top-Right, From Right, and From Bottom-Right.

5. To control when the animation runs, use the controls on the left side of the Timing group:

   • Open the Start drop-down list and choose when to start the animation: On Click (in other words, when you click the mouse), With Previous (at the same time as the previous animation), or After Previous (after the previous animation has finished).

   • In the Duration text box, set the number of seconds and hundredths of seconds you want the animation to run; for example, 1.50 for one and a half seconds.

   • In the Delay text box, set the delay before starting the animation (for example, after the previous animation finishes running). Again, use seconds and hundreds of seconds.

6. To change the order of animations, click an object, and then click the Move Earlier button or the Move Later button in the Reorder Animation area of the Timing group on the Animations tab. PowerPoint displays a number next to each animated item on the slide, so you can easily see the current order.

7. Click the Preview button in the Preview group to preview the animation and see if you need to make further changes.

Changing the Order of Animations

When you apply multiple animations to the same slide, you may need to change the order in which they occur. To do so, choose Animations ➤ Animation ➤ Animation Pane, and then work in the Animation pane. Figure 18-11 shows a slide that contains six animations, including all those applied to the text container.

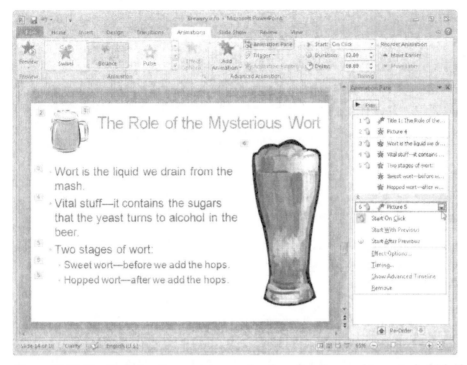

Figure 18-11. *Use the Animation pane to examine the animations and to control which plays when.*

These are the main actions you can take in the Animation pane:

- *Play the animations*: Click the Play button. The Animation pane displays a time readout showing which animation is playing and how long the sequence takes.

- *Change the order of the animations*: Click an animation to select it, and then click the Up button or the Down button in the Re-Order bar at the bottom of the pane.

- *Expand or collapse a container's animations*: Click the light blue bar with two downward chevrons to expand a container's list of animations so that you see them all, or click the two upward chevrons to collapse the list.

- *Change when an animation plays*: Click an animation to select it, then click the drop-down button to display the menu of options. Click the Start On Click item, the Start With Previous item, or the Start After Previous item, as needed.

When you have finished using the Animation pane, close it by clicking its Close button (the × button) or by choosing Animations ➤ Advanced Animation ➤ Animation Pane again.

Using Animation to Display Bulleted Paragraphs One at a Time

When you have several bulleted paragraphs in a text placeholder, you can use animation to display them one at a time. This helps prevent the audience from reading ahead of you and missing the point you're explaining.

To display bulleted paragraphs one at a time, follow these steps:

1. Click the container that holds the bulleted paragraphs.

2. Apply the animation to the container from the Add Animation box or panel. For example, apply the Fly In animation.

3. If the animation offers different directions, choose Animations ➤ Animation ➤ Effect Options, and then click the direction you want. For example, click From Right.

4. Choose Animations ➤ Animation ➤ Effect Options again, and this time click the Sequence option you want:

   • *As One Object*: PowerPoint animates the whole object at once.

   • *All at Once*: PowerPoint animates each top-level paragraph separately but runs the animations all at once. Depending on the animation, this can look very similar to As One Object, but it can also look different.

   • *By Paragraph*: PowerPoint animates each top-level paragraph separately. This is usually the most useful setting.

5. Click the Preview button (choose Animations ➤ Preview ➤ Preview) to preview the effect.

6. If the text has different levels, and you need to control their paragraphs separately, choose Animations ➤ Animation ➤ More, clicking the little button in the lower-right corner of the Animation group. PowerPoint displays the dialog box for the effect.

7. Click the Text Animation tab to display its contents. Figure 18-12 shows the Text Animation tab for the Fly In animation.

Figure 18-12. In the Group text drop-down list on the Text Animation tab of the animation's dialog box, choose the level of paragraphs by which you want to animate the object.

8. Open the Group text drop-down list and choose the animation you want: As One Object, All Paragraphs At Once, or a paragraph level from By 1st Level Paragraphs to By 5th Level Paragraphs. For example, if the container has two levels of paragraphs, and you want to control both separately, choose By 2nd Level Paragraphs.

9. Click the OK button to close the animation's dialog box.

Animating SmartArt Graphics, Charts, and Tables

You can apply animations to SmartArt graphics, charts, and tables just as you can to other objects in PowerPoint. Animations are especially useful when you want to reveal only part of one of these objects at a time, gradually building up to showing the whole object.

Animating a SmartArt Graphic

PowerPoint enables you to animate the component parts of a SmartArt graphic in sequence, so you can choose between displaying the whole object at once, displaying all the objects at a particular level, or displaying one object at a time.

To choose how to display a SmartArt graphic, follow these steps:

1. Select the SmartArt graphic by clicking it on the slide.

2. Apply the animation to the graphic as a whole from the Add Animation box or panel. For example, apply the Fade animation. This makes the whole graphic appear at once with the animation.

3. Apply the animation to the chart as a whole from the Add Animation box or panel. For example, apply the Appear animation.

4. Choose Animations ➤ Animation ➤ Effect Options, and then click the way you want to animate the graphic:

   - *As One Object*: This option displays the graphic as a single object, so it all appears in one animation.

   - *All at Once*: This option treats the graphic as separate objects, but runs the animation on all the objects at once.

   - *One by One*: This option treats each component of the graphic as a separate object. In many cases, this is the most useful option.

   - *Level at Once*: This option treats each level of a hierarchical SmartArt graphic as a separate object. Choose this option when you want to display one level of the graphic at a time.

   - *Level One by One*: This option treats each level of a hierarchical SmartArt graphic as a separate object, and treats each object within the level as a separate object. Choose this option when you want to display the graphic one object of a level at a time.

5. Click the Preview button (choose Animations ➤ Preview ➤ Preview) to preview the effect.

6.   If you need to change the order, choose Animations ➤ Animation ➤ More, clicking the little button in the lower-right corner of the Animation group. PowerPoint displays the dialog box for the effect.

7.   Click the SmartArt Animation tab to display its contents. Figure 18-13 shows the SmartArt Animation tab for the Fade Animation.

Figure 18-13. Use the Group graphic drop-down list on the SmartArt Animation tab of the dialog box for an animation to control how the components of a SmartArt graphic appear.

8.   Open the Group graphic drop-down list, and then click the option you want. The options available depend on the type of SmartArt graphic, but these ones are typical:

   •   *As One Object*: Choose this option to display the whole SmartArt graphic at once.

   •   *All At Once*: Choose this option to display all the components of the SmartArt graphic at once.

   •   *One by one*: Choose this option to display one component at a time

   •   *By branch one by one*: Choose this option to display each branch of a graphic such as an org chart separately, showing one component at a time.

   •   *By level at once*: Choose this option to display each level of a graphic separately, showing the whole level at once.

   •   *By level one by one*: Choose this option to display each level of a graphic separately, showing one component at a time.

9.   If you want to reveal the SmartArt graphic in reverse order, select the Reverse order check box.

10.   Click the OK button to close the animation's dialog box.

Animating a Chart

When you're displaying a chart, it's often helpful to use an animation to show part of it at a time rather than displaying the whole chart at once. To do this, follow these steps:

1. Select the chart by clicking it on the slide that contains it.

2. Apply the animation to the chart as a whole from the Add Animation box or panel. For example, apply the Appear animation.

3. Choose Animations ➤ Animation ➤ Effect Options, and then click the way you want to animate the chart:

   - *As One Object*: This setting displays the chart all at once, so you probably won't want to use it.

   - *By Series*: This setting displays one full data series at a time and is good for contrasting the data series to each other.

   - *By Category*: This setting displays one whole category at a time and is good for comparing the categories.

   - *By Element in Series*: This setting displays each element in a series at a time, then the next element in the series, and so on until the series is finished. This setting is great for focusing on the individual elements in the series.

   - *By Element in Category*: This setting displays each element in a category at a time, then the category's next element, and so on. Use this setting to zero in on the individual elements in the categories.

■ **Note** If you insert a chart as a picture, you can't animate its components.

---

4. If necessary, choose Animations ➤ Advanced Animation ➤ Animation Pane to display the Animation pane, and then adjust the settings. For example, if you've chosen the By Element in Series option, you can set the elements in a series to display automatically one after the other, using a short delay between them.

5. Preview the animation and make sure that the objects appear as you want them to.

Animating a Table

When you're displaying a complex table on a slide, it's often helpful to displays the rows, columns, or even cells one at a time to keep the audience's attention on the data you're currently talking about. PowerPoint's animations don't work for rows, columns, or cells, so you need to take matters into your own hands.

Here are two approaches you can use:

- *Create two or more separate tables*: Create two or more separate tables and position them next to each other so that they appear to be a single table. You can then animate each of the tables separately, giving the effect of animating different parts of the same table. This approach sounds clumsy, but it's easy to do, and it's effective visually.

- *Hide parts of the table*: Create a single table, and then cover those parts you want to hide with shapes (for example, rectangles) colored the same as the slide's background. You can then reveal a hidden part of the table by running an Exit animation on the shape that's covering it.

Keeping Extra Information Up Your Sleeve with Hidden Slides

In many presentations, it's useful to have extra information that you can summon up to deal with points you don't want to cover unless the audience raises them. To meet this need, PowerPoint lets you hide any slide so that it doesn't appear unless you specifically choose to display it.

To hide a slide, right-click the slide in the Slides tab of the Navigation pane or in Slide Sorter view, and then click Hide Slide on the context menu.

PowerPoint indicates a hidden slide by showing around its slide number a box with a diagonal strikethrough (see Figure 18-14) in the Slides tab in Normal view and in the slides area in Slide Sorter view. On the Go to Slide menu in Reading view and Slide Show view, a hidden slide appears with parentheses around its slide number.

Figure 18-14. In Slide Sorter view and on the Slides tab of the Navigation pane, a box with a diagonal strikethrough indicates a hidden slide.

To change a slide back from hidden to normal, right-click the slide, and then click Hide Slide again, turning off the hiding.

Creating Custom Slide Shows within a Presentation

Hidden slides can be great when you want to keep some information in reserve, but if you find yourself hiding many slides within a presentation, you may need to take the next step—creating a custom slide show.

A custom slide show is an arrangement of slides within a presentation. You can choose which of the presentation's slides to include in the custom show, and you can change the order in which they appear. You can create as many custom slide shows within a presentation as you need to.

Opening the Custom Shows Dialog Box

To work with custom shows, first open the Custom Shows dialog box by choosing Slide Show ➤ Start Slide Show ➤ Custom Slide Show ➤ Custom Shows. Figure 18-15 shows the Custom Shows dialog box with a custom show already created.

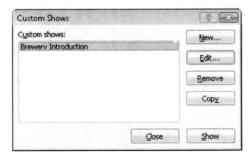

Figure 18-15. *From the Custom Shows dialog box, you can create, launch, and manage custom slide shows within a presentation.*

Creating a Custom Slide Show

To create a custom slide show, follow these steps:

1. Create all the slides for the presentation, or as many of the slides as you can create at this point. (You can add other slides later, but it's easiest to start with all your slides if you've created them.)

2. Choose Slide Show ➤ Start Slide Show ➤ Custom Slide Show ➤ Custom Shows to display the Custom Shows dialog box.

3. Click the New button to display the Define Custom Show dialog box (shown in Figure 18-16 with settings chosen).

Figure 18-16. *Use the Define Custom Show dialog box to name a custom show, add slides to it, and put the slides in the order you want.*

4. In the Slide show name box, type the name you want to give the custom show. Usually, you'll want to make the name as descriptive as possible while keeping it short enough to fit fully in the Custom shows box in the Custom Shows dialog box—40 characters or so at most.

5. In the Slides in presentation box, select the slides you want to add to the custom show, and then click the Add button. After clicking a slide to select it, you can Shift+click another slide to select all the slides between the two, or Ctrl+click individual slides to add them to the selection.

6. Once you've added the slides you want to the Slides in custom show box, rearrange them into the order needed. To move a slide up or down the order, click it, and then click the up arrow button or the down arrow button, as appropriate.

7. When you've finished creating the custom show, click the OK button to close the Define Custom Show dialog box. PowerPoint returns you to the Custom Shows dialog box, where the Custom shows box includes the custom show you just created.

■ **Tip** To create another show based on a custom show you've created, click the existing show in the Custom Shows dialog box, and then click the Copy button. PowerPoint creates a new custom show called *Copy of* and the existing show's name—for example, *Copy of Brewery Introduction*. With the copy selected, click the Edit button to open the copy in the Define Custom Show dialog box. You can then rename the copy and change its contents.

Playing a Custom Slide Show

After you've created a custom slide show, you can play it by opening the Custom Shows dialog box, clicking the show in the Custom shows list, and then clicking the Show button.

Editing or Deleting a Custom Slide Show

To edit a custom slide show, click its name in the Custom shows list in the Custom Shows dialog box, and then click the Edit button. You can then use the Define Custom Show dialog box to change the selection of slides in the show or alter their order as needed.

To delete a custom show, click its name in the Custom shows list in the Custom Shows dialog box, and then click the Remove button. PowerPoint removes the show without confirmation.

Summary

In this chapter, you've looked at how to add graphics, movies, and sounds to your slides. You've also learned how to smooth or dramatize the switchover from one slide to another by choosing a suitable transition to introduce the next slide, and how to bring the elements of a slide to life by applying animations and setting them to run the way you want.

You can now also hide slides that you want to keep in reserve, and create custom slide shows consisting of only some of the slides from a presentation.

By now, you know how to put together a powerful and convincing presentation. The next stage is to deliver the presentation. You'll learn how to do this in the next chapter.

CHAPTER 19

Delivering a Presentation Live or Online

By this point, chances are that you've created a powerful and compelling presentation stuffed with great content. Now it's time to deliver that presentation.

PowerPoint enables you to deliver a presentation in a handful of different ways. The most straightforward way is by giving it live to your audience, showing the slides on a screen. This can be a challenge, but PowerPoint helps greatly by providing Presenter view, which puts your notes and essential controls where you can see them but the audience can't.

To help your audience enjoy your presentation and retain its message, you can create a handout by exporting slides automatically to a Word document that you can then edit as needed. And if you need to distribute a presentation rather than deliver it personally, you can record narration to fit the slides.

At the end of the chapter, I'll show you how to export and share your presentations. Apart from using means of sharing that you already know, such as e-mailing a presentation or saving a presentation to a SharePoint site or SkyDrive, you can broadcast a slide show live on the Web to however big an audience you can muster, or publish slides to a slide library so that your colleagues can work with them.

We'll start by going over how to prepare to deliver a presentation—setting up the display, arranging Presenter view, practicing your presentation, and (if you need to) recording automatic timings.

Getting Ready to Deliver a Presentation in Person

Before you deliver a presentation, you'll need to set up the computer you'll use with the projector or display on which you'll display the presentation. You will likely want to use PowerPoint's handy Presenter view if possible to keep your notes and controls on screen. You will almost certainly want to practice your presentation before you actually have to give it. And you may want to record automatic timings for the slides so that the presentation automatically advances itself while you perform.

Setting Up Your Display and Choosing the Resolution

Start by connecting your PC to the display or projector on which you'll give the presentation, and then get the displays set up. Here's an example using a laptop and Windows 7 (perhaps the most likely scenario):

1. Connect the projector to the laptop's external display port.

2. Turn on the projector.

3. Turn on the laptop and log on.

4. Right-click the desktop, and then click Screen Resolution on the context menu to display the Screen Resolution window (see Figure 19-1).

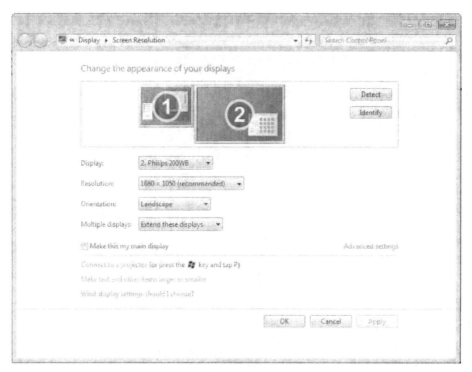

Figure 19-1. Start by setting up the projector or the external display in the Screen Resolution window in Control Panel.

5. Make sure both the displays appear in the Change the appearance of your displays box. If not:

    •   *Projector*: Click the Connect to a projector link or press Windows Key+P. In the Projector panel that appears (see Figure 19-2), click the Extend button to extend your desktop onto the projector (usually best), the Duplicate button to show the same material on the projector as on your PC's screen, or the Projector only button if you want to use only the projector.

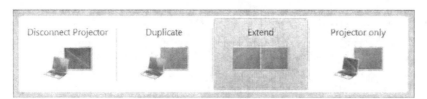

Figure 19-2. In the Projector panel, you'll normally want to click the Extend button so that you can use Presenter view on your laptop's screen while showing the slides on the projector.

- *Display*: Click the Detect button. If you can't tell which icon represents each display, click the Identify button to flash a large number on each display.

6. Drag the display icons to match how the displays are physically positioned. For example, if Display 1 is to the right of Display 2 rather than to the left, drag the Display 1 icon to the right of Display 2.

7. If you need to change the resolution, click the display you want to change, choose the resolution in the Resolution drop-down list, and then click the Apply button.

8. Make sure the Multiple displays drop-down list has the right setting. Normally, you'll want the Extend these displays setting.

9. Click the OK button when you've finished making changes in the Screen Resolution window.

Now that you've got both displays working, you can tell PowerPoint which display you want to use for the presentation. To do so, click the Slide Show tab of the Ribbon, go to the Monitors group (see Figure 19-3), open the Show On drop-down list, and click the display you want.

Figure 19-3. Use the Monitors group on the Slide Show tab of the Ribbon to tell PowerPoint which display to show the slides on, to set the resolution, and to turn on Presenter view.

From the Monitors group, you can also change the display's resolution as needed—just open the Resolution drop-down list, and then click the resolution you want.

Using Presenter View

Next, if you're using two screens and have extended your desktop onto the second screen, turn on Presenter view. This view is perhaps PowerPoint's biggest aid to you in giving an effective presentation. While the audience sees only the slide you're currently displaying in Slide Show view, Presenter view (see Figure 19-4) shows your current slide, the sequence of slides around it in the presentation, and the slide's notes. Normally, you'll use Presenter view on your laptop's screen, so you're the only one who can see it.

To turn on Presenter view, select the Use Presenter View check box in the Monitors group of the Slide Show tab of the Ribbon. Then, when you start the slide show, PowerPoint displays Presenter view on the monitor that's not showing the slides to the audience.

In Presenter view, you can take the following actions:

- *View the current slide*: The current slide appears in the upper-left part of the window.

- *Consult your notes*: The notes for the current slide appear in the upper-right part of the window. You can click the Zoom In button and the Zoom Out button to adjust the text to a comfortable size for viewing.

- *Display another slide*: Click the Next button to move along to the next slide, or the Previous Slide button to move back to the previous slide. To move in bigger steps, you can either click the slide you want in the Slides bar at the bottom of Presenter view, or click the Slide Show button, click or highlight Go to Slide, and then click the slide you want on the submenu that appears.

- *Change the mouse pointer*: Click the Pointer Options button to display a menu of options, and then click the option you want. For example, click Pen to change the mouse pointer to a pen with which you can draw on a slide.

- *End the slide show*: Click the Slide Show button, and then click End Show on the menu.

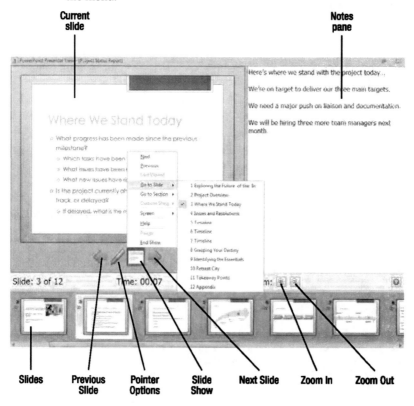

Figure 19-4. When giving a presentation, use Presenter view on a second screen to control the presentation, display your notes, and navigate quickly from slide to slide.

▪ **Note** If you don't have a second monitor for presenter view, you'll need to fall back on traditional means of handling your notes—memorizing them, printing them on note cards, or writing them on the palm of your hand or on your cuff.

Practicing Your Presentation

To make sure that your presentation goes well on the day, practice it until you're confident you know your material and you can speak fluently from the notes you've given yourself. If you find your notes need more detail, rearranging, or other improvements, work on them too.

Ideally, you will rehearse your presentation in the room in which you will deliver the presentation, and using the same equipment. Sometimes you can do this; for example, if you'll be speaking in your company or organization, you may be able to book the conference room for your run-through. But if you will deliver the presentation elsewhere, as is often the case, you will need to practice wherever you find most convenient—preferably somewhere you can speak aloud with interruption or drawing unwelcome attention.

To practice your presentation, use Presenter view (if you'll use it during your presentation) or your notes. You may also want to set timings for slides, as discussed next.

Rehearsing Timings for Slides

For some presentations, you may need to set automatic timings for slides so that you don't need to cue them manually. To set timings, use PowerPoint's Rehearse Timings feature like this:

1. If you will use Presenter view, set it up as described earlier in this chapter.

2. Choose Slide Show ➤ Set Up ➤ Rehearse Timings. PowerPoint starts the slide show and displays the Recording toolbar (see Figure 19-5).

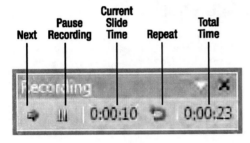

Figure 19-5. Use the controls on the Recording toolbar to set automatic timings for slides or to control the recording of your narration.

3. Use the controls on the Recording toolbar to control the timings like this:

   - *Next*: Click this button to trigger the next animation or display the next slide.

   - *Pause Recording*: Click this button when you need to take a break from practice. Click this button again when you're ready to resume.

   - *Current Slide Time*: This readout shows how long the current slide has been displayed for.

▨ **Tip** To change the time in the Current Slide Time box, click in the box, type the time you want, and then press Enter.

- *Repeat*: Click this button to start recording the timing for the current slide again.

- *Total Time*: This readout shows the total time you've been recording for.

4. When you finish going through the presentation, PowerPoint displays a dialog box (see Figure 19-6) giving the total show time and asking if you want to apply the timings to the slide show.

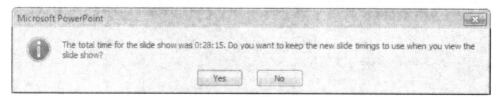

Figure 19-6. Click the Yes button in this dialog box to apply the timings you've recorded to the slide show.

5. Click the Yes button to apply the timings to the slide show.

6. Save the slide show. For example, click the Save button on the Quick Access Toolbar.

Delivering a Presentation to a Live Audience

When you're ready to deliver the presentation live (or when you're practicing), use the commands and techniques explained in this section to start the presentation and display the slides. If necessary, you can annotate the presentation or display a black screen or white screen instead of your slides. You can also run the presentation from the keyboard rather than using a mouse.

Starting a Presentation

When you're ready to launch the presentation, choose Slide Show ➤ Start Slide Show ➤ From Beginning. You can also press F5.

If you need to start from a slide other than the first, select that slide, and then choose Slide Show ➤ Start Slide Show ➤ From Current Slide. You can also press Shift+F5 to start from the current slide.

Displaying the Slides You Need

When giving the presentation, you'll need to display slides in the order you want. The most straightforward way is to start at the beginning of the presentation and run straight through to the end, but in many cases, you'll need to change the order; for example, you may need to go back to an earlier slide, skip ahead to a particular slide by name or number, or display a hidden slide.

PowerPoint provides plenty of different ways to move from slide to slide. The following ways tend to be the most convenient:

- *Run the next animation or display the next slide*: Click the mouse button or press Spacebar.

- *Return to the previous slide*: Press P; or right-click the current slide, and then click Previous on the context menu.

■ **Tip** In Presenter view, click the Slide Show button (the white icon below the current slide) to display the context menu for navigation.

- *Go to a slide by name or number*: Right-click the current slide, click or highlight Go to Slide on the context menu (see Figure 19-7), and then click the slide on the submenu.

■ **Note** Parentheses around a slide's number on the Go to Slide submenu indicate that the slide is hidden.

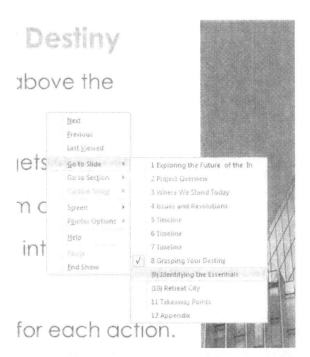

Figure 19-7. The context menu for a presentation includes commands for going quickly to a different slide by name or number, going to a different section of the presentation, or returning to the last slide viewed.

- *Go to a section*: Right-click the current slide, click or highlight Go to Section on the context menu, and then click the section on the submenu.

> ▪ **Tip** To return quickly to the first slide in the presentation, hold down both the left and right mouse buttons together for two seconds.

- *Return to the last slide viewed*: Right-click the current slide, and then click Last Viewed on the context menu.

Annotating the Slides

Sometimes you may want to annotate a presentation to make sure your audience grasps your most important points. PowerPoint gives you the following annotation tools on the Pointer Options submenu, which you can find both on the context menu when giving a presentation and on the Slide Show menu in Presenter view:

- *Arrow*: Choose this item when you want to restore the mouse pointer to its normal arrow so that you can point to items on slides.

- *Pen*: Choose this item when you want to write or draw on a slide. Figure 19-8 shows an example.

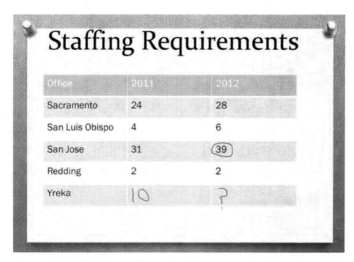

Figure 19-8. You can use PowerPoint's annotation features to mark up slides during a presentation. You can save the annotations afterward if you want.

- *Highlighter*: Choose this item to display a highlighter that you can use to highlight key words or phrases.

■ **Note** To change the color of the pen or the highlighter (whichever you've currently selected), choose Pointer Options ➤ Ink Color, and then click the color you want.

- *Eraser*: Choose this item to display an eraser with which you can erase an annotation by clicking on it. To erase all annotations from a slide, choose Pointer Options ➤ Erase All Ink on Slide.

■ **Note** To hide ink markup, display the context menu or the Slide Show menu, and then choose Screen ➤ Show/Hide Ink Markup. Repeat the command when you want to display the ink markup again.

When you end a slide show that you've marked up with ink annotations, PowerPoint displays a dialog box asking whether you want to keep them. Click the Keep button or the Discard option button as appropriate.

Controlling a Presentation Using the Keyboard

If you're at your PC when you're giving the presentation, you can control the presentation by using keyboard shortcuts. Table 19-1 explains the keyboard shortcuts you can use; you'll find the most useful ones explained elsewhere in the text as well. Several of the actions have two or more keyboard shortcuts. Each works the same; the one I've listed first is usually the easiest; but try them all, and use whichever you find most convenient.

Table 19-1. Keyboard Shortcuts for Running a Presentation

Action	Keyboard Shortcut
Run the presentation from the first slide	F5
Run the presentation from the current slide	Shift+F5
End the slide show	Esc, Ctrl+Break, or – (numeric keypad)
Display the next slide or trigger the next animation	N, Enter, Spacebar, Page Down, Down Arrow, or Right Arrow
Display the previous slide or trigger the previous animation again	P, Backspace, Page Up, Up Arrow, or Left Arrow
Display the next slide if it's hidden	H
Toggle on or off a white screen with no content	W or , (comma key)

Action	Keyboard Shortcut
Toggle on or off a black screen with no content	B or . (period key)
Display the All Slides dialog box for picking a slide	Ctrl+S
Go to a slide by specifying its number	*number key* followed by Enter (for example, 8, then Enter)
Start or stop an automatic slide show	S
Change the mouse pointer to a pen	Ctrl+P
Restore the normal mouse pointer	Ctrl+A
Toggle the display of ink markup on and off	Ctrl+M
Change the mouse pointer to an eraser	Ctrl+E
Erase all annotations from the current slide	E
Hide the mouse pointer	Ctrl+H
Open the context menu	Shift+F10
Select the first or next hyperlink on the current slide	Tab
Select the last or previous hyperlink on the current slide	Shift+Tab
Click the selected hyperlink	Enter
Display the Windows Taskbar (click the slide to hide the Taskbar again)	Ctrl+T

Displaying a White Screen or Black Screen

When you need to focus your audience's attention on you rather than on your slides, display a white screen or a black screen (whichever best suits the lighting conditions under which you're giving the presentation). To do so, open the context menu or the Slide Show menu (in Presenter view), and then choose Screen ➤ Black Screen or Screen ➤ White Screen, as needed.

Press Esc or click with the regular mouse pointer to go back from the black screen or white screen to the slides. (Don't click with a pen pointer—that draws on the black screen or white screen instead.)

Creating a Handout for a Presentation

When you're delivering a presentation live, it's often useful to create a handout that provides your audience with material to browse before you start, to scribble notes on as you proceed, and to take home for further reference afterward. To create a handout, PowerPoint uses Word, to which it automatically exports the slides and other material you choose.

To create a handout, follow these steps:

1. Click the File tab to open Backstage.

2. Click the Share item in the left column to display the Share pane.

3. Click the Create Handouts item in the Share column to display the Create Handouts in Microsoft Word pane.

4. Click the Create Handouts button to display the Send To Microsoft Word dialog box (see Figure 19-9).

Figure 19-9. In the Send To Microsoft Word dialog box, choose the layout and content you want for your handout.

5. In the Page layout in Microsoft Word area, select the option button for the layout and content you want to use:

   - *Notes next to slides*: This layout places the slides on the left of the page with their notes beside them on the right. Use this layout only if all your notes are for public consumption.

   - *Blank lines next to slides*: This layout places the slides on the left of the page with blank lines beside them on the right so that your audience can take any notes they need. This layout gives a moderate amount of space for notes.

- *Notes below slides*: This layout places a slide at the top of each page with its notes below it. Use this layout only if you're sure you want to share all your notes with your audience.

- *Blank lines below slides*: This layout places a slide at the top of each page with blank lines below it on which the audience can take notes. This layout gives more space for notes than the Blank lines next to slides layout.

- *Outline only*: This layout includes only the outline of the presentation, not the slides. You may want to use this layout as the basis for speaker notes.

6. In the Add slides to Microsoft Word document area, choose how to add the slides to the Word document:

- *Paste*: Select this option button to paste in each slide as a graphic. Use this option if you want to be able to move the Word document to a different computer than the presentation is on. The disadvantage to pasting in the slides as graphics is that the Word document becomes large.

- *Paste link*: Select this option button to insert each slide as a link. This makes Word pull in a picture of the slide automatically and helps to keep down the file size. The disadvantage is that, if you move the Word document to a different computer, Word cannot pull in the pictures.

7. Click the OK button. PowerPoint activates Word (if it's running) or launches Word (if it's not running) and creates a document on the lines you've indicated.

■ **Caution** Word may take several minutes to create the document, especially if the presentation contains many slides. If Windows shows the Word window as "Not responding," give it time to finish creating the document and sort itself out.

---

8. Switch to the Word document. For example, click the Word window's icon on the Taskbar. Check that the document has come out the way you want it, add any text needed (for example, add headers and footers with the details of the presentation), and then save the document.

Recording Narration into a Presentation

When you can't deliver a presentation in person, you can record your narration for the presentation and create a file that your audience can play back. This is great for creating a presentation that you will share on the Web or on a CD or DVD.

■ **Note** To record narration, you'll need a suitable microphone. In a pinch, you can use a microphone built into your laptop or your desktop PC's monitor, but such a microphone will usually pick up ambient noise. Usually, you'll be better off using a microphone that you can position freely, such as a handheld microphone or one on a stand, and best off with a noise-canceling microphone mounted on a headset.

To record a presentation, follow these steps:

1. Set up your microphone and check that it's working. For example:

   • Right-click the Volume icon in the notification area, and then click Recording devices on the context menu to display the Recording tab of the Sound dialog box.

   • Check that the microphone appears in the Select a recording device below to modify its settings list box.

   • Speak into the microphone, and make sure that the volume meter next to the microphone registers your voice. If you need to change the input volume, double-click the device to open its Properties dialog box, click the Levels tab, and then drag the level slider.

   • Click the OK button to close the Sound dialog box.

2. Choose Slide Show ➤ Set Up ➤ Record Slide Show > Start Recording from Beginning to display the Record Slide Show dialog box (see Figure 19-10).

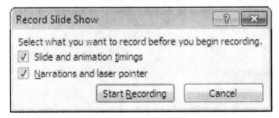

Figure 19-10. In the Record Slide Show dialog box, you will normally want to select both the Slide and animation timings check box and the Narrations and laser pointer check box.

■ **Note** If you want to start recording from a particular slide rather than from the beginning, click that slide. Then choose Slide Show ➤ Set Up ➤ Record Slide Show ➤ Start Recording from Current Slide.

3. Select the Slide and animation timings check box if you want PowerPoint to record when you display each animation and each new slide. Normally, you will want to select this check box so that your narration and the presentation play in sync.

4. Select the Narrations and laser pointer check box if you want PowerPoint to record your narration and the pointer movements. Normally, you will want to select this check box too.

5. Click the Start Recording button to close the Record Slide Show dialog box. PowerPoint starts the slide show from the beginning (or from the slide you specified), displays the Recording toolbar (shown earlier in this chapter), and starts recording your narration.

6. Speak your narration for the presentation, advancing the slides and animations as needed. Use the controls on the Recording toolbar like this:

    •   *Next*: Click this button to trigger the next animation or display the next slide.

    •   *Pause Recording*: Click this button when you need to take a break from recording. Click this button again when you're ready to resume recording.

    •   *Current Slide Time*: This readout shows how long the current slide has been displayed for.

    •   *Repeat*: Click this button to start recording narration for the current slide again.

    •   *Total Time*: This readout shows the total time you've been recording for.

7. When you reach the end of the presentation, PowerPoint automatically stops recording the narration.

Now check how the narration sounds by playing the presentation in either Slide Show view or Reading view. If the narration has come out well enough, save the presentation (for example, press Ctrl+S).

If you find the narration isn't good enough, you can start over either on the current slide or at the beginning. Choose Slide Show ➤ Set Up ➤ Record Slide Show ➤ Clear to display the Clear submenu, and then click the Clear Narration on Current Slide item or the Clear Narrations on All Slides item, as needed. You can then record your replacement narration.

Exporting and Sharing a Presentation

Apart from delivering a presentation in person, PowerPoint gives you several ways to get the presentation to other people across the Internet:

•   *Send the presentation via e-mail*: The most direct way to get a presentation to somebody else is to e-mail it to them, as discussed in Chapter 3. E-mail works well for small presentations, but many presentation files are too large for mail servers to handle. In this case, you're better off using a different means of distribution.

•   *Save the presentation to SkyDrive*: You can save the presentation to a shared folder on Windows Live SkyDrive, as discussed in Chapter 3. Anyone with permission to view the folder can then download the presentation and view it. This is an effective way to distribute presentations across the Internet.

•   *Save the presentation to a SharePoint site*: If you have a SharePoint site, you can save the presentation to it. Anyone with permission to view the folder on the SharePoint site can then view the presentation. In many cases, this is the best way to distribute a presentation within a company or organization that uses SharePoint.

- *Broadcast a slide show*: In broadcasting, you give the slide show live on the Web. Beforehand, you create a link to where you will broadcast the slide show. You send this link to the potential audience, and any of them can click the link to tune in to the slide show at the appointed time. The first section below explains how to broadcast a slide show.

- *Publish slides*: When you need other people to be able to work with the slides in your presentation rather than just view them, you can publish the slides to a SharePoint site or to a slide library. People with access to the site or library can then open the slides, view them, and edit them as needed. The second section below shows you how to publish slides.

Tip When sharing a presentation with people on other computers, it's a good idea to embed in the presentation the fonts it uses in case those computers don't have them—otherwise, the fonts may look strange. Choose File ➤ Options to display the PowerPoint Options dialog box, and then click the Save item on the left to display the Save pane. Near the bottom, select the Embed fonts in the file check box. Below this, select the Embed only the characters used in the presentation option button if the other people won't need to edit the presentation, or select the Embed all characters option button if they will need to edit it. Click the OK button to close the PowerPoint Options dialog box, and then save the presentation.

Broadcasting a Slide Show

When you need to share a slide show with a large audience over the Internet, you can broadcast it. Broadcasting involves you giving the presentation live (or playing back a recorded presentation) at a scheduled time and your audience tuning in to watch it in their web browsers. To provide audio, you can arrange a conference call with the participants.

To broadcast a slide show from PowerPoint, you use Microsoft's PowerPoint Broadcast Service or an equivalent service. The PowerPoint Broadcast Service is free to anyone who has a Windows Live ID, so you'll probably want to try it unless you have a different broadcast service available (for example, one your company or organization runs on its own network).

Note A Windows Live ID is the identifier that Microsoft uses for Windows Live Mail, Hotmail, MSN, and other services. If you have an account with one of these services, you already have a Windows Live ID that you can use for the PowerPoint Broadcast Service. If not, you can sign up for a Windows Live ID using your existing e-mail address; go to http://home.live.com, click the Sign Up link, and fill in the form.

To broadcast a slide show, follow these steps.

1. Open the presentation if it's not already open.

2. Click the File tab to open Backstage.

3. Click the Save & Send item in the left column to display the Save & Send pane.

4. In the Save & Send column, click Broadcast Slide Show to display the Broadcast Slide Show pane.

5. Click the Broadcast Slide Show button to display the Broadcast Slide Show dialog box (see Figure 19-11).

Figure 19-11. Use the Broadcast Slide Show dialog box to set up a slide show broadcast on Microsoft's PowerPoint Broadcast Service or another broadcasting service.

■ **Note** To change to another broadcasting service, click the Change Broadcast Service button in the Broadcast Slide Show dialog box. In the Choose a broadcast service box that the Broadcast Slide Show dialog box reveals, click the Add a new service item to display the Add Broadcast Service dialog box. Type the URL of the service, and then click the Add button to close the dialog box and add the service to the Broadcast Slide Show dialog box. You can then start the broadcast by clicking the Start Broadcast button.

6. Click the Start Broadcast button. If you're using the PowerPoint Broadcast Service, PowerPoint prompts you for your Windows Live ID. Type your e-mail address and password, select the Sign me in automatically check box if you want to use automatic sign-in from now on, and then click the OK button.

7. Next, wait while PowerPoint prepares the slide show for broadcast. This can take several minutes for a slide show with many slides and complex content.

8. When PowerPoint displays the Broadcast Slide Show dialog box shown in Figure 19-12, the slide show is ready to go. You now need to share the link for the slide show in one of these ways:

   • Click the Copy Link item to copy the link so that you can share it; for example, by pasting it into an instant message.

   • Click the Send in Email link to create an e-mail message containing the link and canned text inviting the recipient to view the presentation. You can then add other details as needed (for example, details about the conference call that will provide the audio component of the presentation), address the message, and then send it.

Figure 19-12. From this Broadcast Slide Show dialog box, you can copy the slide show's link or create an e-mail message containing it.

9. If you're providing audio with a conference call, set it up.

10. When you're ready to start giving the presentation, click the Start Slide Show button. PowerPoint switches to Slide Show view (and displays Presenter view on your second screen if you're using it), and you can start giving the presentation.

Tip Until you start giving your presentation, viewers see a blank screen telling them that the presentation will start soon. Instead of leaving them in suspense, create a first slide that shows the time the presentation will start (include the time zone for clarity) and gives some useful information (for example, the URL of your web site). Click the Start Slide Show button in the Broadcast Slide Show dialog box to display this first slide, and leave it on screen until you're ready to start the slide show for real.

11. Deliver the presentation as usual. When you have finished, choose Broadcast ➤ Broadcast ➤ End Broadcast to tell the broadcast service that the presentation is over. PowerPoint display a confirmation dialog box (see Figure 19-13).

Figure 19-13. Click the End Broadcast button in this dialog box to confirm that the broadcast is over.

12. Click the End Broadcast button. Viewers then see a message saying that the broadcast is over.

Publishing Slides to a Slide Library or a SharePoint Site

To make slides available to your colleagues so that they can update them, edit them, or reuse them, you can publish the slides to a SharePoint site or to a slide library.

To publish the slides, follow these steps:

1. Click the File tab to open Backstage.

2. Click the Save & Send item in the left column to display the Save & Send pane.

3. In the Save & Send column, click the Publish Slides item to display the Publish Slides pane.

4. Click the Publish Slides button to display the Publish Slides dialog box (see Figure 19-14).

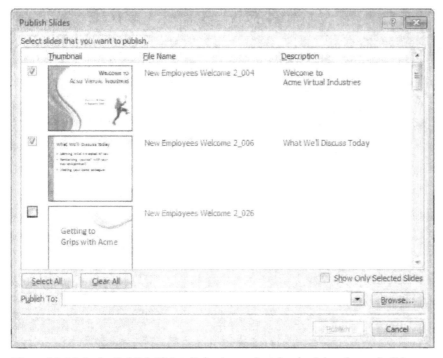

Figure 19-14. *In the Publish Slides dialog box, select the check box for each slide you want to publish, and then choose the site to which you want to publish the slides.*

5. In the left column, select the check box for each slide you want to publish. Click the Select All button if you want to select all the check boxes quickly, or click the Clear All button to instantly clear all the check boxes.

6. If you want to limit the display to only the slides whose check boxes you've selected, select the Show Only Selected Slides check box.

7. In the Publish To box, enter the site or side library to which you want to publish the slides.

    •   The easiest way to enter the address is to click the Browse button, select the location in the Select a Slide Library dialog box, and then click the OK button.

    •   Sometimes you may want to type or paste in the path to the location instead.

8. Click the Publish button. PowerPoint closes the Publish Slides dialog box and publishes the slides without further comment.

Summary

In this chapter, you've learned how to deliver a PowerPoint presentation to a live audience either in person or by broadcast across the Internet. You know how to prepare for the presentation by setting up your displays and using Presenter view, and you can record either timings or full-on narration for the presentation's slides. You can also create a handout for your audience and publish slides to a slide library for your colleagues.

At this point, you're good to go with PowerPoint. In the next chapter, you'll start exploring Outlook, Office's powerful program for managing e-mail, your schedule, and more.

CHAPTER 20

Making the Most of E-mail

In this part of the book, you'll learn to use Outlook, Office's heavy-duty e-mail and organizer program. Outlook covers four main areas:

- *Mail*: Outlook calls it Mail, but most of us call it e-mail—and it's the most important part of Outlook. I'll cover e-mail in this chapter.

- *Contacts*: Outlook provides a digital address book on steroids for storing the details of your contacts and keeping in touch with them. Chapter 21 explains how to work with contacts in Outlook.

- *Calendar*: Outlook can help you keep tabs on your appointments, whether they occur once only or at regular intervals. Chapter 22 shows you how to manage your calendar with Outlook.

- *Tasks*: Outlook provides a robust task list that you can use not only to track your own commitment but also offload them onto your colleagues. Chapter 23 teaches you how to organize your life with tasks.

So in this chapter, you'll learn how to use Outlook to send and receive e-mail and attachments. You'll start by setting up Outlook to work with your e-mail account (or accounts). You'll then take a tour of the Outlook interface, because Outlook packs a host of controls into its window in order to handle all its different roles and tasks.

Once you know what's what, I'll show you how to send and receive messages and attachments; reply to messages and forward them to others; and delete the messages you don't want to keep and file those you do. Then you'll look at how to quickly add standard closings to your messages by creating and using signatures. Finally, you'll learn how to deal with spam, or unwanted e-mail.

Setting Up Outlook

First, you need to set up Outlook to work with your e-mail account. To do this, you need to know your e-mail address and password. You may also need to know which types of mail servers your ISP uses and their addresses.

Note If you've set up Outlook already, go on to the next section.

To set up Outlook, follow these steps:

1. Choose Start ➤ All Programs ➤ Microsoft Office ➤ Microsoft Outlook 2010 to
    launch Outlook. If this is the first time you've run Outlook, the program
    displays the Microsoft Outlook 2010 Startup dialog box.

■ **Tip** If you find Outlook vital to your computing life, either pin the Outlook icon to the Taskbar (or the Start menu)
or set Outlook to launch automatically on startup. See Chapter 1 for instructions on pinning a program or setting it
to launch automatically.

---

2. Click the Next button to launch the Account Configuration wizard, which
    displays the E-mail Accounts pane (see Figure 20-1).

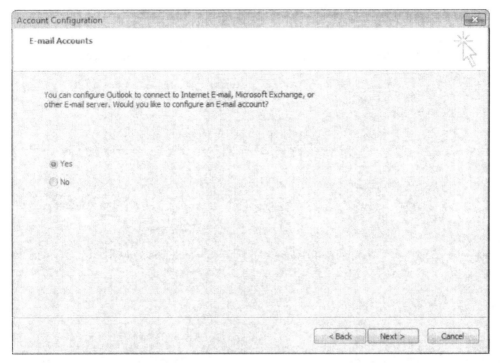

*Figure 20-1. Normally, you'll want to select the Yes option button on the E-mail Accounts screen of the
Account Configuration wizard, which runs when you first open Outlook.*

3. Select the Yes option button, and then click the Next button. The wizard
    launches the Add New Account wizard, which displays the Auto Account Setup
    screen (shown in Figure 20-2 with settings chosen).

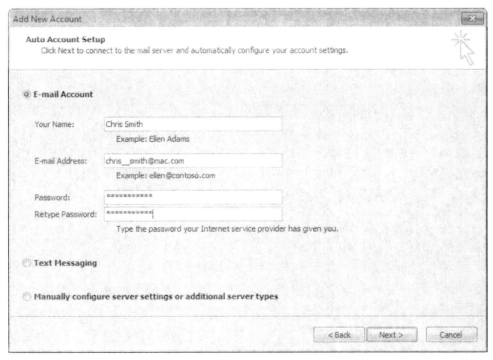

Figure 20-2. On the Auto Account Setup screen of the Add New Account wizard, select the E-mail Account option button and fill in the details of your e-mail account.

4. Select the E-mail Account option button.

5. In the Your Name box, type your name the way you want it to appear in the messages you send; for example, Jonathan A. Smith or Jon Smith.

6. In the E-mail Address box, type your e-mail address.

7. Type your e-mail password in the Password box and the Retype Password box. These boxes display security-conscious asterisks rather than the letters. The Retype Password box is there to ensure that you don't make a mistake in the Password box.

8. Click the Next button. The wizard displays the Configuring screen as it checks the settings you've provided, logs on to the mail server, and sends a test message. If all is well, the wizard then displays the Congratulations! screen (see Figure 20-3).

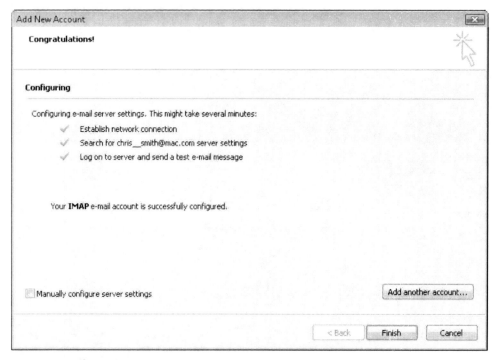

Figure 20-3. If the Add New Account wizard displays the Congratulations! screen, your e-mail account is set up and functional. Click the Finish button to close the wizard.

9. For most e-mail accounts, this is all you need to do, and you can click the Finish button to close the wizard. But if you need to choose further settings, select the Manually configure server settings check box, and then click the Next button (which replaces the Finish button when you select the check box). Then work as described in the next section.

■ **Note** At this point, you can also add another e-mail account by clicking the Add another account button on the Congratulations! screen of the Add New Account wizard, and then going through the setup process again. For example, you may want to add a work e-mail account as well as a home e-mail account.

Changing the Default Settings for an E-mail Account

If you need to change the default settings for an e-mail account, follow these steps:

1. On the Congratulations! screen of the Add New Account wizard, select the Manually configure server settings check box, and then click the Next button to display the Internet E-mail Settings screen (see Figure 20-4).

Figure 20-4. When you need to change particular account settings, display the Internet E-mail Settings screen of the Add New Account wizard.

2. Change the account's settings as needed. These are the settings you're most likely to need to change:

   • *Account Type*: If the Add New Account wizard has chosen the wrong account type, open this drop-down list and choose the right one. Unless you have an e-mail account with a Microsoft Exchange server, the choices are POP3 and IMAP.

■ **Note** POP3 is the acronym for Post Office Protocol, a widely used communications protocol for handling incoming mail. IMAP is the acronym for Internet Message Access Protocol, a newer protocol. If you're not sure which account type you have, ask your ISP or e-mail provider. The biggest difference between the two is that with IMAP your e-mail program keeps the messages on the server, which makes it easy to use various computers to manage your e-mail. By contrast, POP3 normally downloads messages to your PC, which enables you to work with messages even when your PC is offline.

- *Logon Information*: If your e-mail needs a different logon name than the first part of your e-mail address, type the logon name in the User Name box. In the Password box, the wizard enters the password you typed during setup, so you don't normally need to change it.

- *Incoming mail server*: If Outlook has not been able to determine the correct mail server for incoming mail, type the server's address in this box.

- *Outgoing mail server (SMTP)*: If Outlook has not been able to determine the correct mail server for sending mail, type the server's address in this box.

- *Require logon using Secure Password Authentication*: Select this check box if your e-mail provider requires Secure Password Authentication.

- *Remember password*: Clear this check box if you don't want Outlook to store your e-mail password. Normally, it's more convenient to have Outlook store the password so that you don't have to enter it, but you may prefer the security of having to enter the password.

3. Click the Test Account Settings button when you're ready to test the settings. Outlook displays the Test Account Settings dialog box (see Figure 20-5), which displays first the progress of the tests and then the result. Click the Close button when you've finished testing.

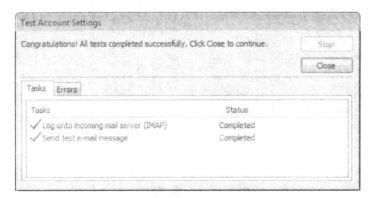

Figure 20-5. If you choose custom account settings, test them to make sure they're working.

4. If you need to customize further settings for the e-mail account, click the More Settings button to display the Internet E-mail Settings dialog box. This dialog box has several tabs of settings (exactly how many depends on the account type), but these are the settings you'll most often need to change:

- *Mail Account*: To change the name Outlook shows for your e-mail account, type your preferred name in this box on the General tab (see Figure 20-6). For example, you may prefer a description such as Home E-mail or Work E-mail instead of the e-mail address (which is what Outlook uses).

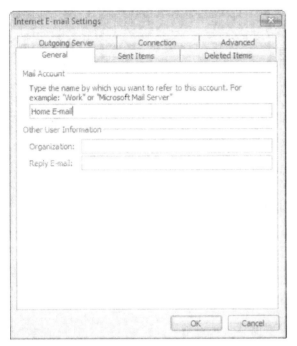

Figure 20-6. On the General tab of the Internet E-mail Settings dialog box, you can change the name that Outlook displays for the e-mail account. You can also set a different reply-to address.

- *Reply E-mail*: In this box, you can set a different reply-to address. When a recipient replies to a message you've sent, the reply goes to the reply-to address rather than the address from which you sent the message. This setting is useful when you use multiple e-mail accounts but need to direct replies to a particular account.

- *Outgoing Server*: On this tab (see Figure 20-7), you can set up authentication for sending e-mail. Select the My outgoing server (SMTP) requires authentication check box, click the Log on using option button, and then type your credentials in the User Name box and the Password box. Select the Require Secure Password Authentication check box if your mail provider requires this authentication. Clear the Remember password check box if you prefer to enter your password manually (for security) than to have Outlook store it for you.

■ **Note** Normally, you'll need to set up different authentication for an outgoing server only if you have to send e-mail using a different ISP than you're using for your incoming mail. For example, some ISPs allow you to send e-mail through their servers only when your computer is connected to the Internet via that ISP. When you connect via another ISP (for instance, when you're on the road), you need to send e-mail using another account.

Figure 20-7. On the Outgoing Server tab of the Internet E-mail Settings dialog box, you can set up Outlook to use use different credentials for sending e-mail than for receiving it.

5. When you've finished choosing settings in the Internet E-mail Settings dialog box, click the OK button to close it.

6. Click the Finish button to close the Add New Account wizard. The main Outlook window then opens.

Meeting the Outlook Interface

When Outlook opens, you'll see a window such as Figure 20-8. Outlook normally displays your Inbox at first, on the basis that you'll want to start by checking your e-mail. If Outlook is displaying a different item, click the Inbox item in the Favorites category in the pane on the left. (If the Favorites category is collapsed to a heading, click the white triangle to its left to expand it.)

■ **Note** This chapter introduces you to the Mail aspect of Outlook's interface. The following chapters show you how to use the Calendar aspect, the Contacts aspect, and the Tasks aspect.

Navigation Pane   Message List   Reading Pane   To-Do Bar

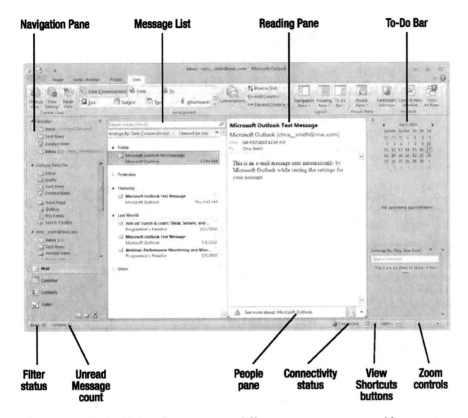

Filter   Unread   People   Connectivity   View   Zoom
status   Message   pane   status   Shortcuts   controls
                count   buttons

Figure 20-8. Outlook's interface uses many different components to provide access to your information and its features.

The following sections explain how to use the main components of the Outlook interface—and how to change those you're most likely to want to change.

Using the Ribbon

Like the other Office programs, Outlook uses the Ribbon across the top of the window as its main control area.

The main part of the Ribbon contains five tabs: the File tab for accessing Backstage, the Home tab, the Send/Receive tab, the Folder tab, and the View tab. Outlook displays other tabs as needed; for example, when you select an e-mail attachment, Outlook displays the Attachment Tools section, which contains the Attachments tab.

The tab contents change depending on the area of Outlook you're using. Outlook displays the same tabs no matter which area (for example, Mail, Calendar, or Contacts) you're working in, but it changes the groups and controls. For example, when you're working with Mail, the Home tab includes the New group, Delete group, the Respond group, the Quick Steps group, the Move group, the Tags group, and the Find group. When you're working with Calendar, the New group and the Find group are still there, but the other groups are the Go To group, the Arrange group, the Manage Calendars group, and the Share group.

Using and Customizing the Navigation Pane

The Navigation Pane appears on the left side of the Outlook window by default. You use this pane to navigate to the items you want to work with.

Normally, your first navigation move is to display the Outlook area you want to work in: Mail, Calendar, Contacts, Tasks, Notes, Folder List, or Shortcuts. To do so, you click the appropriate one of the four main buttons at the bottom of the Navigation Pane.

Once you've displayed the area, the upper part of the Navigation Pane displays controls for navigating about that area. For example:

- *Mail*: The Navigation Pane displays your e-mail folders, so you can quickly click the folder whose contents you want to display.

- *Calendar*: The top of the Navigation Pane displays a date picker that gives you instant access to the days of the current month (or whichever month you choose to display). Below this, the Navigation Pane displays a list of your calendars, so that you can easily switch from one calendar to another.

- *Contacts*: The Navigation Pane displays a folder of your contacts, enabling you to choose the group of contacts you want to work with.

- *Tasks*: The Navigation Pane shows the My Tasks list, so you can pick the task you want to manipulate.

Tip You can switch quickly among Outlook's areas by using keyboard shortcuts. Press Ctrl+1 to display Mail, Ctrl+2 to display Calendar, Ctrl+3 to display Contacts, Ctrl+4 to display Tasks, Ctrl+5 to display Notes, Ctrl+6 to display the Folder List in the Navigation Pane, and Ctrl+7 to display Shortcuts in the Navigation Pane.

Normally, you use the Navigation Pane all the time in Outlook, so it's a good idea to spend some time setting the Navigation Pane up so that you can work quickly in it.

Your first choice is how wide to make the Navigation Pane. You want to strike a balance between being able to read the longest item in the Navigation Pane (whichever area you're working in) and keeping as much space as possible for the rest of the Outlook window.

To change the width of the Navigation Pane, move the mouse pointer over its right border so that the pointer displays a two-headed arrow, and then drag the border to the left or right.

To minimize the Navigation Pane, click the Minimize the Navigation Pane button (the < button) in the upper-right corner of the Navigation Pane. Outlook reduces the Navigation Pane to a narrow strip at the left side of the window. When you click an item that needs more space, it appears on a pop-up panel (see Figure 20-9).

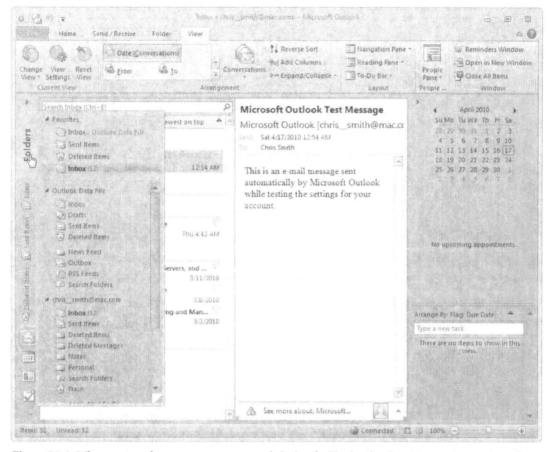

Figure 20-9. *When you need more space, you can minimize the Navigation Pane to a narrow strip at the left side of the Outlook window.*

To restore the Navigation Pane to its normal size, click the Expand the Navigation Pane button (the ► button) that appears in the upper-right corner of the minimized Navigation Pane.

Your next choice is whether to display large buttons or small buttons for the different areas of Outlook. To display large buttons for all items, drag the horizontal divider line above the buttons up toward the top of the pane. This expands the pane, and each of the buttons—Mail, Calendar, Contacts, Tasks, Notes, Folder List, and Shortcuts—grows to its full size, as shown on the left in Figure 20-10.

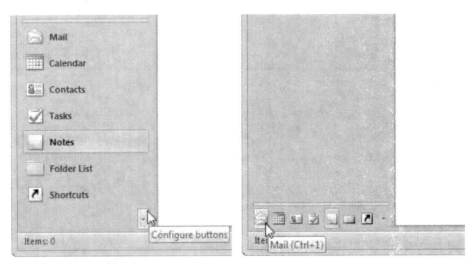

Figure 20-10. *You can drag the horizontal divider line up to increase the size of the Navigation Pane buttons (left) or drag it down to reduce them (right).*

To have all the buttons appear at their smaller size (as on the right in Figure 20-10), drag the divider line down until the buttons appear in a single row at the bottom of the Navigation Pane. This gives you that much more space for working with the other items in the Navigation Pane, and is especially useful on small screens.

To have the first buttons appear at their full size but have the last buttons appear at their smaller size, drag the divider line down or up part of the way.

To choose which buttons appear at the bottom of the Navigation Pane, follow these steps:

1. Click the Configure buttons button (the little drop-down button in the lower-right corner of the Navigation Pane), and then click Navigation Pane Options to display the Navigation Pane Options dialog box (see Figure 20-11).

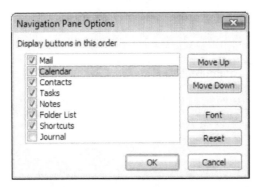

Figure 20-11. *In the Navigation Pane Options dialog box, you can choose which buttons to display and the order in which they appear. You can also change the font—for example, to make the buttons more readable.*

2. In the Display buttons in this order box, select the check box for each button you want to see, and clear the check box for each button you don't want.

3. To change the order in which the buttons appear, click a button, and then click the Move Up button or Move Down button, as needed.

▓ **Note** If you need to restore the buttons to their default order, click the Reset button in the Navigation Pane Options dialog box.

---

4. To change the font used for the button names, click the Font button. In the Font dialog box that opens, click the font you want, and then click the OK button.

5. Click the OK button to close the Navigation Pane Options dialog box.

▓ **Note** To quickly add a button to or remove a button from the Navigation Pane, click the Configure buttons button, click Add or Remove Buttons on the menu, and then click the button you want to add or remove.

Using and Customizing the Message List and Reading Pane

To the right of the Navigation Pane is the Message List, which shows the messages in the selected mailbox (for example, the Inbox). To the right of the Message List is the Reading Pane, which shows the contents of the selected message (or part of the contents). To view a message in the Reading Pane, you simply click it in the Message List.

▓ **Note** Outlook provides the Reading Pane to help you plow through your messages quickly. But you can also open a message in a separate window if you prefer. To do so, double-click the message in the Message List.

Arranging and Sorting the Message List

To enable you to quickly find and read the messages you need, Outlook lets you sort the Message List in several different ways. This section runs you through the main ways of sorting the Message List, but you will want to spend some time experimenting with the various options to see which types of sorting you find most helpful for the tasks you perform with e-mail and the ways you prefer to approach them.

To set up the Message List, you use the controls in the Arrangement group on the View tab of the Ribbon (see Figure 20-12).

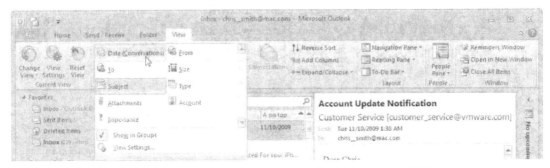

Figure 20-12. Use the controls in the Arrangement group on the View tab of the Ribbon to set up the Message List the way you want it. Usually, you'll want to use the Arrange By control (shown open here) first to choose the overall sort order.

Start by using the Arrange By control on the left of the Arrangement group to choose the overall arrangement. This control appears as a drop-down list if the Outlook window is narrow and as a box with a drop-down panel if the Outlook window provides enough space.

■ **Note** You can also configure the Message List in two other ways. First, you can click the Arrange By bar in the Message List, and then click the setting you want on the pop-up menu. Second, if you can find blank space in the Message List, you can right-click it and then use the Arrange By submenu on the context menu.

In the Arrange By control, choose from the following arrangement settings:

- *Date (Conversations)*: Sorts the items by date and into conversations. (You'll learn about conversations shortly.)

- *From*: Sorts the items by the sender. This setting is good for locating messages from important people.

- *To*: Sorts the items by the recipient's name or e-mail address. This setting is useful if you have Outlook checking different e-mail accounts, as it lets you separate the messages by account. Items sent to you by name (for example, Chris Smith) appear separately from those sent to the e-mail address.

- *Size*: Sorts the items by their size. This setting is handly for quickly locating messages with large attachments. You can also use the Attachments setting (discussed below) to locate all messages with attachments.

- *Subject*: Sorts the items by their subject lines. This setting is useful for locating an item whose subject line you can remember but whose other details you can't. (You can also search for the item, as described shortly.)

- *Type*: Sorts the items into their different types, such as messages and news posts. This setting is helpful for separating e-mail messages from news feeds.

- *Attachments*: Sorts the items into a With Attachments group and a No Attachments group. This setting is good for locating messages with attachments that you need to deal with.

- *Account*: Sorts the items by the e-mail account to which they've been sent. This gives a similar effect to the **To** arrangement, but it uses only e-mail account names rather than your name.

- *Importance*: Sorts the items by their Importance tag into High, Normal, and Low groups. This setting can be useful if your colleagues use the Importance tag sensibly and consistently, but you may find so many people give their messages High priority that the result is meaningless.

Changing the Sort Order

Within each arrangement, you can change the sort order by clicking the right column heading in the Message List and choosing the order you want. For example, if you sort by Date, you can choose between Newest on top and Oldest on top; if you sort by Subject, you can choose between A on top and Z on top; and if you sort by Attachments, you can choose between With on top and None on top.

■ **Note** You can also reverse the current sort order by choosing View ➤ Arrangement ➤ Reverse Sort.

Choosing Whether to Group Items

For each arrangement, you can choose whether to show the items in groups or as a series. The groups vary depending on the arrangement. For example, when you sort by Date, Outlook uses groups such as Today, Yesterday, Last Week, and Last Month; when you sort by From, the groups are the senders (by name when it appears, and by e-mail address when it doesn't); and when you sort by Size, the groups are Tiny, Small, Medium, Large, and Enormous.

To choose whether to group items, choose View ➤ Arrangement ➤ Arrange By (if the Arrange By drop-down button appears) or View ➤ Arrangement ➤ Arrange By ➤ More (clicking the drop-down button at the right end of the Arrange By box), and then click Show in Groups on the drop-down list. If a check mark appears next to Show in Groups, grouping is on, and you click to turn it off; otherwise, click to place the check mark and turn grouping on.

Viewing Conversations

When you've sorted the Message List by Date, which is often the most useful way for regular use, you can view your e-mail messages as conversations. When you do this, Outlook presents each exchange of e-mail messages as a separate section, enabling you to see the sequence of messages clearly and to determine who said what when without having to trawl through your Inbox and other mail folders.

To view messages by conversation, choose View ➤ Arrangement ➤ Arrange By ➤ Date to switch to Date order. Then choose View ➤ Conversations ➤ Show Messages in Conversations to place a check mark next to this item. Once you've done this, each exchange of messages appears as a conversation, and you can expand a conversation by clicking it, and then clicking the white triangle to its left. In Figure 20-13, the Today category contains two conversations, of which the first is collapsed and the second is expanded.

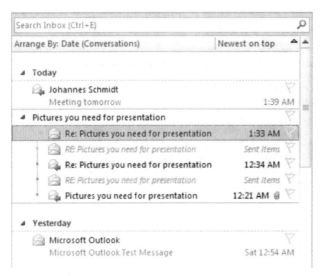

Figure 20-13. When you need to see the sequence of an e-mail exchange, display the messages in conversations. It's usually best to use the Show Messages from Other Folders option and the Show Senders above the Subject option to make the conversation clear, as in this example.

To see the details of a conversation, it's often useful to see the messages you've sent, plus any messages from earlier in the conversation that you've filed in folders. To see messages in other folders, choose View ➤ Conversations ➤ Conversation Settings ➤ Show Messages from Other Folders, placing a check mark next to this item. Clear the check mark when you no longer need to see messages from other folders.

To make the conversations clearer, display the sender above the subject by choosing View ➤ Conversations ➤ Conversations Settings ➤ Show Senders Above the Subject, placing a check mark next to this item.

If you want Outlook to automatically expand a conversation when you click it, choose View ➤ Conversations ➤ Conversation Settings ➤ Always Expand Conversations, placing a check mark next to this item. This behavior lets you work more quickly in the Message List, so you may well want to try it.

If you prefer to have the messages indented to show the different stages of the conversation, choose View ➤ Conversations ➤ Conversation Settings ➤ Use Classic Indented View, putting a check mark next to this item. Figure 20-14 shows a conversation that uses indented view.

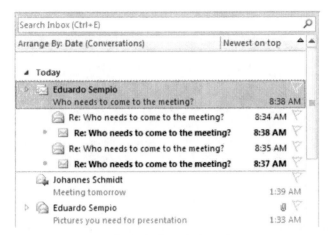

Figure 20-14. *Use Classic Indented view when you want to see the different stages of a conversation indented to different levels, as in the selected conversation here.*

Using and Customizing the Reading Pane

Compared to the Message List, the Reading Pane is straightforward: When you click a message in the Message List, Outlook displays the message's contents in the Reading Pane so that you can read it.

At first, Outlook displays the Reading Pane to the right of the Message List. If you prefer, you can position the Reading Pane below the Message List by choosing View ➤ Layout ➤ Reading Pane ➤ Bottom. Figure 20-15 shows this arrangement. (To put it back, choose View ➤ Layout ➤ Reading Pane ➤ Right.) You may prefer this layout, as it gives you a better view of the Message List (but not as much of it).

■ **Tip** If your PC has a small screen, or if you need more space for the Message List, you may prefer to turn off the Reading Pane and read messages in a separate window instead. To turn off the Reading Pane, choose View ➤ Layout ➤ Reading Pane ➤ Off. To read a message in a separate window, double-click the message in the Message List.

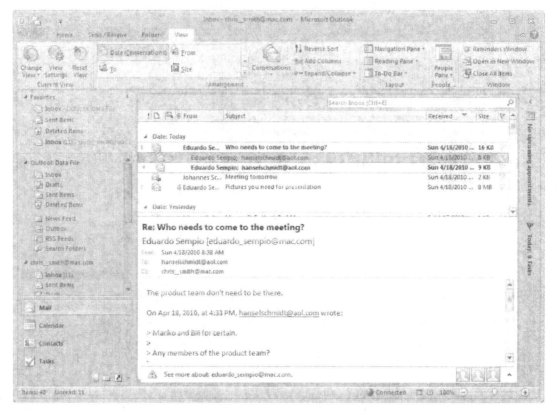

Figure 20-15. *Positioning the Reading Pane below the Message List can make the Message List easier to navigate.*

To control how Outlook interprets your opening a message in the Reading Pane, follow these steps:

1. Choose View ➤ Layout ➤ Reading Pane ➤ Options to display the Reading Pane dialog box (see Figure 20-16).

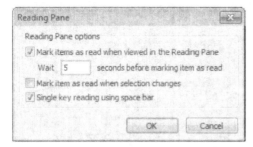

Figure 20-16. *Use the Reading Pane dialog box to tell Outlook whether to mark items as read when you view them in the Reading Pane.*

2. If you want Outlook to mark a message as read when you open it in the reading pane, select the Mark items as read when viewed in the Reading Pane check box. In the Wait *N* seconds before marking item as read box, type the number of seconds Outlook should wait before marking the message read. The default is five seconds, but you may want to use a longer period so that you can glance through a message without having Outlook mark it as read.

Note You can select either the Mark items as read when viewed in the Reading Pane check box or the Mark item as read when selection changes check box, but not both. If one of these check boxes is selected, Outlook clears it when you select the other check box.

---

3. If you prefer to have Outlook mark a message as read when you switch to another message, select the Mark item as read when selection changes check box.

4. Select the Single key reading using space bar check box if you want to be able to press the spacebar to scroll down through the current message and (when you read the end of this message) to display the next message. This feature is usually a great time-saver, so you'll probably want to make sure this check box is selected.

5. Click the OK button to close the Reading Pane dialog box.

Using and Customizing the To-Do Bar

When you're viewing your messages (or your contacts or tasks), the To-Do Bar appears on the right side of the Outlook window, giving you quick access to your appointments and to-do items.

If you're using a narrow window for Outlook, you may want to minimize the To-Do Bar to a strip on the right side of the window to give yourself more space for your messages. To minimize the To-Do Bar, click the Minimize the To-Do Bar button, the ➤ button in the upper-left corner of the To-Do Bar. When you need to restore the To-Do Bar, click the Expand the To-Do Bar button, the < button that appears at the top of the minimized To-Do Bar.

Note If you want to hide the To-Do Bar altogether, choose View ➤ Layout ➤ To-Do Bar ➤ Off. When you want to restore it, choose View ➤ Layout ➤ To-Do Bar ➤ Normal or View ➤ Layout ➤ To-Do Bar ➤ Minimized, as needed.

At first, the To-Do Bar displays a date navigator at the top (the panel showing the days of the current month), a list of your appointments in the middle, and a list of your tasks at the bottom. To remove one of these items, right-click the To-Do Bar, and then click Date Navigator, Appointments, or Task List on the context menu to remove the check mark next to the item (see Figure 20-17).

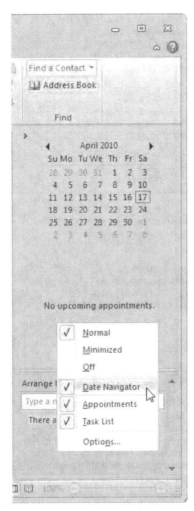

Figure 20-17. From the context menu for the To-Do Bar, you can quickly remove an item, switch the To-Do Bar between its normal sized and its minimized size, or turn the To-Do Bar off altogether.

To choose how many months and which appointments the To-Do Bar shows, follow these steps:

1. Right-click the To-Do Bar, and then click Options on the context menu to display the To-Do Bar Options dialog box (see Figure 20-18).

Figure 20-18. Open the To-Do Bar Options dialog box when you want to change the number of months or the types of appointments that appear in the drop-down button.

2. Select the Show Date Navigator check box if you want the date navigator to appear in the To-Do Bar. In the Number of month rows box, type the number of rows you want (the default is 1).

▨ **Tip** Showing two months in the date navigator is especially useful toward the end of the month, when you may want to start working with the next month.

---

3. Select the Show Appointments check box if you want the appointments section to appear in the To-Do Bar. Then select the Show All Day Events check box if you want all-day events to appear in it. Select the Show Details of Private Items check box if you want private items to appear; otherwise, clear this check box.

4. Select the Show Task List check box if you want the task list to appear.

5. Click the OK button to close the To-Do Bar Options dialog box. Outlook updates the To-Do Bar with your choices.

Using and Customizing the People Pane

Outlook's People Pane gives you quick access to information about the people you work with or exchange messages with. These people can be either on a SharePoint site on your network or on a public network such as LinkedIn, MySpace, or FaceBook.

To set up the People Pane, follow these steps:

1. Choose View ➤ People Pane ➤ People Pane ➤ Account Settings and then click the Next button on the introductory screen to display the Microsoft Outlook: Social Network Accounts dialog box (shown in Figure 20-19 with one social network, LinkedIn, added).

Figure 20-19. You can set up social networks in Outlook by using the Microsoft Outlook: Social Network Accounts dialog box.

2. If the social network you want to use doesn't appear in the main box, click the View social network providers available online link. In the Internet Explorer window that opens, follow through the process of downloading and installing the connector software for the network. You may need to close the Microsoft Outlook: Social Network Accounts dialog box, exit Outlook, and then restart Outlook before you can proceed.

3. Select the check box for the social network you want to use.

4. Type your user name and password for the social network.

5. Select the Remember my password check box if you want Outlook to store your password. Storing the password is convenient but reduces your security a little, as someone else might be able to use your computer if you leave it unattended.

6. Press Enter or click the Connect button. Outlook checks your user name and password, and (if they match) displays a check mark to the left of the social network.

7. Click the Finish button to close the Microsoft Outlook: Social Network Accounts dialog box. Outlook displays a Congratulations! screen confirming that you've added the social network.

8. Click the Close button.

You can now expand the People Pane by choosing View ➤ People Pane ➤ People Pane ➤ Normal or by clicking the Expand the People Pane button (the ^ button) in the lower-right corner of the Outlook window. Figure 20-20 shows the People Pane open for the sender of an e-mail message.

Click the tabs on the left of the People Pane to display the different types of information about the contact:

- *Home*: Click this tab to display a summary of information. This is often the best place to start.

- *News*: Click this tab to see news about the contact—for example, updates to their social-networking profiles.

- *E-mail*: Click this tab to see recent messages from this contact. You can click a message link to open the message in a separate window.

- *Attachments*: Click this tab to see files you've received as attachments.

- *Meetings*: Click this tab to see details of the meetings you had with this contact.

- *Status Updates*: Click this tab to see details of updates to the contact's social networks.

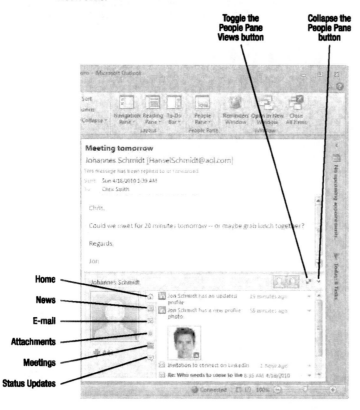

Figure 20-20. The People Pane gives you quick access to the different types of information—news, e-mail messages, attachments you've received, and meetings you've had—about a contact.

Sending and Receiving Messages

When you've got Outlook set up and working right, you'll probably want to start by using Mail. This section shows you how to create and send messages, how to receive messages, and how to read your messages.

Sending an E-mail Message

To send an e-mail message, you create a message, address it, and add contents. You may also want to choose options for the message, such as setting its reply-to address to a different e-mail address than the one you're sending from.

Creating a New Message

To create a new blank message, first choose Home ➤ New ➤ New E-mail. Outlook opens a new message window. The message window's title bar at first shows Untitled, but then it displays the subject line you give the message. Figure 20-21 shows a message window with a new message open. As you can see, the Ribbon in the message window contains the File tab and five other tabs: the Message tab, the Insert tab, the Options tab, the Format Text tab, and the Review tab.

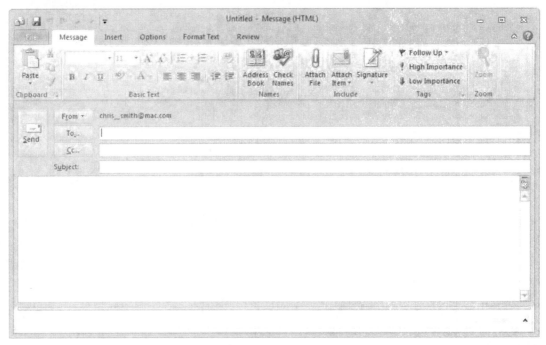

Figure 20-21. A new message opens in a window named Untitled at first.

Tip If you're already working in the Mail area, you can simply press Ctrl+N to start a new e-mail message. The Ctrl+N shortcut creates a new item in the area of Outlook you're using: In Mail, pressing Ctrl+N creates a new message; in Calendar, pressing Ctrl+N creates a new appointment; in Contacts, pressing Ctrl+N creates a new contact; in Tasks, pressing Ctrl+N creates a new task; and in Notes, pressing Ctrl+N creates a new note.

Instead of creating a blank message, you can create a message based on one of Outlook's themes or a stationery design. As in the other Office programs, a *theme* is a coordinated look featuring colors, fonts, and graphical styles that work together. A *stationery design* is a background image that appears in the message, as if you were writing on a piece of paper that bore a design.

To use a theme or stationery, follow these steps:

1. Choose Home ➤ New Items ➤ E-mail Message Using ➤ More Stationery to display the Theme or Stationery dialog box (see Figure 20-22).

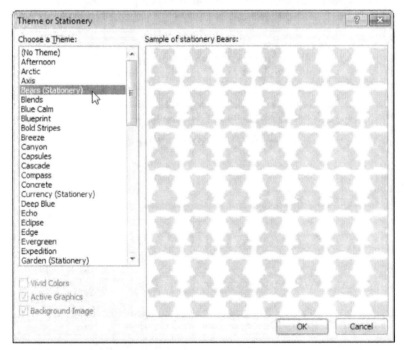

Figure 20-22. *When you need a more colorful message, choose a theme or stationery design in the Theme or Stationery dialog box.*

2. In the Choose a Theme box, click the theme or stationery design you want. Each stationery design has "(Stationery)" after its name; each other item is a theme.

3. If you choose a theme, you can vary its looks by selecting or clearing the Vivid Colors check box, the Active Graphics check box, and the Background Image check box. For a stationery design, these check boxes are dimmed and unavailable.

4. Click the OK button to close the Theme or Stationery dialog box. Outlook starts a message using the theme or stationery design you chose.

Choosing Which Account to Send the Message From

If you have set up Outlook to use multiple e-mail accounts, check which account appears next to the From button. Outlook uses the account you're working in, but sometimes you may need to change account. To do so, click the From button to display the drop-down list of accounts, and then click the account you want.

Addressing the Message

You can add the components of a message in any order that suits you, but what you'll usually want to do is address the message first. To do so, you enter the primary recipients in the To box and any Cc (carbon copy) recipients in the Cc box.

You can enter the e-mail addresses in three main ways:

- *Type or paste in an e-mail address*: If you know the e-mail address, you can click in the box (for example, the To box) and simply type it in. Or if you've copied from a document or a web page, you can paste it in.

- *Type the name and have Outlook complete the address for you*: Click in the box and start typing the name. When Outlook suggests a match (see Figure 20-23), press Enter to accept it. If Outlook suggests several matches, move the highlight to the right one by pressing Down arrow or Up arrow, and then press Enter; or click the right address.

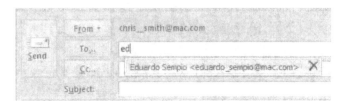

Figure 20-23. Outlook automatically suggests matching contacts for names you start typing.

- *Use the Select Names dialog box*: Click the To button or the Cc button to display the Select Names dialog box (see Figure 20-24), and then work like this:

  1. Choose the address book in the Address Book drop-down list in the upper-right corner.

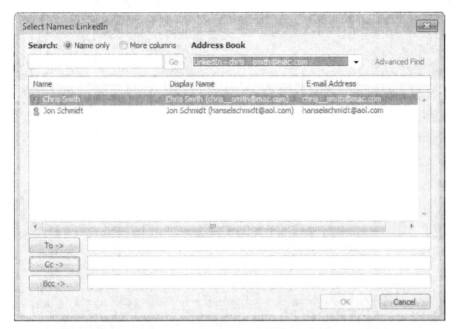

Figure 20-24. Use the Select Names dialog box to select e-mail recipients from your contacts list or from a social network you've added to Outlook (as shown here).

2. Browse for the address or search for it. To search, type text in the Search box. Normally, you'll want to select the Name only option button to restrict the search to names, but if you need to search other parts of the contact data, select the More columns option button. Click the Go button to run the search.

3. Select the address you want.

4. Click the To button to add the address to the To box, click the Cc button to add it to the Cc box, or click the Bcc button to add it to the Bcc box.

5. Click the OK button when you've chosen all the addresses you want.

Outlook enters the recipient's name in the People Pane at the bottom of the message window. You can click the Expand the People Pane button (the ^ button in the lower-right corner of the window) to expand the People Pane (see Figure 20-25) so that you can refer to information about this contact while writing the message to him or her.

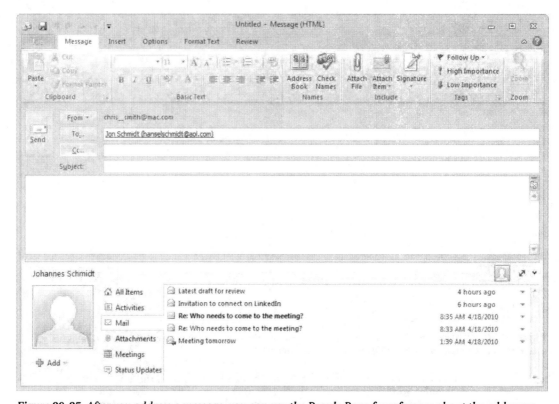

Figure 20-25. After you address a message, you can use the People Pane for reference about the addressee.

Adding the Subject Line and Message Contents

In the Subject box, type the subject of the message. This is the text that appears in the recipient's Inbox to help them identify the message.

▓ **Tip** Make your subject lines as clear as possible while keeping them short enough to fit in the narrow columns that appear in a typical e-mail program window. Your message will most likely be competing for the recipient's attention with many other messages, so making the subject clear will help it get read.

In the main box of the message window, enter the text of the message. Many e-mail messages require only plain text, which you can enter by typing as normal (or by using other standard text-entry techniques, such as pasting text or expanding AutoCorrect entries). Other messages need formatted text, pictures, or other graphical items.

Note Outlook lets you format the message content as plain text, as HTML, or as rich text, by clicking the appropriate button—HTML, Plain Text, or Rich Text—in the Format group on the Format Text tab of the Ribbon. Choose Plain Text when you want the text to have no formatting. Choose HTML when you want to use formatting that is compatible with most e-mail programs. Choose Rich Text for formatted messages only when you're sending to someone you know uses Outlook, as the results may be inconsistent in other e-mail programs.

The Message tab of the Ribbon in a message window provides essential formatting controls, such as font formatting and bulleted lists. To reach the full range of formatting, display the Format Text tab of the Ribbon, which contains everything from font formatting to styles.

Note You can mark a message as being important by choosing Message ➤ Tags ➤ High Importance (or you can choose Message ➤ Tags ➤ Low Importance to mark a message as being unimportant). But be warned that high importance has been so widely abused in e-mail messages that many people ignore it.

The Insert tab of the Ribbon in a message window includes controls for inserting tables, illustrations, hyperlinks, and other objects—even charts and equations if you need them.

Choosing Options for a Message

The Options tab of the Ribbon in a message window (see Figure 20-26) contains a range of options for making a message look and behave differently from normal.

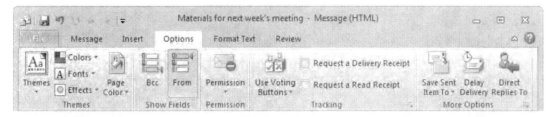

Figure 20-26. The Options tab of the Ribbon in a message window lets you change the message's look and behavior.

Use the controls in the Themes group when you want to change the overall look of the message. For example, choose a different theme from the Themes drop-down panel when you want to change the look of the styles used in the message. Or, if you want to use a background color in the message, open the Page Color drop-down panel, and then click the color you want.

In the Show Fields group, click the Bcc button if you want to display the Bcc field. Outlook automatically displays this field if you add bcc recipients by using the Select Names dialog box, so you'll need to display it only if you want to add bcc recipients manually.

The Permission drop-down panel in the Permission group lets you set restrictions on a message you're sending to another Outlook user on your e-mail system. For example, you can set the Do Not Forward restriction on a message to prevent the recipient from forwarding the message.

■ **Caution** Many of the options on the Options tab of the Ribbon work well—or work at all—only with messages read by someone using Outlook. For example, many e-mail programs routinely ignore requests for delivery receipts and read receipts, because these features otherwise are useful to spammers who want to find out which e-mail addresses are live and which are not.

The Use Voting Buttons drop-down panel in the Tracking group lets you include a pair or group of option buttons to enable the recipients to respond quickly to a message. For example, you can choose Approve;Reject to have an Approve button and a Reject button, or Yes;No;Maybe to have a Yes button, a No button, and a Maybe button. To create your own buttons, click the Custom item, and then enter the text in the Use voting buttons box in the Properties dialog box (see Figure 20-27), separating the button names with semicolons (for example, **Tuesday;Wednesday;Thursday**).

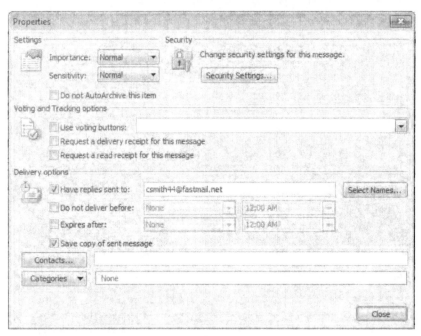

Figure 20-27. The Properties dialog box gives you one-stop access to many of the options for a message, including the directing of replies to a different e-mail address.

Note To reach the full set of voting, tracking, and delivery options for a message, choose Options ➤ Tracking ➤ Message Options (the Message Options button is the little button in the lower-right corner of the Tracking group). Outlook displays the Properties dialog box, which gives you access to all the settings.

Select the Request a Delivery Receipt check box in the Tracking group if you want Outlook to request a receipt when the recipient's e-mail program receives the message. Select the Request a Read Receipt check box to request a receipt when the recipient opens the message.

The More Options group contains these three buttons:

- *Save Sent Item To*: Click this button to display a panel that lets you choose among saving the sent item to the default folder (Use Default Folder), not saving it (Do Not Save), and another folder (Other Folder). In most cases, Other Folder is the most useful choice; in the Select Folder dialog box that appears, select the destination folder, and then click the OK button.

- *Delay Delivery*: Click this button to display the Properties dialog box, and then use the controls on the Do not deliver before line to set the earliest delivery date and time. (Outlook uses this date and time if your PC is awake and online then; otherwise, it sends the message as soon after the date and time as possible.) Click the Close button to close the Properties dialog box.

- *Direct Replies To*: Click this button to display the Properties dialog box, and then enter the delivery address in the Have replies sent to box. This setting is useful when you need the reply to go to a different address than you're sending the message from. Click the Close button to close the Properties dialog box.

Checking the Spelling in a Message

Outlook checks spelling and grammar as you type unless you turn off the Spelling checker and Grammar checker, so you can easily resolve spelling and grammar queries as you create the message.

If you choose not to check spelling and grammar as you work, you can start a check by pressing F7 or by choosing Review ➤ Proofing ➤ Spelling & Grammar. The Review tab of the Ribbon also includes commands for researching the current word or looking it up in the Thesaurus, getting a word count, translating text, and setting the proofing language.

Note See Chapter 3 for instruction on configuring the Spelling checker and the Grammar checker to check only the items you want.

Sending the Message

When you're ready to send the message, click the Send button below the left end of the Ribbon.

Receiving and Reading Messages

Normally, Outlook automatically checks your incoming mail server for messages, and collects those sent to you. You can also force Outlook to check e-mail at any point by pressing F9 or choosing Send/Receive ➤ Send & Receive ➤ Send/Receive All Folders (to get all incoming mail and send all outgoing mail) or by clicking the Inbox and choosing Send/Receive ➤ Send & Receive ➤ Update Folder (to get the mail for this account).

▨ **Note** To control how frequently Outlook checks for new mail, choose File ➤ Options, and then click Advanced in the left pane. Scroll down to the Send and receive heading, then click the Send/Receive button to display the Send/Receive Groups dialog box. In the Setting for group "All accounts" area, make sure the Include this group in send/receive check box is selected. Select the Schedule an automatic send/receive every *N* minutes check box, and then enter the number of minutes in the text box. You can also select the Perform an automatic send/receive when exiting check box if you want Outlook to send and receive when you close the program; this is useful for making sure you don't leave messages unsent. Click the Close button to close the Send/Receive Groups dialog box, and then click the OK button to close the Outlook Options dialog box.

Once you've received your messages, click the Inbox to display them. You can then read the messages either in the Reading Pane or in a separate window. The Reading Pane is often easiest, as it's designed to enable you to quickly triage your messages. Open a message in a separate window when you need more space to concentrate on it or when you need to compare the contents of two or more messages side by side.

Click the message you want to read, or press Down arrow or Up arrow to move the highlight to the message so that Outlook displays it in the Reading Pane.

▨ **Tip** When reading messages in the Reading Pane, press the spacebar to display the next screen of the message. When you reach the end of this message, press the spacebar again to display the next message. You can also press Shift+spacebar to display the previous screen of the current message or (from the beginning of the current message) to display the previous message.

To read a message in a separate window, double-click the message in the Message List. In the message window, you can then display the next message by clicking the Next Item button on the Quick Access Toolbar or by pressing Ctrl+> or display the previous message by clicking the Previous item button on the Quick Access Toolbar or by pressing Ctrl+<.

To close a message window, click its Close button (the × button), choose File ➤ Close, or press Ctrl+F4.

After reading a message, you can reply to it, move it to a folder, or delete it, as discussed later in this chapter.

Tip As discussed in the section "Using and Customizing the Reading Pane," earlier in this chapter, Outlook normally marks a message as having been read after you view it for five seconds (or the number of seconds you set) in the Reading Pane. If you turn off this automatic marking of messages as read, you can manually mark messages as read. From the keyboard, press Ctrl+Q to mark a message as read (or, if it has been read, as unread). With the mouse, right-click the message in the Message List, and then click Mark as Read on the context menu.

Sending and Receiving Attachments

E-mail is a great way of sending messages quickly, but it's also useful for transferring files from one computer to another. To send a file via e-mail, you attach it to a message that you then send as usual; and when someone sends you a file, it comes to your Inbox as part of the message that brings it. You then detach the file from the message and store it in a folder.

Sending a File As an Attachment

To send a file as an attachment, start a message as usual. Then choose Message ➤ Include ➤ Attach File to display the Insert File dialog box, click the file you want, and click the Insert button. Outlook adds an Attached box below the Subject box in the message window showing the file's name and its size (see Figure 20-28). You can then add other files by repeating the process.

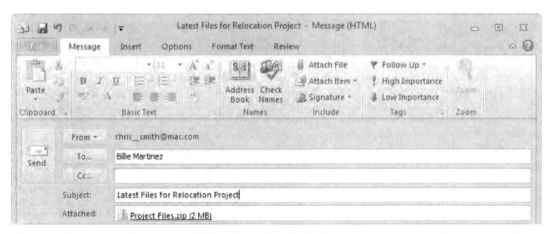

Figure 20-28. Outlook displays the Attached box below the Subject box when you attach one or more files to a message.

■ **Tip** You can also attach a file to a message by dragging the file from a Windows Explorer window to the message window.

Receiving a File as an Attachment

When you receive a file as an attachment, it arrives in your Inbox with its message. You'll see a paperclip icon on the message's listing in the Message List and the attachment's filename at the top of the Reading Pane (see Figure 20-29).

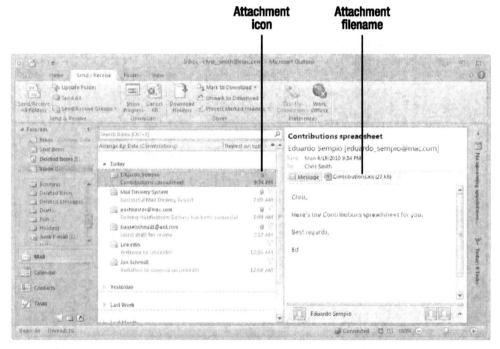

Attachment icon **Attachment filename**

Figure 20-29. The Message List displays a paperclip icon to indicate that a message has an attachment. The attachment's name appears at the top of the Reading Pane.

Click the attachment's name to see a preview of the attachment and to display the Attachment Tools section of the Ribbon (see Figure 20-30).

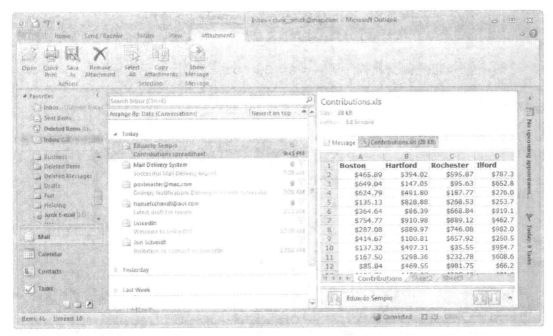

Figure 20-30. *Click the attachment's name in the Reading Pane to display a preview of the attachment and to reveal the Attachment Tools section of the Ribbon, which gives you access to commands for working with the attachment.*

To save the file to a folder, choose Attachment Tools ➤ Attachments ➤ Actions ➤ Save As. In the Save Attachment dialog box that opens, select the folder in which you want to save the file, and then click the Save button. You can then open the file either from a Windows Explorer window or from the program you use for that type of file—for example, Word for a word processing file or Excel for a spreadsheet file.

■ **Caution** The Attachments tab of the Ribbon includes an Open button, but don't open an attachment directly from Outlook. This is because the file opens in read-only mode, in which you cannot save changes you make to the file. You then need to use a Save As command to save the file under a different filename or in a different folder. Saving the file from Outlook and then opening it saves time and confusion.

After you've saved an attachment to a folder, you can either remove it from the message or leave it in the message for reference. Removing attachments is usually a good idea because otherwise your mailbox can become huge, but you may sometimes need to keep attachments in messages as a safety net.

To remove an attachment from a message, follow these steps:

1. Click the attachment in the message.

2. Choose Attachment Tools ➤ Attachments ➤ Actions ➤ Remove Attachment. Outlook displays the dialog box shown in Figure 20-31.

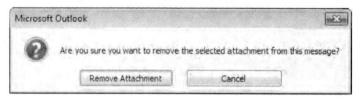

Figure 20-31. *Outlook confirms your removal of an attachment from a message.*

3. Click the Remove Attachment button. Outlook removes the attachment.

Replying to and Forwarding Messages

To reply to a message you've received, choose Home ➤ Respond ➤ Reply or press Ctrl+R. To reply to all the recipients of a message you've received, choose Home ➤ Respond ➤ Reply All or press Ctrl+Shift+R.

Outlook opens a message window for the reply, adding RE: to the subject line to indicate that it is a reply, and showing the original message and sender information below the insertion point (see Figure 20-32). You can then enter the text of the reply—and any other objects needed—and then click the Send button to send it.

To send a message you've received on to someone else, forward it by choosing Home ➤ Respond ➤ Forward or pressing Ctrl+F. Outlook opens a message window containing the forwarded message, adding FW: to the subject line to indicate that the message is forwarded, and placing the original message below the insertion point. You can then address the message, type whatever information you need to add to the forwarded message (for example, why you're forwarding it), and then click the Send button.

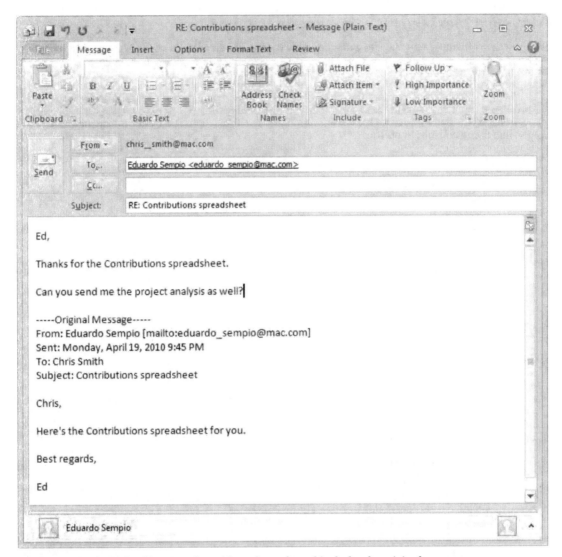

Figure 20-32. Outlook adds RE: to the subject of a reply and includes the original message.

Deleting, Storing, and Organizing Messages

When you don't need to keep an e-mail message, you can delete it by selecting it and pressing Delete or choosing Home ➤ Delete ➤ Delete. But chances are that you'll need to keep many—perhaps most—of the messages you receive. That means creating a structure of folders in which you can place the messages, and then moving each message to the appropriate folder.

Moving a Message to a Mail Folder

The quick way to move a message to a mail folder is to drag the message from the Message List to the folder in the Navigation Pane. This technique works well when you have few enough folders to fit easily in the Navigation Pane; if you have a longer list of folders, you can drag down to the bottom of the Navigation Pane to make it scroll further, but even so, getting to the folder you want can be awkward.

When you have a long list of folders, you may find it easier to use the Move Items dialog box (see Figure 20-33) to move the message to the folder you want. Select the message (or messages), and then choose Home ➤ Move ➤ Move ➤ Other Folder. In the Move Items dialog box, click the destination folder, and then click the OK button.

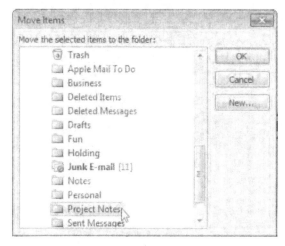

Figure 20-33. *Use the Move Items dialog box to quickly move messages to a folder that's part of a long list.*

Creating a New Mail Folder

To create a new mail folder, follow these steps:

1. In the Navigation Pane, right-click the account in which you want to create the new folder, and then click New Folder on the context menu to display the Create New Folder dialog box (see Figure 20-34).

■ **Note** To create the new folder as a subfolder of an existing folder, right-click the existing folder, and then click New Folder on the context menu.

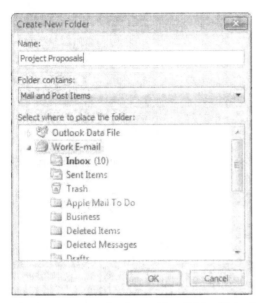

Figure 20-34. Use the Create New Folder dialog box to create a new folder for storing your messages in.

2. In the New box, type the name for the new folder.

3. In the Folder contains drop-down list, make sure that Mail and Post Items is selected. This item should be selected already.

4. If you need to place the new folder in a different folder, choose the containing folder in the Select where to place the folder list box. If you opened the Create New Folder dialog box by right-clicking the folder you want to use, you won't need to do this.

5. Click the OK button to close the Create New Folder dialog box. Outlook creates the new folder.

▥ **Tip** You can also create a new folder from the Move Items dialog box. Click the folder in which you want to create the new folder, and then click the New button to display the Create New Folder dialog box. Then work as described in this section.

To rename an existing folder, right-click it in the Navigation Pane, and then click Rename Folder. Outlook displays an edit box around the name. Type the new name, and then press Enter (or click elsewhere) to apply it.

Adding Consistent Closings to Your Messages with Signatures

When you send a message, you often need to let the recipient know standard information about you—for example, your name and phone numbers, or your company name and address, plus your position in it. To save you having to retype the same information over and over again, Outlook provides a feature called *signatures* that lets you set up one or more standard closings for inserting in your messages.

■ **Tip** If you find signatures awkward, you can create a signature as an AutoCorrect entry and enter it by typing its abbreviation. See Chapter 3 for coverage of AutoCorrect.

To set up your signatures, follow these steps:

1. Choose Home ➤ New ➤ New E-mail to open a new message window.

2. Choose Message ➤ Include ➤ Signature ➤ Signatures to display the Signatures and Stationery dialog box with the E-mail Signatures tab at the front. Figure 20-35 shows the E-mail Signatures tab with a signature being created.

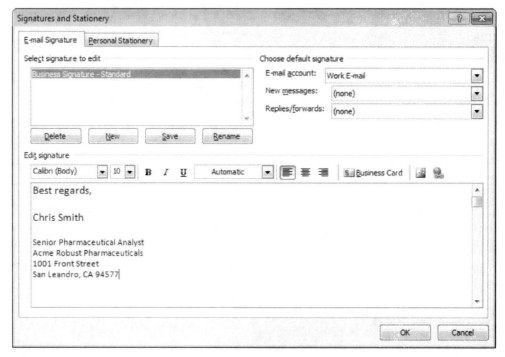

Figure 20-35. *Set up one or more standard signatures on the E-mail Signature tab of the Signatures and Stationery dialog box.*

3. Click the New button to display the New Signature dialog box, type the name for the signature (for example, Business Signature – Standard), and then click the OK button. Outlook adds the signature to the Select signature to edit box.

4. With the signature still selected in the Select signature to edit box, click in the Edit signature box, and then create your signature. These are the main moves you'll need:

   - *Add text*: Type in text as usual, or paste it from somewhere convenient.

   - *Format text*: Use the controls above the Edit signature box to format the text as needed. Alternatively, paste in formatted text.

   - *Add your virtual business card*: To add your virtual business card to the signature, so that the recipient can quickly add your contact details to his or her address book, click the Business Card button. In the Insert Business Card dialog box that opens, click your business card, choose the size at which to show the card in the Size drop-down list, and then click the OK button.

   - *Insert a picture*: To insert a picture in your signature, click the Picture button (the second button from the right above the Edit signature box). In the Insert Picture dialog box that opens, click the picture, and then click the Insert button.

▓ **Caution** Use only small pictures in e-mail signatures; for example, a company logo. Don't include full-resolution photos that will clog e-mail servers and bloat recipients' mailboxes.

   - *Add a link*: To add a link (for example, to your website), click the Hyperlink button (the rightmost button above the Edit signature box). In the Insert Hyperlink dialog box, set up the link using the techniques you learned in Chapter 3, and then click the OK button.

5. In the Choose default signature area, choose when to use the signature:

   - *E-mail account*: Open this drop-down list, and then click the account for which you want to use the signature as the default.

   - *New messages*: To use the signature as the default for all new messages, open this drop-down list, and then click the signature.

   - *Replies/forwards*: To use the signature as the default for all replies and forwarded messages you send, open this drop-down list, and then click the signature.

▨ **Note** Replies and forwarded messages generally don't need a signature. If a particular reply or forwarded message would benefit from a signature, you can add it manually by choosing Message ➤ Include ➤ Signature and clicking the signature you want.

---

6. Click the OK button to close the Signatures and Stationery dialog box.

7. In the new message window, choose Message ➤ Include ➤ Signature, and then click the signature you created to insert it in the message. Check that it looks the way you want it, and then close the message without saving changes.

Dealing with Spam

E-mail monitoring companies report that more than nine out of ten e-mail messages are *spam*, or unsolicited commercial messages. ISPs and e-mail providers generally do a great job of preventing most spam from reaching us, but even so, plenty of spam messages evade the filters and make it to inboxes.

To help you deal with spam, Outlook automatically monitors your incoming mail and puts any suspected spam in the Junk E-mail folder. It's a good idea to visit this folder every day or two to rescue any messages that Outlook has falsely accused and to get rid of the rest.

Removing Non-Spam Messages from the Junk E-mail Folder

If your Junk E-mail folder contains a message that's not junk, click the message in the Message List, and then choose Home ➤ Delete ➤ Junk ➤ Not Junk. Outlook displays the Mark as Not Junk dialog box (see Figure 20-36). If this sender is safe, select the Always trust e-mail from *sender* check box; otherwise, clear it. Then click the OK button to close the dialog box. Outlook moves the message to the Inbox.

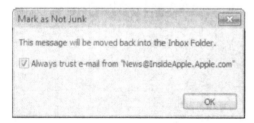

Figure 20-36. When you mark a message as not being junk, you can choose whether to always trust the sender in the future.

After checking that all the messages in your Junk E-mail folder are spam, select them, and then press Delete to delete them.

Marking Spam Messages as Junk

If you receive a spam message in your Inbox, click it, and then choose Home ➤ Delete ➤ Junk ➤ Block Sender. Outlook adds the sender to the Blocked Senders list, moves the message to the Junk E-mail folder, and then displays a dialog box (see Figure 20-37) telling you that it has done so. If you don't want to see this message box when you block other senders, select the Do not show this message again check box. Click the OK button to close the dialog box.

Figure 20-37. *When you block a sender, you can choose whether to have Outlook display this message again in the future.*

Summary

In this chapter, you've learned how to get around the Outlook interface and how to use Outlook's features for managing your e-mail.

You've set up Outlook to work with your e-mail account, and you know how to send and receive e-mail and attachments. You can reply to messages, forward messages to others, delete messages you don't want, and store those you want to keep. You can create and use signatures, and you know how to deal with spam—both identifying messages as spam and recovering those that Outlook has mistakenly sent to the Junk E-mail folder.

In the next chapter, I'll show you how to use Outlook to organize your contacts.

CHAPTER 21

Keeping Your Contacts in Order

In this chapter, I'll show you how to use Outlook to keep your contacts in order.

We'll start by going through how to create contacts either from scratch or by importing your existing contacts from sources such as address books or spreadsheets. After that, we'll examine how to work with contacts: viewing and sorting your contacts to reveal the ones you need, editing contact information when necessary, and quickly creating communications to your contacts.

Creating Contacts

What you'll probably need to do first is create some contacts in Outlook. You can create contacts either from scratch—entering the information manually—or by importing existing contacts from other sources. We'll look at each option in turn.

Creating a Contact from Scratch

If you have a contact's details on a hard copy (for example, a business card or paper) rather than in an electronic form, you'll probably need to enter the details manually. To do so, create a contact from scratch by following these steps:

1. Click the Contacts button in the Navigation Pane if it's not already selected.

2. Choose Home ➤ New ➤ New Contact (or press Ctrl+N) to open a new contact window. Figure 21-1 shows a contact window with a contact's name entered. Until you enter the name, the window's title bar shows Untitled.

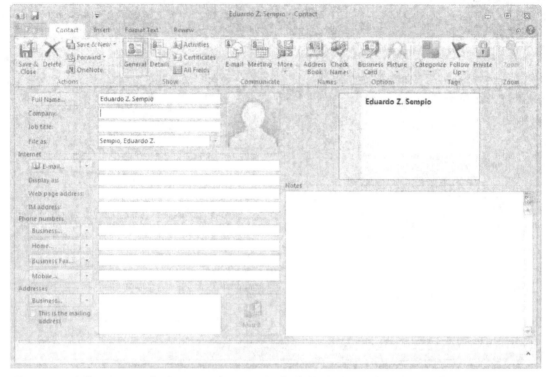

Figure 21-1. When you type in the contact's name, Outlook displays it in the title bar of the contact window and adds it to the preview of the contact's card.

3. Type the contact's full name in the Full Name box—for example, **John Q. Smith**—and then press Tab to move the insertion point to the Company box. Outlook automatically splits the name into its components and enters the name in the File as box with the last name first—for example, **Smith, John Q.**.

■ **Note** If Outlook can't parse the name into its separate components, it automatically displays the Check Full Name dialog box to prompt you to fix the problem. This behavior is usually helpful, but if you don't want Outlook to do this, clear the Show this again when name is incomplete or unclear check box. If you prefer, you can use the Check Full Name dialog box to enter each contact name—just click the Full Name button instead of typing the name into the Full Name box.

---

4. If the version of the name in the File as box is wrongly divided, click the Full Name button to display the Check Full Name dialog box (see Figure 21-2). Fill in the fields the way you want them, including any title (for example, Mr. or Mrs., Prof., or Dr.) and suffix (for example, II or Jr.) needed. Then click the OK button.

Figure 21-2. Use the Check Full Name dialog box to sort out any problems in parsing the contact's name, to add a title or suffix, or simply to enter a contact name the way you want it.

5. Type the company name in the Company box and the job title in the Job Title box. As you add information, Outlook adds it to the preview as well.

6. If the File as box shows a different version of the name than you want to use for filing, click the drop-down button, and then click your preferred version.

7. If you have a photo of the contact, click the Add Contact Picture placeholder to display the Add Contact Picture dialog box. Navigate to the folder that contains the picture, click the picture, and then click the OK button.

8. Enter the e-mail address in the E-mail box. You can do this in any of these ways:

   • *Type the address in*: This is the most straightforward way—provided you don't make a mistake. If Outlook can detect an obvious problem with the address, it displays the Check Names dialog box (see Figure 21-3) to prompt you to examine the address. If the Select the address to use box has the right version of the name, click it. Otherwise, click the Cancel button, and then revisit the address and fix the problem.

Figure 21-3. Outlook displays the Check Names dialog box if there's an obvious problem with an e-mail address you try to enter. This address is missing the @ sign.

- *Paste the address in*: If you have the address in a document or on a web page, copy it, and then paste it into the E-mail box.

- *Use the Select Name dialog box*: Click the E-mail button to display the Select Name dialog box. Navigate to the contact's name, click the e-mail address you want, and then click the OK button.

■ **Tip** You can start creating a contact quickly by right-clicking the sender's name in an e-mail message and then clicking Add to Outlook Contacts on the context menu.

---

9. Whichever way you add the address, press Tab or click in the Display as box to move the insertion point there. Outlook automatically inserts in the Display as box a suggested way to display the name in messages: the full name followed by the e-mail address in parentheses. Having both the name and the address is usually clearest, but you can type a different description if you want; for example, **John Q. Smith (work e-mail)**.

10. If you need to add another e-mail address for the contact, click the drop-down button to the right of the E-mail button, and then click E-mail 2. Fill in the address using the techniques previously described, adjust the Display as text if you want, and then repeat the process if necessary for E-mail 3.

11. In the other fields of the General section of the contact window, fill in the other general information you have for the contact. Most of the fields are straightforward, but here are notes on the ones that have special features:

- *Phone numbers*: You can enter the phone numbers in the Business box, Home box, Business Fax box, and Mobile box by typing or pasting. To add other phone numbers, click the drop-down button next to one of these boxes, and then click the label you want; for example, Business 2, Pager, or Assistant. To enter a complex phone number, click the button, work in the Check Phone Number dialog box (see Figure 21-4), and then click the OK button.

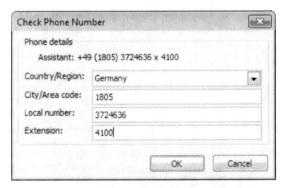

Figure 21-4. Use the Check Phone Number dialog box when you want to enter a complex phone number (for example, including an extension) or have Outlook automatically insert the country code for you.

- *Address*: Open the drop-down list next to the button in the Addresses area, and then choose the address type: Business, Home, or Other. Then type or paste the address in the text box. For a complex address, click the button (which is labeled Business, Home, or Other, depending on your choice), and then work in the Check Address dialog box (see Figure 21-5).

- *This is the mailing address*: Outlook automatically selects this check box for the first address you enter. If you want to use another address for mailing items to this contact, display the address, and then select this check box.

- *Notes*: In this field, enter any notes about the contact (or your dealings with the contact) that don't fit into the other fields. You can format the text in this field by using the controls on the Format Text tab of the contact window. As in Word, it's best to start by applying styles from the Styles group, and then add direct formatting (such as boldface or different line spacing) only for special needs.

Figure 21-5. *Open the Check Address dialog box when you need to make clear to Outlook which part of a complex address is which.*

12. Choose Home ➤ Show ➤ Details to display the Details section of the contact window (see Figure 21-6), and then fill in the information: Department, Office, Profession, and so on.

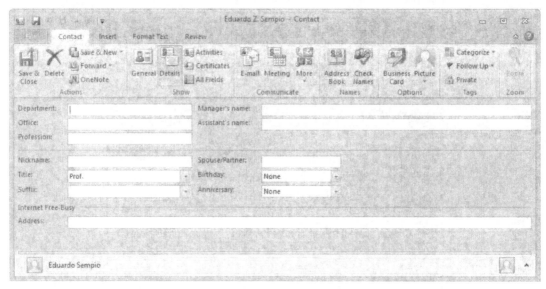

Figure 21-6. *The Details section of the contact window includes fields for further information about the contact's work and personal life.*

> ■ **Note** The intriguingly named Internet Free-Busy box is for entering the URL (the Internet address) of a file server that lets you check whether the contact is free or busy at any given point. You get this URL from the contact (or the contact's company). You can provide your own Free-Busy information to people who have you as a contact by choosing File ➤ Options, clicking Calendar, clicking the Free/Busy Options button, and then specifying the details in the Free/Busy Options dialog box.

13. If you want to assign a contact to a particular category of contacts—for example, Professional, Social, or Family—choose Contact ➤ Tags ➤ Categorize, and then click the appropriate category. Outlook gives the categories color names at first (Blue Category, Green Category, and so on), but you can customize the names by choosing Contact ➤ Tags ➤ Categorize ➤ All Categories and working in the Color Categories dialog box.

14. When you've finished entering the contact's details, choose Contact ➤ Actions ➤ Save & Close to save the contact record and close the window.

> ■ **Note** If you want to create another new contact immediately, choose Contact ➤ Actions ➤ Save & New (clicking the Save & New button, not its drop-down button) instead of Contact ➤ Actions ➤ Save & Close. And if you want to create another new contact from the same company, choose Contact ➤ Actions ➤ Save & New ➤ Contact from the Same Company to create a new contact with the company information already entered.

Importing Contacts from Other Address Books

Often, you'll have contact data in an address book already—so instead of typing it laboriously into new contacts one by one in Outlook, you can import it. This section shows you how to import data from the data sources you're perhaps most likely to have: Windows Contacts, an Excel worksheet containing contacts, Yahoo! Contacts, and Google Contacts.

Broadly speaking, you have three main options for importing contacts:

- *Import an existing address book*: If your addresses are in an address book format such as Outlook Express (the e-mail program that Windows XP and older versions of Windows used), you can import the address book into Outlook.

- *Create a comma-separated values (CSV) file, and then import it*: Comma-separated values, abbreviated to CSV, is a standard format for exchanging data between spreadsheets or databases. The values are separated from each other with commas.

- *Create vCard files, and then import them*: A vCard file is a file that contains the virtual address card of one or more contacts. Outlook works only with vCard files that contain a single contact each.

Importing Data from Windows Contacts

If you have contacts in the Windows Contacts folder, you can add them to Outlook by making vCard files from them. Follow these steps:

1. Create a folder somewhere convenient to put the vCard files. For example:

    • Right-click your Desktop, click New on the context menu, and then click Folder on the submenu.

    • Type a name such as Exported Contacts in the name box for the folder.

    • Press Enter to apply the name.

2. Click the Start button, and then click your user name on the Start menu to open your user folder.

3. Double-click the Contacts folder to open it.

4. Select the contacts you want to export. For example, press Ctrl+A to select all the contacts, or drag a selection box around those you want.

5. On the toolbar, click the Display additional commands button (the >> button), and then click Export to display the Export Windows Contacts dialog box (see Figure 21-7).

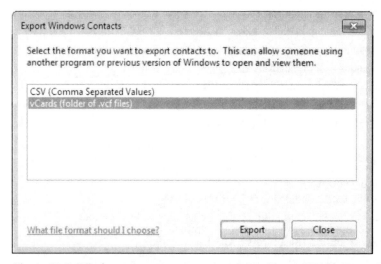

Figure 21-7. *Windows can export your contacts to either a CSV file or to vCard files. Usually, vCards are easier.*

6. Click the vCards item.

7. Click the Export button. Windows Explorer displays the Browse For Folder dialog box.

8. Click the folder you created.

9. Click the OK button to close the Browse For Folder dialog box. Windows Explorer exports the contacts and displays a Windows Contacts dialog box telling you it has done so.

10. Click the OK button to close the Windows Contacts dialog box.

11. Click the Close button to close the Export Windows Contacts dialog box.

12. Double-click the folder to which you exported the vCards to open a Windows Explorer window showing the folder.

13. Press Ctrl+A to select all the vCard files.

14. Drag the vCard files to the Outlook Contacts window. Outlook creates a new contact for each of the vCard files and opens a contact window showing it.

15. For each contact, fill in any other details you want to add (for example, notes), and then choose Contact ➤ Actions ➤ Save & Close to close the contact window.

Importing Contacts from Yahoo! Address Book

If you use Yahoo! Mail, chances are that you have contact information stored in Yahoo!'s Contacts feature. To get this data into Outlook, export it to a comma-separated values (CSV) file by following these steps:

1. Sign into Yahoo! and go to Contacts.

2. Click the Tools button, and then click Export on the drop-down menu to display the Export screen.

3. On the Microsoft Outlook line, click the Export button.

4. On the Please answer the following to verify you are not a robot screen, type the text of the CAPTCHA test, and then click the Export Now button. Yahoo exports the contacts to a CSV file in your Downloads folder.

5. Import the CSV file as described in the section "Importing Contacts from a CSV File," later in this chapter.

■ **Note** The Yahoo! Export screen also offers an option for exporting your contacts to a zip file of vCard files. You can use this option too for getting the contacts into Outlook, but generally, the CSV file is the easier choice.

Importing Contacts from Google Contacts

If you use Gmail or Google Mail, you can export your contact data to a comma-separated values (CSV) file that you can then import into Outlook. Follow these steps:

1. Sign into Gmail or Google Mail, and then go to the My Contacts area.

2. Click the Export link to display the Export screen.

3. In the Who do you want to export? area, select the Everyone (All Contacts) option button if you want to export all your contacts. Otherwise, select the Only option button, and then choose the appropriate group in the drop-down list—for example, Friends.

4. In the Which export format? area, select the Outlook CSV option button.

5. Click the Export button. Google exports the contacts to a CSV file in your Downloads folder.

6. Import the CSV file as described in the next section.

Importing Contacts from a CSV File

When you've created a CSV file containing your contacts, follow these steps to import them into Outlook:

1. In Outlook, click the File tab to open Backstage.

2. Click the Open item in the left column to display the Open pane.

3. Click the Import button to launch the Import and Export Wizard (see Figure 21-8).

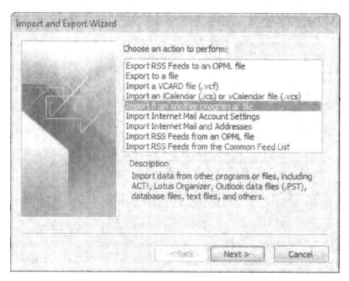

Figure 21-8. On the opening screen of the Import and Export Wizard, click the Import from another program or file item to import a CSV file.

4. In the Choose an action to perform box, click the Import from another program or file item.

5. Click the Next button to display the Import a File: Select file type to import from dialog box (see Figure 21-9).

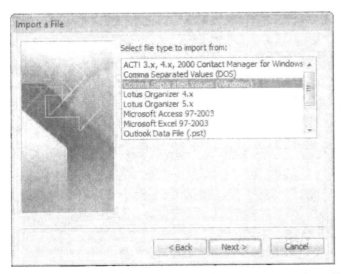

Figure 21-9. *In the Import a File: Select file type to import from dialog box, click the Comma Separated Values (Windows) item.*

6. In the Select file type to import from box, click Comma Separated Values (Windows).

7. Click the Next button to display the Import a File: File to import dialog box (see Figure 21-10).

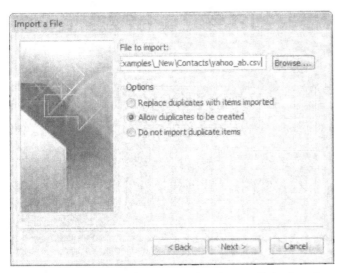

Figure 21-10. *In the Import a File: File to import dialog box, browse to the file you want to import, and then choose how to handle duplicate entries.*

8. In the Options area, choose how to handle duplicate entries by selecting the appropriate option button:

- *Replace duplicates with items imported*: Select this option button to replace any existing duplicates with new items created from the data you're importing.

- *Allow duplicates to be created*: Select this option button to allow Outlook to create duplicates by importing records with the same names. You'll need to go through your contacts afterward and integrate the duplicates (or remove them).

- *Do not import duplicate items*: Select this option button to avoid importing records that duplicate existing names.

9. Click the Next button to display the Import a File: Select destination folder dialog box (see Figure 21-11).

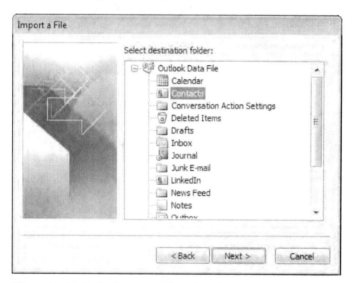

Figure 21-11. *In the Import a File: Select destination folder dialog box, make sure the Contacts folder is selected.*

10. Make sure the Contacts folder is selected in the Select destination folder box.

11. Click the Next button to display the Import a File: The following actions will be performed dialog box (see Figure 21-12).

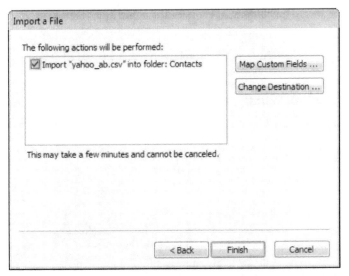

Figure 21-12. In the Import a File: The following actions will be performed dialog box, select the check box for the contacts you want to import. In this case, you have only one option.

12. In the box called The following actions will be performed, make sure the check box is selected for the contacts you want to import. When you're importing a CSV file, you'll normally have only one choice here.

■ **Note** From The Import a File: The following actions will be performed dialog box, you can click the Map Custom Fields button to display the Map Custom Fields dialog box, which enables you to customize which field from the CSV file goes to which field in the Outlook contacts. When you've exported a CSV file of contact data as described in this chapter, the fields have the correct name and order for mapping to Outlook, so you need to change the mapping only if you want to send a field to a destination other than its normal one. See the section "Mapping Custom Fields When Importing Contact Data," later in this chapter, for details.

---

13. Click the Finish button to close the dialog box. Outlook imports the contacts and adds them to your contacts list.

Importing Contacts from vCard Files

When you create vCard files or receive them from others, you can quickly add them to your contacts list in Outlook. Follow these steps:

1. Open Outlook, and then click Contacts in the Navigation Pane to display your contacts.

2. Open a Windows Explorer window to the folder that contains the vCard files.

3. Arrange the windows so that you can see both.

4. In the Windows Explorer window, select the vCard files, and then drag them to the contacts list in Outlook.

Importing Contacts from an Excel Worksheet

If you've created a contact database in Excel, you may need to import contacts from it into Outlook. To do so, follow these steps:

1. In Excel, create a named range that contains the data you want to import. Follow these steps:

    • Open the workbook in Excel.

    • Select the data area, including its header row (if it has one).

    • Choose Formulas ➤ Defined Names ➤ Define Name (click the Define Name button, not the drop-down button) to display the New Name dialog box.

    • Type the name in the Name box. Make sure this name is different from any of the column headings in the header row.

    • In the Scope drop-down list, choose Workbook.

    • Click the OK button to close the New Name dialog box.

2. Still in Excel, save the workbook in Excel 97–2003 format. Follow these steps:

    • Choose File ➤ Save As to display the Save As dialog box.

    • Open the Save as type drop-down list, and then click Excel 97–2003 Workbook.

    • Click the Save button.

    • Choose File ➤ Close to close the workbook, or simply choose File ➤ Exit to quit Excel.

3. In Outlook, click the File tab to open Backstage.

4. Click the Open item in the left column to display the Open pane.

5. Click the Import button to launch the Import and Export Wizard.

6. In the Choose an action to perform box, click the Import from another program or file item.

7. Click the Next button to display the Import a File: Select file type to import from dialog box.

8. In the Select file type to import from box, click the Microsoft Excel 97–2003 item.

9. Click the Next button to display the Import a File: File to import dialog box.

10. Click the Browse button to open the Browse dialog box. Navigate to and select your Excel file of contacts, and then click the OK button.

11. In the Options area, choose how to handle duplicate entries by selecting the appropriate option button:

   • *Replace duplicates with items imported*: Select this option button to replace any existing duplicates with new items created from the data you're importing.

   • *Allow duplicates to be created*: Select this option button to allow Outlook to create duplicates by importing records with the same names. You'll need to go through your contacts afterward and integrate the duplicates (or remove them).

   • *Do not import duplicate items*: Select this option button to avoid importing records that duplicate existing names.

12. Click the Next button to display the Import a File: Select destination folder dialog box.

13. Make sure the Contacts folder is selected in the Select destination folder box.

14. Click the Next button to display the Import a File: The following actions will be performed dialog box (see Figure 21-13).

▓ **Note** If Outlook displays a Translation Error dialog box that says that the Excel file contains no named ranges, one of two problems has occurred. First, the Excel workbook doesn't contain a named range; you need to open the workbook in Excel and create a range as described in step 1. Second, if the workbook does have a named range, this error means that the workbook is still open in Excel—so you need to close it.

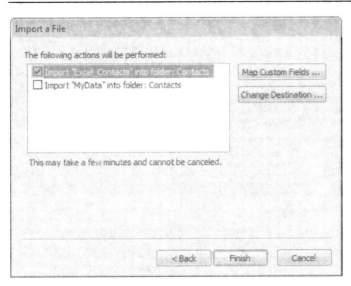

Figure 21-13. In the Import a File: The following actions will be performed dialog box, select the check box for the named range that contains your contacts.

15. In the following actions will be performed box, select the check box for the range that contains the contacts.

16. Click the Map Custom Fields button to display the Map Custom Fields dialog box, and then map the fields as discussed in the section "Mapping Custom Fields When Importing Data," later in this chapter.

17. Click the Finish button to close the Import a File dialog box and import the contact data.

Mapping Custom Fields When Importing Contact Data

When you import data that you've exported to a vCard or another standard format, Outlook has no trouble knowing which piece of incoming data to map to each address field, because the fields use standard names and all the formatting is correct. But when you import data that you have laid out in a spreadsheet or a similar tool, you may need to map the custom fields manually in order to get the data in the right places.

To map the custom data, follow these steps:

1. When you reach the Import a File: The following actions will be performed dialog box, click the Map Custom Fields button to display the Map Custom Fields dialog box (see Figure 21-14).

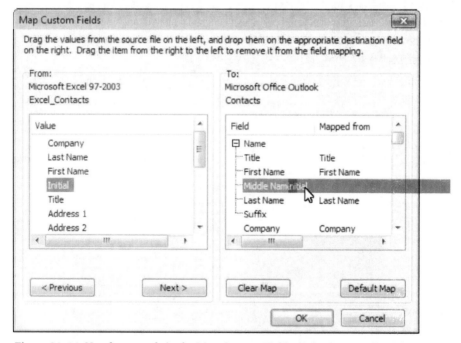

Figure 21-14. Use the controls in the Map Custom Fields dialog box to tell Outlook which field in the incoming data to map to which field in each Outlook contact.

2. In the right box, expand or collapse the listing of fields so that you can see the field you want to map. For example, click the + sign next to the Name item to display the individual fields that make up the name: Title, First Name, Middle Name, Last Name, and Suffix.

■ **Note** If your contact data has a header row, you'll see the field names from the header row in the left box in the Map Custom Fields dialog box. If your contact data has no header row, you'll see the values from the first row of data—the details of the first contact you're importing. You can click the Next button to display the next record or the Previous button to display the previous record (once you've gone forward from the first record).

---

3. Drag the field you want to map from the left box to the corresponding field in the right box, and drop it there. Outlook adds the field's name to the Mapped from column in the right box, so you can see which fields are mapped.

4. When you've finished mapping each field, click the OK button to close the Map Custom Fields dialog box. You can then click the Finish button to finish the process of importing the data.

Working with Contacts

After creating contacts or importing them into Outlook, you can work with them. Outlook makes it easy to view and sort your contacts in different ways, edit the information in a contact record, organize your contacts into groups, and communicate with them.

Viewing and Sorting Your Contacts

To view your list of contacts, click the Contacts button in the Navigation Pane. You can then expand the My Contacts list by clicking the white triangle next to it, and click one of the groups of contacts that it contains. For example, the Contacts screen in Figure 21-15 shows two groups of contacts: the Contacts group in Outlook, and a LinkedIn group imported from the LinkedIn social network.

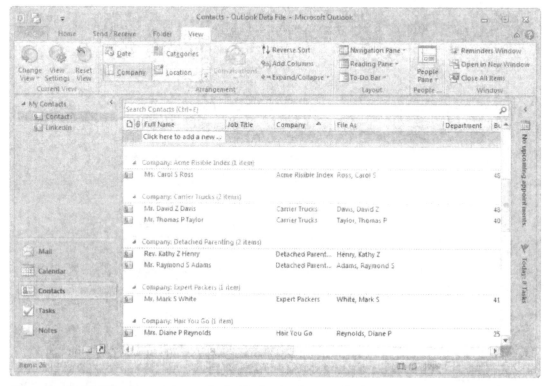

Figure 21-15. Click the Contacts button in the Navigation Pane to display your contacts. You can then expand the My Contacts listing in the Navigation Pane and click the group of contacts you want to display. This screen uses List view.

Changing the View

Figure 21-15 uses Outlook's List view. Outlook gives you four built-in views, which you can switch among by using the View ➤ Current View ➤ Change View drop-down panel:

- *Business Card view*: This view (see Figure 21-16) shows each contact's details on a virtual business card.

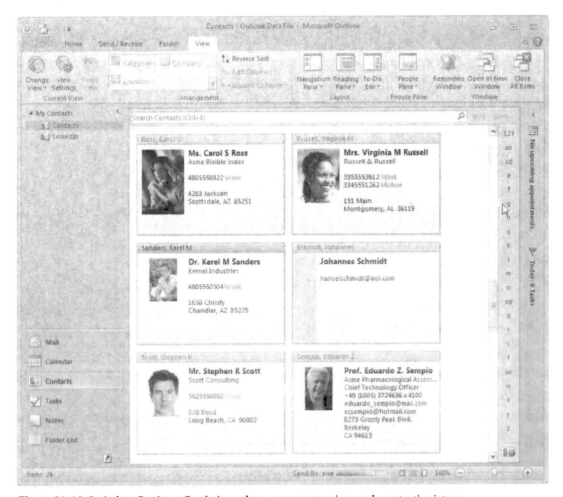

Figure 21-16. Switch to Business Card view when you want to view each contact's picture.

- *Card view*: This view (see Figure 21-17) shows each contact's information laid out on a rectangle with all the fields clearly identified.

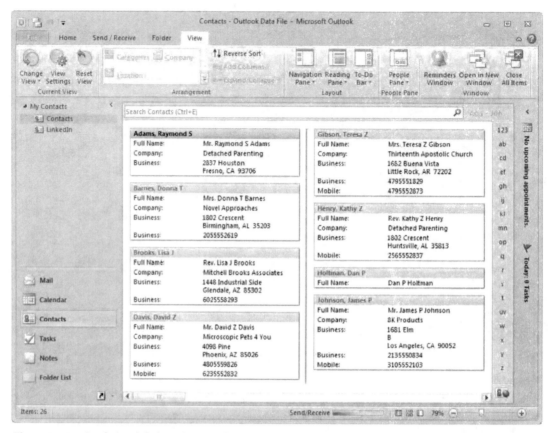

Figure 21-17. Card view labels each item of contact information clearly.

- *Phone view*: This view displays the contacts as a phone list (see Figure 21-18).

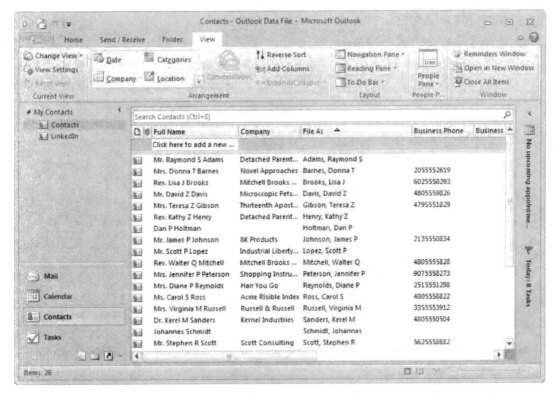

Figure 21-18. Display your contacts in Phone view when you need to quickly find a phone number.

Changing the Arrangement and Grouping

In Phone view and List view, you can use the Arrange By box or drop-down list in the Arrangement group of the View pane to change the way that Outlook arranges your contacts. When the Arrange By box appears, as in Figure 21-18, click the item by which you want to arrange the contacts: Date, Categories, Company, or Location.

For these two views, you can choose whether Outlook displays the contacts in groups within the arrangement. To turn grouping on or off, choose View ➤ Arrangement ➤ Arrange By (if the Arrange By drop-down list is displayed) or View ➤ Arrangement ➤ More (clicking the drop-down button at the right of the Arrange By box), and then click the Show in Groups item to either place a check mark next to it or to remove the check mark.

■ **Tip** For a quick sort, click the heading of the column by which you want to sort.

Searching for a Contact

To search for a contact, follow these steps:

1. Click in the Search Contacts box at the top of the Contacts pane, or press Ctrl+E to select the box with the keyboard. Outlook adds the Search Tools section to the Ribbon and displays the Search pane (shown in Figure 21-19 with a search underway).

Figure 21-19. *When you start a search, Outlook adds the Search Tools section to the Ribbon and displays the Search tab, which contains controls for refining the search.*

2. Type your search term. Outlook displays matching results. You can double-click a search result to open the contact in a contact window.

3. If necessary, change the scope of the search by clicking one of the buttons in the Scope group of the Search tab. For example, click the All Contact Items button to search all contact items instead of just those in the current folder.

4. When you have finished searching, choose Search Tools ➤ Search ➤ Close ➤ Close Search to clear the search and hide the Search Tools section of the Ribbon.

Editing Contact Information

As you interact with your contacts and learn more about them, you'll often need to take notes, add further details, or change the information you've already entered.

To edit a contact's information, double-click the contact record in the list of contacts. Outlook opens the contact in a contact window, where you can edit the information freely.

When you've finished editing a contact record, choose Contact ➤ Actions ➤ Save & Close to close the contact record.

Communicating with Your Contacts

When working in a contact window, you can quickly start a communication with one of your contacts by giving the appropriate command:

- *E-mail*: Choose Contact ➤ Communicate ➤ E-mail to create a new message to the contact.

- *Meeting*: Choose Contact ➤ Communicate ➤ Meeting to start a meeting invitation to the contact.

- *Phone call*: Choose Contact ➤ Communicate ➤ More ➤ Call, and then click the appropriate phone number (for example, Business or Home) on the submenu.

- *Task*: Choose Contact ➤ Communicate ➤ More ➤ Assign Task to start a task request to the contact.

You can also start a communication by right-clicking a contact in the contacts list, and then making the appropriate choice on the context menu (see Figure 21-20); for example, choose Create ➤ E-mail to start a new e-mail message.

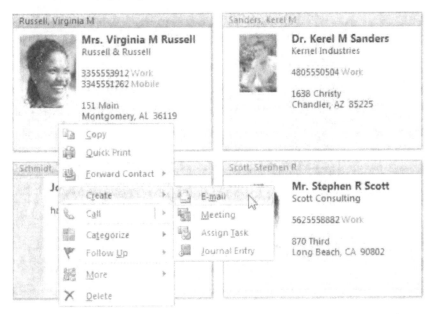

Figure 21-20. *You can start a communication by right-clicking a contact in the contacts list, and then making the appropriate choice from the context menu.*

Summary

In this chapter, you've learned how to work with contacts in Outlook. You now know how to create contacts from scratch or import your existing contact data into Outlook. And you know how to view and sort your contacts, edit their contact information, and quickly and easily create communications to them.

In the next chapter, I'll show you how to use Outlook to manage your schedule.

CHAPTER 22

Managing Your Calendar

In this chapter, you'll look at how to use Outlook to schedule your appointments and keep your calendar in order.

First, you'll meet the Calendar interface, learn to display the dates you want, and customize the calendar settings. I'll discuss the different types of time commitments Outlook uses—appointments, events and meetings—and then I'll show you how to use the Calendar's different views.

After that, we'll go through how to create one-shot appointments (or events) and ones that repeat on a regular schedule. Finally, we'll look at how you use Outlook to schedule meetings and how you respond to meeting invitations you receive.

Meeting the Calendar Interface

To get started working with the Calendar, click the Calendar button in the Navigation Pane or press Ctrl+2. Outlook first displays the Calendar in Day view (see Figure 22-1).

These are the main parts of the Outlook window:

- *Date Navigator*: This area shows the dates in the current month. You can move to the previous month by clicking the left-arrow button or to the next month by clicking the right-arrow button.

Note As usual, you can click the Minimize the Navigation Pane button (the < button at the top-right corner of the Navigation Pane) to reduce the Navigation Pane to a thin strip at the left side of the Outlook window. Do this when you need more space to work on your appointments. Click the Folders button to display a pop-up panel showing the Date Navigator and the Calendars list. When you want to restore the Navigation Pane, click the Expand the Navigation Pane button (the > button at the top of the strip).

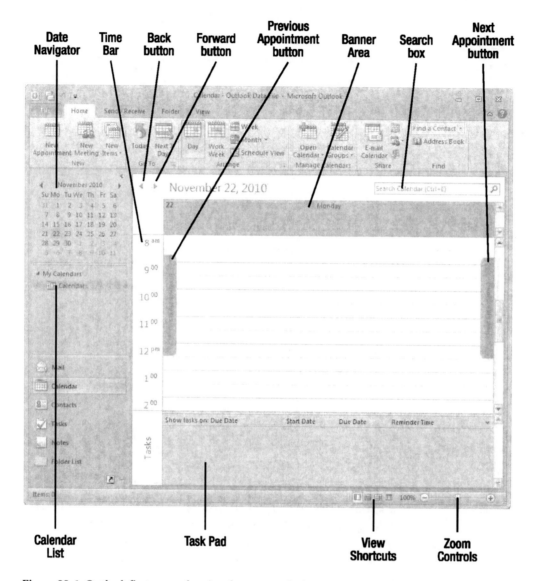

Figure 22-1. *Outlook first opens showing the current day's appointments and tasks.*

- *Calendar List*: This area shows the list of your calendars under the heading My Calendars. Normally, Outlook starts you off with a single calendar named simply Calendar. You can expand the My Calendars list by clicking the white triangle to its left or collapse it by clicking the black triangle that replaces the white triangle when you expand it. You can add other calendars of your own to the Calendar List if needed, or you can add calendars that other people are sharing.

- *Time Bar*: This vertical strip shows the times of day, with the hours marked. At first, Outlook displays each hour divided into two 30-minute slots. You can change these intervals by right-clicking the Time Bar and choosing your preferred interval: 60 Minutes – Least Space for Details; 30 Minutes; 15 Minutes; 10 Minutes; 6 Minutes; or 5 Minutes – Most Space for Details.

- *Back button*: Click this button to display the previous time unit—the previous day when the Calendar is in Day view, the previous work week when the Calendar is in Work Week view and so on.

- *Forward button*: Click this button to display the next time unit—the next day, the next work week, the next month or whatever.

- *Previous Appointment button*: Click this button to display the previous appointment.

- *Next Appointment button*: Click this button to display the next appointment.

- *Banner Area*: This area displays the day name (in Day view) or names (in other views).

- *Search box*: Click in this area and type a search term to search the Calendar.

- *TaskPad*: This area shows your list of tasks from the Tasks folder. You can create a new task by clicking a blank line in the TaskPad and typing the details of the task.

- *View Shortcuts*: Click these buttons to switch among Outlook's four views. See the section "Understanding and Using the Calendar Views," later in this chapter.

- *Zoom Controls*: As with the other Office programs, click the – button to zoom out, click the + button to zoom in, or drag the zoom slider to zoom either in or out.

Displaying the Dates You Want

What you'll probably want to do first is display the dates you need to work with.

First, go to the Arrange group on the Home tab of the Ribbon, and then click the button for the arrangement you want:

- *Day*: Click this button to display a single day at a time. This is what Outlook displays by default until you change it.

- *Work Week*: Click this button to display the days of the work week—Monday to Friday by default, but you can change the days as needed, as you'll see in a moment. This view, shown in Figure 22-2, can be highly useful for planning your time at work.

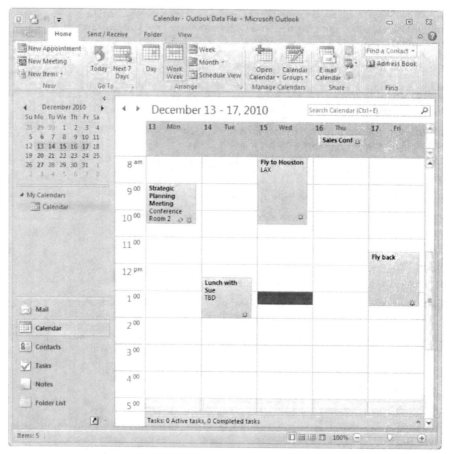

Figure 22-2. Work Week view gives you an overview of your commitments for the working week.

- *Week*: Click this button to display a full week—Sunday through Saturday (you can change the start day of the week as needed).

- *Month*: Click this button (rather than the drop-down button) to display the full month, including any days from the previous month and next month needed to make up the full weeks.

■ **Tip** To change the amount of detail shown in Month view, click the Month drop-down button in the Arrange group, and then click Show Low Detail, Show Medium Detail or Show High Detail, as needed. Low Detail shows only the all-day events; Medium Detail shows all-day events and free/busy information; and High Detail shows all the events and appointments. High Detail is usually most useful if you have only a few appointments; if your schedule is packed, try Medium Detail or Low Detail.

- *Schedule*: Click this button to view the Calendar as a horizontal schedule. This view is good for finding free times on two or more calendars when you need to schedule a meeting. But if you find this view useful for regular work too, you can use it anytime.

Customizing the Calendar Settings

Outlook comes with standard calendar settings, but you can often save time and effort by taking a few minutes to customize the settings to suit your work schedule and your needs. For example, you may need to use different start times and end times for work, change the work week to show different days than Monday to Friday or start the week on a different day than Sunday.

To customize the calendar settings, follow these steps:

1. Choose Home ➤ Arrange ➤ Calendar Options, clicking the tiny button in the lower-right corner of the Arrange group, to display the Outlook Options dialog box with the Calendar category already selected in the left pane (see Figure 22-3).

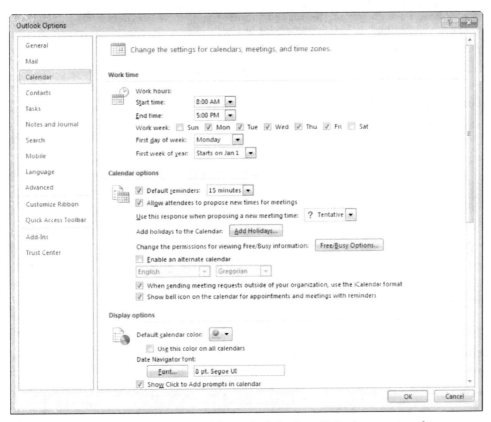

Figure 22-3. In the Calendar category of the Outlook Options dialog box, you can change your work hours, work week, and other essential calendar settings.

2. To change your work hours, set the appropriate times in the Start time box and the End time box. Outlook shades the hours outside work hours to help you avoid scheduling appointments in them (for example, a 3 AM meeting instead of a 3 PM meeting).

3. To change the days Outlook displays for your work week, select the check boxes for the appropriate days on the Work week line and clear the other check boxes. For example, if you work Tuesday through Saturday and have Sunday and Monday off, clear the Monday check box and select the Saturday check box (starting from the regular work week of Monday through Friday).

4. To set the day Outlook treats as the start of the week, open the First day of week drop-down list and click the day you want. For example, choose Monday to start the week on Monday rather than the default day, Sunday.

5. Choose other settings as needed. For example, if your company or organization observes special holidays, click the Add Holidays button, and then select the appropriate check box in the Add Holidays to Calendar dialog box. This dialog box provides check boxes for countries (for example, Andorra, Bolivia and China) and for major religions (Christian Religious Holidays, Islamic Religious Holidays and Jewish Religious Holidays). Click the OK button to close the Add Holidays to Calendar dialog box.

6. When you've finished choosing calendar settings, click the OK button to close the Outlook Options dialog box.

Understanding Appointments, Events and Meetings

Outlook's Calendar uses three different types of time commitments:

- *Appointment*: An appointment is an item on your schedule that requires only you, not other people you need to invite or resources (for example, a conference room or projector) that you need to reserve. The Calendar creates appointments by default unless you choose to create an event or a meeting. An appointment occupies the appropriate time slots in your schedule. For example, if you create a three-hour meeting starting at 10 AM, Outlook displays the appointment taking up the time slots from 10 AM to 1 PM.

- *Event*: An *event* is simply an appointment that lasts for 24 hours or more. Instead of taking up all of a day's time slots by displaying an event right across them, Outlook displays events in the banner area at the top of the schedule.

- *Meeting*: A meeting is an appointment to which you invite other people or for which you schedule resources.

▪ **Note** You can change any of the three types of time commitments to another type by editing its details. For example, you can change an appointment to a meeting by inviting someone else to it.

Understanding and Using the Calendar Views

Outlook gives you four different views for viewing the Calendar:

- *Normal view*: This view (shown in Figure 22-1), displays the Date Navigator in the Navigation Pane and shows the TaskPad below the calendar listing.

- *Calendar and Tasks view*: This view (see Figure 22-4) automatically minimizes the Navigation Pane to provide more space for displaying the calendar listing and the TaskPad. Use this view when you need more space for working on your appointments and tasks.

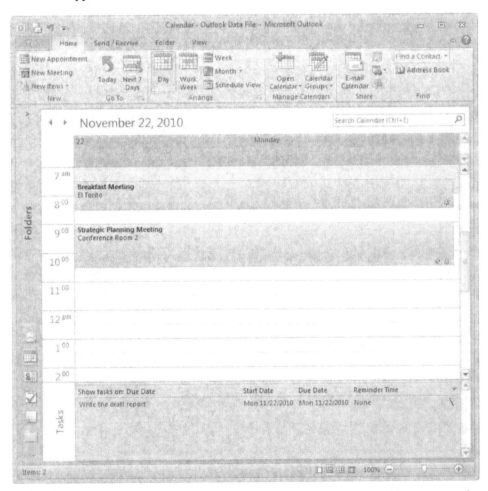

Figure 22-4. *Calendar and Task view collapses the Navigation Pane to provide more room for working with your appointments and tasks.*

- *Calendar Only view*: This view (which looks like Figure 22-4, but without the TaskPad displayed) automatically minimizes the Navigation Pane and hides the TaskPad to give you as much space as possible for working in the calendar listing.

- *Classic view*: This view (see Figure 22-5) shows the To-Do Bar on the right of the Outlook window with the Date Navigator, Appointment list, and Task list in it. This view is useful when you need to see two or more months in the Date Navigator.

Figure 22-5. *Classic view displays the To-Do Bar on the right of the Outlook window. You can customize the contents of the To-Do Bar—for example, you can change the number of months displayed.*

Creating Appointments and Events

This section shows you how to create appointments and events. The following section explains how to schedule meetings.

Creating One-Shot Appointments

In a typical schedule, many of your appointments will occur only once rather than occurring at regular intervals. You can create such one-shot appointments either quickly, providing a minimum amount of information, or by using an Appointment window to enter full details.

Creating a One-Shot Appointment Quickly

To create a one-shot appointment quickly, follow these steps:

1. Click the appropriate slot in the schedule to select it.

2. Type the name of the appointment (or as much detail as you need, but it all goes into a single field).

3. Press Enter to apply the appointment.

4. If you need to change the length of time the appointment takes, drag the lower handle down (to make the appointment longer) or up (to make it shorter). Figure 22-6 illustrates making the upper appointment longer.

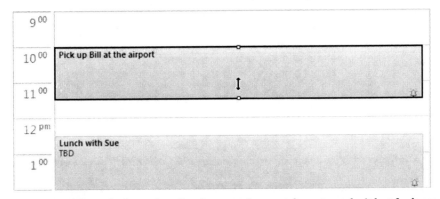

Figure 22-6. Drag the lower handle of an appointment down to make it last for longer or up to make it shorter.

Creating a One-Shot Appointment or Event with Full Details

Creating a one-shot appointment quickly as discussed in the previous section is often handy, but other times you'll need to enter full details for a one-shot appointment. To do so, follow these steps:

1. Choose the time slot and open an Appointment window (see Figure 22-7) in one of these ways:

- *Appointment one time slot long*: To create an appointment the length of a single time slot, double-click that time slot.

- *Appointment multiple time slots long*: To create an appointment that occupies several time slots, click and drag through the time slots in the calendar. Then either right-click in the selection and click New Appointment on the context menu or choose Home ➤ New ➤ New Appointment.

■ **Note** You can also start an all-day event by choosing New All Day Event in the context menu.

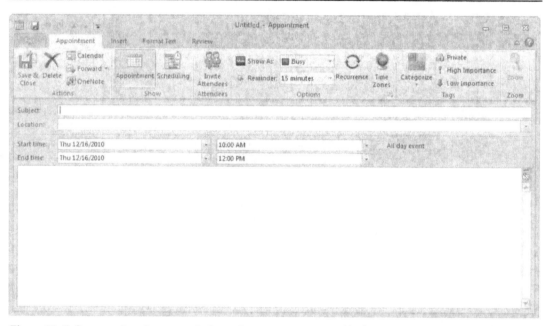

Figure 22-7. Open an Appointment window when you want to specify the appointment's details beyond the subject and the times.

2. In the Subject box, type the subject of the appointment or event.

3. In the Location box, type the location. If it's a location you've used before, you can click the drop-down button at the right end of the box, and then click the location on the drop-down list.

4. If necessary, adjust the start time or end time of the appointment. If you chose the exact times you need in step 1, the Start time boxes and End time boxes will show the right dates and times.

5. If you want to create an all-day event rather than an appointment, select the All day event check box.

6. Type any notes for the appointment in the box at the bottom of the Appointment window. For example, you may need to prepare materials to take with you.

7. In the Options group of the Appointment tab of the Ribbon, choose any options needed for the appointment:

   - In the Show As drop-down list, Outlook automatically selects Busy when you create the appointment. Instead, you can choose Out of Office, Tentative, or Free.

   - In the Reminder drop-down list, choose whether and when Outlook should play a reminder for you about the appointment. The default setting is 15 minutes, but you can choose None to turn off the reminder or any length of time between 0 minutes and 2 weeks.

   - If you need to create a recurring event, click the Recurrence button, and then work as described in the section "Creating Repeating Appointments," later in this chapter.

   - If you need to change the time zone for the appointment, click the Time Zones button. Outlook displays a time zone drop-down list on the Start time line and the End time line. Choose the time zones you need.

8. If you need to categorize the appointment, choose Appointment ➤ Tags ➤ Categorize, and then click the category you want. Outlook starts you off with categories named simply by their colors—Blue Category, Green Category, and so on—but you can change the names to suit your needs.

9. If this is a private appointment, choose Appointment ➤ Tags ➤ Private to prevent others from seeing the appointment's details when you share your calendar.

10. If you need to change the appointment's importance, choose Appointment ➤ Tags ➤ High Importance or Appointment ➤ Tags ➤ Low Importance, as needed. As you'd guess, selecting High Importance turns off Low Importance, and vice versa.

11. Choose Appointment ➤ Actions ➤ Save & Close to save the details of the appointment and close the window.

Creating Repeating Appointments

If your work life involves repeating appointments, you can set them up easily in Outlook. Follow these steps:

1. Open an Appointment window and set up the other details of the appointment as described in the previous section. Or, if you've already set up an appointment and now need to change it to a repeating appointment, double-click the appointment to open it.

Note You can also start a repeating appointment by right-clicking your selected time slot and then clicking New Recurring Appointment on the context menu.

---

2. Choose Appointment ➤ Options ➤ Recurrence to display the Appointment Recurrence dialog box (see Figure 22-8).

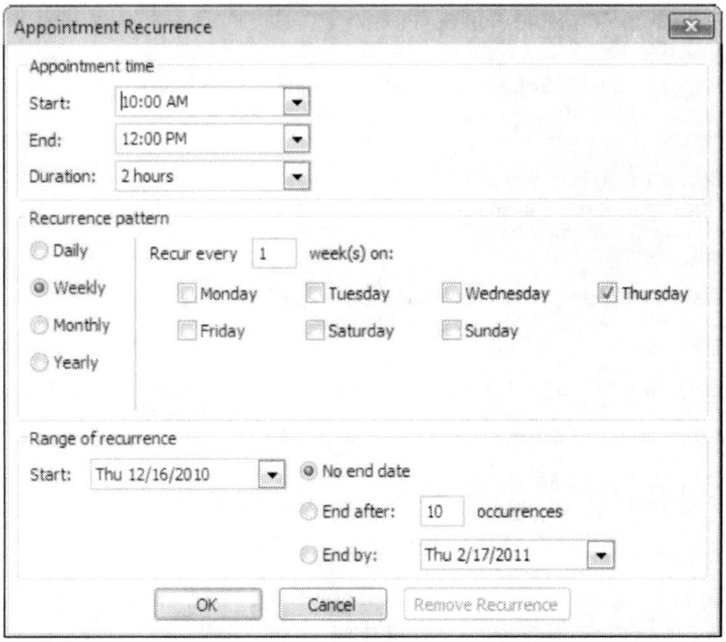

Figure 22-8. *Use the Appointment Recurrence dialog box when you need to create a repeating appointment.*

3. In the Recurrence pattern section of the dialog box, set up the recurrence like this:

   - Select the Daily option button, the Weekly option button, the Monthly option button, or the Yearly option button, as needed. Outlook displays the appropriate controls to the right of the vertical line.

   - Use the controls to the right of the line to set up the recurrence. For example, for a weekly appointment, you can set the number of weeks in the Recur every *N* week(s) on box. For a monthly appointment, you can use the date in the month (for example, Day 16 of every 1 month) or the day of the appropriate week (for example, the third Thursday of every 2 months).

4. In the Range of recurrence section of the dialog box, choose how long the repeating appointment should continue:

   - In the Start box, enter the start date. Outlook uses the date you've specified for the appointment.

   - Select the No end date option button if you want the appointment to run forever. Otherwise, you can select the End after option button and set the number of occurrences in the occurrences box, or select the End by option button and set the date in the drop-down list.

5.   Click the OK button to close the Appointment Recurrence dialog box and return to the Appointment window, which is now called Appointment Series. The Recurrence button in the Options group now appears pressed in to indicate that recurrence is turned on, and the Recurrence line appears below the Location box giving the details of the recurrence (see Figure 22-9). The Appointment Series tab replaces the Appointment tab.

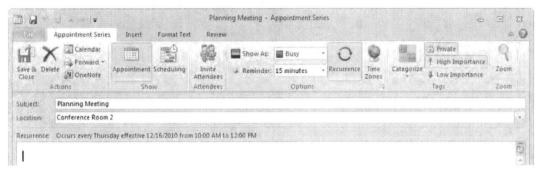

Figure 22-9. *To indicate that the appointment recurs, Outlook selects the Recurrence button in the Options group of the Appointment Series window. The details of the recurrence appear on the Recurrence line below the Location box.*

6.   Choose Appointment Series ➤ Actions ➤ Save & Close to close the window and save the changes.

░ **Note** If you need to stop an appointment from recurring, open the Appointment Recurrence dialog box, and then click the Remove Recurrence button.

Scheduling Meetings

As you'll remember from earlier in this chapter, Outlook considers an appointment that involves inviting other people or scheduling resources to be a meeting. Chances are you'll need to schedule meetings of your own and respond to meeting invitations that other people send you.

Setting Up a Meeting

To set up a meeting, follow these steps:

1.   Select the time slot or slots you will use for the meeting.

2.   Right-click the selected time slot or slots and click New Meeting Request on the context menu, or choose Home ➤ New ➤ New Meeting, to open a Meeting window (see Figure 22-10).

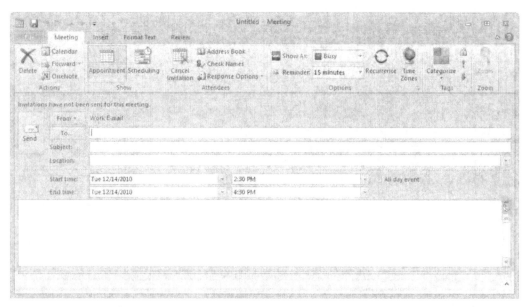

Figure 22-10. Set up the details of your meeting request in the Meeting window, and then send it.

3. Click the To button to display the Select Attendees and Resources dialog box (shown in Figure 22-11 with some settings chosen).

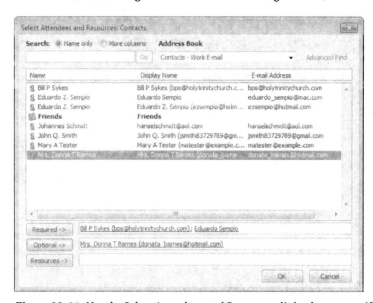

Figure 22-11. Use the Select Attendees and Resources dialog box to specify which attendees you require for the meeting, which attendees are optional, and which resources you need.

4. In the Address Book drop-down list, choose the contact list you want to work with.

5. In the main listbox, click the contact or contacts you want to add as required attendees, and then click the Required button to add them to the Required box.

6. In the main listbox, select any contacts you want to add as optional attendees, and then click the Optional button to add them to the Optional box.

7. If your address book includes resources, select those you need, and click the Resources button to add them to the Resources box.

8. Click the OK button to close the Select Attendees and Resources dialog box. Outlook returns you to the Meeting window, in which it has entered your chosen contacts in the To box.

9. Type the subject for the meeting request in the Subject box; for example, the name of the meeting.

10. Type the meeting's location in the Location box.

11. Type any message about the meeting in the main box. For example, you may want to make clear what the meeting will cover, what attendees need to prepare and so on.

12. If you want to check schedule information, choose Meeting ➤ Show ➤ Scheduling to display the Scheduling pane (see Figure 22-12). Here, you can see the information available about each participant's schedule, which should help you pick a suitable time for the meeting.

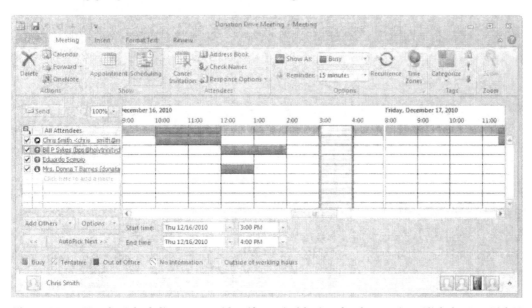

Figure 22-12. *Use the Scheduling pane to identify a suitable time for the meeting. Click the AutoPick Next button to pick the next time available to all required participants.*

13. When you've finished setting up the meeting invitation, click the Send button to send the meeting invitation.

Tracking the Status of Meeting Invitations You've Sent

After you send a meeting request, you receive the responses that the invitees send. Outlook tallies the acceptances and refusals for you. To see a summary of the responses, double-click the meeting in your calendar to open it in a Meeting window, and then choose Meeting ➤ Show ➤ Tracking (see Figure 22-13).

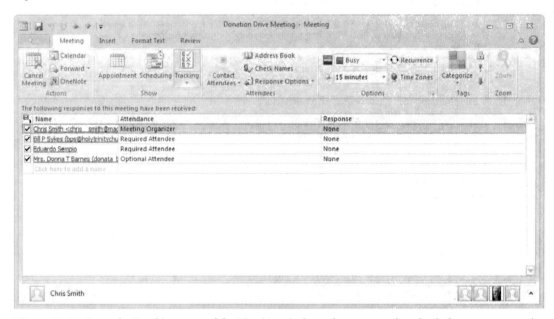

Figure 22-13. Open the Tracking pane of the Meeting window when you need to check the responses you've received to the meeting request.

■ **Note** To remove an attendee from the meeting, clear the attendee's check box in the Tracking pane. When you save the meeting, Outlook displays a dialog box noting that the attendees for the meeting have changed. Select the Save changes and send update option button, and then click the OK button. In the Send Update to Attendees dialog box, select the Send updates only to added or deleted attendees option button or the Send updates to all attendees option button, as needed, and then click the OK button.

Dealing with Invitations to Meetings

When someone sends you an invitation to a meeting, you receive an e-mail message with the details of the message and with a built-in mechanism for replying. Double-click the meeting message to open it in a Meeting window, and then click the Accept button, the Tentative button, the Decline button, or the Propose New Time button, as appropriate. Complete the resulting message with any more information needed, and then send it.

Summary

In this chapter, you've learned how to use Outlook to schedule your appointments and keep your calendar in order.

You now know how to navigate the Calendar interface and make it show the dates you want in the way you want them to appear. You understand the difference between an appointment and an event, and you know not only what distinguishes a meeting from an appointment but also how to set up meetings and respond to meeting invitations.

In the next chapter, I'll show you how to work with tasks and notes in Outlook. Turn the page when you're ready to start.

CHAPTER 23

Working with Tasks and Notes

In this chapter, I'll show you how to work with tasks and notes in Outlook.

Outlook provides strong features for defining tasks you need to complete and tracking your progress on completing them. You can create either one-shot tasks or recurring tasks, record your progress on them, and keep your colleagues informed about what you're doing. You can also delegate a task to someone else and follow her progress with it, even receiving an automatic notification when she marks the task as complete.

Outlook's Notes feature is useful for jotting down information as you work and then sharing your notes with other programs.

Creating Tasks

In this section, you'll learn how to work with Outlook's Tasks feature. You'll meet the interface Outlook provides for working with tasks, create new tasks, and manage your tasks. You'll also see how to assign tasks to other people and deal with the tasks they assign to you.

Meeting the Tasks Interface

To get started with tasks, click the Tasks button in the Navigation Pane or press Ctrl+4. Outlook displays the Tasks folder (shown in Figure 23-1 with several tasks added).

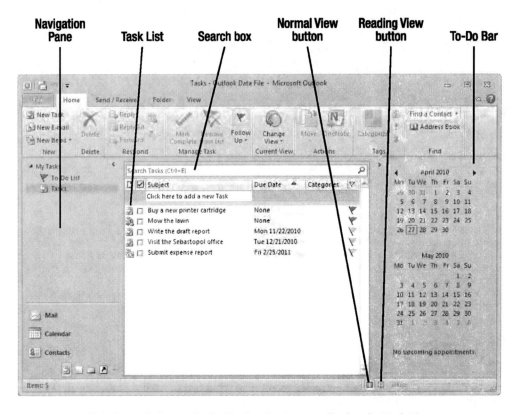

Figure 23-1. Click the Tasks button in the Navigation Pane to display the Task List.

By default, Outlook opens the Task List in Normal view, which shows the Navigation Pane on the left and the To-Do Bar on the right. If you want more space to work with your tasks, click the Reading View button on the status bar to switch the Task List to Reading view (see Figure 23-2), which minimizes the Navigation Pane, the To-Do Bar, and the Ribbon. You can also minimize the Ribbon only by pressing Ctrl+F1 or by clicking the Minimize the Ribbon button at its right end.

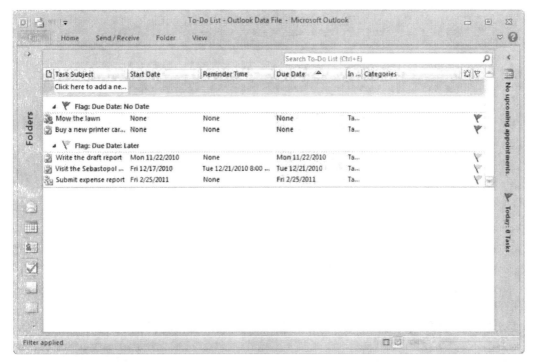

Figure 23-2. *Reading view minimizes the Ribbon, the Navigation Pane, and the To-Do Bar to give you more space to work on your tasks.*

Viewing the Task List

Apart from Normal view and Reading view, Outlook lets you arrange your Task List in nearly a dozen different ways. You can change view by opening the Change View drop-down panel, which you'll find in the Current View group on both the Home tab (see Figure 23-3) and the View tab of the Ribbon, and then clicking the view you want. These are the views:

- *Simple List*: This view shows all tasks, including those you've completed, with a minimal level of detail. This view is useful for general work.

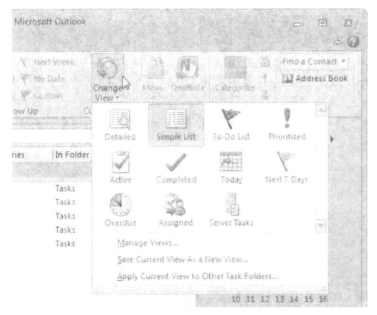

Figure 23-3. You can change view by using the Change View drop-down panel in the Current View group of the Home tab and the View tab of the Ribbon.

- *Detailed*: This view shows all tasks, including completed tasks, with more detail than Simple List view provides. This view works well if you can widen the Outlook window far enough to make space for each column; on narrower screens, this view tends to be too squashed. You can knock out any column you don't need by right-clicking the column heading and clicking Remove This Column on the context menu.

- *To-Do List*: This view displays tasks in your To-Do List. You can arrange them in different ways (for example, first by flag and then by start date) by clicking the column headings.

- *Prioritized*: This view shows tasks arranged by priority. This view is good for focusing on your key tasks rather than getting mired in unimportant tasks that are scheduled for today.

- *Active*: This view shows tasks that you haven't marked as complete.

- *Completed*: This view shows tasks you've marked as complete. Normally, you'll use this view to review the tasks you've performed.

- *Today*: This view shows tasks scheduled for the current day.

- *Next 7 Days*: This view shows tasks scheduled for the next seven days.

- *Overdue*: This view shows tasks whose due date has passed.

- *Assigned*: This view shows tasks you've assigned to others.

- *Server Tasks*: This view shows tasks assigned via Exchange.

Creating One-Shot Tasks

You can create a new task either directly in the Task List or by working in a Task window. Usually, it's easiest to work in the Task List when you need to enter only brief details of a task and to work in a Task window when you need to enter more details.

Creating a One-Shot Task by Working in the Task List

When you're working in a view such as Detailed view or Simple List view, you can create a one-shot task quickly in the Task list without opening a Task window. Click in the "Click here to add a new Task" box at the top of the pane, and then enter the name and details of the task (see Figure 23-4). To keep organized, you'll want to enter at least the subject of the task and its due date.

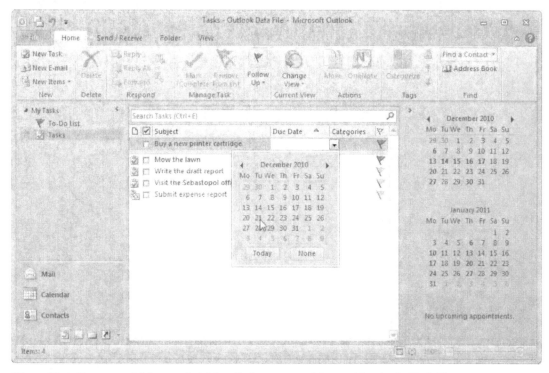

Figure 23-4. You can quickly enter brief details for a new task by working in the Task List.

Creating a One-Shot Task Using a Task Window

When you need to specify more detail for a task than the Task List allows, use a Task window to create the task. Follow these steps:

1. Double-click blank space in the Task List or choose Home ➤ New ➤ New Task to open a Task window. You can also press Ctrl+N. Figure 23-5 shows a Task window with a new task partly created.

▨ **Tip** When you're working in the Mail pane and have the To-Do Bar displayed, you can open a new Task window by double-clicking empty space in the Task List part of the To-Do Bar or right-clicking there and then clicking New Task on the context menu.

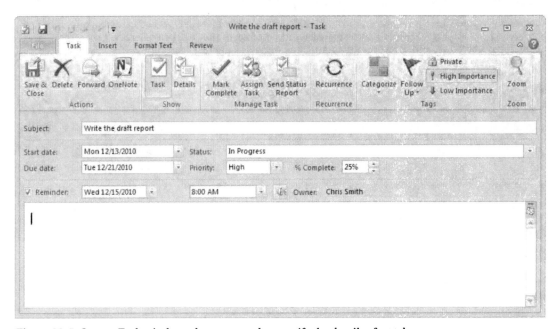

Figure 23-5. Open a Task window when you need to specify the details of a task.

2. Type the task's name in the Subject box.

▨ **Note** If you've created the task already, you can open it in a Task window to add more detail to it.

3. Enter the start date in the Start date box and the due date in the Due date box.

4. If you have already started the task, open the Status drop-down list and then click the appropriate item. Your choices are Not Started (the default), In Progress, Completed, Waiting on someone else, and Deferred. In the % Complete box, set the percentage of the task you've completed. Each click on the buttons changes the value by 25%, but you can type a different value if needed.

5. If necessary, change the task's priority by opening the Priority drop-down list and clicking High or Low instead of the default Normal. You can also choose Task ➤ Tags ➤ High Importance or Task ➤ Tags ➤ Low Importance to change the Priority setting.

6. If you want to set a reminder for a task, select the Reminder check box. Then choose the date in the first drop-down list, and the time in the second drop-down list. If you want to change the reminder sound, click the speaker icon to display the Reminder Sound dialog box (see Figure 23-6). Click the Browse button to open the Reminder Sound File dialog box, click the sound file you want, and then click the Open button. Click the OK button to close the Reminder Sound dialog box.

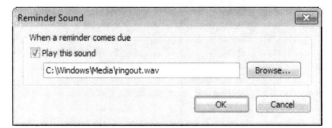

Figure 23-6. Use the Reminder Sound dialog box to set a custom reminder sound for a task.

■ **Tip** You'll find a selection of Windows sounds in the \Windows\Media folder on your PC's boot drive (for example, C:\Windows\Media).

7. Enter any notes about the task in the main box. You can enter large amounts of text or other objects if necessary:

    •   To format text, use the controls on the Format Text tab of the Task window's Ribbon.

    •   To insert a table, picture, chart, or other object, work on the Insert tab.

    •   To check the spelling, get a word count, or use the Thesaurus or other reference tools, work on the Review tab.

8. Choose Task ➤ Actions ➤ Save & Close to save the task and close the Task window.

■ **Tip** If you want Outlook to automatically set a reminder for each task you give a due date, choose File ➤ Options, and then click the Tasks category in the left pane. In the Task Options section, select the Set reminders on tasks with due dates check box, and then make sure the Default reminder time drop-down list shows the default time you want for a reminder. Click the OK button to close the Outlook Options dialog box.

Creating Recurring Tasks

If your job includes tasks that repeat at regular intervals, you can set up recurring tasks to have Outlook remind you of them. Follow these steps:

1.   Create a task as described earlier in this chapter.

2.   Open the task in a Task window.

3.   Choose Task ➤ Recurrence ➤ Recurrence or press Ctrl+G to display the Task Recurrence dialog box (see Figure 23-7).

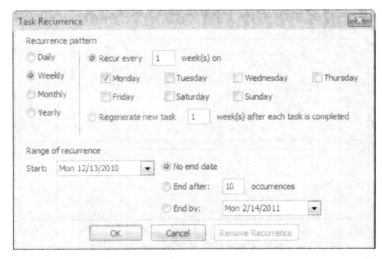

Figure 23-7. Use the Task Recurrence dialog box to set up the schedule for a repeating task

4.   In the Recurrence pattern section of the dialog box, set up the recurrence like this:

   •   Select the Daily option button, the Weekly option button, the Monthly option button, or the Yearly option button, as needed. Outlook displays the appropriate controls to the right of the vertical line.

   •   Use the controls to the right of the line to set up the recurrence. For example, for a daily task, you have three choices: Select the Every *N* Day(s) option button to make the task recur each time that many days pass; select the Every weekday option button to make the task recur every weekday; or select the Regenerate new task *N* day(s) after each task in completed option button to have Outlook automatically renew the task that number of days after you mark the previous instance of the task complete.

5.   In the Range of recurrence section of the dialog box, choose how long the repeating task should continue:

   •   In the Start box, enter the start date. Outlook uses the date you've specified for the task.

- Select the No end date option button if you want the task to run until you stop it manually. Otherwise, you can either select the End after option button and set the number of occurrences in the occurrences box, or select the End by option button and set the end date in the drop-down list.

6. Click the OK button to close the Task Recurrence dialog box and return to the Task window. The Recurrence button in the Recurrence group on the Task tab of the Ribbon now appears pressed in to indicate that recurrence is turned on, and the schedule appears above the Subject box (see Figure 23-8).

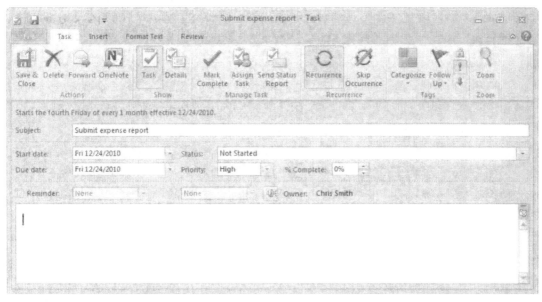

Figure 23-8. The Recurrence button in the Recurrence group of the Tasks tab appears highlighted to show that recurrence is turned on. The recurrence schedule appears above the Subject box.

7. Choose Task ➤ Actions ➤ Save & Close to close the window and save the changes.

Now that you've applied recurrence, the task recurs on the schedule you set. If you need to skip an occurrence of the task without otherwise changing the recurrence pattern, open the occurrence you want to skip, choose Task ➤ Recurrence ➤ Skip Occurrence and then choose Task ➤ Actions ➤ Save & Close.

■ **Note** If you need to stop an appointment from recurring, open the Task Recurrence dialog box, and then click the Remove Recurrence button.

Managing Your Tasks

To keep your task list in order, you'll need to plow through it regularly, adding details to tasks, marking them for follow-up, sending status reports to your colleagues about them, and—when the time comes— marking them as complete.

■ **Tip** After you open a task in a Task window, you can quickly display the next task by clicking the Next button in the Quick Access Toolbar or the previous task by clicking the Previous button.

Adding Details to a Task

To add details such as mileage or working hours to a task, double-click it in the Task List to open it in a Task window, then choose Task ➤ Show ➤ Details. In the Details pane (see Figure 23-9), enter the details in the boxes, and then choose Task ➤ Actions ➤ Save & Close.

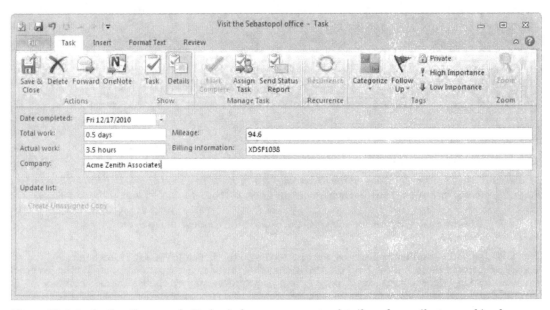

Figure 23-9. In the Details pane of a Task window, you can enter details such as mileage, working hours, or the company involved.

Marking a Task for Follow-Up

If a task needs further action, you can mark it for follow-up at the appropriate time in either of these ways:

- *Task List*: Click the task, go to the Follow Up group on the Home tab of the Ribbon, and then click Today, Tomorrow, This Week, Next Week, No Date, or Custom.

- *Task window*: Choose Task ➤ Tags ➤ Follow Up, and then click Today, Tomorrow, This Week, Next Week, No Date, or Custom.

When you need to set a different date than any of the preset buttons offers, click the Custom item, and then use the Custom dialog box (see Figure 23-10) to set the details of the follow-up.

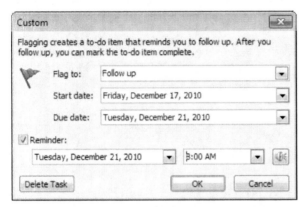

Figure 23-10. Use the Custom dialog box to set a follow-up flag using the exact date and time you want.

Sending a Status Report on a Task

If you perform tasks for someone else, you'll often need to let them know what progress you're making. To give a colleague an update on a task you're working on, you can send a status report like this:

1. In the Task List, double-click the task to open it in a Task window.

2. Make any updates needed to the status.

3. Choose Task ➤ Manage Task ➤ Send Status Report. Outlook creates a message containing the details of the task status and displays it in a Task Status Report window (see Figure 23-11).

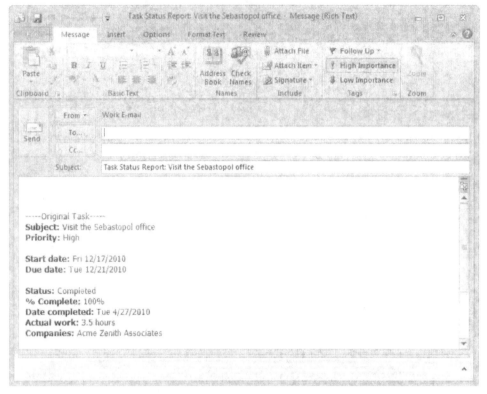

Figure 23-11. You can quickly send a message containing a status report on a particular task to a colleague.

4. Address the message as usual, add any extra text or notes needed, and then click the Send button to send it.

5. Choose Task ➤ Actions ➤ Save & Close to close the Task window.

Marking a Finished Task as Complete

When you have finished a task, select its check box in the Tasks list. If you have opened the task in a Task window, choose Task ➤ Manage Task ➤ Mark Complete to mark the task as complete.

■ **Note** You can delete a task by clicking it in the Task List and pressing Delete or choosing Home ➤ Delete ➤ Delete.

Assigning Tasks to Other People

One way to get ahead in your work is to delegate as much of it as possible to other people. Outlook helps you do this by making it easy to assign tasks to others.

To assign a task to someone, follow these steps:

1. Create the task as usual in a Task window, or create the task in the Task List and then open it in a Task window.

2. Choose Task ➤ Manage Task ➤ Assign Task. Outlook adds a To field to the top of the Task window (shown in Figure 23-12 with settings chosen).

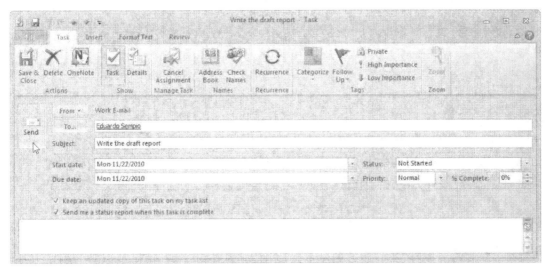

Figure 23-12. To assign a task to a colleague, you simply enter his e-mail address in the To box, choose options and click the Send button.

3. Enter the recipient's address in the To box in one of these ways:

    - Type the address in. Outlook automatically completes the address for you if it's in your Contacts list.

    - Click the To button to display the Select Task Recipient dialog box. Click the recipient's name, click the To button to add the recipient to the To box, and then click the OK button to close the dialog box.

4. Choose tracking options:

    - *Keep an updated copy of this task on my task list*: Select this check box to have Outlook keep this task on your task list and update it so that you can see what (if anything) the recipient has done. This is usually a good idea.

    - *Send me a status report when this task is complete*: Select this check box to make Outlook automatically send you a status report when the recipient marks the task as complete. This too is usually helpful.

5. Type any message needed in the box at the bottom of the Task window.

6. Click the Send button to send the task request.

When the recipient accepts or declines the task request, his e-mail program sends a response that you receive in Outlook.

Dealing with Tasks Other People Send to You

When someone else sends you a task request, it arrives in your Outlook Inbox like any other incoming mail. From here, you can view it either in the Reading Pane or in a Message window (see Figure 23-13), and click the Accept button or the Decline button as appropriate.

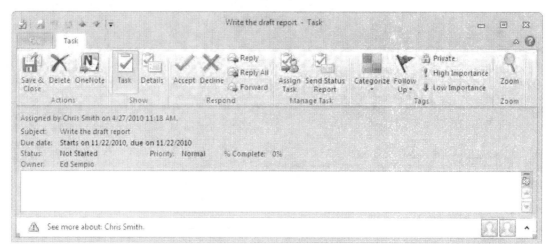

Figure 23-13. When you receive a task request, click the Accept button or the Decline button in the Respond group of the Task tab of the Ribbon.

If you accept the task request, Outlook adds the task to your Task List, where you can work with it just like a task you've created.

Taking Notes

When you're working in Outlook, you'll often find it handy to have a place to jot down scraps of information that you need to deal with later. To do this, you can use Outlook's Notes feature.

Meeting the Notes Interface

To start using Notes, click the Notes button in the Navigation Pane or press Ctrl+5. Outlook displays the Notes pane (shown in Figure 23-14 with two notes created).

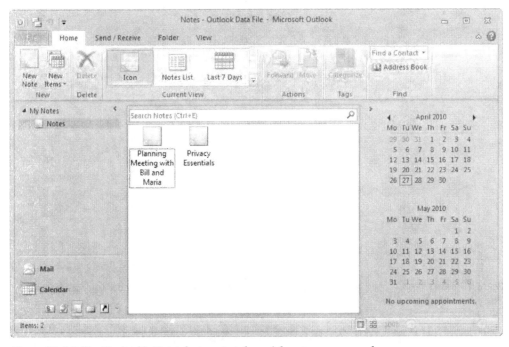

Figure 23-14. *Use Outlook's Notes feature to take quick notes as you work.*

Outlook opens the Notes pane in Normal view by default. To give yourself more space, you can click the Icons Only button on the status bar (the right button in the View Shortcuts group) to switch to Icons Only view, which minimizes the Navigation Pane and hides the To-Do B To-Do Bar.

Creating a Note

To create a new note, press Ctrl+N or choose Home ➤ New ➤ New Note. Outlook creates a new note in a free-floating window (see Figure 23-15). Type the text of your note (or paste in information you've copied), and then click the Close button (the × button) to close the window. The note then appears in the Notes pane.

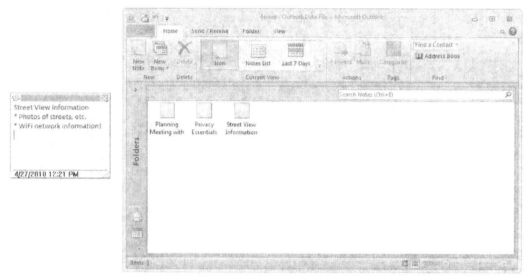

Figure 23-15. Choose Home ➤ New ➤ New Note to create a new note, and then type the information in the free-floating window that opens.

Viewing and Using Your Notes

By default, Outlook displays each note as an icon with its first line beneath it, as in Figure 23-15. When you need to see the text of each note, choose Home ➤ Current View ➤ Notes List to display the notes as a list including their contents (see Figure 23-16).

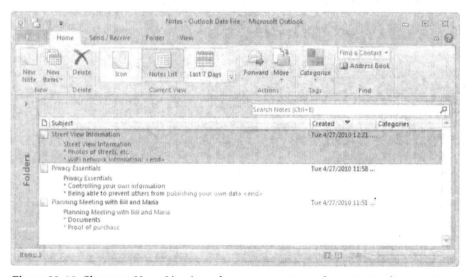

Figure 23-16. Change to Notes List view when you want to see the contents of your notes at a glance.

Tip When you want to view only your recent notes, choose Home ➤ Current View ➤ Last 7 Days. Outlook displays only the notes you've created in the last seven days.

You can use the information you've saved in a note in either of these ways:

- *Copy and paste a note's contents*: Copy the contents of the note, and then paste them into whichever program you want to use them in; for example, Microsoft Word or OneNote.

- *Forward a note*: Click a note, and then choose Home ➤ Actions ➤ Forward to open a Message window with the contents of the note attached. Address the message as usual, type any covering message needed, and then click the Send button to send the message.

Summary

In this chapter, you've learned to work with tasks and notes. You now know how to organize your commitments by creating tasks, managing them, and assigning them to your colleagues. And you can quickly and easily take notes as you work and share them with other programs.

This is the end of this book's coverage of Outlook. In the next (and last) part of the book, you'll learn to use OneNote, Office's powerful program for taking, storing, and making the most of notes.

CHAPTER 24

Taking Notes

When you need to take notes, turn to OneNote, Office's powerful program for recording, storing, and manipulating information. OneNote is great for doing anything from jotting down scraps of information that may come in useful later to recording information in a lecture or seminar. With OneNote, you can collect many different types of data, organize it however you need, and then export finished notes to another program as needed.

This chapter brings you up to speed with OneNote, showing you how to get around the OneNote interface and how to capture and view your information. The following two chapters explain how to organize your information, share it with other people, and export it for use with the other Office programs.

Getting to Grips with the OneNote Interface

OneNote is a database designed to store a wide variety of different types of information. But don't let the word "database" put you off—Microsoft has given OneNote a friendly and flexible interface based on a physical notebook, the ring-binder kind of notebook to which you can add ever more sections and pages. So you don't create a database, or work with forms and records: You just create a file called a notebook, and OneNote handles all the details for you.

Launch OneNote by choosing Start ➤ All Programs ➤ Microsoft Office ➤ Microsoft OneNote 2010, and the program automatically creates a sample notebook named Personal for you so that you can see how things work. The notebook contains sample data that you can either use to try out OneNote or simply delete so that you can use the notebook. Or, if you prefer, you can simply create a new notebook from scratch (you'll see how to do this later in this chapter).

Figure 24-1 shows this default notebook as it'll look the first time you launch OneNote.

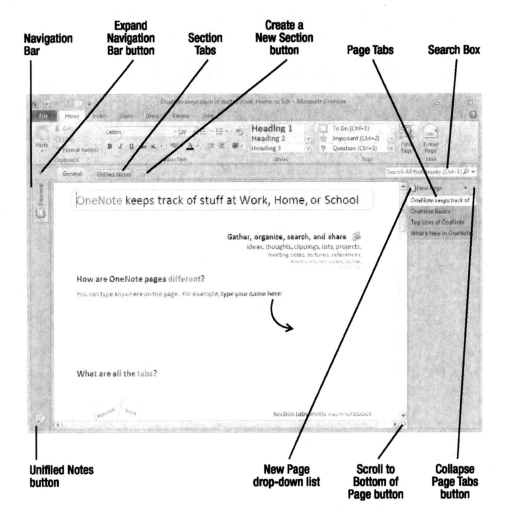

Figure 24-1. *OneNote automatically starts you off with a Personal notebook that includes sample contents.*

■ **Note** Pin OneNote to the Taskbar or to the Start menu so that you can open it easily. Or set OneNote to launch automatically when you log in so that your notes are always just the click of a mouse away.

These are the main elements in the OneNote interface:

- *Navigation Bar*: This is the bar or pane that appears on the left side of the notebook. You can switch between having the Navigation Bar appear as a narrow bar, in which each notebook appears as a vertical button, and as a pane in which each notebook appears as a horizontal bar under which you can display its sections (see Figure 24-2). To switch between the two, click the Expand Navigation Bar button (the > button) at the top of the Navigation Bar or the Collapse Navigation Bar button (the < button that replaces it).

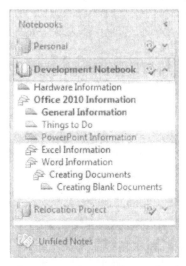

Figure 24-2. *Expand the Navigation Bar to a pane when you want to use it to access the section groups and sections in the workbooks.*

- *Section Tabs*: Click the section tab to display the section you want to see.

- *Create a New Section button*: Click this button to create a new section after the last section in the current section group. (More on section groups in a moment.)

- *Page Tabs*: Click the tab for the page you want to display.

- *Collapse Page Tabs button*: Click this button to collapse the Page Tabs pane to a thin bar. Collapsing the pane is useful when you need as much space for your notes as possible.

- *New Page drop-down list*: Click the button at the top of the drop-down list to create a new blank page after the last page in the section. You can also open the drop-down list and insert a subpage or open the Templates pane and choose a different page type from it.

- *Search box*: Type a search term to start searching for matches.

- *Unfiled Notes button*: Click this button to display your Unfiled Notes section, which is an area for collecting scraps of information without slotting them into particular sections and pages. When you're ready, you can go through your Unfiled Notes section and place the notes where they belong.

- *Scroll to Bottom of Page button*: Click this button to scroll instantly to the bottom of the page. Clicking this button is quicker than dragging the scroll bar.

Working with Notebooks, Section Groups, Sections, and Pages

Let's take a moment to make sense of the different major elements that OneNote lets you create—notebooks, section groups, sections, and pages—and see how to create them.

Working with Notebooks

OneNote's document is called a *notebook*. A notebook is in fact a folder containing various different files and folders, but OneNote presents it to you as a single document.

Looking Around in the Personal Notebook

If you've just launched OneNote for the first time, OneNote will have opened the Personal notebook that it creates for you. You'll see that the Personal tab in the Navigation Bar is selected, and then section tabs named General and Unfiled Notes appear below the Ribbon.

Take a minute to explore the Personal notebook, then decide whether you want to keep it. If you do, delete all the pages in the General section, as discussed later in this chapter. Otherwise, create a new notebook from scratch as described in the section titled "Creating a New Notebook."

Deciding How to Divide Your Notes among Notebooks

When you're starting to use OneNote, you may find it hard to decide how to split your notes among different notebooks. But this isn't a problem, because OneNote lets you quickly move sections or pages from one notebook to another as needed.

At first, you may want to put all of your notes into a single notebook so that no matter which information you need, it's always there for you. Once you see which categories of information you gather, you'll probably want to break it up differently. At that point, you can create each other notebook you need, and then move the information around to where it belongs.

▨ **Tip** If you know you'll need to share some data with colleagues, create a separate notebook for that type of data. That way, you can share some notes with your colleagues without sharing irrelevant or private notes.

Creating a New Notebook

To create a new notebook, follow these steps:

1. Click the File tab to open Backstage.

2. Click the New item in the left column to display the New Notebook pane (shown in Figure 24-3 with settings chosen).

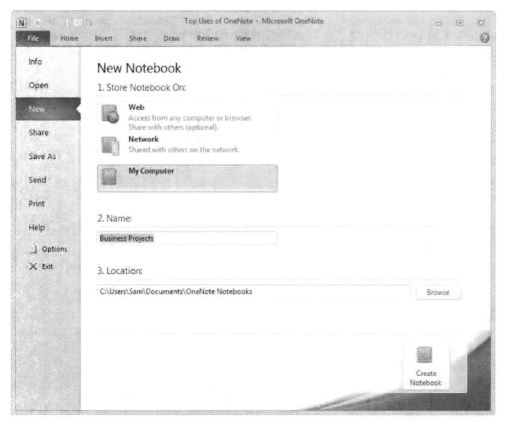

Figure 24-3. In the New Notebook pane, choose whether to store the new notebook on your PC, on your local network, or on the Web.

3. In the Store Notebook On area, click the button for where you want to store the notebook:

- *Web*: Click this button to save the notebook on SkyDrive. See Chapter 25 for information on storing notebooks on SkyDrive.

- *Network*: Click this button to save the notebook on your local network—for example, so that you can share it with your colleagues.

- *My Computer*: Click the button to save the notebook on your PC; for example, because you'll keep this notebook to yourself.

4. In the Name text box, type the name you want to give the notebook. OneNote uses this as the filename when it saves the notebook.

5. In the Location text box, check that OneNote shows the appropriate location. To change the location, click the Browse button, choose the folder in the Select Folder dialog box, and then click the Select button.

▓ **Note** If you choose My Computer in the Store Notebook On area, OneNote suggests saving the notebook in the folder specified in the Save & Backup pane in the OneNote Options dialog box. (See Chapter 26 for instructions on setting the OneNote options.) The first time you choose Network, you will need to use the Select Folder dialog box to identify the network location.

---

6. Click the Create Notebook button. OneNote creates the notebook, saves it, and opens it so that you can start work in it.

Working with Sections and Section Groups

Inside a notebook, you create your notes on pages that take roughly the same role as sheets of paper within a ring binder. The main differences are that the pages can be as long as you want, and you can add subpages to a page. You can even add subpages to a subpage.

As in a ring binder with tabs, you divide your pages into different sections. The Personal notebook that OneNote creates for you contains only the General section and the Unfiled Notes section, but you can add other sections as needed.

Creating a Section

To create a section, follow these steps:

1. Click the Create a New Section button that appears to the right of the last section tab. OneNote adds a section after the last section, gives it a default name such as New Section 1, and adds an untitled page to it.

2. Type the name for the section, and then press Enter. OneNote selects the page title on the page so that you can add that too.

3. Type the title for the page and press Enter again. OneNote creates a text container on the page so that you can start taking notes in it.

Deleting a Section

To delete a section, follow these steps:

1. Right-click the section's tab, and then click Delete on the context menu. OneNote displays a confirmation dialog box (see Figure 24-4).

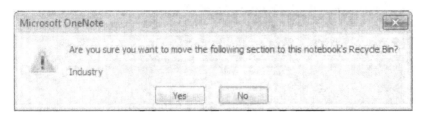

Figure 24-4. To avoid mishaps, OneNote makes you confirm that you want to delete a section.

2. Click the Yes button.

Note When you delete a page, section, or section group, OneNote places it in the Notebook Recycle Bin for the notebook that contained it. If necessary, you can retrieve items from the Notebook Recycle Bin. See Chapter 26 for details.

Renaming and Reorganizing Sections

To rename a section, right-click its tab and choose Rename from the context menu. OneNote selects the current name. Type the new name and press Enter to apply it.

To move a section to a different position in the notebook, click its tab and drag it to where you want it to appear. As you drag the section, the mouse pointer shows a little box, and OneNote displays a downward-pointing black arrow indicating where the section will land. Drop the section when the arrow is in the right place.

Creating a Section Group

When a notebook contains just a few sections, it's easy to keep them organized. But when you've added a couple of dozen sections, you may find you need to break them up further. You can divide the sections up into different categories by using section groups.

Note You can create a section group within another section group as needed, so you can give yourself a whole hierarchy of section groups.

To create a section group, follow these steps:

1. If the Navigation Bar is collapsed, click the Expand Navigation Bar button to expand it.

2. Right-click open space below the last section, and then click New Section Group on the context menu. OneNote adds a new section group and gives it a default name, such as New Section Group.

Note You can also create a section group by right-clicking open space in the section tab bar (to the right of the last tab) and choosing New Section Group from the context menu.

3. Highlight the default name, and then click it. OneNote displays an edit box around the name.

4. Type the name you want the section group to have, and then press Enter to apply it.

Adding Sections to a Section Group

After creating a section group, you can add sections to it by dragging them to it in the Navigation Bar or in the section tab bar. Click the section, drag it until the section group's name is highlighted, and then release it.

To create a new section within a section group, click the section group, and then create the section as described earlier.

Placing One Section Group Inside Another

If you need to keep many different sections in order, you may want to nest some section groups within other section groups. Doing this enables you to create a hierarchy of section groups much like the folder structure you can use to organize your folders in Windows Explorer.

For example, if you have a section group named Home, you can create section groups inside it with names such as Kitchen, Bathroom, Den, Bedroom, and so on. Inside each section group, you can have separate sections for your different projects for those rooms. You can then create pages within the sections to contain your notes.

To nest one section group inside another, click the section group in the Navigation Bar and drag it to the section group in which you want to nest it. You can also move the section group by using the Move Section Group dialog box, as described next.

To take a section group back to the top level in the workbook, follow these steps:

1. Right-click the section group you want to move, and then click Move on the context menu to display the Move Section Group dialog box (see Figure 24-5).

Figure 24-5. *Use the Move Section Group dialog box to move a section group from being nested up to the top level of a notebook.*

2. Click the notebook's name in the All Notebooks list (if the name appears in the Recent Picks list, you can click it there instead). Click the – sign to the left of an item to collapse it, or click the + sign to the left of an item to expand it.

3. Click the Move button to close the dialog box and move the section group.

■ **Tip** OneNote keeps the section groups in alphabetical order in the notebook.

Navigating Among Sections and Section Groups

You can navigate from section to section and from section group to section group by using either the Navigation Bar or the section tabs bar.

If your OneNote window has plenty of space to keep the Navigation Bar expanded, the Navigation Bar is usually the easiest way to get around:

- *Expand a notebook*: If the notebook that contains the section is collapsed, double-click its button in the Navigation Bar to expand it. (You can also click the Expand button at the right end of the notebook's name, but double-clicking is usually quicker and faster.)

- *Expand a section group*: If the section group is collapsed, click the icon to the left of its name to expand it. Repeat as needed to expand a nested section group.

- *Display a section*: Click the section.

Instead of using the Navigation Bar, you can use the section tabs bar. When you've displayed the contents of a section group, the section bar displays the Navigate to parent section group button (a curling up arrow) to the left of the section group at its left end (see Figure 24-6). Click this button to display the *parent section group*, the section group that contains this section or section group. If the section group doesn't have a parent, clicking the Navigate to parent section group button brings you to the notebook itself.

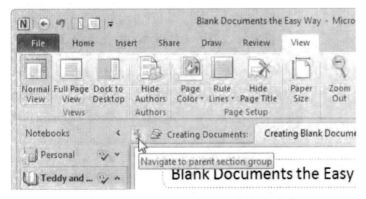

Figure 24-6. *Click the Navigate to parent section group button to move up to the section group that contains the current section group.*

Working with Pages

When you've created enough sections and section groups to be going on with, you can add pages and create notes on them. This section shows you the main moves for working with pages.

■ **Note** When you create a new section, OneNote automatically adds a page to it. After typing the section name, press Enter to move to the page title container. You can then type the page name, press Enter, and start taking notes in the container that OneNote automatically places on the page for you.

Creating a New Blank Page

You can create a new page in the current section in several ways.

If you simply want to add a new page at the end of the section, click the New Page button in the Page Tabs pane or press Ctrl+N. You can leave the page there, or drag it further up the list of page tabs as needed.

To insert a new page between existing pages, use one of these techniques:

- *Use the context menu*: Right-click the page after which you want to insert the new page, and then click New Page.

- *Use the Floating New Page button*: In the Page Tabs pane, hold the mouse pointer over the page before or after which you want to add the new page. OneNote displays the floating New Page button to the left of the page tab with an arrow to show where the new page will go. Move the mouse pointer up or down as needed to make the arrow point before or after the page tab, as needed. Then click the floating New Page button (see Figure 24-7) to insert the page.

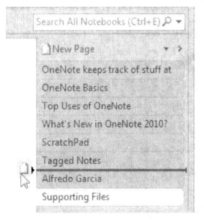

Figure 24-7. *Use the floating New Page button to insert at new page between existing pages.*

Creating a New Page Based on a Template

Instead of inserting a blank page, you can insert a page based on a template. Follow these steps:

1. Click the New Page drop-down list (the downward arrow at the right end of the New page button), and then click Page Templates to display the Templates pane. Figure 24-8 shows the Templates pane open and a page based on the Simple To Do List template already added.

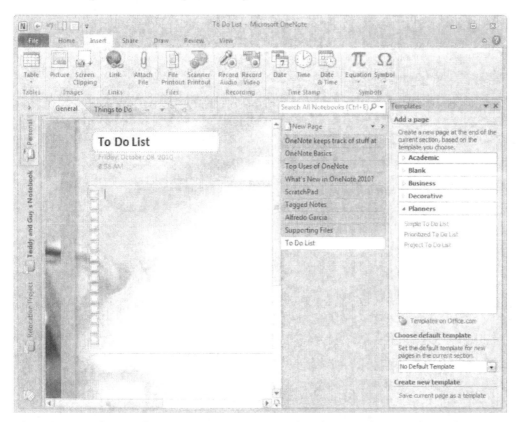

Figure 24-8. *Use the Templates pane to insert a new page based on one of OneNote's templates.*

2. In the Add a page list box, click the heading for the type of template you want to use—for example, Planners. OneNote displays the list of templates below the heading.

■ **Note** To get further templates, click the Templates on Office.com link in the Templates pane. OneNote opens an Internet Explorer window to the Office website, which contains a wide variety of templates that you can download.

---

3. In the list of templates, click the template you want. OneNote inserts a page based on it.

4. Insert other pages based on templates as needed.

5. Click the Close button (the × button) to close the Templates pane. (You can also leave it open for the time being if you have plenty of space in the OneNote window.)

Creating a Page Template That Meets Your Needs

If you frequently take the same kinds of notes, you can save time and effort by creating a custom page template for them. For example, you can create a page for lecture notes, including placeholders for the class name, lecturer's name, and topic, and perhaps containers for audio and video notes.

To create a custom page template, follow these steps:

1. Set up a page that contains the existing information and the containers you need.

2. With this page active, click the New Page drop-down list and choose Page Templates to open the Templates pane.

3. Click the Save current page as a template link at the bottom of the Templates pane to display the Save As Template dialog box (see Figure 24-9).

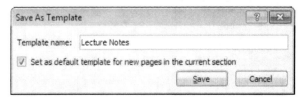

Figure 24-9. You can create a custom page template and use it as the default for new pages in the current section.

4. In the Template name text box, type the name you want to give the template. Make it as descriptive as possible so that you can distinguish it from other templates you create.

5. If you want to use this template as the default for this section of the notebook, select the Set as default template for new pages in the current section check box. This setting can be a great time-saver if the section contains mostly pages of the same type.

6. Click the Save button to close the Save As Template dialog box and save the template.

■ **Note** Your templates appear under the My Templates heading at the top of the Templates pane.

Renaming a Page

To rename a page, first click its tab to display it. Then click in the page name container at the top and either edit the existing name or simply type the new name over it.

Moving or Copying a Page

Often, you'll need to move a page to a different position in the notebook. OneNote makes this easy to do:

- *Move a page within a section*: Expand the Page Tabs pane if it's collapsed, and then drag the page's tab up or down the list of tabs to where you want it to appear. OneNote displays a heavy black line to indicate where the page will land when you drop it.

- *Move the page to another section with the mouse*: Expand the Page Tabs pane if it's collapsed, and then drag the page's tab to the section tab for the section in which you want to put it. Keep holding down the mouse button while OneNote displays that section in place of the one previously displayed. Drag the page's tab back to the Page Tabs pane (which now shows the destination section's page tabs), and drop the page where you want it to appear. Again, OneNote displays a heavy black line where the page will land.

▓ **Tip** If you expand the Navigation Bar, you can drag the page's tab to another section in the Navigation Bar rather than in the section tab bar. Sometimes it's easier to find the tab in the Navigation Bar than in the section tab bar.

- *Move the page to another section or notebook*: Right-click the page's tab, and then choose Move or Copy to display the Move or Copy Pages dialog box (see Figure 24-10). Click the section you want to move the page to, and then click the Move button.

Figure 24-10. You can use the Move or Copy Pages dialog box to move or copy a page to a different section or to a different notebook.

▪ **Note** You can also copy a page by clicking the Copy button in the Move or Copy Pages dialog box.

Working with Subpages

If you need to add extra information to a page without it becoming so long it's hard to navigate, you can add one or more subpages to it. You can even add subpages to subpages if necessary.

To add a subpage, follow these steps:

1. Display the page.

2. Click the New Page drop-down button, and then choose New Subpage from the drop-down list. OneNote inserts a subpage and names it Untitled page as usual.

3. Type the name for the subpage, and then press Enter to create a container on the subpage so that you can start taking notes.

■ **Tip** To create a subpage based on a page template, create the subpage as a normal page, and then use the Make Subpage command to turn it into a subpage.

You can also turn an existing page into a subpage by right-clicking its page tab and then clicking Make Subpage on the context menu. Similarly, you can turn a subpage into a regular page by right-clicking its pane tab and then clicking Promote Subpage on the context menu.

■ **Tip** You can drag a page tab to the right to turn the page into a subpage, or drag it to the left to promote the subpage to a page. You can also promote a subpage to a page by dragging it up or down.

A page or subpage that contains subpages displays a button at the right end of its page tab. You click this button to expand the subpages or to collapse them.

Navigating from Page to Page

In OneNote, you can navigate to a page by clicking its tab in the Page Tabs pane. Normally, you can reach a page in two or three clicks:

1. In the Navigation Bar, click the notebook that contains the page.

■ **Note** If the Navigation Bar is expanded, you can go straight to the section by clicking it in the Navigation Bar—no need to use the section tabs bar.

2. In the section tabs bar, click the section.
3. In the Page Tabs pane, click the page.

Entering Notes on a Page

You now know all you need to know about pages except the most important thing—how to enter on them the wide variety of information that you can store in OneNote. Let's start with a quick overview of all the types of information that you can enter.

Understanding Which Types of Information You Can Save in OneNote

You can save a wide variety of different types of information in a OneNote notebook:

- *Text*: You can store any amount of text, either leaving it plain or formatting it using styles or direct formatting.

- *Tables*: You can create either simple tables (ones with a regular structure) or complex tables (ones that include other tables nested inside cells). Your tables can include text, pictures, and other objects.

- *Equations*: Like Microsoft Word, OneNote includes a full set of equation tools that you can use to construct a wide range of equations, including binomials, Fourier series equations, and quadratic equations.

- *Pictures*: You can add pictures to your notebooks and position them as needed.

- *Screen clippings*: OneNote includes a built-in feature for capturing parts of the screen and including them in your notebooks. This feature is great for documenting computer procedures, but it's also good for quickly capturing information that you want to store. For example, you can capture a screen clipping of a web page for a product you're thinking of buying.

- *Document printouts*: You can print documents from the other Office programs straight to pages in OneNote. This is a great way of pulling together all the information you need in a notebook.

- *Scanner printouts*: If you want to include paper documents in your OneNote workbooks, you can scan them straight in.

- *Audio*: You can record audio straight into OneNote. For example, you can record audio of a lecture to supplement the notes you take.

- *Video*: If your PC has a video camera, you can record video straight into a notebook.

- *Files*: You can attach just about any type of file to a OneNote notebook so that you have it available. For example, you can attach an Excel workbook or a PowerPoint presentation to a workbook. You can't open these files in OneNote, but you can open them from it in the programs associated with them.

Adding Text to a Page

To add text to a page, simply click the point in the page at which you want to start entering the text. OneNote adds a container for the text where you click, and puts the text in the container.

You can enter text by typing it, by pasting it, or by dragging it in from another program and dropping it.

░ **Note** When you drag and drop text (or another object) from one of the other Office programs, OneNote automatically creates a link back to the source document so that you can easily see where the text came from.

Each container works like a mini document, and you can format the text much as you would in Word:

- *Apply a style*: The quick way to apply formatting consistently is to use the styles in the Styles group on the Home tab of the Ribbon. Figure 24-11 shows the Styles panel open for applying a style. OneNote gives you a Page Title style for the page title, Heading 1 through Heading 6 styles for headings, a Citation style, a Quote style, a Code style, and a Normal style for everything else.

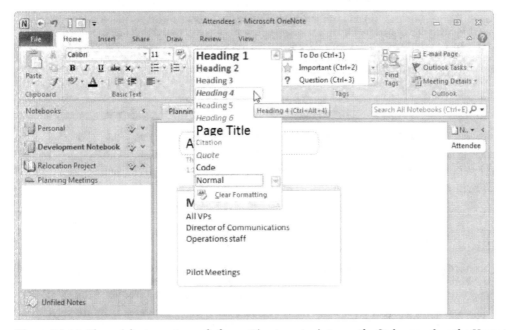

Figure 24-11. The quickest way to apply formatting to notes is to use the Styles panel on the Home tab of the Ribbon.

▓ **Tip** Use styles wherever possible when formatting text-based notes. When you export notes to Word, the text keeps the styles, and you can snap in a different set of formatting in moments by attaching a different template to the resulting Word document. See Chapter 7 for details of how to use styles in Word.

- *Apply direct formatting*: You can apply direct formatting (such as bold, italic, or highlighting) from either the Basic Text group on the Home tab of the Ribbon or from the Mini Toolbar that OneNote displays automatically when you select text.

▨ **Tip** Press Ctrl+down arrow to move from the end of one container to the beginning of the next container. Press Ctrl+up arrow to move from the start of one container to the end of the previous container.

Adding Graphics to Pages

To illustrate your notes, you can quickly add a graphic to a page. Choose Insert ➤ Images ➤ Picture to open the Insert Picture dialog box, navigate to the graphic and select it, and then click the Open button.

After inserting a graphic, you can resize it by selecting the graphic and then dragging one of the placeholders that OneNote displays. Drag a corner placeholder to resize the graphic proportionally, so that the ratio of height to width remains constant. Drag a side placeholder to resize the graphic only in that dimension, distorting the image.

▨ **Tip** You can also add graphics to pages in two other ways. First, you can drag a graphic from a Windows Explorer window to a OneNote page. This method is handy when you're working in Windows Explorer and need to get a graphic into OneNote instantly. Second, you can copy a graphic from a web page or another program, and then paste it into OneNote.

Capturing Screen Clippings in Your Notebooks

If you need to store information about the Office programs, you'll find OneNote's Screen Clipping feature useful. You can insert a full screen or any part of it on the current page. Choose Insert ➤ Images ➤ Screen Clipping, and then drag the resulting crosshair to capture the area you want.

▨ **Note** To control where OneNote places your screen clippings, choose a setting in the Screen Clippings drop-down list in the Send to OneNote pane in the OneNote Options dialog box. See Chapter 26 for details.

Creating Drawings on Pages

If you need to create drawings in OneNote, click the Draw tab on the Ribbon and use the tools it provides. See Chapter 4 for an introduction to these tools.

Creating Tables

A table is often a great way to record information in an organized way, and OneNote makes it easy to add tables to your pages.

The normal way to add a table is to choose Insert ➤ Tables ➤ Table to open the Insert Table panel, and then click the grid square for the table layout you want (for example, ten rows of three columns each).

■ **Note** You can also click the Insert Table button at the bottom of the Insert Table panel to open the Insert Table dialog box, in which you can type the number of columns and rows you need.

You can also create a table quickly by simply typing in a container. Follow these steps:

1. Type the text for the first cell as regular text within the container.

2. Press Tab, OneNote automatically inserts the table with two cells, positioning the insertion point so that you can type the second cell.

3. Type the second cell's contents.

4. Press Tab again to create another cell.

5. When you've ended the first row, press Enter.

6. You can then press Tab to move from cell to cell, and to move to the next row when the insertion point is in the last cell in a row.

7. When you want to end the table, press Enter twice in succession.

Printing to OneNote

You can also send data to OneNote by printing from another program. This is a great way to insert a final copy of a document right into a OneNote notebook so that you can keep it to hand.

To print to OneNote, follow these steps from another Office program (for example, Word):

1. Click the File tab to open Backstage.

2. Click the Print item in the left column to display the Print options.

3. In the Printer drop-down list, choose Send To OneNote 2010.

4. Click the Print button to print the document. The program displays the Select Location in OneNote dialog box.

■ **Note** If you've specified a particular location in the Print to OneNote drop-down list in the Send to OneNote pane in the OneNote Options dialog box, OneNote puts the printout there without displaying the Select Location in OneNote dialog box.

---

5. Choose the notebook and section in which to insert the printout.

6. Click the OK button. The program inserts the printout and displays it.

7. Type the name for the new page.

Sending Outlook Items to OneNote

Outlook makes it easy to send items to OneNote. All you need to do is select the item, and then give the appropriate command:

- *Mail*: Choose Home ➤ Move ➤ OneNote.
- *Contacts*: Choose Home ➤ Actions ➤ OneNote
- *Calendar*: Choose Appointment ➤ Actions ➤ OneNote.
- *Tasks*: Choose Home ➤ Move ➤ OneNote.

If Outlook displays the Select Location in OneNote dialog box, click the section in which you want to put the item you're sending, and then click the OK button.

■ **Note** If you always want to put this type of item in the same section in OneNote, select the Always send *item* to the selected location check box in the Select Location in OneNote dialog box before you click the OK button.

Sending Web Content to OneNote

When you find a web page you want to remember, you can quickly send it from Internet Explorer to OneNote by using the Send To OneNote command, as discussed earlier in this chapter: Open the Print dialog box (click the Print button on the command bar or press Ctrl+P), click the Send To OneNote 2010 button, and then click the Print button.

When you want to save just part of a web page, select it, and then choose Tools ➤ Send To OneNote on the command bar.

In either case, if the Select Location in OneNote dialog box opens, click the section or page you want to add the web material to, and then click the OK button.

■ **Note** You can select the Always send printouts to the selected location check box in the Select Location in OneNote dialog box if you always want to send web pages from Internet Explorer to the same section in OneNote. To change this setting, use the OneNote Options dialog box as discussed in Chapter 26.

Inserting a Scanner Printout

If you need to add a paper document into OneNote, you can scan it in directly. OneNote calls this inserting a scanner printout.

To insert a scanner printout, follow these steps:

1. Position the insertion point on the page you want to use. Often, you'll want to insert a new page to hold the scanned document.

2. Choose Insert ➤ Files ➤ Scanner Printout. OneNote opens a dialog box of options for importing from the scanner.

3. Make sure that OneNote has selected the right device. This is usually a problem only if you have multiple scanners attached to your PC.

4. In the Resolution area, select the Web Quality option button if you want moderate quality. Select the Print Quality option button if you want full quality.

5. If the dialog box includes a Add Pictures to Clip Organizer check box, clear this check box unless you want to add the scanned picture to the Microsoft Clip Organizer.

6. Click the Insert button.

■ **Note** If you've already scanned a document, insert it as a graphic, as described earlier in this chapter.

Performing Calculations

OneNote has an automatic calculation feature, sometimes called "napkin math," that lets you perform calculations quickly and easily in your notes. This feature is great both for informal calculations and for math notes.

To perform a calculation, click in a container, type the calculation followed by an equal sign, and press Enter. For example, type **$.75*23=** and then press Enter. OneNote enters the result.

Here are the characters and text to use for calculations:

- *Addition*: Type a + sign as usual.
- *Subtraction*: Type a – (hyphen), as you'd expect.
- *Multiplication*: Type an asterisk, a lowercase x, or an uppercase X—all work.
- *Division*: Type a forward slash, as in Excel—for example, 5/4=.
- *Percentage*: Type the % sign.
- *Exponentiation*: Type a ^ (caret) followed by the power—for example, 3^4=.
- *Factorial computation*: Type the number followed by an exclamation point—for example, 6!=.
- *Pi and Phi*: Type **pi** or **phi** as needed—for example, 5*pi=.
- *Functions:* OneNote supports the ABS, ACOS, ASIN, ATAN, COS, DEG, LN, LOG, LOG2, LOG10, MOD, PMT, RAD, SIN, SQRT, and TAN functions. Type the function name (lowercase is fine) followed by the argument or arguments in parentheses. For example, type **sqrt(225)=** or **200 mod 8=**.

■ **Note** If the automatic calculation feature isn't working, choose File ➤ Options, click the Advanced category, and select the Calculate mathematical expressions automatically check box.

Using Views, Windows, and Side Notes

To make the most of OneNote, you will need to use the different views it offers. You may also find it helpful to open more than one window at once so that you can view or edit two or more pages of notes at the same time.

Using Normal View, Full Page View, and Dock to Desktop View

At first, OneNote opens in Normal view, which shows the Navigation Bar, the Ribbon, the section tabs, and the Page Tabs pane so that you can navigate easily among notebooks, sections, and pages.

Using Full Page View to See More of Your Notes

When you plan to stay on the page that's currently displayed, and you need as much space as possible to take or work with your notes, switch to Full Page view (see Figure 24-12). You can switch in any of these ways:

- *Quick Access Toolbar*: Click the Full Page View button, so that it appears pressed in.

- *Ribbon*: Choose View ➤ Views ➤ Full Page View.

- *Keyboard*: Press F11.

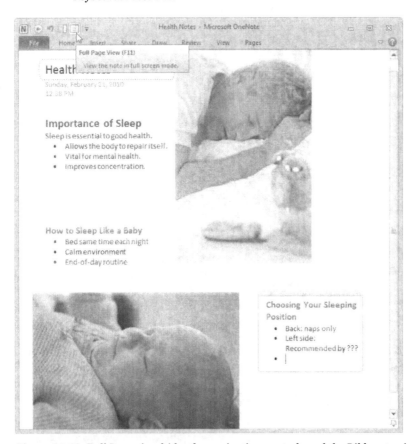

Figure 24-12. Full Page view hides the navigation controls and the Ribbon to give you more space to concentrate on your notes.

To switch back from Full Page view to Normal view, click the Full Page View button on the Quick Access Toolbar again (to un-press it), press F11 again, or choose View ➤ Views ➤ Normal View.

Docking the OneNote Window to the Desktop

When you're working in OneNote, you'll probably want to keep the program window either maximized or at a large size so that you can see as much as possible of what you're doing. But when you're working in another program and you want to keep OneNote handy for taking notes, you may want to dock it to the desktop instead.

Docking the OneNote window to the desktop positions the window at the right side of the desktop and hides the Ribbon, the navigation bar, and the page tabs. You can dock the OneNote window to a different side of the desktop by clicking its title bar and dragging it there. For example, drag it to the top of the screen to dock it across the top of the window. OneNote remembers the docked position and uses it again next time.

To dock the OneNote window, click the Dock to Desktop button on the Quick Access Toolbar or press Ctrl+Alt+D. You can also choose View ➤ Views ➤ Dock to Desktop if you prefer.

To undock the OneNote window, click the Dock to Desktop button on the Quick Access Toolbar or press Ctrl+Alt+D again. You can also choose View ➤ Views ➤ Normal View from the Ribbon.

■ **Note** When you dock the OneNote window, Backstage becomes unavailable. OneNote turns the File tab gray to indicate that it is not available.

Opening Extra Windows

To take down notes about two or more different topics, to compare different pages, or to transfer data from one page to another, it's often helpful to open two or more OneNote windows at once rather than switching back and forth between pages in the same window.

To open a new window, choose View ➤ Window ➤ New Window. OneNote opens the new window to the same page as the current window, but you can then navigate to whichever page you need.

■ **Tip** To give yourself space to work in two OneNote windows at once on a small screen, open a new docked window by choosing View ➤ Window ➤ New Docked Window.

Working with Side Notes

When you need to take a quick note, use a side note rather than starting a new page.

Side notes can be handy and save time, because they enable you to take a note without opening OneNote (if you don't keep it open the whole time) or without moving away from the page you're working on (or opening a new window).

You can create a new side note in any of these ways:

- *Windows notification area*: Click the Open New Side Note icon that OneNote puts in the notification area by default. You can use this method at any time, but it's usually most convenient when OneNote isn't running.

■ **Tip** If you use side notes often, make sure the Open New Side Note icon always appears in the notification area rather than being hidden. Right-click the time and date at the end of the notification area, and then click Customize Notifications on the context menu to open the Notification Area Icons window. In the Select which icons and notifications appear on the taskbar list box, open the Behaviors drop-down list for the Microsoft OneNote Quick Launcher item and choose Show icon and modifications. Click the OK button to close the window.

- *Ribbon*: From OneNote, choose View ➤ Window ➤ New Side Note.
- *Keyboard*: From OneNote, press Ctrl+Shift+M. If you use OneNote extensively, this is one of the keyboard shortcuts that's well worth learning.

When you give one of these commands, OneNote opens a new side note window, which is basically a OneNote window in Full Page view. You can start taking notes as usual, as in Figure 24-13. When you've finished, click the Close button (the × button) to close the window.

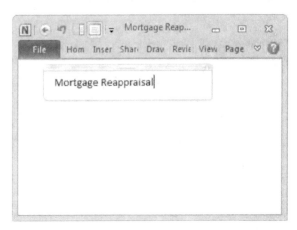

Figure 24-13. Open a side note window when you need to take a quick note either without opening OneNote fully or without moving from the page you're working on.

OneNote adds the side note as a new page in the Unfiled Notes section. You can display this section by clicking the Unfiled Notes button at the bottom of the Navigation Bar, and then edit the page, copy the information from it, or move the page to the section it belongs to.

Summary

In this chapter, you've learned how to start working quickly and effectively in OneNote.

You've grasped what notebooks, sections, and pages are, how they fit together, and how to create each of them. You also now know the most important ways of entering data in your notebooks, from regular text to tables, and from symbols to scanned printouts. And you can make the most of OneNote's different views, open extra windows, and use side notes.

In the next chapter, you'll look at how to organize and synchronize your notes. Turn the page when you're ready to get started.

■ ■ ■

CHAPTER 25

Organizing, Synchronizing, and Sharing Your Notes

Once you've taken stacks of notes, you'll probably need to reorganize them. You can do so by moving pages, sections, and section groups to different locations or different notebooks as needed, by merging sections into each other, or by splitting sections into separate parts.

To find the information you need, you can search any part of your notebooks, from a single page to every notebook. To prevent other people from finding information you don't want them to see, you can protect sections of your notebooks with passwords.

To get the most out of OneNote, you'll probably want to share some of your workbooks with other people. This chapter shows you how to share them, how to work in shared workbooks, and how to review the changes that other people make. You'll also learn to view older versions of pages, recover the versions you need, and clear out old page versions that you no longer require. Lastly, I'll show you how to store your notes on the Web so that you can access them from anywhere.

Organizing Your Pages, Sections, and Notebooks

However neatly you take your notes, you'll probably need to reorganize some of them. You can move pages, sections, and section groups as needed; merge sections together or split them; and merge or split whole notebooks. You can also change the name that OneNote displays for a notebook.

Moving Pages, Sections, and Section Groups

You can move pages and sections by dragging them like this:

- *Move a page to another section*: Click the page in the Page Tabs pane and drag it to the section in which you want to place it.

- *Move a section to another section group*: Expand the Navigation Bar if it's collapsed, and then expand the notebook's heading. Click the section and drag it to the destination section group.

- *Move a page, section, or section group to another notebook*: Expand the Navigation Bar if it's collapsed, and then expand the heading for each notebook. Click the page in the Page Tabs pane, or the section in the Navigation Bar, and drag it to the destination.

If you prefer, you can use the Move or Copy dialog box like this:

1. Right-click the item you want to move, and then click Move or Copy on the context menu to display the Move or Copy dialog box. This dialog box's name shows the item you're moving or copying—it's called the Move or Copy Pages dialog box, the Move or Copy Section dialog box (see Figure 25-1), or the Move or Copy Section Group dialog box.

Figure 25-1. To move an item, you can either drag it to its destination or use the Move or Copy dialog box.

2. Click the + sign to expand the notebook in which you want to place the item.

3. Click the section or notebook in which you want to place the item.

4. Click the Move button. OneNote closes the dialog box and moves the item.

Merging Sections Together

Sometimes you'll find that you need to put all the contents of one section in another section. You can do so by moving the first section's pages, but it's usually easier to merge the sections. Follow these steps:

1. In either the section tab bar or the Navigation Bar, right-click the section you want to merge into another section, and then click Merge into Another Section on the context menu to display the Merge Section dialog box.

2. Expand the notebook that contains the section into which you want to merge the section.

3. Click the destination section.

4. Click the Merge button.

Splitting a Section into Two

At other times, you may need to split a section into two separate sections (or perhaps more). OneNote doesn't provide a command for automating this process, so just create a new section, and then drag into it the pages that you want it to contain.

Merging and Splitting Notebooks

OneNote doesn't provide commands for merging two notebooks together or splitting them, so you need to do this manually:

- *Merge two notebooks*: Open both notebooks in OneNote. Then move or copy all the sections from one notebook into the other. Moving tends to be easier, because you can see all the sections you still need to transfer.

- *Splitting a notebook in two*: Open the notebook, and then create another notebook. Move the appropriate sections from the first notebook to the second notebook.

Changing the Display Name for a Notebook

Sometimes you may want to change the name that OneNote displays for a notebook; for example, because the original name is too short, too long, or not descriptive enough. You can change the display name without changing the file name.

To change the display name, follow these steps:

1. Right-click the notebook in the Navigation Bar and choose Rename from the context menu to open the Notebook Properties dialog box (see Figure 25-2).

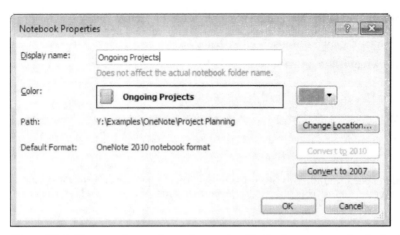

Figure 25-2. *You can change the active notebook's display name and color in the Notebook Properties dialog box.*

2. In the Display Name text box, type the name you want to give the notebook.

3. If you also want to change the color in which OneNote displays the notebook, open the Color drop-down list and click the color you want.

4. Click the OK button to close the Notebook Properties dialog box.

Searching for Information

No matter how well you organize your notebooks, it can become hard to remember where everything is when you've taken a lot of notes. To find what you need, you can use the search field.

To search, click in the search field (or press Ctrl+E) and then type your search terms. OneNote displays a floating panel of search results (see Figure 25-3). Click the result you want to see. OneNote keeps the search results panel open until you click in a page to work with it.

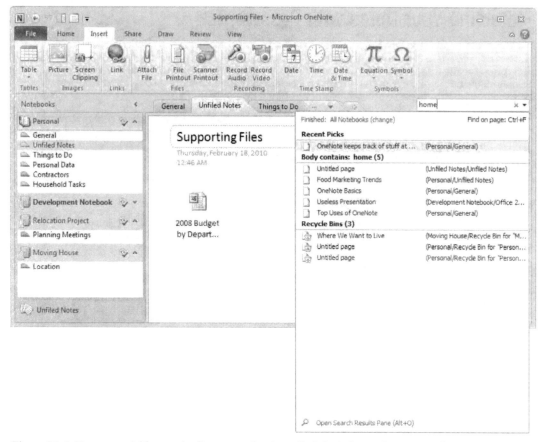

Figure 25-3. *You can quickly search all your notebooks to find the information you need.*

To open a fixed Search Results pane, press Alt+O or click the Open Search Results Pane link at the bottom of the floating search results pane.

To start with, OneNote searches in your default *scope*—the area it's set to search unless you tell it otherwise. The default scope is normally All Notebooks. To change this, click the drop-down button to the right of the search field and choose where you want to search: Find on This Page, This Section, This Section Group, This Notebook, or All Notebooks. To make your choice stick until you change it, click the drop-down button again and click Set This Scope as Default at the bottom, putting a check mark next to this item.

■ **Caution** If you password-protect a section (as described in the section "Protecting Your Notes with Passwords," later in this chapter), OneNote excludes that section from searches. To include the section in searches, you must unprotect it before you begin the search.

Protecting Your Notes with Passwords

Everyone has secrets, and OneNote lets you keep your secrets by protecting sections of a notebook with passwords as needed. OneNote encrypts the data in each section you protect with a password. The encryption means that the data is safe (except possibly against the National Security Agency's unimaginable banks of computers) but that it's essential that you memorize or write down your password—without the password, you won't be able to decrypt your data.

■ **Note** OneNote has several settings that let you control when your passwords take effect and how long you unlock a password-protected section for. See Chapter 26 for details on these settings.

To protect a section of a notebook with a password, follow these steps:

1. Right-click the section's tab, and then choose Password Protect This Section from the context menu. OneNote display the Password Protection task pane (see Figure 25-4).

Figure 25-4. In the Password Protection task pane, click the Set Password button to start protecting the section with a pasword.

2. Click the Set Password button. OneNote displays the Password Protection dialog box (see Figure 25-5).

Figure 25-5. Make sure you remember the password you use for protecting a section.

3. Type the password in the Enter Password text box and the Confirm Password text box.

4. Click the OK button. The Password Protection task pane shows that the current section is protected and displays the Change Password button and the Remove Password button.

5. Click the Close button (the × button) to close the Password Protection task pane.

■ **Note** OneNote doesn't yet let you protect the whole of a notebook with a password.

Unlocking a Password-Protected Section

When you need to work in a section of a notebook that you've protected with a password, you'll need to provide the password to unlock the section.

To do so, follow these steps:

1. Click the section to display it. You'll see the message "This section is password protected."

2. Click this message or press Enter to display the Protected Section dialog box (see Figure 25-6).

Figure 25-6. To work with a notebook section you've protected, type the password in the Protected Section dialog box.

3. Type the password in the Enter Password text box, and then click the OK button. OneNote unlocks the protected section.

■ **Note** How long the notebook section remains unlocked depends on the settings you've chosen in the Advanced pane in the OneNote Options dialog box. See Chapter 26 for details on the security settings you can choose.

Locking Password-Protected Sections Manually

You can lock all password-protected sections of a notebook manually if necessary. Right-click the section's tab and choose Password Protect This Section to display the Password Protection task pane, and then click the Lock All button.

Removing Password Protection from a Section of a Notebook

To remove password protection from a section of a notebook, follow these steps:

1. Right-click the section's tab and choose Password Protect This Section to display the Password Protection task pane.

2. Click the Remove Password button. OneNote displays the Remove Password dialog box.

3. Type the password, and then click the OK button. (You need to type the password to prove that the person removing the protection is you.)

Sharing Notebooks and Creating Shared Notebooks

One of OneNote's strongest features is that you can not only share your notebooks with other people but even work on shared notebooks while other people are editing them. When you share a notebook, OneNote tracks who makes each change and when they make it. You can review the changes afterward and decide which you want to keep and which you want to jettison.

You can either share an existing notebook with other people or create a notebook specifically for sharing

Creating a New Shared Notebook

To create a new shared notebook, follow these steps:

1. Choose Share ➤ Shared Notebook ➤ New Shared Notebook to display the New Notebook pane in Backstage.

2. In the Store Notebook On list box, choose where to store the shared notebook:

    •   *Web*: Choose this item to store the shared notebook on SkyDrive, so that other people can access it over the Internet.

    •   *Network*: Choose this item to store the shared notebook on your local network, so that other people who use that network can share it.

    •   *My Computer*: Choose this item if you've set up a shared folder for other PCs in your workgroup. If not, Web or Network is usually better.

3. In the Name text box, type the name you want to give the notebook. OneNote uses this name as the notebook's file name.

4. See if the Network Location or Web Location text box shows the folder you want to use. If not, click the Browse button to open the Select Folder dialog box, click the folder, and then click the Select button.

5. Click the Create Notebook button. OneNote creates the shared notebook, saves it, and opens it. OneNote then displays a dialog box (see Figure 25-7) telling you that the notebook is shared with anyone who has permission to access the network folder.

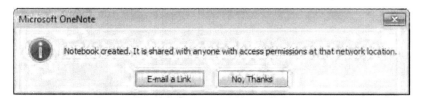

Figure 25-7. After creating a shared notebook, click the E-mail a Link button if you want to e-mail your colleagues to let them know where to find the notebook.

6. If you want to e-mail your colleagues a link to the notebook, click the E-mail a Link button, and then address and send the message that OneNote creates for you in Outlook. Otherwise, click the No, Thanks button, and tell your colleagues in your preferred way where to find the shared notebook.

Sharing an Existing Notebook

If you want to share an existing notebook rather than create a new notebook, follow these steps:

1. Choose Share ➤ Shared Notebook ➤ Share This Notebook to display the Share Notebook pane in Backstage (see Figure 25-8).

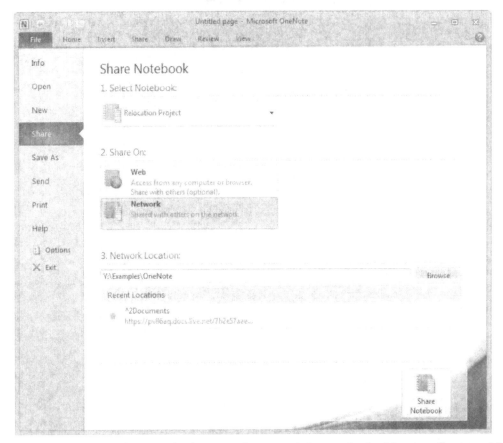

Figure 25-8. *Use the Share Notebook pane to share an existing notebook with your colleagues, either on the local network or on the Web.*

2. Make sure the Select Notebook drop-down list shows the notebook you want to share. If not, open the drop-down list and choose the right notebook.

3. In the Share On area, choose Web to share the notebook via the Internet with SkyDrive. Choose Network to share it on your local network.

4. See if the Network Location or Web Location text box shows the folder you want to use. If not, click the Browse button to open the Select Folder dialog box, click the folder, and then click the Select button.

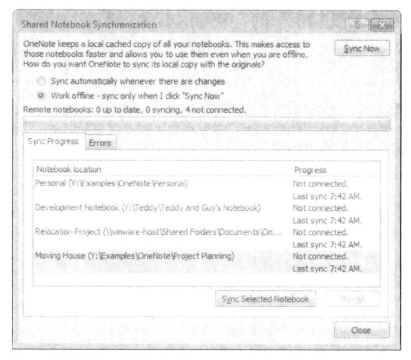

Figure 25-12. Select the "Work offline – sync only when I click 'Sync Now'" option button in the Shared Notebook Synchronization dialog box to take your notebooks offline for editing in peace.

    2.   Select the "Work offline – sync only when I click 'Sync Now'" option button.

    3.   Click the Close button.

When you want to return to automatic synchronization, open the Shared Notebook Synchronization dialog box again, select the Sync automatically whenever there are changes option button, and then click the Close button.

Forcing Immediate Synchronization of a Notebook

If you've taken your notebooks offline, or if you're about to disconnect your PC from the network, you can force synchronization in any of these ways:

- *Navigation Bar*: Right-click the notebook in the Navigation Bar and choose Sync This Notebook Now.

- *Keyboard*: Press Shift+F9 to give the Sync This Notebook Now command for the active notebook.

- *Shared Notebook Synchronization dialog box*: Click the Sync Now button to sync all your notebooks. To sync a single notebook, click it in the list on the Sync Progress tab, and then click the Sync Selected Notebook button.

Using Different Versions of Pages

OneNote stores different versions of the pages it contains, so you can go back to an earlier version of a page as needed. This feature is useful when you find a colleague has deleted material that you need to keep in the notebook—or when you delete material yourself by accident.

■ **Note** OneNote keeps the versions of a page for 60 days and then discards them automatically. If necessary, you can get rid of them sooner, as discussed in the section "Getting Rid of Old Page Versions to Save Space," later in this chapter.

Viewing or Recovering an Earlier Page Version

To see all the different versions of a page, choose Share ➤ Page Versions ➤ Page Versions, clicking the top part of the Page Versions button. (You can also click the lower part of the button and then choose Page Versions from the menu that opens.) The Page Tabs pane displays a list of all the different versions of the page that are available, showing the tabs in gray to indicate that they are versions of the currently selected page.

To view an earlier page version, click the version you want in the Page Tabs pane. OneNote displays the page version, as shown in Figure 25-13. If you want to restore the page version, click the message at the top, and then click the Restore Version command on the menu that appears.

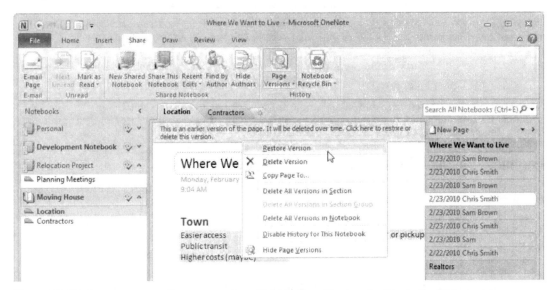

Figure 25-13. To restore an earlier page version, click the Page Versions button in the History group, then click the version in the Page Tabs pane. Click the message at the top of the page, and then click Restore Version.

▓ **Note** From the menu that appears when you click the message at the top of a page version, you can also click the Delete Version command to delete this version or click the Copy Page To command to copy it to a different location. Copying the page to a different location enables you to edit the page and use it further without overwriting the current page version.

Getting Rid of Old Page Versions to Save Space

Keeping the old page versions can greatly increase the amount of space a notebook takes up on a drive and the length of time it takes to load across the Internet. You can clear out old material by using the three Delete commands on the Share ➤ History ➤ Page Versions menu:

- *Delete All Versions in Section*: Give this command to get rid of all the page versions in the current section.

- *Delete All Versions in Section Group*: Give this command to dispose of all the page versions in the current section and its section group. This command is available only if the current section is in a section group.

- *Delete All Versions in Notebook*: Give this command to delete all the versions in the whole notebook. It's usually a good idea to review the whole notebook quickly before doing this, or at least make sure you have a recent backup of the notebook.

▓ **Note** If you find that a notebook is growing too big and unwieldy, you can turn off history in it by choosing Share ➤ History ➤ Page Versions ➤ Disable History for This Notebook or Share ➤ History ➤ Notebook Recycle Bin ➤ Disable History for This Notebook. OneNote then gets rid of old versions and deleted material immediately rather than keeping them in case you need to recover material.

Storing Notes on the Web

If you want to be able to access your notebooks from anywhere using a portable device (such as a mobile phone) or someone else's computer, store them on the Web rather than on your PC or on your local network.

The easiest way to store your notes on the Web is to create a notebook directly on the Web. Follow these steps:

1. Click the File tab to open Backstage.

2. Click the New item in the left column to display the New Notebook screen.

3. In the Store Notebook On area, click the Web item.

4. In the Name text box, type the name you want to give the notebook.

5. In the Web Location text box, make sure that the right folder on Windows Live SkyDrive is selected.

6. Click the Create Notebook button. OneNote creates the notebook and saves it on SkyDrive.

After OneNote opens the new notebook, you can create sections and pages in it as needed. If the material you want to store online is already in other notebooks, copy or move it from them to the new notebook.

If you want to store an existing notebook on the Web, follow the procedure described in the section "Sharing an Existing Notebook," earlier in this chapter. Briefly, choose Share ➤ Shared Notebook ➤ Share This Notebook to display the Shared Notebook pane in Backstage, select Web in the Share On area, and then click the Share Notebook button.

Summary

In this chapter, you've learned how to organize, synchronize, and share your notes.

You know how to move pages and sections both within a notebook and to other notebooks, how to merge sections together, and how to split a notebook into two. You can search for information and protect your notes with passwords.

You've also learned how to share your workbooks with other people, how to work in shared workbooks, and how to review the changes that other people have made in them. You can view older versions of pages, recover the versions you need, and clear out old page versions that you no longer require. You can also store your notes on the Web so that you can access them from anywhere.

CHAPTER 26

Making OneNote Work Your Way

In the previous two chapters, you've learned how to create notebooks in OneNote, add your notes to them, and organize and synchronize your notes. Along the way, you've seen various notes about how you can change OneNote's behavior to suit your needs.

You start this chapter by digging into the options that can make the most difference to your work in OneNote. Once you've chosen settings that suit the way you work, you learn to add audio and video to your notebooks, how to print your notebooks, and how to export data from OneNote to the other Office programs.

Choosing Essential OneNote Options

To get the most out of OneNote, you'll need to configure it. Click the File tab to open Backstage, and then click Options to open the OneNote Options dialog box.

Choose General options as discussed in Chapter 5 and Proofing options as discussed in Chapter 3, and then work your way through the following sections. You'll probably find that you can leave many options with their default settings, but that it's helpful to change others.

Choosing Display Options

The options on the Display screen in the OneNote Options dialog box (see Figure 26-1) let you control how OneNote looks:

- *Place OneNote icon in the notification area of the taskbar*: Select this check box to make OneNote include a OneNote icon in the notification area. This icon lets you open a new Side Note.

- *Create all new pages with rule lines*: Select this check box if you want OneNote to display rule lines on each new page you create. If you clear this check box, you can display rule lines by choosing View ➤ Page Setup ➤ Rule Lines, and then clicking the type of lines you want.

- *Dock new Side Note windows to the side of the desktop*: Select this check box if you want OneNote to automatically dock each new Side Note window you open to the side of the desktop. This option can be helpful for keeping your Side Notes organized. Clear this check box if you prefer to be able to position Side Note windows manually.

- *Page tabs appear on the left*: Select this check box if you want to display page tabs on the left rather than on the right, where they normally appear.

- *Show the floating New Page button near page tabs*: Select this check box if you want OneNote to display the New Page button when you move the mouse pointer over the page tabs. The New Page button lets you quickly insert a page, which is often helpful. Clear this check box if you prefer to insert pages in other ways.

- *Navigation bar appears on the left*: Select this check box (which is selected by default) to display the navigation bar; clear it to hide the navigation bar and give yourself more space to work in.

- *Vertical scroll bar appears on the left*: Select this check box if you want the vertical scroll bar to appear on the left rather than on the right, where it normally appears.

- *Show note containers on pages*: Select this check box (which is selected by default) to have OneNote display a container around each note you place on a page. Clear this check box if you want to hide the containers, so that notes appear simply as text (or whatever they contain) on the page. This setting doesn't affect the page titles—those containers remain displayed.

- *Disable screen clipping notifications*: Select this check box if you want to prevent Windows from displaying a ScreenTip above the OneNote icon in the notification area when you're using the Screen Clipping feature.

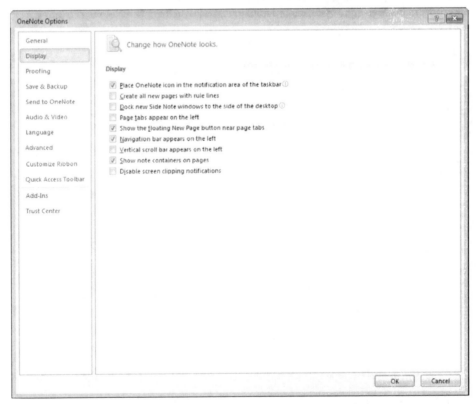

Figure 26-1. The Display options include placing a OneNote icon in the notification area of the taskbar and controlling the placement of the navigation bar.

Choosing Save & Backup Options

The options on the Save & Backup screen (see Figure 26-2) in the OneNote Options dialog box let you choose where to save and how to back up your notebooks. It's worth spending a few minutes setting these options, because they're vital to keeping your valuable information safe—and they can reduce the amount of space your notebooks take up on disk.

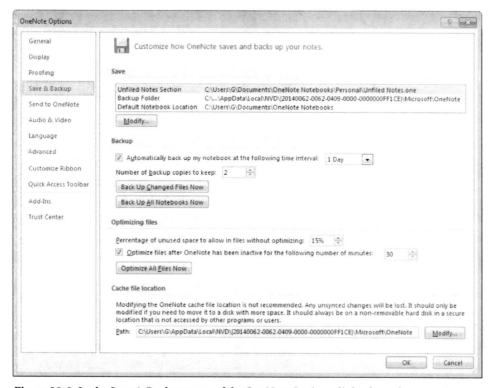

Figure 26-2. *In the Save & Backup pane of the OneNote Options dialog box, choose options for saving, backing up, and optimizing your notebooks.*

In the Save list box, you can choose where to save each of the items that appears: the Unfiled Notes Section, the Backup Folder, and the Default Notebook Location. To change one of these:

1. Click the item in the Save list box.

2. Click the Modify button to display the Select File dialog box (for the Unfiled Notes Section) or the Select Folder dialog box (for the Backup Folder item and the Default Notebook Location item).

3. Choose the file or folder, and then click the Select button to close the dialog box and apply your choice.

In the Backup area, you can choose the following options:

- *Automatically back up my notebook at the following time interval*: Select this check box if you want to make automatic backups—usually a good idea. In the drop-down list, choose the time interval between backups. Your choices range from 1 Minute to 6 Weeks; the default setting of 1 Day is a reasonable medium, but if you use OneNote heavily, you may want to shorten the interval to 12 Hours, 6 Hours, or less.

■ **Caution** In general, keeping frequent backups of your important data is a great idea. But setting one of the shortest intervals, such as 1 Minute or 5 Minutes, in the Automatically back up my notebook at the following time interval drop-down list is overkill. If you try to back up a large OneNote notebook every minute, your PC will be constantly backing up data—and you will gain little advantage.

- *Number of backup copies to keep*: In this text box, choose how many backups of your OneNote notebooks to keep. The default setting is 2, but you may want to increase this to a number in the 5–10 range to give you a better chance of recovering data if you find that your current notebook and the latest backups have been corrupted.

- *Back Up Changed Files Now*: Click this button to back up the OneNote files you've changed.

- *Back Up All Notebooks Now*: Click this button to force a backup of all your OneNote notebooks; for example, because you've had a premonition of impending data loss.

■ **Note** To open a backup file, choose File ➤ Open ➤ Open Backups. OneNote displays the Open Backup dialog box, showing the backup folder set in the Save & Backup pane. Select the backup you want (usually the most recent), and then click the Open button.

In the Optimizing files area, choose how to optimize your OneNote notebooks:

- *Percentage of unused space to allow in files without optimizing*: In this text box, set the amount of unused space you're prepared to tolerate before OneNote optimizes the file. The default setting is 15 percent; you can increase this if OneNote seems to spend too long optimizing your files.

- *Optimize files after OneNote has been inactive for the following number of minutes*: Select this check box if you want OneNote to run optimization automatically after you've left it alone for a period of time. Set the number of minutes in the text box. The default setting is 30 minutes, but if you tend to leave your PC for shorter breaks, you may want to reduce it to start optimization sooner.

- *Optimize All Files Now*: Click this button to run optimization immediately. This button is especially useful if you clear the previous check box, but you can also use it to force optimization at any convenient time (for example, when you're heading off to a lengthy meeting).

In the Cache file location area, you can click the Modify button to choose a different folder for the OneNote cache file location. Normally, you should leave the cache folder in its default place unless your PC's hard disk is running out of space and you need to move the folder to another hard drive. Even then, you should place the folder on an internal hard drive rather than on a removable hard drive (such as a USB hard drive).

Choosing Send to OneNote Options

In the Send to OneNote pane of the Options dialog box (see Figure 26-3), you can tell OneNote how to deal with content you send to it from other programs. Choosing the right destinations for items can streamline your work in OneNote a lot.

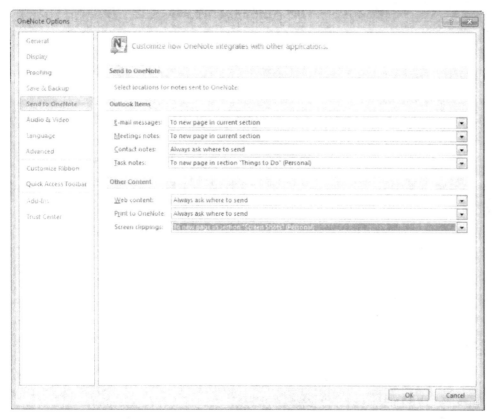

Figure 26-3. In the Send to OneNote pane, tell OneNote how to handle content you send to it from Outlook and other programs.

In the Outlook Items area, open each drop-down list in turn: the E-mail messages drop-down list, the Meetings notes drop-down list, the Contact notes drop-down list, and the Task notes drop-down list in turn. Then choose the destination for each item you send to OneNote using the Send to OneNote command. These are your choices:

- *Always ask where to send*: Outlook displays the Select Location in OneNote dialog box (shown in Figure 26-4 for task notes) to let you choose where to send the item. You can select the Always send *item* to the selected location check box if you want to choose a standard location.

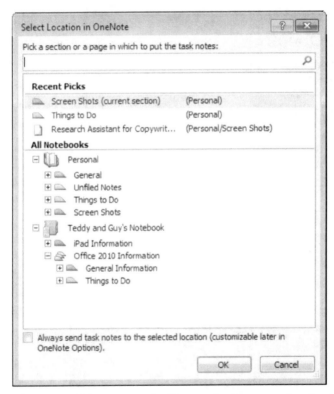

Figure 26-4. *When you use the Always ask where to send option in OneNote, Outlook prompts you to choose the notebook and section in which to insert the item you're sending.*

- *To current page*: Outlook inserts the item on the page you're working on in OneNote.

- *To new page in current section*: Outlook creates a new page in the current section and inserts the item on it. This setting is good for e-mail messages, especially if you send multiple messages at once to OneNote.

- *Set default location*: Click this item to open the Select Location in OneNote dialog box. Choose the notebook and section, and then click the OK button. (If you delete this location, OneNote switches back to the Always ask item.)

In the Other Content area, use the Web content drop-down list, the Print to OneNote drop-down list, and the Screen clippings drop-down list to choose where to place these items too. The destinations are the same as for the Outlook Items discussed above, apart from the Screen clippings drop-down list, which offers the choice To Clipboard only instead of the To current page choice. Select this item if you want to place a screen clip on the Clipboard so that you can insert it wherever it belongs.

■ **Note** We'll look at the Audio & Video options in the section "Choosing Audio & Video Options," later in this chapter.

Choosing Advanced Options

The Advanced pane in the OneNote Options dialog box (see Figure 26-5) contains many options, but you'll benefit from knowing about almost all of them.

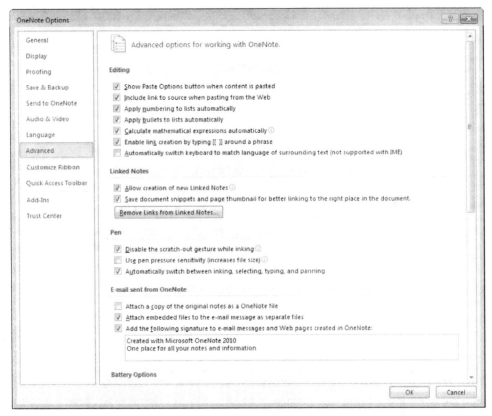

Figure 26-5. *It's worth taking the time to wade through OneNote's Advanced options, because they make a big difference to how easy the program is to use.*

Start by choosing options in the Editing area at the top of the pane:

- *Show Paste Options button when content is pasted*: Select this check box to make OneNote display a Paste Options button when you paste in content. The Paste Options button lets you choose among different ways of pasting the item—for example, as unformatted text instead of formatted text. This button is usually useful.

- *Include link to source when pasting from the Web*: Select this check box to make OneNote automatically build in a link to the Web page from which you pasted in information. For most purposes, this is a great feature, as it gives you an easy way of tracking where you found information.

- *Apply numbering to lists automatically*: Select this check box if you want OneNote to automatically create a numbered list when you start typing a paragraph with a number followed by a period, a closing parenthesis, or a tab. Some people find this helpful; others don't.

▦ **Note** The Apply numbering to lists automatically feature and Apply bullets to lists automatically feature are like the AutoFormat As You Type features in the other programs, discussed in Chapter 3.

- *Apply bullets to lists automatically*: Select this check box if you want OneNote to automatically create a bulleted list when you start a paragraph with a bullet-like character (such as an asterisk) followed by a tab. If you don't find this feature helpful, clear this check box.

- *Calculate mathematical expressions automatically*: Select this check box if you want to use OneNote's automatic calculation feature. You can simply type a sum such as $218*365= and press Enter to have OneNote calculate the formula and fill in the result. This feature, sometimes called "napkin math," is usually helpful.

- *Enable link creation by typing [[ ]] around a phrase*: Select this check box if you want to be able to create a link by typing two brackets before and after a word or phrase. If you type the name of an existing page, OneNote creates a link to it; if not, OneNote creates a new page in the current section and gives it the name you typed.

- *Automatically switch keyboard to match language of surrounding text*: Select this check box if you want OneNote to try to detect changes of language and automatically change the keyboard layout to match.

In the Linked Notes area, choose how to handle Linked Notes:

- *Allow creation of new Linked Notes*: Select this check box if you want to use Linked Notes—notes linked to the program next to which you're working in a docked OneNote window. Linked Notes are usually helpful, but you can clear the check box if you prefer not to use them.

- *Save document snippets and page thumbnail for better linking to the right place in the document*: Select this check box to save this additional information in each Linked Note. Saving this information is usually helpful.

- *Remove Links from Linked Notes*: Click this button if you want to remove the links from Linked Notes. You won't usually need to do this.

In the Pen area, choose how OneNote should respond to pen input:

- *Disable the scratch-out gesture while inking*: Select this check box to turn off the scratch-out gesture (for deleting an item) when you're using ink. This setting helps you to avoid deleting things by mistake and is usually helpful.

- *Use pen pressure sensitivity*: Select this check box if you want OneNote to register pen pressure as well as movements. This is useful when you're drawing, but you'll probably want to turn it off when you're just using a pen for input.

- *Automatically switch between inking, selecting, typing, and panning*: Select this check box if you want OneNote to automatically switch among different types of pen input depending on what you're doing. This feature is intended to save time, but if you find it doesn't work satisfactorily with the way you use pen input, clear this check box.

In the E-mail sent from OneNote area, choose options for e-mail you send starting from OneNote:

- *Attach a copy of the original notes as an OneNote file*: Select the check box only if you want to include a OneNote file containing the original notes when you send an e-mail from OneNote. This feature is sometimes useful, but it's not what you'll usually want.

- *Attach embedded files to the e-mail message as separate files*: Select this check box to have OneNote include separate files of any embedded files that the OneNote notes contain. This is usually a good choice, as receiving separate files enables the recipient to work with the individual files.

- *Add the following signature to e-mail messages and Web pages created in OneNote*: Select this check box only if you want to add a specific signature to e-mail messages you've started from OneNote. If you do use this feature, customize the text rather than including Microsoft's marketing information.

The Battery Options area contains just one setting, the Optimize for the following battery life drop-down list. For a laptop, select the setting for the amount of battery life you want. The choices are Maximum performance, Short, Medium, Long, and Maximum battery life. OneNote reduces its demands by doing fewer background operations such as indexing, text recognition, and synchronization when running on battery life.

In the Tags area, choose settings for handling tags when creating a summary:

- *When using the Tags Summary task pane to create a summary page*: In this area, select the Show original tagged notes as dimmed area if you want original tagged notes to appear dimmed so that you can distinguish them from notes that weren't tagged. The alternative is to select the Leave original tagged notes unchanged option button to leave the notes as they were.

- *Show dimmed tagged notes in the Tags Summary task pane*: Select this check box to have OneNote display the dimmed tagged notes. Clear this check box to have OneNote suppress the dimmed tagged notes.

In the Passwords area, choose how to handle password-protected sections of your notebooks:

- *Lock password protected sections after I have not worked in them for the following amount of time*: Select this check box to have OneNote automatically lock password-protected sections after the length of time you specify in the drop-down list. This setting usually works well once you've chosen the length of time that suits you. Your choices range from 1 Minute to 12 Hours or 1 Day; the default setting is 10 Minutes.

- *Lock password protected sections as soon as I navigate away from them*: Select this check box if you want OneNote to automatically lock password-protected sections the moment you leave them. This makes for tight security but is awkward if you often need to return to protected sections to make further changes.

- *Enable add-in programs to access password protected sections when they are unlocked*: Select this check box if you want to give OneNote add-ins access to the password-protected sections you've unlocked. This setting is normally helpful.

In the Search area, you can click the Install Instant Search button to download and install the Microsoft Windows Desktop Search component. This component adds instant search to OneNote. If Windows Desktop Search is already installed on your PC, the Install Instant Search button is dimmed and unavailable.

In the Text recognition in pictures area, select the Disable text recognition in pictures check box if you don't want OneNote to try to recognize text in pictures so that you can search for it. Whether you should use text recognition in pictures depends on the types of pictures you store in your OneNote notebooks. If you include text-heavy diagrams, having OneNote recognize the text is usually helpful. But if you include mainly illustrative pictures, it's not worth having OneNote devote time and effort to trying to pick out the text in them.

In the Other area, you can choose your preferred measurement unit in the Measurement units drop-down list. Your choices are Inches, Centimeters, Millimeters, Points, and Picas. A point is $^1/_{72}$ inch, and a pica is 12 points, or $^1/_6$ inch.

Choosing Audio & Video Options

If you include audio, video, or both in your notebooks, make sure that OneNote is using suitable settings. Click the Audio & Video category in the left column of the OneNote Options dialog box to display the Audio & Video pane (see Figure 26-6).

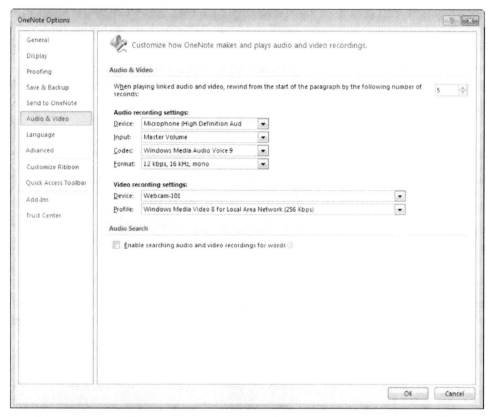

Figure 26-6. *Make sure that OneNote is using suitable settings for the audio and video you add to your notebooks.*

At the top of the pane, set the "When playing linked audio and video, rewind from the start of the paragraph by the following number of seconds" setting as needed. The default setting is 5 seconds, but you may well need to adjust it.

Next, make your choices in the Audio recording settings area:

- *Device*: In this drop-down list, make sure that OneNote has selected your PC's audio input device. If your PC has multiple input devices, such as a microphone and a USB headset, pick the right one.

- *Input*: In this drop-down list, choose the audio input.

- *Codec*: In this drop-down list, choose the codec (the *co*der/*dec*oder software) to use for compressing audio you record. Windows Media Audio Voice 9 is the best choice for recordings of spoken audio. Use Windows Media Audio 10 Professional if you need to make high-quality recordings (normally you would use a different program than OneNote for these).

Note The higher the quality setting you choose in the Format drop-down list, the larger the resulting audio files are, and the larger your OneNote notebook grows. So you need to strike a balance between good enough audio quality and file size. The more audio you record, the more important it is that you strike this balance, especially if you keep the audio notes in the long term (as opposed to creating written notes of the good parts and jettisoning the audio files).

- *Format*: In this drop-down list, choose the quality at which you want to record. For the Windows Media Audio Voice 9 codec, start with the "8 Kbps, 8 kHz, mono" setting, and run a test to see if it gives you high enough quality. If not, increase the setting to "12 Kbps, 16 kHz, mono" and test again; again, move to one of the higher quality settings if necessary. For the Windows Media Audio 10 Professional codec, experiment with the "128 Kbps, 44 kHz, stereo (A/V) CBR" setting for recording music, and choose a higher setting if necessary.

Note CBR is the abbreviation for *constant bit rate*, recording the same amount of data for each second of audio rather than recording more data for more complex audio than for less complex audio (or silence). 44 kHz is the sampling rate used for CD-quality audio; normally, it's not worth using the higher 48 kHz sampling rate, as it takes up more space for very little gain.

Now choose settings in the Video recording settings area:

- *Device*: In this drop-down list, make sure that OneNote has chosen the right video camera. Unless you have multiple cameras attached, the choice will usually be right.
- *Profile*: In this drop-down list, choose the setting at which you want to record video. Start with the Windows Media Video 8 for Local Area Network (256 Kbps), test it, and see if the quality is high enough. If not, choose a higher setting, such as Windows Media Video 8 for Local Area Network (384 Kbps).

In the Audio Search area, select the Enable searching audio and video recordings for words check box if you want OneNote to search your audio recordings and the audio in your video recordings and try to index the words it finds. You can then search for particular words and phrases in the audio recordings and video recordings. This feature gives mixed results, but it's worth testing to see if it's useful to you.

Note If you turn on searching for audio recordings, you will normally need to use relatively high audio quality to get useful search results. The audio quality on any of the Windows Media Video 8 for Local Area Network choices is usually high enough for searching, provided that you position the microphone close to the speaker.

Recording Audio and Video into Your Notebooks

One of OneNote's most powerful features is its ability to record audio and video straight into a notebook. This is great when you need to take multimedia notes.

■ **Note** Before recording audio or video into a notebook, make sure you've chosen suitable quality settings in the Audio & Video pane of the OneNote Options dialog box, as discussed earlier in this chapter.

Recording Audio into a Notebook

To record audio into a notebook, select the page you want to place the audio on, and then choose Insert ➤ Recording ➤ Record Audio. OneNote reveals the Audio & Video section of the Ribbon and displays the Recording tab, creates a container for the audio recording, and starts recording the audio. Figure 26-7 shows an audio recording taking place.

Figure 26-7. *OneNote displays the Recording tab on the Audio & Video section of the Ribbon when you start a recording. The readout under the View tab shows how long the recording has been running.*

While the recording runs, you can continue working in OneNote as needed. OneNote automatically links the notes you take during the recording to the recording as it goes along, so that when you play back the recording, OneNote can automatically display the relevant section of your written notes, as long as it's on the same page. This is great for patching the holes in lecture notes after you were unable to keep up with written notes.

When you're ready to stop the recording, click the Stop button. You can also pause the recording by clicking the Pause button; click the Pause button again when you want to resume recording.

After you end the recording, OneNote displays the Playback tab of the Audio & Video section of the Ribbon. This tab is essentially the same as the Recording tab, but different controls are available for playback than for recording, as you'd expect.

You can play back the recorded audio at any time. When the Playback tab on the Ribbon is displayed, click the audio container, and then click the Play button in the Playback group. You can then use the other buttons—Pause, Stop, Rewind 10 Minutes, Rewind 10 Seconds, Fast Forward 10 Seconds, and Fast Forward 10 Minutes—to control playback as needed. You can also start playback by holding the mouse pointer over the audio file and clicking the play button that appears to the left of the audio container.

If you want OneNote to display the linked sections of your written notes as it plays back the audio file, make sure that the See Playback button is "pressed"—clicked so that it appears orange. If the button looks normal, click it to turn on the See Playback feature. If you don't want to see the playback, make sure the button isn't pressed.

Recording Video into a Notebook

Recording video works in a similar way to recording audio, except that OneNote opens a separate video window so that you can see what the video camera is getting (and adjust it if necessary). To start a video recording, click in the container in which you want to place the recording, then choose Insert ➤ Recording ➤ Record Video. Click the Stop button when you're ready to stop recording the video file.

■ **Tip** You can minimize the Video window if you want to get it out of the way so that you can take notes, but don't close it, as closing it stops the recording.

To play back a video file, click it, and then click the Play button on the Playback tab of the Ribbon.

Exporting or Removing an Audio or Video File

To export an audio file or a video file, right-click the file in its container and choose Save As from the context menu. In the Save As dialog box, choose the folder in which to save the file and the filename to use, and then click the Save button.

If you no longer need an audio or video file, you can remove it from the notebook easily. Just click the audio or video file, and then press Delete.

Searching for Words in Audio and Video Recordings

If you selected the Enable searching audio and video recordings for words check box in the Audio & Video pane in the OneNote Options dialog box, OneNote searches through the recordings when the program is idle and your PC has processor cycles to spare. Depending on how heavily you use your PC, it may be several hours or days before you can search for words in the recordings.

If you haven't turned on searching through audio and video, OneNote displays the Audio Search dialog box (see Figure 26-8) when you stop your first recording, to give you the chance to turn it on. Click the Enable Audio Search button if you want to turn audio search on; otherwise, click the Keep Audio Search Disabled button to leave it off.

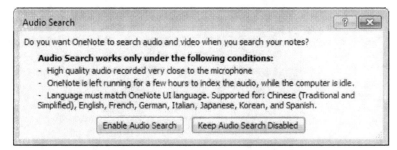

Figure 26-8. *When you stop your first recording, OneNote checks whether you want to enable audio search if it is currently disabled.*

Printing Your Notebooks

Unlike the other Office programs, OneNote doesn't have a print preview feature integrated into Backstage so that you see the preview automatically. If you want to preview a document, you need to launch the separate Preview feature. As this feature has its own Print button for printing directly from it, you may well prefer this means of printing to printing without previewing the document.

Using Print Preview

To preview how a printout will look, follow these steps:

1. Click the File tab to open Backstage.

2. Click Print to display the Print pane.

3. Click Print Preview to open the Print Preview and Settings dialog box (see Figure 26-9).

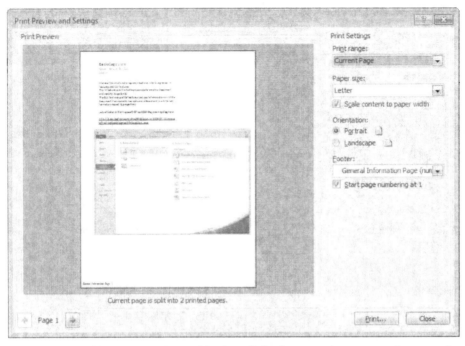

Figure 26-9. *Use the Print Preview and Settings dialog box to make sure your document is set up to print the way you want.*

4. If you need to see the preview at a larger size, drag the dotted handle at the lower-right corner of the dialog box down and to the right.

5. Use the Next Page button and Previous Page button in the lower-left corner of the dialog box to move from page to page as needed.

6. In the Print range drop-down list, choose what to print:

    *   *Current Page*: Choose this item to print the current page. This is often what you need.

    *   *Page Group*: Choose this item to print the group of pages.

    *   *Current Section*: Choose this item to print the whole of the section. Check the readout below the Print Preview box to see how many pages you're about to print.

7. In the Paper size drop-down list, make sure that the right paper size is selected; for example, Letter.

8. Select the Scale content to paper width check box if you want OneNote to automatically resize the content to fit the paper width. Because OneNote pages don't have margins in the way that (say) Word documents do, this scaling is usually a good idea—but always check that the preview looks okay.

9. In the Orientation area, select the Portrait option button to print in a tall orientation or the Landscape option button to print in wide orientation.

10. In the Footer drop-down list, choose the information you want to print in the footer area of the page:

   - *[Page Name] Page (number)*. Select this item to print the page's title, the word Page, and the page number.

   - *Page (number)*. Select this item to print the word Page and the page number.

   - *[Page Name]*. Select this item to print the page's title.

   - *(none)*. Select this item to omit the footer.

11. If you're ready to print the document, click the Print button to display the Print dialog box, and then choose settings as described in the next section, starting at step 4. If you want to return to the notebook to make changes before printing, click the Close button.

Printing a Document

If you're confident that a document will look fine when printed (for example, because you've printed it before), you can simply print without using the Preview feature. Follow these steps:

1. Click the File tab to open Backstage.

2. Click Print to display the Print pane.

3. Click Print to display the Print dialog box.

4. Choose printer settings as described in Chapter 5. For example, choose the printer you want to use and the number of copies to print.

5. Click the Print button to close the Print dialog box and start printing.

Using OneNote with the Other Office Programs

After taking and organizing your notes in OneNote, you'll often want to share them with the other Office programs. This section shows you how to use the many different types of sharing that OneNote offers.

Exporting a Page or Section to a Word Document

When you need to get information into Word, you can export either a page or a section of a OneNote notebook to a Word document.

To export a page from a OneNote notebook to a Word document, follow these steps:

1. Open the page, section, or notebook that you want to export to Word.

2. Click the File tab on the Ribbon to open Backstage.

3. In the left column, click the Save As item to display the Save As screen (see Figure 26-10).

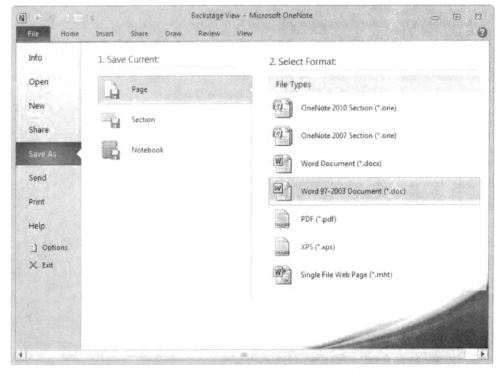

Figure 26-10. Use the Save As screen to save a page or a section of a OneNote workbook to a Word document.

4. In the Save Current column, select the item you want to export: Page or Section. (You can't export a whole notebook to a Word document.)

5. In the Select Format list, click the Word format you want to use:

   • *Word Document (*.docx)*. Use this format for sharing with Word 2010 or Word 2007 for Windows, or for Word 2008 for Mac. Users of Word 2003 (Windows) or Word 2004 (Mac) will need to install file converters before they can use this file format.

■ **Tip** If in doubt, use the Word 97–2003 Document format rather than the Word Document format for sharing OneNote data with Word users. The Word Document format has some technical advantages over the Word 97–2003 Document format, but in the real world, the Word 97–2003 Document format avoids compatibility issues and usually works fine. Most word processors can open the Word 97–2003 Document format, so it's widely useful.

- *Word 97–2003 Document (*.doc)*: Use this format for sharing with any version of Word from Word 97 onward.

6. In the Save As dialog box that OneNote opens, choose the folder and type the name for the Word document.

7. Click the Save button to save the document.

You can now open the document and work with it in Word, or share it with another Word user.

Exporting Data to an Excel Worksheet or a PowerPoint Presentation

OneNote doesn't provide any special commands for exporting data from a notebook to an Excel worksheet or a PowerPoint presentation, but you can use copy and paste or drag and drop freely. For example:

- *Excel*: Right-click anywhere in a table in a OneNote page, choose Table ➤ Select Table from the context menu, and then copy the selection. Switch to Excel, right-click the upper-left cell of the destination area, and then give one of the Paste commands (for example, Match Destination). Excel puts the contents of each table cell in a separate cell.

- *PowerPoint*: Select a picture in OneNote and drag it to the slide on which you want to place it.

Creating an Outlook Message from OneNote

If you have information in OneNote that you want to send using Outlook, you can quickly create a message like this:

1. In OneNote, open the page that you want to send.

2. Choose Share ➤ E-mail ➤ E-mail Page. OneNote makes Outlook create a new message containing the page.

3. If you want to remove any part of the page, select it, and then press Delete to delete it.

4. Address the message, adjust the title as needed, and then click the Send button to send it.

▓ **Note** If you want to send just a single item from a OneNote page, you may find it easier to select the item, copy it, start a message in Outlook manually, and then paste the item into the message.

Creating an Outlook Task from OneNote

When you come across a note that you want to turn into a task in Outlook, you can do so in moments. Right-click the note and choose Outlook Tasks from the context menu, and then click the date or time frame for the task (see Figure 26-11)—Today, Tomorrow, This Week, Next Week, No Date, or Custom. If you choose Custom, Outlook displays the task in a window so that you can choose the date; otherwise, OneNote simply adds the task to Outlook, linking it back to the note. OneNote adds a flag icon to the note so that you can see a task is attached to it.

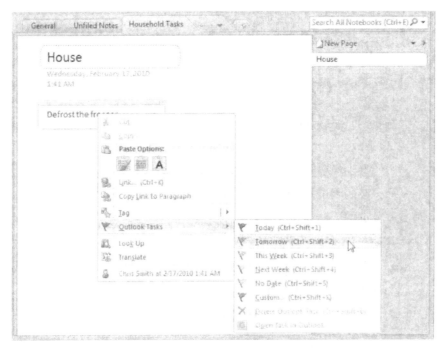

Figure 26-11. You can quickly create a task in Outlook from a note in OneNote.

You can also use the following keyboard shortcuts to quickly create tasks in Outlook. These can be great time-savers if you prefer to use the keyboard. Table 26-1 shows the keyboard shortcuts you can use to quickly create tasks in OneNote.

Table 26-1. Keyboard Shortcuts for Creating Tasks

Create a Task	Keyboard Shortcut
Today	Ctrl+Shift+1
Tomorrow	Ctrl+Shift+2
This Week	Ctrl+Shift+3
Next Week	Ctrl+Shift+4
No Date	Ctrl+Shift+5
Custom Date	Ctrl+Shift+K

Note After creating a task from OneNote, you can choose the Delete Outlook Task from the Outlook Tasks submenu on the context menu to delete an Outlook task directly from OneNote. You can also choose Open Task in Outlook to open the task so that you can work with it.

Transferring a OneNote Notebook to Another PC

When you need to transfer a OneNote notebook to another PC, save it to a OneNote package file from the first PC and import it on the second PC.

Follow these steps on the first PC to save the notebook to a OneNote package file:

1. Click the File tab to open Backstage, and then click Save As to display the Save As pane.

2. In the Save Current column, click Notebook.

3. In the Select Format area, click OneNote Package. OneNote displays the Save As dialog box.

4. Choose a drive or folder you will be able to access from the other PC. For example, use a network drive or a USB thumb drive.

5. Change the name in the File name text box as needed.

6. Click the Save button.

On the second PC, unpack the file like this:

1. Click the File tab to open Backstage, and then click Open Notebook to display the Open Notebook dialog box.

2. Navigate to the folder you saved the file in.

3. In the Files of type drop-down list above the Open button, choose OneNote Single File Package.

4. Click the file, and then click the Open button. OneNote displays the Unpack Notebook dialog box (see Figure 26-12).

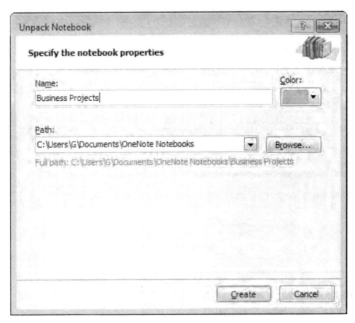

Figure 26-12. In the Unpack Notebook dialog box, choose the folder to put the notebook in and the name to give it.

5. In the Name text box, edit the notebook's default name as needed.

6. In the Color drop-down list, choose the color you want to give the notebook.

7. In the Path box, enter the path you want to save the notebook in. OneNote suggests the OneNote Notebooks folder in your Documents folder, which is often a good choice. To change the path, either type the change or click the Browse button, choose the folder in the Select Folder dialog box, and then click the Select button.

8. Click the Create button. OneNote closes the Unpack Notebook dialog box and opens the notebook.

Retrieving Material from the Notebook Recycle Bin

When you delete material from a notebook, OneNote doesn't get rid of the material in the same way that the other programs do. Instead, OneNote places deleted material in the Notebook Recycle Bin.

Material stays in the Notebook Recycle Bin for 60 days unless you remove it sooner. After 60 days, OneNote deletes the material, and it's gone for good (unless you have backups of it). For security, you may want to empty the Recycle Bin more frequently than this.

To open the Notebook Recycle Bin (see Figure 26-13), right-click the notebook's name in the navigation bar and choose Notebook Recycle Bin from the context menu. You can also choose Share ➤ History ➤ Notebook Recycle Bin, clicking the upper part of the Notebook Recycle Bin button in the History group (the lower part of the button displays a drop-down list).

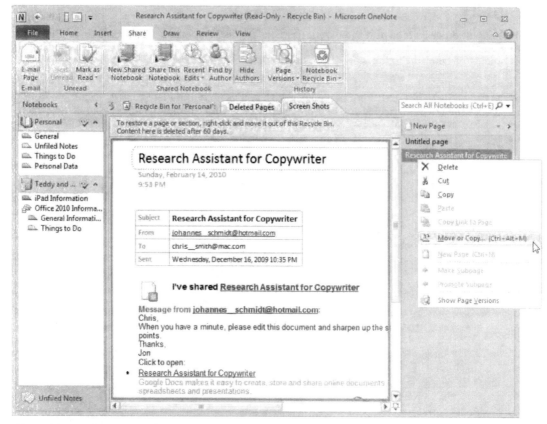

Figure 26-13.When you need to retrieve material you've deleted, open the Notebook Recycle Bin.

You can navigate through the Notebook Recycle Bin using the same techniques as for the rest of OneNote. When you find a section or page you want to retrieve, right-click it and choose Move or Copy to display the Move or Copy Section dialog box or the Move or Copy Pages dialog box. Choose the destination, and then click the Move button to move the section or page there. (You can also click the Copy button to copy a section, but normally you'll want to move material from the Notebook Recycle Bin rather than copy it.)

When you need to reduce the amount of space a notebook is taking up, empty the Notebook Recycle Bin. Click the lower part of the Notebook Recycle Bin button on the Ribbon, click Empty Recycle Bin, and then click the Yes button in the confirmation dialog box that OneNote displays.

To leave the Notebook Recycle Bin, either choose Share ➤ History ➤ Notebook Recycle Bin again (unpressing the Notebook Recycle Bin button) or click a notebook in the navigation bar.

Summary

In this chapter, you've learned how to set options to make OneNote behave the way you prefer, how to record audio and video into your notebooks, and how to print from OneNote. You've also learned how to export notes from OneNote to the other Office programs easily and in the most useful formats.

This is the end of the book (apart from the index, which you've no doubt met by now). Thank you for reading; I hope the book has helped you to bring the powerful Office programs under your control and make them do exactly what you need.

Index

Special Characters and Numerics

#DIV/0 error message, Excel, 356
#N/A error message, Excel, 356
#NAME? error message, Excel, 356
#NULL! error message, Excel, 357
#NUM! error message, Excel, 356
#REF! error message, Excel, 357
#VALUE! error message, Excel, 356
% Complete box, Outlook, 602
Bold and _italic_ with real formatting option,
        AutoCorrect dialog box, 46
+ sign, Word, 225
3-D column chart, Excel, 371
3-D Format category, Excel, 391
3-D option, Borders and Shading dialog
        box, 179
3-D Rotation category, Excel, 391
3-D rotation effects, Office programs, 101
3-D Rotation item, 446
3-D Rotation pane, 446

A

About This Sentence option, context menu, 58
Above Chart item, Excel, 383
Above/below item, Word, 220
absolute reference, Excel, 347
Accept All Changes in Document option, 249
Accept All Changes Shown option, 249
Accept All Changes to the Current Slide
        option, PowerPoint, 435
Accept All Changes to the Presentation option,
        PowerPoint, 435
Accept and Move to Next option, Accept
        drop-down menu, 249
Accept Change option, 249–250
Accept Conflict option, Word, 237
Accept drop-down menu, Word, 249
Account Configuration wizard, Outlook, 512

Account option, Arrange By control, 525
Account Type drop-down list, Add New
        Account wizard, 515
Accounting format, Excel, 319
accounts
    e-mail, changing default settings for, 514
    Outlook, choosing which to send messages
        from, 536
actions, 52
active cell, Excel, 286, 288
Active document option, 146
Active view, Outlook, 600
Add a Digital Signature command, Word, 275
Add a new service item, PowerPoint, 506
Add a page list box, OneNote, 625
Add a Tag field, Save As dialog box, 17
Add Animation box, PowerPoint, 482–483, 485
Add Animation drop-down panel,
        PowerPoint, 479
Add Audio dialog box, PowerPoint, 477
Add Bookmark command, PowerPoint, 471
Add Broadcast Service dialog box,
        PowerPoint, 506
Add Clips to Organizer dialog box,
        PowerPoint, 450
Add Contact Picture dialog box, Outlook, 557
Add Contact Picture placeholder, Outlook, 557
Add Custom Dictionary dialog box, 65, 67
Add Files link, SkyDrive, 30
Add files screen, SkyDrive, 30–31
Add Holidays to Calendar dialog box,
        Outlook, 584
Add New Account wizard, Outlook,
        512–515, 518
Add Printer item, Backstage, 69
Add slides to Microsoft Word document area,
        PowerPoint, 502
Add to Dictionary command, 54, 56, 64, 66
Add to Outlook Contacts command,
        Outlook, 558
Add to Quick Access Toolbar option, 119
Add to Quick Style Gallery, Styles pane, 165

addition calculation, OneNote, 635
Additional Information dialog box, Word, 275–276
Additional permissions for users area, Word, 273
Additional settings area, Word, 274
Address Book drop-down list, Outlook, 536, 593
Address box, Office programs, 114
Addresses area, Outlook, 559
addressing messages in Outlook, 536–537
Advance Slide section, PowerPoint, 478
Advanced category
    OneNote, 635
    Word, 83, 143, 147–148
Advanced Filter dialog box, Excel, 411
Advanced item
    Excel, 290
    Word, 218
Advanced option dialog
    Excel, 290, 295
    OneNote, 663–666
Advanced pane
    OneNote Options dialog box, 45, 646, 663
    Word, 143, 148, 214
After Previous item, PowerPoint, 480
Album Layout area, PowerPoint, 468
Align relative to drop-down list, Word, 206
Alignment category, Excel, 391
Alignment drop-down list, Paragraph dialog box, 174
Alignment group, Excel, 77, 316–317, 320–321, 329
alignment, in Excel, 320
Alignment link, Reveal Formatting pane, 188
Alignment styles, Excel, 329
All at Once option, PowerPoint, 482–484
All Categories option, Outlook, 561
All Commands option
    Categories list box, 146
    Choose commands from drop-down list, 124
    Options dialog box, 121
All Files option, Open dialog box, 148
All Notebooks list, OneNote, 623
All option
    Find and Replace dialog box, 191
    Search drop-down list, 196
All option, Word, 216
All Programs section, Start menu, 11–13
All Reviewers to display comments from all reviewers option, 249
All styles option, Style Pane Options dialog box, 169

Allow all users of this worksheet to box, Excel, 341
Allow drop-down list, Excel, 326
Allow Typing option, View Options drop-down menu, 152, 250
Alphabetical option, Style Pane Options, 169
Always ask where to send option, OneNote Options dialog box, 662
Always AutoFormat area, AutoCorrect dialog box, 48
Always option, Word, 218
Always send item, Outlook, 634
animations, adding to presentations
    adding to objects, 479
    animating charts, 485
    animating SmartArt graphic, 483
    animating tables, 485–486
    changing order of animations, 480–481
    overview, 478
    using animation to display bulleted paragraphs one at time, 481–482
Any value item, Excel, 326
Apply as you type area, Word, 47
Apply Draft Mode command, Excel, 382
Apply Normal Mode command, Excel, 382
Apply Styles pane, Word, 165–167, 183, 186
Apply to drop-down list
    Borders and Shading dialog box, 179–180
    Word, 211
Appointment Recurrence dialog box, Outlook, 590–591
Appointment Series window, Outlook, 591
Appointment window, Outlook, 588–589
Appointments option, context menu, 529
appointments, Outlook
    creating one-time, 587–588
    creating repeating, 589
    defined, 584
arguments, Excel, 360
Arial Black set, Fonts menu, 164
arithmetic operators, Excel, 349
Arrange All option, View panel, 156
Arrange By box, Outlook, 525, 575
Arrange By control option, Outlook, 524
Arrange By drop-down list, Outlook, 525, 575
Arrange group, Outlook, 581
Arrange Windows dialog box, Excel, 306–307
Arrangement group option
    Outlook, 575
    Ribbon, 523–524
Artistic Effects command
    Office programs, 107
    PowerPoint, 466

As One Object option, PowerPoint, 482–485
Aspect Ratio item, Office programs, 110
Assign Task option, Outlook, 609
Assigned view, Outlook, 600
Attachment Tools section, Ribbon, 544–545
attachments
    overview, 543
    receiving files as, 544–546
    sending files as, 543
Attachments option, 524
Audio & Video option dialog, OneNote,
    666–668
Audio & Video pane, OneNote Options dialog
    box, 669–670
Audio & Video section, Ribbon, 669–670
audio icon, PowerPoint, 475
audio, in OneNote, 630, 669–671
Audio recording settings area, OneNote
    Options dialog box, 667
Audio Search area, OneNote Options dialog
    box, 668
Audio Search dialog box, OneNote, 671
Authors icon, status bar, 235
Authors readout, PowerPoint, 431–432
authors, reviewing edits by, 651
Auto Account Setup screen, Add New Account
    wizard, 512–513
AutoCorrect dialog box
    Excel, 401
    OneNote, 45
    Word, 44, 48
AutoCorrect entries, Outlook, 56–57, 135,
    538, 550
AutoCorrect Exceptions dialog box
    Outlook, 50
    Word, 50
AutoCorrect option, 54, 56
AutoCorrect Smart Tag, Excel, 401
AutoCorrect tool
    actions and smart tags, 52
    choosing AutoFormat As You Type
        options, 45–48
    choosing Math AutoCorrect options, 48–49
    choosing options on AutoCorrect tab of
        AutoCorrect dialog box, 45
    creating entries, 49–50
    creating exceptions, 50
    overview, 43–44
AutoFill feature, entering data quickly using,
    293–295
AutoFilter feature, Excel, 406
AutoFilter list, Excel, 406
AutoFit behavior area, Word, 89, 201

AutoFit body text to placeholder option,
    PowerPoint, 48
AutoFit, Excel, 314, 356
AutoFit Row Height command, Excel, 313
AutoFit several columns, Excel, 314
AutoFit title text to placeholder option,
    PowerPoint, 48
AutoFit to contents, Word, 201
AutoFit to window, Word, 201
AutoFormat As You Type options, Office,
    45–48
AutoFormat Column Width command,
    Excel, 314
AutoFormat feature, 48
Automatic bulleted lists option, Word, 47
Automatic numbered lists option, Word, 47
automatic recalculation, Excel, 353
automatically launching with Windows,
    opening programs by, 12–13
AutoPreview item Add Animation drop-down
    panel, PowerPoint, 480
AutoRecover file, 133
AutoRecover files, 131–133, 259–260
AutoRecover settings, 132–133
Autosaved Version bar, Word, 260
AutoSum drop-down list, Excel, 364
AutoText entries
    inserting text with Word, 136–138
    printing with Word, 265
AutoText submenu, 137
Available actions list box, AutoCorrect dialog
    box, 53
Available Templates and Themes pane,
    PowerPoint, 14
Available Templates pane, 14
axes, chart components, 372–373
Axis Labels dialog box, Excel, 386
Axis labels drop-down list, Excel, 385
Axis Options category, Excel, 384
axis titles, adding to chart in Excel, 383

■ B

Background Color drop-down panel,
    Excel, 390
Backstage
    Excel, 283
    Office, 37–38
    OneNote, 637
    overview, 9–10
    PowerPoint, 413–414
Backup area, OneNote Options dialog box, 660
backups, of Word documents, 147–148

Balloons area, Track Changes Options dialog box, 242, 255

Balloons submenu, Show Markup drop-down menu, 249

Banner Area, Outlook, 581

bar chart type, Excel, 374

Base box, Excel, 385

Basic Text group
    OneNote, 77, 631
    Outlook, 78

Battery Options area, OneNote Options dialog box, 665

Before sheet list box, Excel, 303

Behaviors drop-down list, OneNote, 638

Behind Text item, Outlook, 105

Black option, Color scheme drop-down list, 130

Blank document icon, Word, 14

Blank layout, PowerPoint, 441

Blank option, Word, 205

Blank presentation item, PowerPoint, 14, 414

Blank workbook item, Excel, 14, 284

Blocked Senders list, Outlook, 553

Blood Pressure Tracker template, Excel, 285

Body Text style, 160, 163

Bookmark dialog box, Word, 213–215

Bookmark item, Word, 219

Bookmark name list box, Word, 214–215

Bookmark option, 197

Bookmark text item, Word, 220

bookmarks, Word
    deleting, 215
    displaying, 214
    insert, 213
    navigating, 214

Border Color category, Excel, 391

Border lines option, Word, 47

Border style, Excel, 330

borders
    in Excel, 322–323
    in Word, 178–180

Borders and Shading dialog box, 178, 180

Borders and Shading option, 178–179

Borders drop-down list
    Excel, 322–323
    Word/PowerPoint/Outlook, 92

Borders section, Excel, 322

Bottom alignment, Excel, 321

Bottom of page option, Word, 229

Box option, Borders and Shading dialog box, 179

brackets, Excel, 346

breaks for columns, Word, 212

Breaks panel, Word, 204

brightness, of graphics, 106–107

Bring to Front command, Office programs, 113

Broadcast Slide Show dialog box, PowerPoint, 506–508

Browse dialog box, Outlook, 568

Browse For Folder dialog box, Windows, 562–563

Browse Object, Word, 141–142

bubble chart type, Excel, 374

Building Blocks option, 136, 146

Built-in Heading styles option, Word, 47

Bulleted dialog box, PowerPoint, 448

bulleted lists style, 161, 447

Bullets and Numbering dialog box, PowerPoint, 448–449, 451

bullets in styles, Word, 178

Bullets panel, PowerPoint, 448

Business box, Outlook, 559

Business Card view, Outlook, 572–573

Business Fax box, Outlook, 559

By branch one by one option, PowerPoint, 484

By Category option, PowerPoint, 485

By Element in Category option, PowerPoint, 485

By Element in Series option, PowerPoint, 485

By level at once option, PowerPoint, 484

By level one by one option, PowerPoint, 484

By Paragraph item, PowerPoint, 482

By Series option, PowerPoint, 485

▓ **C**

CA (certificate authority), 274

Cache file location area, OneNote Options dialog box, 661

Calculate Now command, Excel, 353

Calculate Sheet command, Excel, 353

calculations, in OneNote, 635

Calendar and Tasks view, Outlook, 585

Calendar area, Outlook, 520, 535

Calendar category, Outlook, 583

Calendar List, Outlook, 580

Calendar Only view, Outlook, 586

Calendar, Outlook
    appointments
        creating one-time quickly, 587
        creating one-time with full details, 587
        creating repeating, 589
        defined, 584
        dates to display, 581

events
creating one-time with full details, 587
creating repeating, 589
defined, 584
meetings
creating, 591
defined, 584
replying to invitations, 595
tracking status of invitations, 594
overview, 579–580
settings for, 583
views in, 585
Capitalize first letter of sentences option, AutoCorrect dialog box, 45
Capitalize names of days option, AutoCorrect dialog box, 45
CAPTCHA test, 563
Card view, Outlook, 573–574
case matching, Word, 191
Categories drop-down list, Word, 216
categories, Excel, 373
Categories list box, Customize Keyboard dialog box, 146
category axis, Excel, 372
CBR (constant bit rate), 668
Cc box, Outlook, 536–537
cell references, Excel, 346
Cell Styles panel, Excel, 330–332, 334
cells, in Excel
alignment, 320
borders and fills, 322–323
copying and moving data with drag and drop, 299–300
deleting, 311–312
editing, 291–292
entering data quickly using AutoFill, 293–295
font formatting, 321
inserting, 311–312
moving active cell, 288–289
number formatting, 317
pasting data into worksheets, 296–299
protection of, 323
selecting and manipulating, 289–290
themes, 320
tools for applying formatting, 315
typing data in, 290
cells, in Word tables, 90
Center Across Selection command, Excel, 320
Center alignment, Excel, 320–321
Centered option, Paragraph dialog box, 174
Centered Overlay Title item, Excel, 382
certificate authority (CA), 274

Change All option, 56
Change box, Word, 273
Change Chart Type option, Excel, 378
Change File Type pane, Word, 277–279
Change Layout box, Office programs, 112
Change Layout drop-down panel, Office programs, 112
Change option, Spelling and Grammar dialog box, 56, 59
Change Styles drop-down menu, 164
Change text box, Word, 273
Change the appearance of your displays box, 492
Change View drop-down panel, Outlook, 572, 599–600
Changed lines drop-down list, 241
Changes group, Ribbon, 249
chart area, Excel, 372
Chart data range box, Excel, 379
Chart dialog box, Excel, 377
Chart Elements drop-down list, Excel, 390–391
Chart Elements submenu, Excel, 389
Chart Name text box, Excel, 390
chart sheets, Excel
changing to from embedded chart, 377
vs. embedded charts, 369
chart title, Excel, 373
Chart Title placeholder, Excel, 383
Chart Tools section, Ribbon, 459–461
charts
animating, 485
in Excel
adding components to, 382–387
applying style to, 381
components of, 371–373
creating, 375–377
custom chart types, 392
data series, 380
embedded, 369, 377
formatting of, 388–391
gridlines to display, 387
layout for, 379
naming embedded chart, 390
numbering of axis, 384
scale of, 384
source data for, 378
switching rows and columns in, 378
types of, 373–378, 392
in slides, 457–462
creating in new embedded workbooks, 458
pasting from Excel into PowerPoint, 460–462
Charts group, Excel, 375–376

Check Address dialog box, Outlook, 559–560
Check Full Name dialog box, Outlook, 556–557
Check Names dialog box, Outlook, 557–558
Check Phone Number dialog box, Outlook, 559
Choose a broadcast service box,
    PowerPoint, 506
Choose a SmartArt Graphic dialog box
    Office programs, 110
    PowerPoint, 456
Choose an action to perform box, Outlook,
    564, 568
Choose commands from drop-down list,
    Excel, 124, 399
Choose File to Merge with Current
    Presentation dialog box,
    PowerPoint, 435
Choose File to Upload dialog box, 31
Choose Theme dialog box, PowerPoint, 468
Circular Reference Warning dialog box,
    Excel, 359
circular references and formulas, Excel,
    359–360
Circular References status bar message,
    Excel, 360
Circular References submenu, Excel, 360
Classic Start menu, 11–12
Classic view, Outlook, 586
Clear Narration on Current Slide item,
    PowerPoint, 504
Clear Narrations on All Slides item,
    PowerPoint, 504
Clear submenu, PowerPoint, 504
Click here to add a new Task box, Outlook, 601
Click to add text, PowerPoint, 420
Click to add title text, PowerPoint, 420
Clip Art icon, PowerPoint, 92–93
clip art, inserting, 93–94
Clip Art pane, PowerPoint, 465
Clip Art task pane, Office programs, 93–94
Clip Organizer program, 93, 95–96
Clipboard, 79–81
Clipboard group
    Excel, 297
    Home tab, 184
    Office programs, 79
Clipboard task pane, Office programs, 79–81
Close command, Backstage, 10, 38
Close Header and Footer option, Word, 207
closing
    document, 17
    program, 21
Codec drop-down list, OneNote Options
    dialog box, 667

collaborating, on PowerPoint presentations
    comparing two copies of presentation,
        435–437
    editing simultaneously, 431
    overview, 430
collapsing and expanding headings in Outline
    view, Word, 223–224
Collated drop-down list, Backstage, 69
colleagues
    editing documents simultaneously
        with, 234
    sharing documents on networks with, 238
    using Track Changes feature, 243
    working on documents with, 233–234
Collect Without Showing Office Clipboard
    item, Office programs, 81
Color Categories dialog box, Outlook, 561
Color drop-down list
    Borders and Shading dialog box, 179–180
    Bullets and Numbering dialog box,
        449–450
    Notebook Properties dialog box, 642
    OneNote Unpack Notebook dialog
        box, 678
    Track Changes Options dialog box,
        241–242
Color drop-down panel, Office programs, 107
Color Saturation section, Office programs, 107
Color Scales panel, Excel, 325
Color scheme drop-down list, Excel, 129–130
Color Tone section, Office programs, 107
Colors dialog box, PowerPoint, 449
colors, of graphics, 106–107
Colors panel, PowerPoint, 417
Column Break expression, Word, 212
column breaks, Word, 212
column chart type, Excel, 374
Column headings, Excel, 286
Column option, Word, 212
Column panel, Excel, 375
Column Width dialog box, Excel, 314
columns
    in Excel, 378
        deleting, 311–312
        freezing, 308
        hiding, 314–315
        inserting, 311–312
        inserting and deleting, 311–312
        width, 314
    in Word, 209–212
Columns box, Remove Duplicates dialog
    box, 405
Columns dialog box, Word, 210–212

Columns panel, Word, 210
Combine Documents dialog box, Word, 257
Comma required before last list item
        option, 63
Comma Separated Values (Windows) item,
        Outlook, 565
commands, giving from Ribbon tool, 35
Commands list box, 146
Commands Not in the Ribbon option, 121,
        146, 399
commas
        Excel, 347
        Word, 200
comma-separated values (CSV) file, 561, 563
Comment on the panel option, 255
Comment option, 141, 197
Comment text box, Excel, 349
comments
        adding, 252–254
        deleting, 256
        viewing and reviewing, 255
Comments option, 152, 248, 298
comments pane, Word, 252–253, 255
common features of Office programs
        Backstage, 9–10
        control menu, 8
        overview, 6
        Quick Access Toolbar, 8
        Ribbon, 9
        status bar, 10
        title bar, 7
Common Symbols option, 146
Compact option, 164
Company box, Outlook, 556–557
Compare Documents dialog box, Word,
        256–257
Compare feature, PowerPoint, 430, 435
Compare group, PowerPoint, 436
Compare Side by Side dialog box, Excel, 308
comparing two copies, of PowerPoint
        presentation, 435–437
Comparison layout, PowerPoint, 440
compatibility of documents, with earlier
        versions of Word, 277
Compatibility submenu, Excel, 365
Completed item, Outlook, 602
Completed view, Outlook, 600
conditional formatting, in Excel, 324–325
Conditional Formatting panel, Excel, 324–325
Confirm Password dialog box
        Excel, 340–341
        Word, 270
Confirm Password text box, 645

Conflicting change between users area,
        Excel, 343
Conflicting changes pane, Word, 237
Congratulations! screen, Add New Account
        wizard, 513–514
Connect to a projector link, Windows, 492
constant bit rate (CBR), 668
contact window, Outlook, 556, 560
Contacts area, 520, 535
Contacts folder, Outlook, 566
Contacts group, Outlook, 571
Contacts list, Outlook, 609
Contacts pane, Outlook, 576
Contacts screen, Outlook, 571
Content with Caption layout, PowerPoint, 441
Context menu
        OneNote, 624
        Outlook, 577
        PowerPoint, 422, 497
contrast, of graphics, 106–107
control menu, 8
conversations, viewing in Message List,
        525–526
Convert Notes dialog box, Word, 229–230
Copies text box, Backstage, 69
Copy and Paste, entering text using, 71
Copy item, Office programs, 95
Copy Link item, PowerPoint, 507
Copy option, 13, 454
Copy Page To command, OneNote, 655
Copy Text from Picture command,
        OneNote, 72
Copy to Collection dialog box, Office
        programs, 95–96
Copy to Collection item, Office programs, 95
copying. See also Cut, Copy, and Paste
        with drag and drop, 299–300
        formulas, Excel, 355–356
        slides from another presentation, 422
        styles from one workbook to another, 333
Correct accidental use of caps LOCK key
        option, 45
Correct TWo INitial CApitals option,
        AutoCorrect dialog box, 45
Corrections command, PowerPoint, 466
Corrections drop-down panel, Office
        programs, 106–107
Corrections panel, PowerPoint, 468
COUNT( ) function, Excel, 360
COUNTBLANK( ) function, Excel, 398
Create a PDF/XPS Document pane,
        Word, 279
Create Custom Dictionary dialog box, 65

Create Handouts in Microsoft Word pane, PowerPoint, 501
Create Handouts item, PowerPoint, 501
Create New Building Block dialog box, 137–138
Create New Folder dialog box, Outlook, 548–549
Create New Style from Formatting dialog box, 165, 170, 181–183
Create PDF/XPS Document item, Word, 279
Crop command, PowerPoint, 470
Crop to Shape item, Office programs, 110
Crop tool, Office programs, 109
cropping graphics, 108
Cross-reference dialog box, Word, 219–220
Cross-reference option, Word, 216, 218–219
CSV (comma-separated values) file
    importing Outlook contacts from, 564
    Windows, 562
Cube submenu, Excel, 365
Currency format, Excel, 318, 351
Currency formatting, Excel, 317
Current keys list box, 146
Current Location list, Backstage, 43
Current Page option, Backstage Print Preview and Settings dialog box, 672
Current Section option, Backstage Print Preview and Settings dialog box, 672
Current Selection group, Excel, 389
Current Slide Time box, PowerPoint, 495, 504
Current View group, Outlook, 599–600
Currently assigned to area, Customize Keyboard dialog box, 147
Custom area, Excel, 332
Custom AutoFilter dialog box, Excel, 408
Custom box, Excel, 307
Custom category, Excel, 330
custom chart types, Excel, 392
Custom dialog box, Outlook, 607
custom dictionaries. See dictionaries, custom
Custom Dictionaries dialog box, 64–67
Custom Format item, Excel, 319, 325
Custom item
    Excel, 327
    Outlook, 607
Custom List dialog box, Excel, 403
Custom List option, Sort dialog box, 403
Custom lists box, Excel, 296
Custom Lists dialog box, Excel, 295–296
Custom mark box, Word, 229
Custom Scaling Options, Excel, 339
Custom shows box, PowerPoint, 488
Custom Shows dialog box, PowerPoint, 487–489

Custom shows list, PowerPoint, 488–489
custom slide layouts, 441
custom slide shows, 486–489
custom styles, 331
Custom.dic dictionary, 64
Customize Keyboard dialog box, 145, 147
Customize Notifications option, OneNote, 638
Customize Quick Access Toolbar drop-down list, Excel, 120, 399
Customize Quick Access Toolbar menu, 118, 120, 399
Customize Quick Access Toolbar option, 119, 121
Customize Ribbon item, 122, 125
Customize Ribbon option, 125
Customize Ribbon pane, 122–123, 126, 145
Customize Status Bar menu
    Excel, 127
    Word, 204
Customize the Ribbon drop-down list, 123
Customize the Ribbon option, 122
customizing Office
    General options pane, 128
    Quick Access Toolbar
        adding Ribbon command to, 119
        moving to below Ribbon, 122
        overview, 117
        sharing customizations of, 125
    Ribbon, 122–125
    Save options
        AutoRecover settings, 132–133
        default file location, 133–134
        default format for, 131–132
        overview, 130
    status bar, 126–127
Cut, Copy, and Paste
    Clipboard, 79–81
    Paste options, 81
    pasting data into worksheets, 296–299
    standard, 79

■ D

data
    entering in Excel database tables, 398–401
    Excel worksheet, creating tables from, 455–456
    labels
        adding to chart, Excel, 386–387
        chart components, Excel, 373
    markers, Excel, 373
    series, Excel, 373–380
Data and Model category, Excel, 331

Data Bars panel, Excel, 325
Data drop-down list End time box, Excel, 327
Data drop-down list, Excel, 327
Data Form command, Excel, 399
Data Validation dialog box, Excel, 326, 328–329
data-entry form, Excel, 394
Date & Time category, Word, 216
Date & Time drop-down list, Excel, 365
Date (Conversations) option, 524
Date and Time dialog box, Word, 216
Date and Time option, Word, 216
Date Filters submenu, AutoFilter drop-down
    list, 409–410
Date formatting
    Excel, 317, 319
    Word, 217
Date item, Excel, 327
Date Navigator and the Calendars list,
    Outlook, 579
Date Navigator, Outlook, 529, 579, 585–586
Day view, Outlook, 579
Decimal item, Excel, 327
Decrease List Level option, PowerPoint, 447
Decrease Text Size option, 151
default file location, Save options, 133–134
Default file location text box, 133
default format, for saving documents, 131–132
Default reminder time drop-down list,
    Outlook, 603
Default style, Style Set submenu, 163
Deferred item, Outlook, 602
Define Custom Show dialog box, PowerPoint,
    487–489
Define styles based on your formatting option,
    Word, 48
Delay text box, PowerPoint, 480
Delete All Comments in Document command,
    Word, 256
Delete All Versions in Notebook command,
    Page Versions menu, 655
Delete All Versions in Section command, Page
    Versions menu, 655
Delete All Versions in Section Group
    command, Page Versions menu, 655
Delete dialog box, Excel, 312–313
Delete from Clip Organizer item, Office
    programs, 95
Delete key, PowerPoint, 422
Delete option
    OneNote, 620
    Outlook, 608
Delete Outlook Task context menu option,
    OneNote, 677

Delete Sheet Columns command, Excel, 312
Delete Sheet Rows command, Excel, 312
Delete Version command, OneNote, 655
deleting
    cells, 311–312
    columns, 311–312
    messages, 547–549
    rows, 311–312
    styles, 334
    worksheets, 301
Deletions drop-down list, Track Changes
    Options dialog box, 241
demoting and promoting, headings in Outline
    view, 223
depth axis title, Excel, 373, 383
Depth Gridlines submenu, Excel, 387
Description area
    Create New Building Block dialog box, 137
    Customize Keyboard dialog box, 146
Detailed view, Outlook, 600–601
Details pane
    Outlook, 560, 606
    PowerPoint, 434
Details to display the Details section,
    Outlook, 560
Device drop-down list, OneNote Options
    dialog box, 667–668
.dic file extension, 64
dictionaries, custom
    adding words to or removing words
        from, 66
    creating, 65
    overview, 64
    turning off, removing, or deleting, 67
Dictionary language drop-down list
    Custom Dictionaries dialog box, 65
    Options dialog box, 61
Dictionary List box, Custom Dictionaries
    dialog box, 65–67
digital distribution, creating documents
    for, 279
digital signature, signing document with,
    274–277
direct formatting
    applying to text and graphics, 76–78
    in Word
        overview, 183
        using Format Painter, 184
        viewing formatting applied to text,
            185–188
        when to use, 159–160
Direction drop-down list, Excel, 290
Disable AutoRecover, Excel, 133

Disable History for This Notebook command, OneNote, 655
Disappear animation, PowerPoint, 478
Display for Review drop-down menu, Word, 248
Display Name text box, 124, 642
display names, changing for notebooks, 641
Display option dialog, OneNote, 657
Display options, OneNote Options dialog box, 658
Display units drop-down list, Excel, 385
Distributed alignment, Excel, 320–321
division calculation, OneNote, 635
Dock to Desktop option, OneNote, 637
Document Automation option, Word, 216
Document Combine feature, Word, 256
Document Compare feature, Word, 234, 256
Document format, Word, 278
Document Information option, Word, 216
Document Inspector dialog box, Word, 266–267
Document Inspector, Word, 266, 268
document printouts, OneNote, 630
Document Properties item, Word, 265
document properties, printing in Word, 265
document type drop-down menu, SkyDrive, 26
Document Updates Available section, PowerPoint, 433
documents
    checking spelling in, 55–57
    closing, 17
    collaborating on, 233–234
    comments
        adding, 252–254
        deleting, 256
        viewing and reviewing, 255
    comparing or combining versions of, 256–259
    copying from PCs to SkyDrive, 30
    creating, 13–14, 26–27
    downloading from SkyDrive to PCs, 30–32
    editing simultaneously with colleagues, 234
    in Office Web Apps, saving changes to, 28
    opening, 18, 27
    printing, 67
    saving, 15–17
        to SharePoint servers, 42
        to SkyDrive, 29, 41
    sending via e-mails, 39–40
    sharing with colleagues on networks, 238

Track Changes feature, Word
    choosing changes, 240
    controlling which changes Word displays, 248
    ensuring colleagues use, 243
    integrating tracked changes into documents, 249–250
    overview, 239
    turning on, 243
    using in Full Screen Reading view, 250
    viewing document's changes and markup, 248
    working in documents, 247
    versions, 259
Documents folder, 16
Documents library, 15
Don't Correct text box, AutoCorrect Exceptions dialog box, 51
Double option, 164
doughnut chart type, Excel, 374
down arrow key, Excel, 292
Down option
    Find and Replace dialog box, 191
    Search drop-down list, 196
download dialog box, SkyDrive, 32
Download link, SkyDrive, 32
Draft and Outline views text box, 168
Draft mode, Excel, 382
Draft view, Word, 149, 154, 167–168, 185, 204, 226–228, 247
drag and drop, copying and moving data with, 299–300
Draw Borders section, Excel, 322
Drawing Tools section, Office programs, 100, 112
drawings, adding to page in OneNote, 632
Due date box, Outlook, 602
Duplicate Selected Slides item, PowerPoint, 421, 441
Duplicate slide option, PowerPoint, 421
Duration text box, PowerPoint, 478, 480
Dynamic Content transitions, PowerPoint, 476

■ E

earlier versions of Word, creating documents compatible with, 277
Edit Field option, Word, 218
Edit Footer option, Word, 207
Edit Hyperlink dialog box, Office programs, 116
Edit Keywords item, Office programs, 96
Edit link, SkyDrive, 29

Edit Series dialog box, Excel, 381
Edit signature box, Outlook, 551
Editing area
    Backstage, 245
    Excel, 290
    OneNote Options dialog box, 664
Editing group, PowerPoint, 472
editing simultaneously, of PowerPoint
        presentations, 431
Editor Options dialog box, 44, 60
Effects drop-down list
    Excel, 320
    PowerPoint, 417
Effects panel, PowerPoint, 417
Elegant style, Style Set submenu, 163
E-mail account drop-down list, 551
E-mail Accounts screen, Account
        Configuration wizard, 512
E-mail Address box, Add New Account
        wizard, 513
E-mail address box, Office programs, 115
E-mail box, Outlook, 557–558
E-mail Page menu option, OneNote, 675
e-mails, sending documents via, 39–40
embedded charts
    changing to chart sheet, 377
    vs. chart sheets, 369
    creating in workbooks, 458
Embedding pane, YouTube, 473
Enclosed Alphanumerics subset, Office
        programs, 74
Encrypt Document dialog box, Word, 270–271
Encrypt PDF Document dialog box, Word, 282
Encrypt with Password option, Word, 270–271
encrypting with password, Word, 270–271
End of document option, Word, 229
End of section, Word, 229
end of word, Find command, 193
End time box
    Excel, 327
    Outlook, 584, 588
Endnote item, Word, 219
Endnote option
    Go To tab, 197
    Select Browse Object panel, 141
Endnotes drop-down list, Word, 229
Endnotes option, Word, 228
endnotes, Word. *See* footnotes and endnotes, Word
Enforce accented uppercase in French option,
        Options dialog box, 61
Engineering submenu, Excel, 365
Enter new password box, Start Enforcing
        Protection dialog box, 246

Enter Password text box
    Password Protection task pane, 645
    Protected Section dialog box, 646
Enter Text dialog box, Insert File dialog
        box, 136
entering
    data in worksheets
        copying and moving data with drag and
            drop, 299–300
        editing cells, 291–292
        entering data quickly using AutoFill,
            293–295
        pasting data into worksheet, 296–299
        typing data in cells, 290
    text
        by scanning document and using OCR,
            71–72
        symbols, 72–75
        using Copy and Paste, 71
        by using speech recognition, 72
Entrance animations, PowerPoint, 478
entries, creating in AutoCorrect tool, 49–50
Equal column, Word, 211
Equation command item, Word, 219
Equation item, Word, 219
Equation menu, Word, 216
Equations and Formulas option, Word, 216
Erase All Ink on Slide command,
        PowerPoint, 499
Eraser item
    PowerPoint, 499
    Word/PowerPoint/Outlook, 89
Even Page Footer item, Excel, 335
Even Page Header item, Excel, 335
Even Page option, Word, 207
events, Outlook
    creating one-time with full details, 587
    creating repeating, 589
    defined, 584
Excel
    exporting OneNote notebook to, 675
    navigating
        moving active cell, 288–289
        overview, 285–287
        selecting and manipulating cells, 289–290
    overview, 2–3
    pasting charts into PowerPoint from,
        460–462
    Save options in
        AutoRecover settings, 132–133
        default file location, 133–134
        default format for, 131–132
        overview, 130

Excel (*continued*)
   worksheet data
      creating tables from, 455–456
      importing Outlook contacts from, 568
Excel Options dialog box, 290, 295, 399, 401
exceptions, creating in AutoCorrect tool, 50
Exit animations, PowerPoint, 478, 486
Exit command, 10, 21, 39
Exit option, Backstage pane, 21
expanding and collapsing, headings in Outline
      view, 223–224
Export All Customizations option, Options
      dialog box, 125
Export screen, 563
Export Windows Contacts dialog box,
      Outlook, 562
exporting presentations, 504–510
Extend mode, Word, 139–140
Extend Selection feature, Word, 139–140
extra arguments, Excel, 361
extra windows, opening in Word, 155

F

Fade Animation, PowerPoint, 484
Fade Duration area, PowerPoint, 472
Fade In box, PowerPoint, 472
Fade Out box, PowerPoint, 472
Favorites category, Outlook, 518
features common to all Office programs
   Backstage, 9–10
   control menu, 8
   overview, 6
   Quick Access Toolbar, 8
   Ribbon, 9
   status bar, 10
   title bar, 7
Field dialog box, Word, 215–218
Field names list box, Word, 217
Field option
   Go To tab, 197
   Select Browse Object panel, 141
   Word, 217
Field properties panel, Word, 217
Field shading drop-down list, Word, 218
fields
   multiple Excel database table, 402
   single Excel database table, 402
   Word, 215–218
File as box, Outlook, 556–557
File Download dialog box, 32
File in Use dialog box, Word, 238–239
File Locations dialog box, 143–145

file locations for templates, Word, 143
File name box, Excel, 392
File Name text box
   Create Custom Dictionary dialog box, 65
   OneNote Save As dialog box, 677
   Save As dialog box, 16
File Now Available dialog box, Word, 239
File Open dialog box, 126
File Save dialog box, 125
File Types area, Word, 277, 279
File types list box, File Locations dialog
      box, 144
Files of type drop-down list, Backstage Open
      Notebook dialog box, 677
Fill category, Excel, 389, 391
Fill Colors drop-down list, Excel, 323
Fill drop-down list, Borders and Shading
      dialog box, 180
Fill pane, Excel, 389
Fill style, Excel, 330
fills, in Excel, 322–323
Final option
   Display for Review drop-down menu, 248
   Show Original/Final Document, 152
Final: Show Markup option, Display for
      Review drop-down menu, 248
Final with Markup option, Show
      Original/Final Document, 152
finalizing document, Word
   and compatibility with earlier versions of
      Word, 277
   for digital distribution, 279
   encrypting with password, 270–271
   marking as final, 268–269
   permissions for, 271–274
   removing sensitive information, 266
   signing with digital signature, 274–277
Financial drop-down list, Excel, 365
Find and Replace dialog box
   Excel, 84–85, 406
   Excel/PowerPoint/Outlook, 85
   keyboard shortcuts, 190
   Office programs, 84, 86
   Word, 86
   Word/Excel/Outlook, 84, 87
Find command, Word
   all forms of word, 192
   case matching, 191
   format searching, 194–195
   highlighting instances found, 191
   ignoring punctuation and white space, 193
   overview, 189–190
   search direction, 191

searching for special characters, 192
searching only part of document, 191
searching only start or end of word, 193
using wildcards, 191
whole word matching, 191
words that sound like other words, 192
Find dialog box, PowerPoint, 84–86
Find feature, Excel, 406
Find option, 141–142
Find Style dialog box, 195
Find what box, Find and Replace dialog box, 194–197, 406
Find what text box, Find and Replace dialog box, 192
First day of week drop-down list, Outlook, 584
First line option, Paragraph dialog box, 174
First Page Footer item, Excel, 335
First Page Header item, Excel, 335
Fit All Columns on One Page item, Excel, 339
Fit All Rows on One Page item, Excel, 339
Fit Sheet on One Page item, Excel, 339
Fit to Slide layout, PowerPoint, 468
Fixed column width option, Word, 201
Flag repeated words option, Options dialog box, 61
Flesch Reading Ease statistic, 62
Flesch-Kincaid Grade Level statistic, 62
Fly In animation, PowerPoint, 482
Folder contains drop-down list, Create New Folder dialog box, 549
Folder List, Navigation Pane, 520
folders, Junk E-mail, 552
Font dialog box, 172–173, 184, 442–443, 523
Font drop-down list
    Office programs, 74, 78
    Ribbon, 442
font formatting, in Excel, 321
Font group
    Excel, 77, 316–317, 321–323, 329
    Home tab, 159–160, 184
    Office programs, 77
    Ribbon, 442–443, 455–456
    Word, 77
    Word/PowerPoint/Outlook, 92
Font list, Reveal Formatting pane, 187
font size, changing in slides, 442
Font Size drop-down list
    Excel, 315
    Office programs, 78
Font styles, Excel, 330
Fonts drop-down list, Excel, 320
Fonts menu, Change Styles drop-down menu, 164

Fonts option, Categories list box, 146
Fonts panel, PowerPoint, 417
Footer drop-down list, Backstage Print Preview and Settings dialog box, 673
Footer from Bottom box, Word, 206
Footer panel, Word, 205
footers
    in Excel, 334
    in Word, 205–208
Footnote and Endnote dialog box, Word, 228–230
Footnote item, Word, 219
Footnote option
    Go To tab, 197
    Select Browse Object panel, 141
footnotes and endnotes, Word
    adding endnote, 227
    adding footnote, 226
    converting, 229
    customizing, 228
    displaying, 230–231
    navigating, 230–231
    overview, 225
Footnotes drop-down list, Word, 229
Footnotes group, Word, 228
For all documents option, Excel Options dialog box, 399
Foreground Color drop-down panel, Excel, 390
Form command, Excel, 399
Form dialog box, Excel, 399–401
Format area, Word, 229
Format Axis dialog box, Excel, 384–385
Format Cells dialog box, Excel, 317–318, 320–323, 325, 329, 332
Format Data Labels dialog box, Excel, 390
Format dialog box
    Excel, 389–391
    Office programs, 103–104
Format drop-down list
    Modify Style dialog box, 183
    OneNote Options dialog box, 668
Format drop-down menu, Find and Replace dialog box, 194–195
Format group, Ribbon, 539
Format item, Excel, 390
Format line, Find and Replace dialog box, 197
Format Painter, Word, 184
Format Picture dialog box, Excel, 335
Format Plot Area dialog box, Excel, 390
Format Shape dialog box, Office programs, 103
Format Text Effects dialog box, PowerPoint, 445–446
Format Walls dialog box, Excel, 389

formatted AutoCorrect entries, Word, 50
formatting, 311–344
    cells, 311–312
    charts, Excel
        copying formatting, 391
        individual elements, 390–391
        wall and floor, 388–389
    columns, 311–315
    conditional formatting, 324–325
    direct, applying to text and graphics, 76–78
    headers and footers, 334
    rows, 311–315
    shapes, 98–101
    with styles, 329–334
    table formatting, 329
    tables, 91–92
    in Word
        direct formatting, 183–188
        overview, 159
        recommended way of, 161
        replacing, 196
        searching for, 194–195
        setting for styles, 172–180
        using styles, 162–171
Formatting area, Track Changes Options
        dialog box, 242, 245
Formatting dialog box, 172
Formatting drop-down list, Track Changes
        Options dialog box, 242
Formatting exceptions area, Paragraph dialog
        box, 177
Formatting icon, Excel, 333
Formatting option
    Show Comments and Changes, 152
    Show Markup drop-down menu, 249
Formatting Restrictions dialog box, 244–245
forms, data-entry, 399–401
Formula bar, Excel, 286, 352–354
Formula result readout, Excel, 366
formulas, Excel
    cell references in, 346
    copying and pasting, 355–356
    and difference from functions, 345
    named cells and ranges in, 348–349
    nesting parts of formulas, 355
    operators for, 349–353
    order of operators evaluation, 354–355
    range references in, 347
    troubleshooting
        circular references, 359–360
        common errors in, 356
        displaying all formulas in worksheet, 358
        seeing error details, 357

    with Trace Precedents command, 358–359
    tracing error source, 357
    using AutoFill, 355–356
Forward option, Outlook, 613
forwarding messages, 546
Fraction format, Excel, 319
Frame shape drop-down list, PowerPoint, 468
Free/Busy Options dialog box, Outlook, 561
Freeze First Column command, Excel, 308
Freeze Panes command, Excel, 309
Freeze Top Row command, Excel, 308
French modes drop-down list, Options dialog
        box, 61
Full Name box, Outlook, 556
Full Page view, OneNote, 636–638
Full Screen Reading view, Word, 150–152, 204,
        209, 250
Full Screen view, Excel, 303–304
Function Arguments dialog box, Excel,
        364–366
Function drop-down list, Excel, 360–361
Function Library, Excel, 364–365
functions calculation, OneNote, 635
functions, Excel
    and arguments for, 360, 365–366
    cell references in, 346
    and difference from formulas, 345
    inserting
        with Function drop-down list, 361
        with Function Library, 364–365
        with Insert Function dialog box, 363–364
        by typing into worksheet, 367
    named cells and ranges in, 348–349
    range references in, 347

■ G

Gallery drop-down list, Create New Building
        Block dialog box, 137
General alignment, Excel, 320
General category, Excel, 315
General command, Excel, 353
General format, Excel, 317–318, 353
General options pane, 128
General section
    OneNote, 618, 620
    Outlook, 558
Glow and Soft Edges category, Excel, 391
Gmail contacts, importing Outlook contacts
        from, 563
Go To command, Word, 197–198
Go To option, Select Browse Object
        panel, 142

Go to Section submenu, PowerPoint, 497
Go to Slide command, PowerPoint, 497
Go to Slide menu, PowerPoint, 486
Go to what box, Find and Replace dialog
    box, 197
Good, Bad and Neutral category, Excel, 331
Google Contacts, Outlook, 561
Grammar & Style option, Options dialog
    box, 63
grammar, checking in Word and Outlook
    choosing grammar and style options,
        62–64
    controlling how spelling checker
        works, 59
    overview, 57–58
Grammar Only option, Options dialog
    box, 63
Grammar Settings dialog box, 63–64
Graphic option
    Go To tab, 197
    Select Browse Object panel, 141
graphics
    adding and formatting shapes, 98–101
    adding to page in OneNote, 632
    adding to presentations, 465–466
    applying direct formatting to, 76–78
    applying style to, 108
    arranging to control which is visible, 112
    brightness, 106–107
    choosing where to insert, 92
    colors, 106–107
    contrast, 106–107
    cropping, 108
    inserting clip art, 93–94
    inserting pictures, 97
    inserting SmartArt, 110
    positioning, 92–103
    rotating, 102
    sharpness, 106–107
    using Cut, Copy, and Paste with
        Clipboard, 79–81
        Paste options, 81
        standard, 79
GREATER THAN box, Excel, 325
gridlines
    chart components, Excel, 373
    of charts, Excel, 387
Gridlines menu, Excel, 387
Group graphic drop-down list,
    PowerPoint, 484
Group text drop-down list, PowerPoint,
    482–483
Growth Trend, Excel, 294

H

handouts for presentations, 501
Hanging option, Paragraph dialog box, 174
Have replies sent to box, Properties dialog
    box, 541
Header & Footer Elements group, Excel, 335
Header & Footer Tools section
    Excel, 334
    Word, 206–207
Header from Top box, Word, 206
Header panel, Word, 205
headers
    in Excel, 334
    in Word
        adding to document, 205–207
        delete, 207
        different, 207
Heading item, Word, 219
Heading option
    Go To tab, 197
    Select Browse Object panel, 141
Heading style, 141, 161, 219
Height box, PowerPoint, 418
height of rows, in Excel worksheets, 313
Help command, Backstage, 39
hidden slides, 486
Hide & Unhide submenu, Excel, 315
Hide Source Documents option, Word, 259
Hide spelling errors in this document only
    option, Word, 62
Hide Window command, Excel, 307
hiding
    columns and rows, Excel, 314–315
    parts of the table, PowerPoint, 486
High Detail option, Outlook, 582
High Importance option, Outlook, 589, 603
Highlight Cells Rules panel, Excel, 325
Highlight Updates option, Show Markup
    drop-down menu, 249
Highlighter item, PowerPoint, 498
highlighting Find command, Word, 191
History group, OneNote, 654, 678
Home box, Outlook, 559
Honeycomb transition, PowerPoint, 477
Horizontal (Category) Axis Labels box,
    Excel, 386
Horizontal alignment, Excel, 320
horizontal axis, Excel, 372–373
Horizontal option, Text Direction panel, 444
horizontal split box, Excel, 304
Horizontal Title item, Excel, 383
hyperlinks, 113, 462–463

I

Icon Sets panel, Excel, 324–325

Icons Only view, Outlook, 611

Ignore All option, 54, 56

Ignore Internet and file addresses option, Options dialog box, 61

Ignore Once option, 56, 58

Ignore Print Area item, Excel, 339

Ignore Rule option, Spelling and Grammar dialog box, 59

Ignore words in UPPERCASE option, Options dialog box, 61

Ignore words that contain numbers option, Options dialog box, 61

Illustrations group, Word, 9

Import and Export Wizard, Outlook, 564, 568

Import Customization File option, 126

Import from another program or file item, Outlook, 564, 568

Importance option, Arrange By control, 525

importing contacts
    CSV file, 564
    Excel worksheet, 568
    Gmail contacts, 563
    mapping custom fields when importing, 570
    overview, 561
    vCard files, 567
    Windows Contacts, 562
    Yahoo! address book, 563

In Front of Text item
    Office programs, 104
    Outlook, 105

In Line with Text item
    Office programs, 104
    Outlook, 105

In Progress item, Outlook, 602

Inbox item, Favorites category, 518

Include in personal view area, Excel, 343

Include non-printing information area, Word, 281

Include this many sheets box drag-and-drop pointer, Excel, 301

Incoming mail server box, Add New Account wizard, 516

Increase List Level option, PowerPoint, 447

Increase Text Size option, View Options drop-down menu, 151

indentation
    Excel, 321
    Paragraph dialog box, 174
    of text, changing in slides, 443

Info command, Backstage, 38

Info pane
    Backstage, 235–236, 243, 260
    Word, 266, 269

Information Management Policy item, 128

Information Rights Management (IRM), 128, 245, 271–272, 282

information, searching for in notes, 642–643

Information submenu, Excel, 365

Initials setting, 130

Initials text box, Options dialog box, 130

Ink option
    Show Comments and Changes, 152
    Show Markup drop-down menu, 248

Input drop-down list, OneNote Options dialog box, 667

Input message box, Excel, 328

Insert and Link command, Office programs, 98

Insert Audio dialog box, PowerPoint, 474

Insert Business Card dialog box, Outlook, 551

Insert Caption command, Word, 219–220

Insert Chart dialog box
    Excel, 373, 376, 392
    PowerPoint, 457–458

Insert Chart icon, PowerPoint, 457–458

Insert dialog box drag-and-drop pointer, Excel, 301

Insert dialog box, Excel, 312

Insert Endnote option, Word, 227

Insert File dialog box, 136, 543

Insert Footnote option, Word, 226

Insert Function dialog box, Excel, 361, 363–365, 398

Insert Hyperlink dialog box, 114
    Outlook, 551
    PowerPoint, 462–463

Insert Media Clip icon, PowerPoint, 92, 469

Insert New Pictures dialog box, PowerPoint, 467

Insert Outline dialog box, PowerPoint, 422

Insert Picture dialog box, 97–98, 107, 112
    Excel, 335, 390
    OneNote, 632
    Outlook, 551
    PowerPoint, 465, 471

Insert Picture from File icon, PowerPoint, 92, 465

Insert reference to drop-down list, Word, 220

Insert Sheet Columns command, Excel, 311

Insert Sheet Rows command, Excel, 311

Insert SmartArt Graphic icon, PowerPoint, 110, 456
Insert Video dialog box, PowerPoint, 469
Insert Video from Web Site dialog box, PowerPoint, 474
inserting
    cells, 311–312
    clip art, 93–94
    columns, 311–312
    files, 135
    graphics
        choosing where to insert, 92
        clip art, 93–94
    page break, Excel, 337
    rows, 311–312
    slides from an outline in document, PowerPoint, 422
    SmartArt, 110
    tables, 88, 199
    text, Word
        from another file, 135
        with AutoText, 136–138
    video file, PowerPoint, 469
    worksheets, 301
insertion point, moving, 75–76
Insertions and Deletions option
    Show Comments and Changes, 152
    Show Markup drop-down menu, 248
Insertions drop-down list, Track Changes Options dialog box, 240
Inspect Document on the drop-down menu, Word, 266
Install the upload tool link, SkyDrive, 31
Internet and network paths with hyperlinks option, AutoCorrect dialog box, 46
Internet E-mail Settings dialog box, Outlook, 516–518
Internet E-mail Settings screen, Add New Account wizard, 514–515
Internet Free-Busy box, Outlook, 561
invitations for meetings, Outlook, 594–595
IRM (Information Rights Management), 128, 245, 271–272, 282

J

Job Title box, Outlook, 557
Junk E-mail folder, Outlook
    marking spam messages as, 553
    removing non-spam messages from, 552
Justified option, Paragraph dialog box, 174
Justify alignment, Excel, 320–321

K

Keep lines together checkbox, Paragraph dialog box, 176
Keep Source Formatting & Embed Workbook option, 461
Keep Source Formatting & Link Data option, 461
Keep Source Formatting item
    Excel, 296
    Word, 83–84
Keep Source Formatting option, 454, 456
Keep Text Only item, Word, 83–84
Key Assignments item, Word, 266
key assignments, printing in Word, 265
keyboard
    controlling presentations using, 499
    controlling Ribbon tool with, 36–37
    navigating with, 75–76
    shortcuts
        Excel, 75, 288, 318
        Office programs, 75, 78–79
        PowerPoint, 499
        Word, 140–141, 145, 166
Keywords dialog box, Office programs, 96

L

Label Changes With text box, Combine Documents dialog box, 257
Landscape item
    Excel, 337
    PowerPoint, 418
Landscape Orientation item, Excel, 339
Language dialog box, 54, 180–181
Language option, 54
larger Mini Toolbar, Excel, 317
larger version of the Mini Toolbar, Excel, 316
Last 7 Days view, Outlook, 613
Last Viewed command, PowerPoint, 498
layout
    for charts in Excel, 379
    layout of slides, 440–441
Layout dialog box, Word/Outlook s, 105–106
Layout view, Word, 227
Left alignment, Excel, 320
Left box, Paragraph dialog box, 174
Left option, Paragraph dialog box, 174
legend, adding to Excel chart, 386
Legend Entries (Series) list box, Excel, 380–381
Legend submenu, Excel, 386
Level at Once option, PowerPoint, 483
Level One by One option, PowerPoint, 483

Line Spacing drop-down list, Paragraph dialog
box, 175
line spacing of text, changing in slides, 443
Line Spacing Options item, Line Spacing
panel, 443
Line spacing, Paragraph dialog box, 175
Link dialog box, OneNote, 115
Link to box, Insert Hyperlink dialog box, 462
Link to column, Office programs, 114
Link to File item, PowerPoint, 469
Link to Previous command, Word, 207
Link to Previous feature, Word, 207
Linked Notes area, OneNote Options dialog
box, 664
Links and References option, Word, 216
List Bullet style, 166
List entries box, Excel, 295
List item, Excel, 327
List of Markup item, Word, 265
List view, Outlook, 572, 575
locating text, 84
Location box
OneNote, 619
Outlook, 588, 591, 593
Word, 228
locking password-protected sections
manually, 646
Logical drop-down list, Excel, 365
Logon Information settings, Add New Account
wizard, 516
Look Up option, context menu, 54
Lookup & Reference drop-down list, Excel, 365
Low Detail option, Outlook, 582
Low Importance option, Outlook, 589, 603

▓ M

Macros option
Categories list box, 146
Choose commands from drop-down
list, 124
Options dialog box, 121
Mactopia Downloads page, 277
Mail Account setting, Internet E-mail Settings
dialog box, 516
Mail area
Navigation Pane, 520
Outlook, 535
Mail category, Outlook, 44, 60
mail folder, 548–549
Mail Merge option, Word, 217
Mail pane, Outlook, 60, 602
Major and Minor Gridlines item, Excel, 387

Major tick mark type drop-down list,
Excel, 385
Major unit box, Excel, 385
Make Available Offline item, Office
programs, 95
Make Subpage command, OneNote, 629
Manage Credentials option, Word, 271
Manage Styles dialog box, Word, 170–171
Manual command, Excel, 353
Map Custom Fields dialog box, Outlook, 567,
570–571
mapping custom fields, when importing
contacts in Outlook, 570
Margin option, Track Changes Options dialog
box, 242
Margin Settings option, View Options drop-
down menu, 152
Margins drop-down list, Backstage, 69
Mark as Final option, Word, 269
Mark as Not Junk dialog box, Outlook, 552
Mark as Read option, 543
Mark selected text as list box, Language dialog
box, 181
marking
documents as final in Word, 268–269
tasks, Outlook, 607–608
Markup Area Highlight option
Show Comments and Changes, 152
Show Markup drop-down menu, 249
Markup area, Track Changes Options dialog
box, 240
markups
printing, 265
viewing, 248
Master Document feature, Word, 225
Match case, Office programs, 86–87
Match Destination Formatting, Excel, 296
Math & Trig drop-down list, Excel, 365
Math AutoCorrect options, Office, 48–49
Maximum box, Excel, 327, 384
Measure in drop-down list, Track Changes
Options dialog box, 242
Measurement units drop-down list, OneNote
Options dialog box, 666
Medium Detail option, Outlook, 582
Meeting window, Outlook, 591–592, 594–595
Meeting window To box, Outlook, 593
meetings, Outlook
creating, 591
defined, 584
invitations for
replying to, 595
tracking status of, 594

Merge & Center drop-down list, Excel, 321
Merge Formatting item, Word, 83–84
Merge into Another Section, context menu, 641
Merge Section dialog box, OneNote, 641
Merge Styles dialog box, Excel, 333
Merge styles from list box, Excel, 333
merging
    cells in tables, 90
    notes, 641
    styles, Excel, 333
Message List, Outlook
    arranging and sorting, 523–524
    changing sort order, 525
    choosing whether to group items, 525
    viewing conversations, 525–526
Message window, Outlook, 610, 613
messages
    adding subject lines and message contents, 538–539
    addressing, 536–537
    checking spelling in, 541
    choosing accounts to send from, 536
    choosing options for, 539–541
    creating, 534–535
    creating new mail folder, 548–549
    deleting, storing, and organizing, 547–549
    moving message to mail folder, 548
    receiving and reading, 542
    replying to and forwarding, 546
    sending, 541
    using signatures, 550
Microsoft Excel. *See* Excel
Microsoft OneNote. *See* OneNote
Microsoft Outlook. *See* Outlook
Microsoft PowerPoint. *See* PowerPoint
Microsoft Word. *See* Word
Mini Toolbar
    Excel, 315
    Office programs, 76
    OneNote, 631
    Word, 76–77, 129
minimizing Ribbon tool, 35–36
Minimum box, Excel, 327, 384
Minor Gridlines item, Excel, 387
Minor tick mark type drop-down list, Excel, 385
Minor unit box, Excel, 385
mixed references, Excel, 347, 356
Mobile box, Outlook, 559
Modify Location dialog box, 144
Modify option
    Quick Style gallery, 183
    Styles pane, 183

Modify Style dialog box, Word, 183
Monitors group, PowerPoint, 493
Month view, Outlook, 582
More Borders item, Excel, 322
More Commands item, Customize Quick Access Toolbar menu, 399
More Functions drop-down list, Excel, 363, 365
More Layout Options, Word/Outlook, 105
More Options group, Ribbon, 541
More Symbols item, Office programs, 73
Motion Path animations, PowerPoint, 478
Move Chart command, Excel, 377
Move Chart dialog box, Excel, 377
Move Items dialog box, Outlook, 548–549
Move or Copy dialog box
    Excel, 302
    OneNote, 640
Move or Copy option, 640
Move or Copy Pages dialog box, OneNote, 627–628, 640, 679
Move or Copy Section dialog box, OneNote, 640, 679
Move or Copy Section Group dialog box, OneNote, 640
Move Section Group dialog box, OneNote, 622
Move to Collection box, Office programs, 96
Move to Collection dialog box, Office programs, 96
Move to Collection item, Office programs, 96
Moved from drop-down list, Track Changes Options dialog box, 241
Moved to drop-down list, Track Changes Options dialog box, 241
Moves area, Track Changes Options dialog box, 241
movies, adding to presentations, 469
moving
    chart to chart sheet, Excel, 377
    data with drag and drop, 299–300
    page to another section or notebook, OneNote, 627
    paragraphs in Outline view, Word, 225
Multiple displays drop-down list, Windows, 493
multiple items, selecting text for in Word, 140
My Calendars list, Outlook, 580
My Computer option, Store Notebook On list box, 647
My Contacts area, Gmail, 563
My Contacts list, Outlook, 571
My Documents folder, SkyDrive, 42
My Folders box, Backstage, 30
My Folders list, SkyDrive, 42

My Tasks list, Navigation Pane, 520
My Templates category, Excel, 392
My Templates heading, OneNote, 626
My templates item
    Excel, 285
    PowerPoint, 416

N

NA( ) function, Excel, 361
Name box, Excel, 568
Name Manager dialog box, Excel, 349
Name text box
    Backstage, 647, 655
    Create New Building Block dialog box, 137
    Create New Style from Formatting dialog
        box, 181
    Excel, 348
    OneNote, 619, 678
named cells and ranges, Excel, 348–349
navigating
    Excel
        moving active cell, 288–289
        overview, 285–287
        selecting and manipulating cells, 289–290
    with keyboard, 75–76
    Word documents
        with Go To command, 197–198
        replacing formatting, 196
        replacing text, 196
        using Find, 189–195
        using Navigation pane, 188–189
Navigation Bar, OneNote, 617–618, 622, 627,
    629, 639, 641, 649, 653
Navigation group, Word, 207
Navigation pane
    Outlook, 520–522, 555, 567, 571, 579, 585,
        597, 599
    PowerPoint, 419–420, 423, 427–428,
        433, 486
    Word, 85, 188–189
nesting
    parts of formulas, Excel, 355
    of tables, Word, 203
Net amount, Excel, 354
Network Location text box, Backstage, 647–648
Network option, Store Notebook On list
    box, 647
NETWORKDAYS( ) function, Excel, 365
New All Day Event option, Outlook, 588
New Appointment option, Outlook, 588
New box, Create New Folder dialog box, 549
New command, Backstage, 39

New dialog box, Excel, 285
New Docked Window option, OneNote, 637
New Folder option, 548
New Formatting Rule dialog box, Excel, 326
New from existing item
    Excel, 285
    PowerPoint, 415–416
New from Existing Presentation dialog box,
    PowerPoint, 417
New from Existing Workbook dialog box,
    Excel, 285
New Group option, 124
New item
    Excel, 283
    OneNote, 618
    PowerPoint, 413
New link, SkyDrive, 26
NEW LIST item, Excel, 295
New Meeting option, Outlook, 591
New Meeting Request option, Outlook, 591
New messages drop-down list, New Signature
    dialog box, 551
New Name dialog box, Excel, 348, 568
New Note option, Outlook, 611–612
New Notebook pane
    Backstage, 647
    OneNote, 618–619
New Notebook screen, Backstage, 655
New Page drop-down list, OneNote, 617,
    625–626
New Page option, OneNote, 624
New pane
    Backstage, 143
    Excel, 283–284
    PowerPoint, 413–414
New Photo Album command, PowerPoint, 466
New Presentation dialog box, PowerPoint, 416
New Recurring Appointment option,
    Outlook, 589
New Section Group option, OneNote, 621
New sheet text box, Excel, 377
New Side Note option, OneNote, 638
New Signature dialog box, Outlook, 551
New Slide drop-down panel, PowerPoint, 440
New Slide panel, PowerPoint, 421
New Subpage option, OneNote, 628
New Task option, Outlook, 602
New Window command, Excel, 306
New Window option
    OneNote, 637
    View panel, 155
    Word, 221
Newsprint set, Fonts menu, 164

Next 7 Days, Outlook, 600
Next Sentence option, Spelling and Grammar
    dialog box, 59
No Paragraph Space option, Built-In
    section, 164
No Scaling item, Excel, 339
None item, Excel, 382, 387
None transition, PowerPoint, 476
Normal mode, Excel, 382
Normal option, Save changes in drop-down
    list, 137, 146
Normal style
    Excel, 334
    keyboard shortcuts, 166
    Style Inspector, 185–186
Normal template, 50, 147–148, 160–161
Normal view
    Excel, 303
    OneNote, 636
    Outlook, 585, 598, 611
    PowerPoint, 419, 422–424, 427–428, 486
Normal View option, OneNote, 637
Normal.dotx template, 50
Not Started item, Outlook, 602
Note item, Excel, 386
Notebook Properties dialog box, OneNote,
    641–642
Notebook Recycle Bin, OneNote, 621,
    678–680
notebooks, 618
    changing display names for, 641
    removing password protection from
        sections of, 646
    reviewing edits by authors, 651
    shared
        choosing how to update, 652–653
        creating new, 647
        opening, 649
        working in, 649–650
    sharing existing, 648
    viewing changes and marking them as
        read, 651
    viewing recent edits, 651
notes
    OneNote
        adding to page, 629–635
        changing display names for notebooks, 641
        choosing how to update shared notebooks,
          652–653
        creating new shared notebooks, 647
        interface for, 615–616
        merging and splitting, 641
        merging sections together, 640

        moving pages, sections, and section groups,
          639–640
        notebooks in, 618
        opening shared notebooks, 649
        pages in, 624–629
        printing to, 633
        protecting with passwords, 644–646
        reviewing changes to notebooks, 650–651
        searching for information, 642–643
        section groups in, 620–623
        sharing existing notebooks, 648
        splitting sections, 641
        storing on Web, 655–656
        using different versions of pages,
          654–655
        views in, 636–637
        windows for, 637–638
        working in shared notebooks, 649–650
    Outlook
        creating, 611
        interface for, 610–611
        viewing, 612
Notes area
    Outlook, 535
    PowerPoint, 423
Notes List view, Outlook, 612
Notes Page view, PowerPoint, 423, 425
Notes pane
    Outlook, 559, 610–611
    PowerPoint, 419–420
Notification Area Icons window,
    OneNote, 638
notification area, PowerPoint, 503
NOW( ) function, Excel, 361
Number Filters submenu, AutoFilter
    drop-down list, 408–409
Number Format category, Excel, 331
Number Format drop-down list
    Excel, 317
    Word, 209, 229
number formatting, in Excel, 317–318
Number group, Excel, 316–317, 329
Number of backup copies to keep text box,
    OneNote Options dialog box, 660
Number of columns box
    Insert Table dialog box, 452
    Word, 201, 211
Number of month rows box, To-Do Bar
    Options dialog box, 531
Number slides from box, PowerPoint, 418
Number styles, Excel, 329
Numbered item, Word, 219–220
numbered list style, 161

numbering
    of axis, for charts in Excel, 384
    in styles, Word, 178
Numbering drop-down list, Word, 229
Numbering panel, Paragraph group, 178

■ O

occurrences box, Outlook, 590, 605
OCR (optical character recognition), 71–72
Odd Page Footer item, Excel, 335
Odd Page Header item, Excel, 335
Odd Page option, Word, 207
Office
    AutoCorrect tool
        actions and smart tags, 52
        choosing AutoFormat As You Type options,
          45–48
        choosing Math AutoCorrect options,
          48–49
        choosing options on AutoCorrect tab of
          AutoCorrect dialog box, 45
        creating entries, 49–50
        creating exceptions, 50
        overview, 43–44
    Backstage tool, 37–38
    checking grammar in Word and Outlook
        choosing grammar and style options,
          62–64
        controlling how spelling checker works, 59
        overview, 57–58
    checking spelling
        custom dictionaries, 64–67
        while typing, 54
        in whole documents, 55–57
    printing documents, 67
    Ribbon tool
        controlling with keyboard, 36–37
        giving commands from, 35
        minimizing, 35–36
        overview, 33–34
    sharing documents
        saving to SharePoint servers, 42
        saving to SkyDrive, 41
        sending via e-mails, 39–40
Office Web Apps
    creating new documents on SkyDrive,
      26–27
    opening existing documents on
      SkyDrive, 27
    overview, 25
    saving changes to documents in, 28
    signing up for, 25

OneNote, 5–6. *See also* notes
    audio in
        exporting from notebook, 670
        recording, 669–670
        removing from notebook, 670
    importing tables from, 454
    and Notebook Recycle Bin, 678–680
    option dialogs for
        Advanced, 663–666
        Audio & Video, 666–668
        Display, 657
        Save & Backup, 659–661
        Send to OneNote, 661–663
    and other office programs
        creating Outlook Message from, 675
        creating Outlook Task from, 675–676
        exporting to Excel, 675
        exporting to PowerPoint, 675
        exporting to Word, 673–675
    printing notebooks, 671–673
    transferring notebook to another PC, 677
    video in, 669–671
OneNote command, Outlook, 634
OneNote Options dialog box, OneNote, 620,
      632–633
one-time tasks, Outlook, 601
Open Backup dialog box, OneNote, 660
Open Backups menu option, OneNote, 660
Open command, Backstage, 10, 38
Open dialog box
    Backstage pane, 19
    PowerPoint, 435
    Word, 257
Open New Side Note icon, OneNote, 637–638
Open Notebook dialog box
    Backstage, 677
    OneNote, 649
Open Notebook pane, OneNote, 649
Open option
    Backstage pane, 19
    Startup folder, 13
Open pane, Outlook, 564
Open Search Results Pane link, 643
Open Task in Outlook context menu option,
      OneNote, 677
Open XML File Format Converter, 277
opening
    documents, 18
    Manage Styles dialog box, Styles pane, 170
    presentation, PowerPoint, 431
    programs
        automatically launching with Windows,
          12–13

by pinning to Start Menu, 12
standard way, 11
Style Inspector, 170
Operation area, Excel, 299
operator precedence, Excel, 354–355
operators, for formulas in Excel
order in which Excel evaluates,
354–355
overview, 349–350
using, 351–353
optical character recognition (OCR), 71–72
Optimizing files area, OneNote Options dialog
box, 660
option dialogs, for OneNote
Advanced, 663–666
Audio & Video, 666–668
Display, 657
Save & Backup, 659–661
Send to OneNote, 661–663
Optional box, Outlook, 593
Options command, Backstage, 39
Options dialog box
Excel, 296
OneNote, 657, 659, 661, 663, 669–670
Word, 280–281
Options drop-down list, Create New Building
Block dialog box, 137
Options group
Excel, 335
Outlook, 589, 591
word, 207
Organizer dialog box, Manage Styles dialog
box, 172
organizing messages, 547–549
Orientation area, Backstage Print Preview and
Settings dialog box, 673
Orientation box, Excel, 321
Orientation drop-down list
Backstage, 69
Excel, 321
Original Document drop-down list, Combine
Documents dialog box, 257
Original option
Display for Review drop-down menu, 248
Show Original/Final Document, 152
Original: Show Markup option, Display for
Review drop-down menu, 248
Original with Markup option, Show
Original/Final Document, 152
Other Authors option, Show Markup drop-
down menu, 249
Outgoing mail server (SMTP) box, Add New
Account wizard, 516

Outline level drop-down list, Paragraph dialog
box, 174
Outline pane, PowerPoint, 422, 436
Outline Tools group, Word, 222, 224
Outline view, Word
closing, 225
developing document in, 153–154
headings in
creating, 222
expanding and collapsing, 223–224
promoting and demoting, 223
moving paragraphs in, 225
overview of outlines, 221
switching to, 221–222
outlines of presentations PowerPoint, 427–428
Outlook, 4–5
attachments
receiving files as, 544–546
sending files as, 543
checking grammar
choosing grammar and style options, 62–64
controlling how spelling checker works, 59
overview, 57–58
choosing grammar and style options for,
62–64
Message List
arranging and sorting, 523–524
changing sort order, 525
choosing whether to group items, 525
viewing conversations, 525–526
messages
adding subject lines and message contents,
538–539
addressing, 536–537
checking spelling in, 541
choosing accounts to send from, 536
choosing options for, 539–541
creating, 534–535
creating new mail folder, 548–549
deleting, storing, and organizing, 547–549
moving message to mail folder, 548
receiving and reading, 542
replying to and forwarding, 546
sending, 541
using signatures, 550
Navigation Pane, 520–522
People Pane, 531–533
Reading Pane, 527–528
setting up, 511–514
spam, 552–553
To-Do Bar, 529–530
using Ribbon, 519
wrapping text in, 104–105

Outlook contacts
communicating with, 577
creating new, 555
editing, 576
grouping, 575
importing from
CSV file, 564
Excel worksheet, 568
Gmail contacts, 563
mapping custom fields when
importing, 570
overview, 561
vCard files, 567
Windows Contacts, 562
Yahoo! address book, 563
searching within, 576
sorting, 575
viewing, 571–576
Outlook Contacts window, Outlook, 563
Outlook Express, Outlook, 561
Outlook icon, 512
Outlook Items area, OneNote Options dialog
box, 662
Outlook Message, creating from OneNote, 675
Outlook Options dialog box
Backstage, 542
Outlook, 583
Outlook Task, creating from OneNote, 675–676
Overdue view, Outlook, 600
Overlay Legend at Left item, Excel, 386
Overlay Legend at Right item, Excel, 386

P

Page break before checkbox, Paragraph dialog
box, 176
Page Break Preview, Excel, 303, 338
Page Color drop-down panel, Outlook, 539
Page Group option, Backstage Print Preview
and Settings dialog box, 672
Page layout in Microsoft Word area,
PowerPoint, 501
Page Layout view, Excel, 336–337
Page Number drop-down menu, Word, 208
Page Number Format dialog box, Word,
208–209
Page number item, Word, 220
Page Numbering area, Word, 209
page numbers, inserting in Word document, 208
Page range area, Word, 281
Page Setup dialog box
Excel, 339
PowerPoint, 418

Page Setup group, Excel, 337
Page Templates option, OneNote, 625–626
Page Versions menu, OneNote, 655
pages
different headers and footers for,
Word, 207
moving, 639–640
in OneNote
copying, 627
creating based on template, 625
creating blank, 624
creating templates, 626
moving, 627
navigating, 629
renaming, 627
subpages for, 628–629
using different versions of, 654–655
Paper orientation in printing option, Track
Changes Options dialog box, 243
Paper size drop-down list, Backstage Print
Preview and Settings dialog box, 672
Paragraph dialog box
Home tab, 173
PowerPoint, 443–444
Paragraph group
Home tab, 159–160, 173, 178, 184
Office programs, 77
Ribbon, 442–443, 445
Word, 77
Paragraph list, Reveal Formatting pane, 187
Paragraph number item, Word, 220
Paragraph option, Borders and Shading dialog
box, 179
Paragraph section, Reveal Formatting
pane, 188
Paragraph Spacing menu, Change Styles
drop-down menu, 164
paragraphs
bulleted, in presentations, 481–482
in Word, 200, 225
parent section group, OneNote, 623
part of document, Find command, 191
Password box
Add New Account wizard, 513, 516
Internet E-mail Settings dialog box, 517
Word, 271
Password Protect This Section option,
644, 646
password protection
removing from sections of notebooks, 646
Word, 270–271
Password Protection task pane, OneNote,
644–646

Password text box
    Excel, 340
    Word, 271
Password to unprotect worksheet text box,
    Excel, 341
password-protected sections
    locking manually, 646
    unlocking, 645
Passwords area, OneNote Options dialog
    box, 666
passwords, protecting notes with
    locking password-protected sections
        manually, 646
    overview, 644
    removing password protection from
        sections of notebooks, 646
    unlocking password-protected
        sections, 645
Paste area, Excel, 298
Paste command
    Excel, 296
    Word/Outlook, 91
Paste operation, Office programs, 81
Paste Options area, Excel, 296
Paste Options drop-down menu, Office
    programs, 82
Paste Options icons, Excel, 296, 455
Paste Options section
    context menu, 461
    Excel, 333
    Ribbon, 454
Paste panel
    Excel, 297–298
    Office programs, 81–82
Paste Shortcut option, 13
Paste Special dialog box, Excel, 296–299, 392
Paste Special icons, Excel, 298
Paste Special submenu, Excel, 297–298
Pasting between documents drop-down list,
    Word, 83
pasting charts, from Excel into PowerPoint,
    460–462
Pasting from other programs drop-down list,
    Word, 84
Pasting within the same document drop-down
    list, Word, 83
PDF files, 205, 279, 281–282
Pen area, OneNote Options dialog box, 665
Pen option, PowerPoint, 494, 498
People Currently Editing area
    Backstage, 236
    PowerPoint, 432
People Pane, Outlook, 531–533, 537–538

Percent style, Excel, 351
Percentage format, Excel, 319
Permission dialog box, Word, 272–273
Permission drop-down panel, Outlook, 540
Permission group, Ribbon, 540
Permissions dialog box, Word, 274
Permissions readout, Word, 270–271
permissions, Word documents, 271–274
Personal Monthly Budget template, Excel, 285
Personal notebook, OneNote, 616, 618
Personal Templates folder
    Excel, 285
    PowerPoint, 416
Phi calculation, OneNote, 635
Phone view, Outlook, 574–575
Photo Album, in PowerPoint, 466
Pi calculation, OneNote, 635
Picture Bullet dialog box, PowerPoint, 450–451
Picture command, PowerPoint, 465
Picture layout drop-down list, PowerPoint, 468
Picture option, 455, 461
Picture Options Area, PowerPoint, 468
Picture Styles group, 108
Picture Tools section, 108
Picture with Caption layout, PowerPoint, 441
pictures. *See* graphics
Pictures in album list box, PowerPoint,
    467–468
pinning to Start Menu, opening programs by, 12
Playback feature, OneNote, 670
Playback group, Ribbon, 670
plot area, Excel, 372
Pointer Options submenu, PowerPoint, 498
Popular Commands option, Options dialog
    box, 120
Portrait item
    Excel, 337, 339
    PowerPoint, 418
Position category, Office programs, 103–104
Position drop-down panel, 104–105
Position group, Word, 206
Position item, Office programs, 103
positioning graphics, 92–103
PowerPoint. *See also* presentations
    exporting OneNote notebook to, 675
    overview, 3–4
    pasting charts from Excel into, 460–462
    Save options in
        AutoRecover settings, 132–133
        default file location, 133–134
        default format for, 131–132
        overview, 130
    slide layouts, 440–441

PowerPoint Broadcast Service, PowerPoint, 505–506
PowerPoint Options dialog box, PowerPoint, 505
Preferred width option, Track Changes Options dialog box, 242
Presentation changes box, PowerPoint, 434
Presentation Views group, PowerPoint, 423
presentations
    adding animations to
        adding to objects, 479
        animating charts, 485
        animating SmartArt graphic, 483
        animating tables, 485–486
        changing order of animations, 480–481
        overview, 478
        using animation to display bulleted paragraphs one at time, 481–482
    adding movies to, 469
    adding pictures to, 465–466
    adding sound to, 474
    adding transitions to slides, 475–476
    adding YouTube videos to, 473
    collaborating on, 430–437
    controlling presentations using, 499
    creating, 413–417
    creating Photo Album, 466
    custom slide shows, 486–489
    delivering
        annotating slides, 498–499
        controlling presentation using keyboard, 499
        displaying slides, 496
        displaying white or black screen, 500
        starting presentation, 496
    exporting and sharing
        broadcasting slide show, 505
        overview, 504
        publishing slides to slide library or SharePoint site, 508
    handouts for, 501
    hidden slides, 486
    outline of, 427–428
    preparation before delivery of
        choosing resolution, 491–493
        practicing, 495
        setting up display, 491–493
        timings for slides, 495
        using Presenter view, 493
    recording narration into, 502–504
    sections in, 428–429
    slides in, 420–422, 439
    views of, 423–427

Presenter view, PowerPoint, 491, 493, 495, 497–498, 507
Preserve area, AutoCorrect dialog box, 48
Presets area, Word, 211
Preview area, Borders and Shading dialog box, 179
Preview box, PowerPoint, 467
Preview feature, OneNote, 673
Preview group, PowerPoint, 480
Preview/Properties dialog box, Office programs, 96–97
Preview/Properties item, Office programs, 96
previous worksheet keyboard shortcut, Excel, 287
Primary Horizontal Gridlines submenu, Excel, 387
Primary Vertical Axis Title item, Excel, 383
Primary Vertical Gridlines submenu, Excel, 387
Print Active Sheets item, Excel, 339
Print command, Backstage, 10, 39
Print Custom Range option, Word, 264
Print dialog box
    Backstage, 673
    OneNote, 67, 634
Print Entire Workbook item, Excel, 339
Print item
    Backstage, 68
    OneNote, 633
Print Layout view
    Excel, 303
    Word, 149, 204–205, 207, 209, 226–227
Print Markup item, Word, 265
Print options
    Backstage, 67
    OneNote, 633
Print pane
    Backstage, 671, 673
    Excel, 335, 339
    Word, 263
Print Preview and Settings dialog box, Backstage, 671–672
Print Preview feature, OneNote, 67, 671
Print range drop-down list, Backstage Print Preview and Settings dialog box, 672
Print Selection item, Excel, 339
Print settings, Backstage, 67
Print to File item, Printer drop-down list, 69
Print to OneNote drop-down list, OneNote, 633
Print What drop-down menu
    Backstage, 69
    Excel, 339
    Word, 263–265

Printer drop-down list
   Backstage, 69
   OneNote, 633
printing
   in Excel
      workbooks, 339
      worksheets, 335–339
   to OneNote, 633
   in OneNote, 671–673
   in Word
      AutoText entries, 265
      consecutive pages, 265
      custom range of pages, 264
      document properties, 265
      individual pages, 265
      key assignments, 265
      markup, 265
      overview, 263
      pages within sections, 265
      range of sections, 265
      sections, 265
      styles, 265
Prioritized view, Outlook, 600
Priority drop-down list, Outlook, 603
Private option, Outlook, 589
Profile drop-down list, OneNote Options
      dialog box, 668
programs
   closing, 21
   opening
      automatically launching with Windows,
         12–13
      by pinning to Start Menu, 12
      standard way, 11
   saving documents from, to SkyDrive, 29
Projector panel, Windows, 492
Promote Subpage option, OneNote, 629
promoting and demoting, headings in Outline
      view, 223
Proofing category
   Backstage, 43
   Options dialog box, 60, 64
   Outlook, 44, 60
Proofing options
   Backstage, 43
   Excel Options dialog box, 401
Proofing pane
   Options dialog box, 52, 57, 60, 62, 64
   Word, 60
Properties dialog box
   Outlook, 540–541
   PowerPoint, 503
Protect Sheet dialog box, Excel, 341

Protect Structure and Windows dialog box,
      Excel, 340
Protected Section dialog box, OneNote,
      645–646
protecting
   cells, 323
   notes, with passwords, 644–646
   workbooks, 340
   worksheets, 341
Protection style, Excel, 330
Public folder, SkyDrive, 42
Publish as PDF or XPS dialog box, Word,
      279–280, 282
Publish Slides dialog box, PowerPoint,
      508–509
Publish Slides item, PowerPoint, 508
Publish To box, PowerPoint, 509
Publish what area, Word, 281
Pulse animation, PowerPoint, 478
punctuation, Find command, 193
Punctuation required with quotes, Grammar
      Settings dialog box, 64

▓ Q

Quick Access Toolbar
   adding Ribbon command to, 119
   and control menu, 8
   Excel, 285, 399
   moving to below Ribbon, 122
   OneNote, 636
   Options dialog box, 119
   Outlook, 542, 606
   overview, 117–118
   PowerPoint, 432
   sharing customizations of, 125
   SkyDrive, 28
   Word, 246
Quick Layout panel, Excel, 379–380
Quick Parts drop-down menu, 136
Quick Parts option, Insert menu, 136
Quick Style box, Styles group, 164–165
Quick Styles box
   Excel, 381
   Office programs, 108, 112
   Word/PowerPoint/Outlook, 91
Quick Styles drop-down panel
   Office programs, 108, 112
   Word/PowerPoint/Outlook, 91
Quick Styles Gallery
   Home Tab, 162–163
   Word, 163–165
Quick Styles panel, Excel, 381–382, 397

R

Raised position, Font dialog box, 173
range of pages, Word, 264
Range of recurrence section, Outlook, 590, 604
range references, Excel, 347
Read box, Word, 272
Readability Statistics dialog box, 62
reading messages, 542
Reading Pane dialog box, Outlook, 528–529
Reading Pane, Outlook, 527–528, 542–545, 610
Reading view
    Outlook, 598–599
    PowerPoint, 423, 425, 486, 504
rearranging worksheets in workbooks, 302
receiving messages, 542
Recent command, Backstage, 39
Recent list, Recent pane, 20
Recent Locations list, Backstage, 43
Recent on the menu option, Backstage, 20
Recent pane, Backstage, 20
Recent Picks list, OneNote, 623
Recent templates item
    Excel, 284
    PowerPoint, 414–415
Recently Closed Notebooks list, OneNote, 649
Recently Used drop-down list, Excel, 364
Recognizers list box, AutoCorrect dialog
    box, 53
Record Audio menu option, OneNote, 669
Record Slide Show dialog box, PowerPoint,
    503–504
Record Video menu option, OneNote, 670
recording in OneNote, 669–670
Recording toolbar, PowerPoint, 495, 504
Recover Draft Versions option, Backstage, 260
recovering earlier page versions, 654
Recurrence group, Outlook, 605
Recurrence line, Outlook, 591
Recurrence pattern section, Outlook, 590, 604
recurring tasks, Outlook, 604–605
Reenter password to confirm text box, Start
    Enforcing Protection dialog box, 246
Reference area, Excel, 286
Reference type drop-down list, Word, 219
Refers to box, Excel, 349
Reject All Changes to the Current Slide option,
    PowerPoint, 435
Reject All Changes to the Presentation option,
    PowerPoint, 435
Reject and Move to Next, Reject drop-down
    menu, 249
Reject Change option, context menu, 250

Reject Conflict option, Word, 237
Reminder drop-down list, Outlook, 589
Reminder Sound dialog box, Outlook, 603
Reminder Sound File dialog box, Outlook, 603
Remote Footer option, Word, 207
Remove All Sections, PowerPoint, 430
Remove Arrows command, Excel, 359
Remove Attachment option, Outlook, 546
Remove Bookmark command,
    PowerPoint, 471
Remove Duplicates dialog box, Excel, 405–406
Remove Duplicates feature, Excel, 404
Remove from Quick Access Toolbar
    option, 119
Remove from Quick Style Gallery option, 165
Remove Page Numbers option, Word, 209
Remove Password dialog box, OneNote, 646
Remove Split, View panel, 158
Remove This Column option, Outlook, 600
removing a section but leave its slides,
    PowerPoint, 430
Rename Folder option, context menu, 549
Rename option
    context menu, 641
    OneNote, 621
Rename Section dialog box, PowerPoint,
    428–429
Reorder Animation area, PowerPoint, 480
Re-Order bar, PowerPoint, 481
Replace as you type area, Word, 46
Replace dialog box, PowerPoint, 84, 86–87
Replace text as you type option, AutoCorrect
    dialog box, 45
Replace the word option, context menu, 54
Replace with box
    Find and Replace dialog box, 196–197
    Office programs, 87
replacing, in Word
    formatting, 196
    text, 86, 196
Replies/forwards drop-down list, New
    Signature dialog box, 551
Reply E-mail box, Internet E-mail Settings
    dialog box, 517
replying to messages, 546
Reset Customizations dialog box, 121
Reset only Quick Access Toolbar option,
    Options dialog box, 121
Reset to Match Style command, Excel, 391
Resolution area, OneNote, 635
Resolution drop-down list, PowerPoint, 493
resolution, for presentations, 491–493
Resolutions group, PowerPoint, 435

Resolve Conflicts dialog box, Excel, 344
Resources box, Outlook, 593
Respond group
    Home tab, 9
    Outlook, 610
Restore Version command, OneNote, 654
Restrict Editing option, Backstage, 243
Restrict Formatting and Editing pane
    Backstage, 243–245
    Word, 243, 246, 252
Restrict Permission by People item, Word,
    271–272
Restricted Access to display the Permissions
    dialog box, Word, 272
Results should be drop-down list, Office
    programs, 94
Retype Password box, Add New Account
    wizard, 513
Reuse Slides pane, PowerPoint, 422
Reveal Formatting pane, Word, 186–188
Reverse Sort option, Outlook, 525
Reviewers item, Show Comments and
    Changes, 152
Reviewers submenu, Show Markup drop-
    down menu, 249
reviewing comments, 255
Reviewing Pane Horizontal option, Word, 254
Reviewing Pane Vertical option, Word, 254
Reviewing pane, Word, 249, 253–256, 258–259
Revised Document drop-down list, Combine
    Documents dialog box, 257
Revisions pane, PowerPoint, 433–434, 436
Ribbon tool, 77
    controlling with keyboard, 36–37
    customizing, 122–125
    giving commands from, 35
    minimizing, 35–36
    OneNote, 636
    Outlook, 519, 576, 598–600, 605
    overview, 9
    PowerPoint, 423, 433, 436, 469–471
    Word, 206, 216–217, 222
Rich Text Format (RTF), 131, 279, 422
Ripple transition, PowerPoint, 477
Rotate all text 90 degrees option, Text
    Direction panel, 444
Rotate all text 270 degrees option, Text
    Direction panel, 444
Rotated Title item, Excel, 383
rotating
    graphics, 102
    text, Excel, 321
Row headings, Excel, 286

Row Height dialog box, Excel, 313
rows in Excel
    and columns in charts, 378
    deleting, 311–312
    freezing, 308
    height, 313
    hiding, 314–315
    inserting, 311–312
RTF (Rich Text Format), 131, 279, 422

▨ S

Sales Report template, Excel, 285
Sample templates
    Excel, 285
    PowerPoint, 415
Save & Backup option dialog, OneNote,
    659–661
Save & Backup pane, OneNote, 620,
    659–660
Save & Close option, Outlook, 589, 605
Save & Send pane, Word, 277, 279
Save As command
    Backstage, 38
    Outlook, 545
    Word, 279
Save As context menu option, OneNote, 670
Save As dialog box
    Excel, 285, 568
    OneNote, 670, 675, 677
    Word, 279
Save As pane, Backstage, 677
Save As screen, Backstage, 673–674
Save As Template dialog box, OneNote, 626
Save as type drop-down list
    Excel, 285, 568
    Word, 279–280
Save Attachment dialog box, Outlook, 545
Save category, Options dialog box, 130
Save changes in drop-down list, Customize
    Keyboard dialog box, 146
Save Chart Template dialog box, Excel, 392
Save command
    Backstage, 10, 38
    Excel, 285
Save Current column, Backstage, 674, 677
Save current page as a template link,
    OneNote, 626
Save in drop-down list, Create New Building
    Block dialog box, 137
Save in the Backstage pane
    File tab, 15
    Ribbon, 17

Save item
    PowerPoint, 505
    Word Options dialog box, 260
Save list box, OneNote Options dialog box, 659
Save options
    AutoRecover settings, 132–133
    default file location, 133–134
    default format for, 131–132
    overview, 130
Save pane
    Options dialog box, 130–131
    Word Options dialog box, 130
Save Selection as a New Quick Style option,
        Styles group, 165, 181
Save Selection to AutoText Gallery option, 137
Save to SharePoint screen, Backstage, 43
Save to SkyDrive pane, Backstage, 29–30
SaveDate field, Word, 217–218
saving documents, 15–17
scale of charts, Excel, 384
Scan text
    OneNote, 135
    Word documents, 135
Scanner Printout option, OneNote, 72,
        630, 634
scanning documents, 71–72
Scatter chart type, Excel, 374
Scheduling pane, Outlook, 593
Scope drop-down list, Excel, 348, 568
Scope group, Outlook, 576
Screen Clipping option, OneNote, 632
screen clippings, adding to page in OneNote,
        630, 632
Screen Clippings drop-down list, OneNote, 632
Screen Resolution window, Windows, 492–493
ScreenTip style drop-down list, Options dialog
        box, 130
ScreenTip style option, Excel Options dialog
        box, 129
ScreenTips, Word, 138, 205–206, 208, 230
Scroll controls, Excel, 287
Search box
    Navigation pane, 188–190
    OneNote, 617
    Outlook, 537, 581
Search Contacts box, Outlook, 576
search direction, Find command,, 191
Search drop-down list, Find and Replace
        dialog box, 191, 196
Search for a Function box, Excel, 363
Search for box
    Office programs, 94
    PowerPoint, 465

Search pane, Outlook, 576
Search Results pane, OneNote, 643, 651
Search text box, Picture Bullet dialog box, 450
Search Tools section, Outlook, 576
searching within Outlook contacts, 576
Section Break, Word, 204
section groups
    moving, 639–640
    in OneNote
        adding sections to, 622
        creating, 621
        navigating among, 623
        placing section group inside another, 622
Section Header layout, PowerPoint, 440
Section item, Word, 204
Section list, Reveal Formatting pane, 187
section, Office programs, 107
Section option
    Go To tab, 197
    Select Browse Object panel, 141
sections
    in OneNote
        adding to section group, 622
        creating, 620
        deleting, 620
        merging together, 640
        moving, 639–640
        removing password protection from, 646
        renaming, 621
        reorganizing, 621
        splitting, 641
    in PowerPoint, 428–429
    in Word
        complex documents with multiple sections,
            203–204
        different headers and footers for, 207
Select a folder to store your files screen,
        SkyDrive, 30
Select a Function list box, Excel, 363
Select a place in this document box, Insert
        Hyperlink dialog box, 462
Select a Slide Library dialog box,
        PowerPoint, 509
Select All command, Styles pane, 170
Select Attendees and Resources dialog box,
        Outlook, 592
Select Browse Object panel, 142–143
Select Data Source dialog box, Excel,
        378–381, 386
Select destination folder box, Outlook, 566, 569
Select File dialog box, OneNote, 659
Select file type to import from box, Outlook,
        565, 568

Select Folder dialog box
    Backstage, 647–648
    OneNote, 619–620, 659, 678
    Outlook, 541
Select Format area, Backstage Save As
        pane, 677
Select Format list, Backstage, 674
Select how list is sorted drop-down list, 169
Select Location in OneNote dialog box
    OneNote, 633–634
    Outlook, 634, 662
Select Name dialog box, Outlook, 536–537,
        539, 558
Select Notebook drop-down list,
        Backstage, 648
Select Picture dialog box, Excel, 390
Select signature to edit box, Outlook, 551
Select Source Data dialog box, Excel, 380
Select Task Recipient dialog box, Outlook, 609
Select the address to use box, Outlook, 557
Select User dialog box, Word, 272
Select where to place the folder list box, Create
        New Folder dialog box, 549
selecting text, Word
    with Extend Selection feature, 139–140
    with mouse, 138
    multiple items at once, 140
Selection and Visibility pane, Office
        programs, 113
Selection pane, Office programs, 113
Send Backward command, Office
        programs, 113
Send in Email link, PowerPoint, 507
Send to Back command, Office programs, 113
Send To Microsoft Word dialog box,
        PowerPoint, 501
Send To OneNote 2010, OneNote, 633
Send To OneNote command, OneNote,
        634, 662
Send to OneNote option dialog, OneNote,
        661–663
Send to OneNote pane, OneNote, 632–633, 661
Send Update to Attendees dialog box,
        Outlook, 594
Send Using E-mail option, Backstage, 40
sending messages, 541
Send/Receive All Folders option, Outlook, 542
Send/Receive Groups dialog box,
        Backstage, 542
sensitive information, removing when
        finalizing document, 266
Sequence option, PowerPoint, 482
Series name box, Excel, 381

Series values text box, Excel, 381
Server Tasks view, Outlook, 600
servers, SharePoint, 42
Service Sign-Up dialog box, Word, 271
Set as Default option, Change Styles
        drop-down menu, 164
Set default location option, OneNote Options
        dialog box, 662
Set Hyperlink ScreenTip dialog box
    Office programs, 115
    PowerPoint, 463
Set Proofing Language option, 54
Settings link, Backstage, 244
Shading drop-down list,
        Word/PowerPoint/Outlook, 92
shading styles in Word, 178–180
Shadow category, Excel, 391
Shadow option, Borders and Shading dialog
        box, 179
Shape drop-down panel, Office programs, 99
Shape Effects drop-down panel, Office
        programs, 101–102
Shape Fill drop-down panel, Office programs,
        101–102
Shape Outline drop-down panel, Office
        programs, 101–102
Shape Styles box, Office programs, 100
Shape Styles drop-down panel, Office
        programs, 101
Shape Styles group, Office programs, 100–101
shapes
    adding and formatting, 98–101
    applying style to, 100–101
Shapes drop-down panel, Office programs, 98
Share column, PowerPoint, 508
Share command, Backstage, 39
Share list, Backstage, 40
Share Notebook pane, Backstage, 648
Share On area, Backstage, 648, 656
Share options, Backstage, 40–42
Share pane
    Backstage, 29, 40
    PowerPoint, 501, 506, 508
Share This Notebook command, OneNote, 656
Share Workbook dialog box, Excel, 342
Shared Notebook pane, Backstage, 656
Shared Notebook Synchronization dialog box,
        OneNote, 652–653
shared notebooks
    choosing how to update, 652–653
    creating new, 647
    opening, 649
    working in, 649–650

SharePoint servers
    publishing slides to, 508
    saving documents to, 42
sharing
    documents, Word
        compatible with earlier versions of
            Word, 277
        format for digital distribution, 279
    presentations, 504–510
        broadcasting slide show, 505
        publishing slides to slide library or
            SharePoint site, 508
    worksheets, 339–344
sharpness, of graphics, 106–107
Show Above the Ribbon option, 122
Show All Revisions Inline command,
    Word, 247
Show As drop-down list, Outlook, 589
Show Below the Ribbon option, 122
Show changes area, Combine Documents
    dialog box, 258
Show Comments and Changes option, View
    Options drop-down menu,
    152, 250
Show document content area, Word, 218
Show Document Content heading,
    Word, 214
Show field, Word, 218
Show Fields group, Ribbon, 539
Show Heading Level, Navigation pane, 188
Show High Detail option, Outlook, 582
Show icon and modifications option,
    OneNote, 638
Show in Groups item, Outlook, 575
Show Legend at Bottom item, Excel, 386
Show Legend at Left item, Excel, 386
Show Legend at Right item, Excel, 386
Show Legend at Top item, Excel, 386
Show Level drop-down list, Word, 224
Show lines connecting to text option, Track
    Changes Options dialog box, 242
Show Low Detail option, Outlook, 582
Show Markup drop-down menu, Word, 248
Show Medium Detail option, Outlook, 582
Show Messages from Other Folders option,
    Outlook, 526
Show Notes option, Word, 231
Show Office Clipboard Automatically item,
    Office programs, 81
Show Office Clipboard Icon on Taskbar item,
    Office programs, 81
Show Office Clipboard When Ctrl+C Pressed
    Twice item, Office programs, 81

Show On drop-down list, PowerPoint, 493
Show One Page, View Options drop-down
    menu, 151
Show Only Comments and Formatting in
    Balloons command, Word, 247
Show Original/Final Document option, View
    Options drop-down menu, 152, 250
Show Printed Page option, View Options drop-
    down menu, 151
Show Quick Access Toolbar option, 121
Show Revisions in Balloons command,
    Word, 247
Show Source Documents submenu, Word, 259
Show Status Near Taskbar When Copying
    item, Office programs, 81
Show Two Pages option, View Options drop-
    down menu, 151
Show Unread Changes in This Notebook item,
    OneNote, 651
Show Windows Side by Side command,
    155–156, 306
Show/Hide ¶ option, Word, 212
Show/Hide Ink Markup command,
    PowerPoint, 499
Shrink & Turn animation, PowerPoint, 478
side notes, OneNote, 637–638
Sign dialog box, Word, 275
Signature Confirmation dialog box, Word, 276
Signature Removed dialog box, Word, 277
Signatures and Stationery dialog box, Outlook,
    550, 552
Signatures item, status bar, 128
signatures, using in messages, 550
Signing as box, Word, 275
signing up, for Office Web Apps, 25
signing Word document, with digital
    signature, 274–277
Silver option, Color scheme drop-down
    list, 130
Simple List view, Outlook, 599, 601
Simple To Do List template, OneNote, 625
Size box, Bullets and Numbering dialog box,
    449–450
Size category, Office programs, 103
Size drop-down list, Excel, 337
Size option, Arrange By control, 524
Skip Occurrence option, Outlook, 605
SkyDrive
    copying documents from PCs to, 30
    creating new documents on, 26–27
    downloading documents to PCs from,
        30–32
    opening existing documents on, 27

saving documents from desktop office programs to, 29
saving documents to, 41
Slide changes box, PowerPoint, 434
Slide pane, PowerPoint, 419, 433, 436
Slide Show menu, PowerPoint, 498–499
Slide show name box, PowerPoint, 488
Slide Show view, PowerPoint, 423, 426, 486, 493, 504, 507
Slide Sorter view, PowerPoint, 421–424, 486
slides
  add content to, 420
  adding, 421
  adding hyperlinks to, 462–463
  adding SmartArt graphics to, 456
  charts
    creating in new embedded workbooks, 458
    overview, 457
    pasting from Excel into PowerPoint, 460–462
  deleting, 422
  formatting text
    changing font, font size, and alignment, 442
    changing indentation and line spacing of text, 443
    using bulleted lists, 447–448
  layouts of, 440–441
  orientation of, 418
  planning in presentations, 439
  rearranging, 422
  size of, 418
  tables in
    creating, 452
    creating from Excel worksheet data, 455–456
    importing from Word or OneNote, 454
    overview, 451
Slides bar, PowerPoint, 494
Slides group box, PowerPoint, 418
Slides in custom show box, PowerPoint, 488
Slides in presentation box, PowerPoint, 488
Slides pane, PowerPoint, 419, 421–422, 436
Slides sized for drop-down list, PowerPoint, 418
smaller Mini Toolbar, Excel, 316
smart tags, 52
SmartArt graphics, 111–112
  adding to slides, 456
  animating, 483
  inserting, 110
SmartArt Styles group, Office programs, 112
SmartArt Tools section, Office programs, 111–112

software as service
  Office Web Apps
    creating new documents on SkyDrive, 26–27
    opening, 26–27
    opening existing documents on SkyDrive, 27
    saving changes to documents in, 28
    signing up for, 25
  overview, 23–25
  SkyDrive
    copying documents from PCs to, 30
    downloading documents to PCs from, 30–32
    saving documents from desktop office programs to, 29
Sort & Filter group, Ribbon, 402, 406
Sort by drop-down list, Sort dialog box, 403
Sort dialog box, Excel, 402–404
Sort On drop-down list, Sort dialog box, 403
Sort option, AutoFilter drop-down list, 407
Sort Options dialog box, Excel, 403–404
Sort order drop-down list, Manage Styles dialog box, 171
sound, adding to presentations, 474
Sound dialog box, PowerPoint, 503
Sound drop-down list, PowerPoint, 477
Source box, Excel, 327
source data, Excel, 378
Spaces required between sentences, Grammar Settings dialog box, 64
Spacing area, Paragraph dialog box, 443
Spacing before and after paragraphs, Paragraph dialog box, 175
Spacing box, Word, 211
spam, 552–553
Spanish modes drop-down list, Options dialog box, 61
speaker icon, PowerPoint, 475
special characters, Find command, 192
Special drop-down list, Paragraph dialog box, 174
Special drop-down menu, Find and Replace dialog box, 193
Specific items in the list drop-down list, AutoFilter drop-down list, 410
Specifying a Custom Range of Pages to Print, Word, 265
speech recognition, entering text using, 72
Speech Recognition settings, Windows, 72
spell checking
  controlling, 59
  in messages, 541

spell checking (*continued*)
    while typing, 54
    in whole documents, 55–57
Spelling & Grammar in a message window
       option, Outlook, 55
Spelling & Grammar option, Word, 55
Spelling and Grammar dialog box, Word,
    55–59
Spelling dialog box, 55–56, 59
Spin animation, PowerPoint, 478
Split boxes, Excel, 287
Split Cells dialog box,
    Word/PowerPoint/Outlook, 90
Split command
    Excel, 304
    View panel, 156
Split option, Word, 221
split panes, of windows, 156
splitting
    cells in tables, 90
    notes, 641
Square item
    Office programs, 104
    Outlook, 105
Stacked option, Text Direction panel, 444
Start After Previous item, PowerPoint, 481
Start box
    Excel, 327
    Outlook, 590, 602, 604
    Word, 229
Start drop-down list, PowerPoint, 472, 480
Start Enforcing Protection dialog box, Word,
    245–246
Start menu, opening programs by pinning
       to, 12
start of word, Find command, 193
Start On Click item, PowerPoint, 481
Start Recording from Current Slide command,
    PowerPoint, 503
Start time boxes
    Excel, 327
    Outlook, 584, 588
Start time line, Outlook, 589
starting creating a new style, Styles pane, 170
Statistical submenu, Excel, 365
status bar
    customizing, 126–127
    Excel, 303–304, 307
    overview, 10
    PowerPoint, 423, 428
    Word, 204, 221
Status drop-down list, Outlook, 602
stock chart type, Excel, 374

Stop item, Excel, 329
Store Notebook On area
    Backstage, 647, 655
    OneNote, 619–620
storing messages, 547–549
style, applying to graphics, 108
Style area, Grammar and style options list box,
    63–64
Style dialog box, Excel, 331–332
Style drop-down list
    Borders and Shading dialog box, 180
    Excel, 329
Style for following paragraph drop-down list,
    Create New Style from Formatting
    dialog box, 182
Style Includes (By Example) area, Excel, 332
Style Inspector, Word, 185–186
Style list, Borders and Shading dialog box, 179
Style name box, Excel, 332
Style Name drop-down list, 166
style options, choosing for Word and Outlook,
    62–64
Style Pane Options dialog box, 169
Style Set submenu, 163
styles
    in Excel
        applying to charts, 381
        formatting worksheets with, 329–334
    in Word
        Apply Styles pane, 165–166
        applying to shapes, 100–101
        board, 166
        creating by example, 172–181
        custom, 172–183
        managing with Manage Styles dialog box,
          170–171
        managing with Styles pane, 168–170
        modifying existing, 183
        overview, 162
        printing, 265
        Quick Styles Gallery, 163–165
        viewing styles used in document, 167–168
        when to use, 160–161
Styles group
    Home tab, 162, 164
    OneNote, 631
    Outlook, 559
Styles item , Word, 265
Styles option, Categories list box, 146
Styles pane
    Modify Style dialog box, 183
    Styles group, 165
    Word, 168–170

Styles panel, OneNote, 631
Subject box
    Office programs, 115
    Outlook, 538, 543, 588, 593, 602
subject lines, adding to messages in Outlook, 538–539
Subject option, Arrange By control, 524
Subset drop-down list, Office programs, 74
Subtle category, PowerPoint, 476
Subtle Emphasis style, Find and Replace dialog box, 194
Subtle transitions, PowerPoint, 476
Suggest from main dictionary only option, Options dialog box, 61
Suggestions list box, 56
SUM( ) function, Excel, 345, 360–361
Switch Windows command
    Excel, 306, 346
    View panel, 156
switching rows and columns, Excel, 378
Swivel animation, PowerPoint, 478
Symbol box, Rename dialog box, 124
Symbol dialog box, 72–75, 449
Symbol drop-down panel, Office programs, 72–73
symbols, entering, 72–75
Sync Status icon, OneNote, 649
Sync Status indicator, OneNote, 652
Sync This Notebook Now command, OneNote, 653
synchronization, in notebooks, 652–653
Synchronous Scrolling command, Excel, 308

T

Tags area, OneNote Options dialog box, 665
Task List option, context menu, 529
Task list, Outlook
    creating one-time task in, 601
    views for, 599
Task List part, Outlook, 602
Task Options section, Outlook, 603
Task Recurrence dialog box, Outlook, 604–605
Task Status Report window, Outlook, 607
Task window, Outlook, 601, 604–609
Taskbar ScreenTip option, 12
TaskPad, Outlook, 581, 585–586
Tasks area
    Navigation Pane, 520
    Outlook, 535
Tasks category, Outlook, 603
Tasks folder, Outlook, 597
Tasks list, Outlook, 608

tasks, Outlook
    adding details to, 606
    assigning to other people, 609–610
    creating one-time, 601
    creating recurring, 604–605
    interface for, 597–598
    marking, 607–608
    overview, 597–598
    sending status report on, 607
    sent from other people, 610
    views for Task List, 599
Template format, Word, 278
Template name text box, OneNote, 626
templates
    in OneNote, 625–626
    in Word, 13, 143
Templates item, Excel, 392
Templates on Office.com link, OneNote, 625
Templates pane, OneNote, 625–626
Test Account Settings dialog box, Outlook, 516
text
    adding to page in OneNote, 630–631
    applying direct formatting to, 76–78
    converting to table, 199–200
    entering
        by scanning document and using OCR, 71–72
        symbols, 72–75
        using Copy and Paste, 71
        by using speech recognition, 72
    formatting in slides
        changing font, font size, and alignment, 442
        changing indentation and line spacing of text, 443
        using bulleted lists, 447–448
    hyperlinks, 113
    inserting, 135–138
    moving insertion point, 75–76
    selecting, 138–140
    tables
        adding content to, 90
        drawing, 89
        formatting, 91–92
        inserting, 88
        merging and splitting cells in, 90
    using Cut, Copy, and Paste with
        Clipboard, 79–81
        Paste options, 81
        standard, 79
    using Find and Replace with, 84–86
    wrapping, 104–105
Text Box pane, 445–446
Text direction drop-down list, 446

Text Direction panel
  PowerPoint, 444
  Ribbon, 445
Text drop-down list, Excel, 365
Text Effects dialog box, PowerPoint, 445
Text Filters submenu, AutoFilter drop-down
    list, 407–408
Text from File command, 135–136
Text Layout area, 446
Text length item, Excel, 327
Text option, Borders and Shading dialog
    box, 179
Text recognition in pictures area, OneNote
    Options dialog box, 666
Text to display box
  Insert Hyperlink dialog box, 463
  Office programs, 115
Theme or Stationery dialog box, Outlook,
    535–536
themes
  in Excel, 320
  in Outlook, 535
  in PowerPoint, 417
Themes box, PowerPoint, 417
Themes group
  Excel, 320
  PowerPoint, 417
  Ribbon, 539
Themes item, PowerPoint, 416
Themes panel, PowerPoint, 417
Through item, Office programs, 104
Tight item, Office programs, 104
Time Bar, Outlook, 581
Time format, Excel, 319
Time item, Excel, 327
Timing group Add Animation drop-down
    panel, PowerPoint, 480
Timing group, PowerPoint, 480
title, adding to chart, 382
Title and Content layout, PowerPoint, 440
title bar, 7
Title Below Axis command, Excel, 383
Title box, Excel, 328
Title Only layout, PowerPoint, 441
title placeholder, PowerPoint, 420
Title Slide layout, PowerPoint, 440
Titles and Headings category, Excel, 331
To book drop-down list, Excel, 303
To box, Outlook, 536–537, 593, 609
To Clipboard only option, OneNote Options
    dialog box, 663
To current page option, OneNote Options
    dialog box, 662–663

To field, Outlook, 609
To new page in current section option,
    OneNote Options dialog box, 662
To option, Arrange By control, 524
TODAY( ) function, Excel, 360–361
Today view, Outlook, 600
To-Do Bar Options dialog box, Outlook,
    530–531
To-Do Bar, Outlook, 529–530, 586, 598–599,
    602, 611
To-Do List, Outlook, 600
To-Do List view, Outlook, 600
Toggle Field Codes, Word, 218
Top alignment, Excel, 321
Top and Bottom item
  Office programs, 104
  Outlook, 105
Top/Bottom Rules panel, Excel, 325
Total row drop-down list, Excel, 398
Total Time box, PowerPoint, 496, 504
Trace Dependents command, Excel, 359
Trace Error command, Excel, 357
Trace Precedents command, Excel, 358–359
Track Changes area, Excel, 342
Track Changes feature, Word
  choosing changes, 240
  controlling which changes Word
      displays, 248
  ensuring colleagues use, 243
  integrating tracked changes into
      documents, 249–250
  overview, 239
  turning on, 243
  using in Full Screen Reading view, 250
  viewing document's changes and
      markup, 248
  working in documents, 247
Track Changes option, View Options drop-
    down menu, 152, 250
Track Changes Options dialog box, Word, 240,
    242–243, 247, 255
Track Changes readout, 243
Tracking group, Ribbon, 540–541
Tracking option, Outlook, 594
Transition Scheme box, PowerPoint, 476–477
transitions, adding to slides, 475–476
Translation Error dialog box, Outlook, 569
Trim Video dialog box, PowerPoint, 471–472
troubleshooting formulas, Excel
  circular references, 359–360
  common errors in, 356
  displaying all formulas in worksheet, 358
  seeing error details, 357

with Trace Precedents command, 358–359
tracing error source, 357
TwelveBrowse Objects, Word, 141
Two Content layout, PowerPoint, 440
Type option, Arrange By control, 524
Type the document title placeholder,
     Word, 206
Type your text here window
     Office programs, 111–112
     PowerPoint, 457

U

Unfiled Notes section, OneNote, 617–618, 620,
     638, 659
Unfreeze Panes command, Excel, 309
Unhide command, Excel, 315
Unhide dialog box, Excel, 307
Unhide window command, 307
unlocking password-protected sections, 645
Unpack Notebook dialog box, OneNote, 677–678
Unprotect Workbook dialog box, Excel, 340
Untitled Section, PowerPoint, 428–429
Up option
     Find and Replace dialog box, 191
     Search drop-down list, 196
Update changes area, Excel, 343
Update Folder option, Outlook, 542
Update Style Name to Match Selection option,
     Styles group, 183
updating the presentation, PowerPoint, 432
Upload Blocked dialog box, PowerPoint, 433
Upload Failed bar, Word, 237–238
Upload Failed dialog box, PowerPoint,
     432–433
Use Balloons drop-down list, Track Changes
     Options dialog box, 242
Use Destination Styles option, 84, 454, 456
Use Destination Theme & Embed Workbook
     option, 461
Use Destination Theme & Link Data
     option, 461
Use separator drop-down list, Word, 209
Use this font drop-down list, Excel, 315
User Information option, Word, 217
User Name box
     Add New Account wizard, 516
     Internet E-mail Settings dialog box, 517
     Options dialog box, 130
User templates folder, Word, 143
User templates item, File Locations dialog
     box, 144
using bulleted lists, in slides, 448

V

validation of data, in Excel, 326
VBA (Visual Basic for Applications), 390
vCard files
     Outlook, 561–563, 567
     Windows, 562–563
     Yahoo!, 563
VeriSign company, 274
versions
     documents
          comparing or combining different, 256–259
          Word, 259
     of pages
          getting rid of, 655
          getting rid of old page versions to save
               space, 655
          viewing or recovering, 654
Versions area, Backstage, 260
Versions readout, Backstage, 260
Vertical alignment drop-down list, 446
Vertical alignment, Excel, 321
vertical axis, Excel, 372–373
Vertical Title item, Excel, 383
Video Options group, PowerPoint, 472
Video recording settings area, OneNote
          Options dialog box, 668
Video Styles box, PowerPoint, 471
Video Tools section, PowerPoint, 471
videos
     adding to presentations, 473
     OneNote, 630, 669–671
View Footnotes dialog box, Word, 231
View Options drop-down menu, 151, 251
View pane, Outlook, 575
View Side by Side command, 308
viewing comments, 255
views
     in Excel, 303
     in OneNote
          Full Page view, 636–637
          Normal view, 636
     in Outlook Calendar, 585
     of presentations, PowerPoint
          Normal view, 419–423
          Notes Page view, 425
          opening extra windows, 427
          Reading view, 425
          Slide Show view, 426
          Slide Sorter view, 423–424
     for Task List, Outlook, 599
     Word
          Draft, 154
          Full Screen Reading, 150–152, 250

Views (*continued*)
    Word (*continued*)
        Outline, 153
        Print Layout, 149
        selecting, 149–154
        Web Layout, 152
        and windows, 155–156
Visual Basic for Applications (VBA), 390
Volume icon, PowerPoint, 503

W

Web Layout view, Word, 152, 204, 226–227
Web Location text box, Backstage, 655
Web option, Store Notebook On list box, 647
Web, storing notes on, 655–656
white space, Find command, 193
Who has this workbook open now list box,
        Excel, 342
Whole document, Word, 211
Whole number item, Excel, 327
whole word matching, Find command, 191
Width box
    PowerPoint, 418
    Word, 211
Width drop-down list, Borders and Shading
        dialog box, 179
width of columns, Excel, 314
wildcards, using with Find command, 191
Windows Contacts dialog box, Windows, 563
Windows Contacts, importing Outlook
        contacts from, 562
Windows Contacts, Outlook, 561
Windows dialog box, Excel, 306
Windows Explorer window, 13, 19, 133, 144
windows, in Word, 155–156
Windows Live, 430–432, 504–505
Windows Security dialog box, 30
Windows sounds, PowerPoint, 474
Windows startup, automatically launching
        programs with, 12–13
With Previous item, PowerPoint, 480
Word
    checking grammar
        choosing grammar and style options for,
            62–64
        controlling how spelling checker works, 59
        overview, 57–58
    choosing grammar and style options for,
        62–64
    controlling which changes are
        displayed, 248
    documents, versions, 259

    exporting OneNote notebook to, 673–675
    importing tables from, 454
    overview, 1–2
    Save options in
        AutoRecover settings, 132–133
        default file location, 133–134
        default format for, 131–132
        overview, 130
    setting Paste options in, 83
    wrapping text in, 104–105
Word icon, PowerPoint, 502
Word Options dialog box, Word, 83, 119, 130,
        143, 145, 147, 163, 214, 218, 260
words, adding to or removing from custom
        dictionaries, 66
workbooks. *See also* worksheets
    creating, 283–284
    embedded, creating charts in, 458
    navigating
        moving active cell, 288–289
        overview, 285–287
        selecting and manipulating cells, 289–290
    printing, 339
    protecting, 340
    rearranging worksheets in, 302
    saving, 285
worksheets
    cells
        deleting, 311–312
        inserting, 311–312
    columns
        deleting, 311–312
        hiding, 314–315
        inserting, 311–312
        width, 314
    deleting, 301
    displaying
        changing window and arranging open
            windows, 306
        comparing two windows side by
            side, 308
        freezing rows and columns, 308
        opening extra windows, 306
        viewing separate parts of worksheets,
            304–305
        views, 303
        zooming, 307
    entering data in
        copying and moving data with drag and
            drop, 299–300
        editing cells, 291–292
        entering data quickly using AutoFill,
            293–295

pasting data into worksheet, 296–299
    typing data in cells, 290
formatting
    conditional formatting, 324–325
    headers and footers, 334
    with styles, 329–334
    table formatting, 329
inserting, 301
navigating
    moving active cell, 288–289
    overview, 285–287
    selecting and manipulating cells, 289–290
printing, 335–339
protecting, 341
rearranging in workbook, 302
rows
    deleting, 311–312
    height, 313
    hiding, 314–315
    inserting, 311–312
sharing, 339–344
using data validation to check for invalid
    entries, 326
Wrap Text panel, Word/Outlook s, 105
wrapping text, in Word and Outlook, 104–105
Writing Style drop-down list
    Grammar Settings dialog box, 63
    Options dialog box, 62–63

 X

X Y chart type, Excel, 374
X-axis, Excel, 372
XPS Document options area, Word, 282
XPS files, Word, 205, 279, 282
XPS viewer, 282

 Y

Yahoo! address book, importing Outlook
    contacts from, 563
Yahoo! Contacts, Outlook, 561, 563
Yahoo! Export screen, Yahoo!, 563
Yahoo! Mail, Outlook, 563
Y-axis, Excel, 372
Year placeholder, Word, 206
Your Name box, Add New Account wizard, 513
YouTube videos, adding to presentations, 473

Z

Zoom Controls, Outlook, 581
Zoom dialog box, Excel, 307
Zoom slider
    Backstage, 68
    Excel, 307
Zoom to Selection command, Excel, 307
    zooming in Excel, 307

CPSIA information can be obtained at www
Printed in the USA
LVOW09s0153010815

448488LV00008B/208/P